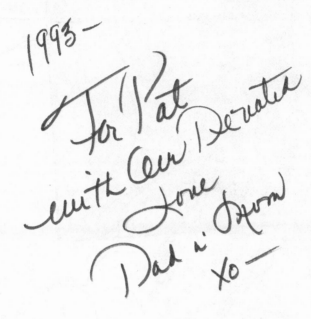

1993 —

For Pat
with our Deepest
Love
Dad & Mom
xo —

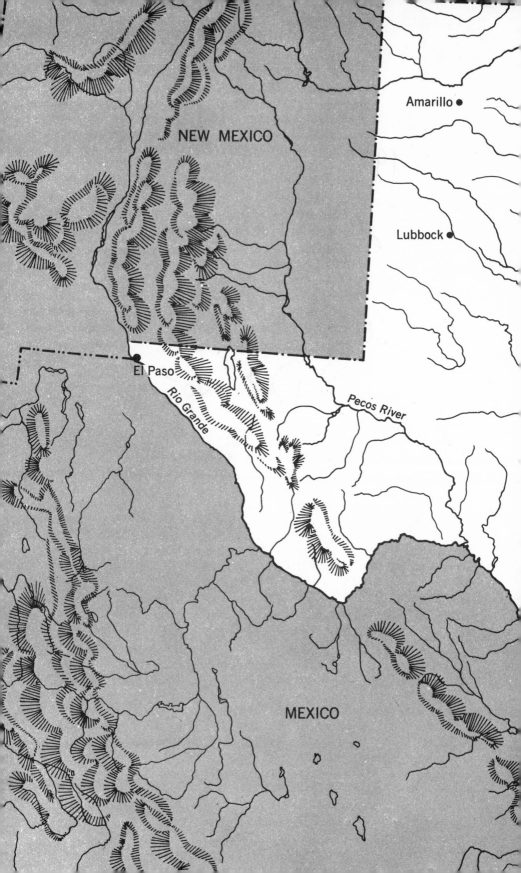

Books by T. R. Fehrenbach

LONE STAR

FDR'S UNDECLARED WAR

THIS KIND OF PEACE

THE SWISS BANKS

THIS KIND OF WAR

CROSSROADS IN KOREA

FIRE AND BLOOD

LONE STAR

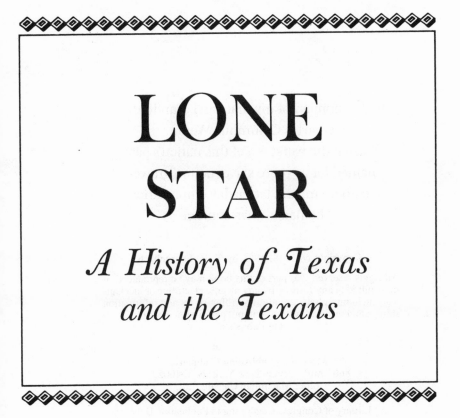

LONE
STAR

*A History of Texas
and the Texans*

T. R. FEHRENBACH

COLLIER BOOKS
A Division of Macmillan Publishing Company
NEW YORK

To the memory of my maternal grandfather,
Charles Columbus Wentz:
Born in the worst era of this nation's past,
named for a Negro slave; cotton grower,
cattleman, and latter-day empresario;
he had always courage.

Macmillan Publishing Company
866 Third Avenue, New York, N.Y. 10022
Collier Macmillan Canada, Ltd.

Library of Congress Cataloging in Publication Data
Fehrenbach, T. R.
Lone star.
Bibliography: p.
Includes index.
1. Texas—History.   I. Title.
F386.F4   1980   976.4   80-10576
ISBN 0-02-032170-8

First Collier Books Edition 1980

10   9   8   7

Macmillan books are available at special discounts for bulk purchases for sales promotions, premiums, fund-raising, or educational use. For details, contact:
Special Sales Director
Macmillan Publishing Company
866 Third Avenue
New York, N.Y. 10022

Printed in the United States of America

CONTENTS

PART IV. THE CONFEDERACY AND THE CONQUERED

PART V. UNTIL DAY BREAKS AND DARKNESS DISAPPEARS: THE LAST FRONTIER

PART VI. THE AMERICANS: NEW DREAMS FOR OLD

FOREWORD

The foreword of the first edition of *Lone Star* quotes the eminent Texas historian Walter Prescott Webb as follows: "The historian whose work is to stand the test must deal with facts as if they were remote, with people as if they were no longer living, and with conditions as they are or were and not as they should have been." In this regard, my purpose in writing the book was to neither buttress nor destroy Texas myths, but to cut through to the reality underneath all "national" myth, and in so doing not to write from a present-minded and problem-oriented viewpoint but to put things in a broad perspective. This approach is no doubt at risk in a modern America whose social sciences are so overwhelmingly oriented in this way, and whose practitioners of history seem increasingly intellectually and emotionally removed from the ancestral frontier that made Texas and the Texans what they are.

Lone Star was culled from an enormous number of scattered and sometimes conflicting sources: general histories published in the United States and abroad; documents, manuscripts, and archives in English, Spanish, German, and French; historical and scientific quarterlies; private journals, family records, and letters; 19th-century newspapers, and official papers of several governments. I have also drawn on specialized works on subjects ranging from anthropology to zoology, geology to firearms, and I generally have followed published works; notation of any unpublished source is made in the text. And because this is a general work, the flow has not been interrupted with footnotes.

A great deal of Texas historical material exists, including county, city, and regional histories aside from the general histories and the usual documents; there are also biographies of almost every prominent Texan in every field, as well as histories of most industries, including the major oil companies, railroads, and cattle ranches. If every waterhole has its history, most have their mention in print. All this varied writing contains bits of exciting information and occasional gems of insight, but it tends to be drowned in detail, littered with trivia, and constricted in perspective. Texans have continually tried to capture the vision that created the broad plantations, giant oil corporations, and baronial cattle spreads, as well as the hundreds of thousands of frontier farms. But the state is so wide and varied, and so rich in ceaseless action, that the student trying to grasp the "feel" and meaning of Texas' place in American history is often baffled. Modern general histories are few. *Lone Star* was written in an attempt to fill this void and correlate the whole.

I think that *Lone Star* has withstood the test of time, and the Texans themselves. Fashions of the 1950s, fads of the 60s, and funks of the 70s have come and gone, while the state and her people, and the factors that made them both, have endured. When the book was first envisioned, Texas was still merely the prospect of an empire; today it has become an empire indeed, a truly "imperial" state whose economy, resources, wealth, politics, people, and attitudes (for better or worse) increasingly impinge upon and affect the greater American nation. Whatever Texas is, whatever Texans may be or how they may be seen by others, the state is now too important to be regarded as quaint, provincial, eccentric, or "different." After all, the state's history is the history of America, at the very core of the history of fully one-quarter of the nation's people. Without Texas there would be no American West, and the nation would be unthinkable in its present form. Texas and Texans cannot be understood without first understanding the people-making processes of our past, from the massacres of the Texas Revolution to the bloody aboriginal wars, and from the lonely sojourn as a sovereign nation to the unending bitter struggle for and upon the soil. Most Texans sense this history even when they can't articulate it. Others need to know it.

In this, our Sesquicentennial Year, 150 years after the birth of the Republic of Texas in blood and iron, both Texans and others are realizing that there is something special about this people and their land, just as there is something special about France and Frenchmen, or Israel and the Jewish people. Our past, like theirs, is part of humanity's trek across this globe. For this reason, *Lone Star,* this vision of the Texas past that made the Texas present, has been committed to film, a documentary series that will be shown nationwide on PBS beginning in December 1985 and will eventually be seen over most of the world.

T.R.F.
June 1, 1985

Old now is earth, and none may count her days.
Earth might be fair, and all men glad and wise.
Age after age, their tragic empires rise,
Built while they dream, and in that dreaming weep:
Would man but wake from out his haunted sleep,
Earth might be fair, and all men glad and wise.

OLD HUNDRED TWENTY-FOURTH

Part I

COMANCHES AND THE KING'S MERCIES

1

THE AMERINDS

I live, but I shall not live forever.
Mysterious Moon, you only remain,
Powerful Sun, you alone remain,
Wonderful Earth, only you live forever.

DEATH SONG OF THE TEXAS KIOWA

In the beginning, before any people, was the land: an immense region 265,000 square miles in area rising out of the warm muck of the green Gulf of Mexico, running for countless leagues of rich coastal prairies, forests, and savannahs; reaching out hugely 770 miles from boundary to boundary south to north and east to west, to enclose a series of magnificent, rising limestone plateaus, ending in the thin, hot air of blue-shadowed mountains. Geologically, this was a New Land, thrusting westward from the sea across three major geophysical provinces of North America, the Atlantic-Gulf coastal plain, the Great Plains, and the Rocky Mountain system. Therefore, it was a land of sudden and dramatic change.

No human beings were native to the New World; every race of men entered as invaders. The date of the first intrusion is not known. But it came tens of thousands of years before the dawn of recorded history, during the last great Ice Age. Immense glaciers covered the Northern Hemisphere, and because the earth's water supply is constant, the oceans shrank. A land-bridge rose out of the northern seas to connect Asia and Alaska, and the first men to see America almost certainly crossed this narrow strip.

They were not Indians. Another and very different race first took possession of Texas soil.

This race passed down the few unglaciated valleys of the north, seeking

3

the sun, and the grass and game that followed the sun. These early men reached both the Atlantic and Pacific coasts, but their true home was the High Plains. They left their greatest concentrations of relics and fire sites high on the limestone plateaus of Texas, and here the oldest remains of man in the New World were found. Modern radiocarbon tests proved charred wood from one such camp site to be beyond the dating range of the carbon-14 technique—and this process can search back 37,000 years. Man in Texas was not, as scientists once believed, a late arrival. Fluorine analysis of ancient human bones found in Texas limestone showed that these were contemporary with the bones of the ages-extinct Pleistocene horse, uncovered beside them. Archeologists, who once firmly thought that Indians were the first proprietors of North America, grudgingly named these original Texans Paleo-Americans, or simply, Old Americans.

They were biologically true men—the half-men, such as the European Neanderthal, had died out long before they left the Old World. They were not Mongoloid. The skulls they left behind are longheaded, more longheaded than any race of modern men. They had massive teeth, and their leg bones were flat and curved. They were more unlike American Indians than white men are different from Chinese, and they may have been a Caucasoid race that roamed east out of Central Asia in the human dawn.

The Old Americans entered Texas with hundreds of thousands of years of human evolution and social development behind them. They were erect, gregarious, symbol-and-weapon-using, and therefore intelligent. They had fire, wore fur and skin garments, and made tools of flint and bone. They chipped beautiful stone spearheads, thousands of which they left behind. They were mentally and physically equipped to conquer new worlds.

Like all Pleistocene or Ice Age men, they were hunters. They roamed across the High Plains, leaving their tools and bones from Clovis, New Mexico, to Abilene, Texas, and from Abilene east to the banks of the Pedernales, just above the Balcones Escarpment. Their favorite hunting ground was the Llano Estacado, the Staked Plains—the home of the ancient American elephant.

Magnificent animals lived on the high plateaus in those times: the awe-inspiring *Elephas columbi* or Columbian elephant, the mammoth, the mastodon, the ground sloth, and the ancient bison, a beast twice the size and probably four times the weight of the modern buffalo. The Old Americans must have been an incredibly tough, almost inhumanly courageous race; they pursued and killed all these animals with flint-tipped spears. They roasted meat in great kitchens or middens in the limestone; they flaked new flints around their fires, and they must have roared great hunting and victory songs to the Pleistocene moon. They left no "old" bones. Life was hard and incredibly dangerous; men probably rarely lived beyond eighteen or twenty years, and females not much longer.

They may have made flutes and drums, and they may have worshiped their God or gods, but nothing more of their culture has survived—with one fantastic exception. These were the great stone heads found in the bed of the oldest trace of the Trinity River, seventy feet above the present flood plain. Paleontologists consider these heads the most exotic relic unearthed in North America.

The heads, discovered among the bones of the Columbian elephant and the giant mastodon, were tooled from rock. One weighed 135 pounds, one 60, and the third an even 100. The first two massive heads are recognizably human: one frowns, one smiles. The third, and largest—weird, inhuman— can only represent some unknown force or beast.

The Old Americans wandered across the high plateaus for many thousands of years. But nature is never constant, and the world is never made. The land changed. The vast ice sheets retreated north; the rivers dug deeper into the earth, and the lakes dried. The lush land that had been Texas grew hotter, harsher. The woolly mammoth disappeared. Something happened to the elephant. Perhaps, like the ground sloth and the mastodon and small native horse, it was pushed on its way to extinction by Paleo-American spears. The Pleistocene ended, and the Pleistocene animals died. The Old Americans vanished with them.

Whether the race died out, or merely changed so much over the millennia as to be no longer recognizable, is unknown. But there were already new conquerors, new proprietors, on the land. Before the land bridge sank, other men crossed from Asia and pushed out across the Great Plains. Some went east, and some west, and some did not stop until they had climbed the Andes, thousands of miles to the south.

The new men were definitely Asian. They were Mongoloid in skin shade, hair form and color, and other ways. These were the Amerinds, or American Indians, as Europeans later named them. They called themselves, in hundreds of different tongues, merely the People, or sometimes, the Real Humans.

Like the Old Americans, the Amerinds came as hunters and gatherers. But besides their racial stock, they differed from the Paleo-Americans in many ways. The Old Americans apparently came in a single invasion, over a relatively short period of years. There were never very many of them, and they preserved a certain cultural unity; Old American spear points, for example, never varied much from place to place, or over thousands of years.

The Amerinds came in a long series of invasions, a genuine *Völkerwanderung* that had not completely ceased by historic times. By about 5000 B.C. these invasions were in full swing, and they continued for thousands of years. The ice was gone; instead of a few unglaciated routes, the Amerinds could choose a thousand corridors south. Some remained for long periods in the north before they left, and some never roamed at all. The Amerinds —most of whom in North America showed almost identical racial or physical characteristics, with only minor variations of height or color—became differentiated culturally. They split into linguistic stocks, and then adopted mutually unintelligible languages within each linguistic group. They made their tools and artifacts in different ways: the early Amerinds left twenty-seven different kinds of dart points on the Edwards Plateau of Texas alone.

They carried a great assortment of stone and bone tools: axes, knives, drills, pipes, scrapers, picks, and gravers. Their principal weapon was still the spear, but they had developed the atlatl, or throwing stick, to give them extra range. They came out of Asia with domesticated dogs.

Culturally varied, speaking different languages, nomadic and constantly impinging on each other, the hundreds of bands of Amerinds could only follow the oldest human logic: they made war. Each new folk wandering from the north invaded already appropriated hunting grounds, and the first wars stemmed from the most logical of reasons, the defense of territory. But a constantly roaming, constantly colliding people soon imbedded the idea and act of warfare deep in their cultural heart. All men except the Real Human Beings—kith and kin—were enemies. The fighting was not racial, but internecine, as in modern Europe; the center of society and most important member was the warrior. There was a place for women, because warriors were too occupied to work; there was a place for priests or shamans, and both the young and old, but no place at all for the weak or cowardly.

Civilized men, caught in their modern traps and pressures, have often looked longingly toward the seeming freedom, and barbaric majesty, of the Stone Age, nomadic Amerind male. Females did his bidding; he seldom soiled his hands with labor. But the division of labor, and the culture that grew up around it, was cruelly logical. The warrior had to hunt and fight. He had to kill the elusive deer, the dangerous bear, and the powerful buffalo with a flint spear, or the tribe went hungry; he had to defend his soil, and—the culture soon demanded it—carry war and raids to the enemy, for women and spoils. He had to prove his courage from the day of manhood until he died, and sometimes prove it while dying. The fiendish custom of torturing captured males—captive children were enslaved or adopted, and women were equally useful—probably originated as a courage rite. The tortured captive had to prove his courage at the stake; the tormentors had to gain moral superiority by breaking it. Significantly, whatever sadistic pleasure they got out of it, almost all Amerinds considered it an evil omen if a prisoner defied their tortures and died well.

Virtually all Amerind peoples took scalps from the bodies of their enemies, living or dead, and every warrior lucky enough to secure them wore or displayed them in various ways. These were, certainly, more positive proof of courage or success in war than the medals or decorations of more civilized man.

Amerinds spread through the forests of the eastern seaboard of North America; they poured down into Mexico and beyond, and some of them scattered across the High Plains and central plateaus of Texas. Now, the land was taking its modern form. The lushness and the great waterholes that had supported mastodon and elephant had long vanished. Across the plains the rain fell less and less, in a marked progression from east to west. The violent, harsh contrasts between timbered country in the east, savannah in the south, and endless prairie to the west appeared. The dense growths of the limestone plateaus became arid, cedar-sprinkled hills. The land lay far south, and there were rivers of palms on its southern fringe— but it was also in the center of the great North American continental land mass, where icy winds could sweep down from the Pole. Such regions are always varied, and subject to violent natural change.

Warm, moist breezes blew out of the Gulf; they moved inland over leagues of endless, bending grass until they turned hot and searing. Arctic winds at times howled off the roof of the world, roared across the High Plains and whistled over the decaying limestone formations of the central plateaus, plunging into the dry savannahs beyond. In spring, warm and cold winds met and warred, with brilliant electricity, ice rains, and dark funnels that dipped and tore the ground. Nature was always hard, and frequently at war with itself.

Over the whole land the sun burned, not the distant, friendly orb that filtered light through European forests, but a violent, brassy engine that browned the earth and made the hillsides shimmer with heat. The moon hung low and silver cold beyond the ephemeral night clouds against a back-blaze of stars. On each successively higher prairie or plateau the land stretched out, fairly level, further than any living eye could see. There were few boundaries anywhere, and then sharp ones: where the trees ended and the land became an ocean of soughing grass; where the high mesa turned to blue-mountained, dusty desert; where the rolling, grassy, mesquite-studded savannah etched up into the flinty Balcones Scarp. The regions were wider than modern European nations; the subregions larger than Atlantic seaboard states. Over it all the wind blew, now south, now north. Endless land, and eternal wind—it made all animal life restless, long-visioned, volatile, and free.

The Amerinds who entered this harsh, changeable country may have seen no beauty in it, nor learned to love it, until a generation had been born there. The tribes who scattered through it in the Amerind Archaic Age were not notably successful. They were tough and hardy, but they were on foot. They were in open country, armed with flint knives, stone axes, and flint spears; for some thousands of years they did not have the bow and arrow. Bison dotted the plains, but even this modern buffalo, a fraction of the size of the ancient, Pleistocene bison, was a formidable beast to attack on foot, at arm's length. More important, it was impossible for the tribes to follow the buffalo on their great migrations north and south over the arid plains. The hill country, where the ancient limestone formations frayed out above the Balcones Escarpment in spectacular scenery, supported deer and bear and smaller game. But there was not enough of this, nor sufficient easily killed animal flesh upon the grassy savannahs to the south, for Texas tribes to live off the fat of the land. There was, simply, very little fat, and the campsites of the early Amerinds have revealed mortars and pestles, seeds, and the remnants of roots among their small bones, as well as cracked human femurs. Broken and sucked human marrow bones have been discovered preserved in the ancient muck of the coastal prairies in great quantity—proof that where the Old Americans had been able to live well on mastodon and elephant meat, the aborigines who displaced them came to depend on other foods. In modern times all Texas tribes except one—the late-coming Comanches—practiced at least some form of ritual cannibalism, a grisly, ceremonial residue of a harsh past.

The land was too big, too harsh, too restless in climate for man to dominate, or even carve a stable niche for himself, with the tools the archaic Indians possessed.

This era, which paleontologists call Archaic, lasted for some thousands of years across all America. The invention of the bow, about the time of Christ, did not make life much easier, except that now birds, and more small game, were added to the Amerind diet. The great change, which ushered in the Neo-American Age, was the Agricultural Revolution. In America, as everywhere on earth, this was the greatest social and economic revolution mankind ever experienced, beside which the Industrial Revolution was a mere change of phase.

Several thousand years before Christ lived—certainly long before 2500 B.C., for radiocarbon-dated seeds have been discovered in New Mexico as of that date—the Amerinds of Middle or South America discovered how to domesticate maize, or Indian corn. Just as all mammalian life is dependent, in the final analysis, upon water and grass, all human civilization is based on the controlled growth of some cereal grain, whether rice, or wheat, or corn. No civilization could exist without cities—the words are synonymous —and no stable populations could live without a dependable food supply. When the Amerinds of Middle America learned how to grow corn, and along with this development to domesticate a few animals, the basis for a genuine American civilization was firmly laid.

True city-based civilizations began to rise in Middle America, in the same latitudes and in no way inferior to the ancient civilizations of Egypt, Babylon, and Ur of the Chaldees. Their centers were in Middle America and the slopes of the Andes, and in time they sent dim reflections to the ends of both American continents. There was no single Amerind civilization, but a series of connected cultures, which in the hands of different peoples, rose, flourished, withered, and were restored. The Aztecs of the Valley of Mexico, and the Incas of Peru, were merely the conquerors and stabilizers of what was already a very ancient culture, and both took command within recent pre-Columbian times.

In Mexico, many miles to the south of the Texas plains, a succession of Mayan, Toltec, and other cultures farmed the soil, grew large populations, and erected vast cities, comparable to ancient Memphis, and not much inferior to Imperial Rome. Immensely disciplined, hard-working and imaginative, these Amerinds evolved a highly sophisticated social and political organization, with complete divisions of labor, classes, and castes. They built immense palaces and pyramids out of carved stone. They developed mathematics, writing, and astronomy—their calendar was superior to Cortés'—and pursued fine arts. They worked gold, silver, and copper with brilliant mastery. The fact that they did all these things without smelting metals only adds luster to the accomplishment—though this lack, when they were taken by unexpected disaster from across the Atlantic, probably more than anything else sealed their doom.

Had Cortés and the conquistadores met metal-armed and armored men, the fate of Mexico might have been startlingly different.

Where the civilization of this Nuclear America might have gone can only be conjectured. The Spaniards, on arrival, did not commit genocide, but something probably worse: culturicide. In almost a single night the Europeans, who sacrificed men and women to their God by burning them alive, justified the extinction of Amerind culture because of the Mexic addiction to ceremonial human sacrifice, the cutting out of living victims' hearts with stone knives. The dominant Amerind aristocracy was exterminated, their temples razed, and their palaces purified. The conquerors even erased the memory of their Mexican slaves. Ironically, the racial descendants of the Aztecs first learned authoritative facts about their vanished heritage from the excavations of North American and European archeologists in recent times, who stumbled upon abandoned Amerind cities the Spaniards never found. Even then, the memory was blighted, because no cultural bridge survived.

Had the discovery of America been delayed a few centuries, the history of Middle America would have been much more like that of modern Asia. Europeans might have conquered, but they could not so easily have destroyed, and essential Amerind culture would have survived. When Columbus sailed, the Mexic civilization was on a par with 14th century Europe, and certain other tribal groups of North America were culturally contemporary with the Germans of Tacitus' time. As it was, the Amerind contribution to the world was profound: three-fifths of the value of all the earth's agriculture in the 20th century came from crops the Americans planted first: maize, "Irish" potatoes, yams, tobacco, beans, squash, pumpkins, peanuts, tomatoes, chocolate, rubber, and long-staple cotton. Amerind discoveries were essential to modern American civilization.

Though Amerinds tamed the llama, alpaca, turkey, duck, guinea pig, and dog, again in one crucial field—animal domestication—they fell behind. They had good reason; in the New World the horse, pig, cow, and sheep did not exist.

Between 2500 B.C. and Columbian times, the use of corn spread northward. When the first white men came, the planting of maize had reached its geographic limits. But this great cultural revolution bypassed Texas, or rather, surrounded it on each side. The cause was geophysical, and obvious. For several hundred miles on either side of the Rio Grande the country was virtual desert—not "true" desert, like the Sahara or Kalahari, but Lower Sonoran plain, dry, dusty, almost waterless, with less than twenty inches of annual rainfall. When the tremendous Amerind invasion went north, it could have more easily marched through the southern part of Hell than crossed South Texas.

But agriculture crept up the spine of Mexico and created a pallid reflection of Aztec splendor among the Uto-Aztecan peoples of the Rocky Mountain system. On the high plateaus of New Mexico, Arizona, and Colorado the Puebloan culture evolved, one of the two true barbaric civilizations of North America. The Puebloans—again, there was a series of tribes and peoples, at different times and over a wide area—farmed cotton and corn, beans, tobacco, and squash. They also ate sunflower seeds. They built spacious houses out of slabs of stone, which they chinked with adobe and covered with hides or thatch. They made beautiful ornaments and garments and pottery. They discovered social organization; both men and women worked in the fields. The practice and notion of war declined in their culture, and the peaceful farmer, rather than the savage warrior, became the nucleus of society. They organized colorful pageants and ceremonials; the Puebloans rose out of savagery to barbaric civilization.

About A.D. 1000 the Pueblo (the word comes from the Spanish for "village") culture seemed to expand. Versions of it spread into the High Plains of Texas, and a Puebloan tribe built fine stone dwellings along the Canadian in the Panhandle. Other feelers of civilization inched down the Rio Grande into the Trans-Pecos region. Here, on the ruins of other semiagricultural tribes, such as the cave-living Basket Makers, the Jumanos put together a definite, though struggling, Amerind nation. But here, as on the edge of the Great Plains far to the north, the agricultural advance stopped. The Puebloan remained a civilization of the upper Rio Grande.

Meantime, far to the east, certain events still clouded in mystery were taking place. The archeology of the American Southeast is much less advanced than that of the Southwest; the wet climate and the inundation of the white man destroyed sites and ancient evidence still preserved in the thinly settled, arid High Plains. But around the year 500 of the Christian Era, a vital new Amerind culture was spreading up from the Mississippi basin. It began on the Gulf of Mexico, reached the Great Lakes, and followed the curve of the sea so far as the forests ran. Thus, it spilled over into Texas, crossing the Sabine with the western edge of the great Southern pine forest. This barbaric civilization has been called the Mound Builder, from the eroding remnants of the immense earthen pyramids they left behind.

The Mount Builders showed strong Mexican cultural influences. Otherwise, they were a Circum-Caribbean Amerind culture, building pole houses not unlike those found on the islands or the coasts of Venezuela. It seems likely they entered the present United States by water, though archeologists dispute this. No evidence of their passage across Texas has yet been found. The Mount Builders raised dirt pyramids fifty feet high, faced them with log stairs, and erected temples—presumably to a sun-god—at the top. The similarity to the Mexic culture is unmistakable; the Mound Builders used mud and logs because they lived in a country with little stone. The Amerinds also wore feathered robes, and they were divided sharply by class; their chieftains were borne about on litters, like Aztec or Mayan lords. The smell of the Middle American civilization lies all across this Mississippi pattern, as archeologists have described it.

Although this new culture spread widely along the Gulf and up the Mississippi, something happened to it long before the Europeans came. This reinforces the idea of invasion; the Mound Builder culture was foreign, and it did not quite take root in a vastly different land. But in modern times it left behind a barbarian civilization within the borders of historic Texas, the Caddo Confederacies of the Piney Woods, once the most numerous and powerful Indians within the state.

A haunting feeling of having descended from something greater still pervaded the Caddo nation when the first Europeans arrived. It was not truly indigenous to Texas; it faced East rather than West, and it halted abruptly where the pine woods ended, far short of the central plains. The Caddoan language, even, was linguistically bound not to the prairies, but to the lower Yazoo. Caddos resembled Choctaws, Cherokees, and Creeks; they unquestionably had a common cultural ancestor.

The Caddoan peoples—there were two great confederacies, the Hasinai and the Kadohadacho, and more than two dozen tribes—still maintained the forms not of a blood kinship but of a former political ascendancy. There was a genuine bureaucracy: minor officials, subchiefs, tribal chiefs, who reported to each other, and finally, to the great chief of all the tribes, the Grand Caddi. They had a priesthood, which outranked the secular officialdom in standing.

The high priest, or Xinesi, was responsible for the eternal flame in the central Caddo temple. All the various tribal temple fires had to be lit from this central, holy flame, a pontifical organization with recognizable manifestations.

The Caddoans lived in a country of abundant rain, with rich soils. They enjoyed complete economic self-sufficiency; they hunted game much as the Anglo-Saxon settlers did, more as a supplement than a staple. They grew two varieties of corn and a whole assortment of vegetables, including pole beans. They lived in small villages, made up of large timbered houses, domed and thatched. These houses were airy and comfortable, furnished with colored rugs, baskets, and pottery. The villages were organized on a communal-kinship basis; both men and women worked the soil, and house-raisings were public affairs.

The Caddoans made bows of a superior wood, Osage orange or bois d'arc, which was greatly in demand on the plains and in the far west. They must have carried on an extensive commerce with the west, because Puebloan cottons and pottery, as well as Plains buffalo hides, were often found in their houses. In this commerce the Jumanos of the Trans-Pecos acted as middlemen. Caddos occasionally hunted the bison, but they had no great enthusiasm for moving out on the plains. War had declined among the confederacies, and society no longer revolved about the cult of the warrior, as it had in the Archaic Age. The village official, the priest, or the peaceful husband had become the social ideal. These had developed into hereditary classes.

These peaceful Amerinds had developed other traits, or had degenerated them, showing civilized origin. Though they no longer built temples or pyramids to the sun-god—or even knew why these once were built—they practiced a ritual torture unknown to North American tribes. Captives were stretched on racks to face the morning and evening sun; the ritual, and torture, was carried on for days, before the prisoners were killed and eaten, not for food, but ceremonially. The Caddos had torments far more exquisite, and lengthy, than the fiendish, savage, but relatively quick executions of the Plains Indians.

Unlike other Amerinds, the Caddoans shed tears easily. They wept and wailed on almost every occasion, especially meeting or parting. White enemies were often warned of an impending massacre, in historic times, by the fact that the Caddos went into sobs and fits of weeping. Uniquely, the Caddos mourned their victims while they prepared to kill them.

The cult of courage, at the base of most Amerind culture, was not important to the Caddos. A warrior who triumphed, or gained loot by treachery or stealth, or who fled the scene of battle with some gain, was still a hero. The Caddoan practice of war, however, was not really sophisticated: it was replete with moves, actions, delays, and ceremonials that no longer made sense even to the participants; they were fixed by custom. All war preparations, for example, required eight days, and ended with a ceremonial burning of a house. In all this can be sensed the dead hand of a former military tradition—much as the love of close-order drill has persisted in European armies in the Atomic Age.

Because they were agricultural and war was no longer a central part of their culture, the Caddoan tribes were remarkably amiable to white men in the first years of contact, with disastrous results to themselves. It was not accidental, though ironic, that the first French and Spanish who encountered Caddos appreciated them more, found their culture more related to theirs than that of any other Texas Amerind, and also destroyed them most easily.

Between the Puebloan civilization of the upper Rio Grande and the decadent barbaric grandeur of the Sabine Hasinai Confederacy, the vast reaches of Texas remained what anthropologists call with some justice a cultural sink. Mexic and Circum-Caribbean influences reached Texas, but only on the fringes. On the hot, dry, harsh sweeps of the high mesas, the limestone plateaus, and the rolling coastal savannah, the numerous tribes never culturally left the Amerind Archiac Age.

Racially all Texas Indians were quite similar, except for minor differences of height and skin shade. In their tribal customs, habits, and economies, however, they were as differentiated as Frenchmen and Chinese. Nor were the land and peoples stable.

It is impossible to reconstruct the history of these peoples with any accuracy, and since a majority of the Texas tribes died out or had decayed to impotency by early historic times, their history had little importance to what came after. Its pattern merely suggests a continuing, endless rhythm of periodic aggression from the north, with sporadic internecine warfare at all times.

South of the Caddo Confederacies, along the Gulf Coast, lived a number of small Atakapan tribes. These were a wretched reflection of the Caddos in some respects; their name was a Choctaw word for "man-eater."

Further south along the coast, from Galveston to Corpus Christi bays, the Karankawa tribes had a more formidable reputation as cannibals— though their man-eating seems to have been as much of a ritual nature as for dietary benefit. This people early acquired a name for peculiar savagery, as well as bestiality. An early Spanish traveler wrote: "They are cruel, inhuman, and ferocious. When one nation makes war with another, the one that conquers puts all the old men and old women to the knife and carries off the little children for food to eat on the way; the other children are sold. . . ."

Several Spaniards described Karankawa tortures and cannibal feasts— though naturally none of these men were eyewitnesses. The most notable fact about the Karankawas was that they avoided all contact with Europeans; they refused to cooperate with them in any way, and attacked any incursion of their territory with fury. In return, no Amerind tribe was ever described in worse terms or exterminated with greater relish or sense of justification.

West of Karankawa country, on a line ranging through San Antonio to Del Rio and south to the mouth of the Rio Grande, was the territory of a great number of small bands of Coahuiltecans. This was cactus and brush country, arid, rolling stretches of semidesert, dry savannah at its best, which the Spanish called *brasada* or *monte*. The bison did not come below the Balcones Scarp because of the heat, and there were no large game animals in sufficient numbers to support a true hunting economy. Few regions of America were less bountiful for primitive man, without irrigation techniques or the use of domesticated cattle. The Coahuiltecan culture was one of digging and grubbing, with an occasional economic windfall such as a jackrabbit in the pot.

Yet, such is human ingenuity that no other species ever used the resources of a country more fully: the Coahuiltecans consumed spiders, ant eggs, lizards, rattlesnakes, worms, insects, rotting wood, and deer dung. They caught fish when they were beside a stream, roasted them whole, then set them in the sun for several days, collecting flies and maggots. The enriched food was eaten with gusto. They utilized almost every plant that grew in South Texas. They made flour from agave bulbs, sotol, lechuguilla, and maguey. They roasted mesquite beans, and ate these with side orders of earth. One peculiar source of food—which a Spaniard, Cabeza de Vaca, described as "indescribable"—was the Second Harvest: whole seeds and similar items picked out of human feces, cooked and chewed.

The Coahuiltecans also discovered uses for local plants not wholly scorned by civilized man. They concocted a drink, mescal, from maguey leaves. This was intoxicating, and in a slightly refined form, is the principal intoxicant of the Mexican peasantry today. The Coahuiltecans also dissolved ground red Texas laurel beans in mescal, and produced real firewater. They ate the fruit of the prickly pear, and from another cactus, peyote, they produced what can only be called a very unusual tea.

These tribes were all completely nomadic, moving constantly, erecting only temporary shelters of mud, skins, or brush. They did not seek war, but fought if their territory was violated. The tribes or bands were all patrilineal, but band fought band. They frequently killed female or girl-child captives, and practiced infanticide, because, in their eyes, the land was already overpopulated.

Inhabiting, for the Amerinds, the least fruitful part of Texas, the Coahuiltecans perhaps had a more glorious history in former times. They were of Hokan linguistic stock, and the only other Hokan, or Yuma, tribes in modern centuries lived in California. Paleontologists have envisioned a broad band of Hokan peoples, stretching from Pacific to Gulf at one time, split by waves of hardier Uto-Aztecans, who appropriated the southern sierras and poured into Mexico in prehistoric eras. The Hokan-speaking tribes, perhaps, were driven into brutal, inhospitable country—South Texas and the similar Arizona-California border. Certainly, no Amerind people would have settled there by choice.

Above the country of the Coahuiltecans, over the Balcones Escarpment, lived the Tonkawas, whose name for themselves was Tickanwatick, or "the most human of men." They ranged across the great Edwards Plateau to the Brazos valley. The Tonkawas were not one tribe, but a group of tribes; their language was apparently unrelated to any other Amerind stock, but perhaps derived from Hokan. So far as can be told, Tonkawas had lived on the central plateau from time immemorial; they may have replaced the first Old Americans. They lived by hunting, fishing, and gathering fruits, nuts, and berries. The Tonkawa culture was that typical of the pre-horse southern Plains Indians; they lived on the edge of bison country, in buffalo-hide tepees, and they used large dogs as beasts of burden. They had evolved the clan organization, with both civil and military authorities. Like most Texas natives, they tattooed their bodies, wore breechclouts and long hide moccasins; in winter they donned buckskin shirts and warm buffalo robes. They carried bows, their principal weapon, and long Plains lances, and they dipped their dart heads in mistletoe juice—presumably in the hope of poisoning them. Fray Morfi, a Spanish priest who wrote about Tonakawas in the middle of the 18th century, called them "a terrible and bellicose nation . . . they live for warfare, robbery, and the chase."

The Tonkawas, however, did not hunt or raid very high on the Texas plains; they were confined to the Edwards Plateau. Another, fiercer tribe was lord of the rich buffalo grounds.

At some recent but unknown date, a new race appeared out of the north to harry the spreading Puebloan cultures of the Rocky Mountains. The new men spoke Athapaskan, a language whose traditional homeland was the far Northwest, Canada and Alaska. These tribes must have wandered for many years south across the Great Plains, finally entering the eastern Rockies. In the passage they had become exceedingly warlike and unusually fierce and skilled at fighting. These were the Apaches, who looked on all other Amerinds as enemies.

The Apache invasion of the Southwest caused reverberations that still lingered in tribal wars and tribal hatreds until the last years of the 19th century. Apaches raided through a vast region, from modern Kansas to Arizona to deep in Mexico. They pushed out some of the former tribes, exterminated others, and settled down in their new homeland to ceaseless warfare with the rest. They split into two great divisions, the Eastern and Western Apaches. The Western tribes, Navaho, San Carlos, Chiricahua, and Mescalero, carved out a place in the southern Rockies; they became Arizona- and New Mexico-based. They ceased to be wholly nomadic; they learned rudimentary agriculture from the various Puebloan cultures which they continually harassed, but they never lost their traditional warlike spirit. They remained raiders and marauders to the last.

Each Apache tribe or group was influenced by its new locale. The Eastern Apaches—Jicarillas, Palomas, Carlanas, Lipans, and others—apparently destroyed the Puebloan cultures of the Texas Panhandle, forced the town-dwellers back into the mountains of New Mexico, and made themselves masters of the High Plains. They ranged as far north as the Dismal River in Nebraska, and south into Mexico. They harried all the surviving Puebloan tribes, and began to exterminate the Jumanos of the Trans-Pecos Texas area. They kept Tonkawas and others far to the east and south, away from the richest of the bison plains. Halfway between the endless plains and the eastern Rockies, they made semipermament settlements. One tribe, the Jicarillas, even began to use irrigation on their fields of corn. But, above all else, the Eastern Apaches learned to live off the buffalo.

As during the Pleistocene, the richest game area in North America lay on the High Plains that ended almost indiscernibly in the central Texas plateau. Here there were millions upon millions of American bison, as well as elk, deer, and antelope. Each spring and fall the bison congregated on the southern plains, moving north in a seemingly aimless pattern during the summer. Anthropologists believe that the typical buffalo-hunting cultures of the Plains evolved first in Texas, then spread north; the Eastern Apaches were certainly the dominant prototype.

The plainsman based his life and culture—aside from war, which was already deepseated—upon the bison. The great hunts took place in spring and fall, when small herds were surrounded by men on foot and shot with arrows until all beasts were dead. The bison was a remarkably vulnerable animal in many ways. It did not frighten or stampede unless it smelled the scent of an enemy, and men downwind from a herd could sometimes kill hundreds of beasts in one spot; the sight of falling buffalo, or the odor of blood, did not start the rest. Sometimes herds were deliberately stampeded into canyons, or over deep furrows in the ground, where the trapped or injured animals could be killed and skinned at leisure.

Immediately, the dead bison were opened with flint knives, and raw livers and other delicacies eaten on the spot. This work—in fact, all work —was done by women, either of the tribe or slaves; men's labor was confined to the hunt or war. Buffalo carcasses were then roasted. The intestines were often cooked whole, as a special treat. Some lean flesh was sun-dried, or jerked, to carry over the winter or on the trail. Buffalo guts were cleaned out and used as bags to store precious water. Buffalo bones made picks and tools.

The hides were used for shelter, clothing, and blankets. The Apaches made comfortable and ingenious tepees of buffalo skins, with light frames of sotol poles. These tents, actually dryer, warmer, and more airy than log cabins, were flapped with bearskins for doors, and open at the top for escaping smoke. Four to twelve people lived in one tepee. Wood or dung fires were built in their centers, and they were furnished with hide blankets spread over soft beds of dry grass. Tepees shone red and white against the sun, and the bison hide was tanned so fine that rain could not penetrate or even stiffen it.

In the hot months Apaches wore very little—breechclouts or buckskin skirts and moccasins. Their coppery skin, like that of all Amerinds, was sun-resistant. In winter they put on deerskin shirts or wore heavy buffalo robes. Outside of his clothing, his flint-edged weapons, and his tents, the Apache owned nothing. It was simple, a matter of minutes, to strike his tents and move, and so far as possible, during the hunting seasons, the tribes formed long caravans and followed the migrating bison herds. Shaggy dogs pulled the ingenious Plains travois, while scouts and warriors ranged far ahead.

But Apaches on foot were simply not equipped to exploit the Plains to the fullest. The High Plains were beautiful and flowering in spring or after the widely scattered summer rains, but other times, and in summer, they turned to broiling near-desert. The water holes dried and the grass withered. The buffalo followed the rain and grass, and in the hottest months, heavy-hided, they went north to avoid the terrible sun. The herds moved too far and too fast across endless, almost waterless country for walking hunters to follow. The Apaches prized deer, antelope, and bear for their meat and fine hides, and the bear especially for its fat. But these animals, while numerous, were not so easily killed as the staple buffalo.

Therefore, the first Plains Amerinds had to supplement their economy with other foods. They learned rudimentary agriculture from the harassed Puebloan cultures of the upper Rio Grande, and planted beans, maize, squash, and pumpkins, usually on small plots alongside the infrequent rivers and streams. While these crops ripened, Apache bands settled down for long periods in tent villages beside the waters. The Spaniards gave these semipermanent camps the name *rancherías,* which clung, just as they gave the Athapaskans the title Apache, from the Puebloan Zuñi word meaning "enemy." A Spanish explorer claimed to have seen a *ranchería* of "five thousand souls" on the headwaters of the Arkansas—probably a gross exaggeration.

Although they had one foot on the Great Plains and the other imperfectly affixed to the land, the Apaches clearly were the lords of high Texas. They dominated the region, and their power extended so far as they cared to bring it. Apache bands roamed as far as the Red River in northeastern Texas, and warred with the Tonkawas along the Balcones Escarpment. The areas they did not penetrate (the barren Karankawa coastal bend, the pine woods of the Caddos, and the Coahuiltecan southern triangle between the Gulf and the Rio Grande) they simply did not want.

The Apache society never climbed to true barbarism, but remained savage throughout its independent history. The borders of the rich bison plains acted as a brake upon agriculture. The culture continued half hunting, half farming, unable, or unwilling, to make the most of either way of life.

More important, Apache society was remarkably fragmented, even by Amerind standards. The "nations" the Spaniards continually wrote about were nations only in the Spanish descriptive term: they could not even be called true tribes. These uncommonly fierce warriors took no orders, not even from their own kind. Their social organization never evolved beyond the kinship band, nor political organization beyond the warrior and his sometime leader, the band chief. The T'Inde, or People, were only several thousands of men, women, and children who shared a common language and a common way of life—and in the Southwest, even these began to shatter and separate. The Navajos soon ceased to consider themselves Apaches, though they were still nomadic and Athapaskan-speaking. Important cultural differences developed between the Eastern and the Western tribal groups.

In this intensely democratic way of life all warriors were not only theoretically but actually equal. The center of society was the warrior and his personal family group: wives, children, slaves. Each family group was self-sufficient; brothers espoused dead brothers' wives, because in a society devoid of organization there could be no orphans or widows. There were both civil and war chiefs, but no one appointed them. A warrior became a chief through exploits, experience, and his prestige, which might attract other warriors around him. Warriors obeyed a chief implicitly on the war trail—a taboo with discernible logical roots—but they joined his war party purely at their own option. A chief who failed, or made unwise decisions, was quickly abandoned. Any male who disliked or disagreed with a band leader could find a more congenial band, or start his own. Thus chieftainship in the Apaches was elective in the truest sense.

Women were not exactly chattels, though they did the labor and were expected to serve warriors. They had to be protected and provided for. The Apaches, like most tribes, often found wives by raiding other Amerinds; children as well as girls were frequently carried away into captivity to augment the numbers of a band. While the first Europeans, accustomed to chattel slavery, called the Apache captives slaves, these prisoners were usually adopted into the tribe with full rights. Women were married to warriors; young males were allowed to become Apache warriors. Ironically, this Amerind lack of prejudice dismayed and horrified European women captives as much as the Apache custom of physical torture of captured males.

Apaches had strict moral codes and taboos, which made as much sense, in their circumstances, as such codes everywhere. Children were treated permissively until they began to develop; then they were taught the disciplines of work or war, according to sex. Boys were trained and hardened for the chase and fighting. Boys became warriors when they were old enough; the words man and warrior were synonymous.

The Apaches had a vague belief in a supreme being, but their religion was largely shamanistic and revolved around certain folkloric deities, such as the Killer of Enemies, a powerful, supernatural creature that befriended Apaches. The Apaches were children of the sun, sprung from mother earth, finely attuned to the mysterious world around them. They were more influenced by the land than by ideas. They did have a supernatural horror of the dead, or the spirits of the dead, an Athapaskan cultural residue carried down from the gloomy Northwest.

The only genuine socializing acts of the Apaches were the hunt and war, because here numbers and cooperation counted. But both were sporadic actions, and never cemented the bands together. Families and bands of Apaches lived beside each other along streams, or on the hunting grounds, but always in individual states of splendid isolation. The Apaches feared nothing that walked or breathed, and thus there was no external force, even danger, to hold the tribes together or to keep the People strong.

2

CORONADO
AND COMANCHES

I have done all that I could possibly do to serve Your Majesty and to discover a country where God our Lord might be served and the royal patrimony of Your Majesty increased. . . .

FROM THE REPORT OF DON FRANCISCO
VÁSQUEZ DE CORONADO TO THE KING OF SPAIN

IN the burning midsummer of the year 1540 a new and powerful invader burst into the American Southwest, not from the north but out of Mexico. This was the fateful expedition of Francisco Vásquez de Coronado, Governor of Nueva Galicia, who rode in golden armor at the van of a powerful army: more than three hundred Spaniards in shining steel, accompanied by conquered Mexican Indian allies and women, with priests walking in the apostolic fashion, and with the red and gold banners of Spain, and the Cross, going on before.

This, with Hernando de Soto's expedition proceeding further east, was the last and largest of the great *entradas* of the *conquistadores*. It was an extension of the Spanish conquest of Mexico, and for many decades afterward marked its limits.

The Spanish conquest of the New World began in the islands of the Caribbean discovered by Columbus. Here also began the Spanish colonization policy based on the *encomienda*. This was a grant of land, usually huge, to the Spanish conqueror who defeated the American Indian inhabitants and created a *tierra paz,* "pacified country." The grant included all the inhabitants as well as the land; they were to work for the *encomendero*

19

and provide him with revenues, a part of which went to the Spanish Crown. The system was an obvious extension of the social organization of feudal Spain, incorporating the far older Mediterranean concepts of latifundia, modernized by the newly powerful, centralized authority of the Crown. Because, from the first, Spanish exploration and colonization were both subsidized and rigidly controlled by the Crown, colonization became one of conquest, never settlement, which was always expected to return a profit to the central authority, and which was jealously guarded.

The islands of Cuba and Santo Domingo were conquered and enclosed in encomiendas, but immediate problems developed with the conquered Indians, who were supposed to work the land in the style of European peasants. The Circum-Caribbean tribes died rapidly under such treatment, both from Spanish barbarity and their own cultural inability to adjust to such a form of serfdom. The Spanish discovery of Mexico was the result not of a search for gold but of a hunt for new Amerind slaves.

While the economic needs of the island encomiendas were eventually filled by the importation of African slaves, the discovery and conquest of the Valley of Mexico turned the Spanish toward a new preoccupation: the hunt for gold. Vast quantities of gold were found in Tenochtitlán, the city of the Aztecs. This, however, was the accumulation of centuries; Cortés and others were disappointed to find that Mexico did not possess extensive gold deposits. But the chagrin was soon ameliorated by the discovery of virtually inexhaustible silver lodes, at Potosí and elsewhere. A stream of metal eventually amounting to billions of dollars was begun to Europe. Shortly afterward, Pizarro entered the Inca empire of Peru, and found a real storehouse of virgin gold, and the search was on again.

Thousands of Spaniards, eager for fame and fortune, accumulated in the New World. Spreading out from the central valley of Mexico, Spaniards quickly reduced the agricultural civilizations of the Middle American plateaus. The reduction was characterized by brutalities that with the passage of time historians tend to ignore, but in the end it was complete, and final. All traces of the higher Amerind culture were destroyed, though millions of Mexican Indians continued to live on in various stages of Spanish servitude. The efforts of genuine Spanish humanitarians, such as the gentle Bishop of Mexico, Juan de Zumárraga, to improve the harsh treatment of Indian serfs failed, and could not help but fail, in the face of Spanish nature and the *de facto,* if not always admitted, needs of the Crown. Both Charles V and his son, Philip II of Spain, were increasingly desperate for money to finance their enormous European wars.

It was not really possible to bring crippling pressures against the *encomenderos,* who operated mines and plantations with the sword and lash but who also fed millions of silver pesos into the treasury of the Crown. The Indians would not have performed these services without the severest repression, and Spaniards of the 16th century were enormously successful at adjusting humanitarian theory to economic reality. Nor was the policy without its genuine rationale, a rationale that kept the Spanish then and later from any sort of trauma.

All the Spanish conquistadores were marked in unusual degree by four dominant characteristics. They were ferociously courageous and audacious; they were the most successful explorers the world had ever seen. They were rapacious for fame and gold—but not, curiously, avaricious, because they seldom held what they seized but spent gold prodigally. They were utterly racist in an unconscious way, never doubting Spanish superiority, not even bothering to theorize it—but making the practice of their superiority none the less terrible to the victims. Finally, as a heritage of the Moorish wars, the Spanish were filled with the juices of religious crusade, the most hideous of all human conflicts. The bigotry that fueled the Counter-Reformation and applauded the Inquisition was frequently turned against French or Italian Roman Catholics—something not always understood; it was not a purely Catholic, but a remarkably Iberian, phenomenon that differentiated the Spanish Church from every church in Europe. The Moors left something behind in Spain besides the Alhambra and the Afro-Asian mustang: an unconscious cultural impulse toward expounding religious faith with the sword. To the Spaniard, intellectualism was for German monks; rationalism for cowardly Italians. The Spanish were not unique, or even peculiarly detestable, though a long line of Anglo-Saxon chroniclers have tried to make them so. Every age has a people or a culture that believes the shortest distance between dreams and goals is a bomb, a bullet, a gas oven, or a keen Toledo sword and burning stake.

Because the Spanish faith was real, and America had two continents filled with heathen, even the Spaniard who came for lands, riches, or to raise his station in life arrived with a ready, and unshakable rationale for conquest. It gave him a sort of moral superiority that not only dominated the battlefields of Europe for more than a century but lasted and stood the test of time. Destroyed empires and millions of dead Amerinds never haunted the Spanish conscience, because even the enemies of the Spanish were willing to give crimes against humanity committed with an ideological basis higher status than those done with no such excuse.

A superior culture—superior in the realities of organization and power —always has attempted, and always will attempt, domination of other cultures upon which it impinges. The means can be in question; the practice, never. Even Bartolomé de Las Casas and Juan de Zumárraga, who blenched at the documented atrocities done to *Indios,* never questioned the propriety of the conquest itself, or the inherent value of the advance of European civilization. They would have preferred that it be carried out in gentler ways.

Conquerors who question themselves or their values soon cease to be conquerors, whatever else they become. When Vásquez de Coronado, for example, who was known among the conquistadores as something of a legalist, asked his chaplain about the ethicality of impressing several Indian girls into his wife's service, he was told that while the captives were not technically subject to the Crown or laws of Spain, but free agents, if they were allowed to go free they would remain heathen and unquestionably burn in hell forever. However, under Doña Beatriz, the girls would learn both European civilized values and adopt the true faith, ensuring their eventual entry into Paradise. The real crime would not be in enslaving them, but in letting them go free. Coronado was satisfied; the girls were kept in bondage, and passed from recorded history.

Those who regarded this Spanish attitude as magnificent sophistry, however, had to face the fact that the Spanish were fully prepared to back it up with hot blood and cold steel, to the ends of the earth. Not only the Aztec and Inca states but the kingdoms of Europe quailed when the Spanish *tercios* of massed infantry received the *Adelante!* (Forward!), and the cavaliers of Salamanca kissed the cross-hilts of their swords and shouted the *Sant'Iago!* calling upon the patron saint of Spain. To the world of the 16th century, the phrase "fought like Spaniards" meant "fought like devils," and was the fighting man's supreme compliment.

Besides ferocity, battle skills, and an ultimate sense of moral superiority, the Spanish invaders were equipped to invade America in other ways. Accustomed to an arid homeland (most of the true conquistadores came from Salamanca), which was essentially a high plain devoid of timber and lacking large rivers, the Spanish found the mountains, deserts, and high plains of Middle America different only in degree. They left no record, as other Europeans did, of finding the Southwest particularly unlovely or forbidding; it was a land in which they could feel at home. More important, they were mounted, and rode the Spanish mustang, not the heavier, grain-fed northern European horse. *Caballero* and gentleman were the same word in Spanish, as in no other European language. Spaniards were horsemen, and they had a horse that could live in the new land.

The Spanish horse was a relict of the Moorish occupation. It had a strong dash of Arabian blood, crossed with North African barb; it was desert-bred and hardy. It could feed entirely off grass, and live from waterhole to waterhole.

It could carry the Spanish armor across the plains and high mesas, thus giving the invaders mobility and military advantage. In a pinch, the mustang could, and did, serve as food. Mounted on Spanish mustangs, armored, and armed with Toledo steel, a Spanish *entrada* could cut through any American Indian "nation" that lived.

Two events called forth the Coronado expedition of 1540. Spanish conquest and pacification of Mexico had reached nowhere near the Rio Grande, but New Spain was filled with adventurers eager to find new kingdoms in America. After all, Cortés had found Mexico, and Pizarro Peru. No one believed the possibility of conquerable empires was exhausted. Further, the Crown was insatiable in its demands for specie, which poured through Madrid without lasting benefit, to enrich the Flemish and German bankers who financed Spanish wars. The viceregal government of New Spain not only believed in the existence of more golden cities, but was prepared to implement the belief. When Álvar Núñez (who preferred to use his matronimic of Cabeza de Vaca, because it denoted higher social rank) returned to Mexico from his shipwreck on the Texas coast, after six years of wanderings among the Amerind tribes, he brought rumors of great cities in the north and west, and he reported to the Viceroy, Mendoza, that he had seen "signs of gold, antimony, and iron." Cabeza de Vaca had not actually seen gold or silver, and he had in fact suffered incredible hardships in captivity among the Karankawas and Coahuiltecans, who had not yet learned the expediency of killing a white man on sight. The "cities" the Texas Indians had told him about were the terraced cliff dwellings of the Puebloan culture of New Mexico. But the Spaniards, with the fresh evidence of Tenochtitlán and Cuzco, were easily led astray.

Mendoza sent a priest from Nice on the French-Italian coast, Fray Marcos, to investigate Cabeza de Vaca's rumors. His report was the second event that assured the Coronado invasion. Marcos had had vast experience in the New World: he had been on Santo Domingo during the final extermination of the natives, accompanied the brave Alvarado on his sweep through Guatemala, and claimed to have been with Pizarro in Peru. He was considered an old hand, who could recognize gold when he saw it, and he was ordered to scout the northern country with a Negro slave who had returned with Núñez.

Fray Marcos de Niza traveled an incredible distance, through modern Arizona and New Mexico, then fortunately relatively devoid of Apaches. Eventually he came to a city, which he scouted from a great distance. On his return, he informed Mendoza of a "land rich in gold, silver, and other wealth . . . great cities . . . and civilized people wearing woolen clothes." He had seen the wealthy city of Cíbola rising out of the desert, with walls and gates, surrounded by domestic animals whose names he did not know. Cíbola was larger than Tenochtitlán—which, before the Spanish swords and smallpox epidemics, had contained 300,000 Amerind souls.

Marcos did not claim to have entered Cíbola or any of the other six cities of that fabulous land. But before retiring he had piled a cairn of stones on a hill overlooking the Cíbola plain, and on the rocks erected a small Cross, taking "possession" of Cíbola and "the kingdoms that lay beyond it" in the name of God, King Charles V, and the Viceroy, Mendoza. No one in New Spain questioned the validity of that title, and Mendoza himself was enthralled.

From his own purse Mendoza put up the equivalent of two million dollars to finance an expedition to claim these northern kingdoms. The choice of commanding it—there were many claimants—fell on Francisco

Vásquez de Coronado, thirty years of age, already distinguished in rounding up *Indio* slaves and pacifying areas of Mexico, and more to the point, wealthy enough through his wife's inheritance to raise 50,000 *excelentes* to defray the costs. Thus Coronado and Mendoza, between them, invested almost four million modern dollars in this quest for gold. Coronado also seemed a reasonable choice in other ways. Not a great combat leader, he was still high-minded, and with a strict legalistic sense. As Governor of the Mexican province of Nueva Galicia, he had been an enormous improvement over the conquistador human beast, Núño de Guzmán, who once nailed a man to a post by his tongue, for insolence.

With an army of 321 Spaniards, five Portuguese, two Frenchmen, two Italians, a German, and one Scot, several hundred tamed Indians, several women, and some religious (the Spanish term for assorted clergy) including Fray Marcos of Nice, Coronado moved north. After five months of marching through the *despoblada,* hot, dirty, and hungry, on July 7, 1540, the army arrived on the upper Rio Grande, outside the city Fray Marcos had claimed was Cíbola.

Cíbola proved to be a sun-bleached rock pueblo of Zuñi Indians, containing perhaps two hundred dwellings all told. In front of this village several hundred Zuñi warriors were disposed warily for peace or war.

The army's notary, Bermejo, rode forward in armor to read a proclamation to the astonished Puebloans. They were decreed subjects of his Spanish Majesty beyond the sea, and further informed that they were now under the King's protection, with nothing to fear. Here, for the first time, a ceremony was enacted on North American soil that was to have many counterparts over the years.

The unimpressed Zuñis rejected the King's protection with a shower of arrows, all badly aimed. Coronado again tried for peaceful submission, but the Indians mistook this for temporization, and attacked. Coronado, tried beyond patience, sounded the charge. Flint-tipped arrows rattled off Spanish armor, but Toledo steel struck home. After two dozen Zuñis were killed, the others scampered up the ladders of their rock dwellings, and pulled the ladders up behind them, leaving the angry Spaniards temporarily baffled.

The Zuñis, and other Puebloan culture tribes, were not warlike. They were agricultural workers; they tended their beans and squash, and fought, rather ineptly, when Apaches or others failed to leave them alone. Their main defense was their stone houses, terraced into rock cliffs or hills. These had no doors or entrances on the lower floor. Upper stories were entered through trapdoors, and behind these walls the Puebloans had managed to survive.

The Spanish, however, pushed a siege with much more determination than Apaches. By means of a captured ladder they carried the bottom story after a bruising battle against arrows and stones. Coronado himself was struck down and saved from death only by his golden armor. But now, seeing the issue lost, the Zuñis made terms, and were allowed to retreat out of "Cíbola" to another fortress, to which their women and children had already gone. In the captured village Coronado found some food, which a chronicler admitted the expedition was then in greater need of than gold.

Coronado was enraged and heartsick with the disillusionment of the reality of Cíbola, which was actually the pueblo of Hawikuh. He and his cavaliers rained curses on Fray Marcos' head, if not to his face; and the priest was sent back to New Spain with a report to Mendoza. Shortly afterward, Fray Marcos suffered a stroke and died in disgrace, which most of the conquistadores considered was God's justice.

However, Coronado was not prepared to return to Mexico as a failure. Too much money and effort had gone into his expedition. There still might be kingdoms beyond Cíbola or gold somewhere in the country; even the *Indios* possibly could be a source of slaves. He determined to stay the winter and explore the land.

The Spaniards did explore, with almost incredible persistence. One of Coronado's lieutenants actually reached the Grand Canyon of the western Colorado after tracking across New Mexico and Arizona. Another expedition journeyed far to the east, across the Panhandle of Texas, and contacted a party of Caddoan Indians. These were Hasinai, but the Spaniards called them Tejas, from the Caddoan *Teychas,* meaning "allies" or "friends." This word was spelled "Texas" frequently in old Spanish, in which the "x" was substituted for a "j" sound, and from this mistaken tribal name the land derived its name. The Spanish seized all the Texas Indians' buffalo robes, at which the Indians wept.

Meanwhile, the Spaniards wreaked a bloody havoc on the Puebloan culture of the upper Rio Grande. Coronado proclaimed that the Hopis and other tribes were annexed in the name of the Crown; and those Indians who did not submit to the "will of God and the King" were treated as rebels.

On one occasion, after a Spanish rape of Hopi women, the Indians began to kill Spanish horses and mules. Coronado's lieutenant, Cárdenas, the same officer who had reached the Grand Canyon, reduced the rebellious pueblo with ferocity, and acting on Coronado's orders "to take no one alive, in order to impose a punishment that would intimidate the others," had two hundred stakes erected outside the Indian town. Then some two hundred Puebloan captives were brought forward. Realizing Cárdenas was going to burn them alive, the prisoners broke en masse. The Spanish cut down more than one hundred, and in the end only thirty unfortunates died screaming at the stake, in front of women and children witnesses. Coronado also sent over some chiefs or headmen from other villages to watch Spanish justice, and embraced Cárdenas after the executions.

During the winter of 1540–41 Coronado continued to reduce Puebloan settlements and partially destroyed or depopulated at least twelve. In one case fierce Spanish hounds were turned on a chief, in an attempt to make him confess to having gold. Though severely bitten, the Indian was unable to produce any precious metal.

Through these measures, the Coronado expedition broke all Indian resistance, and Coronado was able to proclaim the area along the upper Rio Grande *tierra paz,* or pacified country.

He found a Pawnee, from a tribe far to the east, in one of the Puebloan towns. This Indian, whom the Spanish named El Turco because he looked like one, talked about a great empire in the east, called Quivira. Here there were table services "of silver and gold." El Turco was probably party to an Indian plot with two aims: to get the murderous Spaniards lost on the Great Plains, or at least out of the Pueblo country. El Turco, though a Pawnee captive, was not a slave in the sense the Spaniards thought; he had been adopted, with full rights, into the tribe. But Coronado and his captains were eager to believe in hidden kingdoms, and in the spring of 1541 they set out, marching east.

They approached and climbed onto the vast escarpment thrusting up from the lower mesas of New Mexico and Texas like a palisaded wall. Coronado called this the *Llano Estacado,* which was unfortunately translated as "Staked Plains" by later English-speaking explorers, losing the real Spanish meaning of stockaded or palisaded high plain. Fortunately for him, Coronado entered the Llano Estacado early in the year, when the country was flowering and the water holes still full, and the bison herds covered the grass as far as the eye could see. Later in the year, the Llano became an arid semidesert, and had Coronado tried to cross the plains in summer he might well have left his golden armor gleaming about his bleached bones. But although the Spanish, guided by El Turco, more than once became lost on the Great Plains and had to march by compass as on the sea, they escaped serious hardship.

After marching for many days, the dirty, ragged Spanish came to Quivira. It turned out to be a miserable grass-thatched village of tatooed Wichita Indians. It was probably in modern Kansas, though some historians think that Coronado did not leave Texas. Coronado remained here more than a month, avoiding serious trouble with the Plains Indians, investigating about twenty other villages—all of which were mere accumulations of hive-shaped mud and grass huts.

The Spanish disillusionment was terrible. El Turco was tortured until he confessed he had lied to Coronado, and although he screamed out promises of another, richer kingdom further east, Coronado ordered him garroted.

After claiming the entire Wichita country in the name of the King, Coronado gloomily returned to the Rio Grande, this time led on a shorter path by Wichita guides. Unknowingly, he was at this time only about three hundred miles west of Hernando de Soto's contemporary *entrada,* which was seeking "Cíbola" from the east. De Soto had landed at Mobile Bay, fought his way through Indian tribes to Texas, finally raiding the graineries of the Caddoan Confederacy, which was as helpless before the warlike Spaniards as the Hopis. De Soto, unlike Coronado who had narrow escapes, was killed and buried in the river he discovered, the Mississippi. His party, reaching the Great Plains on the edge of Caddo territory, recoiled from them and returned east.

Back in Pueblo country, Coronado's men spent a cold and hungry winter. The Indians had fled to the mountains; they offered no services or assistance, and the Coronado expedition nearly starved. In April, 1542, Coronado, who had now been injured in a fall and who was sick mentally and physically, mumbled the order to return to New Spain.

The three priests with his army—whatever their cruelty and intolerance, they were entirely sincere—chose to remain to convert the Indians. None was ever heard from again.

On his way south, Coronado slaughtered some rebellious Mexican Indians in the Sonora Valley, then reported to Viceroy Mendoza. His reports, and his official letter to King Charles V, written in New Mexico, profoundly affected Spanish policy toward the north.

Coronado found Texas and the Plains a "country of fine appearance," not unlike Spain. It was "full of cattle" in numbers impossible to estimate —bison, which the Spanish ironically came to call *cíbolos*. It was potentially rich for farming, especially the lands of the Wichitas to the east. But Coronado warned that there was no gold or any other metal, and the Indians were uniformly a poor lot, who owned nothing and spent their miserable lives following the "cows." There was nothing to be exploited or turned to ready cash; thus there was nothing in it for the Crown.

The effect of this was that, although there were several *contra bandos* or unauthorized expeditions in the following years, Spain officially ignored the Cíbolo-Quivira country for many decades, and abandoned any attempt to colonize the Texas plains for 150 years. The violent, colorful, and cruel *entradas* into the land were successful explorations, but nothing more. They left a series of romantic accounts and a country dotted with exotic place-names, but in the 16th century Spanish ardor implanted no European seed in Texas soil.

Francisco Vásquez de Coronado, a magnificent failure as a conquistador, was relieved of his office of governor and brought to trial on charges of gambling, financial peculations, and "great cruelties upon the natives." The first two charges were patently trumped up, and ridiculous; the third was a crime under Spanish law, but not under the polity of an expanding Spain. A royal *audiencia* acquitted Coronado of all charges, and permitted him to die in bitter and disappointed peace.

In 1598, when the memory of Coronado's rape of the upper Rio Grande was only a legend among the Puebloans, the *Adelantado* Don Juan de Oñate, future Governor and Captain-General of the province of New

Mexico, which he officially named while pausing at the site of present El Paso, again carried Spanish power north. Again, Spanish armor, banners, crucifixes, and swords came into the land. Oñate repeated much of Coronado's old explorations, but he brought something new. Old Mexico was relatively "pacified" now, and Spanish civilization was creeping north, following the path of Indian corn thousands of years before. Four hundred soldiers and priests accompanied Oñate, the first to catch *Indios* and the second to Christianize them; but far more important, 130 families of soldiers went along. This was to be a permanent colonization, to set a Spanish peasantry in North American soil.

Most important of all, though Oñate could not have known it, were the seven thousand domestic animals in his train, which included three hundred Spanish colts and mares. Oñate was introducing European cattle, and the Spanish mustang, to the Great Plains.

The long history of the brutal conquest of the Puebloan tribes, the founding of Santa Fé and numerous missions, the dotting of the New Mexican country along the upper Rio Grande with Spanish villages and *ranchos,* the great revolt of the missionized Indians in 1680, and the hideous reconquest in the 1690's by Vargas, which implanted a stultified Mexican-Spanish culture, half Christian, half Indian, upon New Mexico for centuries, had little importance to the development of Texas. Oñate's introduction of horse herds in the Southwest did.

Because the Puebloan cultures were fixed to the soil, and the gardening Indians were already bound to labor, the Spanish conquest was feasible and relatively successful. Puebloans, unlike the more savage tribes, allowed themselves to be captured, and also to be enslaved, either by the friars at the missions or by *rancheros* who needed hands. Oñate himself, however, turned up something ominous when he ventured out on the Plains to the east. The Spanish struck a war party of Wichitas, and although the armored, mounted Europeans won through a bloody battle, the Wichitas neither surrendered nor showed any fear of Spanish might. They could be killed, but not, like the Puebloans, easily cowed. The only real advantage the Spaniards enjoyed over these more warlike people was the fact that they were mounted; they had both mobility and the terrifying shock of the cavalry charge.

No historian any longer believes that the *entradas* left horses among the Indians. Coronado and others lost horses, some of which went wild, and some of which were undoubtedly eaten—but the Indians learned to ride only when a permanent colonization of New Mexico placed a horse culture in close proximity to the High Plains. The Spaniards forced "tame" Indians to tend their horses, and such Indians naturally learned horsemanship. And some escaped into the mountains or plains, and took skills and stolen horses with them. In the first half of the 17th century, both passed into the hands of the Apaches and other tribes. What now happened was an absolute revolution on the Great Plains of North America.

The hardy Afro-Arabian Spanish mustang was a small, unlovely beast, rarely more than fourteen hands high. It was shaggy, and often looked ill-proportioned—but no horse on earth was more admirably suited to life on the semiarid, grassy mesas. It was incredibly hardy, unbelievably swift, used to little water, and could thrive on a diet of grass alone; the European horse required gentler handling and regular feedings of grain. Thus the bison country and the Spanish mustang were beautifully matched; no region in the world was better suited than the warm Southwestern prairies for such a steed. Either domestically or wild, they multiplied.

Sometime between 1600 and 1650, the entire horse knowledge of the Spanish was transmitted to the Apache tribes. And something else had happened: while the Spanish and Plains Indians at first were at peace with each other, the ancient feuds of the Apaches and the Puebloans were inherited by the conquerors, now living on the land of, and being the "protectors" of, the Puebloan Indians. In 1659, the appearance of a new, ominous cloud on the Spanish colonial horizon was first recorded—one that all the power of Spain in America never dispelled: Apaches—on horseback—were raiding Spanish-Indian settlements from both the northeast and west. Apache horsemen now could raid fast and far, striking deep into Spanish territory, and then run back to safety on the endless plains before they could be pursued. On one raid alone in the 1650's, Apaches carried off three hundred horses. They also made wholesale incursions on Spanish cattle, which they liked as much as buffalo.

The authorities of New Mexico mounted many an expedition in reprisal —but out on the vast and unmarked plains of Texas these punitive raids had no success. One expedition penetrated halfway across Texas, without finding Indians, who obviously did not care to be found. Another, ironically, had its own horses stolen and nearly perished. The fearful Spanish *Adelante!* was one thing to Puebloans or even Aztecs drawn up in ranks on foot with clubs or bows; it was laughable to Indians who could ride away in all directions. The Spanish war cry *Santiago!* was swallowed in the vastness of the endless West Texas plateaus.

For the first time in history, American Indians were equipped to meet European invaders on equal, and even superior, terms, on their own land. The history of the Southwest, so very different from that of Mexico or the English-settled Atlantic coast, was the result. Here, on the edge of mountain and semidesert, Amerinds were to hold out, and even conquer, for three hundred years.

The Puebloans had survived intermittent Apache warfare for many years, perhaps centuries, but now the conflict reached a new intensity. Apaches did not breed their own horses; with considerable common sense they came to look upon the Spanish *ranchos* as a permanent source of supply. Their sudden swoops and raids harried the conquered Puebloans unmercifully. Puebloan villages subject to the Spanish were wiped out. Mission Indians in some localities were exterminated. Caught between

Spanish priests who ordered them whipped if they failed to work or ran away and Apaches who tortured and killed them whether they ran or stayed, the Puebloans finally rose in one last, despairing revolt in 1680. One reason was the forced imposition of Christianity and the suppression of their age-old customs, such as the rain dance. More important was the failure of Spanish protection.

The Spanish fled the upper Rio Grande amid scenes of massacre and horror; only eleven priests and about 2,000 Europeans escaped. They left many thousands of sheep, cattle, and horses behind. The Puebloans had no need for horses, and the evidence is that these herds were traded to, or seized by, marauding Indians from the north and east. When the Spanish, ten years later, returned with fire, sword, burning stake, and smallpox, not only were the horses gone but many of the southern Pueblo villages were already wiped out by Apache terror.

On their vengeful return, the Spanish pragmatically solved the religious problem by closing their eyes to Amerind religious customs practiced alongside the Mass; the majority of the Pueblo tribes were thus never fully Christianized. *Apachería,* however, as they called the dread stretches away from the Rio Grande, could not be handled so simply. The ironic fact was that it was not the European Spaniards but another American Indian people who destroyed the power of the Eastern Apaches, drove them from the plains, and pushed the Western Apaches deep into the mountains of Arizona.

With the great horse dispersal of 1680, all the Texas tribes had learned about horses; the knowledge reached the Caddo country. But the knowledge, and the use, spread. A generation later, certainly by 1750, mounted Indians were common as far north as Saskatchewan in Canada. The seat of the horse culture, however, remained in the Southwest, near the Spanish *ranchos* on the edge of the Texas plains. Like a magnet, this area began to draw Amerind tribes, who heard of the new wealth to the south. In the year 1705 the first Utes appeared from out of the Rocky Mountains of Colorado, begging horses from the Spanish. With these Utes came a few representatives of another mountain tribe—who, significantly, stole a horse herd before they left, and thus rode victoriously away, and into bloody history.

The mountain Utes called these people by a word meaning "enemy." They called themselves The Human Beings. They were alien to the Southwest, speaking Shoshone, the language of the Rocky Mountains of the north; they lived somewhere beyond the headwaters of the Arkansas, in old Wyoming. They were a poor tribe, fruit- and berry-pickers, wanderers, and living off the scant game of the eastern Rockies. Their life was probably better than that of the Coahuiltecans in only small degree, and it was undoubtedly made worse by the bitter winters.

The designation in the universal Plains sign language for these people was a backward, wriggling movement of the index finger, meaning "snake." The Spanish did not call them the Snake People, but named them from the Ute word *Komantcia,* or Comanches.

The horse made the Apaches infinitely more dangerous to the Spanish frontier, but it completely revolutionized the entire life of the Comanches. They took to horseback as few people in history ever did; they not only rode, they made a fetish of the horse; man, woman, and child virtually lived in the saddle. Like certain other tribes that had lived on the fringes of the Great Plains—Dakotas, Cheyennes, Crows, Kiowas—they abandoned their old homelands and moved out on the plains themselves. The horse gave them freedom to become completely nomadic and follow the buffalo on its peregrinations; the buffalo gave them complete economic freedom. It became their food and clothing, meat and drink. Buffalo carcasses, hides, and bones, even buffalo chips, supplied everything the Plains Indian's primitive culture required, except the horse itself. Ironically, despite the popular belief, the horse created certain economic problems for the Comanche tribes. Horses became wealth, the only medium of value or exchange the Indians knew, and the Comanches never completely settled the growing problems of horse dowries and above all, horse inheritance, before their extinction on the plains. Understandably, the Comanches became the greatest horse thieves of them all, a palm universally granted them by every other tribe.

The Comanches had never planted a seed, and they departed their cold mountain meadows—a country of incredible beauty but equal harshness for primitive people trying to eke a living from it—with no signs of regret. Instead, they gloried in their horses, and in the Plains. The new horse culture was intoxicating, for both the hunt and war. Astride a fleet horse, the skulking hunter and berry-picker now had both freedom and power. The horse gave many Amerind tribes a deep sense of pride and superiority, but apparently no people absorbed this feeling more thoroughly than the Comanches.

Now, bands could gallop across the vast plains in the full panoply of war, or thunder alongside the fleeing buffalo herds, killing prime animals at will. Mounted, with horsedrawn travois, the entire tribe could take to the plains, follow the bison winter and summer, and live permanently, exhilaratingly, on the move. The new culture, the new technique, as so often happens, was now exploited not by tribes who had lived with one foot on the plains, but by people who had no vested interest in their old way of life. Utes and Wichitas and Apaches learned to ride; Comanches came to live on horseback.

The Comanche horse culture was assiduously copied from the Spanish. The Indians mounted from the right, a habit the Spaniards had acquired from the Moors; they used crude replicas of Spanish bits, bridles, and saddles, made of bison hide. The only new—and deadly—development of the Comanches was the adoption of a thong by which a warrior could drop

over the side of his horse while thundering in the circling charge, concealing and protecting himself from an enemy's shaft or bullet.

No one, not even the scientists who study them, knows why human
cultures develop in certain ways, and diverge along strikingly different
lines. All peoples seem to start at one time with about the same potential;
yet, even within subspecies of man, development rarely follows a similar
path. Anthropologists call these differences "cultures" and let it go at that.
The possibilities for cultural difference have been proven infinite, and climate or habitat is not determining, only limiting. Men make cultural
choices by band, tribe, and nation, then live or die by them.

Some cultures make fatal, if logical, mistakes. The Apaches had acquired a taste for beans and corn, and even after the coming of the horse,
they continued to live in their comfortable *rancherias* beside rivers and
streams. They sent warriors out to hunt the buffalo, but the tribes themselves did not cast loose their territorial anchors and move into the sea of
grass. And now once again, just as when the fearsome Eastern Apaches
had come upon the nascent Puebloan culture of Texas like a deadly plague,
there were bloody scenes of cultural life and death on the High Plains.

The stunted Comanches—they were always the shortest and smallest of
Texas tribes—reveled in new riches. There was suddenly meat for all, a
never-ending supply of food that only need be ridden down. A chief or
strong warrior who had had one woman now could take two, or three, or
four. There were few hungry winters, and no more infanticide. The dozen
Comanche bands swelled. Soon each could mount five hundred or more
warriors, and they pushed south toward the richest prize of all—the southern bison plains.

They brushed certain other tribes, Wichitas and Pawnees, out of their
way. Hardened by this skirmishing, the Comanches rode south, away from
the Eastern Rockies, following the herds and the sun, driving deep into
Apachería.

The Comanche hordes debouched on the Texas plains around the year
1725. They came like a thunderbolt; one historian compared them with the
mounted hordes of Genghis Khan. Man, woman, and child, they were
among the finest horsemen ever known. They were armed with the long
Plains lance and bison-hide shield, hard enough to turn a musket ball, and
they could fire a shower of arrows with deadly accuracy from the gallop.
There were probably more Eastern Apaches in those days than Comanches, but the Athapaskans were fragmented, and worse, they lived in
scattered, semipermanent villages. Comanches rode to war by the light of
the moon; their favorite tactic was to strike deep into enemy territory, two
or even three hundred miles or more away, kill, despoil, take prisoners, and
gallop back to the trackless plains.

Indian wars are sometimes thought of as a sort of game, courage rites in
which not much damage was ever done. Since Amerind society was not
highly organized anywhere, its warfare could not be highly organized or

regimented, either. Like all warfare, it developed customs and taboos, such as counting coups (touching an armed enemy in battle), taking scalps, and assessing the portents of one's "medicine," or luck. But this did not mean it was not vicious or bloody, or not fought for a basic purpose: to kill or despoil the enemy with the least damage to oneself, and to assume control of the hunting grounds, or land. The sum of a hundred small war parties in Apachería was the same as the result of pitched battles in Europe: someone won, someone lost, some people died or were driven away, some tribe took over the richest ground.

Disaster out of the north overtook the Apaches, who had been lords of the plains from the Balcones Escarpment to Colorado, and who had had villages in far Nebraska. Entire tribes, known to the Spanish in New Mexico, suddenly disappeared from history. Others lost their separate identities. All Apaches were driven from the plains.

The Western Apaches moved further into the *despoblada* of the Southwest, Arizona and New Mexico; the Eastern tribes were nearly exterminated. The Eastern remnants abandoned the High Plains. Some were pushed deep into the bare and ugly mountains of the Trans-Pecos region, and others scattered along the fringe lands just above the Balcones Escarpment. These survivors ceased to be a Plains tribe. They became hill and mountain Indians, and the remnants of several bands became the Lipan Apaches, or *Ipa 'Nde,* the people of Ipa's Tribe. They lost none of the primordial Apache fierceness, but they no longer possessed the former Apache power.

Ironically, however, pushed into greater proximity to the Spanish and other weaker tribes, such as the Coahuiltecans, they now became an even greater scourge to these neighbors. They had lost the rich hunting lands; now the Lipan Apaches had to live more and more by raiding. But their numbers were in decline, and the Lipans were already heading toward their final status, a despised, impoverished border tribe, before eventual extinction.

The hard-riding Comanches had seized a vast new kingdom: all the high plains and central plateaus of Texas.

This land, from the Llano Estacado to the Balcones Scarp, had the highest concentration of large game on the continent. The Llano itself was an eastern-sloping high mesa or tableland, rising out of the Great Plains. It began south of the Canadian River in the Panhandle; it was bounded on the east and north by another escarpment, the Cap Rock, and on the west by the beginnings of the Rockies. This was an immense, high, flat region, broken only by infrequent rivers such as the Brazos, the Colorado, and the Red. Its broad plains held scattered playa lakes, or ephemeral ponds, and here and there rose sand dunes.

To its south, the Llano Estacado merged imperceptibly into another plateau, the Edwards, which spread for hundreds of miles south and east, and which finally ended in the mountains of the Big Bend country—part of the Rocky system—and fell away along the Balcones Escarpment, below which there were coastal prairies and rolling savannah plains. The fringes of this great plateau formed the Texas hill country, where the streams and rivers carved deep canyons and dramatic scenery through the fraying limestone. On the southern end, the plateau was covered less with tall grass than with brush and cedar brakes on the rolling hills.

North of the Edwards Plateau, east from the Cap Rock to the Cross Timbers (west of Fort Worth), was a vast stretch of dark, level prairie land, ending in the belts of oak on the east.

All this area was part of the Great Plains of North America, which swept down from Canada to the Gulf. It was a rich section of the great American sea of grass, and it comprised the Texas bison range, one of the most splendid big-game regions upon the earth. Between the timber on the east, the mountains on the west, and the increasingly hot, dry savannahs of the south, this series of plateaus and prairies, hills and valleys, was incredibly fertile for grazing animals.

Over most of this land rain seldom fell more than twenty inches per year, and even this rain was scattered widely, randomly. There were wet years, also severe drouths. But the winters were mild, compared with the North, and the ground was endlessly green and flowering in the spring, or after summer rains. In late summer the oceans of deep grass—buffalo, bunch, needle, and gramma—burned off; the shallow lakes dried, and the country appeared desertlike, only to flower again. The bison roamed over immense distances, following the scattered rains and the grass.

Coronado was the first European to see the bison on its home range; the Spaniards were impressed with the incredible numbers. Coronado wrote that the number was "impossible even to estimate." There were certainly many millions of beasts; there were even individual herds that ran into the millions.

Besides buffalo, there were enormous numbers of other species: hundreds of thousands of pronghorn antelope, bounding and skittering over the grass; varieties of deer, peccary, hares and rabbits, turkeys and squirrel. The game drew predators, wolves, coyotes, and several varieties of cat, including the cougar or mountain lion. There were tall elk in the high river valleys, and lurking bear as well.

The Comanches scorned the snakes, rodents, birds, and smaller game. They killed deer for hides, bear for fat, but real men hunted the buffalo. They carved up this immense buffalo hunting ground into regions or territories for their several bands or tribes. The Penatekas (Honey-Eaters) took the southern fringe, the area lying north of the Balcones Escarpment. To their north, the Wanderers, Wasps, Liver-Eaters, and Buffalo-Eaters hunted. In the far north the Yap-Eaters (named for a Shoshone root) held sway. The Llano Estacado itself, perhaps the richest grounds, was the preserve of the Antelope Band, or Quahadis, known as one of the fiercest of Comanche peoples.

Within all these hunting regions the Comanches continually roamed.

They never erected fixed villages, and some parts of their domain were not visited for years. They did not have to stand on their land. Their reputation was sufficient to keep both Spaniard and Apache out.

Meanwhile, the horse revolution of 18th-century America set other tribes on the march. North of Texas, the Wichitas, a tribe with Caddoan roots, found themselves caught between the rising Comanche tide and aggressive Osages to their east. The Osages were now armed with French muskets, supplied by traders in Louisiana. The Wichita tribes gave up their grass-hutted villages in Kansas and drifted south, into east-central Texas. Fortunately for them, a French trader was able to arrange a truce between Wichitas and Comanches, and the Wichitas were permitted to settle just beyond the eastern limits of the Texas buffalo range. The main tribe located near the present Fort Worth. Other Wichita bands, Tawakonis and Wacos, moved further east, settling along the Brazos. The Wichitas, although mounted and buffalo-hunting, never made the complete leap culturally to the Plains. They continued to live in houses and planted corn; they were a people part way between the Comanche and the Caddoan culture.

Even further north, another great migration was taking place. The Kiowas, a small but very warlike people, had come out of the mountains of Montana and roamed the Black Hills of South Dakota. Here they came into collision with the terrible Dakotas, or Sioux, then moving west. The Kiowas, harassed by Sioux on the east and Cheyennes on the west, began to drift south. Like the Comanches, they had become a wholly Plains-living, bison-hunting tribe. Moving with them were the Kiowa Apaches— an Eastern Apache band that had, in the *Völkerwanderung,* remained Athapaskan-speaking but adopted Kiowa culture and alliances, probably in self-preservation. In the late 18th century, Kiowas rode into Comanche country.

There was war, but mutual extermination was avoided, almost by accident. In 1790 a party of Kiowas arrived at a Spanish trading station in New Mexico, to find a band of Comanches already dismounted and dickering. The European trader, probably out of sheer desperation, persuaded both tribes to agree to a truce. Out of this shaky agreement grew an enduring alliance; Kiowas and Comanches shared the High Plains hunting grounds, and soon were riding the warpath together against their common enemies, Apaches and Spaniards.

The Kiowas never moved entirely into Texas territory, but in a terrible sort of way they became a true Texas tribe: they were noted, even more than the Comanches, for distant raiding. Kiowas pushed war parties many hundreds of miles into hostile country, harrying both Indians and Europeans. One war band raided so far south they brought back descriptions of monkeys and parrots. They had reached either Guatemala or Yucatán.

By 1750, the Comanches had entered their golden age. The Apaches had abandoned the Plains, though they apparently became more warlike when they were forced into the borderlands near the Spanish settlements—the Spanish began to have even more trouble with them. The once-dangerous Tonkawas were badly dispersed along the Balcones Escarpment. The Wichitas lived on the edge of buffalo country by Comanche sufferance. The two other powerful tribes in Texas, Caddos and Karankawas, were no threat to the lords of the plains. Caddoans were well fed in their forests, and rarely ventured out; Karankawas were confined to the marshy, fever-ridden coast. The Coahuiltecans of the southern savannahs hardly counted.

Although the Spanish soon came into painful contact with Comanches, both in Texas and New Mexico, it is clear that they did not understand at first the full extent of the revolution that had occurred on the High Plains. It would soon be a Comanche boast that the warrior tribes permitted Spanish settlements to exist on the fringes of Comanche territory only to raise horses for them.

The Spanish in New Spain, however, only dimly aware of conditions on the northern frontier, were much more concerned with the advance of an old European enemy, France.

3

FLEUR-DE-LIS
ON THE FRONTIER

*The purposes of the French enemy seem to be to penetrate
little by little inland. This country is very suitable for doing
this. . . .* THE REPORT OF THE GOVERNOR OF NEW MEXICO,
DON ANTONIO DE VALVERDE COSINO, TO THE
MARQUÉS DE VALERO, VICEROY OF NEW SPAIN

FRAY Marcos de Niza and Francisco Vásquez de Coronado were not the last Europeans to hold aloft a crucifix, wave a sword, and take titular possession of the immensity of Texas. In the year 1682, the Frenchman René Robert Cavelier, Sieur de La Salle, added greatly to the romantic folklore of North America by navigating the Mississippi from the Ohio Valley to its mouth on the Gulf of Mexico. In the process he claimed ownership not only of the mighty river but of all the lands and territories within the river's and its tributaries' watershed, comprising two-thirds of the present continental United States, and some of Texas. La Salle, unaware that Hernando de Soto had already discovered and named the river the Espíritu Santo, called the country Louisiana, after Louis XIV, and the river the Colbert, for the French minister, thus covering all bets. The Indians, however, continued to call the stream *Misi Sipi,* or Big River.

La Salle returned to France, where he was uncomfortable after years in the woods, to find Versailles already fired by the schemes of a renegade Spaniard from New Mexico. This man, Peñalosa, had been badly abused by the Inquisition, and he petitioned Louis XIV for an expedition to take New Spain from the Spanish. However, it was La Salle, French, famous, and the greatest explorer that nation ever produced, who received a royal commission to return to Louisiana, build a fort at the mouth of the "Colbert," and to establish a French empire in the Southwest, so that "the cause of God may be advanced" among the Indians and "great conquests may be made for the glory of the King, by seizures of provinces rich in silver, and defended only by a few indolent and enervated Spaniards."

La Salle was far-visioned and indomitable. And the country did lie open; the Spanish had shown little interest in the lands between Florida and the River of Palms (the French term for the Bravo, or Rio Grande) since the time of Coronado and De Soto. Under the futile Charles II, Spain was rapidly declining in Europe, and the Puebloan revolt kept it thoroughly occupied in the west. However, Louis XIV, the richest and grandest monarch of Europe, was poorly prepared to give La Salle what he needed to make this dream come true. Almost no Frenchmen were desirous of seeking fame and fortune in the gloomy forests of the New World, and the French gentry much preferred to win honors by fighting Spain and Austria closer to home. La Salle received four ships from the King. But his army consisted of thirty "gentlemen adventurers" with nothing better to do, three friars, three priests, "some girls seeking husbands," and a hundred or so men dragged out of taverns, "the scum of the French ports." With this command, Sieur de La Salle sailed for America in the summer of 1684. The expedition was ill-fated from the start, but the fault, as always, lay in the men themselves and not their stars.

Robert Cavelier was brave, strong, and capable, thoroughly knowledgeable of the American frontier. But he was also dogmatic and introspective, shy and hard to get along with, qualities dangerous in a great leader of men. His associates thought him cold, arbitrary, and haughty above his station, because unfortunately La Salle was not born into the nobility of France. The naval commander of his expedition, De Beaujeu, and many of the aristocrats resented him as a self-made man. From the first, La Salle could not maintain full discipline among his officers—and his rank and file were men of the worst stamp that could be impressed in France.

La Salle and Beaujeu argued most of the way across the Atlantic. At the French island of Santo Domingo, Beaujeu disobeyed an order and put into a different port from the one La Salle picked out. It was a bad choice, "an evil place and with evil fruits," as Henri Joutel, La Salle's most loyal lieutenant, wrote. "The scum of the French towns" and "local females who were worse" engaged in "dissipation and vice," which left many of them with "loathsome diseases." Even the aristocrats were not immune; one, the Marquis de Sablonnière, tottered back on board with a raging case of syphilis. When the expedition set sail again, it was riddled with venereal maladies and tropical fevers.

One ship never arrived at all. The *St. François* was picked off by the Spanish navy. All its valuable tools and stores were lost, and worse, the crew gave the expedition away under judicious Spanish interrogation.

The King of Spain had issued an edict against all navigation by foreigners in the Gulf of Mexico. La Salle did not dare make too many landfalls; he sailed directly for what he hoped was Louisiana. But he was not a great navigator, and he forced De Beaujeu to bear too far west. The remaining three ships made land on the Texas coast at Matagorda Bay, missing the mouth of the "Colbert" by four hundred miles.

Here one of the ships was wrecked. La Salle, preferring to explore the country on foot, moved inland and built a wooden stockade, surrounding six small log cabins and one large one, on Garcitas Creek. He hoisted the fleur-de-lis, and called his post Fort St. Louis. He could not have selected a worse site. The coast held plenty of wild game and fish, but it was low, marshy, and unhealthy for an already sick and weakened company. Even worse, Garcitas Creek lay in the very heart of Karankawa country, who were utterly unlike the relatively civilized Caddoans and Natchez Indians of Louisiana.

From the very first day there was trouble with the local tribes. La Salle overawed them at first by ship's cannon, fired over water, and with musket shots—the Karankawas were unused to firearms. But the Indians were not cowed, nor could La Salle make friends with them. There was mutual robbery and murder; the Indians skulked about in the marshes, and picked off several Frenchmen. Some of these were probably ritually cannibalized in the *mitote:* tied to stakes, pieces of their flesh sliced off, roasted, and eaten before their eyes.

La Salle made explorations. He found a river, which he hoped was the Mississippi but was only the Brazos. Sickness and dissension increased in the company, and La Salle was able to maintain control only with the harshest and most arbitrary discipline. With supplies low, in hostile country, only the highest discipline and self-sacrifice could have saved the expedition. La Salle, with all his great qualities, could not evoke this spirit. Finally, realizing his situation was desperate, on January 7, 1687, La Salle gathered almost all the able-bodied men, who were not eager to go, and started on a difficult march to reach the Mississippi, then travel on to find French outposts in the Illinois country. He left Fort St. Louis under the command of the Sieur Barbier, with the sick and the women and children, including the Marquis de Sablonnière, who could no longer walk. Also left behind were the poor French girls who had come seeking husbands.

On the march, the "scum" of La Salle's party mutinied; some wanted to stay behind, others wanted to become "squaw-men" with the Indians. La Salle was treacherously shot from ambush. After fighting, in which several more French were killed, Joutel and seven others escaped, and these eight miraculously eventually reached the Illinois country.

Here, the courageous Italian-French captain, Henri de Tonty, who had been supposed to join with La Salle on the Mississippi, immediately set out with a party to rescue Fort St. Louis. He searched the Texas coast, but was unable to find anything. Sorrowfully, he returned north in 1690. Even had he found Fort St. Louis, he would have been too late.

Meanwhile, there had been considerable debate about the French expedition among the "indolent and enervated" Spaniards. The Viceroy of New Spain was aware of La Salle's invasion even before the Frenchman reached Matagorda Bay. A ship was sent to search the coast, but it was wrecked. This, and the continuing troubles in New Mexico, delayed positive action. In 1686 a land expedition was despatched. Hugging the coast, this party found the wreckage of one of La Salle's ships, but did not go inland in the area of Garcitas Creek.

In 1688, however, a filthy, bearded Frenchman dressed in skins staggered into a Spanish presidio in northern Mexico. He said he was Jean Henri, a deserter from La Salle. This arrival—the Spanish were incredibly sensitive toward any foreigners in their territory—galvanized Don Alonso de León, Governor of Coahuila, into action. Formerly, he had not discovered any use for Texas, which at this time the Spanish called New Philippines—but this did not mean that His Most Catholic Majesty's men were prepared to surrender the country to the Most Christian King without a fight.

Don Alonso marched up the Texas coast with one hundred soldiers and the indomitable military chaplain, Padre Damian Masanet. He crossed the Bravo (as the Spanish called the Rio Grande), then the Nueces, the Hondo, the Medina, and the Guadalupe, all of which he named. In April, 1689, the Spanish reached Fort St. Louis.

The stockade still stood, eery and deserted in the sunlight. Eight small ship's guns, still on their carriages, covered the approaches. As the Spanish cautiously approached, they stumbled over three rotting skeletons outside the palisade. One was female. Swords drawn, muskets cocked, they went in through the open, sagging gate. Inside was a scene of utter desolation.

Chests had been broken open and looted, furniture smashed. Some expensive, leatherbound books lay mouldering on the ground. Here and there was a broken gunstock. Crossing himself, Don Alonso ordered Padre Masanet to say the proper words and burn the place to the ground.

The Governor of Coahuila was diligent. An empty fort did not mean there were no French in the vicinity, and he began a search among the Karankawa tribes. In one filthy village he found two Frenchmen, who had deserted La Salle soon after arrival. They had gone native, smearing themselves with stinking fish oil like the Indians for protection against mosquitoes. Both men refused to join the Spaniards, and since the Indians were restive, Don Alonso let them be.

Further away, on the Brazos, De León discovered two more Frenchmen, this time in a village of the peaceable Caddoan Hasinai. These men told Don Alonso they had deserted the fort before a "massacre," after which they had returned and buried fourteen bodies. The Spaniard had these men put in irons.

In all, two more white boys and one Frenchwoman were found and rescued by the Spanish. De León pieced together a tragic story, from the youngest survivors, of the last days of Fort St. Louis.

After La Salle took the men and left, the settlement was consumed with despair. Smallpox broke out. With only invalids and women, the Sieur Barbier realized he must make friends with the Karankawas to survive. One day, when five Indians approached the fort, Barbier took a great, but he thought necessary, risk. He opened the gates to them and offered them hospitality.

As soon as the gates were open, however, a larger party of Indians who had been concealed in the bushes rushed the fort. The whites had no chance. Barbier and Sablonnière were hatcheted, all the other men killed. The whooping Karankawas carried off the children and many of the young Frenchwomen, who, to their horror, at last found husbands in the New World. For years the Spanish heard rumors of white women in Indian villages, but rescued only one.

De León destroyed Fort St. Louis so thoroughly that its exact location remained in dispute until recent years, when the site was rediscovered by archeologists. A steel spearhead was found nearby, stamped with the fleur-de-lis. That was all that remained of the French presence in Texas.

De León was still concerned over the danger of French intrusion. In 1690 he returned to East Texas with a larger party. Avoiding the unhealthy Karankawa coast, he erected a mission in the pine-wooded Caddo country along the Trinity River. This was called San Francisco de los Tejas, from the name the Spanish gave the Hasinai. European diseases, however, broke out among the friendly "Tejas" and the mission soon failed, which should have been an ominous warning for future efforts.

No further French threats arose, and in 1692 the Spanish again withdrew from Texas. But once again, French activity pulled them back, into the land they really did not want.

The accession of a Bourbon king to the Spanish throne had no effect on the bitter rivalry between French and Spaniards in the West. The Spanish remained intensely jealous of their fabulous empire, now measured in continents. But Spanish power was clearly on the wane, and Spain was not able to prevent French seizure and settlement of the Gulf coast, from Mobile to the Mississippi. D'Iberville placed the French flag here permanently. In 1713 the Sieur de Cadillac, Governor of the new province of Louisiana, sent the Canadian St. Denis up the Red River, to build a fort on "Spanish" soil. France's claims to Texas had never been officially relinquished.

Louis Juchereau de St. Denis, a Quebeçois, was to become a remarkable figure in the old Southwest, and a living legend to both the French and Spanish. Ironically, this Frenchman did more to bring Spanish colonization of Texas than any Spaniard of the time.

To understand the actions of St. Denis and Cadillac, it is necessary to understand the French approach to their Gallic empire of Louisiana. They were more interested in trade than territory; they were not much concerned with converting, incorporating, or pushing the natives off their land. Thus

their aims and approach were entirely different from either English or
Spanish in America. They did desire to keep the other powers out, and
they generally tried to use the Indians to their advantage in this. By the
18th century, the French had traders and officers voyaging from Canada
and Louisiana over the entire central part of North America, agitating
Indians and encouraging them to resist the other Europeans.

Louisiana was always envisioned not so much as a colony as a trading
enterprise. The settling of French peasants was accidental: the English
displaced French settlers in Nova Scotia, or Acadia, and these "Cajuns"
had nowhere else to go. Mobile and New Orleans were established as
trading posts, and St. Denis built his fort of Natchitoches in the Red River
Valley for the same purpose.

The French were far more successful than either English or Spanish in
getting along with North American Indians. The reason was obvious, since
the French approach neither displaced nor enslaved the natives. The
French were also aided by a curious characteristic, a tendency to blend into
the forests and even adopt much of the Indian way of life. They became the
greatest traders, trappers, and squaw-men of them all. Unlike other Europeans, they freely sold the Indians guns. Their influence over most tribes,
naturally, became very great.

Trading with Indians was profitable, but Louis de St. Denis envisioned
far greater profits for Louisiana—if the Spanish built settlements in Texas.
All trade between Spanish colonies and foreigners was strictly forbidden, of
course, but on the frontier such regulations were not only ridiculous, they
could not be enforced. St. Denis, and to some extent, Cadillac, were hopeful of a much more lucrative business if permanent Spanish garrisons could
be induced to remain in Texas.

Soon after founding Natchitoches, the young Canadian, who was always
described as gay, brilliant, and utterly charming, rode boldly across Texas
and appeared at Spanish settlements in New Spain. Though his arrival
caused consternation, he avoided arrest and even married the daughter of
an important military official. Then he talked the Spanish authorities into
the reentry of East Texas. In 1716 St. Denis, his wife, his father-in-law,
and a large party of priests and soldiers marched into Texas to found four
new mission-forts, including one at Nacogdoches, across from Natchitoches on the Red.

Although Governor de Cadillac was as charmed as the Spanish with St.
Denis, he and other French officials became a little concerned about the
young man's initiative. Cadillac wrote dryly that St. Denis seemed to be
acting in his own service as much as that of the King. Cadillac himself,
however, was on the payroll of Crozat, the French merchant who had been
granted a trading monopoly for Louisiana, and St. Denis undoubtedly was
prepared to include the Governor in whatever "smuggling" profits that
accrued.

Now St. Denis, from Natchitoches, set up a smuggling (as all trade with the Spanish had to be classified) business with his father-in-law across the more or less accepted boundary between Louisiana and Texas. St. Denis, actually, did more than anyone else to define this boundary. Both French and Spanish claims widely overlapped, but despite continual tension a sort of gentleman's agreement came about. The Sabine was considered the eastern limit of active Spanish influence, while French power halted at the Red. St. Denis himself was wholly unconcerned with the Most Christian King's rights to Texas; on one occasion he unilaterally offered to cede to the Spanish all territory west of the Mississippi—a cession quite beyond the powers of the commander of Natchitoches.

But the regime he had charmed in New Spain changed; a new viceroy and a new governor of Coahuila took office. On a visit to Texas on business St. Denis was rudely arrested for trespass, and sent under guard to the City of Mexico. Here it was decided to incarcerate him in Guatemala. St. Denis, however, made a daring escape, stole a horse, and galloped north to Texas. He stopped at his father-in-law's post long enough to pick up his wife, then crossed the Louisiana border. Cadillac happily reinstated him to his old command. St. Denis had tremendous influence among the Caddoan tribes of the Red River Valley; this neither the Spanish nor the French authorities ever forgot.

Because of this power among the Indians he kept the Spanish in continual alarm. He also traded the Indians a large quantity of guns and ammunition, and this caused them more than alarm. In 1720, the French-armed and allied Pawnee defeated a Spanish expedition on the Platte, in the Nebraska country. A not very serious border war broke out, and on one occasion St. Denis captured a Spanish fort with only seven men. The Spanish maintained far more troops in East Texas in these years than the French had across the river, but French influence with the Caddoans—who came armed at St. Denis's call—more than made up for the difference.

St. Denis continued to harass, frustrate, and trade with the Spanish on the sly for more than twenty years. He made an enormous fortune and lived in grandee style. Louis XV knighted him a Chevalier of St. Louis. Dozens of legends grew up about him, none of which were important to history, including the story that the Viceroy of New Spain, the Conde de Fuenclara, cried out *"Gracias a Diós!"* (Thank God!) when he was dead. Louis de St. Denis, who only wanted to keep the Spanish off balance and doing business, died in bed in 1744.

His place in Texas history was secured, not by his daring or smuggling, or even his establishment of borders, but because he directly caused the King of Spain to found a number of Texas forts and missions. One of these eventually came to be called the Alamo.

4

THE FAITH AND
THE FAILURE:
THE MISSIONS

I see that for a century the faith has been planted in these provinces, and that nothing has prospered . . . if we had only expended the money that we spent fighting the Apaches, since God took them to be an instrument to punish our sins, in building new establishments, where would not be raised the standard of the holy cross?

PADRE FRANCISCO GARCES, DIARY OF THE YEAR 1775–1776

Most Excellent Señor: The time has come when the Supreme Powers simply must understand that the Comanches, Lipan Apaches, Wichitas, and other small bands of savages have not only hindered the settlement of Texas . . . but for two centuries have laid waste to the villages and committed thousands of murders and other crimes. . . . These depredations have dressed whole families in black, and filled their eyes with tears.

The Government must realize, that with utterly baseless hope and with paralyzing fears, the cowardly governors and ecclesiastical councils have· presided over enormous crimes, under the deliberate and infantile notion that some day these barbarians will be converted to the faith, and reduced to their dominion. To this perverse view and policy, countless victims have been and are still being sacrificed.

THE REPORT OF THE OFFICIAL, TADEO ORTIZ

THE Spanish empire in America was an empire very much in the ancient Roman sense. The Spanish came, conquered, displaced the Amerind ruling hierarchies, threw a patina of Hispanic civilization over the masses, and incorporated new provinces into the Spanish state. Wherever the natives had already been broken to division of labor or the plow, as in Mexico or Peru, the Spanish installed themselves as a new elite. The system was successful. Lima and the City of Mexico had brilliant societies in the 17th century, and the Spanish empire accomplished everything possible for an empire to do. It defended itself adequately against outside enemies; it lasted three hundred years; and it passed on to a vast area the Spanish language, ethic, and religion. It left its successor states immense problems: in class structures, theory of government, land tenure, and church-state relationships. But these were all problems of Hispanic society itself since the Middle Ages. Spain could only transmit its own values. It could not impart to the New World ideas, ethics, or practices Spaniards themselves did not value or possess.

But the Spanish system was incorporation, not colonization. When Hernán Cortés was offered land in Cuba, he snarled that he had not come to the New World to till the soil like any peasant. This angry statement summed up both the philosophy and the polity of the Spanish conquest. Spain never intended to send out large numbers of settlers—emigration was rigidly controlled—and except in rare cases, those who arrived expected to live not off the soil but off the resources of a subject native population.

Although ultimately under the authority of the Crown, the early *entradas* and conquests wreaked enormous havoc among the hapless Indian civilizations. The mass cruelties of the conquistadores in Mexico and Panama had never had the sanction of the Church, and over the centuries the Spanish Church worked assiduously to prevent the wholesale extermination of new Christians by exploiting *encomenderos*. The Church did not question the conquest; this would have been foreign to its value system, and it did not dispute the undeniable fact that incorporation of Indians at best permitted them only third-class citizenship within the Spanish state. Hispanic civilization was rigidly class-structured, hierarchically centralized; ethnocentrism —the notion that one's own culture is immensely superior to all others— neither began nor ceased with imperial Spain. Spanish clergy did not and could not represent values foreign to Spain; at all times and in all places it is not possible for a clergy to be really different from the society from which it springs.

The form of incorporation in Mexico, the *encomienda* (later, *hacienda*), worked brilliantly for the Spanish in south-central Mexico on the wet, fertile plateaus of the older Indian civilizations. By 1575, there were more than 500 *encomiendas,* producing 400,000 silver pesos per year in revenues, and another 320 estates yielding 50,000 pesos directly to the Crown. But as Spanish power worked north, beyond the limits of the older Aztec sphere of influence, the *encomienda* became only marginally successful. Although it was adapted to include the *estancia de ganado,* or cattle ranch, the great problem was that the system was running out of amenable Indians.

In 1720 the *encomienda* was officially abolished, although the great estates it had created remained, then and later, as an enormous social problem for Mexico, not so much because of their size but because of their peculiar, two-class human structure. The new colonial system was essentially an adaptation of the old—cross and sword, but without the slave-herder.

Since settled, agricultural Indian societies capable of Hispanicization and incorporation did not exist on the northern frontier of Mexico, the aim of Church and State, synonymous now in Spain, was to create them. Presidio-missions were to be erected beyond the frontier of settlement. The mission, conducted by members of a religious order, had several tasks: to get the Indians to congregate around it, to Christianize them, and to teach them a new, settled, agricultural way of life. The presidio, or garrison-fort, accompanied the mission to afford the religious and new Christians protection from the as-yet-untamed, and also to help keep the mission Indians in hand. This system was called, in Spanish, "reducing," and Indians civilized through it *reducidos,* or the "reduced." When a tribe was sufficiently reduced to become useful subjects of Spain, then other Spaniards could be sent among them to perform the functions of the middle classes and the elite; a town could be built, and a potentially wealthy new province arise. It was considered that the initial process would require about ten years.

Just as the early incorporation of New Spain was based entirely upon the Indian at the bottom, the incorporation of Texas into New Spain was completely dependent upon finding available savages to reduce.

The mission was thus not a private organization, but fully an agency of the State, and the missionary priests were agents of the Crown. The Crown in fact completely subsidized them, as well as sending and paying the essential soldiery. The Crown would receive its own reward when the reduced were hard-working, tax-paying citizens, subject to military service and other duties, with about the same privileges and status as the peasants of Old Spain.

The various ecclesiastical councils of Spain and Mexico were enormously proud and hopeful of this system, which was certainly a humanitarian improvement over the former creation of *tierra paz* in the New World. It should be noted that even in the late 17th century the Spanish military, particularly those who had seen service on the northern frontier, were not very sanguine about making peaceful shepherds out of Apaches. But the ecclesiastics argued forcefully that soldiers always took this attitude, and their counsels carried.

The Spanish colonial system of the 18th century has always won a certain admiration, and it has been regarded sentimentally because it was the only system that ever envisioned any place for the Indian. It was carefully thought out; the Spanish put more attention, money, and effort into it than any contemporary European power gave its own system. But at its inception it was a triumph of ideology over reality. The Spanish ecclesiastics made assumptions that were false. It was a beautiful, humanitarian idea, designed to create a lovely, paternalistic Spanish-Indian culture, and it was an idea that never really died in Spanish-Catholic hearts. But, whatever its eventual social faults, there was one thing wrong with it. In Texas the Spanish would come in contact with types of Amerinds they had never had to face before, and all their dreams and illusions about savage mankind—and the nature of civilizing European man—would fall to crashing ruin.

Enormous responsibility rested upon the Spanish missionary priests and friars. They were not only expected to be men of God, but persuaders, teachers, civilizers, and law-givers. Theirs was the burden of not only carrying the Cross into heathen lands, but also the whole fabric of Western civilization. They, not the soldiery, held ultimate responsibility for planting the lions-and-castles, the red-gold banner of Leon and Castile, over a vast new empire. For generations they had argued and pleaded for the chance. Now, at the dawn of the 18th century, with secular Iberia in steep decline, they represented the last, best push and promise of Hispanic civilization; they certainly possessed more vigor and determination than any other Spanish class. Probably they deserved a better fate.

The first missionary effort in Texas came in 1690, following the furor caused by La Salle's landing at Matagorda Bay. It was abortive. But its results were studiously ignored in later years in the ecclesiastical councils where concepts, not experience, remained dominant. But in its appalling prophecy for later years, it is worth exploring.

De León returned to East Texas in 1690 with a large body of soldiers and priests, determined to found a permanent colony to halt further French exploration. He constructed a log mission, San Francisco de los Tejas (from the name by which the Spaniard mistakenly called the confederacy of the Caddoan Hasinai), in just three days. This structure was raised on the Trinity River, about fifty miles south of Nacogdoches, deep in the pine forests.

The Hasinai had many villages in the vicinity, where they lived in relative comfort, planting corn and vegetables in spring, hunting and fishing in the rich region in other seasons. The Hasinai lived a secure, basically lazy life. They did not often venture out on the dangerous plains to the west, and they were the most numerous tribe in Texas. They were raided now and then, but their existence was hardly in question. Horsemen did not care to plunge into the dense, dank forests; Hasinai and the Plains tribes lived in utterly different worlds, which hardly impinged.

Secure and basically unwarlike, the Hasinai welcomed the Spaniards into their country. Hundreds came to watch the priests dedicate the mission, and to celebrate the colorful Mass. A people with a strong, but rudimentary, sense of pageantry, they were impressed. They listened gravely to the priests, presented the soldiers with corn and other foods, and promised to give thought to the matter of becoming mission Indians.

But they gave it interminable thought, which made the dedicated religious orders restive. Hasinai seemed more amused than frightened at the idea of year-round work in the fields, and at the argument that they should cease being warriors altogether, now that the soldiers were on hand to protect them. They lived in an essentially timeless world, and while they agreed the Spanish arguments had merit, they appeared in no haste to begin making changes.

Now, a difficult kind of problem arose, complicating relations. The Spanish soldiery, many months on the march and away from the comforts of New Spain, began instructing the Caddoan girls in things other than the Christian faith. This put the garrison in bad odor not only with the Indians but with the friars, and there were many bitter recriminations.

Then, the Spanish unintentionally transmitted a lethal epidemic to the neighboring villages. What the Europeans called normal childhood diseases, such as measles, were fatal pestilences to all Texas Indians. The nearby Hasinai were decimated. The survivors simply avoided the mission, and those who had congregated melted back into the forests.

The priests requested the soldiery to bring them back, but now the soldiers did some procrastinating of their own. The Caddoans were getting restive, and they began to steal horses and cattle from the garrison.

The departure of the friendly Indians precipitated crisis. Not only was the purpose of the mission failing, but the mission was dependent upon the natives for its food. The supply bases in New Spain were many hundreds of miles to the south. The priests' job did not include farming for the garrison, and most of the soldiers had entered the King's service precisely to avoid that kind of labor. The military grew increasingly unruly and angry, and as the religious reported, "arrogant and intractable." They wanted to go out and skewer a few of the Hasinai to teach the rest hospitality.

While the two groups of Spanish elite argued bitterly over ways and means, the Caddoans died of disease or disappeared. The French menace, meanwhile, seemed to have evaporated. In 1692, by full agreement between the religious orders and the military, the mission of San Francisco de los Tejas was abandoned, and the Spanish marched back to Mexico. Both parties forgot about Texas for more than twenty years.

Again, it was the French who incited action. St. Denis's appearance in New Spain may have interested his father-in-law, Captain Ramón, in potential smuggling profits, but it stirred the Marqués de Valero, the Viceroy, into calling again upon the orders to reenter Texas. Again, the Crown raised soldiers, put up money, and authorized an extensive colonization project.

This time the Spanish presence was to be permanent. A great semicircle of presidio-missions was planned to stretch up from northern Mexico, generally reaching across the middle area of Texas on a line from Laredo to the Sabine River. Both the Great Plains and the fever coast were avoided by the Spanish; both were unhealthy. At this time, the Gulf Coast of northern Mexico was not settled by the Spanish, for climatic reasons, and the impetus of Spanish colonization came up through central Mexico to skirt the central plateau of Texas along the Balcones Escarpment.

One mission was planned and planted on'the north Texas coast, at the mouth of the Lavaca, with two purposes, to reduce the Karankawas, and to provide the Spanish with a settlement near the sea. This site, however, was quickly moved inland, though still in Karankawa country.

Three missions were organized for the Hasinai area. The Caddoans were the most civilized of Texas Indians, and therefore held the most promise for quick reduction; also, their territory overlapped that of the French in Louisiana. East Texas required greater attention.

A mission was sited in the Tonkawa territory, midway between the East Texas presidios and the way-station mission of San Antonio de Valero, built in 1718 near the headwaters of the San Antonio River, some 150 miles northeast of the borders of Coahuila. The San Antonio mission was not at first considered important, except as a feeder-station and backup for the main effort further east.

Two more missions, Rosario and Refugio, were planted in south Texas, along the crescent coastal bend.

The planning showed that each known Texas tribe (Caddoans, Tonkawas, Karankawas, and Coahuiltecans) was considered in the scheme of things. At this time, in the first years of the 18th century, there was no real contact between the Spanish and the Apaches of the higher plains in Texas.

Although many of them were pushed with great persistence, backbreaking labor, and heartbreak, all but one of these missions failed utterly. Each had a detailed and sometimes romantic history. But in the sweep of important events, they can be bypassed briefly: none achieved its primary mission of reducing any important Indian tribe, or increasing Spanish power.

The three missions among the Hasinai were balked by two problems. The Caddoans refused to adopt Christianity and Spanish serfdom of their own will, and the French, with considerable cleverness, gave them both arguments and the power to resist. French traders freely sold the Hasinai firearms, and the Spanish military always decided against trying to congregate the confederacies by force. This trade greatly embittered the Spanish, whose policy was always to deny Indians firearms, even their allies. But there was nothing they could do about it.

So long as St. Denis lived, he exercised great influence over the Hasinai, and kept them from adopting Spanish ways. Afterward, other Frenchmen took up the task. But meanwhile, ominously for the Caddoans, both French and Spanish diseases were debilitating the sedentary tribes. There was no stopping the spread of measles, smallpox, and other European maladies so long as foreigners moved among the Indians. By the middle of the 18th century the Caddoans were in rapid decline, and by the end of the century they had almost disappeared. Unwittingly, and certainly unwillingly, the good friars helped exterminate the people they had come to save.

The Tonkawa mission never attracted any Indians at all. The nomadic Tonkawas ignored it, and the soldiers with the mission avoided locating Tonkawas for the padres to proselyte.

The two missions on the south brought a few of the grubbing Coahuilte-can bands together. But these Indians tended to stay so long as they were fed or offered gifts. When they were put to work, they either died out quickly or ran away.

The Karankawa mission, Espíritu Santo, actually persuaded a number of the fierce coastal tribe to gather about the fort. This attention, however, was rewarded by the now usual lethal infusion of epidemics. The Karanka-was fled back into their coastal marshes, and killed any Spaniards who came after them. The Karankawas ever afterward avoided all contact with Europeans, but they had already received a fatal blow. European disease had been introduced, and, like the Caddoans, the Karankawa numbers were soon in rapid decline.

In east Texas, especially at Nacogdoches, across from Natchitoches (the French rendition of the same Hasinai name), tiny Spanish settlements did take hold around the forts. But these were based on Spanish, or Spanish-Mexican, settlers who emigrated to them and built small, struggling communities. Without an infusion of Hispanicized Indians, these could not grow large, and they were crippled by the Spanish intransigence toward any kind of legitimate trade with their French neighbors. This Spanish determination to direct all commerce in Texas back toward New Spain, hundreds of miles away across unsettled and savage territory, made any kind of economic growth around the presidio-missions impossible.

Had Spanish settlement in Texas been allowed to seek and make contact with its natural economic partner, Louisiana, history might have been somewhat different. But the Spanish wanted the best of all possible worlds: a purely Hispanic province of Texas, from which all profit accrued to their own Church and State.

The tiny mission of San Antonio de Valero, founded in the same year the French began New Orleans, developed differently from the failures all around it. San Antonio de Valero (named for the Viceroy) started with certain advantages. One was its location, the closest of all Spanish missions to New Spain, only 150 miles away from border to border, though in real terms—settlement to settlement—this distance was doubled.

San Antonio lay at the headwaters of the San Antonio River, in a region that rose up out of the dusty, cactus-studded lower Sonoran plain like a green oasis. A Spanish friar described it eloquently as "the best site in the world, with good and abundant irrigation water, rich lands for pasture, plentiful building stone, and excellent timber." The area lay just below the Balcones Escarpment, which gave it several advantages; a mild, dry, healthful climate, with pleasant winters and unhumid, quite bearable summers, somewhat similar in fact to the climate of Spain; and it was the hunting ground or preserve of no powerful tribe of Indians. It was the more or less permanent territory of a Coahuiltecan band, but Coahuiltecans were no danger to Spanish friars.

With plenty of water, numerous groves of trees around the streams and springs, solid native limestone for building, and several miles of rolling, rich soil between the edge of the rocky Edwards Plateau on the north and the stretches of dry *brasada* to the south, the area at the headwaters of the San Antonio was a sheer delight to the Spaniards. They never intended San Antonio, with its admittedly sparse native population, to become the nucleus of their northernmost province, but it was no accident that this happened.

Although a Mass had been said in the area in 1692, the first permanent settlement began in 1718, when St. Denis and his bemused Spanish cohorts passed back through. A mission was established, to be a way station between New Spain and the East Texas missions that St. Denis inspired. The friars who founded San Antonio were Franciscans, but the mission itself did not begin there. The clergy, and the commission, had been moved around from several different sites in northern Mexico, called variously for St. Joseph and St. Francis, before the Marqués de Valero decided to dispatch them across the Bravo into Texas. In Mexico, the religious had picked up a considerable band of Coahuiltecans, of the same blood and language as the Texas tribe. These accompanied the mission to San Antonio de Valero. They gave the Franciscans an immediate advantage—they were already in business, with tame Indians, who could tell the others about the good things attending the Spanish-Indian way of life. The partly Hispanicized Coahuiltecans did bring some others into the new mission.

In the furor that followed St. Denis's arrest and escape from Mexico in 1721, Valero took action that strengthened his namesake mission. He incorporated the area around San Antonio into the province of Coahuila— thus removing it entirely from New Philippines, or Texas—and sent a force of 54 soldiers to build a strong fort, or presidio, nearby. With the soldiers also arrived a total of four Spaniards, who came north to stay, as settlers.

Nine men and a corporal were assigned to guard the mission, while the rest of the soldiery began, with no great enthusiasm, to erect a stone fort, a few miles away. They named it Fort San Antonio de Béjar (alternately Béxar), after the Duke de Béjar, a brother of the Marqués de Valero, killed fighting the Turks. (All Spanish names in the area were to include that of St. Anthony of Padua, because the first Mass said by Spaniards here was dedicated to this Italian.) As a matter of fact, during the next century this fort was never completed, though the friars, with much greater zeal and energy, put up a series of stone missions along the San Antonio River.

The San Antonio complex, mission and fort, continued to collect people from here and there. By 1726, there were two hundred men, women, and children in the area, not counting Indians. Those Indians who had come in from the alternately hot and cold drab Sonoran plain were progressing nicely, or so it seemed. They showed no great interest in steady work, and some of their free-and-easy sexual customs were distressing to the stern padres, but, as one said, Rome was not built in a day.

The Franciscans felt so optimistic—they alone of all the Texas missions were going to meet their ten-year deadline—that they petitioned the Viceroy and King Philip V to send settlers into the country, to found a true Spanish town to grow up contemporaneously with the adjoining fort and mission.

What occurred in San Antonio from 1718 onward is vital to the understanding of all Spanish-Mexican history in Texas. With the hindsight of history, it is easy to mark the mission concept of colonization as a failure; but what took place in the San Antonio region for the next century showed all the virtues, and all the inherent faults, of the entire Spanish colonial effort in North America.

By the 18th century, the Spanish religious orders in the New World had had long experience with the Spanish military establishment, and also a long period of trouble in the presidio-mission colonization of north Mexico. All the lessons of the East Texas fiasco of 1690–1692 were not forgotten. When the Franciscans at San Antonio de Valero wrote the Viceroy requesting a Spanish garrison, they made it very clear they wanted a particular kind of soldier for the Texas mission frontier. He must be of the pure Spanish race (this should not be laid wholly to prejudice; the mixed bloods at this time had an anomalous social and legal position in the New World, and could not be expected to make the best soldiers); of irreproachable moral character, and married. Families should accompany the troops. The friars did not want more mixed bloods bred on the frontier, especially out of their Indian charges. They also specified they wanted no *lobos* or *coyotes,* nor any *mestizos.*

Settlers sent from Spain should also be of high character; otherwise, they would have a bad effect on the new Christians.

Of course, it was quite beyond the powers of the Marqués de Valero to find a garrison wholly composed of men of high moral character, in New Spain or anywhere else. All Mexican soldiery was now mercenary, usually having joined the ranks to escape some worse fate, such as hanging or hard work, and by this time the martial ardor of the gentlemen of Spain had largely cooled. The ranks of the Viceregal army were filled with a combination of gutter-Spanish and "so-called Spaniards"—the Marqués de Rubí's bitter phrase for Mexicans who were certified as Spaniards. The infusion of Indian blood was very noticeable; and much worse, the discipline of Spain was considerably less than that of other European powers. The conquistadores had been an undisciplined lot, but they made up for it with fierceness, fanaticism, and a real taste for war. Walter Prescott Webb compared the blood of 18th-century Mexican soldiery to ditchwater, which may be going too far; but certainly, the cutting edge of Spanish fury that had accompanied Coronado was gone.

The record shows the Franciscans of San Antonio de Valero were much chagrined by the quality of the garrison they got. They informed the head of their order in Mexico that half of the soldiers arrived unmarried, and most of those who were had conveniently left their families behind. Furthermore, there were definitely "half-breeds, outlaws, and no-goods" among them.

The troops themselves were hardly enchanted. The padres refused to allow the mission Indians to perform services for the garrison; in fact, they banned all contact. Denied labor, the garrison never did get a presidio built—while the missions themselves put up impressive and enduring stone edifices—and when the Franciscans moved San Antonio across the river to give the Indian women more security, relations completely deteriorated.

Meanwhile, the Coahuiltecan Indians, who at first had been amenable and shown so much promise, became a great exasperation to the strong-willed, hard-working friars. The Coahuiltecans did not resist conversion, and while some ran away, most were willing to congregate. They were placed under the stern Spanish-Catholic moral code; the men were taught to hoe the fields, and the women practical handicrafts. The Franciscans were men of energy, and no little talent—but from their letters and reports, it is apparent that the Indians simply could develop no initiative, or any joy in their work. At all times, to get anything done, friars had to stand over them, and punishments for malfeasance or laziness were frequent. The Coahuiltecans could understand punishment, but they seemed unable to grasp the need, or rationale, for constant, disciplined labor. From time immemorial, the tribes had eaten well in fat years, starved in the lean. Ten years—or two hundred years—were too few to erase Coahuiltecan tribal memory or to bring them into agricultural civilization. The paternalism of the padres was also deadly—but this was second nature, both to the Church and Spanish nature, and no Franciscan recognized it as such.

The most alarming fact of all, however, was that the Coahuiltecans, once they were congregated into clean stone barracks at the missions, began to die. The death rate rose; the birth rate consistently fell. Disease had some bearing, but most probably this was the result of a terrible failure of morale. The Coahuiltecans were simply overwhelmed; their old way of life was being destroyed, and like many barbarians whose tribal structures and ethos are proven wanting in the face of superior power, they became apathetic. Mission life was miserable, with its incomprehensible moral strictures and eternal, backbreaking labor; if the Indian ran away, the soldiers would bring him back; if he ran too far, the Apaches would surely get him. Death was the only escape.

By the middle of the century a total of five separate missions had been built in the San Antonio area, and at this time each mission had more than two hundred Indians. But this was the high water mark. There was never any successful second generation of mission Indians. Strength could only be maintained by recruitment of new Coahuiltecans from the brush, and the supply, always meager, soon gave out. Though ten-year plan after ten-year plan failed to produce a responsible, responsive native population, the friars grimly held on, and they got their concessions renewed time after time through the free use of their immense influence with the Royal government.

The Spanish orders of the 18th century were probably the strongest and most vigorous element of their declining society, but even their determined refusal to accept reality was a symptom of a general Hispanic decline. While some of the best minds in Spain and New Spain investigated the Texas situation and reported that the missionary effort was failing, clerical influence continually prevailed, certainly for many decades after everyone knew all hope for success had gone.

Generations of missionary priests and friars came out, grew old and died, and were replaced. There is no question that most of them came to hate their charges with what they themselves recognized was unchristian lack of charity. They wrote letters and reports filled with distaste. The passive Coahuiltecans were described as "vile, cowardly, treacherous, and lazy." They could not be trained to defend themselves or to help hold off the wilder Indians above the Escarpment. Ironically, one Spanish missionary, Fray Morfi, who wrote a history of the period, came to look upon the terrible Comanches with much friendlier eyes. With perfect, though unconscious, logic, the Spanish conquerors felt a greater affinity for the powerful warrior tribes than for the poor skulkers who came begging to their missions.

The Spanish settlers requested by the Franciscans arrived in 1731. They were a group of ten families and five newly-marrieds, subsidized by the Crown and sent from the Canary Islands. There were fifty-six Spaniards in all. The origins of this group are obscure; apparently they were people who had been exiled to the Canary Islands from Spain, for political reasons. Life in these barren islands induced them to volunteer for the Texas frontier, at a time when almost no Spaniards could be persuaded to go. The King was pleased to grant their request; the government paid the entire costs of passage, and they were to be the vanguard of between two hundred and four hundred families in all.

But in addition to the transportation costs, the King granted each settler the honor of *hidalgo* (from the old Spanish *Fijo d'Algo,* or son of someone important), which was a genuine title of gentility, to be held by him and his descendants in perpetuity. While this honor and reward was in accord with the Spanish desperation to settle the frontier, it was a considerable mistake. At this period pride of birth was taken more seriously in Spain than anywhere in Europe, with the possible exception of Ireland, and the Canary Islanders took their new titles completely to heart.

Being *hidalgos* in Spain, or even New Spain, was a considerable social asset—but at one swoop it removed the recipients from the nonaristocratic working classes and created a ridiculous situation on the San Antonio frontier. Men with the dignity of hidalgo were not expected to do common labor—but the Canary Islanders were sent to Béxar specifically to be farmers and raise crops to support the Spanish garrison. This meant they had escaped a hardscrabble life as dirt farmers in the Atlantic only to adopt a role equally difficult and barren.

The Canary Islanders refused it. They arrived in the San Antonio region expecting to find a town, and a subservient population over which they might become an elite. They found instead they were expected to build the town, or villa, and to plant crops, all without Indian labor, which the padres icily refused to let them use. They arrived convinced they were an upper class, but totally without funds, and found there was no lower class that could be induced to support them. The attitude of the settlers is indicated in one's signature: "I, Juan Leal Goraz, Spaniard and noble settler by order of His Majesty (whom God guard) in this Royal Presidio of San Antonio de Véjar and Villa of San Fernando, Province of Texas, or New Philippines, and present Senior Regidor of the said Villa, also farmer." The occupation, dirt farmer (*labrador*), is tacked on at the end, almost as an afterthought, and also where it would do the least social damage. Unfortunately for the colony, Goraz and the others approached their function in the same way.

Fray Morfi told the story of one settler who observed to his son that in this mild Texas region the rabbit made no burrow, and this meant that there was no need for men to build houses or cultivate fields. From that day forward the son did no labor, and he raised his own children in the family philosophy.

Instead of carving a flourishing community out of the wilderness, the new settlers tended to go native. They became hunters, fishers, loafers, and in some cases, thieves. It was possible to raise a few beans without much effort, and also the ubiquitous Spanish cattle now dotted the fields around Béxar. The Spanish could eat without great difficulty, and meanwhile, enjoy what was indeed a splendid climate, amid beautiful scenery.

The two-sided war between missionaries and soldiers now became three-cornered. The Canary Islanders wrote bitter letters to the Viceroy, protest-ing the fact that the religious hogged most of the good land, and also unreasonably kept the tame Indians out of the labor economy and even let their cattle roam about untended. The friars wrote that the settlers were "indolent, given to vice" and unworthy of the blessings of this new land. The Franciscans were particularly incensed that the Crown had spent 80,000 pesos bringing the Canary Islanders to San Antonio—such govern-ment monies could have been better spent on the Church. The settlers slyly reported back that the friars weren't getting anywhere with the Indians, and what went on in the missions should be thoroughly investigated. Although there were several mission churches in the vicinity, they demanded their own parish church, and priest.

There were other additions to the population. A few Indians became sufficiently Hispanicized to take up a life similar to that of the elite. Some settlers wandered north from New Spain, mostly "so-called Spaniards." More than one soldier was forced by the friars to wed an Indian woman, and the *mestizo* community slowly grew.

The Canary Island elite tended to marry only within itself, and quickly deep social cleavages, which hardly reflected economic status, opened up. These were actually no more than an extension of the intricate class and caste systems of Spanish America, which by the 18th century were ap-proaching India's in complexity. Spaniards born in the old country out-ranked everyone else, though they themselves were graduated according to birth and station. Next came *criollos* of pure race, unfortunately born in the colonies, also graduated. Below the undeniably Spanish elites, there opened up a bewildering complexity of various kinds of mixed bloods, with pure *indios,* not theoretically, but actually, at the bottom. There were also people officially listed as Spanish, but not socially accepted as such. The Spanish census listed each person by rank and supposed racial mixture with what can only be called appalling clarity; not accidentally, the offi-cial terms used by the Spanish empire eventually became regarded in themselves as insults.

Isolated, unable to trade with French Louisiana by official decree, and unable to make an Indian base upon which to expand an agricultural community, the admitted gem of Spanish Texas held its own but hardly flourished. It stayed deeply divided, among missionaries, soldiers, settlers, and villagers of differing degrees of *Hispanidad.* After two generations of original settlement, a Spanish census listed the population as 1,700. Be-tween three and four hundred were Spanish, loosely interpreted; the rest were Indians, *mestizos,* and *culebras.* This last was a Spanish word for mulatto, but it most likely referred to an admixture of Spanish, or Spanish-Mexican, with Coahuiltecan. There were more *culebras* listed than *mes-tizos,* but there were almost no Negroes on the Spanish frontier. *Mestizo,* meanwhile, was gradually coming to mean a Hispanicized Mexican Indian, regardless of racial origin. The biggest difference between a *mestizo* and a true Indian was the use of Spanish, and his clothes.

In the 1770's, Fray Morfi described the Royal Presidio and Villa as a group of wretched shanties, with a "few good buildings." The Commandant General of the Interior, De Croix, reported that the settlers of San Fernando "live miserable lives because of their laziness, captiousness, and lack of means of support, all of which defects show themselves at first sight." De Croix found no start at any kind of public education, and no professional men. There was neither doctor nor lawyer. A series of Spanish government officials visited or inspected what was now the capital of Spanish Texas, and few had much good to say about it.

Life for the average man in Spanish Texas was probably summed up succinctly and with unconscious brilliance by an 18th-century resident of San Antonio, who described his youth in these words: "We were of the poor people . . . to be poor in that day meant to be very poor indeed, almost as poor as the Saviour in His Manger. But we were not dissatisfied. . . . There was time to eat and sleep and watch the plants growing. Of food, we did not have overmuch—beans and chili, chili and beans."

English-speaking historians have been as fascinated with the inner contradictions and inner social weaknesses of Spanish Texas as other schools of observers have been with the internal decay of the Roman Empire.

Certainly, the weaknesses of a declining Spanish state, a clerically influenced society, a rigid and at times ridiculous class and caste structure, economic ineptitude, the reluctance of families to emigrate to the frontier, and the determination to be an elite of those who did, all played an immense part in the failure to incorporate the New Philippines, or Texas. There were other problems as well. Spanish centralism broke down in practice, if not in theory, when extended over vast distances. The wonderful Spanish-colonial phrase, *Recibidas, obedicidas, y no cumplidas* ("Received, obeyed, and not carried out") of the governors and viceroys showed what happened to even sensible instructions of distant authority.

Furthermore, Texas was not in reality a contiguous province of New Spain. In the 18th century Spanish settlement had not yet reached the Bravo, or Rio Grande, when fear of the French sucked missions and presidios north. Several hundred miles of *despoblada,* burning brush and cacti-studded near-desert, separated Spanish civilization in Mexico from the Texas oasis and capital of San Antonio. Settlement had to leap a very harsh frontier, which was not much populated even by the 20th century. Then, Spanish settlements were isolated. Only a forest-and-farm-oriented race could have spread through the thickets and hills of Texas. The Spanish were Mediterranean, and thought in terms of *colonias,* or town-sites, in the Roman pattern. Economically, these could not be supported.

But what is too often overlooked is the single, major reason for Spanish failure to hold Texas—just as a French historian pointed out that it is generally overlooked, in delving into Rome's internal woes, that the Empire was assassinated. The Spanish transmitted the horse to Apachería, and through it, to the Comanches, and unhappily created the most fearsome light cavalry—the Plains Indian—the world had ever seen.

The Spanish never even began to solve the Indian problem on their northern frontier. In fact, over the years it grew worse. Eventually, every frontier community from New Mexico through Texas lived in intolerable danger, both from the bold strokes of far-riding Comanches and the incessant guerrilla warfare of the scattered Apaches. The settlement of Texas was halted, and the settlement of New Mexico and great parts of northern New Spain was delayed and harassed for generations. Hundreds of Spanish colonists were killed in the north, and more thousands along the fringes of Old Mexico. Indian war parties were plunging as far south as Jalisco by the mid-18th century. Literally hundreds of thousands of horses and cattle were stolen or destroyed.

This was a problem the Spanish themselves never liked to face. By 1720 they had more armed men stationed in Texas than they had employed for both the conquests of Mexico and Peru, empires that had contained millions of natives. The fact that some twenty to thirty thousand horse Indians could not only halt but rip and shred the power of Spain was hardly to be admitted. Yet this, again and again, was exactly what the most far-seeing men Spain sent out to the frontier tried to get the authorities to concede.

These men were aware that the frontier was not advancing—it had already begun to retreat. The Marqués de Rubí, writing his report from the inspection of 1766, desperately tried to get the government to distinguish between the real and the "mythical" frontier. There was a tremendous difference between what Spain claimed and what Spaniards held.

The great failure of the missions was twofold. First, they could only be planted among the nonwarlike tribes, and instead of forging them into a strong, Hispanic base able to defend the land, contact with Spanish culture soon exterminated these. Second, the Spanish success in Mexico and Peru had come about because the Spanish were able to conquer the dominant people, or Amerind tribe, who already overawed all the rest. The dominant tribes in Texas were the Apaches and Comanches. The Spaniards were never able to conquer the first, and the second gave them the greatest defeat they ever suffered at the hands of natives in the New World.

A party of mounted Comanches visited San Antonio de Béxar (as the community of San Antonio de Valero, San Fernando de Béxar, and nearby missions was coming to be called) soon after it was founded, but the first real trouble came from the Apaches, now being pushed back down on the Edwards Plateau. Soon, Lipan Apaches were harrying the wretched Coahuiltecans, and undoubtedly Apache pressure forced many to accept mission life. Then, in 1730, a large band of Lipans attacked the garrison of the presidio. Two soldiers were killed, thirteen wounded, and the survivors driven into the villa. The Apaches ran off sixty head of cattle and enjoyed an enormous barbecue.

Reprisals were called for; the Spanish always made a policy of answering an Indian raid with a punitive expedition, to demonstrate the power and implacability of imperial Spain. Commandant Bustillo y Cevallos surprised an Indian camp west of San Antonio, probably on the San Sabá River, a branch of the Colorado. Bustillo attacked, and a great many women, children, and warriors were killed. Bustillo claimed "two hundred," but Fray Morfi sneeringly called this report "exaggerated" in his *History of Texas*.

This did not end the Apache troubles. San Antonio was continually raided; horses and cattle were lost, individuals picked off. The Spanish retaliated when they could, and captured a number of Apache women and children. Then, a party of Lipan Apaches came boldly into the mission at San Antonio. They would have nothing to do with the Spanish Long-knives, but they wanted to treat with the Brown Robes, the padres.

The Apaches told the priests that they desired a mission in their own country, which was on the San Sabá, far to the northwest. They wanted only peace. They offered to buy back the captives they had lost, and asked the padres' good services with the soldiers. The missionary priests were overjoyed—there had never been a chance of planting a mission in Apachería before. Although the soldiery grumbled, nothing could dampen the clerical enthusiasm, and in a few years viceregal authority was granted for a new presidio and mission: San Luís de las Amarillas, to be erected in the country of the *Lipanes*.

In April, 1757, soldiers under Colonel Diego Ortiz de Parilla and five priests set out from San Antonio for the San Sabá. Here, in the heart of what was considered Apachería, the mission was built of logs, surrounded by a palisade, and the presidio erected a few miles away. This expedition seemed to have three purposes. One was to convert the Lipans, to reduce and remove a great threat to settlement; another was to extend Spanish power further out from San Antonio. A third hope is explained by the persistent rumor of rich silver mines in the vicinity—a rumor of the Lost San Sabá Mines that has never entirely died away. Supposedly, some silver was mined and freighted on muleback to San Antonio. But then and later, no conclusive evidence ever existed. Coronado was not the last man to believe in mythical treasures.

The Lipan Apaches had been meek enough in Béxar, but now, in their own country, they put the Spanish off. They stated they could not congregate just yet; it was the hunting season. Later, it was something else. The priests persisted, and hopefully, kept the mission open. The Indians seemed to be waiting for something, and the Spanish, with very limited intelligence of what was actually happening on the far frontier, decided to be patient.

In retrospect, what was happening was very clear. The Apaches, mauled by Spanish power on the south and shredded by a terrible force from the north, with keen intelligence hoped to get both their enemies involved. They had lured a presidio-mission not just into Apachería but beyond the vague borders of Comanche country. They were eagerly waiting to see what the Comanches would do about it.

A few months after the San Sabá mission was established, a friendly Indian brought word of a terrible calamity that was going to befall. Worried, the Spanish alerted their entire frontier—but when nothing happened during the summer and fall, they relaxed. Winter passed, the grass sprang out green and lush across the plains to the north, and early in March, 1758, the moon waxed huge and full. Both priests and soldiers were delighted with the ephemeral beauty of the land. Neither knew Comanches— or that when the grass was full and thick, and the moon threw light to ride by, Comanche warriors could range a thousand miles.

Then, something happened. Every uncooperative Lipan Apache suddenly disappeared. No one saw an Indian—but one morning, there were shrieks and shouts, and a rush of horsemen swooped down on the Spanish horse pasture, between the mission and the fort. Sixty horses disappeared.

Colonel Parilla put all his men on the walls, and he sent a messenger requesting the padres to move at once to the presidio. The padres refused. Parilla waited a few days—but nothing happened. He went personally to the mission and argued with Padre Terreros, the priest in charge, to seek safety, and to bring all the sacred articles in the mission with him.

Terreros halfheartedly agreed to move the following day; he told Parilla it was incredible that any unseen Indians would wish the padres harm. Parilla left seventeen soldiers with the priests, and departed.

Early next morning, March 16, Padre Terreros conducted the usual Mass; he was determined that the orderly routine not be disturbed. But before the Host was lifted, there was a booming yell outside the palisade.

The soldiers ran to the walls and cocked their muskets. Padre Terreros and another priest, Padre Molina, climbed to the parapet. What they saw made them speechless. Two thousand Comanches, all on horseback, were deploying slowly around the mission walls. Molina was frightened, and now said so. But his superior stammered that these men must be friendly— the priests had done no one any harm.

The soldiers waited to fire, but Terreros refused to give the order. He seemed hypnotized by the barbaric splendor of the savages, who were painted black and red—war paint, though the Spanish did not recognize it—and wore impressive headgear of buffalo horns, deer antlers, and eagle plumes. All were armed with lances and bows, and at least a hundred carried French-made muskets.

A Comanche warrior boldly walked up to the palisade gate and opened it, while Padre Terreros hesitated. After that, it was too late—the Indians poured inside the compound. Terreros and the other priests began to bring out gifts of tobacco and beads with shaking hands.

In the sign language, the Comanches now demanded that Terreros send a message to the presidio, that it be opened to them, too. A quaking friendly Indian translated, and a message was written out by Terreros for Colonel Parilla. A large party of Comanches took the message and rode off.

But meanwhile, another mission Indian had seen the Comanches arrive and had fled to tell Parilla. The colonel immediately ordered a detachment of troops to reinforce the mission. These men mounted and rode off. They rode directly into the party of Comanches coming from the mission with Terreros' message. The Comanches charged; the Spanish never had a chance. In a few seconds every soldier was shot or lanced. Only one, badly wounded, was able to crawl away.

At the mission, the Indians had thrown off all restraint. They no longer waited for gifts to be offered, but began to sack and wreck the Spanish storerooms. The Europeans gathered in a little knot in the middle of the enclosure.

When the party that had killed the soldiers returned suddenly, yelling and waving fresh scalps, the killing began. Before they could even fire, the Spanish soldiers were shot down or filled with arrows. One priest was stabbed, and his head cut off. Two Comanches seized Terreros and started to carry him off, probably for torture. Fortunately for him, another Comanche shot him dead with a musket as he was pulled away.

Padre Molina was able to break away, and with a few others hid in the *padre presidente's* quarters. Now, the Comanches set fire to the mission, and Molina, wounded, soon had to come outside again, smoking and gasping for air. By a miracle, as he thought—the Indians were too busy burning, looting, and celebrating, to notice—Molina's few survivors reached the mission church, which was made of green logs and did not burn. Here they remained, cowering and praying, until the last whooping Comanche rode away.

Sometime after midnight that night, Molina and the others reached the presidio. It was only three days later, when scouts reported that the Comanche horde had left the area, that Parilla and Molina returned to San Sabá. Terreros and the others were found and given Christian burial. After that Parilla retreated to San Luís, and asked for help.

The destruction of San Sabá caused consternation and rage at the capital, San Antonio de Béxar. The Spanish government and ecclesiastical authorities felt strongly that the burning of a mission and the murder of priests must not go unpunished. When the presidio at San Sabá was raided again by Comanches in 1758, a conference was called at San Antonio. A punitive expedition was planned. All the presidios in Texas were called upon for soldiers, and a large number of Indian allies were raised. The plan was approved by the Viceroy in Mexico. In August, 1759, Colonel Parilla was placed in command of six hundred men, with orders to sweep the Indian country north of Béxar.

Only part of Parilla's army was composed of Spanish soldiers. He commanded a number of Coahuiltecan and other Mexicanized Indians, and 134 Lipan Apaches who joined the Spaniards for a Comanche war. He was furnished two field guns and a supply train for an extended campaign. This was the greatest Spanish expedition ever mounted in Texas, and Parilla had more men than either Cortés or Pizarro.

Parrilla did not march for the heart of the Comanche country, which lay to the northwest. Reluctant to put his army out on the Great Plains, he went almost due north, through the fringes of the Comanche range. He did not meet Comanches. He did find a Tonkawa village, and the Spanish frame of mind was clearly shown: Parilla attacked it, killing fifty-five Indians and seizing 150 women and children, for forcible "reduction" and conversion. He went further and further north, until by October, 1759, he approached the Red River, the northernmost boundary of Texas.

Here he found Indians. Apparently a vast, ephemeral alliance was formed by some of the Plains tribes, Comanches, Witchitas, and several others. Colonel Parilla's own account stated that he fought 6,000 warriors who displayed the French flag, and who were probably commanded by French officers.

Though authorities disagree, and it is true that French agents were among the Indians trading and selling firearms, no real evidence of French participation in the Indian alliance was ever revealed. This claim, like the obviously exaggerated numbers, was probably made to make the Spanish defeat appear in a better light. It was one thing to be beaten by other Europeans, but quite another to be routed by savages.

For Parilla suffered the worst military catastrophe dealt to Spanish arms in Texas. When he attacked the massed Indians, his civilized Indian allies ran for their lives instead of at the enemy, and his Lipan Apache allies disappeared. Parilla fought his way out of an Indian encirclement with very small losses in numbers of Spaniards—but he abandoned his two cannon and all his supplies, and a few weeks later reappeared at Béxar after a precipitous retreat. Few Spaniards were killed, but Spanish power was dealt an enormous psychological defeat.

Some years later a Spanish writer stated bitterly: "The memory of this event remains yet on the . . . frontier as a disgrace to Spaniards."

Colonel Parilla was court-martialed in Mexico. His lost cannon were not recovered for twenty years, and then, ironically, were gotten back by a French agent in the Spanish service.

The San Sabá mission-presidio and the Parilla expedition were the high water marks of Spanish power. Never again was a mission authorized for the warlike tribes of the interior; never again was a serious campaign mounted against the Comanches. There was a subtle but terrible change on the Mexican-Spanish frontier; the balance of power had turned over, and from 1759 forward the Spanish were on the defensive.

The Lipans continued to terrorize the frontier communities, and the Comanches began to raid and plunder deep into New Spain. The presidial soldiery, clinging to their forts, were ineffective to halt the menace—in many cases they refused to venture out in pursuit of Indians. The Spanish had a cluster of missions and settlements in East Texas near the Louisiana border, a few barely surviving missions and forts along the south Texas crescent, and the capital at Béxar. Other than that there was no settlement of the land, and nothing on the northern frontier except Santa Fé, hundreds of miles to the west in New Mexico. The true state of affairs is shown plainly by the fact that if a Spaniard wanted to travel between San Antonio de Béxar and Santa Fé, he had to go far south into Mexico, west to Durango, then up the Rio Grande. It was considered perilous for even a full company of soldiers to try to cross the Apache-Comanche plains.

Once the warlike tribes learned the vulnerability of the Spanish, the Indian problem was primary. It was a classic case of guerrilla warfare along a poorly defined frontier of vast spaces and immense distances. The Apaches, and even more so the Comanches, enjoyed a privileged sanctuary on the trackless plateaus, onto which the Spanish dared not penetrate too far. The Indians could ride far and fast; the Comanches could range a thousand miles. They galloped into Spanish territory, raided and killed and plundered, then galloped away into the wilds. War bands then split into many tiny groups, making effective pursuit impossible. If a punitive expedition did press far into Indian country, then the war bands came together again, in superior numbers. Colonial Spain had neither the resources nor the will to fight this kind of war.

Meanwhile, ranches, haciendas and struggling frontier settlements on the northern fringes of Mexico, all through Sonora, Coahuila, and Durango, lived in perpetual fear and harassment. The full moon of summer, and the greening of spring grass, upon which the Indian horses could forage, brought a sense of terror. As Toynbee wrote, when the frontier between a more advanced culture and a barbaric one becomes stationary, the balance usually does not accede to the advanced civilization. The more aggressive culture, in fact, tends to become "superior."

The idea of reducing the Indians through mission-presidios, and thus forming an Hispanicized core to populate and hold Texas, died slowly and painfully. Mission after mission failed, as Indians died out or moved away, or became bitterly hostile. Some were moved to new locations, but with little better success. After the middle of the 18th century the congregation of missions at Béxar began to wither away, too. Yet the idea was so strong, and in decline the rigidity of the Spanish mind so great, that one new mission was founded in South Texas as late as 1792, long past the time when either the military or the secular powers had any faith in the system.

In 1793, after continual requests by the citizens of Béxar backed up by the military commanders, the mission of San Antonio de Valero was secularized; that is, the lands of the mission were distributed, and the mission building itself turned over to the military. At that date, after seventy-five years of continual effort, San Antonio de Valero contained only forty-three settled converts, and none of the other four missions in the area had any more. The total population of Spanish Texas was less than three thousand, including all converted Indians and garrison troops.

By the second half of the 18th century, thousands of men and women on the Spanish-Mexican frontier, who each year lost cattle, horses, and loved ones in continual, cruel warfare, had come to curse both the ecclesiastical councils and the Crown.

5

THE KING'S MERCIES

The country should be given back to Nature and the Indians.
FROM THE REPORT OF THE MARQUÉS DE RUBÍ
TO THE KING OF SPAIN

Two of the enduring myths concerning the Spanish colonization of America are: it was never Spanish policy to exterminate Indians; the Spanish were less rigid about racial matters than other peoples. Neither of these myths can stand inspection, but their origin is understandable. Where the Spanish found adaptable Indians, they always worked to incorporate them into the state as third- or fourth-class citizens to form a laboring class. And while the position of all except Spaniards born in Spain was always anomalous in the empire, and blood castes were rigidly defined if not always enforced, after the Spanish departure the soon-to-be-dominant *mestizo* groups naturally preferred never to dwell much on the notion of racial descent. It was impossible for all but a handful in New Spain to prove a racial purity that other European colonists took for granted. But class distinctions, always sharply drawn in Hispanic civilization, remained.

Significantly, in the light of later events on the Great Plains, in the last half of the 18th century Spanish policy in Texas underwent a great change. Secular and ecclesiastical authorities had long been locked in a bitter battle over the best way to manage the northern frontier; but the impetus and desire to incorporate Texas had always come from the fear that the French in Louisiana would usurp the Spanish claim. In 1762 this French pressure was removed. As a gambit to keep the Louisiana territory out of the hands of the victorious English, France ceded the Louisiana country to Spain, and this transfer was ratified at the close of the Seven Years War in 1763. Up to this time Louisiana had been hardly more profitable to the French

65

Crown than Texas had to the Spanish; both provinces were a constant worry and a constant drain.

The removal of the French threat called for a reassessment of the situation in Texas, and in 1766 the King sent out an inspector general, the Marqués de Rubí, to examine the whole northern frontier of New Spain, map the territory, and make recommendations for future policy. The new Spanish king, Charles III, was the ablest and most enlightened of the Bourbon line, and he was creating incisive reforms in the Spanish state. These were extended to the New World, and after 1759 a series of capable officers were dispatched to the Spanish frontier. Spain had good men in Texas in the last half of the century: the Frenchman Athanase de Mezières, El Caballero (Chevalier) Teodoro de Croix, the Baron de Ripperdá, and the Marqués de Rubí. Unfortunately, this handful of far-seeing and enlightened aristocrats were unable to reverse the situation. Spain and New Spain simply did not possess the will and the resources, or, above all, a growing, disciplined, homogenous population, which was required to cement and push back the frontier.

Rubí and his map-making engineer, de la Fora, spent three years traveling the frontier from Louisiana to Baja California, covering some 7,000 miles. Rubí arrived determined to understand and correct a colonial system that obviously was not working. The civilized Indian population of Texas was declining instead of growing, and the danger of Indian warfare was rapidly increasing. By the time he arrived in Texas, in 1766, not only the mission at San Sabá but the presidio of San Luís in the area and the forts at Orcoquisac on the lower Trinity River and El Cañón on the upper Nueces were being intolerably harassed by Comanches. The garrisons for all practical purposes were pinned behind their walls and defending cannon, and the missionary effort in the areas was hopeless. San Antonio de Béxar itself was in constant danger; the Comanches as well as the Lipans were now riding to Béxar with impunity.

Rubí quickly discovered the basic failures of the mission-colonization scheme, and he further saw something that the various officers and governors of Texas had reported but had never been accepted by higher authority. The scattered presidios, filled with only a few hundred soldiers, could not police the country—they could not even maintain or defend themselves. Rubí was disgusted with some features of the presidial system: the use of "so-called Spaniards" instead of the pure race as soldiers, and the corruption of the local commandants, who were permitted to act as paymasters, sutlers, and commissaries for the garrisons. Prices on the frontier were exorbitant for the soldiery, who were paid some 450 pesos per year; some garrisons were in rags, and improperly mounted and armed. In other places, soldiers were being used to work on private lands of officials rather than guard against the Indian menace. The deep social decay into which New Spain had fallen permeated Texas, and it turned out to be impossible to eradicate.

Rubí saw something else: that the supposed frontier of Spanish power in Texas was wholly imaginary. The string of scattered, far-flung presidios from East Texas to San Sabá did not give Spain control of the country; the soldiers hardly controlled the ground on which the forts were built. This advanced line did nothing whatever to prevent or punish the incessant, tragic plundering of the "real" frontier—which was the line of Spanish-Mexican settlement in New Spain, and which had not yet reached the Bravo, or Rio Grande.

Rubí quickly was made to understand that many of the Texas Indians posed no threat to Spain. The Hasinai, Karankawas, Tonkawas, and others were not incorporable, but they were either dying out or were reasonably friendly. The Spanish could control these tribes by treaties or by force. But the Comanches and the Apaches seemed to be completely beyond control. Rubí did fall into the trap of adopting a mistaken notion popular on the Spanish frontier: that the Spanish trouble with the Comanches stemmed from Spanish dealings with Apaches, as at San Sabá. It was not yet understood that the Comanches and their allies were the greatest raiders in North America, to whom plundering and horse stealing had become a way of life. The Apaches had been driven down in close proximity to Spanish settlement, against which they were waging a bitter, interminable guerrilla warfare. Rubí, and most Spanish officers, mistakenly felt that it was only the Apache presence that pulled their enemies, the Comanches, into the Spanish sphere.

In a series of comprehensive and very clear reports, the Marqués sent home a number of suggestions, which added up to a radical change of Spanish Indian policy in North America. He requested the following alterations on the frontier:

The abandonment of all missions and presidios in Texas except two: those in the San Antonio de Béxar region, and La Bahía, which lay below Béxar on the San Antonio River and provided an outlet on the coast.

The strengthening of Béxar by the removal of all Spanish settlers in East Texas to San Antonio, which, with Santa Fé in New Mexico, would remain as the two solitary outposts of Spanish power north of the Bravo.

Recognition of the real frontier, by establishment of a line of some fifteen forts stretching across northern Mexico from just below Laredo to the Gulf of California. This was an immense withdrawal, and it was the recommendation for a purely military response to the Indian problem. All the country north of this line, including all Texas (except the outpost at San Antonio) was to be returned to "Nature and the Indians," at least for the time being.

The institution of a deliberate war of extermination against the Apaches, in which alliances with the Wichitas, Comanches, and other northern tribes should be sought. To secure these alliances, both the abandonment of the country and "French methods" of dealing with the Indians would be helpful. If any Apache women or children survived, they were to be removed to

New Spain and civilized by being reared in slavery. With the Apaches removed forever, Rubí thought it would be possible to make peace with the Plains tribes.

With the exception of the possibility of peace with the Comanches, the Rubí reports were clear-cut reflections of Spanish reality in Texas. With the forces available, nothing else was possible. And in fact, the war against the Apaches, while accepted wholeheartedly by officialdom, was already beyond Spanish power to support.

In 1772, substantially all the Rubí recommendations were promulgated by the King, in a "New Regulation of the Presidios."

The New Regulation for the frontier thus marked a Spanish retreat. Ironically, one of the incidents connected with its implementation pointed up the whole nature of the Spanish Texas dilemma—unconquerable Indians, lack of colonists, governmental ineptitude—and unwittingly almost destroyed one of the few genuine Spanish roots in the province.

The Baron de Ripperdá, who arrived in San Antonio de Béxar as Governor of Texas in 1770, inherited the task of removing the Spanish presence in East Texas to the capital. He marched to the Sabine with a party of soldiers in 1772, with orders to close the four moribund missions in the region and to escort all Spaniards to San Antonio.

Ripperdá found the presidials and the missionary clergy ready enough to leave. The forts and missions were stripped of valuables and set afire. But since Rubí had inspected the area in 1767, the small Spanish community clustered near the forts had begun to take root and grow, on its own, completely without aid or even the knowledge of the Crown. It already numbered about five hundred persons.

These people had become small farmers and herders in the rich pine woodlands. The Caddoans left them alone; the Comanches and Wichitas had never smelled them out, and they had created a comfortable life. They raised corn and beans and the ubiquitous rangy Spanish cattle and pigs. They were doing well, and they had no desire to leave their farms and homes in East Texas and move to what was admittedly a less hospitable and far more dangerous frontier.

Baron de Ripperdá sympathized. Quite probably he saw the removal of these families as a mistake; but he also understood the complete impossibility of getting the orders changed. The Spaniards were routed out with soldiers, their goods and livestock gathered together, and their settlements burned. Protesting and weeping, the settlers were marched to Béxar.

But settled on new lands along the San Antonio River, they continued to complain. The best lands were admittedly sequestered by the missions, or already appropriated by officials or Canary Islanders. They hated the dry climate and the thin, rocky soil they were allotted, and they were terrified of Apache-Comanche raids, which were admittedly bad. At this time

Ripperdá was writing florid, dramatic reports about the Indian terror to out-lying farmers and ranchers, and begging for more troops.

Two leaders of the East Texans, Gil Ybarbo and a man named Flores, petitioned the Viceroy for permission to return to their old homes. This petition, understandably, caused consternation, embarrassment, and some confusion in official circles. Finally, at Ripperdá's suggestion, Ybarbo was told his people were not to return to their former settlement, but they were permitted to emigrate in that general direction. They were not to approach closer than 100 leagues to Natchitoches in Louisiana, now a Spanish fort.

Ybarbo and the East Texans pushed their mandate to the limit. They packed up and left Béxar and picked a new settlement site on the Trinity River, about as far east as they could go. Ripperdá agreed to this site, since the land was fertile, with good rainfall, and it was east and south of the Wichita and Tonkawa ranges. Both of these tribes were now friendly toward the Spanish, and Ripperdá thought they would create a buffer between Ybarbo and the Plains Indians. The new settlement was named Bucareli, like all the forts, missions, and settlements in Texas, after a prominent Spanish official, a lieutenant general of New Spain, who founded the National Pawnshop of Mexico.

For four years Bucareli thrived. Then, in May, 1778, a Comanche war party rode past and stole some horses. Ybarbo, with considerable courage, formed a posse and pursued. He came across a few Comanches and killed them. When he reported this incident to Béxar, he was gravely adjudged to have done the correct thing, since it was considered that no Comanche would be in the vicinity of a Spanish settlement for friendly reasons. However, Ybarbo's people became frightened and called for troops. There were none to spare.

Then, in the Indian summer of October, 1778, a howling horde of Comanches swooped down on Bucareli. They did not kill anyone, but took away 276 horses. Ybarbo sent a new appeal to San Antonio, while some friendly Indians pursued the Comanches, but without success. The Bucareli priest, Padre Garza, wrote that now no Spaniard dared step outside the village, even to plant his crops or to go hunting, unless all the men went along. The whole town was on guard and in constant terror night and day.

Gil Ybarbo decided not to risk another Comanche spring.

Defying his orders, he took the Bucarelians back into the East Texas timberlands, to the site of the old presidio of Nacogdoches, arriving in April, 1779. Here, they were in familiar territory, and deep enough into the woods to be free of Comanche terror. Ybarbo and his five hundred put down new roots. The Royal Government accepted this fait accompli, and the descendants of these folk were still living in the region in the 1960s.

If there had been more like Ybarbo and his followers, Hispanic civiliza-tion might have dominated the land and altered history. As it was, they remained a tiny, isolated outpost in a vast area, soon to be overwhelmed by a new invasion from the east.

Meanwhile, at Béxar, Ripperdá got more troops, but he was never able to make the country secure. The planned war of extermination against the Lipan Apaches proceeded with massive slowness, always a characteristic of 18th-century Spanish bureaucracy. In 1776, the year the English colonies on the Atlantic seaboard declared themselves independent, all the northern frontier provinces of New Spain were placed under Teodoro de Croix, whose headquarters was at Chihuahua, in north-central Mexico. The new commandant-general—his office was primarily a war post—began his planning the next year. He held three major war councils, at Monclova, San Antonio, and Chihuahua, during 1777–1778. He asked each of these councils sixteen questions, and got substantially the same answers, as follows:

The Apache terror had existed since the first Spaniards entered the country. Each year, instead of seeing improvement, was worse than the last. The Apaches numbered 5,000 fighting men, armed with bows, lances, and guns. They always made war by surprise, and fought like guerrillas— that is, they only attacked when they had the advantage. The Comanches were their enemies, and if an alliance could be made, "by God's grace" they would soon be destroyed. There were not enough troops on the frontier for either attack or defense. There should be a campaign against the Eastern Apaches. *It would require at least 3,000 soldiers.* The friendship of the Comanches should be cultivated, and the war should proceed. On these statements, virtually all Spanish officers agreed.

Meanwhile, Spain was employing a new, and temporarily very effective, weapon in the north. Frenchmen from Louisiana, now under Spanish control and citizenship, were used to win friends and influence tribes on the far-northern frontier. The principal architect of this plan, originally conceived by Rubí, was Athanase de Mezières, who significantly enough was a son-in-law of Louis de St. Denis, as well as a brother-in-law of the Duc d'Orleans. In 1769 he had been appointed lieutenant governor of the Natchitoches district. He had lived on the Louisiana frontier for some thirty years.

De Mezières traveled to north Texas, and with all the French genius for blending with the land and reaching rapport with the savages, by 1771 he had buried the hatchet with the Wichitas, former allies of the Comanches, by making separate agreements with each Wichita subtribe: Taovayas, Wacos, and Tawakonis. In 1772 he recovered Parilla's lost cannon and sent them on to Bucareli. He voyaged up the dangerous Brazos more than a hundred miles, skirted the regions of the Red, and finally came to Béxar. He was even able to secure a fleeting peace with one Comanche band, in 1774. He worked closely with Ripperdá, and for a time it seemed that the Marqués de Rubí's master plan for a two-front war against the Lipans was taking shape.

De Mezières enthusiastically supported the concept. His reports on Texas Indians north of the San Antonio region revealed that these fell into three broad groups: the maritime (coastal) tribes; the eastern inland nations; and the frontier, or northern bands. De Mezières stated that the coastal tribes, such as Coahuiltecans and Karankawas and Atakapans, were useless to Spain and should be ignored. Of the Eastern, inland tribes —the Caddo confederacies—two had been virtually wiped out by disease and vice, and the remaining, which he called the Tejas, were on friendly terms, but not much use for war. The third group, the frontier Indians that included the Tonkawa and Wichita tribes and the Comanches, were all warlike and dangerous to the Apaches. Of these, only the Comanches were hostile to Spain, and he was working on this problem.

The Spanish authorities were much impressed by this Frenchman, who was the best European frontiersman in Texas since St. Denis. He was permanently transferred to Texas, and appointed governor to succeed the Baron de Ripperdá. This was an enormous concession by the jealous *hidalgos* of Spain, who rarely permitted even highborn Spanish colonials to hold office. Unfortunately for Spain, however, he died before he could take office. His great work, which might have created an enduring alliance between the Spanish-Mexican civilization and the Plains tribes against all comers, was never completed.

Teodoro de Croix, councils completed, now drew up his plan of campaign. All the Spanish troops that could be scraped up from the frontier, including settlers and militia from New Mexico and the northern settlements of New Spain, were to advance on Apachería from the west and south. All the presidial soldiers in Texas, and the allied northern tribes (including, it was hoped, Comanches) making up the strongest contingent, were to attack from the north. The Apaches were to be swept up and pressed into a trap along the Rio Bravo. Three thousand troops in all were to be used.

De Croix did not believe that such a campaign would actually exterminate the Apaches, but he did think it would "secure the happiness of the province." At the very least, it would further reduce the Lipans, damage their spirit, and teach respect for the power of Spain. He ordered that the war must come to the enemy as a surprise, and to achieve this both the Commandant-General and the governing councils agreed that sincere-sounding protestations of peace and friendship be sent immediately to the Apaches to throw them off guard.

De Croix stated that once the Apaches were reduced, he had hopes of straightening out the embarrassingly bowed frontier. In the future it would run directly from Louisiana along the Red River on a line with Santa Fé. At one swoop, he would secure a country larger than the size of Old Spain. The new frontier along the Red would still be a "frontier of war," but Hispanic settlement could pour freely into the vacuum, and Béxar and all northern Mexico would be relieved of Indian wars.

The grand plan of Apache extermination was never carried out. The reasons were several: the alliances with the northern tribes were never cemented; there were bureaucratic delays; and most important, De Croix could never find the men and money for operations of the magnitude required. A few minor military expeditions were mounted, sometimes with Indian allies, and a few peace treaties were made with various Comanche bands. Both produced ephemeral results.

Significantly, in the year 1780 Domingo Cabello, who took Ripperdá's post as Governor of Texas, wrote the Viceroy: "There is no instant by day or by night when reports of barbarities and disorders from the ranches do not arrive. Totally unprotected as we are, this can only result in the complete destruction and loss of this province."

The frontier communities could survive, clinging to a stultified Spanish-Mexican ranching culture at Béxar and at Santa Fé. They could not grow or flourish. Meanwhile, their simple maintenance cost the Crown millions of gold *escudos* and returned nothing. Hoping to ease the military threat, the authorities now tried a policy Spain had never resorted to before, that of giving presents to the Indians to buy peace. Trade goods and gimmicks were distributed to Apache and Comanche chiefs, but the raids did not cease. Actually, Indian social organization was such that this practice could not succeed. No chief had that kind of control over the warriors, who raided when they either needed horses or felt like it. In 1792, a new Governor, Manuel Muñoz, reported that peace treaties and lavish gifts were having no beneficial results at all.

The presidio at Béxar was materially strengthened, however. At one time, as many as eight companies of troops were dispatched from New Spain. These were supposed to form powerful, mobile units capable of pursuing and defeating Apache and Comanche raiders. One detachment of Spanish troops was sent from a post in northern Mexico, which was called Pueblo de San Carlos del Alamo de Parras, or in the Spanish fashion, Alamo for short.

The commander was horrified to find that over all the years, no one had ever gotten around to building a genuine presidio at Béxar. Soldiers had always merely been billeted in the villa. This officer appropriated the old mission of San Antonio de Valero, just east of the San Antonio River from the town proper, which had just been secularized. The few Coahuiltecan squatters who were still clinging to the grounds were driven off by force.

Here, as in a few other places surrounding Béxar, the Franciscans had erected a strong compound and chapel out of native stone. The walls had fallen into disrepair, but were easily put right. The living quarters of the mission were turned into a barracks, and the chapel into an armory. This new presidio was called the Alamo by the soldiers, in nostalgic recollection of the post in Mexico where they had served. In this way, the generations-old work of the missionary friars passed into the hands of the military, and even the name of San Antonio de Valero was forgotten.

The outbreak of a general European war in 1793 brought further interest in development by the Spanish Crown to an end. A century of Spanish colonization had resulted in a population of about 4,000 citizens, of which 1,000 were soldiers, in an area larger than Spain itself.

The historian Richardson wrote that Spain suffered most "because of a lack of realism in her policies"—the presidio-mission was doggedly retained, although it soon proved useless in Texas; trade was never permitted with Louisiana, Texas' natural commercial partner; firearms were never sold to friendly Indians, thus making them allies not of Spain but of the French; and to the last the fiction was maintained that poorly paid officers commanding isolated posts would be both vigorous and honest. Another Texas historian, Walter Prescott Webb, laid most of the problem to the savage and incorrigible Indians, which Spain, for the first time in its history, could not conquer, convert, or destroy.

Rigid adherence to outmoded ideas—always the mark of a society in decline—certainly played a major role in Spanish failure. In Texas Spain met new and different conditions, and the Spanish secular and ecclesiastical mind was never able to adjust.

The Texas tribes could not be tamed or Hispanicized; they could not be used to populate the land. Only an expanding, pragmatic, decentralized, adaptable culture could have penetrated the region and put down roots in the face of the Apache-Comanche threat. And this was precisely what Spain lacked. Spain failed to put people in Texas. Gil Ybarbo's five hundred, acting on their own initiative, showed what several thousand Spanish peasants, had they moved into the fertile forest areas, might have done.

The violent *entradas* and explorations, the friars, the council-calling civil servants, and generations of presidio soldiers left only romantic legends and a dotting of Spanish place names. A few attractive structures of native stone survived around Béxar, for the Franciscans did build for the ages. But the quiet, gentle beauty of these crumbling mission walls remained the principal monument to the dreams of Spain.

Ironically, while millions of *pesos duros* were spent keeping soldiers and missionaries in Texas, a separate Hispanic advance occurring at the same time was to have vastly more influence on North America.

The 18th-century Spanish-Mexican frontier, as the Marqués de Rubí saw, still lay far south of the Rio Grande. But along this frontier a genuine Mexican civilization, differentiated in many ways from the Spanish, was beginning to take shape and expand. A way of life, and a value system, were evolving that would eventually reach as far north as Calgary in Canada.

The dry, mountainous, thinly populated regions of northern New Spain had never been suited for the hoe or for the *encomienda*. Here the Spanish met conditions similar to those they would find further north. Before the close of the 17th century, the *encomienda* had become valueless, and after this colonial system was officially abolished in 1720, the frontier was pushed north in other ways. The presidio and mission played a big role, and a more successful one, in New Spain than they did in Texas. But even here they could not adequately populate or hold the land. Conquered and converted Indians were not declared free subjects of Spain until almost the close of the 18th century, but there was already a large class of Mexican peasants or laborers who were not slaves but were bound to the hacienda system. Their status—peonage, or debt slavery—was eventually codified into Mexican law, probably inevitably, because of the class, caste, and paternalistic trends of Hispanic society. No worker or servant could leave a master to whom he was in debt, and most Mexicans of the lower class were almost literally born into debt.

The *hacienda,* or agricultural estate, was strong in Yucatán and on the south-central plateaus, but in the rougher and less fertile regions to the north it soon gave way to the *estancia de ganado,* or *rancho* (which always denoted a relatively small estate) devoted to cattle raising. The first Spanish cattle were brought to Mexico in 1521; Cortés and the importer Gregorio de Villalobos were responsible for the first acts leading to a new way of life.

The great conquistador was the first man to use brands—not on his livestock but on his Aztec slaves. Captive Indians were branded with the letter "G" (for *guerra,* signifying prisoner of war) on their cheeks with a hot iron, and thus marked as personal property. Many of these men were put to herding their masters' cattle, and the transfer of the personal identifying mark, or brand, from man to beast came about soon afterward. The brand, in New Spain, took on both legal and symbolic connotations. It became sacred.

Spanish law at first expressly forbade any Indian slave to ride a horse. But this rule was obviously unworkable, especially as cattle ranches pushed north into arid, open country. On the broad semideserts of the Sonoran Plain, and in the mountains, a man on foot was helpless herding cows. As the Indians became more Hispanicized they were mounted, and the emerging Mexican became a horseman.

Spanish-Mexican cattle were lean, rangy, longhorned, ugly, and incredibly tough. Like the Afro-Arabian horse, however, they were splendidly suited for the country. Left to roam wild, they flourished and increased. With such stock, and possessed of almost unlimited grazing land, the Mexican cattle industry became entirely different from animal husbandry in Europe. Cattle were branded for identification, turned loose on what was virtually open range (though it was owned by someone, usually a large *hacendado*), and they were protected from wild Indians, rounded up, and branded or slaughtered by a new breed of laborer, the *vaquero,* "cowman." Such cattle were not much good for beef, but in a very poor frontier society, such as was developing in the north, they could be raised profitably for hides.

Open spaces, a rough frontier where there were still dangerous Indians, both from the north and the mountains to the west, and labor performed almost entirely on horseback began to create those attitudes and values known in New Spain as *charro.* The *charro* was not just a horseman or a cowboy; he represented a genuine, if somewhat limited culture and way of life. The new breed was subtly different from the cowed and captive hoe-men of the old Aztec empire. The *vaquero* might still be legally and so-cially a peon—but he rode horseback, and this changed his outlook. There was an old saying: to be a *vaquero* was to be a hero; to be a *ranchero* was to be a king.

It took a better breed of man to be a *vaquero,* who had to ride inde-pendently, who worked with wholly wild, often dangerous animals, and who regularly faced the Indian peril on his own. The country, the cattle, and the requirements of living on the frontier began to force certain adap-tations to the land, creating both a culture and a powerful tradition and mythology. The basic attitudes of the *charro,* or cowman hero, were origi-nally social or economic necessities, which became genuine folk-culture. These were bravery and disregard of personal danger; comradeship with peers; an almost mystical loyalty to the hacienda and its brand; the deter-mination to ride any horse that lived; skill with the rope; and utter disdain for any kind of work that could not be done in the saddle. The man who embodied all of these was the ideal.

The deep class cleavage of all Hispanic society remained between *hacendado* and *vaquero,* owner and worker, but the frontier produced a loyalty both up and down that had already passed out of the European experience. Mexico, like almost all frontier, seminomadic societies, began to develop a new culture with strong overtones of feudalism—but the genuine feudalism of early Hellenic or Iranic culture rather than the decay-ing, rigid class structures that still characterized most of Europe.

The attitudes, even the distinctive costumes of this society were well marked by the 18th century: the immense *sombreros,* or hats, broad leather belts with silver buckles, buckskin jackets with (when possible) silver buttons, the tight, canvaslike horseman's trousers, the half-boots, and chaps, or *chaparreras.* The *charro* culture even used its own jargon, which every modern English-speaking person will recognize: *corral, bronco, loco, arroyo; lazo, la reata, rodear, adobe, pinta, caballado, rancho.* Other words passed into English with changes: *mesteño* (mus-tang), *jáquima* (hackamore), and *vaquero* (buckaroo).

This cattle culture was already old and well developed when the govern-ment of New Spain took steps to expand the contiguous frontier to the Rio Bravo.

In 1746 Colonel José de Escandón, a Spaniard from Santander, with Royal approval, was commissioned by the Viceroy to move people north and plant settlements along the Rio Grande. By November, 1748, Escandón had gathered 755 soldiers and 2,513 Spanish-Mexican colonists at Querétaro, a town 165 miles north of Mexico, and 650 south of the Bravo. From Querétaro, picking up more adventurous spirits along the way, Escandón marched north, into the modern state of Tamaulipas. Here he began to select the sites for future townships. He founded twenty towns in all.

By March, 1749, Escandón had laid out both Reynosa and Camargo, on the south bank of the Rio Bravo; he also left capable settlers and leaders to put down roots. Blás María de la Garza Falcón commanded at Camargo; *Capitán* Carlos Cantu at Reynosa. Thus historic families were founded, as well as towns, planting names that would someday be carried by thousands of border people, many of whom were not actually descended from the great men.

Escandón avoided the coast. The entire Gulf was still a fever area in the 18th century, though the richest lands lay in the lower delta of the Rio Grande. The settlements were sited far up the river, in the drier and presumably healthier climate from Reynosa west. But the soils were thinner and rockier, and rainfall insufficient for agriculture without extensive irrigation in this region. Therefore, Escandón unwittingly saw to it that the Mexican cattle culture, and not the one-crop hacienda, was planted beside the Rio Grande. Regarding the country as best suitable for ranching, Escandón returned to Querétaro, and brought back a number of *rancheros,* with their *vaqueros* and thousands of longhorned Mexican range cattle. These were scattered across the arid lower Sonoran plains both north and south of the river.

Revilla (later Guerrero) was founded in October, 1750, Mier in 1753, and Laredo on May 17, 1755. This last town Escandón placed on the north bank of the river, which spot he considered best. In all, Escandón settled 3,600 Spaniards, and 3,000 "Christian converts" throughout his new province, which with the usual lack of imagination of the developer he called New Santander. The borders of New Santander did not stop at the Rio Bravo; they went north to the Nueces, near Corpus Christi, then west and north to the Medina, then south again on a line along Laredo to the eastern slopes of the Sierra Madres, deep in Mexico.

Soon afterward, as Spaniards measured time, Royal surveyors and officials arrived to legally parcel out the land. The Crown had determined generous subdivisions for the cowmen moving north. Since Mexican law already recognized the primacy of water possession in land tenure (who controlled the water controlled the land), the *porciones* marked off for colonists were laid out at right angles, north and south of the Rio Grande. An average grant, called a *merced* (literally, "The King's mercy"), contained a half mile of river front, extending many miles inland. Thus each grant had access to the river, with the riparian right.

The King's *mercedes* were quite merciful. Escandón, created Count of Sierra Gorda for his services, was awarded a colonization grant of 100 miles of riverfront beginning at the mouth of the Bravo, following the south side of the river west. This merced contained 645 leagues, or

2,850,000 acres in all. Around Camargo, beginning with the inevitable church square in the central plaza, 10,000 *varas* were granted on each side to the town, or four square leagues of 4,428 acres each. Eleven *porciones,* 1500 varas wide and up to 20,000 varas deep, were alloted to the gentlemen colonists of the new town, on each bank of the river. The gentry at Reynosa received 80 very similar grants.

The territory north of the river nearest the Gulf, considered unfit for permanent towns, was reserved for wealthy hacendados and "Spaniards of reliability." Such reliable men received huge land grants that reached from the Bravo as far north as 100 miles, or to the very borders of the new province. Three of these, the Espíritu Santo, the San Juan de Carricitos, and the San Salvador de Tule *mercedes,* each contained between 250,000 and 500,000 acres.

Some of these lands were resold at reasonable prices. The Count of Sierra Gorda put up some thousands of acres at 10 *duros* per league. There were some small holdings, principally around the towns. But the movement to the border was not the advance of an antlike army of small settlers; it was the carefully controlled march of feudal trains. The *patrón,* or *latifundista,* laid out his lands, received his title, and moved his cattle and his peons onto his new dominion. It was an organic, paternalistic, and quite rigid society that took hold of the Rio Grande and spilled over into Texas. It was permanent. The *ranchero* or *hacendado* and his *vaqueros,* both Indian and *mestizo,* rode together to the frontier to have and to hold, each according to his station, from this day forward. Both put a solid stamp on the south Texas frontier that was to last and last.

Settlement remained mostly confined to the south bank of the river, but cattle by the thousands spilled over and roamed north. Here, in the grassy savannahs along the Nueces, cattle and cattlemen found an unexpected refuge. The climate was mild, the land open and rich in feed, and the Indians scarce. Apaches and Comanches did not care to enter the south Texas triangle, the old Coahuiltecan grubbing grounds. Compared to the north, game was scarce. Bison did not go below the Balcones Escarpment because of the increasing warmth. The lack of fixed settlements made it a poor country for raiding, compared to the areas further west. And the position of the garrison at Béxar, in the raiders' rear, made far-ranging war parties uncomfortable. Indians, expert at ambush, knew how to avoid one.

There was nothing but lean Spanish cattle and a few *vaqueros* along the Nueces; all Indians preferred to scout a Mexican settlement or mission than to make war on a mounted, mobile, and armed Spanish-Mexican cattle ranch.

Therefore, on the savannahs just north of the Rio Grande, vast herds of cattle grew by natural increase, while Béxar and other Spanish settlements barely clung to life.

Life was also hard for the new towns along the Rio Grande. Like virtually all frontier societies, this was a poverty-stricken culture in both thought and goods. There were priests and peons, and Falcóns or Garzas who could ride their own acres for days, but there were almost no carpenters, or artisans, or men with professional skills. There was no education, except for those rich enough to leave to seek it. There was no money—but few men needed it. Sheep and goats and cattle and beans provided food enough for all classes to live.

The Indian peril never ceased. Apaches struck out of the blue-shaded mountains just to the west. Comanches rode down a well-marked trail in spring and fall. The localities furthest west suffered most; they were nearest the Indian path to Mexico. In 1771, Indians forced the township of Laredo to move to the south side of the river. For the whole border, 1792 was a terrible year, with burnings, killings, and torturings. Complaints to King and Viceroy brought promises but seldom any action.

Spanish officials and leaders held countless councils with the Indians; it was estimated that the governor at Béxar gave presents to nearly two thousand Apaches or Comanches in a single normal year. None of these brought relief to the baronies along the Rio Grande. But in a courageous, hardy, if stultified way, the culture clung. Neuvo Santander, reaching from Tampico to Corpus Christi Bay, and westward again to Laredo, contained 15,000 Spanish-speaking souls in 1800. All but a few hundred still lived south of the Rio Bravo.

This Mexican colonization of the Rio Grande affected Texas more than all the missions. It did three things, each of considerable historic importance. It carried the seeds of *charro* culture north; Mexican cattle kingdoms entered North America. It established land titles, and with them certain features of Spanish law, north of the Bravo, putting a permanent imprint upon the region. And finally, for future trouble, it seeded a breed not of Spanish priests or half-breed soldiers but tough Mexican frontiersmen along both banks of the Rio Grande, who came to stay.

But the advance of this colonization ebbed at the river. It scattered seeds, but not swarms of people, over the north bank. Beyond the river, the land remained *tierra despoblada,* populated only with lean and longhorned cows.

The first successful Hispanic colonization of Texas was not to come until much later, in the 20th century.

Part II

BLOOD AND SOIL:
THE TEXANS

6

THE ANGLO-CELTS

The Anglo-Saxons—lacking grace
To win the love of any race;
Hated by myriads dispossessed
Of rights—the Indians East and West.
These pirates of the sphere! Brave looters—
Grave, canting, Mammonite freebooters,
Who in the name of Christ and Trade
(Oh, bucklered forehead of the brass!)
Deflowered the world's last sylvan glade!

WALT WHITMAN

THE Spanish arrived in the New World in the hope and assurance that God would provide, and for some centuries they were not disappointed. They found unbelievable deposits of gold, silver, copper, and rich plantation lands and millions of potential slaves. The 18th-century Spanish empire was the world's largest, richest, and however ironical it might seem to later generations, the world's most envied. Britain and France, in this bullionist age, acquired no lands with mineral wealth and were forced to create riches through their economies. But they envied, and dreamed of wresting away, the wonderful Spanish possessions. It was not easily apparent that the flood of precious metals was having a lethal effect on the fossilizing society of Spain.

At the end of the 18th century, the Spanish empire in Middle and North America presented a glittering vista. New Spain alone contained seven million people, almost as many as Great Britain, and the City of Mexico, with 150,000, was the metropolis of the hemisphere. The life of the privileged classes was as opulent and sybaritic, if not as brilliant, as any in the world. Mexico was a great capital, presiding over a very respectable empire, which had at least twice the population of the Anglo-American states on the Atlantic seaboard.

Reaching northward from this imperial base, Spain held legal title to almost all the lands of the present United States west of the Mississippi, plus Florida and most of the Gulf coast. The Spanish flag had replaced the French over the vast Louisiana Territory. Texas, New Mexico, and Arizona, though largely *tierra despoblada,* had been Spanish for centuries. Spanish garrisons and missions, sparked into activity by Russian explorations, were moving firmly up the California coast, from San Diego to Monterey.

Anyone looking at the map of the last years of the 18th century would have predicted a vastly different future for North America, if the prediction were based on geographic factors alone. But geography, in human affairs, is usually limiting but rarely determining. North of the Bravo, the Spanish lions-and-castles flew over a vacuum which the Spanish Crown, despite valiant and expensive efforts, could not fill.

There was far more enlightenment, anticlericalism, and even good humor in Spanish officialdom under Charles III and Charles IV than is usually recognized. These men had considerable vision and a reasonable grasp of the empire's problems. If they were unable to do anything, it was because social tensions were too far gone, and there was an incredible amount of obstructive machinery in their way.

The society of New Spain was not composed of citizens. When the Indians were finally granted "citizenship" in the 1790's, this was an empty act. Hispanic society was frozen into a series of human corporations—classes, state, and church—each with its own bureaucracy, and most mutually hostile. It was rigidly centralized in theory by the power of the Crown, which in the face of the corporations was often powerless. New Spain strongly resembled Roman society in the days of the Dominate and suffered from the same flaws. In a structure so organic, even the concept of citizenship failed. Only the symbol, and the legitimacy, of the Crown held the whole fragile framework together, as much by centrifugal force as anything else.

Spanish officialdom in New Spain during the last quarter of the century was aware Spanish power was sitting on a local volcano. The *criollos* were disaffected; the *mestizo* element was restless; and even the Hispanicized Indians were showing signs of rebellion. The governors and officers in North America were beset with the generations-old wild Indian problem, and a newer problem that frightened them considerably more: the ominous approach of another outside people toward their empty landscapes. For within seven years after Spain had erased the French danger with the acquisition of Louisiana, the English-speaking settlements that had been confined to the Atlantic seaboard for two hundred years began to move toward the Mississippi, in one of the greatest armed migrations of all time.

If Spain built rigidly in its own image in the New World, the British Isles tended to spin off a haphazard swarm of dissidents, diehards, and refugees to America. If cavaliers and assorted gentlemen came to build estates or seek their fortunes as did the *hidalgos* of Spain, vastly more Britishers emigrated because the home country was, for various reasons, unbearable. The first Massachusetts settlers were middle-class refugees from the gaudy episcopacy of Laud and Hooker; they were followed, in other areas, by persecuted Roman Catholics, and during the Civil Wars of the 17th century, conquered adherents of the Crown. Following the Restoration, hundreds of Cromwell's officers sailed, with whatever fortune they possessed, to the middle Atlantic colonies. Other dissidents, religious or economic, followed.

Two characteristics of this American immigration stood out: the people left mainly for ideological reasons, not to seek their fortunes; therefore, few ever had any intention of returning. Second, the emigration was never controlled, certainly not in its decisive years. For long periods the various governments of Great Britain paid only minimal attention to its Atlantic dominions. This, plus the long-developed traditions of county government in England, allowed the scattered colonies to build viable local societies of their own.

To understand the pattern of sudden Anglo-American expansion after the middle of the 18th century, it is necessary to understand that English-speaking society between the Atlantic and the Appalachians was not a cohesive whole. In modern times, the differences between Puritan New England and the plantation South have been thoroughly explored. Actually, these differences were probably not so great in the 18th century as a century, or two centuries, later. If the "aristocratical spirit" reigned south of the Mason-Dixon Line, still Pennsylvania, New Jersey, New York, and Delaware had evolved a tight and interrelated landed and mercantile elite. The local affairs of Massachusetts Bay were not in the hands of Yankee small farmers. A Middleton or Rutledge of South Carolina was perfectly able to room with, or communicate his views to, New England's Hancock or Sam Adams in the Continental Congresses at Philadelphia.

By the year 1750 the British colonies in America had evolved into a newly prosperous, Protestant, inherently liberal "deferential society" in the seaside counties and towns. One enormous difference between America and Europe was that on this side of the Atlantic there was almost no poverty on the European scale. Underpopulation had something to do with this, but human poverty seems to be more often the result of social forces than the nonavailability of resources. In Europe, with an abundance of the richest soils on earth, millions still went hungry; on the rock-scrabble soil of Massachusetts no one, after the first few winters, starved.

The social structure of British America and the position of the landed and mercantile elite could best be described as that of an oligarchy or squirearchy, with limited powers. Institutions as they developed on the coast were remarkably free. Local governments were elected by mass ballot. The laws of most colonies required electors to be freeholders or to own land, but this requirement does not seem to have been strenuously enforced. George Washington as a young squire was returned to the Virginia Burgesses by "cheerful, rumpot elections" in which he bought the barrel. But the clusters of men and families colonial America deferred to possessed a remarkable ethical sense. A Washington, Jefferson, Richard Stockton, Livingston, or Hancock, from Virginia to Massachusetts Bay, did not sit in the seats of power due to law or caste, but more by use and wont and demonstrated ability. In this squirearchy America had a gentry fully equal to its role.

This elite was fully influenced by the enlightenment and rationalism of the century, and they inherited the Enlightenment without the crippling weight of the customs, traditions, and establishments that plagued older societies. Because it was rational and ethical, the American leadership was inherently liberal, and these men were optimistic, as men who believe in the rationality of mankind must be. The one dark cloud on this rational and optimistic horizon was the institution of Negro slavery, which was early established in all European colonies where it was economically feasible, English, Spanish, and French. This troubled the Jeffersons, Rutledges, and Lees apparently more than it did the New England squires in the 18th century, since they saw it at close hand. There was general agreement that the institution should not be permitted to spread, but beyond that there seemed to be no workable economic or social solution. No one was less fitted by rationale to make human chattels of other men than Anglo-Americans, but the problem was horribly complicated by economics, social factors, and race.

The important differences, and real tensions, within the British-American community were not between North and South in the 18th century, but between East and West, tidewater and foothills, Cohee and Tuckahoe. New England and the South did not then impinge on each other. They pursued separate ways, culturally, economically, and politically, with the only common focal point the British Isles. Atlantic America looked outward, not inward. It was part of the greater 18th-century world, and it was essentially a maritime world. The mercantile establishments of New England and the Middle Atlantic were geared to European or Caribbean trade. Even the landed estates to the South were mercantile in nature; they raised and sold produce primarily for foreign markets. A high percentage of the American gentry were educated in England, or traveled there. The Benjamin Franklins, Morrises of New York, and Southern planters never thought of themselves as anything but a part of the maritime British world. When they revolted against the home country in 1775–1776, they were not so much turning their backs on Europe as demanding new and more favorable arrangements with the Old World. Washington, in reestablishing economic ties with Britain, made this very clear. The Anglo-American leadership, after independence, did not want political connections or political involvement. They had a cold and clear understanding America did not have sufficient power to play that role.

In this essentially Atlantic orientation, the dominant view of the English seaboard was different from the outlook of the backwoods frontier. The people who had pushed to the blocking range of Appalachia by 1750 had a different culture, world view, and even racial origin from the coast. The predominant strain, and dominant ethic, of the up-country or frontier was that of the Presbyterian, or Scotch-Irish.

Nineteenth century American historians, who exhaustively sifted American evidence but rarely delved deeply into European sources or documents, were once converted to the idea that the Western frontier and free lands shaped American individualism, self-reliance, democratic ways, optimism, and the notion of virtually unlimited material or economic opportunity. The concept, really the hope, that Americans created something uniquely new on this continent is understandable, if no longer supportable. The best evidence indicates that only the sense of unlimited material opportunity derived from the frontier, for obvious reasons. For decades, the land was limitless. The other ideas and qualities were European transplants.

The background and ethic of the Scotch-Irish who emigrated to America is quite important to understanding the process of Anglo-American expansion out of the Atlantic slope, and of the dominant ethic of all inner America itself. It is a valid question, whether the long frontier shaped Anglo-America, or whether attitudes, prejudices, and ethics brought from Europe shaped the American frontier. Interestingly enough, almost all modern foreign observers, from France to Brazil, believe the latter. One band of European emigrants created Hispanic-American civilization. Very different men, facing reasonably similar conditions in many places, made the United States.

The Scotch-Irish were once Scots borderers in the British Isles, the mixed race of Dane, Gael, and Saxon of the Teutonic Scottish south. They evolved as a tough, stubborn, dour people, conditioned to border war. They fought the English for generations, though they themselves were English-speaking from the Middle Ages. The great break in their history came in the 16th century, when they took up the teachings of John Knox.

Knox brought a stunning new vision of God, man, and the world from Calvin in Geneva. This doctrine was far more than a mere reformation of the rites, and rebellion against the authority, of Rome. At bedrock, it was a rejection of the whole mysterious panoply of the medieval world, and all the pageantry of medieval British life. The Scots of the south swept the religious attic bare not only of Popes and prelates but of the concepts of hierarchy and organic society. When the priest was transformed into the preacher, not only the Church but the entire structure of Christendom was starkly changed. As always, the polities of the new religion became more important than its policies and theology, which grew stale.

Scots Presbyterianism had a common root with English Puritanism of the 17th century. But the Puritans south of the border were dominantly members of the English middle class, the tradesmen, merchants, and artisans of an already highly organized society. The Pilgrims who fled to Plymouth Rock maintained a similar world view to the border Presbyterians, but with one difference: the Scots were still a rural, and for some centuries a warrior, race.

"Freeholders and Tradesmen are the strength of Religion and Civility in the land," trumpeted a spokesman for both parties in the 17th century, "And Gentlemen and Beggars and servile Tenants are the strength of Iniquity." The social outlook of frontier America can be traced to that feeling. The idea that gentlemen were superfluous and pernicious and beggars were to be despised permeated the American frontier, but it was not born there. The statements, arguments, and atmosphere surrounding the Puritanism that failed to triumph in England and peeled off to British America show more than a hatred of social hierarchy and dependency. They indicate a strident insistence that everyone was, or should be, middle-class.

The religious wars of England's 17th century eroded Laud's insistence on the organic state of State and man, but Calvinism did not win. Modern England was to be a compromise between organic Anglicanism and Protestant Puritanism. Attitudes that were abortive in England fled to, and took root in, America. Merrie England eventually broke out of the Middle Ages keeping many of its social and religious toys intact. The Scots Covenanters made no such deals.

Hating prelacy almost as much as popery, the Scots took part on Cromwell's side in the Civil War. By one act of political genius, the Lord Protector of Great Britain transported some thousands of them to the turbulent province of Ireland. This served two ends: he removed a hardcore, armed, and dissident ethnic group away from the English border, where they were bound to cause trouble, and he delivered that trouble to the rebellious native Irish. In their new home the Scots picked up the name "Scotch-Irish," transferred their blood feuds with the Saxons to the Celts, and carved out Ulster, the greatest pale of all.

These transplanted Presbyterians were unable to become a settled peasantry in Ireland; their surprisingly middle-class ethic, and their hatred of both Irish Papists and Ascendancy Anglicans made this impossible. When the bloody battlefields of 17th-century Ireland faded into the gray, futureless landscape of the next century, the Scots had lost their function. Thousands began to look for a new border, a new frontier. Family after family packed up their Bibles, old fiddles, rusty broadswords, pewter utensils, and bleak, bourgeois ethical baggage, and set sail. By 1730, they were arriving in America by the thousands.

They left an enclave behind; the Scotch-Irish were always leaving enclaves behind. In their three major migrations—from Scotland, from Ireland, and from Appalachia—there may have been something of natural selection. The evidence indicates that those who went were more vigorous than those who stayed behind.

The Scots landed on the wharves at Philadelphia and Charleston with certain convictions firmly fixed. They were enormously self-disciplined, both by their Puritan ethic and the warlike borderer's life. They had three public virtues: thrift, because they had always been poor and Knox taught poverty was a disgrace; self-reliance, because in the new Reformed world every man felt himself something of an island; and industry, agreeing with St. Paul that who did not work should not eat. They interpreted the New Testament mainly as a moral destruction of aristocracy and beggardom. The quality of social mercy was not strained, but the idea made Scotch-Irish uncomfortable. Calvin, through Knox, extolled material success and despised human weakness. He had destroyed the old Christian concept of a station in life and built a new cosmos in which men and women should have no place, but functions. The act of being was thus meaningless; action was everything, and the worth of any man could only be judged by what he did.

The Scotch-Irish, like all English-speaking Puritans, were thus driven to material success, and whether they enjoyed this or not, they were not permitted to translate success into social class. This last was to confuse foreign observers, and Anglo-Americans themselves, for generations. Calvinists were always uneasy and rebellious at the concept of the gentleman, even when they hungered for rank. Status in society, which is much less definable than class, became their goal.

A code this practical and functional had almost no room for art as it had evolved in Europe, but it did for learning, or at least literacy. Each man and family head was expected to read, and interpret, his own Bible. The Scotch-Irish had another religious distinction; they believed that as a matter of right they should elect their own clergy, and support no other. In these attitudes, and the distrust of social rather than functional station, some historians, probably rightly, have seen the seeds of American middle-class democracy.

Like all truly successful emigrants, these Anglo-Celts abandoned a world in Europe they at heart hated. They were Israelites leaving Egypt. They had already burned most of their bridges to the traditional culture behind them when they sailed for America, but they were bringing their own brand of civilization with them. They were bound for the Wilderness, on an Old Testament trek to build the new Jerusalem. All such peoples, throughout history, have been the most fitted to seize new ground, because peoples, like children, must first sever their umbilical cords before they can stand alone. Those who would rather remain in Egypt tend to make poor pioneers.

The invasion of the Anglo-Celts between 1700 and 1740 was decentralized, uncontrolled, and uncoordinated. Apparently, Ireland was content to see them go. America was indifferent to their arrival. No government either aided or hindered them so far as can be ascertained. Yet there was a strange order, almost a pattern, to their actions in America. The Scotch-

Irish were the only major immigrant group in American history that completely avoided all existing civilization and settlement. They passed through no coastal screen, but headed for the western, Indian frontier.

There were several reasons. Lands close to the coast were largely taken; and it was already an American custom to obtain legal title to country that lay beyond present development; speculation was already old. Only the frontier, which might be legally owned by a British company or seacoast squire, had open lands. Indians or the wilderness still had possession, and few people on the Atlantic slopes were disposed to dispute this. The valleys up against the Alleghenies were untaken. There was no other place to stake out thousands of small, free farms.

The newcomers did not have to seek the frontier; all the other immigrants did not. Labor was in short supply. But the Anglo-Celts had not crossed the sea to become servile tenants. Both the Anglican South and Congregational New England had established churches and levied land taxes. For all these reasons, and probably for another, more important— the borderer instinct, which no historian can measure—the Scotch-Irish went beyond the effective jurisdiction of the colonial establishments, up against the Indian frontier. Even then, they did not go far enough to suit many of them; they were soon in continual tension with tidewater legislatures, sheriffs, and men who had no desire to fight Indians but did understand how to get legal possession of ground they had never seen through the courts of law. This tension, then and later, caused some bloodshed.

In the rolling, wooded, well-watered valleys of the Alleghenies and Appalachians, which are a single chain, the new borderers found a country admirably suited to their ethic and mythology. Conditions everywhere were much the same. Every man started equal. The Scotch-Irish staked out small farms, with the ridge lines serving as boundaries in between. They knocked down trees and burned out stumps. They cleared the hillsides and scratched open the reddish earth. They quickly learned a local agronomy from the Indians, and raised corn, squash, melons, and beans. Fruit trees they brought from Europe. They did great damage to this land, but this was neither reckless nor unreasoning in their eyes. The land seemed limitless; it would never be exhausted in their time. They were functional men, not trained to see or dwell on beauty. Later Americans would know only from French and other European travelers' accounts that western Pennsylvania, which was the Anglo-Celts' great nurturing ground in America, and particularly the river junction where Pittsburgh now stands, was perhaps the loveliest region in all the primitive continent.

With a Calvinistic, potentially urban ethic, the Scotch-Irish could only regard land as a commodity. They could not become affixed to it, like Quebecois peasants. They acquired it and spent it; hungered for it, used it, left it. Within one generation, thousands of Anglo-Celts born in Pennsylvania were moving on, side-slipping down the barrier mountains to the south. They filtered through western Virginia and met another stream, those Scotch-Irish who landed at Charleston, in the foothills of the Carolinas. The two streams joined and formed a solid, Anglo-Celt population between the inner Indian country and the coast.

These people built rude log cabins, rougher and less comfortable than Indian lodges, and ephemeral beside the adobe houses of the dry Southwest. They did not make towns, at first. They created small forts and trading posts out of necessity, and scattered their farms around them. The heavy stockades were inhabited only in times of Indian uprising, or danger. No soldiers manned them. The frontiersmen were their own warriors. These forts and stockades later became the nucleus of towns.

Society was thus ridge- and valley-bound, deep in the forest, and rural and far-flung. It was cohesive mainly because it was a society at war; defense against Indian raids demanded cooperation. But cooperation did not normally extend much beyond the valley or the settlement. Although the land and the people were everywhere much the same from Pennsylvania to the Carolinas, the frontiersmen were suspicious toward men they didn't know. The farms and the frontier produced a real sense of isolation, which would have appalled some races but which the Anglo-Celt was easily prepared to endure.

The extended 18th-century family, almost a clan, which might comprise fifty or more persons, under these conditions broke down. The settlers were spreading out, moving on, even if only laterally. The economic basis became the small farm, and under this condition the family group narrowed, to husband, wife, dependent children, and those old folks who survived past their prime. With open lands, children married and moved away. Clans grew together in some valleys, but the more vigorous human stock wandered away. Thus, in America, the family group fragmented long before the Industrial Age.

Men were farmers, fathers, hunters, and soldiers. Women inherited all the incredible backbreaking labor of the primitive frontier. The Anglo-Celts arrived with perhaps a few spoons, an axe, and only the most essential minor tools. They were forced to buy a rifle and metals and salt. Almost everything else they made themselves. It was in no sense an easy life, and it was one that never should have been romanticized. In its time and place, like most successful institutions, frontier life was necessary.

Children were not particularly ornamental, but useful. They were needed for the secondary tasks about the farm. Whenever possible, they were given essential schooling: the Bible, some writing, and simple arithmetic. Oddly, even frontier America in the mid-18th century was more literate, in the literal sense, than the old country. But children quickly had to put aside childish things. When a boy was big enough to hold a gun, he was taught to shoot. When a girl was big enough to marry, she was often considered old enough. There seems to have been little rebellion inside the Anglo-Celt family; in any event, children were pushed on their own soon enough. Family tension, like problems of social order, required a certain amount of affluence or leisure to sprout. The frontier family was functional, and maturity came earlier than it would probably ever arrive again. Work, hunger, danger, and terror could not be kept or disguised from young people. It was impossible for a boy or girl to create a false, or romantic, vision of the world. In terms of its own reality, the Allegheny world was vastly sophisticated. No Anglo-Celt child reached physical maturity without seeing babies born and people hurt, animals slaughtered and old folks die.

In Ireland, the native Scots had acquired some Huguenot and Irish blood. Crossing Pennsylvania and congregating against the barrier Appalachians, the strain became more mixed. There was an infusion of both Germanic and English stock. Here, actual national origins blurred. The Huguenot name Maury was soon thought of as English. Surnames like Boone, Frisbe, Forbes, Crockett, Reed, and Houston lost their Scottish connotation. Many Pennsylvania Dutch joined the clans, and became Celticized as Rohrbaugh or Ferenbaugh. The old American names of Wentz and Utterback seemed to cease being German. All of these, American English-speaking, Puritan Protestant, and culturally Calvinistic, were blending into a great population mass of Northern stock that would finally be termed Anglo-Saxon in the United States.

They tended to be a tall, very Caucasoid race, more rawboned than wiry. They filled the ridges and valleys with fair-skinned people and blue-eyed children, and two centuries later huge enclaves of their stock would still remain. Their birthrate was phenomenal, by any standard. Life was hard, but the climate was moderate; food was plentiful most years, and the valleys were far from pestilential cities and human crowding. Two generations before Europe learned of sanitation, Appalachia was enjoying certain of its effects. Ten children to a family were common, and the majority survived. The Anglo-American population increase, in the 18th century, was far higher than the birthrates of Spain, Britain, or even fertile France. It was higher than that of any region in the 20th-century world, including the Orient or Middle America. Here, on the threshold of what a French historian called the "Anglo-Saxon centuries," this remarkable increase was regarded by the Latin world with despair.

In 1750, almost all frontier people who professed a religion, or were churched, claimed Scots Presbyterianism. But the formal persuasion was eroding in the backwoods, and not more than a small minority of the American-born generations were churched. The Church itself suffered enormously in this century, not only from theological contradictions but from an inability to adjust itself to its people on the frontier. Presbyterianism was essentially urban in outlook, and it was not to inherit the American frontier. The newer denominations of Baptists and Methodists soon took the region for their own. But the Anglo-Celt polity and outlook suffused those religions and stamped them immutably; Baptistry and Methodism, on the frontier, were very much Puritanism reorganized to fit society. The Calvinistic code remained. Even Episcopacy, when it leaped the mountains at last, seemed to absorb an indelible Calvinist stain. The striking puritanism of the inner South, so odd against the easy Anglicanism of the tidewater coast, did not, as some supposed, suffuse down from New England. It came from Ireland, via Pennsylvania.

If the old Church fragmented in the Cumberlands, it still achieved immortality of a sort, for its ethic dominated. Organic Anglicanism was left behind.

As the second half of the century began, a tremendous American-born generation of Scotch-Irish frontiersmen was crowding its valleys to capacity. As land was then used, eroded, and abandoned, and as the hated writs from the coastal counties began to appear, the Appalachian region was threatening to explode. The excess could have drifted back to the tidewater, or added to the growing cities. There was more than enough room in this still-dawning America. But the backwoods generation was unequipped, and more important, mentally unprepared, to enter Deferential Civilization. Jammed between the endless forest, the savage unknown beyond the mountains, and encroaching Anglo-America in their rear, they had only one place to go. The New Jerusalem, whatever each man sought, did not lie behind him.

The Presbyterian Irish—never "Irish" and no longer Presbyterian—of America had turned their backs on the whole panorama of their cultural history. They retained only its tools and an ethic, abandoning bishops and baronets, pageantry, paganism, and Bach. The world they abandoned was already in a crisis of rationale, stretching from Koenigsberg to Philadelphia, when they departed with their 17th-century values intact. But they would be only dimly affected by either Paine or Rousseau. They were withdrawing from European time, and from ideas as remote from their experience as dance steps at Versailles or Hampton Court.

They were not going to retreat. They were poised to attack, a tough, hungry, numerous, riotous, and yet curiously disciplined horde. They were moving out of cultural time, to devour limitless space. They had no banners, armies, or grand leaders, no real rationale for conquest. They had their long rifles and sad songs, their fiddlers and graybeards, their chopping axes and their essentially gloomy grasp of life. McAfees, Bryans, McGees, McConnells, Harlans, Boones, Logans, and Clarks; Maurys, Autrys, Wetzels, and Wentzes—De Riencourt, the French historian who was both fascinated and appalled by these folk, tried to describe them:

> Strong, inhumanly self-reliant, endowed with an ecstatic dryness of temper which brushed aside the psychological complexities of mysticism, these puritans were geared for a life of action. They shunned objective contemplation and were determined to throw their fanatical energy into this struggle against Nature . . . they fought their own selves with gloomy

energy, repressing instincts and emotions, disciplining their entire lives . . .
remorselessly brushing aside all men who stood in their path.

No Anglo-Celt would have understood the elegant Riencourt. They had
no real intention of destroying the Wilderness, or any people who lived in
it. Their own sayings were "God helps them who help themselves," "there's
no such thing as luck," and "Devil take the hindmost," and they were going
West.

7

THE WAY WEST

. . . The West became the mainstay of American power and vigor, the home of an Americanism that looked down on the slightly decadent Easterners who stayed behind.

AMAURY DE RIENCOURT

IN the folklore of inner America the real history of the United States did not begin at Philadelphia; it commenced when a thirty-five-year-old Anglo-Celt named Daniel Boone crossed over the barrier mountains and scouted the grasslands of Kentucky, in 1769.

Boone was not the first Anglo-American to see Kentucky or to reach the Mississippi. The Cumberland Gap had already been found and named. Other men had put outposts along the river. But Boone went back to North Carolina and brought his family and a party of pioneers across the mountains, who came to stay. He was big, sinewy, and typical, born in Pennsylvania in 1734, reared in Carolina, a restless child of the old frontier. He was a great man in his way. There were a hundred, maybe a thousand, Boones nurturing in Appalachia—but he was the first to break a permanent trail and to create a settlement beyond the mountains that was completely isolated from the East. He was instrumental in founding this colony, and in preserving it during some desperate years.

Kentucky was a country of striking beauty, green limestone hills, broken forests, and meadows rich with buffalo, bear, and deer. It lacked the gloomy, endless forests farther south, or the sullen, black-soiled prairies to the north and west. Boone and his people, who were more hunters and trappers than real farmers, fell in love with the country.

The land south of the Ohio was not closely held by any Indian tribe. It had become a sort of buffer and battleground between the mountain Cher-

93

okees and forest Creeks below the Tennessee, and the less civilized but more warlike Algonkian Amerinds to the north. The really dangerous tribes, Wyandots, Miamis, and Shawnees, lived north of the Ohio. All these made forays into the lands between. Kentucky was dangerous ground.

The desperate distances involved and the dangers of carving settlements out of this wilderness have faded with time. The people who remained East, even the frontiersmen up against Appalachia, stayed in another world. This world could not even assist the pioneers in the crucial years; in fact, embroiled in its troubles with the British, it paid them little attention. The tremendous Trans-Appalachian empire between the mountains and the Mississippi was won almost unnoticed by the people on the coast.

Historians have accumulated many theories as to what made Boone's people go. But it seems safe to say that the migration was due as much to the Anglo-Celtic borderer instinct as economic reasons or the press of population. There were no fortunes to be made in the wilds by frontiersmen. There was no gold or silver or precious minerals. There was boundless land, but a man could only use the land he worked himself. Boone's people wanted to see the other side of the mountain; they had no strong ties with Anglo-American civilization, and they were not afraid of war.

Certainly, the armed migration westward was no part of the Enlightenment or rational theories of human government evolving on the coast. As its manifestos clearly show, 18th-century America was not imperial. The invasion of the Trans-Appalachian West was no result of policy of any government, American or British. In fact, this human explosion was in many ways contradictory to American thought and theory as it was being formulated in the East. The Anglo-American historical experience was to be this: the people moved outward, on their own, and they sucked their government along behind, whether it wanted to go or not. This experience, from the first, was radically different from either the Spanish or the French.

No iron-willed Washington or idealistic Jefferson, pledged to defend the rights of man forever before the altar of God, guided or shaped this emigration. They had the keen good sense, in time, to take advantage of it. And even then, the notion that Anglo-America should dominate its continent, and take all the owned, but empty, lands from sea to sea for its own advantage and protection, was not universally adopted or admired by millions in the East.

However, more and more anthropologists believe that the desire to expand, to seize territory and hold it, is a human instinct easily aroused, and one that requires no rationalization. It is only when the rationalization is attempted that hypocrisy enters in. Ironically, the Amerinds understood blood and soil; many of the people who destroyed them did not. In fact, if many of the ideas and arguments expressed in Anglo-America concerning peace and human rights had been dominant, it is not inconceivable to contemplate a United States still cramped behind the Alleghenies, complaining to world opinion about Amerind raids.

The way into Kentucky was hard. Even the passage was disputed; Boone's oldest son was killed coming through the mountains, in 1773. This pattern was repeated; the accounts of many early parties show that they had brushes with the Indians coming through. If the frontiersmen had not already had considerable experience fighting Indians, the early Kentucky and Tennessee settlements could not have survived. But Indian wars had been endemic on the borders of Anglo-America since the first white men pushed their way onto the continent, and it had not been many years since Massachusetts and other colonies had paid bounties for all Indian hair. All Appalachia had been Indian ground when the Scotch-Irish moved up against it; Indian fighting was part of the folk culture of Daniel Boone.

However, the first Trans-Appalachian generation was isolated as no other. It was not so much an extension of civilization beyond a continguous frontier as an armed intrusion into hostile territory. The experience certainly shaped this generation, and the one that followed. The men born in the late 18th century and the early 19th on the middle border were probably the toughest, and toughest-minded, in American history. As Toynbee and other historians pointed out, life in direct proximity to the Indian frontier was savage, and the frontiersman could not help but be brutalized. Yet this brutalization was held within reasonable limits, because with the exception of Kentucky the fighting frontier proved to be ephemeral, and the English-speaking peoples developed a unique attitude toward the native Amerinds.

The Indians were not considered human beings by the average frontiersman. In this way their title to the land was obviated without any need for ideological reasons such as the Spanish employed, and their suppression could be carried out without moral qualms. Killing Indians, to the frontiersman, was hardly more meaningful than killing catamounts or bears. They were all natural obstacles to his full development and enjoyment of the land.

However, there was no notion of deliberate extermination among the whites. They wanted two things: to be left alone by Indians, and for the Indians to move out of the way. The warlike traditions of the Indians and the white determination to preempt the land of course made war inevitable.

Indian warfare buttressed the frontier people's moral case. It was based on stealth, treachery, guerrilla tactics, and marked by ferocious cruelty to its victims. There were no humanizing codes or protocols, and few prisoner exchanges. Captives of the Indians were normally mutilated, emasculated, and burnt alive. It was one thing to hold a rational discussion about the brotherhood of man over a glass of Madeira in Philadelphia, but quite another to look on the blackened results of an Indian atrocity. Sympathy for the Indians existed in a marked progression back from the frontier. The frontiersmen's outlook was simple and followed a pattern. When he was weak or outnumbered, he tried to make peace with the Indians. When he was stronger, he sought to have them removed. In virtually every case the frontier people were successful in their basic aims. The true hypocrisy rested with a long succession of United States governments.

The Anglo-American frontierspeople were completely successful in establishing the moral superiority this protracted warfare required. They themselves suffered no trauma or self-doubt. They did leave a certain trauma to their descendants, and to Americans without a frontier heritage, because they never bothered to develop a ready rationale.

The frontier folk were splendidly equipped for the struggle. They had the inherited experience and organizational skills of European civilization. They had basic organizational discipline and the understanding of long-term goals, which the Indians completely lacked. The Indian's society was utterly democratic; no man had to obey any chief's orders for long or suffer if it did not suit him. The whites in time of danger could voluntarily forgo their freedoms and cooperate. The fact that during Indian uprisings no man could fail to muster was not entirely due to understanding the demands of common defense—frontier society did not tolerate any other course.

The Indians understood the country better, but the Anglo-American white was immensely adaptive. It was already an American characteristic to avoid rationales for action but to do what came naturally in the most pragmatic fashion. The Anglo-Celt might have been stubborn in his basic convictions toward the world, but he changed artifacts and techniques easily. These Americans took agronomy from the Indians, and quickly adapted their warfare to the foe. Men like Boone or Wetzel, a legendary Indian-killer, could track like Indians, and meet the savages tomahawk to tomahawk. They saw the advantages of the Indian tomahawk over pike or sword in the forest, and soon made better ones of iron. But the characteristic weapon of the frontier was also borrowed from outside the British experience. This was the Central European rifle.

The rifle had been used as a hunting and target weapon in the Central European forests and mountains for generations, and it was carried to Pennsylvania by German immigrants. The Scotch-Irish immediately saw its superiority for their purposes over the smoothbore musket and created an enormous demand. Thousands were forged in Pennsylvania, and it was also made as far south as the Carolinas, wherever the frontier ran.

This Pennsylvania (later called Kentucky) rifle was very heavy and very long, as tall as a man. It was smallbored, about .32 caliber, and forged from soft iron and fitted with a short, awkward, wooden stock. It was ungainly but immensely accurate up to 200 meters or more. The rifle's characteristics made it unsuited for formal military use, because of the tactics adopted at the time. It was difficult to load, and most effective when fired from a rest. It was perfectly suited for the western hills and forests of America, where combat was decentralized and individual, where there was plenty of cover, and men fought from concealment, lying down. This weapon made the American frontiersman the most formidable fighter and predator, on his own ground, of the time.

The rifle remained purely a frontier weapon. The tidewater militias, like continental armies, were armed with smoothbore muskets, some dating back to Queen Anne's day. New Englanders first saw the Pennsylvania rifle when Dan Morgan's Virginia backwoodsmen marched to the siege of Boston in 1775.

Although the invasion of Kentucky was unplanned and unpremeditated on any national scale, everywhere at this time the frontier began to burst. Robertson and Sevier moved with others into Wautauga, or Tennessee. All these frontier people were probably as remote from their centers of government, or even the recognition of government, as any in civilized history. Government, either British or colonial, did not impinge upon their lives. But while many of them consciously wanted to remain outside the jurisdiction of the governments they knew, they were not anarchical. They had that cohesion and sense of order that seems peculiar to the English-speaking. The Kentuckians rejected the authority of Virginia, and the weak regimes in North Carolina were despised along the Tennessee, but the frontiersmen quickly formed their own governments. Already in the 18th century, the parameters of social action, and cohesion, were outside the concepts of even elective government. Characteristically, frontier society made government, and not the other way around.

At the same time Boone founded Boonesboro, several other fortified settlements were established in Kentucky, at Harrodsburg, St. Asaph's, and Boiling Springs. Other new forts were soon built: McGee's, Bryan's, McConnell's, and more. Heavy stockades were thrown up, but only a sort of headquarters—usually the trading post—stayed permanently within these walls. The settlers cleared fields, and built crude log cabins, in the forts' proximities. Family units were scattered over wide areas. But in these extremely primitive conditions a certain order was established. The erection of forts, desperately needed in times of Indian forays, took cooperation, and around these forts the nucleus of county, not city, government was formed. Frontier Kentucky in the 1770's consisted of three more or less organized counties, whose legitimacy stemmed from the House of Burgesses in Virginia, although Burgesses had no effective control. Thus the legitimate political unit in the West became the county, under the state, something that would cause rising urban communities grief much later on.

The needs of organization were few: an arrangement for militia, which rarely went beyond agreement for all males to assemble on call, under an already elected leader; a justice of the peace to issue writs; and a clerk and sheriff at the court's disposal. The immense difference between this and the Latin-American colonies was that the initiative came from the frontier. There were no appointed officers, responsible to a distant rear.

While the Kentuckians considered themselves "independent" counties of Virginia, the Tennesseans went much further. The first free and independent commonwealth in North America was formed in 1772 in what is modern Tennessee. Here the frontiersmen created a civil government, complete with courts responsible to no others, and five commissioners to set the law. The Commonwealth of Wautauga made its own treaty with the Cherokees, the ultimate exercise of sovereignty. These county governments, and the spirit that brought them forth, were nothing new; they came directly from centuries of British tradition. But the frontier people showed they were adaptive, psychologically independent, and capable of running their own affairs. The movement west, in 1769, revealed a beginning American "revolution" some years before 1776.

A marked feature of Western county governments, incorporated into the Wautauga "constitution," was a psychological disestablishmentarianism, both toward the organic English law and organized religion. The return toward social or folk law was of course abortive; the desire for religious freedom was not. Eastern lawyers crowded the frontier long before churches could be organized.

By 1775 Anglo-American settlement was firmly fixed across the mountains. But the situation of these scattered, struggling colonies was extremely difficult. The American Revolution both robbed them of potential Eastern support and turned a terrible tide of Indians against them. It was deliberate British policy to arm and incite the Indians against Americans on the frontier, but this act of dominant British policy (once vehemently and angrily denied by British authorities in the 19th century) backfired. It made the Westerners, who were none too loyal to the rebellious coastal colonies themselves, violently anti-British. British officers leading Indians and the "hair-buyers" in Detroit, who paid for white scalps, were the renegades supreme, traitors against both white civilization and the white race. British Indian policy, which might have made sense to gentlemen safely ensconced in London, fired a smoldering, and lasting, hatred of Great Britain across the entire Middle Border.

Though Boonesboro was under siege again and again by British-incited Algonkians, the policy had to fail. Each year during the Revolution, almost unnoticed everywhere except by British officers in the West, 20,000 Anglo-Americans crossed over the mountain frontier. This population stream cemented the West to Anglo-America in a way the ephemeral victories of George Rogers Clark in the Northwest never did. When the British ceded the region to the United States at Paris in 1783, they were merely acknowledging, and the Americans accepting, a fait accompli.

Kentucky's worst times came late in the war years. In 1782 Indians and British rangers marauded through Kentucky, burning and killing. This summer, against Boone's sage and cool advice, a large band of armed settlers under Hugh McGarry, Harlan, Trigg, and Todd attacked the more numerous British and Indians at Blue Licks. The result of this battle was disaster. Although Boone, a militia captain, fought well himself, his son Israel was killed here, and seventy Kentuckians were slain. Seven more were captured and burned alive. The whole frontier was in flames, and in despair. Thirty-seven more whites were carried off in one raid. But if the frontiersmen were not able to meet the war parties and beat them in the forests, they were able to hold their fortified outposts with relative ease. The Indians were not equipped, and had no stomach, for protracted siege.

And there were too many whites now south of the Ohio. George Rogers Clark raised four hundred Kentucky volunteers and went into the Miami and Shawnee country north of the river. He was able to burn most of the Miami villages and destroy the Indians' corn just as the winter descended. All of the Amerinds east of the Mississippi were primarily agricultural, unable to live on game alone. This gambit, which worked against the Iroquois in New York earlier and years later against other Ohio tribes and the Creeks of the south, ended the Indian danger. The tribes starved, and the frontier had uneasy peace for a few more years, though Indian raids were again endemic by 1787.

The horde of sturdy hillbillies, pacifying the frontier, pulled the United States along behind them. The United States claimed the Mississippi as its western boundary, knowing that some thousands of its claimed citizens were already there. Even those policy-makers in the East who had no interest in, or a distaste for, the savage West, realized that history had already been made since 1769. The pacifistic Thomas Jefferson, clear-sighted in the power of the White House, understood that once a hundred thousand Anglo-Americans were in the Mississippi drainage, the United States must control New Orleans or lose that land and people, even if the nation had to go to war. By a fortuitous historical accident, Jefferson was able to acquire the Louisiana Territory in 1803, and thus push the inevitable Anglo-Latin conflict further west. The people went first across the mountains; dominant American policy only followed. Government pursued its people, and under the American system, was responsive to them.

This was a rhythm of cause and effect that later Latin American and European observers never quite understood, because they did not understand the makeup or ethic of Anglo-American frontier society. They saw the machinations of the American independent government easily—its attempts to buy more territory to the west, its support of the movement west with roads, harbors, military posts, and surveys. Americans of the frontier, even while vociferously demanding help and protection from the more powerful East, tended to overlook this support for natural emotional reasons. Again and again the western regions were able to force a reluctant government to move the remaining Indians out with troops, from the Ohio country to Texas. The historic support for Amerind rights, both in North and Hispanic America, invariably came from the distant governments. Both Washington and Madrid would have preferred to civilize the Indians under gentler terms. Ironically, Spanish policy failed in large measure because of Royal control of colonization, while Anglo-American, almost against the will of its nominal rulers, proved eminently successful.

The Spanish, for centuries, put forts and villas and missions in the wilderness, only to be frustrated by the failure of Hispanic populations to attack the frontier. In 20th-century South America, the same process was going on. Governments build roads into the interior, and sometimes, as with Brasilia, even cities, only to see the people, with no frontier instinct, move the other way, crowd already crowded coasts, and congregate into insupportable slums.

When the Peace of Paris was signed in 1783, most men thought it would require another thousand years for Anglo-America to fill the region between the Appalachians and the Mississippi. This estimate was intelligent, based on the slow progress of British America over two hundred years. It reckoned without either the birthrate of 18th-century Anglo-America or the restless ferocity of the Celtic borderers. Hundreds of veterans of the Revolutionary War left their bones in graves beside the inner river, and no government or power then on earth could have held them back.

What was not inevitable was the course of the organic expansion of the United States. Kentucky and the other regions, remote, distant, and disaffected in many cases from Burgesses and Congress, might easily have solidified into separate English-speaking commonwealths, with national as well as local sovereignty. Or they might have become affiliated with countries such as France or Spain. The West seethed with separatist sentiment and conspiracies, from Sevier's State of Franklin to Burr's grandiose dreams; Spain, through James Wilkinson and others, worked mightily to separate the Trans-Appalachian West. These regions found both Eastern establishments and taxes insupportable; they distrusted the deferential society and its gentry, and its writs and land laws more. They made their own local government and were determined to stand by it.

The solution was by any standard brilliant, and a credit to the continuing political instinct of the English-speaking race. To this time no nation on earth had ever treated a colony, or extension of its citizenry into new lands, as an equal. Colonies might be treated badly or well, but they were always dependencies, subject to metropolitan rule. The Northwest Ordinance of 1787, which laid the basis for new territories to be granted entry into the Union as equal, sovereign states, subject to only the broadest of limitations, broke new ground. It created a pattern that permitted the United States to absorb, with only minor difficulty, Kentucky and Tennessee. Statehood offered the western regions—even before national sentiment was fixed and firm, in the next century—enormous material advantages, both economically and for defense. Political union, as the legal equal of Old Virginia, was irresistible to all except a few by 1787, and in 1792 Kentucky became a state. At this point, probably, the doom of Hispanic empire on the continent was sealed.

By 1784, pending these arrangements, the inrush of settlers across the mountains had become a torrent. The grim Anglo-Celt hunter had torn an irreplaceable breach in the forbidding frontier, and as Theodore Roosevelt wrote in his *Winning of the West:*

> All men who deemed that they could swim in troubled waters were drawn toward the new country. The more turbulent and ambitious spirits saw roads to distinction in frontier warfare, politics, and diplomacy. Merchants dreamed of many fortunate adventures, in connection with river trade or the overland commerce by pack train. Lawyers not only expected to make their living by their proper calling, but also to rise to the first places in the commonwealths, for in these new communities as in the older States, the law was then the most honored of professions, and that which most surely led to high social and political standing. But the one great attraction for all classes was the chance of procuring large quantities of fertile land at low prices.

The western regions were still struggling, and conditions were still bad, when the rush began. Colonel William Fleming of Virginia, who later helped the settlers break with Virginia and form their own state, left a vivid description of Kentucky in 1780. Boonesboro and Harrodsburg were unlike the clean and beautiful valleys of 18th-century Appalachia; they were filthy settlements, where human offal and dead animal skins littered the ground. The water was polluted, and people were sickly. Many children died. Because of the Indian problem, corn and vegetable food was scarce; the people lived almost exclusively on smoke-cured buffalo meat, which they cooked by boiling without salt. In the outlying cabins where families still lived, conditions were even worse. But with a grim, almost instinctual tenacity, the people were holding on. They were forted up, and they had come to stay.

Five years later, things were remarkably different. New people were coming in. These not only helped, but immeasurably changed, the old frontier. Already, by the 1780's, there was a definite pattern of colonization in Trans-Appalachia, one which with regional variations held true for a hundred years.

The first white men in new country were hunters and trappers. French Canada produced thousands of these, but on the fringes of Anglo-America this type was usually Scots or Anglo-Celt. This vanguard sometimes traded with the Indians, but never adopted Indian ways; they blended neither with the natives nor the forest. If they wintered with Indians, and begat half-blood offspring, they usually abandoned these, thus maintaining racial purity of a sort. Boone himself was of this class: explorer, hunter, warrior, and finally, trader.

These men were borderers, a filter between the wild frontier and the farmer-hunters, who came next. They were skilled in forest lore and knowledgeable about the Indian enemy. They were leaders in the worst of Indian years, and their advice was often sought, if not invariably followed. Many of them—and again Boone was one of these—had a certain respect and admiration for the Indians. But their gravitation was back toward civilization, and their own kind. They might try to prevent an Indian war, but when it came, blood called to blood, and their skill and ferocity was decisive on the settler side. Few became renegades, or "Indian-lovers," the most despised terms on the whole frontier.

The borderers were extremely able warriors in their own milieu. They were entirely different from the farmer militia (which came in their wake and with which later Americans sometimes confuse them). These were the kind of men who won the timely victory at King's Mountain, and marched to New Orleans with Jackson from Tennessee. They should not be confused with farmer militia of these times. The farmer militiaman was of sturdy stock, but he only took down his gun in time of war, and marched in some semblance of military battalions. This industrious militia had as little discipline as the backwoodsman, but it totally lacked his forest skills, as St. Clair's defeat on the Ohio in 1790 proved. The real frontiersman lived with his rifle in his hand, and he could smell an Indian ambush miles away.

He was not totally admired by the more civilized frontier. Boone and Wetzel took scalps as a matter of course, and if Boone left evidence that he could live in Indian country all alone and kill a bear, he could spell neither "killed" nor "bear." Hunters planted corn only intermittently and with reluctance, and the true settler pioneer soon crowded them. By the 1780's many of the survivors of Kentucky's worst years were pushing on, toward the Illinois. Boone's own descendants moved on, hunters still, till they reached the western ocean.

Close on the heels of the hunter-trapper came the hunter-farmer, sometimes so closely that the two were hard to tell apart. This group also lived with rifle in hand, but the rifle was a supplementary, not the primary, source of food or income. The hunter-farmer did not range far ahead of his womenfolk and children; he needed them on the farm. This class was bred both to frontier conditions and easy, endless land.

They staked out small farms, cleared them haphazardly, and planted corn. Their stock, if any, was allowed to graze wild. The clearings around their cabins were usually marred with burned-out places and stubborn stumps. The cabins themselves were crude, things of neither beauty nor cleanliness. They had hard-packed dirt floors. The first farmers had only the most rudimentary tools beside the axe. They were, on the frontier, jacks of all trades—there were few stores, and fewer dollars still to buy anything—but rarely masters of any. These peoples were self-sufficient; they had to be; but they seldom lived in any comfort. There was land lying all about them in the shaded forest, but they were desperately, even stubbornly, poor.

They divided their time among hunting, fishing, and backbreaking work, and like the pure hunter, they were crowded by more industrious neighbors. When the Indians were gone, and the country settled up, with newer, richer settlers rising all around, this class tended to sell out or move out, heading on. These men were adventurous, restless, and in terms of organized society, shiftless; but they were stubbornly proud and Calvinistic for all of that. They were freedom-loving. They scorned to work for wages or to be tenant to another man. In fact, they probably worked harder and gained less with the rifle than they might have done with the plow, and they held themselves to be equal with any man.

Again and again, the hunter-settler packed up his few belongings, his grubby children, and his gaunt woman and wandered on. He rarely changed his condition but merely repeated his former life. He carried certain dreams, and certainly a certain heartbreak, with him where he went. He tended to despise the successful gentry, the lawyers, the merchants, and their airs. This man, like the trapper before him, was a true pioneer; he helped break a savage land, but he paid a savage price. His kind made up the mass of poor whites on the Southwestern frontier.

The people who crowded out the Boones—the farmer-settlers—tended to be more industrious than adventurous. They were the normal strain of civilized men—not afraid to fight but much preferring to avoid an Indian war. They normally did not arrive in large numbers until the Indians were crushed; then, if there was more trouble, they were instrumental, politically, in having the Indian remnants pushed on, but by federal forces. They voted and paid taxes, and within a few years of arrival took control of the country away from the frontier leaders, the old Indian-fighters. They came for opportunity, which meant land to clear and to hold. Their outlook and reason for existence were almost wholly economic. They spoke of getting ahead—though they also claimed to be making a place for their children, and children's children. They were a part of the Anglo-Celtic stream, though now heavily reinforced with English and other extractions. They sprang not so much out of the old Cis-Appalachian frontier, but the more settled lands behind it. There were restless, but they tended to move less, and to put down roots. They hunted—all frontier Americans hunted—but they hunted as a supplement, or sport. They were above all else farmers.

At first there was little to distinguish one of their cabins from those of the tribes that preceded them. But Tocqueville saw through this class of American pioneer:

> Nothing can offer a more miserable aspect than these isolated dwellings. The traveler who approaches one . . . towards nightfall sees the flicker of the hearth flame through the chinks in the walls; and at night, if the wind rises, he hears the roof of boughs shake to and fro in the midst of the great forest trees. Who could not suppose that this poor hut is the asylum of rudeness and ignorance? Yet no sort of comparison can be drawn between the pioneer and the dwelling that shelters him. Everything about him is primitive and wild, but he is himself the result of the labor and experience of eighteen centuries. He wears the dress and speaks the language of cities; he is acquainted with the past, curious about the future, and ready for argument about the present; he is in short a highly civilized being, who consents for a time to inhabit the backwoods, and

who penetrates the wilds of the New World with the Bible, an axe, and some newspapers.

There was as little of the European peasant in these farmer folk as in the preceding hunter-trappers and hunter-settlers. The farmer-settlers were enormously industrious, however; their instinct was not merely to conquer the frontier but to destroy it. They put their sweat into their farms, and their first painful capital into barns or new improvements. They gradually erected comfortable frame houses and filled them with clean-lined if plain furniture they made themselves. They quick-burned timber, to get a crop in, but then they year by year tore out the rocks and stumps. The American farmer-settler was stubborn, intelligent, literate, self-reliant almost to a fault, and suffused with what was now a discernible middle-class, democratic bias. These farmers considered themselves the salt of the earth.

They worked very hard, for the most part; they "got ahead" and could see the visible results of their work, and despised most people who did not or could not do the same. They rarely got rich. A man could only work so much good land, and hard money, always, tended to be extremely scarce on the older frontier. Landowners, even if small, they much preferred money inflation to more sober times. They grudgingly respected those richer than they, but remained suspicious or derisive of the gentry or any whose success gave them social airs. They became the backbone of the countryside; they planted a strong, cohesive, eminently successful if colorless Anglo-Saxon culture in the land.

Besides the corn, melons, and squash raised for food, beef, wheat, and tobacco began to be produced in surplus. Cotton—at first always a crop for capitalistic enterprise—came later. Horse culture came very early across the mountains, and flourished particularly in Kentucky. Tobacco, some sold upriver as evil "stogies," and horses soon created an economy in which there were a few more luxuries than the first two emblazoned forever on the American frontier: the bowl of cherries and an apple pie.

Schools, demanded by the Puritan instinct, were established everywhere. Few communities were unable to support a young New Englander with some learning, or perhaps an Irish immigrant who had seen better days. Boys and girls went to school together. They learned everything their society required them to know: reading the Testament, spelling, and simple figures. Schoolteachers were almost always immigrants from outside, usually young, usually going on to better things—almost a tradition on the American frontier. They enjoyed universal respect in this consciously building society.

The Western frontier, strangely, did not so much loosen social bonds as remake or re-cement them. The first stock into the old Southwest was not truly "Southern"; most of it came originally out of Pennsylvania. People from every state in the original thirteen followed. One of the phenomena of the frontier South, however, was that it quickly created its own American patina, its own folklore, and its own dominant ethic. There were no real cities to enhance but at the same time fragment culture, and conditions on the early frontier did not permit the formation of enclaves. Everyone was thrown together. Lutherans were buried in Methodist cemeteries; the few Roman Catholics who wandered to the frontier married into, and were lost in, the Puritan mainstream. This mixed people, basically British and at least one-quarter Celt, became everywhere very much alike, over wide distances.

If the Scotch-Irish disintegrated as a distinct race, they stamped their ethic, their notion of democracy, their biases, and their energy across the whole region, which was immortality enough. What was continued was the remarkable Anglo-American culture of intense order without formal restraint. An early settler of Kentucky, who had become a judge, wrote James Madison:

> We are as harmonious among ourselves as can be expected of a mixture of people from various States, and of various Sentiments and Manners not yet assimilated. In point of Morals . . . the inhabitants are far superior to what I expected to find in any new settled country. We have not had a single instance of Murder, and but one Criminal for Felony. . . . I wish I could say as much to vindicate the character of our Land-jobbers. This business is attended with much Villainy.

In this increasingly tribal society on the vanishing frontier, there was one deep flaw, generally as unpalatable to later Americans as the pattern of Indian warfare. Land was the source of most wealth, but it was also the source of most trouble. Land speculation, in a "land-poor" region, was continuous. Land ownership was often difficult to define. Paper money was issued by state wildcat banks, not on the basis of solid deposits but on acres of undeveloped land. There was continual litigation, land booms and busts, which ruined many families and forced many others to move on. Some of this speculation in public lands—everything up to the Mississippi became "public" lands in 1783, and twenty years later the Louisiana Territory entered the federal soil reservoir—had national implications and effects, and one financial panic was instrumental in sending the first American colonists to Texas.

Men acquired public lands in various ways, mostly by buying up legitimate government purchases or grants; then they speculated wildly in them, without developing them, ruining credit and currency, destroying established prices. There was more land, most of the time, than the economy could afford. A lasting American class, the land speculator (ironically often called a "developer"), was soon born.

But the settlers who were able to put down roots prospered reasonably. Nowhere was there much luxury, or one-tenth the specie that passed through the City of Mexico, until the last great class of immigrants from the seaboard passed over the Appalachians.

These were the people of means, who in the 18th and 19th centuries referred to themselves as gentlefolk. These were the planters, successful

merchants, and lawyers. There was a lasting American tradition that this
class, if it could be called a true class, itself sprang up or arose on the
frontier. But this was rarely the pattern. The rich merchant usually came
with merchandise and mercantile instinct from somewhere else, often
Pennsylvania; he was sometimes Scotch-Irish, but not the trader who had
first opened a primitive post on the stockaded frontier. The lawyers, who
were indispensable once the West had joined the States, brought their
education with them from the older regions. The planters, who more than
anyone else resembled a true social class rather than a status elite, invariably carried capital, in the form of acquired land titles and Negro slaves,
from the English tidewater, or at least the area behind the hills. The
merchant and the lawyer came West for obvious reasons, just as the lawyer
and merchant, in colonial America, had frequently left the New England or
Middle Atlantic States for the far South. In a new, building country opportunity was greater. But the plantation agriculture of the South, with its
tobacco, was also ruining miles of lands. There were new empires that a
man with know-how, connections, and a handful of slaves could create
beyond the blue mountains.

All these groups, which formed the commercial, legal, and educated elite
any highly organized society required, came looking for good situations
in the West. They came after the war whoop and the screams of Indian
victims had passed away, but not so far behind that they could not be
considered true pioneers or makers of the land. Some came from families
"already high on the Atlantic slope"; many merely claimed to. If a man
said he came from Virginia and displayed civilized manners, his claim to
gentility was honored. The Anglo-Celt vanguard rarely mentioned, and
actually had forgotten, its antecedents. Few of the first pioneers, after a
generation or two, could trace their ancestry behind the Cumberland Gap,
or wanted to.

The new elite, which filled a void and in a rather hostile world clung
instinctively to itself, did bring education, skills, capital, and manners to
the middle border. It also brought less popular things: Negro slavery and
uneasy concepts of social class.

The mercantile and professional elite sought the burgeoning sites of
future cities, while the planters acquired suitable lands. The groups tended
to merge. Successful lawyers married into plantation families, and rich
merchants deliberately, following ancient English social instincts, purchased land. Even in America the manure pile had a more genteel odor
than the countinghouse. The coming elite, then, did not settle everywhere.
The plantation economy required flatlands. The planters acquired acres in
the grasslands, in the river bottoms, or in the black belts. The hardscrabble
hills were left to the hunter-settlers, huge enclaves of which held fast in
western Virginia and eastern Kentucky and Tennessee. But the governments, the tone, and the manners outside the mountain regions, and of the
states themselves, gradually became dominated by the planter class. They

had the money, the assurance, and the time to devote to politics. Their understanding of, and connections with, important men in the old states gave these men definite advantages. The settlements might, and frequently did, elect representatives in coonskin hats, but the beaver-topped planter dominated the community.

In a country where men were very similar and conditions of life much the same, the planters and mercantile elite differentiated themselves in several annoying ways. They created, or tried to, limited genteel social circles, on the order of Williamsburg or York. They built imposing houses and introduced a custom until then utterly foreign to the frontier: the concept of hospitality. The Anglo-Celt tended to be suspicious of strangers, and even churlish to people outside his clan or ken. The planters imported clothes and furnishings from the East or even Europe. They made a fetish of sending their children back across the mountains to school.

If the lawyers were invaluable to the organic continuance of the community, and essential once the West began to enter the Union as states, they also aroused antagonisms. The frontiersman had needed no legal talent to face the requirements of his existence. The lawyers brought social history and familiarity with the concepts of Anglo-Saxon law and justice. But they also carried along land titles, law suits, and a whole frightening bag of tricks that frequently dissolved the frontiersman's possession of his blood-won ground. Noticeably, in the folklore of both the old and the later West, the lawyer, like the banker, is rarely cast as hero. The small farmer and pioneer detested the orator who could neither plow nor fight Indians, who inevitably dominated political offices, and who invariably sided with the most-propertied class.

The merchant came closest, in modern social parlance, to being a class enemy to the farmer. The merchant made possible the arrival of goods and the rise of comfort on the frontier and filled a very necessary void, but the antagonism of a people who never quite had enough money to buy is understandable. The feeling was more psychological than political.

All of these inheritors of the old frontier were perhaps envied, but not disliked for their material success. The functional Anglo-America of the West already had a great respect for, and mythology about, material success. It was perfectly proper to build two-story brick houses; the real tension between planter and dirt farmer was the former's pretensions to social class. In a Puritan ethos there was no real place for the role of the gentleman. What emerged was a sort of uneasy compromise. The planter adopted, quietly, his pretensions to gentility; the strongly puritanical majority of the country studiously ignored the pretensions, and only became furious if they were flaunted in their faces.

The planter, however, was not so much a gentleman as a working capitalist. He bought land, raised cash crops, and with the surplus quickly produced, invested in more land, to the extent of his luck, ability, and desire. The blot on this successful agriculture was the planter's employment of and dependence on Negro slaves. Strangely, by the turn of the 19th century human slavery was firmly imbedded across what was one of the most egalitarian areas of earth. The frontierspeople who went west both above and below the Ohio were initially very much the same. But slavery, and the quick imposition of a capitalist plantation economy in the South, created very different societies. The first prosperity, on the surface, was won handily by the South, which was soon a surplus-producing region, with a viable upper class. But the Northwest Territory had two advantages. The Ordinance of 1787 forbade slavery, and its climate was unsuited for the then richest cash crops. The old Northwest Territory was to be spared the social residue of Negro slavery for almost two hundred years.

Slavery eroded certain values on the formerly free frontier. It also produced race hatred. The frontiersmen disliked human slavery both in theory and practice, and it took no great effort to extend this feeling to the slaves, with whom they were hard put to compete. When the first planter in a new community came to a cooperative house- or barn-raising, and watched while his "niggers" sweated shoulder to shoulder with a throng of poorer whites, a stain was thrown over the whole frontier. The free farmers disliked planters, but hated Negroes, somewhat illogically fixing the victims with the system's blame. Negroes were hated next to Indians, because the frontiersmen found it harder to hate people that they much more despised. The Indian seemed to have some admirable qualities; the unfortunate black, to white frontiersmen, had none.

Except for the institution of slavery, the rising gentry on the border South would have been unable to establish caste. They were not, and never would have been, an aristocracy in the European sense. They might be mainly Episcopalian, but they were not free from the Calvinistic pressure of cause and effect. Theodore Roosevelt's description of this class is significant, in a way he himself, a conscious member of the old American gentry, probably never understood:

> Their inheritance of sturdy and self-reliant manhood helped them greatly; their blood told in their favor as blood generally does tell when other things are equal. If they prized intellect they prized character more; they were strong in body and mind, stout of heart, and resolute of will. They felt that pride of race which spurs a man to effort, instead of making him feel he is excused from effort. They realized that the qualities they inherited from their forefathers ought to be further developed by them as their forefathers originally developed theirs. They knew that their blood and breeding, though making it probable that they would with proper effort succeed, yet entitled them to no success which they could not fairly earn in open contest with their rivals.

The planters of Kentucky and Tennessee were, like the rest of Americans, a driven class; they concerned themselves with matters such as success, which no true aristocrat would understand. Under Roosevelt's biases, the truth comes through. These were whiskey-drinking Puritans, as deeply imbued with the American ethic as the hard-nosed, farming middle class.

The Southern frontier, then, like a vast horde of jungle ants, moved inexorably toward the Mississippi. There was order in the seemingly chaotic march. And, common to all English-speaking societies, there was something of the anthill in its industriousness, its internal order, and its individual discipline, which differed from those of the American North only in slight degree. Nowhere was there anything of the stubborn mysticism of the Spaniard, or the individualism of the French, both of which required imposed restraint. The Anglo-Saxon built his own prisons and lived in them cheerfully.

First came a swarm of free frontiersmen, more belligerent and daring than ambitious. They were followed by a larger swarm, narrow-minded in its economic preoccupation, but industrious. Finally, there arrived a growing class that styled itself as an elite. This class stamped manners, thought, and custom, but otherwise hardly impinged upon the others. Meanwhile, the frontier experience threw these separate ethnic and social components together, making one common people out of many.

A permanent, and lasting, single people was created along the Southern frontier, out of shared experience and a sense of common destiny. A true nation was made. Unfortunately, as history unfolded in other parts of the Anglo-American continent, this Southern frontier was to become something of a nation within a larger nation. All Americans did not share its outlook and experience. The great majority of people never left the East while there was a frontier, and other millions, by coming late, avoided the struggle for the continent altogether.

It was no part of their history; they took little pride in it, and were never influenced by the sense of race, blood, and common soil it engendered.

An American historian in the 19th century described the frontier vanguard in the following words:

> Thus the backwoodsmen lived on the clearings they had hewed out of the everlasting forest; a grim, stern people, strong and simple, powerful for good and evil, swayed by gusts of stormy passion, the love of freedom rooted in their hearts' core. Their lives were harsh and narrow; they gained their bread by their blood and sweat, in the unending struggle with the wild ruggedness of nature. They suffered terrible injuries at the hands of the red men, and on their foes they waged a terrible warfare in return. They were relentless, revengeful, suspicious, knowing neither ruth nor pity; they were also upright, resolute, and fearless, loyal to their friends, and devoted to their country. In spite of their many failings, they were of all men the best fitted to conquer the wilderness and hold it against all comers.

The Anglo-American 18th-century frontier, like that of the Spanish, was one of war. The word "Texan" was not yet part of the English language. But in the bloody hills of Kentucky and on the middle border of Tennessee the type of man was already made.

8

THE FILIBUSTERS

*In 1806, the only towns . . . in Texas were San Antonio,
numbering about 2,000 inhabitants, Goliad with perhaps 1,400,
and Nacogdoches with nearly 500. In spite of the dangers that
constantly threatened them, many excellent American families
had settled near Nacogdoches, and these, with the officers in the
Mexican army, formed the higher circles of society. Elaborate din-
ner-parties were given, at which the conversation was bright and
sparkling, the toast-speeches witty and eloquent: toasts were always given to the King of Spain and the President of the United
States. In San Antonio lived many descendants of aristocratic
Spanish families; the army officers were generally men of polished manners, as they often came from the Vice-Regal Court of
Mexico; the priests were men of learning and refinement. The
governor made frequent receptions, while each night on the public
square the people met to dance, to converse, to promenade, and
to visit. Captain Pike, who (in 1805–6) was sent out by our
government on an exploring tour, reported San Antonio to be
one of the most delightful places in the Spanish colonies.—*

ANNA J. HARDWICKE PENNYBACKER,
in *A History of Texas for Schools*, 1895

To Spanish officers holding the west side of the Mississippi, the vision of
this cold, dry, graceless, and restlessly aggressive race helping themselves
to the continent was frightening. There was a historic antagonism between
the Hispanic and the English-speaking worlds, rooted in the collapse of the
Middle Ages. The Puritan frontiersmen still told tales of the Spanish Inquisition and thought of the King of Spain as the archtyrant; Charles III's
officials were appalled at the energy and the Mammonite tendency to what
they called "piracy" of the Anglo-Saxon horde. *Anglosajón,* in Spanish,

had always a pejorative connotation, standing at best for men without manners, and at worst for rapists and looters.

The French dream of North American empire was exploded in the gunsmoke at Quebec, but Spain had inherited France's superb strategic position athwart the Mississippi. The red and gold of Leon and Castile flew over New Orleans, and Spanish cannon dominated the river. In this era before rails or efficient land transport, Spain controlled all inner America's outlet to the sea. But Spain suffered from the same deadly weakness that made the French presence in the Ohio country ephemeral. Spain ruled only some 20,000 Europeans in the entire Louisiana Territory, and most of these were Canadian French.

A few cannon and a few thousand French-speaking subjects did not make Spanish power secure. There were no troops, or even the will, in metropolitan Spain to keep a firm grasp on this outpost of empire. Spain's legal title to Louisiana was recognized by all powers, but as Spanish colonial officials well knew, history rarely turned on legality alone.

Don Francisco Bouligny, a Spanish officer commanding in Upper Louisiana, or Missouri, was the first official to recommend a rather dangerous step: to fight the Anglo-Saxon population increase by trying to incorporate it within the borders of Spain. In 1776 Bouligny recommended that immigration be opened to Anglo-Americans who were willing to change citizenship. He saw that Boonesboro and other settlements in Kentucky were now firmly fixed, and there was even an English-speaking outpost on the river, at Manchac. If the east bank became solidly English, Bouligny argued, the English would eventually dominate the country. His purpose was to suck all new settlement west of the river, under the Spanish flag. Spain would have to allow freedom from restriction and give liberal grants of land. The price the immigrants would have to pay would be loyalty to Spain.

The ethnic homogeneity of the empire had already been broken, with the incorporation of thousands of ethnic French. Most of these had made loyal subjects. Bouligny proposed that English-speaking Roman Catholics be given land grants. The law of Spain required all citizens to be Catholic and permitted no other form of worship. Bouligny's first proposal was that only Catholic Englishmen should be admitted freely, and supplied with Irish curates in the pay of the Crown.

Whatever the supply of Irish priests, however, the stumbling block was that there were no Roman Catholic Anglo-Saxons on the Mississippi frontier. In fact, there were only about 30,000 English-speaking Catholics in all British America, and none of these were in the West or could be induced to go there. Bouligny now went further: he wrote that immigration should be opened to "any individual, whatever his nation, especially if he comes with his family and his negroes." He ignored the delicate question of religion. However, Governor Gálvez understood and agreed. Louisiana officials had no power to change the law, but to create a viable community of immigrants they would have to ignore it. This, carefully never put in writing, they agreed to do. Unknown to most Anglo-Americans, or for that matter even to their own countrymen, many Spanish officials were themselves in violation of the law. They were freethinkers, or at least, Freemasons.

The American Revolution threw a stream of refugees, mostly Tories, across the Mississippi. Some even built a town along the Amité River. These people were not molested by Spanish soldiers, and in 1779 Gálvez even paid them an official, friendly visit. When it was apparent that the United States had won its independence, most of them took the oath of allegiance to the King of Spain. In 1783, Gálvez was able to secure a Royal edict that all refugees into His Most Catholic Majesty's dominions should enjoy the right to stay. Many did.

Gálvez, and his successor, Miró, were now actually building a pluralistic society in a most unusual place, a colony of Spain.

By 1787, Miró was actively pursuing two courses of action. The Spanish Minister at Philadelphia was empowered to recruit Anglo-Americans for the Missouri country, while General James Wilkinson of Kentucky, one of the oddest and most successful scoundrels ever to wear an American uniform, was paid to separate the western settlements from the United States. As part of the conspiracy, Wilkinson secretly took an oath of allegiance to Spain and tried to foment a war between Virginia and Kentucky.

The Spanish policy of recruitment was more successful. One Revolutionary veteran, Colonel William Morgan of New Jersey, contracted to settle a number of American families at the mouth of the Ohio, at a town called New Madrid. The Spanish offered lucrative deals to responsible men who could recruit and found a colony at their own expense. They were granted the title *empresario* and given enormous acreages of free land. The families they brought with them were also well rewarded. Spain granted rich land—leagues of it—under terms immensely better than those administered under the public land policies of the new United States. Missouri had other advantages: the French, long before, had already wiped out the powerful Indian tribes through a combination of warfare, smallpox, and venereal disease.

Several thousand American citizens emigrated to Missouri. Among these were a number of men who later became prominent in the state. Although these colonists agreed to become Roman Catholics, they were officially assured they would be left in peace. Miró, in a private audience, smilingly insisted that it was quite all right for one family to continue being Protestant. They did, however, all become citizens of Spain.

The Louisiana governor's plans were almost upset by the unexpected arrival of a Capuchin priest, Padre Sadella, who was sent out by the Inquisition, in Spain still a law unto itself. As reported in an official document of 1789, Miró acted quickly. He had Father Sadella arrested and shanghaied aboard a vessel bound for home. The arrest was carried out at night, and Miró pretended he had never arrived. He was quite concerned that the news of the Inquisition's interest in the affairs of Louisiana would leak out.

Angrily defending his action to the King, Miró wrote: "His Majesty ordered me to foster an increase in the population, admitting inhabitants from the Ohio country. These people were invited with the promise they would never be molested . . . the mere mention of the name of the Inquisition would stop all immigration, and cause those already here to depart." As Miró well knew, it would also have caused a riot among the Catholic, but not particularly pious, French of New Orleans.

The Anglo-American settlements in Upper Louisiana generally prospered. Despite the clash of cultures, there was no real trouble. The problems of religion was scrupulously avoided, and the problems caused by Spanish customs law were evaded by all concerned. Spanish officers either "took their bite (*mordida*)" or turned their backs; at any rate New Madrid and other communities did a flourishing business with Pittsburg and other trading posts on the Ohio. Under the *de jure* tyranny of Spain, a handful of enlightened officials had created a *de facto* free society comparable to that of the United States. They considered their policies eminently successful. Missouri was filling up, with Spanish subjects whose only fault was that they still spoke English. Miró felt that a generation or two would bridge that gap, but in this he was much too sanguine, for the English-speaking would have soon predominated.

The only trouble at all came over local self-government, and this was prophetic. As *empresarios,* Morgan and his kind were Spanish officials; they were granted vast powers over their colonies. They were expected to run them in the manner of hidalgos. Morgan, wisely, let New Madrid hold elections and generally run itself. Although the Anglo settlers caused no trouble, Morgan's granting of self-rule aroused Spanish suspicions and fears. Miró and his officers, all aristocrats, had no trust at all that ordinary subjects could govern their own affairs. In Spanish eyes, Morgan's system was tantamount to anarchy.

Two things brought the Spanish dream of a great new Mississippi empire to an end. First, the United States was able to hold the western settlements in Kentucky, and through the device of statehood, begin its rapid, organic growth. Now, Spanish threats to close the Mississippi to Anglo shipping did not cow Kentucky, but brought the danger of a U.S.–Spanish war. Second, the fatal weakness of metropolitan Spain brought all Bouligny's, Gálvez's, and Miró's work to an ignominious end. In 1800 Napoleon, First Consul of the powerful French Republic, his ambitions blocked in Egypt, reconceived the old notion of a Gallic American empire. Napoleon forced the King of Spain to cede him Louisiana, in return for some petty Italian territory.

At this transfer Napoleon made a solemn covenant that the French would never alienate Louisiana or let it fall into the hands of an English-speaking power. But Napoleon had broken promises before, and would again.

The British Navy, and a Negro revolt in the French possession of Haiti, again blocked the French dictator's dreams of overseas empire. By 1803, Napoleon was drawn back to brewing continental war, and he realized that the resumption of conflict with Great Britain would endanger French control of Louisiana. Almost at the same time that the French flag formally replaced the Spanish over New Orleans, Napoleon abruptly sold the whole territory, with its people and its historic claims, to the government of the United States.

The Spanish experiment with pluralism and free immigration ended abruptly in 1800, for reasons beyond Spain's control. But the policy was to influence later history, for two reasons. One was that everyone concerned considered it a great success; Napoleon's commissioner for Louisiana, after investigation, had even recommended its continuance to the Anglo-Saxon-hating leader of the French. Spain would be tempted to try it once again, in Texas. A precedent was set.

The other reason was that one of the Americans who took up lands in Missouri, and became a loyal citizen of Spain, was a Connecticut Yankee named Don Moses Austin. He and his son, as *empresarios,* were to bring the first Anglo-Saxon colony to the country north of the Rio Grande.

At the close of the 18th century, an exhilarating sense of opportunity pervaded the entire Anglo-American frontier. The Indians had been pushed back into northwest Ohio; settlers were in Illinois. Kentucky was a prosperous state, and only the friendly Chickasaws still held extensive lands in Tennessee. Georgia had acquired title, under federal law, to all its former Indian territories. Everywhere, thousands of settlers were pouring west, and the Territory of Mississippi was being organized. The Amerinds of the old Southwest were in their tragic half-century of full retreat toward the dessicated lands of Oklahoma.

It was now being shown that the free citizens of an egalitarian republic could exercise a far more energetic imperialism than the most corrupt ministers of a monarchical state. But Anglo-American imperialism, if that were the proper word for it, was a folk imperialism: it was largely individual enterprise. The various governments only entered the picture when a task arose too big for private citizens—such as removing all remaining Indians from their lands within the boundaries of a new state. The purpose of government, in Anglo-American thought, was not to hinder but support. And because this was a free society of white citizens, with freely elected officials, the governments were and had to be acquiescent and responsive. No ukase out of the national capital could protect the Amerinds or halt the steady encroachment west.

Jefferson's purchase of Louisiana was more in the nature of support of this movement, than of its shaping or control. In the same fashion, a few years later Americans were going into Florida, whether with Jackson in pursuit of Indians or as settlers running down fleeing slaves, and the better part of valor was to secure the land by diplomacy or purchase to avoid the risk of war.

The Americans of the Southwest had a taste of territorial expansion, and both a sense of far horizons and ethnic superiority—a feeling that then pervaded the whole English-speaking world. They were also belligerent, a lasting American folkway that seems to have formed its base in the old Southwest.

These attitudes, coupled with a lasting distaste and sense of separation from the Old World, bordering on xenophobia in some cases, were useful in the erection of a powerful and dominant United States. They did not, in intellectual terms, create for many Americans what historians call a "usable past." Hypocrisy and confusion entered into the American concept of history when the attitudes and practices of the expanding frontier were correlated with the 18th-century Atlantic manifestos, to which thousands of frontier folk never subscribed.

The British government still played its disastrous game with medals and firearms for Indian chiefs, hoping to contain the American advance. This containment effort was far too little and too late. The West was determined on three goals: more land, dominion over the continent, and expansion of its folk. The War of 1812, which established American independence beyond doubt and helped crush the Southern Indians, was entirely popular in the West. It was perhaps significant, however, that Massachusetts, still mercantile and Atlantic-oriented, almost chose secession in preference to a British war. The border was not much concerned with freedom of the seas. It was determined to have freedom of action.

The national government was frequently painfully caught between Eastern pacifism and Southwestern expansionism and belligerency, swinging one way or the other, depending on where the immediate power lay.

At the close of the 18th century, besides the wood choppers and plantation makers of the border West, another class of expansionists was rising in the land. These were the men called filibusters, who cut a brief but bloody swath across the old Southwest.

The term filibuster, derived from the old English word freebooter, by which Anglo-Saxons invariably described Sir Henry Morgan and the various looters of the old Spanish Main. The word had semantic significance. Drake, Morgan, Dampier, Rogers, and Shelvocke went beyond the recognized international law. Morgan had raided the Caribbean coast and looted Panama with only the flimsiest license. But the English freebooters, in most Anglo-Saxon eyes, served a national and ethnic as well as a personally profitable purpose. The freebooters did not, or were supposed not to, attack their own kind; they confined their damage to the King of Spain—an ancient, historic, religious, and ethnic, if not always admitted, enemy.

Sir Henry Morgan, the freebooter supreme, was considered to have done necessary things his own cowardly government would not, or could not, approve. The French had this same class of entrepreneur in the Gulf and Caribbean and called them *boucaniers,* and in the 17th and early 18th century French and English buccaneers often were allied. Freebooter came into the French language as *flibustier,* and then, through a curious process, back into American English as filibuster. It carried all its emotional connotations intact. Significantly, Spanish never adopted a term for freebooter or buccaneer. All such men were called simply *piratas,* or pirates. When *filibustero* came into Spanish usage, it referred to American insurgents against the Spanish Crown.

The first of the American filibusters was Philip Nolan, mistakenly named by Edward Everett Hale as "The Man without a Country." Nolan was an educated man, who immigrated to the frontier from Ireland, with a love both for far horizons and the main chance. In the year 1785, he was known in Texas, from where he engaged in a highly dangerous and completely illegal trade with Natchez on the Mississippi. If Louisiana encouraged Anglo immigration and allowed free trade, the Governor of Texas, Manuel Muñoz, emphatically did not.

Nolan's business was mustanging—gathering wild horses in Texas and selling them to the burgeoning market in the South. He scouted Texas thoroughly and was the first English-speaking person to make an accurate map. In his business and his map-making, Nolan saw Spanish weakness, and smelled the heady scent of empire. Already, there was something about the open spaces of Texas that strongly affected the Anglo-Celtic mind.

In 1797 Nolan presented the Baron de Carondelet, Governor of Louisiana, with a copy of his Texas map and received a contract to sell horses to a Louisiana regiment. Both men knew his operations were in Texas, and therefore, illegal. Carondelet and his Texas colleague, Muñoz, were not always on the best of terms. More important, Nolan also entered into a secret compact with General James Wilkinson, commander of the United States Army. Wilkinson suggested that Nolan get together some good men and detach Texas from New Spain, with the General's clandestine support.

In October, 1800, Nolan reentered Texas with a party of about twenty armed Americans and some personal slaves. This was ostensibly to be just another mustang raid. But the new Texas governor, Juan Bautista de Elguezábal, was gripped by an attitude approaching phobia toward all Anglo-Americans. This feeling was rapidly becoming dominant on the Spanish-American frontier. Elguezábal, aware that there were already American squatters in parts of east Texas, issued orders that all North Americans whose conduct was the least suspicious should be arrested. Nolan fully qualified; in fact, the Spanish claimed to have evidence that he planned to foment a revolution and make himself King of Texas.

Standing orders were issued to "put Nolan out of the way" if he ever again returned to Texas.

Nolan met a Spanish patrol in east Texas but was able to face these men down. He got as far as the Brazos River and had assembled three hundred horses, before a full company under Lieutenant Musquiz tracked him down. Musquiz surrounded the American camp by night and attacked it at dawn.

In a brief, sharp fight, Nolan was shot and killed. Peter Ellis Bean took command of his forces, but, outnumbered and almost out of ammunition, Bean surrendered to Musquiz, on his own assumption that the Americans would be sent back to the United States. The Spanish officer instead marched them into Mexico, after noting in his journal: "Nolan's negroes begged permission to bury their master's body, which I granted after causing his ears to be cut off in order to send them to the Governor of Texas."

Nothing was known in the United States of Nolan's fate for many years. His men were held in Mexico pending a Royal decision on what should be done with them. This did not arrive, with Spanish slowness, until 1807. The King decreed that every fifth man should be hanged as a pirate, and the rest sentenced to ten years' hard labor.

Meanwhile, all but nine of the party of twenty had died of prison or hardship. The Spanish official empowered to execute the King's orders took this as a mitigating circumstance, and decided only one American should be hanged. The survivors were assembled on their knees before a military drum, blindfolded, and threw dice from a crystal tumbler. The lowest, and fatal, number was thrown by Ephraim Blackburn, who, Spanish records show, was duly hanged. The rest were marched to Acapulco, which then was hardly an Anglo-American resort.

The fate and even the names of all except Peter Ellis Bean were lost. Bean was a recalcitrant but remarkably resourceful prisoner. He once threw his plate in a Spanish priest's face; he tried to escape several times; and he was once tortured by being placed in stocks and left for fifteen days. When revolution against the Crown broke out in Mexico in 1810, Bean at once volunteered to join the Royal army and fight. He was released. At the first opportunity he deserted to the revolutionary general Morelos, and talked Morelos into sending him back to the United States to win American sympathy and aid. Bean arrived again in New Orleans in 1814, in time to fight the British in Andrew Jackson's army. Surviving all this, he returned to Mexico a few years later, after independence, and was made a colonel in the Republican army. He married rich, and died in bed.

Meanwhile, Nolan's sponsor, General Wilkinson, was busy with many things. Wilkinson was another of that series of fantastic figures of the Southwestern frontier. Like St. Denis, he wore his nation's uniform—but his service was always strictly for himself. He was not typical—but not entirely unusual for the times. Neither the American army nor diplomatic service was yet professional; men went in and out of offices as their influence allowed, but few thought in terms of a federal career. Wilkinson became one of the greatest double agents—but not quite traitors—of all times.

Before he assumed command of the U. S. Army, he had been part of conspiracies against George Washington, George Rogers Clark, Mad Anthony Wayne, Kentucky, Virginia, and the United States itself. In 1787 Wilkinson traveled down to New Orleans. While in command of the Kentucky militia, he made a secret concordat with Spain. He became a Spanish citizen, promised to separate the Western counties from the United States, and went back north with Miró's gold. He almost fomented a war between Kentucky and Virginia, but survived with reputation intact and was rewarded with command of the army. When he took command in Louisiana, after Jefferson's purchase, he was still a citizen of Spain, and drawing Spanish gold in return for regular reports on what the *anglosajones* of the North were plotting next. At the same time, he spoke regularly to important Americans about the possibility of detaching Texas from New Spain.

When Wilkinson and United States forces entered Louisiana on the authority of the Purchase, there was an extremely delicate diplomatic situation. At first, the Spanish refused to evacuate; the return of the province to France in 1800 had been kept secret, and the French tricolor had gone up just shortly before. Finally, Spain gave in—only to be stunned once more.

The United States government insisted that it had bought not only Louisiana, but everything north and east of the Rio Grande as well. The French, to sweeten the Louisiana pot, had revived their old claims to Texas, and sold them as part of the Purchase. President Jefferson indicated to Spain that he expected their people to evacuate Texas, with great popular support. Now, there was extreme tension on the Texas-U.S. border. Spain responded by throwing more troops into east Texas, and by standing fast. They argued that even Napoleon could not sell a province he had never owned.

With Texas unresolved, there was another, more immediate problem. Since the days of St. Denis, the actual border between Texas and Louisiana had never been surveyed or defined; it had been a matter of gentleman's agreement between the Spanish and the French. But the new Yankees on the border were much more difficult to reason with than the French. Spain put soldiers across the Sabine, at the old post of Los Adaes; the Americans demanded their removal, and before they were removed, there was almost open war. The Americans now insisted the boundary was along the Sabine; the Spanish held it extended south directly from the Red.

Wilkinson arrived on this messy scene and personally took charge. He opened a lengthy protocol with the Spanish over the boundary question, and while this was going on, dispatched a New Jersey officer, Lieutenant Zebulon Pike, to scout New Mexico. Whatever Wilkinson's motives— probably to foment a war of nerves—this action was remarkable in light of the touchy diplomatic situation.

Wilkinson had other irons in the fire. He informed the British government about a possible Anglo-American invasion of New Spain. When he had the British interested, he informed the Spanish ambassador that Great Britain was plotting against Spain. Spain increased his pay. Meanwhile, Wilkinson pulled his greatest coup of all; he caught the imagination of the Vice-President of the United States, Aaron Burr.

Wilkinson mentioned the possibility of detaching Texas, New Mexico, and perhaps even Mexico itself from Spain. The original idea was Wilkinson's, but Burr, who whatever his faults was a man of action, "matured it." Making, as he thought, a secret compact with Wilkinson that the general would resign and join his project at the proper time, Burr made a trip west in 1805, seeking support, raising men and arms and shipping to carry them down the Mississippi. By this time, Burr had left the office of Vice-President.

What the result of this grand design would have been can only be conjecture. Wilkinson had overplayed his hand. He was having difficulty in keeping federal politicians off his back, and the Spanish themselves were getting suspicious. If Spain revealed his secret dealings—or even the fact he was a Spanish subject—Wilkinson would be a candidate for a firing squad. Now, realizing his schemes could no longer be sustained, Wilkinson extracted himself with brilliance, if utter immorality.

He wrote President Jefferson that he was on the trail of a great conspiracy. Having caught Jefferson's interest, he next revealed the traitor's name: Aaron Burr. For Jefferson, and for a great part of the country, he could not have named a more fortunate choice. Burr was unpopular; now he became an arch-ogre. To defray his great expenses in tracking his conspiracy down, Wilkinson asked the President for a large sum of money, and collected.

With great cunning, Wilkinson did not accuse Burr of conspiring against Texas or New Spain. That sort of filibustering was not quite treason. Instead, he personally preferred charges that Burr was out to separate Kentucky and the Louisiana Purchase from the United States. He personally ordered Burr's arrest. Wilkinson was the sole source of this charge, and he was to be the principal witness at Burr's ensuing treason trial. Whatever else this did—Burr was acquitted on a technicality—it effectively silenced Burr, who otherwise might have talked and brought Wilkinson down in his own destruction. The Burr Conspiracy, and James Wilkinson, have always been unhappy subjects for the historian. One capable scoundrel can cause enormous riptides in the currents of history, which makes rational study dangerous. There is strong evidence to suggest that all Wilkinson's plots and counterplots were done for only one reason: to frighten Spain and therefore permit him to extort money from Spain for information. Having shaken the United States government to its roots by accusing Burr, Wilkinson sent pertinent parts of the story on to Madrid, and in return for revealing this great danger and quickly scotching it, he received a handsome sum of gold.

Then, in 1806, before quitting Louisiana and journeying to Burr's trial, Wilkinson called a conference with General Herrera, in command of the east Texas forces of Spain. He proposed the border situation be settled amicably; he agreed to accept a buffer or neutral zone between the Sabine and the Arroyo Hondo, a tiny tributary of the Red. This moved the U.S. boundary seven miles to the east. Neither Herrera nor Wilkinson had the least authority to negotiate a treaty, but Wilkinson proposed that it was stupid for them, as professional soldiers, to fight over something their respective governments would soon work out. Herrera gratefully agreed, and, since the protocol was favorable to Spain, he was upheld.

Wilkinson might have been in serious trouble for giving United States territory away. But Wilkinson, again, had read Thomas Jefferson rightly; he knew the last thing the Administration wanted was a Spanish war. He was commended for his actions. He passed out of history peacefully, like the Chevalier de St. Denis.

The Neutral Ground, as it was called, proved a legacy of trouble, not from the Spanish, but from the swarm of outlaws that quickly congregated there. Neither Spain nor the United States had jurisdiction, and under the terms of the protocol, neither could send in its officers or troops. For six years, some of the worst desperadoes the old border had ever known, thieves, murderers, and smugglers, found it a perfect haven. The situation, from the American side, became intolerable when the 1810 Revolution against the Crown broke out in Mexico, and quickly spread to Texas. Law and order dissolved west of the Sabine. Many Mexican revolutionaries fled into the Neutral Ground. Finally, Lieutenant Augustus Magee of the United States Army was authorized to clean the strip out.

Magee, who was a hardheaded frontier officer, quickly broke up the robber gangs. Some inhabitants of the strip were killed in fighting, a few were hanged, and Magee, to show the United States meant business, had the prisoners his men took tied to posts and flogged. The strip did not again cause trouble.

But now Augustus Magee, looking across the Sabine to Texas, caught the heady scent of empire. In New Spain, the Revolution had failed: the powers of the Crown, Church, and Army had killed Hidalgo and crushed his Indian and *mestizo* followers. But Texas and Mexico still seethed with frustrated Republicans, and some of these had sought refuge in the Neutral Ground. Magee met some of these men, who were both educated and idealistic, and they implanted the notion in him that the Royalists in Texas were both corrupt and ripe.

Magee, who was no idealist, also was familiar with Zebulon Pike's experiences in the West. Pike had ventured into New Mexico on Wilkinson's orders, and deliberately, it seems, planted the United States flag at a little fort beside the Upper Rio Grande. It is not known what Wilkinson's intention was, except perhaps further to frighten Spain.

If so, he succeeded. Spanish documents show that the civil, military, and ecclesiastical authorities in New Mexico felt consternation at the appearance of the U.S. flag on their soil. A detachment of soldiers was sent to arrest Pike. But he was an entirely different proposition from the piratical Nolan: Pike was an officer on the regular service of a bordering and quite truculent power, and there was no question of hanging him. The governor of New Mexico hit upon the happy idea that Pike had merely lost his way, which Zebulon Pike, surrounded by Spanish soldiers, let stand. Pike was taken to Santa Fé, wined, dined, shown the extreme courtesy of which highborn Spaniards were capable, and sent back to New Orleans via Chihuahua and San Antonio de Béxar. Shortly afterward, the Spanish government sent three companies of troops on a march from Béxar to Santa Fé, directly across Comanche country, probably as a show of force to prove to the Americans that Texas was still theirs.

Pike kept a clear, trained eye on his travels through New Mexico, Texas, and New Spain. His puritanical Yankee soul was astounded at the luxury of Spanish officialdom—Spanish officers traveled about with burros loaded with delicacies and wines. But he also saw and reported the rags and indiscipline of the common soldiery. Spanish culture had frozen on this frontier. Spanish cavalry was armed with shield and lance. The militia carried old musketoons and even crossbows. If it came to war, this country was ripe for plucking, or so many Americans thought.

Lieutenant Magee was already toying with the notion of empire when his own government made up his mind. Although he had a good record, he failed promotion to captain. Convinced that the cause of Republican liberty in Texas was being lost mainly because there was no competent soldier west of the Sabine to lead it, Magee resigned his commission in January, 1812, and appointed himself a colonel in the "Republican Army of the North," which he now proceeded to raise.

These were extremely confused and bloody times in New Spain, or Mexico. For a generation social tensions had been rising in the Spanish empire, based on poverty, political oppression, racial antagonism, and the clash of castes. The ideas of the American and French revolutions touched a few highly educated or prominent men and created republican sentiment. However, the first real crack in the structure came when Napoleon, invading Spain, forced the Bourbon King off his throne, in 1808. This caused a guerrilla war in Spain, and it paralyzed the Americas. All power, and all initiative, rested with the Crown, which was suddenly and disastrously defunct. No council, governor, or viceroy in America recognized French rule or Joseph Napoleon—but Ferdinand VII, for a time in French hands, could not rule either. In America, in a time of great tension, there developed a fatal interregnum. The whole, overcentralized structure of Spanish government rapidly crumbled.

In 1810 a *mestizo* priest, Hidalgo, raised the *grito* or shout of revolt against the government in Dolores. This was much more a social insurrection than either a republican movement or a national rebellion against Spain. With a horde of Indians and *mestizos* of the lower castes, some of whom were soldiers, Hidalgo seized the city of Guanajuato, looted it, and set up a provisional government. Soon afterward, he captured Guadalajara, and the provinces of Nuevo Santander and Coahuila—on the Texas border—went over to him. The civil insurrection was now a full-scale revolution.

But this revolt divided, rather than unified, the population of Mexico. The traditional arbiters of the Spanish state, the *latifundistas* or landowners, the army, and the Church, and most of the professional and merchant middle class stood with the Crown. Significantly, the revolutionaries came predominantly from the lowest classes, and most of their leadership came from the lower orders of the Catholic clergy. This was a people's revolt against intolerable conditions, not a declaration of independence on the North American order. The threat of social revolution threw most property-tied and educated Mexicans on the Spanish side; this alliance doomed Hidalgo and his horde. The revolution failed to take the capital, and one by one its leaders were captured and shot by the superior Spanish soldiery.

The Spanish people of Texas at the outset declared loyalty to the King. But then, volatile, the Bexarites revolted, seized General Simón Herrera and Governor Manuel María de Salcedo—then reinstated them. The entire social order of New Spain, with the power of the Crown gone, resembled nothing so much as a headless chicken, floundering about.

The execution of Hidalgo, Matamoros, and other leaders did not stamp out the revolution. A smoldering guerrilla warfare continued. One of the leaders of this was Bernardo Gutiérrez de Lara, a wealthy citizen of Revilla in Nuevo Santander, just south of the Rio Bravo. Gutiérrez was a man of profound republican feeling, and he fled to the United States to whip up sentiment for the revolutionaries. He spent time in Philadelphia and New Orleans, unsuccessfully, and then set up a sort of headquarters in exile at Natchitoches on the Texas-Louisiana border. Here he carried on a correspondence with the Texas republicans and suddenly interested Augustus Magee. Magee and Gutiérrez planned to invade Texas, with Gutiérrez in command for obvious political reasons, but with Colonel Magee and his Army of the North doing the dirty work. Gutiérrez began to flood Texas with pamphlets and broadsides; Magee went to New Orleans to recruit men.

Magee soon raised a remarkable army of drifters, borderers, idealists, and men of good family. He enlisted a large number of the men he had driven out of the old Neutral Ground, and even some Indians. But this was not a desperado army in the main; almost all Americans passionately believed that Texas rightfully belonged to the United States, like Louisiana, and they were opposed to the ruthless oppressions of the King of Spain. Most of Magee's recruits were adventurers, but, as they thought, in a good cause. To those who needed further motivation, Magee offered forty dollars per month, and a league of Texas soil.

This conglomerate republican army of Americans, Louisiana French, Mexican rebels, and Indians went across the river to Nacogdoches in August, 1812. The Spanish soldiery fled. The population, the descendants of Gil Ybarbo's people, met the liberators with a procession. With Nacogdoches secured, the army moved on, about eight hundred strong, with Gutiérrez in nominal command, but with Magee in actual control. Almost all Magee's officers—Kemper, Lockett, Perry, Ross, and Gaines—were American.

The invaders marched south, toward La Bahía. Here Governor Salcedo stationed about 1,500 troops and planned to hold Magee and Gutiérrez north of the Guadalupe. Magee, however, skillfully flanked and by-passed the waiting Spanish army, struck La Bahía by surprise, and captured the presidio with its stores and cannon. Inside, Magee also found the Spanish army's commissary and military chest. Magee was paying his motley forces in good silver when Salcedo and the enraged Spanish raced back to besiege him.

The filibusters, secure behind the walls of La Bahía, with food and artillery, laughed at Salcedo's demands for surrender. A four months' siege ensued. During this time, in February, 1813, Magee died. There are several versions (as with almost every event in Texas history for the next generation) how this happened, because the veterans of these gaudy times widely embellished or told different tales. It is possible he committed suicide, but the most accepted version is that Magee died of disease. Samuel Kemper, his second in command, assumed the rank of colonel and took command of the so-called American Volunteers.

Salcedo, desperate, now ordered an attack on La Bahía. Kemper repulsed this with heavy casualties to the Spanish, and in March, 1813, Salcedo retreated northwest toward San Antonio. The news of this victory spread across Louisiana and jumped the Mississippi. Americans in the Southwest spoke glowingly of the glorious deeds of the American Volunteers fighting for Texas liberty. Dozens of young men, among them the son of General Wilkinson, rode south to participate in these great events. It was firmly held that Kemper's Volunteers were fighting not only for freedom, but to destroy the outmoded claims of a polite, but quite inferior, race.

Reinforced, Kemper followed Salcedo to San Antonio. In another sharp battle, the garrison at the Alamo was driven back. Salcedo asked for terms, and Kemper gave them: if the Spanish surrendered, all the soldiers would be merely disbanded, and the Royalist officers released on their own parole. The Royalists surrendered approximately 1,200 men. The Republican Army of the North, or *Ejército del Norte,* marched into Béxar, "took possession of all treasures, rewarded all soldiers, and released all prisoners found in San Antonio."

This was enormous success. All Royalist forces in Texas were now destroyed, and the Mexican population was coming over to the Republican revolution. The American Volunteers, on April 6, 1813, issued a "Declaration of Independence of the State of Texas"—a document that drew its inspiration almost entirely from the American Declaration of Independence, and which incorporated the liberties Anglo-Americans now took to be self-evident. Kemper and Major Lockett, his principal officer, kept their troops in good control and discussed the imminent possibility of Texas joining the United States.

Now, however, there was trouble. With the destruction of the military danger, Bernardo Gutiérrez and his group of political leaders demanded full control. They informed Kemper the American Volunteers were on Mexican soil, and the Mexicans proceeded to draw up a Texas constitution that Kemper and his officers considered a vicious burlesque of republican liberalism. It followed the ancient Spanish pattern of government slavishly —quite logically, since Gutiérrez knew nothing else—but substituted a governor and a ruling *junta* for the King, with dictatorial powers. The *junta* was not elective, nor was it to be responsible to any people. Loyal revolutionaries filled all the posts.

The Anglo-Americans were particularly stunned with a clause in this constitution: *the State of Texas forms a part of the Mexican Republic, to which it remains inviolably joined.* Since Gutiérrez de Lara and all his principal associates were citizens of Mexico, not Texas, this was inevitable, but it showed that communication, somewhere, had broken down.

Then, the terrible pattern of social revolution that had begun in Mexico, with atrocity and retaliation, could not be damped in Texas. One of Gutiérrez' officers, *Capitán* Delgado, begged his chief for revenge against Governor Salcedo, who had ordered Delgado's father executed some time before. Whatever his personal feelings, Gutiérrez entered into a plot with Delgado. He told the American Volunteers that the captured Governor and his Spanish officers should be sent to New Orleans to be paroled. Kemper acquiesced.

The Governor and his officers who refused to join the revolution were dispatched toward the coast, guarded by a file of Mexican soldiers under Delgado. A few miles outside of Béxar, he stopped the march, told Salcedo to "expect death," and had all the prisoners bound hand and foot. Then, with great cruelty, Delgado cut their throats.

This murder was quickly discovered. In the uproar Gutiérrez was deprived of his command. Kemper and Lockett were enraged because their word of honor had been violated, and the high-minded Americans among the Volunteers were sickened. They regarded the attachment of Texas to the United States an act of duty, if not piety, but the callous murder of Royalists was too much. Kemper, Lockett, and most of the idealistic adventurers deserted the revolution and returned to the United States. General Simón Herrera and twelve other Spanish officers who had joined the revolt went with them. These facts, and some of the events that followed, are still controversial among Texas historians.

A man named Henry Perry assumed Magee's old command, and a Spaniard, José Álvarez de Toledo, took Gutiérrez' place. Most of the Americans who remained seem to have been common cutthroats, and while Toledo was an idealist, he had some of this breed among the Spanish.

The Americans were now reduced to freebooters, and the leadership of Toledo created problems among the Mexicans. Don José was a Republican, banished from New Spain, but he was also born in the Indies to an aristocratic family of the pure Spanish race. He was a *gachupín,* and the ordinary Texas Mexican citizenry hated *gachupines,* whatever their liberal political views. Although the Army of the North had now swelled to 3,000, there was dissension in the ranks. However, Perry was able to defeat the Spanish General Elizondo at Alazán Creek, near Béxar, in June, 1813.

The defeat of Elizondo resulted in the march northward of General Joaquín de Arredondo, who was both an experienced and a clever commander. Arredondo gathered up the remnants of Elizondo's force, and made a camp some six miles south of the Medina River, in the oak forests about fifteen miles from Bexar.

There was a great deal of argument in the revolutionary camp. Toledo insisted on taking full command. Perry's Americans refused to obey his orders in battle; they also demanded a fight. Toledo wanted to hold the north bank of the Medina and make the Royalists come to him, but the Volunteers pushed him into crossing the river and falling on Arredondo's lines. On August 18, 1813, the Army of the North crossed the Medina and tried to take Arredondo in the flank.

What was repeated was a version of Senlac Hill, in reverse. When the revolutionary vanguard charged, whooping and yelling, the Spanish general, on prearranged orders, had several companies fall back, apparently in disorder. The American Volunteers broke into a run, and immediately ran into a trap. Arrendondo's forces opened into an enormous V, with the Americans in the middle, enfiladed from each side.

Toledo gave an order to retreat. The Mexicans and most of the Indians in the force obeyed. The other wing, all American, of his army, emotionally stood its ground. Someone shouted: "Goddamit, we *never* retreat!" There was a great roar of approval, and in this way the fate of 850 American Volunteers was sealed.

At that, the frontier rifles among the Americans almost counterbalanced Arredondo's cunning and the regulars' discipline. The Volunteers inflicted heavy losses on Arredondo's 2,000 men, until disorder and a lack of ammunition broke their ranks. Slaughter followed. Only ninety-three Americans of the entire Volunteer force survived; these escaped into the woods and straggled back across the Medina. Colonel Perry was one who got away.

Toledo, who was badly wounded in the battle, eventually made his way to Louisiana. Finally, he took an oath of allegiance to the Spanish King, and was made Ambassador to the Court of Naples. Ever afterward, he retained, as he said, an awe of American irregulars. If he'd had 2,000 at the Medina, he claimed, he would have conquered all Mexico.

Now, atrocity bred atrocity. Knowing the fate of the Spanish Royalists the Army of the North had captured, Arredondo ordered no prisoners be taken. The broken elements of the Republicans were hunted through the woods. About eighty men surrendered at a place called Spanish Bluff. These men were marched, hands bound, in groups of ten to a cypress tree lying across a huge mass grave. Among those shot here was the bloodthirsty *Capitán* Delegado.

The battle at the Medina effectively destroyed the Republican cause in Texas. Arredondo and Elizondo, veterans of the social wars in Mexico, followed up the victory with the determination to stamp out rebellion forever. The Royalist soldiery swept the whole province, executing any citizen who was suspect.

In San Antonio de Béxar, the rebel capital, Arredondo arrested three hundred townsmen who had supported the revolution. They were crowded into a single adobe building overnight in August, and eighteen died of suffocation. The next morning most of the survivors were shot without trial. About five hundred of the wives, daughters, and other female relatives of these traitors were rounded up and put to work for the Royalist army, making thousands of *tortillas,* or Mexican corn cakes, daily for the soldiers. General Elizondo pursued refugees from Béxar as far as the Trinity River, and returned with a large number of women and children captives on foot. The property of suspected Republicans was confiscated. Afterward, Nacogdoches suffered a similar fate. Some hundreds of Texas residents fled across the Sabine to the United States. Although Arredondo had pledged to kill every Anglo-Saxon found on Spanish soil, a few Americans flushed out later were merely deported. No similar mercy was shown native rebels.

Outside of Béxar, Texas was virtually depopulated by the purge, and San Antonio itself was reduced to the population of some twenty years before. In fact, as Arredondo wrote dryly, when the new, liberal Spanish Constitution of 1812 was received in Texas (and became law), he was unable to fill any of the offices because there were not enough "suitable" persons left.

Simón Hererra and a few Republicans were able to survive on Galveston Island. This island, off the north Texas coast, had been named for the Conde de Gálvez, the former Governor of Louisiana, and it was still the haunt of some Karankawa Indians. Hererra, with his aides Aury and Mina and joined by Colonel Perry, organized a miniature "Republic of Mexico" and chartered a few dubious ship captains to sail against Spanish commerce as privateers.

At first this venture was surprisingly successful; several rich Spanish ships were taken. However, the Republicans made two mistakes. They attacked other than Spanish ships in a couple of cases, and one of the leaders, apparently Perry, engaged in the slave trade. By this time the United States Navy was beginning to dominate the Gulf and Caribbean, pledged both to destroy piracy and the now illegal importation of Negroes into America. In 1817, to avoid a war with the United States, Hererra and Perry decided upon a descent on the Central American coast. The buildings they had erected on Galveston Island were burned, and the Republic of Mexico took ship for the south. Neither it nor Perry survived this fili-buster.

A new buccaneer took over: the legendary Jean Lafitte. Lafitte was born in France, emigrated to New Orleans, and became a blacksmith. He first entered history in 1807, when he became the known agent for smugglers violating the U.S. Embargo Act on the Louisiana coast. A dozen legends exist about his early past—including his dispossession and the rape of his wife by officers of Spain, romantic duels, and the like—but only one thing is certain: he had and held a hatred for the King of Spain. He always insisted he was not a pirate, but a buccaneer in the style of L'Ollonois, Louis le Golif, Montbars, and Pierre le Grand; it is a claim his adopted countrymen, the Americans, have sentimentally granted.

But Lafitte was not, in his early career, an American hero. He estab-lished a base at Grand Terre, or Barataria, about sixty miles from the Mississippi, and from this directed the smuggling operations on the coast. This caused the U.S. Governor of Louisiana, William C. C. Claiborne, to offer $500 for his head. With the flair all successful rogues must have, Lafitte made the Governor a laughingstock by offering $15,000 for Clai-borne's capture in return.

Considerably more humiliating, Lafitte surrounded and captured a party of armed revenue agents in the swamps, then turned them loose with rich gifts. However, this provoked the U.S. Navy to bombard Barataria severely, and for a few years Lafitte quietly dropped from sight.

The British, in a diplomatic blunder, revived him. In 1814, when the British were preparing to invade Louisiana and take the mouth of the Mississippi from the United States, they approached Lafitte for aid. They promised him British citizenship, the command of a Royal Navy frigate with the rank of post captain, and £30,000 to make war against the United States. Lafitte, who always maintained that while he broke its laws he was a loyal "citizen" of the United States, sent documentary proof of this offer, and an offer of assistance, to the State of Louisiana. He was at once romantically received by New Orleans society, and he and his crew joined Jackson at the battle of New Orleans. For this, Lafitte received a full pardon for all crimes signed by the President of the United States.

His smuggling and his agenting for pirates, meanwhile, had suffered. Inspired by Hererra's example, Lafitte secured letters of marque from the rebel regime in Venezuela to sail against the Spanish, and in April, 1817, moved to Galveston Island and founded a town he called Campeachy. Within a few months he attracted a thousand men. To strengthen the legality of his position, Lafitte also organized a "Republic of Mexico" on the island, created a titular government, and forced his men and all newcomers to Campeachy to take an oath of allegiance to it. He professed it a matter of great disappointment when American newspapers, detailing his activities on the Spanish Main, labeled him the "Pirate of the Gulf."

Lafitte was a man of splendid appearance and considerable courtesy and dignity. He built a fine home at Campeachy, lived in baronial style, and entertained visitors royally. A very significant number of men prominent in the Gulf region visited him at one time or another. Lafitte continually professed that the United States was his adopted country, and let it be known that his privateers had strict orders not to molest American shipping, only Spanish. Some of the sea wolves sailing under his commission, however, were not scrupulous in their choice of victims. Lafitte did great damage to Spanish and other shipping on the Gulf of Mexico, and a considerable store of treasure was brought back to Galveston Island. From one such "haul" Lafitte garnered the chain and seal of a Mexican bishop, robbed on his way to Rome. This prize was given as a present to Rezin Bowie, a member of the Louisiana family deeply engaged in the smuggling and slave-running trade.

The continuing tension between the American and Spanish governments had not been eased by the succession of filibusters originating in the United States. So long as Washington maintained an official claim to Texas, each entry of American "volunteers" seemed part of an official conspiracy. While the United States government itself did not conspire against Spain, the activities of officers and men like Wilkinson, Magee, and even the buccaneer Lafitte made Spanish officials quite confused over where public policy ended and private enterprise began. Washington's protests that it had little control over the filibusters was politely disbelieved. Finally, after years of wrangling, both governments reached agreement. The United States purchased Florida, and as part of the treaty the Neutral Ground became Louisiana territory and the American claim to Texas was abandoned. This treaty was signed in 1819 and soon afterward ratified, but only over great opposition in the American Southwest.

It was vehemently held along the Mississippi that Congress had no right, or power, to sell, exchange, or relinquish an "American possession." Hundreds of angry letters were mailed to Washington. Dinner talk on the subject was violent, and there were a number of protest meetings, which were attended by prominent men. One center of opposition was the frontier town of Natchez, Mississippi.

In the spring of 1819 the people of Natchez organized and equipped an expedition, "to invade Texas and establish a Republic." Dr. James Long, who had gained a reputation fighting at New Orleans, was a favorite of Andrew Jackson, and had married a niece of James Wilkinson, was elected to lead this filibuster. Dr. Long, taking along his lovely young wife and infant child, marched west from Natchez for Nacogdoches in June, 1819, with eighty men. By the time he reached the Texas border his force had swelled to three hundred, and among these was the old revolutionary, Bernardo Gutiérrez de Lara.

Long easily took Nacogdoches, which was almost deserted after the earlier revolution and Royalist counterrevolution. Here a solemn convention was held. Texas was declared a free and independent republic and Dr. Long was elected its President. Long then offered Texas' public lands put up for sale on generous terms, and sent men to establish posts on the Brazos and the Trinity.

Now, in September, 1819, the new President of Texas set out for Galveston Island to seek assistance from the real power in the region, Jean Lafitte. On the way Long heard that a Spanish army had left Béxar for east Texas, and he sent back orders for his wife to cross over to Louisiana, while his officers were to "concentrate their forces." Then he rushed on to Galveston.

The Pirate of the Gulf received Long cordially and wished him success. But Lafitte, who had already helped another illegal expedition (some exiled Bonapartists under Generals Lallemand and Rigault, who tried to settle 120 Frenchmen on the Trinity in 1818, but were driven away), absolutely refused to become involved. He told Long coolly that no mixed group of Mexican revolutionists, American land seekers, and republican idealists could win without a large, well-disciplined army, which Long did not have.

Returning disappointed to Nacogdoches, Long learned that the Spanish General Pérez had defeated his forces, killed his brother, and captured some of his settlers. Nacogdoches itself was deserted, everyone had fled. Long crossed over into the United States, joining his wife and child.

But James Long had caught the filibuster fever. He made his way to New Orleans, talking of a new expedition. He found supporters to finance him and get him new supplies, and he fell in with Don Felix Trespalacios, a well-known Mexican Republican exile. In 1820, Long and Trespalacios, styling themselves the "Patriot Army," led an expedition by sea against the Texas coast. Mrs. Long, now with two small children, went along.

At a place called Point Bolivar, the Patriots built a tiny fort. Trespalacios then sailed down to Mexico, to spread revolution, while Dr. Long took some men and marched inland to La Bahía. Once again the old town fell to American invaders. But Royalists quickly surrounded Long's men, and the Patriots were forced to surrender. Long would have been shot, but the political climate of New Spain was now in complete flux. The leaders of the Royalists were going over to the idea of independence, and Long was, after delays, sent south to the City of Mexico.

In Mexico Long found that the Royal government had fallen; Iturbide was in power, and soon to make himself Emperor; his comrade in arms, Trespalacios, had just been appointed Governor of Texas. Dr. Long created a problem for the new regime, which did not know whether to treat him as a Republican hero or an Anglo-Saxon pirate. In the end he was shot, ostensibly as an accident, though many of his friends claimed Don Felix Trespalacios himself had given the order.

Jane Wilkinson Long, meanwhile, had remained in the tiny fort at Point Bolivar on Galveston Bay. When news of Long's capture reached there, the small garrison of Patriots voted to go back to New Orleans. All the men sailed away, leaving Jane Long, her two tiny children, and a single Negro girl behind. Mrs. Long was not yet twenty-one years of age.

The two women and two children survived the winter of 1812 mainly through courage. For some time their only food was oysters the slave girl clawed up from Galveston Bay. Once Indians appeared. Jane Long loaded and touched off one of the small cannon the Patriot Army had abandoned at the fort. The savages sheered away.

At last, a Mexican messenger rode into this deserted stretch of coast, with news that Dr. Long was dead. The indomitable Jane Long now rode to Béxar, and from Béxar to Monterrey, many hundreds of miles. She was determined to have her husband's killer punished. Finally, she realized that, despite the protestations of sympathy polite Mexicans gave her everywhere, nothing was going to be done. She went back to Mississippi on horseback.

Years later she returned to Texas and settled at Richmond near the coast. She died in 1880, honored by most of the people of the state as a heroic pioneer.

The treaty of 1819 between Spain and the United States finally ended two decades of hostility, confusion, and bloodshed. As part of the price of acquiring Florida, the United States officially renounced its claim to Texas. Disturbed by the constant intrusion of Americans into Spanish territory, President Madison had ordered American citizens not to enter Texas; however, the fact that Mexico declared independence from Spain, thus destroying the professed rationale of the filibusters, did more to bring the era to its end. Long was the last of the true filibusters in Texas.

The warlike expeditions, and the Mexican revolution of 1810, had a disastrous effect upon the province. In effect, most of the Spanish progress of the preceding century was destroyed. General Arredondo executed or exiled one thousand people, approximately one-third the Texas Spanish population. In the aftermath of Long's filibuster, royal officers drove away more settlers. Much of the improved farmlands around San Antonio, and in east Texas, went back to waste. Travelers crossing Spanish Texas faced a risk of starvation, and for some years even at Béxar food was scarce. The great problem was underpopulation. There were 30,000 untamed Indians in the province, but fewer than 4,000 Europeans, when the era of the filibusters closed.

In 1821, the United States Navy forced Jean Lafitte to halt his buccaneering operations in the Gulf. Lafitte abandoned his base on Galveston Island and disappeared from history. Some said he died a few years later on the high seas, at the hands of Spain. There were lasting rumors that Lafitte buried an enormous treasure on one of the sandy islands off the Texas coast. But, like the rest of the filibusters, Lafitte left nothing but romantic and bloody legends behind.

9

THE EMPRESARIOS

They are a strange people, and must be studied to be managed. They have high ideas of national dignity, should it be openly attacked, but will sacrifice national dignity, and national interest, too, if it can be done in a "still" way, or so as not to arrest public attention. "Dios castiga el escándalo más que el crimen" (God punishes the exposure more than the crime) is their motto. The maxim influences their morals and their politics. I learned it when I was there in 1822, and I now believe that if I had not always kept it in view, and known the power which "appearances" have on them, even when they know they are deceived, I should never have succeeded to the extent I have done in Americanizing Texas.

STEPHEN F. AUSTIN, ON MEXICANS

THE Texas filibusters strongly captured the imagination of a large part of the people of the southwestern frontier. The survivors of the expeditions spread their tales around, undoubtedly exaggerated, of American heroism, Hispanic cruelty, fortresses taken and lost, dramatic councils of war, and chests of silver coins. The miserable, struggling Spanish towns became cities rich in gold and lovely, dark-eyed women. The soil of the coastal prairies was said to be far superior to that in the United States, and the climate the best in the world. Through these tales shone the shimmering image of a fabulous empire, of broad vistas and plateaus where a man could see for miles, of barbaric Indians and millions of buffalo and cattle hardly less wild. This was country where a man could be a man, and a good man make himself a king. In these years a lasting legend was born.

But in the year 1820 an era seemed to be closing, rather than great opportunities opening. Anglo-America, after three-quarters of a century of almost incredible growth, had almost everywhere reached what seemed its natural limits. The Southwest beyond the Sabine was Spanish, and was so recognized by formal treaty. The United States, with the purchase of the Louisiana Territory, extended to the Rocky Mountains, and, in addition to Texas, Jefferson had claimed the Northwest Pacific, too. But up against the barriers of the mountains and Great Plains, the United States appeared to be entering a period of consolidation. Since 1800, its territory had more than doubled.

While there were still appetites for raw land in the West, there were very real evidences of actual opposition to any new expansion in the northern and eastern States. The question of the extension of chattel slavery in the Union was becoming difficult. The Missouri Compromise, worked out with some trouble, showed that, as President Monroe wrote the aged Thomas Jefferson, "the further acquisition of territory to the west and south involves difficulties of an internal nature which menace the Union itself."

There was a diehard contingent in the South and West, like Henry Clay and Thomas Benton of Missouri, who denounced Monroe and John Quincy Adams, the Secretary of State, for having signed away American "rights." But after Dr. Long's disastrous expeditions, vocal argument died away. Even Andrew Jackson, who had forced the Administration's hand on Florida by invading it and humiliating the Spanish garrison, stated that "for the present we ought to be content with the Floridas."

But Americans were still pressing west as individuals, and the story of the next two decades was only an outgrowth of processes that had gone on before.

One of the Americans who had emigrated to Missouri when it was a Spanish province was Moses Austin, a Connecticut-born lead mine operator in Virginia. In 1796, Austin's lead mines were played out, but there were reports that rich deposits had been found near St. Genevieve, in Upper Louisiana. Austin, who had the Yankee characteristic of going where the business was, got written permission from the Spanish Minister to the United States to investigate; leading a party of his miners and slaves, he set out for far Missouri. Moses Austin, however, was not a dreamer. He was just past thirty, already successful, and possessed of a keen political instinct.

At St. Louis, Austin halted his group, dressed himself and his men in their finest, then rode into the mud-streeted town. Austin, in a long, blue, scarlet-lined mantle, with lace at his throat and sleeves, and on a fine horse, cut an imposing figure. He deliberately led his procession past the Spanish commandant's house, and this gentleman, convinced Austin was a man of rank, immediately received him with great courtesy. Here began negotiations that ended with Moses Austin being granted a *sitio,* or square league of land, and the lead mines discovered at "Mine A Burton," near St.

Genevieve, in January, 1797. He was also granted the right to settle thirty families from the United States.

Moses Austin created the first permanent settlement in Washington County, Missouri, erected smelting furnaces, and developed the lead deposits. He was a prominent leader, and regarded as an excellent Spanish subject, when Upper Louisiana entered the United States in 1804. After his return to American citizenship, Austin prospered even more. He became one of the founders and principal stockholders of the Bank of St. Louis.

Then the first great national panic, or depression, as it was later called, struck the United States. The problem was related to the closing of the United States Bank, but the underlying cause was land speculation. All frontier banks followed a pattern: they loaned money extensively to land speculators (usually having it printed, too) who were engaged in selling public lands to emigrants moving west. The loans, and the money issues, were thus covered only by the value of undeveloped land. For a while, prosperity and inflation ensued, which in 1818 was followed by a crash. Land values, especially speculative land values, fell. Banks everywhere collapsed, including the Bank of St. Louis. Moses Austin, at the age of fifty-four, was wiped out. He was where he had started twenty years before.

The Arkansas country was opening up to the south, but Moses Austin was not a settler or cotton planter. He was an empresario and businessman. It was perfectly natural that a dream grew in him that once again he could repeat his former career, by following the Spanish frontier. After discussing the question with his son, Stephen, Austin set out, this time alone, for Texas. He rode 800 miles, and entered San Antonio de Béxar in the fall of 1820.

He entered a town still quivering from the reverberations of James Long's last filibuster. General Arredondo, the Commandant of the eastern internal provinces, or Interior, had made a career in Texas of stamping out Anglo-Americans. Arredondo was convinced, rightly, that his major troubles in Texas came from Anglo-Saxon filibusters, not local revolutionaries. He had recently given Texas Governor Martínez the most explicit orders that no *Norteamericanos* be permitted to enter Texas on any pretext, with the hint that any failure to follow them might have serious conquences, for Martínez. Arredondo, the man who had captured and killed the rebel Hidalgo and destroyed the Republican Army of the North, was a power unto himself in northern New Spain. He reported not to the Viceroy, Apodaca, but to the King.

Under these circumstances, Moses Austin's unannounced arrival at Béxar caused consternation at the governor's palace. Austin called on the Governor, and tried to talk to him in French. When Austin admitted he was an American, Martínez refused to converse any longer, nor would he look at the papers Austin carried proving he had been a citizen of Spain. Martínez' orders were unequivocal: Austin was to leave Béxar and recross the Sabine. If he remained overnight in Béxar, he would be placed under arrest.

Utterly dejected, the aging Austin left the palace and crossed the plaza to his horse. What now occurred was a genuine accident that changed history. Austin met an old friend.

Felipe Enrique Neri, Baron de Bastrop, as he was known in Texas, was a Hollander who had once been in the Prussian service. He had emigrated from Europe during the turmoil of the French Revolution, and Carondelet, the Spanish Governor of Louisiana, gave him a land grant. He founded the towns of Bastrop and Mer Rouge in Louisiana, but when Napoleon reacquired the territory, he crossed over into Texas. Bastrop preferred to remain a citizen of Spain.

At San Antonio the Baron de Bastrop was very poor, living in a single adobe room. But he had the claim and appearance of gentility, and under Spain this counted more than wealth. He was welcome at the governor's palace, and because he was a staunch Royalist, even Arredondo liked him. And back in Spanish Louisiana he had known Don Moses Austin very well, especially as a gentleman and loyal subject of the King of Spain.

Almost as important, Bastrop immediately understood what Austin wanted; from his Louisiana experience, he prepared to argue both for the American and for the feasibility of letting him bring Anglo-Americans to Texas. Bastrop readily agreed to serve as Austin's agent. Within a week, he obtained a petition approved by Martínez and the *ayuntamiento,* or governing council, of Béxar, to Arredondo and the provincial council at Monterrey, requesting permission for Austin to settle three hundred families in Texas.

Bastrop used three arguments, besides his own and Austin's vouched-for reliability:

The Indian danger in Texas would never be ended until the country between Béxar and the Sabine was colonized. The Comanches were riding into Béxar and acting as if they owned it.

After several centuries, no Spaniards or Mexicans were coming to Texas; in fact, more were leaving it.

Anglo-Saxon colonization, properly handled, had been a success in Louisiana. Here, as there, there was no other way to put people on the land.

On January 17, 1821, General Arredondo notified Governor Martínez that the petition in the name of Moses Austin had been granted, with the full approval of all councils. Arredondo had become convinced of two things, both military in nature. A band of American colonists in Texas might create a buffer between the Spanish settlements and the Indians, and the right sort of North Americans, loyal to the Crown, would prevent future filibusters. The Royalist authorities felt that colonists who were also landowners and slaveholders—"the right sort"—would hardly be revolutionaries, because they would have an immense stake in the land. In these assumptions, so far as they went, Arredondo was not mistaken.

Moses Austin never saw his grant. He rode out of Béxar for Missouri in January, 1821. He had to cross some of the wildest country on the entire frontier. Austin ran out of food; he was robbed; he caught cold, and his health broke. He reached Missouri only in time to die, but with the knowledge that he had a Royal Commission to settle three hundred families in Texas, and was once again an important man. He begged his son Stephen to carry on when he was gone.

Stephen F. Austin needed no urging. In the failure of the St. Louis Bank he saw his own career damaged, if not destroyed. Young Austin, at twenty-seven, was both in political instinct and education a cut above the public figures of the frontier. After Missouri had become U.S. territory, in 1804, he had spent four years in the best private schools in Connecticut; later, he had graduated from Transylvania College in Kentucky. In his teens he was elected to the Territorial Legislature of Missouri, won the admiration of Thomas Hart (Old Bullion) Benton, and became a director of his father's bank. While his father went to Texas to plead with the authorities, Austin staked out some land in Arkansas, separated from Missouri when the former territory became a state. He was appointed a territorial circuit judge, but he had no capital, and he also now had a great dislike for the land system of the United States.

While the Spanish system, such as it was, rewarded colonization, the public lands of the United States were sold strictly for revenue. This system fostered speculation, and land speculation had ruined the Austin bank. Stephen Austin saw that a man without money, but with an official grant, had a much better chance to succeed in Spanish territory than on American soil.

Austin rode to Natchitoches, where he met the Spanish commissioners, Juan de Veramendi and Erasmo Seguín. The commissioners quickly acknowledged him as the heir to his father's grant, which Martínez at Béxar also confirmed. Martínez gave Austin the formal papers from Monterrey, and the resolution of the Provincial Council, which read in part:

> . . . Therefore, if to the first and principal requisite of being Catholics, or agreeing to become so, before entering Spanish territory they also add that of accrediting their good character and habits . . . and taking the necessary oath to be obedient in all things to the government, to take up arms in its defense against all kinds of enemies, and to be faithful to the King, and to observe the political institution of the Spanish monarchy, the most flattering hopes may be formed that [Texas] will receive an important augmentation in agriculture, industry, and arts by the new immigrants, who will introduce them.

To this Martínez added a letter of his own:

> I shall also expect from the prudence which your actions demonstrate, and for your own peace and prosperity, that all the families you introduce shall be honest and industrious, in order that idleness and vice may not pervert the good and meritorious who are worthy of Spanish esteem and

the protection of this government, which will be extended to them in proportion to the moral virtue displayed by them.

Stephen F. Austin and the Spanish authorities had a clear understanding on two matters: one, that the American colonists would be substantial, law-abiding people; and two, that the requirement of the Roman Catholic religion would not be enforced. Neither Austin made any secret of the fact that they were Protestants, and Stephen Austin never ceased to be one, as a Mexican official. The understanding with Martínez and other officials was verbal; very soon Austin began to learn the subtle intricacies of keeping up appearances while the law was fractured. Austin did enforce the requirements of character on his colony but not religion. As the settler Linn reported, not one-tenth of the American immigrants ever adopted the Catholic faith; the few who did, did so for either politics or appearances. When the American colonization began, in fact, the Church itself was extremely weak in Texas. There were only three churches—at Béxar, La Bahía, and Nacogdoches; in 1840 Father Odin, who became the first Catholic bishop, wrote in his diary that confessions had not been held anywhere for fourteen years. The major functions of the few clergy were baptisms, marriages, and burials of the dead, for which, in the Mexican manner, "exorbitant fees were charged." Many of the Spanish and Mexican officials, *pro forma* Catholics, were in fact members of the Masonic order.

Governor Martínez seemed impressed by young Austin, and he offered him time to survey the country and choose a site for his colony. During the summer of 1821 Stephen Austin explored. He went from Nacogdoches in the far north to La Bahía southeast of San Antonio, with a small party of Americans, to pick his land. At Nacogdoches Austin noticed that there were only about three dozen inhabitants all told, with five houses and a church. He did see certain Anglo-American squatters, settlers who had moved across the border and built cabins in the forest, on Spanish soil. Among these people were the Ambersons, Cartwrights, Englishes, and J. H. Bell. A few miles beyond Nacogdoches the land became virgin wilderness, with no break to the outskirts of Béxar. Traveling the Camino Real or Royal Road, which was more a trace than a highway, Austin's party ran into Mexicans who told of finding fresh corpses along the way—one Spanish and two American. Indians were raiding even in San Antonio, killing several men and stealing horses and mules. La Bahía, like Nacogdoches, showed evidence of Magee's invasion. The old town surrounding the presidio had not been repaired, and there had recently been an Indian raid. Austin wrote in his journal: ". . . the Spaniards live poorly. The inhabitants have a few horses and cattle and raise some corn." He also noted they ate with spoons and their fingers, having neither knives nor forks.

The most impressive region Austin found lay south of the Camino Real, between the Colorado and the Brazos. These rich river bottoms were part of the Southern coastal plains, with good rainfall, accessible to the Gulf. Austin described this country as the best in the world, "as good in every respect as man could wish for, land first rate, plenty of timber, fine water —beautifully rolling." The Brazos bottomland was perfectly suited to the American plantation economy. Austin could not have made a better choice.

The site also lay outside of dangerous Indian country. It was inland from the disappearing, but still dangerous, bad-smelling Karankawas of the coast, and separated from the fierce Comanches by a buffer of two friendly Wichita tribes, the Wacos, and Tawakonis.

When Austin returned again to Louisiana, to advertise for settlers, he found around a hundred letters awaiting him at Natchitoches. The word was already out: Land and Texas, and the price of foreign citizenship seemed no obstacle in the applicants' way.

In the fall of 1821 Austin was back in Texas, and he found some applicants for his colony already there, awaiting him. Others began to arrive every day, though one party, on the schooner *Lively,* became lost and never did find the mouth of the Colorado, which Austin had picked as his marshaling point. The first settler to enter Austin's colony proper, Andrew Robinson, crossed the Brazos in November. Here he stayed and began to operate a ferry, on the site that became Washington-on-the-Brazos. Three days later the three Kuykendall brothers came by with families, then Josiah H. Bell, who had decided to become a legal colonist and deserted his holdings in east Texas. Others followed rapidly. In January, 1822 Jared E. Groce, planter, lumberman, and capitalist of Georgia by way of Alabama, rumbled in with fifty wagons and ninety Negro slaves. One of the colonists wrote down for posterity that about this time he saw six sailing ships in Galveston Bay.

The oath these colonists took has been preserved in Spanish records; it was later changed slightly to meet the circumstances of Mexican independence:

> In the name of God, Amen. In the Town of Nacogdoches before me, Don José María Guadiana, appeared Don Samuel Davenport and Don William Barr, residents of this place, and took a solemn oath of fidelity to our Sovereign, and to reside forever in his Royal Dominions; and to manifest this more fully, put their right hands upon the Cross of our Lord Jesus Christ, to be faithful vassals of His Most Catholic Majesty, to act in obedience to all laws of Spain and the Indies, henceforth adjuring all other allegiance to any other Prince or Potentate, and to hold no correspondence with any other foreign power without permission from a lawful magistrate, and to inform against such as may do so, or use seditious language unbecoming a good subject of Spain.

In return for this oath each colonist received title to land at terms unheard of in the United States. The rich river bottoms along the Brazos,

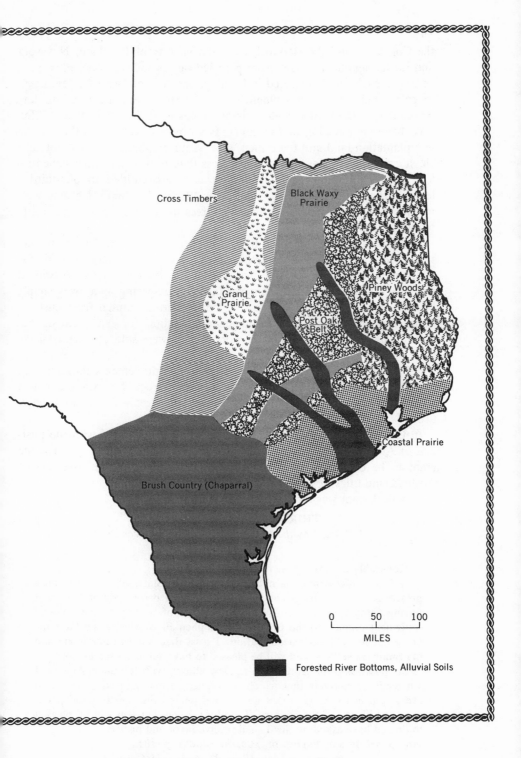

Cross Timbers

Black Waxy Prairie

Piney Woods

Grand Prairie

Post Oak Belt

Coastal Prairie

Brush Country (Chaparral)

0   50   100
MILES

Forested River Bottoms, Alluvial Soils

Regions of Vegetation in Eastern Texas

the Colorado, and the Bernard, from the vicinity of Brenham, Navasota, and La Grange to the Gulf, were parceled out as follows: one *labor* (177 acres) to each family engaged in farming; one *sitio* or *legua* (4,428 acres) to each family head who planned to raise stock. Spanish-Mexican law, unlike that of the United States, already recognized the fundamental difference between ranching and farming. For obvious reasons—although this was plantation land and these men were Southern planters—most colonists classified themselves as stock raisers. Less than twenty land titles called for less than a square league. Single ranchers were entitled to one-third a league, or about 1,500 acres—and some twenty-six "family" grants went to bachelors who joined up in twos or threes to create a family and satisfy the letter of the law.

The colonists were supposed to pay Stephen Austin a *medio,* or one-half silver *real* ($0.125), per acre, but most of this was later remitted; the government charged a flat title fee, part of the money going to Austin. It was also Austin's boast that he never turned a deserving man away simply because he could not pay. By law, colonists were exempted from customs duties for seven years and from general taxation for ten. Leaving out customs duties and taxation, these bottomlands were sold at a tenth of the price of public lands in the United States.

Substantial men were given extra acres for improvements they planned to build, or for the importation of slaves. Jared Groce, for example, got in all ten *sitios* or leagues. Austin, as empresario, received title to twenty-two.

In this fashion the Baron de Bastrop, who was rewarded with the position of Austin's land commissioner, issued 297 titles. The law required the grant to be developed within two years. Only seven of the first 297 of Austin's land titles were forfeited for cause.

A typical grant was recorded as follows:

THIRD SEAL: Four Reales ($.50)
Validated by the Mexican Nation for the Year 1824.
No. 235.

Honorable Commissioner the Baron de Bastrop:

I, Arthur McCormick, a native of the United States of America and a present resident of the province of Texas, appear before you and say that having come to this place with the intention of settling in the colonial settlement granted to the Empresario Stephen F. Austin by the Supreme Government of the Mexican Nation: I trust that you will admit me and my family as settlers, and will be pleased to have surveyed for me and put in my possession the land which the law allows, with the understanding I am ready to cultivate that which is assigned to me, subjecting myself in every respect to the laws that govern and defend the rights of independence and liberty of the country. Therefore, I beg that you will be pleased to do as I have asked; in this I shall receive favor and justice.

THE TOWN OF SAN FELIPE DE AUSTIN. AUGUST 7, 1824.

(Signed) *Arthur McCormick.*

Honorable Commissioner:

. . . . I say that the petitioner, Arthur McCormick, is worthy of the favor he solicits, and can be admitted as a resident of this new colony because of good qualities and circumstances, and his well-known application to agriculture, cattle raising, and industries. In consideration of this a league of land may be granted to him.

SAN FELIPE DE AUSTIN. AUG. 7, 1824.

Estévan F. Austin (Rubric)

In the Town of San Felipe de Austin on the 9th day of the month of August of the year one thousand eight hundred twenty-four: The Baron de Bastrop, sixth member of the most excellent deputation of the Province of Texas, Commissioner of the Government, and Estévan F. Austin, Empresario. In virtue of the Commission which the Governor of this Province, Lieutenant Colonel Don Luciano García conferred on the former . . . and of the order of the political chief of this province, Don José Antonio Saucedo . . . and of the powers granted to both by the order of the Superior Mexican Government, ratified by the decrees of the sovereign Congress, and that of the Commandant General of these Provinces, Brigadier Don Felipe de la Garza issued to said Empresario Don Estévan F. Austin: Exercising these powers and considering the merit of the petitioner Arthur McCormick, according to the preceding, by these presents, we grant and concede in the name of the Mexican nation to the said Arthur McCormick, his heirs and successors, a league of land situated on the west bank of the San Jacinto River. . . .

The Baron de Bastrop   *Estévan F. Austin*
(Rubric)   (Rubric)

The said commissioner the Baron de Bastrop and Empresario Estévan F. Austin, the witnesses, the adjoining owners . . . the surveyor, and the interested party repaired to the tract we have granted . . . [described]. We put the said Arthur McCormick in possession of said tract, taking him by the hand, leading him over it, telling him in loud and clear voices that in virtue of our Commission and Powers, in the name of the Government of the Mexican nation, we put him in possession . . . and the said Arthur McCormick in token of finding himself in real and personal possession . . . shouted aloud, pulled up grass, threw stones, fixed stakes, and performed the other ceremonies fixed by custom. He was warned of the obligation to cultivate it within two years. And for proof we certify our signatures below, in the Town of San Felipe de Austin on the 10th day of the month of August, 1824.

El Baron de Bastrop   *Estévan F. Austin*
Witness: Witness:
David McCormick   *Samuel M. Williams*

Austin's first settlers, although actually only 297 land grants were made, were called the "Old Three Hundred." These families were able to choose some of the best farming land in Texas. Not all of them prospered or survived, but out of this group came the first Anglo planter-gentry in the province. Most of these people came as farmers from the United States, but a substantial number arrived as men of means. Ancestry traced to the Old Three Hundred names, such as Bell, Borden, Kuykendall, McCormick, McNair, McNeel, Varner, or Rabb was to become a mark of Texas pride. With only a few exceptions, all these names came from the British Isles.

These people were not frontiersmen or mountaineers. Austin did not want "leatherstockings." The rules of his colony provided that "no frontiersman who has no other occupation than that of hunter will be received —no drunkard, no gambler, no profane swearer, no idler." These rules were enforced. Austin drove a number of families out of his settlements as undesirable, and on more than one occasion ordered some such unwanted immigrant into his plantations publicly whipped. Thus Austin's colony— but not, as it turned out later, the state—was kept free of certain characteristic classes of the Old Southwest. Only four of Austin's Old Three Hundred were not literate or possessed of some education.

These Americans, who were characteristic of all the land-grant immigrants, came overwhelmingly from the Trans-Appalachian South. Records show that the most common states were, in order, Louisiana, Alabama, Arkansas, Tennessee, and Missouri. Of some 776 colonial families examined, 669 registered from the Border South, and only 107 showed their origin in the East. Many people born east of Appalachia came to Texas, but very few had reached maturity there. The Texas population was part of the immense stream moving west.

The vast majority emigrated to Texas for no other reason than economic opportunity: the chance to get cheap land. Some left debts behind in the States, but most brought some form of capital: seeds, equipment, stock, or slaves. After 1820, the minimum price for public lands in the United States was $1.25 per acre, and because of the recent speculations, credit-buying was no longer allowed. For the price of 80 acres of plantation ground in the South, a Texas settler could acquire a square league, or 4,428 acres. The original price of $0.125 per acre was greatly reduced, and Austin himself lent generous credit.

The first year of the colony, 1822–23, while Austin was forced to stay in Mexico defending his commission before a succession of new, independent Mexican governments, was incredibly rough. A disastrous drought ruined the first crops. The Karankawa Indians attacked and killed a large number of settlers. Emigration to Texas stopped, and some families already there went back. But upon Austin's return, in the summer of 1823, matters quickly improved. Austin organized a militia and scoured the Karankawas completely out of his colony; some finally sought protection of the padres at La Bahía, far to the south. He made treaties with the friendlier tribes, Wichitas and Tonkawas. Some of these Indians were caught stealing horses in the colony; Austin did not hang them but had them flogged. Whatever this did to warrior pride, it effectively stopped further horse raids along the Brazos.

The colony was subject, of course, to all the laws, rules, regulations, of intricate governmental bureaucracies, first of Spain, then of independent Mexico. But actually, the Anglo settlements lay completely outside Mexican Texas. They were planted on completely empty ground, hundreds of miles from the nearest historic town or fort. By their location, high up on the Texas coastal plain, they were removed from and outside the economic sphere of San Antonio de Béxar. Lack of money and the absence of good roads handicapped trade with San Antonio; the Anglo colonies looked back north, toward the United States. Nacogdoches began a rapid growth, as a way station and trading center between the Brazos and Louisiana. The cessation of customs duties granted by the Mexicans permitted this commerce to continue.

The economy, in the small Anglo communities and trading centers that grew up, was based on barter. The books of an early merchant, the Austrian immigrant George Erath, show an intricate listing of goods balanced against other goods: clothing made in Europe traded for hogs, horses exchanged for corn, an ox for a sow, a feather bed for three cows with calves, a gun for a mare. These items were valued in a dollars-and-cents money of account, but money never changed hands. Local taxes, of which there were a few, were also often paid in kind, at the rate of a cow with calf at $10. Interest rates, when credit was allowed, were enormous.

The exports of the colony of farmers were, in Austin's words, "cotton, beef, tallow, pork, lard, mules, etc." All of these went to the United States. The only commerce with Mexico amounted to a little salt, and sometimes horses. The Texans bought anything they needed—and luxuries were almost nonexistent—from the States, usually through New Orleans. Cotton was by far the most important money crop. Ten years after Austin granted his first land, a Mexican official listed Texas exports at $500,000. Cotton accounted for $353,000 of this; furs, hides, and cattle the rest. These figures were probably guesses and too high, but they showed the pattern. This commerce with Europe and the States was hampered by the lack of decent harbors on the Texas coast.

Another indication of the cotton economy was the proportion of whites to blacks in Austin's colony in 1825: 443 slaves and 1,347 whites.

Removed by enormous distances and commercial patterns from the Mexican economy, the region between the Colorado and the Brazos was also outside the Mexican body politic. For some years there was no constitutional provision for Anglo-colonial government—Governor José Felix Trespalacios, Dr. Long's old compatriot, gave the colony local self-government by decree in 1822, and Don Luciano García made it clear to Stephen Austin that the empresario was expected to manage his people and not bother the authorities with their problems. García was friendly, and gave Austin sanction to establish a town or municipality on the Brazos, called San Felipe de Austin. This became the colony's capital.

After 1825 Texas was a department of the State of Coahuila, ruled by a political chief appointed by the Governor. This officer, really a subgovernor, resided at Béxar. The major unit of local government under the Hispanic system was the municipality. A municipality could include several towns and thousands of square miles; in other words, the principal town ruled the countryside. The *ayuntamiento* was the governing council of a municipality, combining the functions of both the North American city council and county commissioners. The chief executive officer of the *ayuntamiento* was the *alcalde,* who was a sort of mayor, judge, and high sheriff, all combined. The *regidores* were members of the council; the *síndico* was something like the present American city attorney. The *alguacil,* appointed by the *alcalde,* was the principal law enforcement officer. Municipalities were divided, if necessary, into precincts or *distritos,* with a presiding commissar, whom Americans preferred to call a justice of the peace.

Austin's colony was unofficially made a municipality, which was divided into two districts, or precincts, the Colorado and the Brazos. Austin allowed two *alcaldes* to be elected; these magistrates were to have real problems struggling with their decisions in the light of Mexican law, of which they were ignorant.

The court system of this government, in American eyes, was impossible. Both the commissar and the *alcalde* could hear cases, but neither was allowed to rule on them. The testimony had to be transmitted to the state capital at Saltillo, a distance of more than four hundred miles. A Mexican magistrate called the *asesor general* then examined the testimony and issued his *dictamen,* or ruling. This then had to be approved by the Mexican Supreme Court. Any error in the written accounts vitiated the whole process, which could go on for years. Only two things made the legal system supportable in Anglo-Texas: there was almost no crime (all observers agree on this), and what little there was the empresario handled outside the courts. San Felipe de Austin never built a *cárcel,* or jail.

In this system the empresario had enormous powers; Austin was in reality a theoretical despot. He could appoint all his officials if he chose. Since the colony was excused from state and national taxes, church tithes, and customs duties, and was created in Mexican eyes to defend Northern Mexico and itself at its own expense, in its crucial formative years official Mexico had no real interest in it. Austin in his early years was warned repeatedly to govern and defend himself and not to let his colony be a nuisance. For this purpose the empresario was commissioned a lieutenant colonel in the Mexican Army, made military and political commander of his colony, and Austin was even permitted to develop and codify his own laws. He did this, following the Mexican Constitution of 1824 so far as he thought wise.

Although Austin knew better than to act as a petty potentate, his duties and responsibilities were still enormous. He delegated such local government as seemed needed to the *alcaldes, alguaciles,* and *comisarios* his settlements chose to elect; his settlers, unable to pronounce these Arabic-derived titles, stubbornly called their officials mayors, sheriffs, and justices of the peace. Austin's real function was to deal with the state and national Mexican governments, which were often unsympathetic and remained foreign. He had to stand between these and his Anglo-Saxon planters, who might be self-reliant, hardy, and law-abiding, but were also usually prejudiced, stubborn, ignorant of the true situation, violently jealous of what they considered inherent American rights, and determined to find fault with anyone in authority, particularly the empresario. Austin had to pass on every settler; he was responsible to the state for every colonist. The Baron de Bastrop merely signed his name to the land titles; Austin had to see to the surveying and all the details. The *alcaldes* whom the people elected carried out rules and regulations, civil and criminal, that Austin drafted first. His power and position were resented fiercely by many colonists who came begging land.

At one stage the settlers revolted against the twelve-and-a-half-cents-per-acre fee Austin was supposed to collect, not because it was unfair or exorbitant, but because it was making Austin "rich at their expense." The subgovernor remitted this fee, and henceforth charged colonists only a small, set title price. Austin received a part of this, but his potential profits were enormously reduced.

Austin's efforts for his colony, meanwhile, as one observer wrote, "could not be exaggerated." He was the greatest colonial proprietor in North American history. But he was also something more. He was a politician of exquisite skill, who seemed to understand almost any kind of mind he came in contact with—Mexican, planter, or the various frontier types. He found out people's weaknesses and worked on them, with the utter pragmatism the Anglo-American frontier mentality called forth. Austin had no ideology, and he was entirely sincere; otherwise he could not have survived an incredible succession of Mexican Royalists, Imperialists, Republicans, and dictators. He began in Missouri as a businessman, but he became something immensely more important: he was a visionary, capitalist, developer, and Father of his People, all in one. Somewhere along the line, Austin lost interest in his personal fortune and developed an obsession to "redeem Texas from its wilderness state by means of the plow alone, in spreading over it North American population, enterprise, and intelligence." Austin had no notion—not for many years—of taking the land away from Mexico. What his Mexican colleagues, totally lacking in such instincts, could never comprehend was his sincere and boundless joy at the destruction of the wilderness. Each crashing tree along the Brazos gave Austin pleasure; each mud-paved town hammered together in the middle of nowhere instilled in him a sense of destiny fulfilled. In this, Stephen Austin was not unusual. Destroying nature and creating civilization as they knew it was already a fetish in North American minds. Austin merely had more vision and far more ability than most.

The wilderness, beautiful but economically barren, was an offense in Anglo-American eyes. Only when the land was tamed and all the resources of Nature put to man's use would Nature's plan be complete.

In all, there were twenty-six empresarios in colonial Texas. Austin was immeasurably the greatest, not because he was the first, or most powerful, but because he saw his role as something more than merely selling land.

Don Estévan Austin, as he was called, was essentially a civilized man, and a civilizer. He was never a frontier hero. He was slender, rather handsome, charismatic, especially to Latins, and very much the gentleman. He was really the creator of Anglo-Texas, but he was not to be the Texans' greatest hero. Austin was not a man on horseback. He was appalled by conflict and preferred to save his people by more devious ways than war.

Austin never married; he devoted his life to his cause. He took on hundreds of informal tasks beyond his position as empresario. Prospective colonists were put up at his house, and shown about, at his expense. Planters called on him to act as a collection agency, and also as their agents for commercial transactions in the United States. Men badgered him for loans, and to settle personal disputes. Parents in the South wrote him continually to find, or look out for, strayed, lost, or emigrating offspring. Austin carried all these burdens voluntarily and well.

After his first three hundred patents were used up, he applied for and got more. His colony was gradually enlarged, beginning in 1825. In ten years, Austin located more than 1,500 American families, and these became the heart of Anglo-Texas. In a single decade, these people chopped more wood, cleared more land, broke more soil, raised more crops, had more children, and built more towns than the Spanish had in three hundred years.

The various laws and decrees that permitted Austin to open Texas for colonization applied only to him. But on August 18, 1824, the Republic of Mexico, continuing Spanish practice, issued a general colonization law. This national law had four key provisions:

Public lands were remanded to the Mexican States for administration.

State land codes must conform to the Constitution.

No person could acquire more than eleven leagues (48,708 acres) for colonization.

No foreigner was to be granted land; immigrants must become citizens.

The Republican Constitution of 1824 was federalist in concept, a strong break with Spanish centralist tradition. Austin himself had something to do with this, as he recommended certain key provisions to important men in Mexico. A federal Act of May, 1824, made the former Spanish provinces into supposedly sovereign states, on paper at least, on the North American order. Coahuila and Texas were incorporated into one state, with its capital at Saltillo. The act provided that Texas might become a state when its population grew sufficiently; the Mexican mood at that time was to grant the northern colony a definite measure of independence within the greater nation. The legislature of Coahuila in 1825 passed a colonization law for Texas, in conformance with the federal enabling act. The provisions of this law were that Texas was to be opened to Roman Catholics who could prove Christian belief, morality, and good habits. Immigration could be by individuals, or through empresarios. New empresarios were commissioned with territories bordering Austin's. They could continue to grant up to one *sitio* per family, and they were to receive five *sitios* and five *labores* of land for every 100 families settled, up to a limit of 800.

Native-born Mexicans could simply buy up to eleven *sitios* for a small fee. The decrees remitting state taxes, church tithes, and customs duties were continued.

The year 1825 saw an explosion in empresarios and immigration into Texas. Twenty-five empresario commissions were granted in all, but only a few of these had any permanent effects. Although native Mexicans could acquire land in Texas under much more favorable circumstances than Americans, and the relaxation of taxes and tithes applied to them also, very few families went north. The push to this still wild frontier came almost entirely from the United States, with a few families arriving from Europe.

Next to Stephen F. Austin in importance as an empresario was Green DeWitt of Missouri. DeWitt had gone to Mexico at about the same time as Austin, for the same reasons. His contract was authorized in April, 1825, for 400 families to be located south of Austin's colony, on the Guadalupe, San Marcos, and Lavaca rivers. DeWitt laid out Gonzales, his headquarters town, named for the current Governor of Coahuila, a few months later. However, in July, 1826, a serious Indian attack pushed the Gonzales settlers down toward the coast. This drew them into conflict with Martín de León, who had in peculiar circumstances been granted empresario lands that overlapped the Missourian's.

De León originally was commissioned not by Coahuila but by the provincial government of Texas at Béxar in 1824. He settled between 100 and 200 families, almost all Mexican, along the lower Guadalupe River. This area was shortly afterward granted to DeWitt, but De León proved belligerent in defending his position.

De León's Mexican birth counted heavily for him, and the Governor of Coahuila confirmed the fact that he should be given first choice under the law. De León laid out his small capital, Victoria, while DeWitt's people, led by James Kerr, a Missouri state senator, returned west of the Colorado to Gonzales. By 1828 Kerr and DeWitt had Gonzales firmly established, with blockhouses and a small fort. DeWitt was able to issue and have confirmed 166 land titles, but most of his allotted lands remained vacant. The Gonzales settlers felt they had been treated unfairly by De León, and by the law. There was hostility between Gonzales and Victoria, which might have resulted in feuds and war. Austin himself took on the role of peacemaker, and his efforts finally damped the quarrel. José Antonio Navarro, through Austin's help, confirmed the Gonzales colony's holdings in 1831.

Another contractor, Haden Edwards, secured permission to build a colony in east Texas near the Sabine. Here, conflicting claims with earlier Mexican settlers did produce a war, which was one of the preludes to the Texan Revolution. Edward's colony failed.

In 1830 the Mexican government halted all immigration, only to renew it again in 1834. After this year, the Galveston Bay and Texas Land Company acquired the rights earlier secured by David G. Burnet, Joseph Vehlein, and Lorenzo de Zavala in east Texas. This company originated tactics that were used in the West for many years: it advertised irresponsibly in the United States, sublet large tracts to fly-by-night subcontractors, and sold scrip on 7,500,000 acres of Texas land at from one to ten cents per acre, though it did not legally own the land. Stephen Austin was very bitter about this company; he felt it was bringing all the abuses of the old American land-speculation fever to Texas. The government at first refused to recognize any Galveston Bay claims, but the company, through a judicious use of influence and payments, finally secured land titles for one thousand holders of its scrip.

Another company, the Nashville Company, was better known by the name of its agent, Sterling Robertson. Robertson acquired lands north and northwest of Austin's colony, sold scrip, and generally damaged honest immigration. The Mexican government voided Robertson's contract and turned the region over to Austin and a partner, Williams. However, after the revolution the government of Texas returned to Robertson premium lands for 379 families.

Arthur G. Wavell, an Englishman, was commissioned to settle 500 families in deep northeast Texas. Wavell's partner, Benjamin Milam, succeeded in locating some families, but ran into a boundary problem with the United States, which claimed his grant lay east and north of Mexican Texas. No premium lands were ever secured.

Two colonies were begun with the idea of settling families direct from Europe. James Power, an Irishman, and James Hewetson, an Irish-born citizen of Monclova, Mexico, got special approval to locate a settlement within the federally reserved coastal strip between the Lavaca and Nueces rivers, immediately south of De León. Evil fortune dogged these two Irishmen and their settlers. They became involved in legal difficulties with the irascible Martín de León; their capital, Refugio, on the site of an old mission, unfortunately brought them within the jurisdiction of the *ayuntamiento* of one of the three Mexican towns in Texas, La Bahía. Two shiploads of hopeful people setting out from Ireland were struck by cholera; seventy of these had to be abandoned at New Orleans as unfit for Texas, while many others died and were buried at sea.

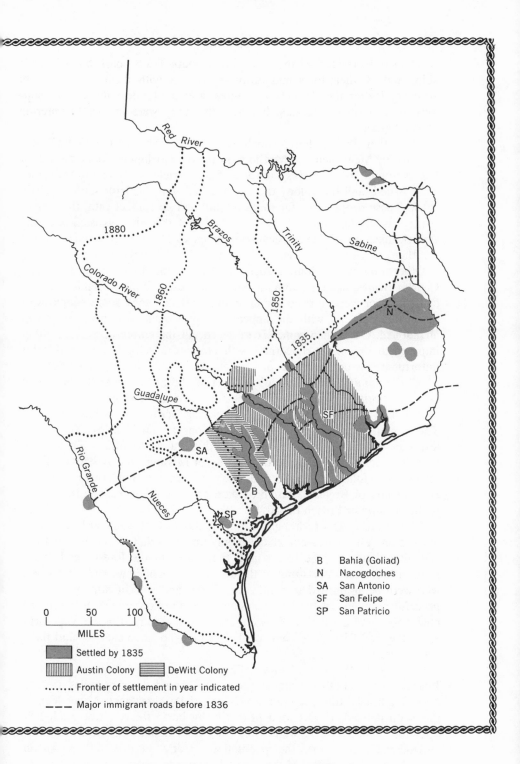

The Settlement of Texas, 1820-1880

The survivors reached the inhospitable south-Texas coast, but lost their ships and all their tools and farm implements with them. After a grim struggle, Power and Hewetson granted 200 land titles; these were supposedly to Irish immigrants, but actually many were in fact to entering North Americans.

The other Irish colony, which was called "The Irish Colony," was founded by McMullen and McGloin, in the old Coahuiltec country south of San Antonio. Its town was known as San Patricio. Only eighty-four titles were issued, and the colony did not succeed, but the Irish settlers grimly stuck. These people were far south of, and had no contact with, the Anglo-Americans farther north and east. In spite of this, they assisted with the Americanization of Texas because they spoke English; eventually, except for their religion, they were indistinguishable from the frontier mass.

Other proposed colonies, such as that of the Englishman Dr. John Charles Beales, came to nothing. Many of these comprised lands unfit for cultivation or were in deep Indian country. Beales took some people west of the Nueces, but with the appearance of Comanches this colony was abandoned. Other than some six or seven, all the empresarios were either impractical dreamers, concerned with creating a refuge in the wilds for unfortunates or oppressed peoples, or else speculators hoping to get rich.

All the immigrants in this colonial period did not come at the invitation of the authorities. Even before Moses Austin rode to San Antonio, a trickle of English-speaking people were wandering across the Sabine or Red. These men wanted nothing to do with dons or empresarios. The Texas historian Strickland accurately described them as follows: "They came from Kentucky and Tennesse by the way of Missouri and Arkansas. Their fathers had followed Boone and Harrod over the Wilderness Road to Harrodsburg or Bryant's Station or pioneered with Sevier along the waters of the Holston or French Broad."

They were part of the grim, tough, Anglo-Celt vanguard, eternally moving on. They came out of the mountains with their hatchets and rifles and filtered through the forest until they came to the forest's end. They lived in Indian country—that of the also-moving Choctaws and Cherokees, who were being pushed west into east Texas and who in turn pushed the peaceful remnants of the Caddoans out into the borderlands between the pine woods and the Plains. They cut clearings and hunted in the wilderness along the Red River, and some of the people who came close behind them planted corn.

By 1815 the Wetmores had a trading station at Pecan Point on the Red. Jonesborough, another frontier town, was founded thirty miles further west. Trammel's trace, a road which linked this area with Nacogdoches, was soon defined. It was used primarily by horse thieves, who raided in Missouri. By 1821 there were some 80 settled families in these squatters' settlements; after 1825 the population greatly swelled. When Austin formed his colony, a few of these people chose to move south and legalize their claims, and the Gillilands, Robinsons, and Varners became part of the Old Three Hundred. But the majority of these hunter-trappers lived in splendid isolation, like their forebears. Not for many years were they brought into the jurisdiction, to become a part, of Texas.

By 1825, then, both planter and frontiersman were firmly ensconced within the boundaries of Mexican Texas. Each would make, in his own way, his own abortive culture, live and die, and leave his descendants and legends in the land. The dynamic dualism—Old South and Old Frontier— that was to characterize the history of the state was established early. The foundations of the Cotton and Cattle kingdoms were already laid.

After a decade of the empresarios, there were 20,000 Anglo-Americans, with their slaves, in Texas. This exceeded the Spanish-speaking inhabitants by 5 to 1. Gradually, the principal problem of Don Estévan Austin, the great empresario, became not how to tear down the wilderness but how to stand between the sovereign Republic of Mexico, to which he was politically loyal, and a swarm of his own race who were rapidly re-creating Spanish Texas in their North American image. Austin, an intelligent and perceptive man, had a foot in both worlds and saw values in each. In the best sense, he was loyal to both sides. But a profound clash of cultures had already begun, which Austin never anticipated and which proved to be beyond even his powers, and his great good will, to solve.

10

THE CLASH OF CULTURES

This is the most liberal and munificent Govt. on earth to emigra[n]ts—after being here one year you will oppose a change even to Uncle Sam.
STEPHEN F. AUSTIN, IN A LETTER TO HIS SISTER, 1829

Mexicans! Watch closely, for you know all too well the Anglo-Saxon greed for territory. We have generously granted land to these Nordics; they have made their homes with us, but their hearts are with their native land. We are continually in civil wars and revolutions; we are weak, and know it—and they know it also. They may conspire with the United States to take Texas from us. From this time, be on your guard!
FROM A SPEECH TO A SECRET SESSION OF THE
MEXICAN CONGRESS, 1830, THE SENTIMENTS OF WHICH WERE
WIDELY ECHOED IN MEXICAN PAPERS AND PRONOUNCEMENTS

The strongest cause in bringing the Texas Revolution, however, was the lack of sympathy between the Mexican people and the Anglo-Saxon colonists. They could not understand our methods of government and we could not endure their idea of a republic.
FROM A HISTORY OF TEXAS USED IN 19TH-CENTURY TEXAS SCHOOLS

THREE major facets illuminated and determined the continuing struggle for the North American continent between Hispanic and Anglo-American civilization in the early-19th century. The first was the dissolution of the

Spanish empire into successor states, and the enormous crisis of order into which these states, like the entire Hispanic world, now passed. The second was the serious national suspicions and rivalries between the two new republics of the United States and Mexico. The third, which probably made conflict inevitable, was the ethnic clash between two very different peoples and ways of life as they met in Texas.

In the summer of 1821, when Stephen Austin was exploring the Texas coastal plains for the best site to plant his American civilization, word reached Texas that Mexico was now free of Spain. A shout of *Viva Independencia!* went up—for the announcement was not of a new revolution but of a *fait accompli*. But then, for almost a year, nothing changed. No one in distant Texas really knew what had happened to the south.

In the middle of organizing his colony in March, 1822, Austin received bad news from the last Royalist Governor, Don Antonio Martínez. Officials of the new government at Monterrey had revoked Austin's commission. Further, the government of the Mexican nation was preparing a new colonization law for Texas and the Californias. Martínez, who was soon to be replaced, advised Austin to go at once to the capital and protect his interests. This Austin immediately did.

What had happened in New Spain was never easy for Anglo-Americans, who knew the society dimly, to understand. Padre Hidalgo's revolt in 1810 did not, like the stirrings of the American Revolution, attract the support of substantial men. Its leaders were primarily people's priests, who saw the anguish of the poorest classes, and its masses were a swarm of ragged Indians. Here and there a genuine *rico,* such as Bernardo Gutiérrez, with genuine republican sentiments, joined the cause. But Hidalgo, Mier, Morelos, and Matamoros led a screaming horde with enormous grievances but with no real hope of success. The army, the Church, the bureaucracy, and the *hacendados,* all the foundations of the Spanish state, sided with the Crown. One by one, the rebellious priests were defrocked, hunted down, imprisoned by the Inquisition, and stood against a wall. Their followers were massacred.

The revolution did not die. A few leaders, the most important Vicente Guerrero and Ignacio Rayón, and Gutiérrez through Magee in Texas, kept guerrilla warfare and a spark of resistance alive. But real revolution was so completely crushed that by 1819 the Viceroy, Apodaca, informed the King there was no more need for troops.

Now, the situation completely swung about. A revolution broke out in metropolitan Spain, based in part upon the crushing taxes and thousands of soldiers raised in the home country to put down rebellion in the empire. Spanish liberals came briefly to power; they dominated the *Cortes,* or parliament, and made a virtual prisoner of the King. The liberals forced Ferdinand VII to restore the liberal Constitution of 1812, which he had voided, and began to dismantle the enormous privileges of the Spanish Catholic clergy. Monasteries that sprouted all over Spain like mushrooms were closed; the lands of the orders were sequestered, and the higher orders of the clergy reformed by civil law. Thus began a Church-State struggle in Hispanic civilization that was to continue for more than a century. The liberals in Spain were soon crushed by a Catholic reaction and by the invasion of foreign troops from Bourbon France, but not before the shock of a revolutionary regime at home wreaked historic damage in New Spain.

These events, wrote the American Minister to Mexico, "were viewed with dread by the clergy" and also the upper classes. The Mexican Church, the landowners, and a large part of the army went over to independence. The first successful revolt in Mexico came not to end, but to preserve, the old regime.

The Royalist general Agustín de Iturbide, who had equaled Arredondo's efforts to stamp out the unrest, now made a deal with Vicente Guerrero's surviving forces in the south. Guerrero and Iturbide met, talked, and issued a proclamation called *El Plan de Iguala,* in February, 1821. This was a compromise, or was meant to be, between the Royalists and liberals in New Spain. Mexico was proclaimed an "independent, moderate, constitutional monarchy." The Roman Catholic religion, with all privileges of the clergy, including its enormous property, and racial equality were both guaranteed. Although in perspective this proclamation looked like something of a Royalist plot, it temporarily reunited all classes. When the new Spanish Viceroy, Juan O'Donojú, arrived in Mexico in July, he quickly realized the cause of Spain was lost. He tried to salvage something for the Bourbons by working out a new deal with Iturbide, in which a regency council was formed. The "moderate, constitutional" throne was to be offered first to the King, Ferdinand VII, and then to members of the Royal family in turn. Under these provisions, conflict ceased, and Iturbide and the Republicans entered the capital, Mexico City, in September, 1821.

But O'Donojú soon died. The *Cortes* in Madrid repudiated his treaty with Iturbide, pending its own solution to colonial problems, and this left the field to a power struggle between Generalissimo Iturbide and a group of uneasy Republicans. When Stephen Austin reached Mexico, he found the regency council quarreling bitterly within itself, and Iturbide quietly increasing his real power.

In July, 1822, the general instigated a sergeants' revolt, and a march on the palace by the Mexico City mob, a coup out of the gaudiest days of the Roman Empire. "Army and people" thus proclaimed Iturbide Emperor of Mexico. On August 1, Augustine I abolished the Mexican legislature and replaced it with a handpicked *junta,* or council, of forty-five. Here legitimacy, which had at least held the Mexican elite together, was lost, and it remained lost for another century.

Stephen Austin lived in the capital during these months, learning the Spanish language as rapidly as he could, listening and learning about Mexican politics. He became aware that he was now moving in a different world from the American frontier—a glittering capital of now rapidly shifting loyalties and balances, where intrigue was the normal way of doing business, where appearances were everything and plain talk was dangerous and rarely done. Austin learned to speak facile Spanish with all the proper phrases of gentility, and "to beat about the bush," as he called it, with the best of them. Austin had that rare ability, which most capable leaders have, of being both clear-sighted and without illusions, while at the same time entirely sincere. He had determined on and adopted loyalty to his new country, Mexico, but without blinding himself to realities of its governments. These two qualities allowed him to perform a minor miracle: he talked with every man of the Imperial *junta,* including the Emperor, and was able to get his empresario commission confirmed.

But with his decree in hand, Austin dared not leave the capital. Iturbide's power was growing less every day. Several generals came out in opposition to him, were imprisoned, but escaped. The Republican opposition finally staged its own coup. Iturbide fell and was exiled, and Mexico was now proclaimed a republic. All imperial decrees were voided, and now Austin had to do his work all over again. Again he performed a miracle and persuaded the new Congress to confirm his privileges, even before a new colonization law was prepared. In all, Austin was forced to stay in Mexico for a full year, and during this period, 1822–23, his colony on the Brazos almost failed.

The Mexican Republic resembled that of the United States only slightly, although the Constitution of 1824 created a federal system of sovereign States. Mexico had no tradition of strong, local governments; the Spanish tradition was strongly centralist in both theory and practice, and the Hispanic love of regulating equaled or surpassed the Anglo-Saxon tendency to legislate. The Republic of 1824 was the result of a temporary liberal ascendancy in Mexico, and a liberal experiment with new theories imported from the north. Mexico now entered, as did many of the Hispanic successor states, a long period of tension between Federalists and Centralists, who preferred to establish an all-powerful Presidency and Congress to regulate, in minutest detail, the entire domain.

Although republican ideas enjoyed a great vogue, Mexico faced two enormous problems with republican governments even its own intellectuals did not understand. In Mexico there was no citizenry in the North American or European sense. There were only subjects of different degrees. And there was no tradition, such as had originated in the British world, that governmental powers originated in and with the people. There were no "people" in the fashion of the United States or France. In 1820, 18 percent of the Mexican population were pure European, or nearly so; 22 percent were mixed, or *mestizo;* 60 percent, the great mass, were Indian. This was almost the exact opposite of the racial composition of the United States in 1820, where 82 percent were white, and 18 percent Negro. The Mexican whites tended to think of themselves as Spanish, with nostalgia for the past.

The Indian masses were illiterate and possessed no national sense. The idea of a Mexican nation was centered in the *mestizo* group; even here it took a century more to jell.

Mexican society went from Viceregency to Republic almost unchanged. The Church was preserved. The *hacendado* class retained its lands, with peonage intact. Racial discrimination was abolished by law, but it could not be abolished in fact. The one great and dangerous vacuum created was the empty space left by the abolition of the Crown—and again, this vacuum was not to be successfully filled for a hundred years, until the Mexican Presidency finally acquired legitimacy.

In a republic without citizens, although there were thousands of men with genuine republican feelings, it was inevitable that the age of *caudillaje* began. The *caudillo,* or military dictator, was perhaps a necessary phase, since there was no possible way to hold such a society together except by some use of force. In a state divided severely by class, with tension between Church and State, and with an illiterate majority living in intense poverty, only a balance of forces could preserve the whole. The *caudillo* was a military adventurer, who gained control of the army, the largest disciplined body within the state, and balanced off the rest through a combination of cajolery and fear. The *caudillo* or man on horseback was frequently vicious and intolerable; but without him there usually developed an anarchy that was worse. The *caudillo* was inevitably a Centralist, backed by army, Church, and landed elite. The republican or Federalist leadership came both from the elite and mixed class, but it could rarely establish more than an ephemeral regime out of its middle-class and Indian support.

The *hacendados* ruled the masses on the local level, but they had been denied a political role by the Spanish. They did not adopt one now. So long as its privileges were guaranteed, this potentially powerful group remained inert. Politics became more and more the preserve of the more vigorous, and discontented, *mestizos* of the educated professional classes. Professionals, such as lawyers or doctors, in Mexico represented a middle, not an upper, class. Faced with a landed elite, this class was often revolutionary. Political struggle tended to become a power struggle between opposing cliques or factions, without real social meaning, however, since the *hacendados* were too powerful to be disturbed, and the Indians, except for local disturbances, too inert.

Every military ruler or *caudillo* tried to preserve republican appearances while exercising an actual despotism. He was aided not by consensus, because a true concensus in this kind of setting was impossible, but by the tensions between landowners and Indians, *mestizo* professionals and the Church, army and Republican politicos. He employed bribery, and also a vitally useful strain of force. The result was an almost continual civil strife, damped only when an unusually powerful *caudillo* seized control, until the pot boiled over again. The so-called revolutions, which occurred with monotonous frequency, and which shed some blood, were more or less palace revolutions. The men in power changed, but institutions were in no way altered or damaged.

This long period of virtual anarchy that began in Mexico in 1821 had fatal effects on the Mexican empire north of the Rio Grande, and, more than any other single cause, cost the Mexican nation its possessions from California to Texas. The Mexican problems with government, above all, convinced North Americans that the Mexicans were an inferior race. It was impossible for Anglo-Americans to respect a people who could not rule themselves—and again and again, in crucial years, Mexicans had no real sense of national destiny, or could not unite.

When Stephen F. Austin went back to Texas from Mexico in 1823, the last thing in his mind was the thought of potential conflict between his adopted country and the United States. The 1819 treaty, by which the United States renounced Texas, seemed to end the possibility for all time. Austin saw correctly that only North Americans could tame Texas, but he did not foresee that there would be terrible strains trying to accomplish this within the framework of the Mexican Republic. Nor did he see that factions in both the United States and Mexico would make the task difficult. Austin was a clever politician, but he had very little ethnic animosity or ideology, and he did not sufficiently perceive the phobias of others.

Two great underlying problems made relations between the Republic of Mexico and the United States prickly and difficult. The first was that a large body of Americans, primarily in the Southwest, were expansionist; they wanted Texas and all the land to the Pacific Ocean for the United States. The second trouble was that almost all educated Mexicans hated, distrusted, or feared the rapidly burgeoning power of their northern neighbor. Americans were proud of the explosive growth of their country, and extolled their national vigor. They failed to see the other side of the coin— the effect that American expansion was having on the Mexican mind. All educated and upper-class Mexicans were aware that between 1800 and 1820 the Anglo-Saxon United States more than doubled its land area by the acquisition of the Louisiana Territory and Florida.

These territories were purchased, but there had always been a strong threat of violence underlying the peaceful negotiations for acquisition. The United States government had made it crystal clear that it would never permit the Spanish authorities in Louisiana, sovereign or not, to close the mouth of the Mississippi. General Andrew Jackson willfully ignored the Spanish border of Florida while pursuing marauding Indians. The entire expansion of the United States in its early years came at the expense of the Spanish-speaking world. Few Americans thought about it in this way, but all Mexicans did. They knew that all these changes came about only because of basic Spanish weakness.

Thus the Anglo-American settlement of Texas, in itself a great drama, was played out upon a larger canvas, which was the struggle between the English-speaking Americans and the Spanish successor state of Mexico for domination of the North American continent.

In such circumstances, the historic tides of Mexico's Hispanic centralism and Henry Clay's obsession to acquire Texas made Stephen Austin's apparently logical dream of an English-speaking, autonomous, federal state within a Mexican confederacy impossible.

The United States Presidential election of 1824, indirectly, had enormous effects on American-Mexican relations. In this year John Quincy Adams and Henry Clay drew 121 electoral votes between them, against Andrew Jackson's plurality of 99. The election was thrown into the House of Representatives; deals were made. Adams emerged President, while Clay became Secretary of State.

The Massachusetts patrician, Adams, had no real taste for western expansion. But he did want to improve his popularity beyond the Appalachians, and he was willing to appease the western states by attempting to purchase Texas. The slavery question had not yet become an overriding moral issue. Adams was to become perhaps the most fanatical foe of Texas annexation, but during his Presidency he pursued that course, with lip service, if not with enthusiasm. The Missouri Compromise did allow the acquisition of Texas as slave territory, and Adams authorized Clay to work for revision of the 1819 Spanish-American treaty, which Mexico inherited. To move the western boundary of the United States south of the Brazos River, Adams was prepared to offer $1,000,000 and a commercial treaty.

This offer was not made immediately. In 1825 the American Minister to Mexico wrote Clay that American interests would best be served by delay. His letter stated that "most of the good land between the Sabine and the Colorado" was filling up with grantees or squatters from the United States, "a population the Mexicans would find difficult to govern."

When the province became thoroughly American and unruly, the Minister believed the Mexican government would be glad to cede it to the United States.

To say that neither Americans nor Mexicans really understood the psychology of the other would be an understatement. The leadership of each nation operated on a different plane of thought. Americans always made two basic assumptions: the American nation was more vigorous and certainly superior to the Mexican; and that the western lands in question were useless to Mexico, which had been unable to settle them. Americans expected Mexicans to accept both assumptions reasonably. But in reverse, the American assumption of superiority lacerated the immense Latin pride of the Mexicans, and the fact that their empire north of the Rio Grande *was* vulnerable suffused Mexicans with such fear and suspicion that it became almost phobia among the upper classes. No matter what the United States proposed, it was assumed to be part of a *Yanqui* plot.

The open suggestion that Mexico "alienate" a portion of its "sacred soil" by selling it to the United States frightened and infuriated so many Mexicans that the few pragmatic souls willing to be rid of Texas could not operate. In a very real sense, Austin was already "alienating" Texas, and many Mexican officials knew this. But this was being done in a covert—or "still"—way, without popular feelings of territoriality or pride becoming involved. Austin's great advantage was that he intuitively understood the labyrinths of Mexican politics and the Byzantine Mexican mind. Never once did Austin broach his request for a colonization grant in public. He met quietly with powerful officers, talked things out politely with *junta* members. Afterward, decrees were issued. The great mass of Mexicans never were aware of what took place. No demagogue or ambitious opposition politician was able to use Austin as a target for popular emotion.

Compared to Austin, Joel R. Poinsett, the first American Minister to independent Mexico, was a bungling meddler. Poinsett should have been knowledgeable. He had lived in Mexico, served in other Latin countries, spoke Spanish, and knew the Spanish social niceties. But Poinsett was apparently utterly impervious to understanding the Mexican national psychology. He persisted in trying to do business like an American. He was contemptuous of "acting in Rome like the Romans."

Poinsett had one other tremendous liability, which Austin lacked. Austin had no ideology. He wanted to Americanize Texas as part of a great development scheme. He dealt with despots, potentates, dictators, generals, or republican liberals with equal courtesy and finesse; he would deal with anyone to serve his purpose. Poinsett, however, was deeply prejudiced in favor of the Mexican liberals, who, unfortunately from his point of view, were not in power. His biases led him to choose sides in purely domestic matters in Mexico, and to make moves that destroyed his usefulness to his own government. He was among the first, but certainly not the last, American diplomat of his kind.

Significantly, Poinsett, on his first public appearance in the City of Mexico in 1825, at first drew a great ovation from an audience made up of Mexican congressmen and other notables by eulogizing Mexican independence and American friendship. Then, in mid-speech, Poinsett broached the idea that the 1819 treaty should be changed. He had not mentioned this to anyone in Mexico beforehand.

As a British observer wrote, the effect was much as if he had thrown a bomb among his listeners. They were outraged and shocked. Poinsett had tossed a delicate mission out before the public, and the public was hostile. A little feeling of his ground would have told Poinsett this. Furthermore, his abrupt action alienated those politicians who might have entertained the notion.

With this great gaffe, Poinsett actually convinced many Mexican government officials that the United States was preparing to take a hard, or aggressive line against the territorial provisions of the 1819 treaty. A few quiet words would have ensured they understood the real situation—that Adams was making a *pro forma* offer, to please the American West, and actually was not disposed to push the issue.

Some Mexicans believed the age of filibusters was reopening. These men had never been convinced that the American nation had not actively supported the earlier invasions, or believed that the expeditions had been purely private enterprise the Presidents of the United States had been powerless to stop. Magee had been a regular army officer, and there was suspicion that his Volunteers were really not volunteers. All of the filibusters had been able to recruit men and raise money and supplies along the border, and as soon as they had crossed it, they proclaimed the sovereign independence of Texas from the Spanish-speaking world—with great support by certain American newspapers. Not understanding the American social or governmental system, Spanish minds fell prey to pervasive suspicions.

Austin was able to proceed only because the treaty of 1819 seemed to remove Texas as a legitimate American goal; the United States renounced Texas "forever." When Poinsett seemed to reopen the issue, this was to have a far-reaching effect. Some Mexicans believed the United States government again favored schemes to separate Texas from Mexico.

Poinsett found the ruling conservatives in Mexico frosty to his overtures. He delayed, and advised Clay to delay, hoping for changes in Texas due to immigration, or in Mexico due to a change in government. The formal offer to buy Texas was not tendered until 1827. When it was made, this move merely threw oil on smoldering fires.

Meanwhile, Poinsett proceeded to disaster in other ways. Angered by the attitude of the clerical and monarchical-minded Mexican conservatives, he tried to "promote republican principles," as he called it. He had discovered that Freemasonry had an immense hold on the educated classes, and actually formed the basis for a political club in Mexico. But there were certain enormous differences between Mexican and North American Masons. Freemasonry had been introduced into the Hispanic world in Bourbon times as an aristocratic organization, composed of men of birth and wealth. Up to this time, as in France and Spain, Masonry in Mexico was anything but politically liberal in the Anglo-American sense. The Scottish Rite, or *Escoseses,* instead formed a genuine political vehicle for the ultraconservative cause. The liberal-minded republican Mexicans were also strongly attracted to Masonry, but could not break conservative control of the order.

Poinsett had what he felt was a brilliant inspiration. He introduced the York Rite into the capital, offering it to the liberals as their vehicle to compete with the *Escoceses.* Poinsett believed he was serving both the cause of liberty and his country, but as the *Yorkinos* became a secret society plotting against the existing regime, the true effect on the ruling party can easily be imagined. Poinsett became *persona non grata.*

Aside from the irritation and anger aroused by such meddling in the affairs of a foreign power, Poinsett, and many other Americans in government, had made dangerously false assumptions about both the Mexican liberals and the effects of American immigration into Texas. As George Lockhart Rives wrote in his monumental study of United States–Mexican relations between 1821 and 1848, "a government whose existence depended in any degree on popular opinion had never been known to part with territory, except as the result of unsuccessful war."

The Mexican liberals did not favor selling Texas; they were as vehement as the conservatives, or more so, where national sovereignity was concerned. After Mexico became independent, there was never the faintest chance that sovereign Mexico would sell Texas, or its North American possessions, voluntarily.

This atttitude annoyed Poinsett. He wrote President Adams, "They regard the United States with distrust and the most unfounded jealousy . . . It is vain that I represent the disinterested and generous conduct of the United States toward these countries and assure them that so far from our regarding their property with envy (as they, with unequalled vanity, suppose) we are most desirous that the Mexican state should augment in wealth and in power, and that they may become more profitable customers and more efficient allies . . ." He put down the Mexican reluctance to part with Texas as a dog-in-the manger attitude, and never understood how even his disclaimers tended to infuriate the Mexicans.

Mexico, like all new nations, was developing a heady nationalism, although this emotion had not yet produced national unity. The ruling groups were actually most united on the determination to hold Texas. Remote, unpopulated, and unconquered as the province was, it was still Mexican soil, and such soil, everywhere in similar circumstances, tends to acquire mystic symbolism. Such territory could be bought with blood, but never with money.

Poinsett and Clay, meanwhile, simply could not comprehend the matter of Mexican pride. Mexico—in fact, the entire Hispanic world—was tyrannical, clerical, and backward by 19th-century American notions. The Mexicans, unlike North Americans, had been able neither to form a free government, nor a viable government. Anglo-Americans took pride primarily in the fact that they were free men, and their contempt for any men who could not achieve a similar system of government was both genuine and unavoidable. Americans did not understand cultural pride—a lack of comprehension that was to color all Anglo-American relations with Hispanic societies.

La raza, as Mexicans were beginning to call themselves, did not mean "race" in the sense of the English word. It was a cultural thing, actually untranslatable into American English. *La raza* referred not to blood in the veins, but to an entire cultural heritage that extended back to Rome, and to a value system every Mexican felt was as valid as, if different from, the values prized by the English-speaking. The concept was symbolic and mystical, and held by a race that valued mysticism. And it pointed up a separation that had existed since the days when Nordics crashed against the Latin Roman Empire. If Nordics saw Latins as somewhat degenerate, tyrannical, slavish, and cruel, Latins considered the Northerners arrant barbarians.

This deep-seated pride, and the American failure to understand it, acerbated all American-Mexican dealings.

Ironically, the British Minister to Mexico, Henry Ward, saw the real state of affairs better than any American. Ward wrote Canning in September, 1825:

"... Six hundred North American families are already established in Texas; their numbers are increasing daily, and though they nominally recognize the authority of the Mexican government, a very little time will enable them to set at defiance any attempt to enforce it."

Ward also reminded the British Foreign Secretary that the Americans were "backwoodsmen—a bold and hardy race, but likely to prove bad subjects, and most inconvenient neighbors." The British government, of course, had had some experience with this kind.

The British Minister further illuminated the difference between Mexican attitudes toward Texas, and the reality of what Mexican officialdom was actually doing. "... Were but one-hundredth part of the attention paid to practical encroachment, which will be bestowed upon . . . verbal cession, Mexico would have little to fear."

Thus, while·the capital buzzed with tales of American plots, and public speeches denounced Poinsett, Adams, Clay, and the American nation, Austin brought 5,000 Anglo-American settlers into Texas, and loose Mexican administration permitted thousands of others to filter over the border. Worse, for the eventual destiny of Mexico, many Mexican citizens exercised their option to buy up eleven leagues of Texas lands; they never settled in Texas or had any intention of settling, but they sold these land rights to North Americans for handsome profits.

This was the reality that caused Stephen Austin to make his biting comment—over which Mexican historians still writhe—that Mexicans would sell their birthright if appearances could only be preserved. The majority of Hispanic historians have always accorded Austin the honor of being honest, and of being a gentleman whose loyalty to Mexico was true until it was put to unbearable strains.

The question of the Texas Purchase smoldered without action through the Adams Administration. Mexico demanded that the United States again officially renounce Texas, as a preliminary to further treaties. Adams accepted this in 1828, but this new treaty was not ratified by the Senate. When Adams left office in 1829 the United States not only had failed to acquire Texas, but had deepened suspicion and distrust as to its intentions below the Rio Grande.

In these years Austin was the real ruler and power in Anglo-Texas. He summed up his own experience in these words, in a letter of 1829: "I had an ignorant, whimsical, selfish, and suspicious set of rulers over me to keep good-natured, a perplexed, confused colonization law to enforce, and a set of North American frontier republicans to control, who felt that they were sovereigns, for they were beyond the arm of the government, or of the law, unless it pleased them to be controlled." By sheer skill, Austin kept both the capital and his unruly frontiersmen in good humor.

But there were other empresarios who lacked Austin's tact and skill. Haden Edwards, a Kentuckian, was granted a tract in east Texas for the purpose of settling 800 families. Edwards arrived at Nacogdoches, which was to be his seat, in October, 1825. Although Edwards' title from the State of Coahuila seemed clear enough, he inherited a very confused situation around the town. He was required to respect the rights of earlier settlers who held legal land titles in the area, but did not have to honor squatters' rights. The trouble was that many people in east Texas, old Spanish, Mexicans, and rough border Americans, had no legal certificates or standing of any kind. All these people, including many Indians, were actually on Edwards' grant.

Edwards announced that settlers claiming land under old Spanish grants must present their papers to him; this alarmed everyone, Mexican and American alike. The Mexicans were particularly resentful of a North American empresario being placed over them. Edwards next arbitrarily ordered an election for *alcalde* for the district, and tried to swing the post to his son-in-law. This election, however, was set aside by the political chief at San Antonio; Norris, the "Mexican candidate" was installed, and Edwards' colonists found that apparently they could not win a disputed land case against an old settler.

Edwards was required to return to the United States on business. He left his colony in charge of his brother, Benjamin. Ben Edwards, acting on Austin's advice, wrote Governor Blanco of Coahuila-Texas a full explanation of the troubles, and requested clarification. Blanco's reply was to begin by stating Edwards' letter showed a lack of "respect for superior officials," and to decree the annulment of the empresario contract, and expel both Edwards brothers from the Mexican Republic.

Haden Edwards had spent some $50,000 bringing Americans to east Texas, and many of his colonists also had gone to great expense. Mexicans around Nacogdoches now claimed title to the lands Edwards' colonists had settled. Benjamin Edwards, understandably angry with this incomprehensible government that granted lands with one hand and withdrew them with the other, raised the standard of revolt. On December 20, 1826, the "Republic of Fredonia" was declared. The Republic divided Texas into two spheres, American and Indian, because Edwards was trying to make an alliance with the Cherokees, now moving strongly into the province. Edwards, who had about two hundred supporters, wrote Stephen Austin for aid.

But Austin refused any part in the revolt. In fact, his colony sent a hundred men to aid the Mexican force that pushed north under Colonel Ahumada. Peter Ellis Bean, the old filibuster who was now in the Mexican service, successfully separated the restive Cherokees from the Fredonians. Although Austin got Ahumada to issue a proclamation of amnesty to any rebel who surrendered, Edwards fought on, hopelessly. In January, 1827, the Fredonians fled to the United States. Again, through Austin's pleading, those of Edwards' people who stayed behind were treated reasonably well by the Mexican authorities, though the Edwards grant was divided between two other empresarios.

The Fredonian revolt caused a sensation far beyond its actual importance. American newspapers played it up—"200 Men Against a Nation!" —and expressed sympathy, while these "apostles of democracy were crushed by an alien civilization." In the Mexican capital, when the first confused reports arrived (actually, while the rebellion was being cleaned up on the spot), the Congress authorized massive measures "to repel invasion." Mexican opinion claimed the Fredonian affair was part of a greater North American plot. The President, General Guadalupe Victoria, knew better, but he also knew better than to express in public unpopular views. The Mexican government, through its Minister to Washington, Obregón, asked the United States to disclaim any part in the Fredonian revolution. Henry Clay did this, and was believed by those Mexicans actually in power. But neither Clay nor President Adams could control American newspapers. Obregón saw, and wrote home, that American sympathy was with the rebellion, and advised there would be trouble in days to come if American colonization of Texas were allowed to continue.

The fact that Austin's colony had supported the legal government, and that North Americans had fought against Edwards, was overlooked in Mexico and widely disapproved in the United States.

There had arisen in Mexico a group of officials who were deeply concerned with the American danger. This attitude was as much ethnic as national, and most of this anti-Americanism centered in the educated Hispanic elite. They feared the Anglo-American value system was producing a relentlessly aggressive national neighbor to the north, and they were determined to defend the Mexican way of life. They hoped to make their countrymen see the danger. This faction included such important men as General Don José María Tornel, General Don Manuel Mier y Terán, and the Mexican Minister of Foreign Relations, Don Lúcas Alamán.

General Mier y Terán investigated Texas during 1828–29 for the government. He wrote a most disturbing report. According to the messages he sent the President, the Mexican presence "disappeared" beyond San Antonio. The ratio of Mexicans to *Norteamericanos* was 1 to 10, and Mexicans were becoming the very lowest class. The foreign immigrants had their own schools (the Mexicans had none), and their older children were sent back to the United States to be educated. With these schools, and their terrible energy and enterprise, the foreigners were bound to take over the country. There was already resentment between the North Americans and local Mexicans, and this could lead to trouble and plunge the whole nation into revolution. The President was warned to take "timely measures," or lose the province forever.

Mier y Terán made several specific recommendations, which show both Mexican fear and helplessness: The government should send ethnic Mexican colonists to Texas; encourage Swiss and Germans to colonize; encourage trade between Texas and the Gulf coast of Mexico; garrison more troops in Texas, using convict conscriptees who after their term of service might be forced to settle in the province.

Terán's inspection resulted in several attempts to curtail the American colony. General Tornel prevailed upon the new President, Vicente Guerrero, to sign a decree abolishing slavery in the entire republic; since there was no chattel slavery in Mexico, this was aimed at weakening Austin's people and discouraging more Americans from immigrating. Other Mexican officials, however, saw to it that Texas was exempted. Actually, the whole Mexican legal attitude toward slavery was confusing in the extreme. On several occasions during the 1820's and 1830's, the Mexican government curtailed or abolished slavery and peonage contracts, only to reinstate them with convenient loopholes in the law. The Texas colonists brought approximately 1,000 Negro slaves into the region, and their status was always uncertain. Two things were certain, however; the North Americans generally ignored whatever decrees the capital issued, and these were never enforced.

Lúcas Alamán, meanwhile, presented Terán's proposals to the Congress, in a secret session. This resulted in the Decree of April 6, 1830, which in Article 11 expressly forbade any further colonization of Mexican territory by citizens of adjacent countries—meaning the United States. The decree also prevented any foreigner entering Texas "from the North" unless he possessed a passport made out by a Mexican consular agent in his own country. Importation of slaves was again prohibited.

Alamán's recommendations to the Mexican Congress went much further, and these too were adopted as policy, although not officially made public in a decree:

To settle Mexican convicts in Texas.

To introduce colonists from nations that differed widely from the Anglo-Saxons, to dilute and offset the English-speaking colonization.

To collect customs and supervise trade, so as to make Texas trade with Mexico rather than the United States.

To place Texas directly under the control of the central government so that the province could be closely observed.

To dispatch competent persons to Texas to gather information—in short, to keep government spies in the province.

Alamán's pervasive ethnic hostility to North Americans precipitated these acts and became a significant part of Mexican policy toward Texas from this time forward.

The Decree of April 6, 1830, and the other actions were taken to "meet an emergency" caused by "imperious circumstances," Alamán stated. The emergency at this time was almost entirely in the anti-American cabal's mind. The United States had no overt aggressive intentions toward Texas. The overwhelming majority of Anglo-Texans were loyal to Mexico, though in their own fashion. Alamán and the others, however, very effectively created a genuine emergency in the ensuing months and years.

The colonists had sworn allegiance to Mexico and promised to obey its laws, and this was an argument and a justification that Mexican historians and apologists were to hammer upon for the next century. However, the most notable feature of the Mexican colonization program in the 1820's was its munificence and liberality. In effect, the colonists were promised exemption from virtually all duties and laws—anything to get them to settle the land and create a buffer against the marauding Indians. The statement of a Nacogdoches land commissioner summed up the state of affairs in Anglo-Texas during its formative period: "Come what may I am convinced that Texas must prosper. We pay no taxes, work no public roads, get our land at cost, and perform no public duties of any kind."

While Mexicans were subject to military service, taxes, customs duties, and mandatory church tithes, Anglo-Texans were not. Their government was left to the empresarios, who let them regulate themselves. However, this munificence was no sacrifice to the Mexican Republic; the colonists were given no military protection or government services of any kind. The Anglo-Texans were simply allotted lands the Mexicans had never been able to use, and within ten years they were chipping out a sort of Jeffersonian paradise: a commonwealth rich in natural resources, where every man with a white skin was more or less equal with his league of land, and hampered by no distant government, beneficial or otherwise.

Even aside from the fact that Anglo-Americans belonged to two different civilizations, with different value and manners systems, the reintegration of such a republic within a republic must have caused enormous problems. No band of pioneers, grown used to such an environment, would willingly tolerate the sort of regulation that was normal to Mexico.

The status of religion and the Indian problem in Texas give some indication both as to Mexican motivation in allowing the colony, and their disappointment with it. Although Mexico was by law a Roman Catholic nation, for a full decade Austin was unable to secure a curate for his colony. There was no one to baptize, marry, or bury, according to Mexican law. Austin complained regularly. The problem was not a shortage of priests but one of footing the costs. The Texans had been relieved of all taxes and church tithes for ten years, so any clergy had to be supported by the central government. Finally, in the 1830's, Austin's people received a priest, an

Irish curate named Muldoon. Father Muldoon was a kindly man who did not inquire too closely into the state of the colonists' religion, but, as one Texas historian wrote euphemistically, he "did not always live up to the standards of piety which Anglo-Americans held up for the ministry." Among other things, he had an alcohol problem. Actually, there was no overt religious trouble. The settlers left their formal churches at the Sabine, and although a few itinerant Protestant preachers wandered Texas, occasionally getting in difficulty with the authorities, the religious problem was really a part of the ethnic problem. The colonists did not bring new temples, but they brought a completely Protestant ethos, in attitudes toward work, money, art, God, state, and man, while Mexican officials who detested the clergy, who had not been inside a church in years, and were members of the Masonic Order remained unconsciously but utterly Catholic in their culture. Every President of the Mexican Republic was a Freemason, but almost every one of them instinctively distrusted heretics.

The Indian situation in Texas deeply frustrated the Mexicans. The single biggest reason for allowing foreign immigration was to create an Indian buffer. But Austin's people were only up against tribes who were no problem for the Mexicans. With the dread Comanches Austin was able to make a very real peace. The Comanches recognized the Anglo-Texans as a separate people from the Mexicans and did not bother them, while they continued to harass the Mexican ranches at Béxar and along the Bravo. Inevitably, the Mexican authorities came to look upon this peace with the Comanches as a North American plot, a prelude to an Indian alliance that would seize all Texas. Austin's failure to engage in all-out conflict with the Comanches is understandable, but this was not what the Mexicans had hoped. Oddly, in the light of future history, in 1836 a Scots-American traveler wrote truthfully that the settlement of Anglo-Texas had been accomplished with the killing of fewer white men than any other American state, with the exception of Pennsylvania. The writer did not class Spaniards and Mexicans, of course, as white. So long as Austin's colony remained east of the Colorado, it was safe, but the Mexicans to the west were continually burned out, killed, or carried off.

The Mexican mistake, beyond the original allowing of a large horde of self-disciplined, armed land seekers to cross the borders, was in permitting the Anglos to create, without hindrance, their own community within nominal Mexican territory. The immigrants did abandon their own homeland and its sovereignty. But, as Yoakum wrote, these Americans "brought with them here, as household gods, their own first lessons in politics, morals, religion, and business, and they wished not to unlearn those lessons to learn others." In other words, the immigrants never had any real intention of becoming Mexicans—in fact, they had no opportunity to do so. Only Austin and certain other Anglo officials, who were in direct contact with Mexicans, ever learned the Spanish language.

The settlers could not learn Mexican culture and the Mexican language in schools, because the only schools were the ones the colonists started themselves.

That this was not seen at first as a problem was due to the fact that the Austins and the Spanish officials who negotiated the colonization were all born into the 18th century, before modern nationalism was strong. But by 1820, both American and Mexican nationalism were becoming virulent, in a way many leaders did not yet fully understand.

The real, underlying cause of the Texas Revolution was extreme ethnic difference between two sets of men, neither of whom, because of different ideas of government, religion, and society, had any respect for the other. Added to this was the inherent distaste of Anglo-Americans for the racial composition of the Mexican nation. This attitude was not peculiar to Americans; every European traveler of the time, including Spaniards, commented openly on the vices of a mixed, or *mestizo,* race. The 19th century was quite intolerant of mixed blood, and very honest about it. As Rives wrote:

> They [the Texans] were, in fact, always ready to conform to laws which they understood, but that had been their custom and the custom of their fathers for many generations. They would never submit to the domination of a race they regarded as inferior. They despised Mexicans as they despised negroes and Indians.

In short, it was perfectly possible for Anglo-Texas to fly the Mexican flag and be legally a part of the Mexican nation—most substantial settlers were happy with the arrangement, since they fared better under the liberal colonization laws than they would have in the United States—but only as a self-governing commonwealth. This goal seems to have been what everyone originally had in mind, both Austin and the framers of the Mexican Constitution of 1824. But they reckoned without the inherent Hispanic centralist drive, and the underlying ethnic hostility and fear of the United States of men like Lúcas Alamán. Mexico, fatally, was unable to create another North American empire along the pluralistic lines of the nation it disliked most.

If the underlying reason for revolt was ethnic hatred on both sides, the immediate cause was Mexico's determination, after 1830, to bring Anglo-Texas under the national authority and to integrate the province under Mexican terms. Legally, Mexico had every right to attempt this. Morally, the colonists had every right to resist. What was coming was deep cultural conflict, in which two peoples clashed, and as anthropologists have shown again and again, in cultural conflict there is seldom any clear-cut right or wrong. Men are moral or ethical only in terms of their own values, and no one else's.

In failing to comprehend, or in rejecting, the fact that Anglo-Texans were loyal only so long as they were left to themselves, the Mexican government was hardly unique. A British ministry had made a similar error two generations before.

The Edict of April 6, 1830, was received with consternation in Anglo-Texas. It was seen, correctly, as a calamity. The colony was now really beginning to grow, and the prosperity of many of its citizens was based on growth. Immigration meant more towns—there were already thirteen municipalities, predominantly Anglo—more stores, more cotton ginned, more commerce and increasing values of every kind. The whole Anglo ethos centered around this growth, this tearing down the wilderness and planting more producing, consuming people. The end of immigration meant the stagnation of Texas. Worse, it separated families, denying entry to some who planned to come. Finally, the Texans regarded it as all immigrants would—a gratuitous insult to their kind.

Meetings were called, protests were issued. Understandably, the Mexican authorities at San Antonio and other places saw these as seditious, because peaceful assembly had never been an Hispanic trait.

But if the cessation of immigration stunned Texas (Austin and De Witt, cleverly, were able to get around the law on a technicality for two years), the other actions of the central government began to infuriate the Texans.

The settlement of convicts and deserters among them was never successful—Mexico could not make even this kind of people pioneer—but the idea rankled among Austin's peaceful planters. Mexico did send special battalions of convict soldiers, however, to the far frontier, with eventually disastrous results.

The time allowed for freedom from customs duties and taxes now expired. Taxes were levied on Texas, and customshouses built. These in themselves were not unreasonable nor unfair. While there was a certain element in Texas—as in every country—determined to ignore these levies and to bring in luxuries duty free, the evidence is clear that Austin and most substantial citizens counseled compliance with the law. But the methods the government used to enforce its rules were regarded by all Anglo-Texans as humiliating. Old Mexico itself, in these days, was rapidly coming under military dictatorship. Vicente Guerrero failed to gain reelection in 1828; he raised the standard of revolt, took the government away from Gómez Pedraza, the legally elected President, and was inaugurated in 1829. Nine months after assuming office, Guerrero was deposed and executed by his own Vice President, Anastasio Bustamante. Then, Gómez was restored through the efforts of a popular military hero, Don Antonio López de Santa Anna, who had repulsed an attack on Tampico by Spain. The Constitution of 1824 was hanging now in shreds, as *yorkinos* and *escoceses,* Federalist liberals and conservative Centralists, battled with armies for control. The armies, and their leaders, were the only winners, and generalship had become synonymous with government.

The collapse of Mexico into political anarchy and *caudillaje,* with military rule imposed everywhere by garrisons, caused a dangerous situation in

Texas. Instinctively, the ruling authorities sent army garrisons north of the Bravo, twelve in all, to hold the province under the central government. Texas was *not* being especially subjected to military domination; the army garrison was becoming the real power structure everywhere in Mexico.

Texas was placed under the command of the able, scholarly, and American-hating Don Manuel Mier y Terán. Colonel Don José de las Piedras and 350 soldiers were stationed at Nacogdoches. Captain Juan Bradburn with 150 men built a post at Anáhuac, on Galveston Bay. Under Colonel Don Domingo de Ugartechea, another 100 garrisoned Velasco, at the mouth of the Brazos. There were smaller forces at the Presidio of Terán, on the Neches, and at La Bahía, which was now renamed Goliad, an anagram of the revolutionary priest Hidalgo's name. The standing troops at San Antonio (which the Anglos still called Béxar) were increased. This was, as every Anglo-American immigrant believed from his own folk-history, a "martial array." And in William Barret (Buck) Travis, a young firebrand lawyer from Alabama, Texas was to find its Patrick Henry.

No people on earth were less amenable to military rule at this time than Anglo-Americans. They would have detested any soldiery placed over them, but they detested this "foreign" soldiery particularly. The commanding officers were imperious dons, and the rag-tag ranks were dark-skinned and culled from the lowest classes. Knowing they were the balance of power, the troops swaggered about obnoxiously; the commandants arrested civilians or declared martial law under the flimsiest pretexts. All this had become the practice in revolt-torn Mexico, and Mexican law allowed imprisonment without specific charges. But Anglo sensibilities and morality were outraged.

Trouble flared in late 1831. In this year, the state government in Coahuila changed; the new governor, Letona, reopened settlement under the old colonization law of 1825 to Americans who were already in Texas by 1830—thus setting aside some provisions of the 1830 Decree. With Letona's approval, a number of late-comers were granted land titles in east Texas, and organized the town of Liberty, not far from the military garrison at Anáhuac.

General Mier y Terán was outraged. Asserting military authority, he ordered Captain Bradburn to arrest the Coahuilan land officials responsible for issuing the new titles. Bradburn, a peculiarly arrogant officer, went even further than his orders. He marched troops into Liberty, officially abolished the community, ignored all civil authority in the region, and redistributed the land grants himself. He treated all civilians, Mexican and Anglo alike, with contempt. Bradburn was especially detested by the settlers, for three reasons. He was the most arbitrary of all Mexican officers, utterly lacking in tact or courtesy; his main duty was enforcing customs regulations on the coast; and he was an American, a Kentuckian, by birth. Anglos considered him a turncoat, a racial traitor.

The action against Liberty caused a public complaint within the municipality. Bradburn answered this by ordering all the ports except Anáhuac closed. A group of colonists assembled at Brazoria on December 31, 1831, and vowed not to submit to such tyranny. Although Bradburn reopened the ports, relations between him and the local citizens deteriorated rapidly.

In May, 1832, Bradburn suddenly declared ten leagues of the coast under martial law and arrested several civilians, including William B. Travis and one Patrick Jack. The prisoners were jailed in an old brick kiln; no charges were filed; and Bradburn refused to turn them over to the civil law. There is no question that Travis and Jack had been making trouble for Bradburn. They had passed insulting remarks, and while not openly treasonous, they had apparently manufactured spurious messages concerning plots and armed revolts and sent these on to Bradburn, probably hoping to goad him into some ill-considered action. They succeeded. But almost every Anglo-Texan felt that their punishment by imprisonment was extreme.

Patrick Jack had a brother, William. When William Jack was unable to secure a release, he rode angrily to San Felipe. Here he found that Stephen Austin was in Saltillo on some official business, and there was no one else in authority who could help. Jack began walking the streets of San Felipe, bitterly telling everyone about his brother's plight.

By this time, there had arisen a distinct new element in Anglo-Texas. The Decree of April 6, 1830, had created a large group of late immigrants who had failed to get lands; some of these were legitimate colonists frustrated by circumstance, others merely border drifters who had wandered to the Brazos. Their status was ambiguous, and many were actually now classed as illegal immigrants. Further, the new restrictions put into effect in 1830 had created great hardships for Anglo lawyers and merchants newly arrived in Texas. Most of these people now had no legal right to work in Texas; Travis himself was one of these. All these men, frustrated or balked in various ways, formed a potential unruly element. Bradburn's tyranny gave their resentment a focal point. When William Jack harangued crowds on the streets of San Felipe, rebellion suddenly burst.

Jack shouted that he intended to return to Anáhuac to free his brother, and asked the citizenry to join him. Dozens of armed men fell in behind him, openly urging an attack on Bradburn's fort. Then, a larger assembly was held at the site of the abolished town of Liberty. Here, most of the people were aggrieved. Both honest farmers and drifters began to appear with their rifles.

Riders spurred through the settlements, spreading rumors and resentment. Everyone hated Bradburn, and although a majority of the older colonists considered Travis and Jack troublemakers, feelings ran high. John Austin, no relation to the empresario but a former member of Dr. Long's filibuster, gathered 90 men at Brazoria and marched to Liberty. He sent for cannon, of which there were several along the coast.

Actual insurrection was beginning.

While John Austin and his men were seeking the cannon, Colonel José de las Piedras arrived at Liberty with a handful of men. The Nacogdoches commandant realized the situation was volatile. Things were much worse than he had thought; his small force was outnumbered. Piedras, with considerable courtesy and skill, offered to negotiate. He promised to hear all grievances, and said he would require Bradburn's prisoners to be remanded to the civil law, and would review the land disposals the Kentuckian had made, and even ask to have Bradburn removed. This mollified the Liberty residents, although it enraged Bradburn. He resigned.

The rebellion at Liberty was damped, and shortly afterward the Anáhuac garrison was called away. They were needed for a new revolution in Mexico, this one begun by General Antonio López de Santa Anna against the supreme government.

However, most of the real troublemakers had gone to Brazoria with John Austin. This group of about 160 Anglos was unaware that Piedras was negotiating. They loaded three small cannon on a ship, then sailed down the Brazos to attack Anáhuac from Galveston Bay. However, the fort at Velasco blocked the armed schooner's passage downriver.

At Velasco, Colonel de Ugartechea stood to arms, and when Austin demanded that the Mexicans stand aside, the Colonel refused. John Austin ordered an attack to reduce Velasco. It was to be a two-pronged affair; the schooner would engage from the river, while riflemen dug themselves in close around Velasco's walls.

The Texas schooner stood off the fort, firing its cannon, while riflemen along its deck, sheltered by cotton bales, took aim at the Mexican gunners manning the fort's heavy artillery. At the same time, the land party poured a blistering fire upon Velasco's ramparts. This deadly rifle fire was decisive.

Velasco had been built so that its cannon commanded the river, but it had not been planned to withstand a land attack. Ugartechea's gun positions were exposed to the Texan ground fire. The Texan sniping knocked down gunner after gunner; men were killed by balls through the head, or staggered back to cover screaming with smashed arms or wrists. The Mexican soldiers, unable to retaliate, at last refused to work the guns. Although Don Domingo de Ugartechea himself gallantly loaded and fired one cannon several times, he was forced to capitulate.

In a short but blazing fire-fight, he had lost a large part of his men.

John Austin triumphantly granted the Mexicans the honors of war; the garrison was allowed to march out on a promise to return to Matamoros, across the border of Mexico. Then, just as Austin was marshalling his force to move on against Bradburn at Anáhuac, word arrived that the crisis there had been negotiated and ended peacefully by Colonel Piedras. Austin's army melted away; the Anáhuac war, as it was called, was over. Shortly afterward, John Austin died from illness; he never again figured in Texas history.

The sudden rebellion against Anáhauc showed that a strong wind of resistance to Mexican authority was blowing along the Texas coast. Now, both Anglo-American and Mexican blood had been shed on Texas soil. The seeds of anger had been sown; and there was much talk in the colony that every Mexican garrison must be removed, by force if necessary. Colonel Piedras, understanding the ticklish situation, evacuated Nacogdoches; and the presidio at Tenoxtitlán on the upper Brazos was also abandoned. Since Anáhuac and Velasco had already been evacuated, this left no Mexican soldiers in Anglo-Texas.

In the summer of 1832, it seemed certain that all Anglo-Texas would pass into a state of rebellion and open war, just as the American colonies had passed from scattered resistance to open rebellion in 1775. Logically, the Supreme Government of Mexico would react harshly to this rebellion and ouster of its troops, and the issue would be joined.

But this did not happen in 1832; the final crisis was delayed. There were two reasons. The first was that the Great Empresario made his last strenuous, valiant efforts to keep the peace. More important, certainly, was the fact that events in Mexico paralyzed the struggle and confused the issues for three more years.

11

REVOLUTION

> *The plans of the revolutionaries of Texas are well known to this commandancy, and it is quite useless and vain to cover them with a hypocritical adherence to the Federal Constitution. The constitution by which all Mexicans may be governed is the constitution which the colonists of Texas must obey, no matter on what principles it may be formed.*
> GENERAL DON MARTÍN PERFECTO DE CÓS,
> MILITARY COMMANDANT OF COAHUILA-TEXAS,
> TO THE *Jefe Político* AT NACOGDOCHES, AUGUST, 1835

> *War is an ugly thing, but not the ugliest thing: the decayed and degraded state of moral and patriotic feeling which thinks nothing worth a war is worse. . . . A man who has nothing which he cares about more than his personal safety is a miserable creature who has no chance of being free, unless made and kept so by the exertions of better men than himself.* JOHN STUART MILL

THE Texas Revolution in many ways resembled the revolt of the British colonies against King and Parliament in 1775–1776. Both Texas and the colonies were remote from the central authority. Both during their early years were ignored by a government concerned with other matters. Both regions were permitted to exercise local self-government, defend themselves, and build viable social institutions on their own. Both grew increasingly prosperous. Trouble came in each case only when the central government began to insist upon taxation and collection of customs. Fights with customs officers and the quartering of troops at colonial expense

174

aggravated the situation. The determination to enforce complete obedience, and the dispatch of an army, in 1775 and 1835, brought the colonials flocking to arms.

The Texas situation had three major differences: the Anglo-American settlers arrived in Mexican territory with certain constitutional principles already formed, and so took no time to forge them. They came into Texas cocked for crisis, when they entered a country with traditions and customs they did not approve of or understand. Potential trouble was given tremendous impetus by tensions between Mexico and its northern neighbor, the United States. Most difficult of all to assess was the deep ethnic hostility that pervaded both sides. This feeling made much of the legalistic arguments on each side meaningless. Some Mexican officials repressed Texans because they hated or feared the United States or detested Anglo-Saxons. Many Texans revolted simply because they refused to be ruled by people they despised.

As in 1775, there was both a War and a Peace party, with some colonists standing in between. Planters and men of property generally did not want war. Few of the Old Three Hundred desired independence. Newer immigrants, with fresher ties to the United States, pushed Texas independence, as a prelude to Union. But there were no political parties in colonial Texas, and no single dominant opinion. All the confusion, hesitation, and equivocation that marked the American war for independence scarred the Texas Revolution.

Right was not entirely on either side. The Anglo-Texans, like their forefathers of 1776, won both the propaganda war and the final military victory on the field. After that victory, they tended to forget their faults and frights, their crashing errors and their own atrocities, and accepted what happened as the will of Providence. This was an American trait even before the first English-speaking people crossed the Sabine. The triumph in Texas only reinforced it. It was perhaps this very characteristic that made later Americans look back on the triumph as inevitable and bought at little cost, and so, perhaps, to be despised. But the war that won the West was a near thing, and there was nothing inevitable about its outcome.

The motives, facts, and feelings of many of the principal figures of the Texas Revolution are unclear. It is significant for the art of history as a whole that Texan and Mexican accounts tell different tales. The results are clear, however. They can be measured on maps, and in populations and power. And that, aside from the fact that the world is ceaseless struggle, is probably the major story history has to tell.

In the summer of 1832 hotheads and some men with honest grievances precipitated an insurrection at Anáhuac. A Mexican garrison was attacked and captured, and several more driven out of Texas. This rebellion endangered the continued existence of the colony between the Colorado and the Brazos. Twenty thousand farmers were in no position to challenge Mexico's millions. Mexico was not a major power, but it was a very considerable one. As European observers pointed out, it was hardly inferior in population or resources to the United States. It possessed a vastly larger and more experienced army. The weaknesses of Mexican society, which North Americans scented rather than understood, were not easily seen. Retribution and disaster would have fallen on Texas after Velasco, except for the fact that those inner weaknesses were now in full play. Mexico was having another revolution of its own.

Of all the *caudillos* or military chieftains who rode across Mexico, none was more remarkable than Antonio López de Santa Anna Pérez de Lebrón. No leader ever seems to have understood his people or his times so well, or gambled on his luck so heavily and won. Certainly, none ever did Mexico more intrinsic damage, and not only lived, but was honored for it. Even Santa Anna could not destroy sturdy, stubborn Mexico, but he presided over the end of its northern empire.

Santa Anna was born in Jalapa, in the mountains above Vera Cruz, in 1795. His father was Spanish, his mother a *criolla* of the pure race; he was apparently a member of the lower elite. At about sixteen, he entered a Royal Spanish regiment as an officer cadet. The revolt of 1810 soon broke out, and Santa Anna won his commission, and promotion, in the field. He was a superb soldier as a youth. He served in Texas under Arredondo as a full lieutenant, learning Arredondo's wily, flexible tactics and another lesson—brutality to the vanquished. Both of these lessons stood Santa Anna in good stead.

Santa Anna returned from the slaughter in Texas with a decoration for bravery under fire, and a love of hard campaigning he never lost. Fighting in the Royalist forces, he won a captaincy and two more medals by 1821. In that year he was campaigning under Iturbide against Guerrero in the south. When the future Emperor and the old Republican warrior met to issue the Plan of Iguala, Santa Anna not only survived the leap to independence but emerged a brigadier. Here Santa Anna learned another lesson, one that was being absorbed all across the Hispanic world: the way to high office in times when legitimacy fled was not devotion to a soldier's duty but the choice of the proper side.

He accepted honors from Iturbide, then jumped to the Republicans when it became apparent Iturbide must fall. He backed the swing to Federalism in the Constitution of 1824—though he was arrested, and almost shot, because he jumped too soon. But Santa Anna, personally brave, with the Latin gambler's nerve and fatalism, could smell the wind. Through chaos and convolutions, he survived.

In 1828 the *criollo* Gómez Pedraza won the Presidency by election from his fellow *yorkino,* General Guerrero. This caused a fatal split in the temporarily dominant Republican faction, along personal and racial lines. Guerrero was *mestizo.* The election was not allowed to stand. Gómez was declared an enemy of the true revolution by many army officers; among these was Santa Anna, who had been marked for courts-martial by the President. When Vicente Guerrero agreed to armed intervention, Gómez Pedraza fled. Guerrero made Santa Anna a general of division.

In 1829, Spain made one last attempt to reconquer Mexico. Santa Anna commanded the patriot forces that defeated the Spanish landings at Tampico. The Hero of Tampico was now a national figure, much admired by the soldiers everywhere. By his stand with Guerrero, he was known as a staunch Republican.

Nine months later, Anastasio Bustamante, the Vice President, ousted Guerrero and seized control. Bustamante was reactionary, and a tyrant; it was a Mexican custom to couple presidents and vice presidents of different ideologies in the hope of gaining wider support, a custom not unknown in the United States. Sensing Guerrero was lost, Santa Anna sat this revolution out. He retired to the large hacienda he had acquired at Jalapa. He did not rebel, but neither did he accept offers or honors from the Bustamante regime. This course met with enormous popular approval; even American and British newspapers reported his integrity and unswerving liberalism. The Bustamante government sent General Mier y Terán and Captain Bradburn to Texas on the recommendations of another crony, Lúcas Alamán. Therefore, in Texas Santa Anna was looked upon as a hero, and a possible savior.

In January, 1832, Santa Anna raised the *grito* of revolt in Vera Cruz. The steps of a Mexican revolution had already become as ritualistic as those of the bullring. First came the *grito,* "shout," which was a denouncement of the existing government. If the *grito* went unopposed after a short time, the *pronunciamento* was issued. This was a detailed list of grievances, with some suggestions for redress. With a *pronunciamento* the revolution was in full swing; it had gained momentum and attracted support. Then, invariably, was issued the *plan,* which set out the revolutionaries' proposals for a new government. It usually ended with a pledge by the signers to die in its behalf. Every major city in Mexico eventually had its *plan,* which was always named for the site of issue.

Santa Anna's *plan* called for the restoration of the Constitution of 1824, benefits for the common people, and justice for all races. This was the extreme liberal position at the time. Since the Constitution of 1824—more honored in the breach over past administrations—called for a federal system of government like that of the United States, with severely limited Presidential power, an autonomous Congress, and sovereign states, it was understandable that in Anglo-Texas, public opinion swung quickly to Santa Anna's revolt.

Bustamante was still favored by the Mexican elite, but Santa Anna was the darling of the army. Revolt sputtered throughout Mexico, with Bustamante daily losing strength. By midsummer, most of the army garrisons in Texas had declared for Santa Anna. This revolt against Bustamante saved Texas from retribution for John Austin's boldness at

Velasco, because Stephen Austin and other prominent men were able to pass the disturbances off as demonstrations for Santa Anna.

The assault on Velasco had aroused considerable antagonism among the more conservative planters, but everyone saw that it was essential for Texans to stand together, since they would all suffer under Mexican punishment.

Matamoros, just south of the Bravo, was captured by Santanista forces under Colonel José Antonio Mexía in July, 1832. Here Mexía heard of the insurrection up the Texas coast. Immediately he proposed a truce with his ministerial or Bustamante opponent in the area, Colonel Guerra. Mexía argued that despite the internal quarrel, patriotic Mexicans must save Texas for the nation. Guerra agreed, and the Bustamante and Santanista troops were pooled. With four hundred men Mexía marched north toward the Colorado.

What would have happened if Stephen Austin, who had been in Saltillo, had not rushed over to Matamoros to join Mexía can only be conjecture, but it seems certain that Austin prevented bloodshed. He wrote the Mexican authorities long letters of explanation, and he argued forcefully with Mexía that the events at Velasco and Anáhuac in no way were a rebellion against the Mexican nation, but only an uprising against Bradburn and his superiors, Mier y Terán and Bustamante. Since it was the official Santanista position that Bustamante was a tyrant, this was an effective gambit. Austin's statement, "There is no insurrection of the Colonists against the Constitution and Government, neither do they entertain ideas endangering even remotely the integrity of the territory," was accepted, particularly since Stephen Austin sent word ahead to prepare a lavish reception for the invading Mexican army.

Mexía was greeted at the mouth of the Brazos with a cannon salute, and reception committee after committee assured the Colonel of Texas' loyalty. John Austin entertained him in his home; a huge ball was thrown at Brazoria, which was described as "large, cheerful, and convivial." Mexía had his suspicions, but he was convinced that the Texans were loyal to the Constitution of 1824, and to Santa Anna, if not to the Mexican nation, come what may. It was impossible to make war on colonists who treated him like a hero. Meanwhile, the Bustamante party in Texas collapsed. Mier y Terán committed suicide, and the loss of this distinguished general was a blow to Bustamante. Mexía gathered up the remaining Mexican garrisons in Texas, and, assured that the province was safe, took these troops back to the wars below the Rio Grande.

In this assumption Colonel Mexía was absolutely correct: the province was safe so long as his leader ascribed to the Constitution of 1824, which gave Texas the hope of eventual sovereign statehood within a Mexican confederation.

In Mexico, there was no real bloodshed between Bustamante and Santa

Anna. Bustamante continued to lose power, and in the fall proposed a truce. Santa Anna accepted. Under this convention Gómez Pedraza was recalled and placed in the President's chair, because his constitutional term under the election of 1828 ran till April, 1833. This making peace with the tyrant he had denounced and placing the aristocrat, Gómez Pedraza, back in office, astounded some of Santa Anna's followers. But it brought him even greater acclaim—here seemed to be an officer who put principle before personality or even personal gain. It was overlooked that Gómez had no real power, and that Santa Anna had led the revolt that turned him out of office in the first place. General Santa Anna controlled the army, which meant he was the ruler of the nation.

Santa Anna consented to stand for the office of President. He chose a liberal of impeccable reputation, Valentín Gómez Farías, as his running mate. The ticket was overwhelmingly elected, and probably honestly, though it was already noticeable that the faction controlling the polls on election day invariably won. Then, instead of assuming the Presidential office, Santa Anna turned the executive power and duties over to Gómez Farías and returned to his estates. Again he was praised as a Republican of Roman virtue, but instead Santa Anna was once more sniffing the wind. He had his doubts about the future of liberalism in Mexico. Although none of his contemporaries saw this, he was letting Gómez Farías send up the trial balloons, by demanding and inaugurating a broad spectrum of reforms.

In addition to restoring the powers and privileges of the States, Gómez Farías asked reduction of the powers of the army and the Church. Recognizing the problems with a citizenry who could not read or write, he emphasized a broad literacy program. The Vice President was one of those sincere, and tragic, liberal figures of Hispanic history. He knew what the nation required in order to make a true republic on the order of the United States or France. But he immediately displeased the army, and his literacy aims frightened both the landowners and the Church. Since he was not a demagogue, he talked over the heads of his real friends, the lowly Indians and *mestizos.* They might have supported a revolution that gave them immediate freedom and bread, but they could not comprehend his long-range plans. Opposition to Gómez Farías and the liberal position rapidly swelled. And, as Santa Anna suspected, the traditional bases of Mexican power, the army, the *hacendados,* and the Church hierarchy, were entirely too strong to be legislated out of existence.

The ins and outs, the plots and counterplots engineered by Santa Anna from retirement at Jalapa were typical but hardly important. In time, the General succeeded in doing what he had in mind all along: he returned to power and resumed his office with the entire backing of the forces in the nation he now realized were strongest. He was hailed as the country's savior. The Church praised him; Te Deums were sung. Officers toasted him, and the *latifundistas* breathed a sigh of relief and turned to more enjoyable things. Even the ragged populace, who had never understood the coldly intellectual Gómez Farías, cheered the nation's greatest hero. Santa Anna now began to be proud of his new title: *El Napoleón del Oeste,* "the Napoleon of the West." It was no longer necessary to keep his ambitions concealed.

Meanwhile, the Anglo-Texans, like the ministers of many nations, were misunderstanding the true state of affairs in Mexico. Mexía and his soldiers had departed with good cheer in the summer of 1832. The true, liberal Constitution was officially restored: Santa Anna made the temporary President, Gómez Pedraza, swear to it before having his three months in office. The liberal hero, hailed in Europe and the United States, was in power. It seemed the time to press for liberalization of the Texas government, and to secure what most Texans felt were their inalienable rights. Few greater miscalculations were ever made.

However, the great mass of colonists had absolutely no idea of making a rebellion or war. Colonel Juan Almonte, who was sent to Texas by Gómez Farías as a combined goodwill ambassador and Presidential spy, was surprised to find the atmosphere different from what he had been led to expect. In the capital it was widely stated that the Texans were plotting to detach the province; Almonte found only goodwill and loyalty to the Constitution. After making an exhaustive survey, Almonte realized the settlers had no dark aims against the Mexican nation, *but they did expect to live in Texas as Americans, with all the North American individual privileges and rights.* This, most Mexicans failed to understand, or understanding logically, emotionally rejected. Almonte, rather liberal, recommended that Texas be given the concessions, such as statehood, they demanded, but he offset this by recommending the province be well stocked with Mexican troops. It was virtually impossible for even a Mexican of goodwill to comprehend the fact that Anglo-Americans were capable of regulating themselves.

For this reason, the moves now made by the colonists were misunderstood by both Mexican liberals and conservatives alike. On their own initiative, the settlers of the *ayuntamiento* of San Felipe called a convention to meet on October 1, 1832. Sixteen Anglo-Texas districts responded; only Goliad's delegation arrived too late.

This convention chose Stephen Austin as its President and passed a number of draft resolutions addressed to the Federal government and to the government of the State of Coahuila. These resolutions asked that, among other things, new land titles be supplied, new *ayuntamientos* be created for self-government, that the colonies be exempted from customs duties for three more years, that customs officers be appointed by local, not national, authorities, and that land be set aside for the support of schools. The convention also approved a uniform plan for organizing all Texas militias, and drew up plans for Indian defense.

Most interest and emphasis centered on two resolutions to be sent to the federal capital: a petition for repeal of the decree of April 6, 1830, on immigration, and a request to be separated from Coahuila and granted full sovereignty within the confederation as a state.

Each of these resolutions was emphatically preceded by professions of loyalty to the *Mexican Confederation and the Constitution.* These were wholly sincere. But what the Texans were asking for was cultural pluralism, under Mexican sovereignty, and pluralism was not only foreign to the Hispanic nature but, in the light of the phobia against the United States that suffused most Mexicans, impossible to be weighed on merits. In fact, the very assemblies, so peaceful and so natural to the English-speaking experience and tradition, were entirely extra-legal under Mexican law. In Mexico, no initiative, except riot and insurrection, ever began with the people. Both liberals and conservatives, in office, ruled by decree. In this light, every Mexican official in Texas and in Mexico could only view the convention as some sort of enormous plot, aimed at the foundations of the nation.

The October resolutions at San Felipe de Austin were never presented to the state or federal authorities. The Coahuila Governor ordered the political chief at San Antonio to remind the colonists that their meeting was a violation of the law and "represented a disturbance of good order." Santa Anna, when he heard of the convention, denounced it and remarked there seemed to be a tendency among the foreigners to try to be independent.

This action by authority weakened Stephen Austin and other leaders whose whole aim was to secure Texas liberties within a loose framework of Mexican sovereignty. A pattern very similar to the conventions of the American Revolution emerged: more radical men, who did not proclaim allegiance and subservience to the Mexican nation quite so loudly, began to come to the fore. Semisecret committees of "safety" or "vigilance" were set up throughout Anglo-Texas, a complete and conscious inheritance of the events of 1775 and 1776. In January, 1833, the central committee called for a new assembly at San Felipe to meet on April 1. This convention deposed Austin as chairman and elected William H. Wharton, a settler whose position was that there was a limit to argument with Mexicans who never seemed to understand.

This second convention got to the point quickly. It passed resolutions setting forth grievances against customs duties, legal inequities, and military rule, and again petitioned for the resumption of immigration and a state government of, by, and for Anglo-Texans. Then it proceeded onward and actually framed a proposed state constitution, on the American pattern, which was to be presented to the Federal Congress for approval.

In this every historian will recognize the normal process of Anglo-American government; every state that entered the Union beginning in 1792 followed almost an identical process.

Drafting this constitution and forwarding it to the federal authority for ratification was the North American way of doing things, and the San Felipe convention did it instinctively. But understandably, this looked to

Mexicans precisely like a *pronunciamento,* followed by a *plan.* Almost all Mexican historians believed there was always a well-conceived plot to separate Texas from Mexico, and this cannot entirely be denied. The majority of the settlers were not involved, but certain leaders now pushing to the front had either lost confidence in Mexico, or had never had any. Among these were Wharton, David G. Burnet, and a newcomer who had merely drifted into Texas but who had enjoyed great prominence in Tennessee—Sam Houston. Houston was a known protégé of Andrew Jackson, now President of the United States, and he was made chairman of the constitutional committee of Texas, although he was not even a legal resident. Houston's motivation was to bring Texas eventually into the United States.

However, the burden of presenting this plan to the Mexican government fell to the empresario Austin, a man of proved loyalty and common sense. Somewhat unhappily, Austin agreed, and on April 22, 1833, took the long and arduous journey to the capital. He arrived at Mexico City early in July. At this time Gómez Farías was Acting President, with Santa Anna biding his time in the wings.

There are several versions of what now occurred. The government was in a turmoil of reform and confusion, and cholera had broken out in the city. But apparently Gómez Farías received Austin cordially and agreed to submit the petition to the House of Deputies. Also, through Lorenzo de Zavala, a Spanish Republican who had been exiled from Madrid and was now a Mexican cabinet minister, uniquely friendly toward Americans, he got a promise that the offensive Article XI, forbidding Anglo-Saxon immigration, would be revoked.

But the Mexican regime had problems it considered more pressing than Texas, and though Austin stayed in the city through the epidemic no action was taken on his petition. Sometime in September, 1833, Austin again saw Gómez Farías. At this interview he tried to convince the President that delay was dangerous, and that if the Mexican authorities failed to act, the Texans were in a frame of mind to organize a state government without sanction. Austin spoke bluntly, and Gómez took this as a threat. Both men were angry when the discussion ended. Probably Austin had failed to understand that a Mexican liberal could be as suspicious of foreigners, and more nationalistic, than a member of the *escocés* elite.

For the first time in his career Austin now moved somewhat rashly. He wrote the *ayuntamiento* at San Antonio (whose members, although wholly Mexican, were eager for statehood) on October 2 that the municipality should take the lead in peacefully making preparations for a government distinct from Coahuila. This letter was written, as Austin admitted, "in a moment of irritation and impatience," after he had been cooling his heels in the capital for months.

When this letter arrived at San Antonio, the political officer considered it treasonous, so marked it, and sent it back to the Acting President at Mexico City.

Meanwhile, Austin and Santa Anna, who returned to the capital, conferred on November 5. De Zavala and three other cabinet ministers were present. Santa Anna seemed friendly. He stated he would not approve separation of Texas from Coahuila—and here Santa Anna was on firm ground, because the Constitution of 1824 required a territory to have 80,000 inhabitants before becoming a state. But he agreed to every other request the convention at San Felipe had made: repeal of the ban on immigration, better mail service, a modification of the tariff. He also promised to try to influence Coahuila to institute trial by jury in Texas—something more and more Texans vociferously demanded.

Santa Anna, however, still suspected the Texans of revolutionary tendencies, and in letters to other officials made the statement. He insisted to Austin that 4,000 Mexican soldiers must be stationed in Texas "for the protection of the country." Austin argued that Texas was prepared to collect its taxes and guard its frontier without such government assistance. Only de Zavala backed him, and he got nowhere. However, he wrote home that he was well pleased with Santa Anna. "All is going well. . . . General Santa Anna has solemnly and publicly declared that he will sustain the federal representative system, as it now exists. . . ."

Austin now witnessed the repeal of Article XI. Although the refusal of self-government would be a blow, he knew the opening of immigration would be joyfully acclaimed. Reasonably content, he departed Mexico City on December 10. In January, he stopped over at the Coahuilan capital of Saltillo to transact business with the Governor. Here he was suddenly arrested on a Presidential order and escorted back to Mexico. His letter to San Antonio had been received by Gómez Farías, who was angered and ordered Austin taken to the ancient Prison of the Inquisition. He was held there *incomunicado,* which meant he was deprived of books, writing implements, visits by friends, and even walks in the prison courtyard. He was kept in solitary for some weeks.

Austin demanded a trial, but was denied one on the grounds that no Mexican court would accept jurisdiction. His only triumph in this period was that he was able to hide a small journal from his jailers, in which he kept the thoughts of an educated and sensitive man condemned to solitary confinement.

News of his arrest caused great concern in Texas. Two attorneys, Peter Grayson and Spencer Jack, raised money and petitions for Austin's release and rode to Mexico. These two men were able to accomplish only one thing: to get him released on bail on Christmas Day, 1834.

Now, while Austin languished, the liberal but politically unwise Valentín Gómez Farías, who alternated with Santa Anna in the Presidential chair, decreed himself into oblivion. Church appointments were given to the state; the clergy was forbidden to preach on politics or to enforce tithes, and the list of army officers was greatly deflated. Although Gómez Farías kept Austin in prison, the atmosphere of his regime did assist Anglo-Texas. In these months of 1833–1834 immigration was again permitted, and the State Legislature at Saltillo passed a number of liberal measures. Naturalized citizens for the first time were allowed to engage in retail trade. Texas was allotted three deputies to the Coahuila congress. The Texas government was revised into three more efficient departments, at San Antonio, San Felipe, and Nacogdoches. The English language was first recognized for official business. A superior court—with the privilege of trial by jury— was authorized for Texas. Finally—and this actually in contravention to the Federal Constitution—religious toleration was granted.

All these were honest attempts by Coahuila to satisfy its unwilling partner. But at the same time, greatly to the disgust of substantial men in Texas, the state opened land speculation. Thousands of leagues of land were granted to various promoters, both Mexican and American. One grant was in return for 1,000 soldiers being raised to fight Indians. Not a single soldier was armed, but many men grew rich. Liberalism had its drawbacks; speculators and promoters flocked to Saltillo, and land scrip was sold wildly in Texas and the United States. During this period some thousands of Americans crossed over into Texas. Some were honest land seekers. Others were drawn by the scent of opportunity.

Then, in April, 1834, Santa Anna took over the government at the capital. Gómez Farías was ousted for the last time. But this was a new Santa Anna, who now thought he knew the heart of Mexico. He repudiated liberalism publicly and dissolved the republican Congress. He dismissed all cabinet ministers but one, and by decree, abolished all local legislatures and *ayuntamientos* in the nation. The laws confining the clergy was declared void. This was a new Napoleon, indeed. Lorenzo de Zavala fled to Texas.

A new and subservient Congress one by one legalized all Santa Anna's acts. Finally, in October, 1835, the Constitution of 1824 was officially voided. Something identical to the old Spanish system of government replaced it. Mexico was declared a centralist state, in which the President and the national Congress held absolute powers. But this was only official recognition of what had already taken place, in 1834—Santa Anna already appointed every governor and official in the land. He was king, and more than a king, since he owed responsibility neither to the people nor God. There is much evidence that the mass of the population, although they did not approve of every whim of the General, breathed easier under the old system than under a federal republic no one could make work, and which only a few imported intellectuals understood.

The people of Zacatecas, a state where liberalism had a strong hold, revolted when the regional militias were reduced in favor of the standing army. Santa Anna's regulars defeated and destroyed a Zacatecan force of

5,000. Then, as he had learned in his days with Arredondo, Santa Anna disdained to be burdened with prisoners and permitted his troops to rape and plunder the state capital.

Word of these events reached Texas, but very little of what was happening was understood. Santa Anna still had a good reputation. Much progress had been made during 1833–1834, and the compromising party was now ascendant. The hint of trouble crossed the Rio Grande only in April, 1835, when Santa Anna sent an army to reduce Coahuila.

Coahuila, under the federal system, had fallen into chaos. Self-government here had turned into confusion. After passing a number of liberal acts affecting Texas, the legislature had begun to fight among itself, over the issues of location of the state capital and the question of land speculation. The Governor and certain other officers seemed mainly concerned with becoming rich. The official capital was removed to Monclova from Saltillo, but the citizens of Saltillo erected a rival government. The issue provoked a small civil war.

Santa Anna entered the quarrel and decreed the capital should remain at Monclova. In April, 1835, the legislature issued a bitter criticism of this interference in their war. Under his new system of centralism Santa Anna sent his brother-in-law, General Martín Perfecto de Cós, to break up the local government and render it obedient to the President. Governor Viesca was arrested, and a few state officials along with a "swarm of land speculators" dashed for safety north of the Rio Bravo. Once again, as in the troubles of 1810, Texas was becoming the refuge for Mexicans with anti-government sentiments.

In Texas, the events of the crucial year 1835 somewhat resembled the troubles of 1832. In January, the central government once again sent customs officers to Anáhuac and Velasco on the coast. Once again there was trouble, shots were fired, and two prominent citizens jailed. General Cós, mopping up in Coahuila, got word of this. He determined to reinforce the Texas garrisons and sent a dispatch rider north to Captain Don Antonio Tenorio at Anáhuac to stand firm and "be of good cheer"—the Mexicans were coming.

In these weeks the war party in Texas again came to life. These were men who for a great variety of reasons felt that life under the rule of Mexicans was unendurable. Again, these people were mostly newcomers who had failed to get land grants, merchants who found it impossible to operate under Mexican law, and lawyers who were particularly outraged by the non-Anglo-Saxon features of Hispanic codes, such as jailing citizens without trial. The great majority of the farmers and planters were busy with their crops and unconcerned with revolution. When the war clique or party seized the saddlebags of General Cós' courier at San Felipe and intercepted his message to Tenorio, most Texans condemned this act. But the nature of Cós' correspondence drove the war group into even more drastic action.

A group met, elected J. B. Miller, the political chief of the Department of the Brazos, as chairman and passed a resolution that authorized the hotspur William Barrett Travis to capture Anáhuac. Buck Travis was not only willing but eager. He gathered about two dozen followers, mounted a small brass cannon on a sawmill truck, deployed in front of the fort of Anáhuac, and demanded its surrender. On June 30 Captain Tenorio, although he commanded forty-four Mexican soldiers, complied. Travis immediately paroled these men, and there was no violence.

This seemingly senseless attack aroused enormous opposition throughout the colony. Travis was denounced as a fool, a traitor, and a dangerous idiot. Seven Texas communities passed formal resolutions to the effect that they did not require their rights defended in this manner. During the entire month of July, 1835, a definite majority of the settlers expressed loyalty to Mexico, denounced the notion of conflict with the central government, and even J. B. Miller, who had headed the radicals in June, sent a conciliatory letter to General Cós, who was now poised at Matamoros. Several "peace commissioners" were elected from the communities in a meeting at San Felipe and sent south to confer about the recent trouble with Santa Anna's brother-in-law.

General Cós, however, was not in a conciliatory mood. He had several demands on the colonists before he would consent to treat with them: the arrest of Lorenzo de Zavala, the former cabinet minister who was somewhere in Texas, and the arrest and submission to the military of a group of prominent men of the radical or war clique. In an episode Texans later preferred not to talk about, some of the extreme conciliatory or peace party had handed Colonel Ugartechea, now commanding at San Antonio, a list of names. These included Travis, F. W. Johnson, a notorious land speculator, Robert Williamson, who was known as "Three-Legged Willie" and was like Travis a Patrick Henry of this revolution, and Sam Williams. The peace party felt that if these men were removed, the trouble would subside, and they were willing to sell the hotspurs to the Mexican government in return for peace.

Now, an ironic but perfectly logical turnabout occurred: Cós' demand for these men to be arrested by their own kind and turned over to him shocked and angered the majority that had been, in meeting after meeting, condemning them. There was considerable understanding in Texas of Mexican military tribunals; the Mexican authorities played their politics in different ways from Anglo-Americans. No matter what Travis had done, no Anglo-Texan was prepared to see him put before a military court and shot. Cós, who had good intelligence and monitored the sentiments of the colony, felt his suspicions grimly confirmed by this sentiment. These people, who kept professing loyalty to the Mexican Constitution, were not really loyal to the Mexican nation or people. He made his famous statement, which summed up the Mexican attitude perfectly, and which was perfectly logical: that the Texans were citizens of Mexico, and they must submit to the government of Mexico, no matter on what principles the Constitution might be construed from day to day.

Given the attitudes, prejudices, and folkways of the Anglo-Texans, this was impossible. They thought of themselves as free men, only minimally subject to any government, and if the central authority construed this as insurrection or anarchy, a large party of them were prepared to defend their position with arms. Thus, as Richardson wrote, did the season for conciliation pass.

A few committees of correspondence, in the manner of 1774, had already been formed. Now, in the summer of 1835, these proliferated, with Cós and his army standing just below the Rio Grande. Call after call for a general convention to "discuss the public safety" went out. On August 15 William H. Wharton, who was openly calling for action, presided over a meeting at Columbia, which sent out a call for a consultation of all Texas citizens. A great convention was planned for Washington-on-the-Brazos for October 15. This message stated that the aim of the convention was to secure peace *if it could be obtained on constitutional terms,* and if not, to prepare for an inevitable war.

While the planters were busy harvesting their cotton, the towns and municipalities were buzzing with talk of war. Significantly, the newest towns and communities in Anglo-Texas no longer took the names of Mexican officials; there were no more Goliads, Victorias, and Mexías, but Columbias, Libertys, and Washingtons. During this period, the last great inrush of immigration unquestionably heightened tensions. Perhaps 10,000 Anglo-Americans passed over into Texas after 1830, making the population approximately 30,000, with not more than 10 percent of this Negro slaves. The older planters still had memories of a "munificent and liberal" Mexico; the new men were fresh from the ways and ideals of the United States. There is no question that many men, frontiersmen, now came with the idea that a war was brewing, and that Texas would soon become a part of the United States. In the Southwest the old dream never died.

One great question in the legitimate settlers' minds was, what did Colonel Austin think? Austin had not ruled Anglo-Texas since 1828, but he had represented the region at Saltillo, and his influence with the older faction was still very great. What Austin would or could have done during the hot summer of 1835 can only be conjecture, because he was still held *incomunicado* in a Mexico jail. His arrest, in fact, was a large factor making the planter group uneasy. This imprisonment, on specious charges and without being brought to trial, violated all Anglo-American notions of justice.

Nothing was more indicative of the state of Mexican law and justice in these years than the fact that although Gómez Farías fell from power in April, 1834, Austin was still held more than a year later. No Mexican court or Mexican judge would accept responsibility, either for freeing him or shooting him. Finally, on July 13, 1835, Austin was released under a

general amnesty—one of those peculiarities of Hispanic justice no American could understand. He was neither pardoned nor cleared, but set free
with an assortment of prisoners and criminals of every kind. Before he
could quit the country, he was forced to travel to Jalapa and seek Santa
Anna's permission. The dictator gave it, apparently on the assumption that
the former empresario would be a temporizing factor with the colonists; at
this time Santa Anna did not know how far revolutionary sentiment in
Texas had gone. Austin was given a passport to take ship to New Orleans.
He left the country fully aware of the radical changes the Napoleon of the
West was making, and with his trust in the Mexican President completely
destroyed.

At New Orleans, Austin wrote a revealing letter to his cousin, Mrs. Holley. During eighteen months in prison, while constitutionalism in Mexico
was extirpated, Austin's sense of ethnic Americanism was enormously enhanced. His ideas of a pluralistic commonwealth under the Mexican flag
were dead. He was now utterly convinced that Texas must separate from
Mexico.

In his letter Austin stated that Texas must be fully Americanized, remain a slave country, and hinted it should come under the American flag.
He indicated that he was going to continue to keep up appearances, not to
"become a very Mexican politician in hypocrisy" but because such a course
was prudent. He felt that Santa Anna would move against Texas in the
coming spring or summer. He could not, of course, know that events were
moving much more rapidly. He wrote that the "great law of nature—self-
preservation—operates, and supersedes all other laws . . . in all countries,
one way or another, a few men rule society," and he was out to convince
those men, in Texas and the United States, of the great benefits that would
"result to the Western world by *Americanizing* Texas." His aim was to
keep the trouble damped and the Mexicans unsuspicious, while a hoped-for
massive immigration of Americans flooded Texas:

> A great immigration from Kentucky, Tennessee, etc., *each man with
> his rifle* . . . would be of great use to us—very great indeed. . . . I
> wish a great immigration this fall and winter from Kentucky, Tennessee,
> *everywhere; passports or no passports, anyhow.* For fourteen years I have
> had a hard time of it, but nothing shall daunt my courage or abate my
> exertions to complete the main object of my labors to *Americanize* Texas.
> This fall and winter will fix our fate—a great immigration will settle the
> question.

With enough Kentucky and Tennessee rifles in Texas, Austin had no fear
of Santa Anna and his Mexicans.

Mexican historians took this letter as proof that Austin from the first
planned the basest treason against his adopted country. This view ignores
Austin's arbitrary and illegal imprisonment, the bald pronouncements by the

Mexican military that Texans would have to endure whatever kind of government the central regime decreed, and the bloody record of Santanista duplicity. The very adoption of the title "Napoleon of the West" was ominous to Texans, because Napoleon, in all English-speaking lands, was never looked upon as a great law-giver, but only a military tyrant of the bloodiest and most maniacal kind. The dominant Mexican view was legalistic, and in point of fact, entirely legal under international or any other kind of law—Texas was recognized Mexican soil, and the Mexican nation had the right to impose any kind of government it chose. This fact was recognized, however reluctantly, even by President Andrew Jackson of the United States. But the Mexican outlook completely ignored not only Santa Anna's tyranny, but the fact that every Anglo-Texan was born with the notion he possessed inalienable rights. He could not give these up simply by taking Mexican citizenship or slough them off at the Sabine. Americans of the 19th century frequently were wrong, but very few had any moral doubts. Austin himself had none. He had created an Anglo-Saxon society in Texas, and as he wrote, the first duty of any society was to survive.

The call for a massive and illegal entry of armed Americans was not so much a plot to join Texas to the United States as it was Austin seeking, from the most logical source, all the help he could get—just as Israelis, beset by Arabs, called upon Jewry all over the world. Neither Texas in the 19th century, nor Israel more than a century later, had any doubt of their right to defend themselves. What was at stake was more than mere boundaries.

After issuing a call for help, Austin rode back across the Sabine to the Brazos. He reached San Felipe in September. Here, he found matters far gone, and the call for a consultation of all Anglo-Texans had already gone out.

Austin approved the call. As colonel of the militia, he took the chair of the San Felipe municipal Committee of Safety. A few days later, a hard-riding courier from Béxar brought word that General Cós had crossed the Rio Grande with a large army, bound for San Antonio. Stephen Austin, who no longer signed himself "Estévan," now put out a general call for Texans to stand to arms: "War is our only resource. There is no other remedy. We must defend our rights, ourselves, and our country by force of arms."

Thus the acts of Mexican Constitutionalists and Mexican reactionaries, taken together, had finally created the very monster Mexicans had always feared.

12

BLOOD AND SOIL

. . . *We consider death preferable to disgrace, . . . opening the door for the invaders to enter the sacred territory of the colonies. We hope our countrymen will open their eyes at the present danger. . . . I fear it is useless to waste arguments upon them. The thunder of the enemy's cannon and the pollution of their wives and daughters—the cries of their famished children and the smoke of their burning dwellings, only [this] will arouse them. . . . For God's sake and the sake of our country, send us reinforcements.*

LT. COL. WILLIAM BARRET TRAVIS, COMMANDING
THE ALAMO, TO GOVERNOR SMITH, FEBRUARY, 1836

. . . *To suppose that such a cause will fail when defended by Anglo-Saxon blood and by Americans, and on the limits and at the very door of this free and philanthropic and magnanimous nation, would be a calumny against republicanism and freedom, against a noble race.*

FROM STEPHEN F. AUSTIN'S SPEECH TO THE
CITIZENS OF LOUISVILLE, FEBRUARY, 1836

God and Texas—Victory or Death!

THE CLOSE OF TRAVIS' LAST LETTER FROM
THE ALAMO, MARCH 3, 1836

. . . *It sealed forever the title of the Texans to the soil of Texas. The blood of Travis, of Bowie, of Bonham, of Crockett and the rest, consecrated the soil of Texas forever.*

LOUIS J. WORTHAM, LL.D., *A History of Texas*

Austin's call to arms went out to the Texas *ayuntamientos* on September 19. Other letters went out from San Felipe, making the colonists' position clear: Cós, representing the Supreme Government, as the Mexicans now called it, demanded the surrender of the proscribed agitators, and the unconditional submission of the colonists to any changes in the law or government made by the Supreme Government. No consultation or colonists' assemblies would be permitted or recognized. To ensure this compliance, Cós was moving garrisons into Texas, making San Antonio his headquarters beginning September 16. The Anglos could submit or fight; it was a matter of supreme indifference to the General.

Cós also said, and this was widely circulated by Austin from the Brazos to Nacogdoches, that it was time to break up "foreign settlements in Texas."

The call to arms united almost the entire population, but only upon two things: that the consultation must be held, and Cós' troops should be kept out of Texas. The evidence is very clear, from statements and letters of the planters, that a majority of the people had not adopted any notion of independence. The landowners and cotton planters had seen crises come and go, and there was great confidence that this one would blow over, too, if only Texans stood by their rights.

Nor did all Texans stand to arms immediately. This was the season of the harvest east of the Colorado, and the bulk of the stable population were farmers. Austin and other leaders had to write broadside after broadside to arouse the country: "There must be no half-way measures! War in full! The sword is drawn and the scabbard must be put on one side until the military are all driven out of Texas."

By general consent, Austin assumed the high command and the rank of general. Couriers were sent pounding down the dusty roads and trails, carrying the news and spreading the alarm. The coastal strip that was Anglo-Texas was thinly settled and the word took time to spread. But the little, straggling communities and towns were filled with rumor, and anger at "military despotism." An account went out that Cós carried 800 pairs of iron hobbles, in which Texans would be marched back to Mexico. Bands of armed men—every Anglo-Texan at this time went armed—began to gather along the trails and at the crossroads, to defend the Constitution, and what most of them considered immensely more important: their own soil. The Mexicans regarded these men as foreigners, but the colonists saw the Mexicans as invaders, and by the often unhappy logic of history, both parties were correct.

The first bloodshed came for the same reason the shots heard 'round the world were fired at Lexington. Mexican policy was now to seize arms and military stores in Texan hands before real trouble started, and in doing so among a population of this kind, they started it. When Cós took ship from the Rio Bravo to sail to the Texas coast, and from there to march to Béxar, Colonel Ugartechea at San Antonio sent a file of cavalrymen riding south to Gonzales. Green DeWitt's colony had been issued a small brass cannon, a six-pounder, for defense against Indians some years before.

Andrew Ponton, the Gonzales *alcalde,* received the order for the surrender of the gun, signed by the political chief at San Antonio. Ponton stalled for time, supported by the citizens. He demanded an order from the political chief of the Department of the Brazos before releasing it. The noncommissioned officer in charge of the Mexican cavalry left his men camped at Gonzales and rode back to Béxar for further instructions. Meanwhile, Ponton buried the cannon, and sent runners to the surrounding area for armed assistance. Messengers reached Bastrop and the plantation of J. H. Moore, on the Colorado.

Now, the eighteen men in Gonzales able and willing to fight organized, removed all boats from the Guadalupe River, and hid the ferry in a bayou north of town. The next step was to capture the handful of Mexican soldiers waiting near the town. This was done—but one man got away, and rode hallooing back to Béxar.

On October 1, 1835, Captain Francisco Castañeda arrived from San Antonio with something less than two hundred men. Ugartechea intended a show of force. Casteñeda, blocked by the Guadalupe, demanded the ferry be restored, and the cannon handed over. There was some parleying, a demonstration by the Mexican cavalry near the town, and considerable yelling and taunting by the Texans, who were now steadily being reinforced by a swarm of armed men filtering from the backwoods into town. During this Mexican stand-off, Castañeda's troopers took no action except to strip a watermelon patch.

Now, John Moore, the big man of the neighborhood, arrived and was elected colonel. Moore decided to attack the Mexicans at daylight. The buried cannon was unearthed and mounted on a wagon. A blacksmith shop busily forged some ammunition—iron scraps and lengths of chain. Some inspired soul made a flag: two yards of white cloth, painted with a cannon and the words COME AND TAKE IT.

Before the dawn, in the morning fog of October 2, Moore's militia went out to find the Mexicans. They blundered into the Mexican pickets, but in the dark and fog there could be no war. Everyone drew back and waited until daybreak.

Daylight showed both forces drawn up on an open prairie. The Gonzales cannon fired, without doing any damage, and Castañeda immediately requested a parley. He asked why he was being attacked.

Colonel Moore explained that the Captain had demanded a cannon given to the Texans for "the defense of themselves and the constitution and the laws of the country," while he, Castañeda, "was acting under the orders of the tyrant Santa Anna, who had broken and trampled underfoot all the state and federal constitutions of Mexico, except that of Texas," which last the Texans were prepared to defend.

Castañeda answered that "he was himself a republican, as were two-thirds of the Mexican nation, but he was a professional officer of the government," and while that government had indeed undergone certain surprising changes, it was the government, and the people of Texas were bound to submit to it. Castañeda further stated that he was not here to cause a war; if he was refused the cannon, his orders were simply to take up a position nearby and await further instruction.

Moore then suggested to the Captain, if he was a republican, he should join the revolution against tyranny by surrendering his command, which might then fight in the common cause. Captain Castañeda replied stiffly that he would obey his orders. At this, Moore returned to his own lines and ordered the Texans to open fire. There was a brief skirmish, and the Mexican force immediately abandoned the field and rode toward San Antonio. There is no question who fired first in the Texas Revolution.

By now, the word was out that there was shooting at Gonzales; hundreds of men from the Colorado and beyond were pouring in. Calls for a stand went out signed by prominent planters, such as Bryant, Archer, and Mc-Neel. At Brazoria, William H. Wharton distributed a broadside, which began:

Freemen of Texas

TO ARMS!!!   TO ARMS!!!

"Now's the day, and Now's the hour!"

Communication after communication went out. Most were inflammatory, some repeated gaudy rumors, but all took up the constitutional question. A number were printed in Spanish, for the Mexican population, which was traditionally Republican in Texas. Three hundred men gathered at San Felipe, then went on to Gonzales.

In San Antonio, Colonel Ugartechea received the report of Captain Castañeda grimly. Cós was now at Goliad, having landed earlier at Cópano Bay, and Ugartechea knew he would soon be reinforced by the Commandant General's army. But he made an attempt to stop the fighting before it got worse. He sent a letter to Stephen F. Austin, appealing to this influential citizen to avoid an irreparable break.

Ugartechea asked for peace, but on the already stated terms: surrender of the cannon, and the proscribed citizens. He also promised something he patently could not deliver: there would be no garrisoning of troops if the colonists subsided. He professed friendship for Austin and the Texans, and asserted he would behave towards them as a gentleman, even though they had not behaved well toward Mexicans. But if the colonists did not submit, he would act militarily, and the dignity of the Mexican nation would be upheld.

This letter was significant, because it showed clearly the attitude of the vast majority of Mexican officials toward the Anglo-Americans, and especially those, like Ugartechea, who were genuinely friendly. Ugartechea himself, and almost every Mexican officer, in recent years had at some time or another taken up arms against one or another Mexican regime, in the name of some constitution. But this was a pastime reserved for ethnic Mexicans. Any attempt at resistance by Anglo-Texans, even though they were full-fledged citizens under the law, was instinctively regarded as a North American plot or an insult to the nation. This of course was an attitude toward alien immigrants peculiar neither to Mexicans nor to that time and place, but it infuriated even the peace party in Texas.

Meanwhile, Cós marched from Goliad to Béxar, arriving on October 9. He left a small detachment behind to hold Goliad, which was the Mexican gateway to the sea. At San Antonio, the Mexican Commandant General now had 800 soldiers. These men were regulars, and they should have been more than enough to pacify the country.

But the Mexican army in Texas, like the British regulars sixty years earlier, was facing men and conditions outside its experience. The oak-studded plains southeast of San Antonio were aswarm with riflemen. Ugartechea made one rather feeble demonstration outside Béxar; running into dangerous numbers of Texans, he retired. By October 24, the Mexican forces in San Antonio were under a genuine state of siege.

After the "victory" at Gonzales, a tremendous euphoria swept the countryside. A few days later, Captain Collinsworth and a few militiamen took Goliad, a small victory, but one which had a bad effect on Cós' morale. A force of 300 assembled at Gonzales. The inevitable shout was raised: "On to San Antonio!"

An attack on San Antonio seemed to make good sense. The town was the heart of Mexican Texas, and at the moment, it was where the troops were. If San Antonio fell into the hands of the Anglo rebels, they would control the entire state. Stephen Austin, now General Austin, arrived to take command of the "Army of the People," a job he did not particularly want. Austin was not a military man, and his health had been destroyed in the Prison of the Inquisition.

In straggling but happy order, the army took the road to San Antonio, the "Old Cannon Flag" of Texas flying at the head, the Gonzales "artillery" rumbling at its rear, pulled by two yokes of longhorn steers. Noah Smithwick, one of the volunteers, described the march in colorful terms:

> Words are inadequate to convey an impression of the appearance of the first Texas army as it formed in marching order . . . it certainly bore little resemblance to the army of my childhood dreams. Buckskin breeches

were the nearest approach to uniform and there was wide diversity even there, some being new and soft and yellow, while others, from long familiarity with rain and grease and dirt, had become hard and black and shiny. . . . Boots being an unknown quantity, some wore shoes and some moccasins. Here a broad-brimmed sombrero overshadowed the military cap at its side; there the tall "beegum" rode familiarly beside a coonskin cap, with the tail hanging down behind, as all well-regulated tails should do. Here a big American horse loomed above the nimble Spanish pony . . . there a half-broke mustang pranced beside a sober, methodical mule . . . in lieu of a canteen each man carried a Spanish gourd. . . . A fantastic military array to a casual observer, but the one great purpose animating every heart clothed us in a uniform more perfect in our eyes than was ever donned by regulars on dress parade.

In this army the frontier element predominated; they did not look like an army, but they were grimly and deadly efficient for all of that. Each man carried his long rifle, made in the United States, and these were the grandsons of the men who had fought at King's Mountain, and broke over the Cumberlands into Kentucky and Tennessee. They were not soldiers in any accepted sense, but they were the deadliest and most efficient predators the continent had ever known.

The army moved slowly up the road to Béxar. The famed Gonzales cannon did not make it; the wheels broke down and it was abandoned at a place called Sandy Creek. Texas roads were unfitted for artillery, and cannon, or the lack of it, was to play a great role in this war.

The Army of the People started with about three hundred, but on the way it picked up more and more. Armed men from the region above the Brazos now came in. The Texans reached San Antonio, and flowed around the villa like a horde of hungry soldier ants. Whatever advantage the Mexicans had was surrendered by General Cós. His regulars could best have met the Texans in the open fields, on the march to San Antonio. Here regulars were at their best, and frontiersmen at their worst, since they fought as individuals, without any real notion of command or discipline. But Cós was cautious; he pulled his men into San Antonio, and begged for reinforcements. Ugartechea, whose personal courage is unquestionable, had seen his troops punished by rifle fire at Velasco. Neither officer desired to risk a full-scale clash. In the town, the Mexican army rapidly ate up its provisions, and worse, its morale steadily sank.

At the same time, the Texan army, camped outside the town, sank into its own form of confusion. Austin wanted to treat with the enemy and negotiate Cós out of Texas; others wanted to fight; no one had much command or control. The Texas militia had marched to Gonzales and San Antonio at a propitious time; the crops were in, and the farmers had nothing else to do, and they were as content hunting Mexicans as squirrels and bear. But the call of service had only been for two months, and after half the time expired, some where already restless; by early December they were thinking of spring planting. Austin, who understood the deficiencies of his army, tried to improve things but without much success. Austin was a diplomat, not a field commander. On one occasion, when he ordered an attack on San Antonio, there was no response.

When Austin was relieved by the Consultation that meanwhile met at San Felipe, with orders to proceed to the United States to seek American aid, there is evidence that both he and the army were pleased. Austin left on November 25. The troops held an election, and passed the command to Colonel Edward Burleson.

Despite the fact that on November 26, in a sharp exchange called the "grass fight," some fifty foragers sent out by Cós for desperately needed hay were killed, vast discouragement pervaded the Texan army. They lacked artillery, and most of the officers were reluctant to assault San Antonio and the presidio of the Alamo without artillery support. Significantly, many of the Americans with military training, notably Sam Houston, tried to stop the San Antonio expedition altogether. When the weather in late fall turned bad, conditions in the Texan camp became miserable. There was insufficient clothing; most of the men who turned out in late summer had not even brought coats with them; and food was not only poor but irregular. There was no organized commissary or service support of any kind. The "army," irregular enough at the start, was rapidly degenerating into a grousing mob.

Its composition was changing also. The Texan farmers and planters began to dribble away, back to families, warm homes, and their more pressing affairs. By December, most of the Texas militia had deserted the siege—a siege being probably the most difficult operation of all for a purely amateur army to conduct. But in these weeks, a new element of reinforcement swelled the Texas ranks. Hundreds of men were pouring into the region from the southwestern United States.

The news of war had reached New Orleans and traveled up the Mississippi. Adventure and fighting in Texas appealed strongly to many men along the American frontier. In small groups, sometimes singly, they began to drift across the Sabine. Formal volunteer units were quickly organized in several southern states. One of these, the smartly turned-out New Orleans Grays, sailed to the Texas coast and marched inland from Goliad.

Austin's wish for a great immigration from Kentucky, Tennessee, "everywhere," with their rifles, was in part coming true. These men came for every motive in the world: adventure, idealism (because many Americans thought the conflict in Texas was "their" war), and the sheer love of violence. No matter how many historians prefer to gloss over the fact, the first Trans-Appalachian-born or -bred generation was an extremely tough and violent race. Texas was where the action was. It became a lodestar, pulling an enormous number of the men—Sam Houston, Davy Crockett, James Bowie, and others—who were already in some way legends on the old frontier. As one historian wrote, Texas seemed to cast some sort of spell, to make men who were cold, pragmatic, and opportunist in the main, want to go and die.

At first, the American increments pouring into San Antonio increased the Texan army to considerably more than Cós'. Then, when the Texans began to leave, this force shrank. By December 3, the Americans outnumbered the native fighters, and the whole army numbered somewhere between three and five hundred. Nobody kept an accurate roll.

A consultation of officers held by Burleson agreed to abandon the siege, although some men argued this would destroy the entire Texas army. The goal of San Antonio was all that held it together. The men were paraded on December 4, and orders issued for a retreat to Gonzales. It was not received with great enthusiasm in the ranks—many men, miserable as they were, had come to Béxar to fight.

The baggage wagons were already loaded when a random spark reignited the war. A Mexican officer, a deserter, passed into the Texan lines. Burleson was forced to conduct his interrogation of this man in front of the whole army, and wild excitement spread. The Mexican lieutenant advised that Cós' army was disheartened, hungry, and that San Antonio could be easily seized. Colonel Frank Johnson, the adjutant general, the one officer who had held out for continuing the siege, remarked to Colonel Ben Milam, standing beside him, that perhaps a call should be raised for volunteers.

Ben Milam, an old empresario agent, whom bad luck had dogged all his life and who had barely escaped with his life from Cós' conquest of Coahuila—where he had been best known as one of the biggest land speculators—suddenly raised a shout: "Who will go with old Ben Milam into San Antonio? Who will go with old Ben Milam into San Antonio?"

A great cry went up. "Then fall in line!" Milam roared. Two hundred men stepped forward. There was nothing Burleson could do but go along. He agreed to hold the rest of the army outside the gates, while Milam's volunteers assaulted San Antonio. But when Milam assembled his troops at an old mill, just outside of town, he counted three hundred and one. Milam had the heart and the command of the army, and his part to play in history.

Instead of putting his troops entirely in the old presidio, with its strong fortifications, Cós had divided his command into two divisions. One held the Alamo, east of the San Antonio River. The other was quartered in the town to the west, and strongly entrenched in the two plazas with their stone buildings. Both divisions had artillery.

Milam's assault began at three in the morning, December 5. His men broke through the Mexican pickets and filtered into San Antonio. Now, house to house, a hot and bloody battle began. It was small-unit fighting, house to house and man to man. It was the kind of warfare that American frontiersmen, taught to take cover and shoot to kill, loved best. It was one in which Mexican regulars, who like most Latin troops were better in the assault than defense, were nibbled to death. House after house, plaza after plaza, were cleared by deadly sniping; the Mexicans fell back, and Cós began to panic.

On the third day of this bitter, close-in fighting, old Ben Milam, who for these hours had been a colonel indeed, exposing himself and leading the bloody advance from house to house, was shot dead. The Masons in the army, with ceremony, buried his body in the courtyard of the Veramendi house, almost where it fell. Milam was now immortal, the first in a long pantheon of Texas heros.

Then, amid the flat crack of American rifles and the duller boom of the Mexican *escopetas*, or flintlock muskets, another election was held. Johnson was chosen commander, with Major Morris of the New Orleans Grays as his second in command. The assault went on. Some houses were reduced room by room. Battering rams, made of logs brought in from the sawmill, knocked down doors, and rifle butts smashed in Mexican faces. The Mexicans responded with heavy cannonades, which knocked down walls but killed few Texans. Although on December 8, Cós was heavily reinforced, with about six hundred men from the south, his nerve was gone. One hundred and seventy-nine men, with six officers, deserted and fled toward the Rio Grande. On December 10, 1835, Cós surrendered eleven hundred and five officers and men, and his fortress, the Alamo.

By any standard, this victory of a force that never numbered more than 350 over three times its number entrenched in defensive positions, with artillery support, was a brilliant achievement. It was hailed with rejoicing back along the Brazos. But it was to be almost fatal to the Texas cause; it convinced many men the war was over and made them hold the Mexican army in far too much contempt.

Burleson, who took command again as the shooting ended, gave Cós the honors of war. Cós signed a covenant of surrender, in which he pledged that he would never fight again against the colonists, or the Constitution of 1824. He was allowed to march out toward Monclova, south of the Rio Grande.

Now, in the chill December sunlight, the Texas army held both Goliad and the Alamo at Béxar—two strong presidios on the San Antonio River guarding Anglo-Texas from southern attack. Texas was completely cleared of Mexican soldiers. Convinced the war was over at least till the coming summer, the Texas residents in the army drifted away, back to farms and homes. Even Colonel Edward Burleson left his command, passing it on to Johnson.

To understand the approaching tragedy, this victory euphoria and the failure of the Texans to create a strong government must be understood.

Until this time, self-government in Texas had really meant the absence of government. In a province where everyone had land and there was little crime, no government was needed to clear the wilderness and plant cotton. Texans had three great disadvantages now in trying to form a viable government for the whole state: Texas society was a society of relative new-comers, in which, since no Anglo-Texan was allowed to hold higher than a municipal office, no political experience or leadership had developed. Although Anglo-Texas was ethnically solid—Mexican settlement did not exist north of the San Antonio River, and the old Spanish colony at Nacogdoches was already beginning to speak English—the various grants and districts did not form any kind of commercial or political entity. Austin's and DeWitt's colonies had had only the sketchiest relations, and both were remote from deep East Texas. Finally, there was a strong streak of independence and opportunism in almost every man who had braved the Sabine. An enormously self-reliant group had colonized Texas; now, that very self-reliance made it hard for these men to cooperate easily. The average Texas was determined to take no orders from Mexicans, but he also took few willingly from his own kind.

In an atmosphere without political parties or political traditions, politics rapidly coalesced around personalities, with explosive and tragic effects.

The first state government was the so-called Permanent Council, which organized at San Felipe in October, 1835. This was a rump regime, but so far as it could go, it organized well. This Council elected Richard Royall of Matagorda as its president, commissioned privateers, sent some supplies to San Antonio, set up a postal system, and halted all land surveying and speculation. It also authorized one Thomas McKinney to go to the United States and borrow $100,000.

On November 3 the Permanent Council was dissolved because the planned general consultation of all the districts convened. Delegates to this were elected by twelve municipalities and two departments. The convention was immediately badly divided; the question was the nature of the war, and how it should be conducted. What were Anglo-Texans fighting for? In defense of their rights as Mexican citizens under the Constitution of 1824, or for independence from a corrupt Mexico?

The committee appointed to study the question was hopelessly dead-locked, and the question was thrown before the general convention. As Gail Borden, Jr., who was to become better known for his condensed milk than for his efforts as a Texas politician, wrote, the question was debated for three days with animation, "yet coolness and moderation prevailed."

A large majority of the delegates opposed outright independence. There was a split here between older settlers and the new. The planter party insisted on incorporating the Texas Revolution into a Mexican civil war. It was known that General Mexía, the old Santanista, was planning a revolt against the dictator. The older group preferred to enlist the Republican sentiment in Mexico in the Texas cause, rather than let it devolve into an outright Texas-Mexico war, in which the Mexican millions and trained army would be brought to bear with crushing force.

The attitude of the United States toward the struggle was a big factor. That nation was bound by a treaty with Mexico regarding the inviolability of Texas. The brother-in-law of the U.S. Secretary of State wrote Texans, advising them to follow a legal and constitutional course, which would appear well in international law. Some Texans found the U.S. attitude hard to comprehend, but it was this: the government was prepared to assist a band of civil rebels fighting for a constitution unofficially, but it refused to become involved, because of appearances, in anything that looked like a plan to join Texas to the Union. President Jackson himself held this official legalistic view; he branded a Texas declaration of independence a "rash and premature act" as late as April, 1836.

The newer arrivals, who had never developed a sense of Mexican citizenship, and who had gotten so far only trouble from the Mexican authorities, were much less patient. Some of these last had emigrated to Texas during 1834–1835 with the deliberate idea of splitting the province away from Mexico. This group, although not dominant, was strong.

The final declaration of purpose by the November Consultation was a compromise. It attacked Santanista tyranny, upheld "natural rights," and stated Texans fought for the Constitution of 1824, thereby "laying the cornerstone of liberty in the great Mexican Republic." But it was also stated that Texas had the right to establish an independent government if Mexico discarded the Federal system. This compromise was obsolete before it was issued. Mexía's attempt to arouse Mexicans in defense of republicanism was utterly abortive. On October 3, 1835, Santa Anna's subservient Congress voided the old constitution and legalized the centralist state. The attitude of American citizens beyond the Sabine was that, whatever their government's position, they were hardly interested in assisting in a Mexican civil war, and the Texas emissaries quickly shifted their sails to this wind.

Austin, when he arrived in the States in December, 1835, began to describe the Revolution as a "sub rosa" American war, a successful outcome of which would be in the interests of the United States.

Finally, something resembling an ethnic conflict was already taking place. The signs were ominous. When Governor Viesca of Coahuila escaped to Texas and tried to join the anti-Santa Anna forces around Béxar, he was brushed aside with suspicion, even contempt. The *alcalde* of the Mexican settlement in Victoria, in de León's colony, complained that the Texas militia, which now seized the town, treated all Mexicans, even those who declared for the Revolution, as virtual enemies. Some Texas natives did join the revolt. The Spaniard Lorenzo de Zavala, the old land commissioner Seguín, Don Juan Antonio Navarro, Placido Benavides, and a handful of *rancheros* either declared for Texas or fought in the Texan army. But the majority of the some 4,000 ethnic Mexicans in Texas either were hostile or held aloof. This doomed the illusion of civil conflict between Mexicans of different ideologies from the start.

The Consultation created a provisional government. This consisted of a Governor, Lieutenant Governor, and a Council. Henry Smith, an irascible settler who had proven his patriotism by taking a bullet at Velasco in '32, was elected Governor. Stephen F. Austin, William H. Wharton, and Branch T. Archer, the Consultation president, were appointed Commissioners to the United States. This last was probably a serious error. These three were the only recognized leaders in Texas and badly needed at home. In fact, many of the Old Three Hundred families considered the appointment of Austin to be part of a plot to get him out of the country and out of the way of more ambitious men. Somewhat ironically, the more radical war group felt Austin was dangerously "pro-Mexican."

The Consultation also appointed Sam Houston of Tennessee commander in chief of the army, but it failed to raise a regular force for him to command, although it was much discussed. Actually, it was beyond the Texans' powers to raise a permanent army. There was no money to pay it, and there were as yet no men available to enlist. At this time, November, 1835, the whole community was far from aroused. Not one man in four had reported for the militia call, and those who did were released within two months. As Wortham wrote, "In November, 1835 . . . a good percentage . . . were giving more attention to gathering their cotton crop than to the revolution." In all, no more than one hundred men were ever enlisted in the "regular" army, and this was to add its weight to the coming terror.

On November 14, the Consultation adjourned. Public affairs were left to Governor Smith and his Council. Unfortunately and incredibly, the powers of neither had been defined, and personal hostility was already brewing.

At Béxar and Goliad, the Texan army now consisted almost wholly of American volunteers. Only a few officers were Texas residents or could claim the legitimate title of "Texian." And the one thing a volunteer army, imperfectly organized, supplied, and led could not do was to sit and wait the Mexicans out.

The only advantage Texas had in this war was geography. Scarred as Mexico was by civil wars, the nation had a hard, blooded, professional army, an adequate treasury filled by its silver mines, and in Santa Anna, remarkably energetic leadership. The Texans could not possibly raise as many soldiers, and they had no money or industrial or supply system at all.

But several hundred miles of virtual desert, without roads, separated Anglo-Texas from the Mexican centers of population. The problem of maintaining a campaign hundreds of miles north of the Bravo, in an age of muscle power and wagon transport, was tremendous. Further, the two fortified positions the Spanish had left along the northern frontier now worked against Mexico in reverse. The Alamo and the presidio at Goliad were genuine barrier forts blocking the southern flank of Anglo-Texas. The Texas coast was not nearly so vulnerable as it seemed. The rebels held all the existing ports and harbors, commanded now by captured cannon. The rest of the shallow, shoaling coastal waters had never been charted. Almost every past expedition to Texas had lost ships on those sandbars and reefs; no Mexican admiral could take in a hostile flotilla now.

If Texas' aim was independence, the most logical strategy was to continue to recruit men and money from the citizenry of the United States, and wait. In the north, far from its bases, even a superior Mexican army might be pinned against the barrier fortresses and destroyed. So long as these key positions were held, no Mexican force could operate with impunity east of the Colorado, leaving armed men at its rear.

But the volunteers at Béxar were composed of many men who could not wait. One such was Dr. James Grant, who had fled Mexico ahead of General Cós. Grant had never been a Texas resident, nor owned an inch of Texas soil. He had lost vast estates in northern Mexico. Dr. Grant devised a grand scheme to carry the war below the Rio Grande. He argued that by marching south and seizing Matamoros, the major Mexican city on the border, two things might be gained. One would be to give the republicans to the south moral support, by a demonstration of force. The other would be to damage Santa Anna by carrying the war to him.

Actually, a demonstration against Matamoros—a hit-and-run raid— made strategic sense, but only if the Texans were strong enough to mount and direct such a campaign capably. General Houston opposed the notion of any wholesale invasion of Mexico, but he agreed to a raid, provided it was commanded by a man for whom he had deep respect: James Bowie.

Dr. Grant took his Matamoros Expedition strategy before the government at San Felipe. He split the government in two. Smith, Houston, and most of the Texans who had no interest in Mexican politics were strongly opposed to Grant's proposal that the whole army move south. A majority of the Council, for a great variety of reasons ranging from idealism to personal spite, favored it. Some wanted to seed Mexico with Anglo-Saxon liberties through this army. Others wanted to put the Governor, and his high cockalorum General, Houston, in their places.

On January 3, 1836, the Council authorized Dr. Grant and Colonel Frank Johnson, now commanding at Béxar, to capture Matamoros. But Johnson, momentarily troubled by Governor Smith's opposition, declined the command. The Council then appointed James W. Fannin, Jr., to take command in Johnson's place, and after hearing Dr. Grant's declaration that Burleson had intended to pass the command to *him,* also appointed the doctor Commander-in-Chief of Volunteers. Since almost the entire army consisted of volunteers, this meant that Grant and Fannin held co-equal, and mutually nonresponsible, commands. Then, a few days later, the Council compounded this consummate military folly by reinstating Colonel Johnson, who professed a change of heart. The other appointments were allowed to stand, and the Texas army now had four supreme commanders. General Houston, in fact, was not even advised of these new appointments.

These moves and appointments were passed over the Governor's veto, there being no definition of either conciliar or gubernatorial powers. When Smith received a message from Lieutenant Colonel J. C. Neill, who now commanded the fortress of the Alamo, that Grant and Johnson had stripped that fort of its cannon, supplies, and clothing for the expedition, Smith exploded. On January 10, he issued a statement that denounced these acts and vilified the Council in extremely personal terms. He further demanded an apology from the Council for its villainy, and suggested it must either agree to cooperate with him or else dissolve until after March 1, 1836.

The Council in return vilified the Governor, impeached him, and elevated Lieutenant Governor Robinson to the executive chair. Again, whether the Council possessed such powers was moot; no one knew. Smith refused to vacate. He seized the State archives, kept the official seal, and promised to shoot "any son of a bitch" who tried to take it from him. He continued to act as Governor as best he could; Robinson's efforts to operate the office were futile.

Then, on January 17, the Council itself was unable to raise a quorum. In effect, the government of Texas disappeared. All this in fact provoked not only anger but some amusement among the watching Texans, most of whom were now preparing for spring planting. But, however amusing it might appear, the results of this fiasco were tragic. Because the provisional government collapsed, some thousands of men were doomed to die.

Governor Smith had the loyalty of General Houston, Lieutenant Colonel Neill at San Antonio, and his recruiting officer at San Felipe, William Barret Travis, now a regular lieutenant colonel. The majority of the army, inflamed with the notion of seizing the strategic site, silver, and *señoritas* of Matamoros, claimed to be following the orders of the Council. Actually, it seemed to be acting on its own will.

Smith commanded Houston to proceed to Goliad, take command of the army there, and talk some sense into it. Failing that, he was authorized to advance upon Mexico. Houston met up with Grant and Johnson's force at Refugio.

Meanwhile, he received an urgent dispatch from Neill at the Alamo, asking for reinforcements. Houston detached Colonel James Bowie with a handful of men to march from Goliad to San Antonio on January 17. Houston's battle plan had been to garrison the two fortresses, but since Grant and Johnson had removed the army from Béxar to the Goliad area, Houston wanted a capable officer to inspect the situation at the Alamo and make a decision whether the northern post should be held or abandoned. Houston did not give Bowie orders to abandon San Antonio; he left this to Bowie's discretion. But it is evident that he anticipated a decision to withdraw.

Johnson and Grant had gathered about 500 volunteers at Refugio. Almost all of these were American citizens from the southern states. At this time, January 20, 1836, Fannin, also authorized to advance against Matamoros, sailed from Velasco to Cópano Bay near Goliad with what was called the "Georgia Battalion" and about twenty-five Texas volunteers, in all some 450 men. Fannin, Johnson, and Grant were each conducting separate operations. Houston soon found that none of them, commissioned by the Council, intended to place themselves under his orders.

Houston was informed that his authority applied only to the "regulars," and Fannin declined to accept him unless he placed himself under the orders of the Council. The commissions given Grant, Johnson, and Fannin utterly destroyed Houston's authority over the only troops in being. Houston advised the rank and file to give the expedition up, and departed. In a letter to Governor Smith on January 30 he washed his hands of the Matamoros affair, impuned the leaders' motives, and predicted that whether Matamoros fell or not, the expedition could only bring disaster to the Texas cause. The smell of piracy hung over the entire operation. Houston further revealed the complete inability of a logical, responsible military mind to comprehend the way things were being run in Texas. He withdrew from the army, furloughing himself until March 1, and went north to treat with the potentially dangerous Cherokee Indians in east Texas.

Houston in one way was not entirely unsuccessful. Most of Grant's men departed with him, leaving the doctor only about 150 all told, most of whom were the remnants of the New Orleans Grays. The Grant-Johnson expedition moved a few miles south to San Patricio. While waiting here, many of the men took up mustanging, or catching wild horses on the coastal plain.

Fannin's larger force camped at Goliad, making preparations for the march south. Fannin wanted to go by sea, but could not find the ships.

At about this time, Governor Smith ordered one of the few men he could rely on to obey orders, Lieutenant Colonel Travis, to cease recruiting duties for the regular army at San Felipe, and to proceed to the Alamo in support of Colonel Neill. Travis thought this meant he was to command that fortress, and he hastened south with all the men he could raise, some thirty.

At San Antonio, Bowie found Neill had only 104 men. They had weapons and a few cannon, but were short of supplies and powder. None of these 104 was Texan, except nine ethnic Mexicans who had joined the Revolution. Two-thirds were men born somewhere below the Mason-Dixon Line, the largest group from Tennessee, but there were men born in almost every American state, and a sizable contingent from the British Isles. In many ways the point of origin was misleading. At this time most frontiersmen were actually born in the East, but nurtured in the West. Almost all these men, including the six from Continental Europe, had spent some time on the American frontier. Between them, Travis and Bowie brought in about fifty more, and these were mostly "Texians."

Perhaps oddly, very few of this Alamo garrison of 150-odd were farmers. The larger part were hunter-trappers by past profession, and the rest professional men, doctors and lawyers. Why the original one hundred remained at the Alamo with Neill is not known. Some planned to return to the United States; some merely lacked inclination to march to Mexico. None had received promised pay for service.

Shortly afterward, David Crockett of Tennessee arrived at San Antonio with an entourage of twelve rifles.

Bowie came to a careful decision. He estimated that the Alamo fortress required a thousand men to be secure. But apparently, he never seriously considered giving it up. The brooding walls of the old mission seemed to cast a spell over every North American who came under them. On February 2, 1836, Bowie wrote Governor Smith:

> The salvation of Texas depends in great measure on keeping Bexar out of the hands of the enemy. It stands on the frontier picquet guard, and if it was in the possession of Santa Anna, there is no stronghold from which to repel him in his march to the Sabine. Colonel Neill and myself have come to the solemn resolution that we will rather die in these ditches than give them up. . . .

Meanwhile, General Santa Anna, the Napoleon of the West, had been stung into an enormous rage by the defeat and surrender of his brother-in-law at Béxar. Showing energy that no Texan gave him credit for, he rode clattering into Saltillo on or about January 20, 1836. He had an army in northern Mexico now of 6,019 men. Santa Anna, never more cheerful or energetic than when on campaign, issued staccato orders: the 1,500-man brigade under Ramírez y Sesma, form the vanguard and advance to San Antonio; the 1,600 men and six guns of Gaona, at Saltillo, the 1,800 men and six guns of Tolsa at Monclova, and Andrade's 437-man cavalry brigade, form the main body and prepare to march; General Don José Urrea, with 300 infantry, 301 lances, and one four-pounder, proceed to Matamoros, join with the battalion en route from Campeche, and cross the Bravo. Santa Anna had excellent intelligence supplied by Mexican *rancheros* in the south. Urrea was to find the Matamoros Expedition, destroy it, then roll up the Texan flank at Goliad, while President Santa Anna himself led the main force on a direct assault through San Antonio.

These plans had been made as early as the previous summer. The disgraceful conduct of Cós at San Antonio, which Santa Anna felt reflected upon his own honor, triggered him into quicker action than any Texan thought possible. Santa Anna did not wait for the end of the winter rains or the coming of the green spring forage grass. He was a professional soldier, not a Comanche.

His Texas policy had already been ratified by his Congress. Every colonist who had taken part in the rebellion was to be executed or exiled. Those who had not were to be removed to the interior. Never again would any North American be permitted to enter Texas. Texas would pay for all

expenses of the campaign, through the sequestration of lands, to be real-
lotted to the Santanista soldiery. Every foreigner found in arms in Texas,
or who aided the revolt in any way, was to be treated as a pirate. The
North American presence was thus to be extinguished.

This was perfectly in accord with internal and international law, if
harsh; the province was in revolt. Armed Americans on Texas soil were
devoid of legal rights. Historically, these measures made good strategic
sense. A large minority allied by ethnic background with a powerful neighbor was a dangerous luxury on the Mexican frontier. Santa Anna intended
to remove the Anglo-Saxon peril forever.

The President, in personal command, drove his brigade columns north
without mercy. He arrived on the Rio Grande near Laredo in mid-February, 1836; this was a remarkable pace, but he had paid a price. Hundreds
of horses and some men had been lost; far more important, Santa Anna
had been forced to abandon his heavy artillery to the muddy roads. The big
guns followed far behind. When the Mexican columns came in sight of San
Antonio, they dragged with them only two batteries of small six-pounders.

Santa Anna was surprised, though not alarmed, to find the Alamo
fortress defended. The population of Béxar, which now flocked to his
banner, gave him accurate information about the foreigners. They had only
150 men, and while there were more than a dozen cannon on the Alamo
walls, the defenders had very little powder. This was important, since the
long eighteen-pounder burned twelve pounds of gunpowder with each shot.
Santa Anna was also told that the Anglos had stripped the town of all its
corn, and driven thirty beeves within the walls.

He had in fact almost taken them by surprise; Bowie and Travis had
barely got their men inside before the Mexican cavalry wheeled into San
Antonio on February 23.

It is still a matter of controversy which flag, if any, the Texians hoisted
over their walls. Official Texan accounts claim the national red, green, and
white emblem of Mexico was flown, on which were superimposed the
numerals 1 8 2 4, showing the rebels fought not against the Mexican
nation, but for the liberal constitution. Other, contemporary accounts indicate this was not so. However, there is no dispute about Santa Anna's
banner. Here the President made his first great historic mistake in Texas.

His decision to reduce the Alamo made military sense. But he ordered
flown from the towers of San Fernando Church, the tallest building in
Béxar, a long, flapping, blood-red banner which could easily be seen from
the Alamo. This was a sign that no quarter was to be given. Now, with
historic irony, the legitimate Mexican army went to battle on Mexican soil
underneath the pirate flag.

Human folly is far easier to explain than human valor.

The Texan government at this time was gripped by chaos, dissension,
and rivalry; the people of Anglo-Texas were still mostly concerned with

their private affairs. The volunteers camped at Refugio and Goliad were dreaming of loot below the Rio Grande. Life east of the Colorado went on almost as before. No Texan really believed that Santa Anna was anywhere near Texas with an army, until Travis' couriers rode splashing winter mud and shouting alarm through the Colorado-Brazos country. Governor Smith, who held the title but actually governed nothing and no one, did try to raise a force for Travis. In the time remaining, he failed.

In all this, there was nothing new to history. The Texans seemed to be following an old and often-trod path to defeat and destruction.

But at the Alamo history was altered. It is not easy to explain exactly why. The complete details of the battle, like those of all the battles of the Texas Revolution, simply are not known, or agreed upon. Few wars of such eventual historic importance have been so poorly documented or reported. Myths have sprouted, and legend has embellished fact. The story has been well told; it needs no retelling. But certain perspectives of the battle are often ignored.

There is no question but that Travis and his conglomerate force of Texians, Americans, Scots, Englishmen, and Texas-Mexicans could have escaped from the Alamo had they chose. Long after the siege began, the Mexican net was not tight. Couriers came and went on horseback to the very end. Yet 150 men stayed on stubbornly to fight an army; no one ran away, unless the tale of the mercenary Rose is credited. No competent Texas historian really believes that Travis actually drew his line on the ground with his sword and invited his men to leave or stay. This was not Buck Travis' style. He intended to keep his command on the walls regardless of what the men wanted. He was consciously guarding the ramparts of Texas.

Bowie and Travis, together, for a time in co-command, agreed to hold the Alamo. The reasons must have been a combination of strategy, stubbornness, and not to be overlooked, sheer exaltation. There was a core of barbarian hardihood, and barbarian warlikeness, in each of these men, different as they were. At first, there were problems of command. Colonel Neill, called home on business in mid-February, scrupulously passed the command to Travis, the only regular field officer present. This angered Bowie's following. The Texians in the fort accepted Travis' commission, but the majority of the American and other volunteers claimed Bowie was the better man. They obeyed his orders only. Certainly, Bowie's reputation as a fighting man far exceeded Travis'.

Travis burned for the honor of commanding the most dangerous post in Texas. When some of the men looked to Bowie after every order, he almost resigned and returned to the Brazos. He did not, because William Barret Travis, on the surface a fiery, almost unstable rebel, was in his deepest soul a traditionalist. He was a regular Texas officer, and immensely proud of it. The Governor had ordered him to the Alamo. Honor, loyalty, and military dignity were important things to Travis; he stayed. He was surrounded by paladins, who insisted on fighting as paladins. The whole Revolution was marked and marred by commanders and men who fought with fierce independence, ignored orders, sulked in their tents, and with their coteries freely came and went. But Travis, according to his lights, was a soldier. He had been trained at an academy in the state of his birth, South Carolina; it was typical of the man that he was thrown out of school for inciting a student revolt but retained the values he had learned.

The greatest measure of his ability was not the bravery he had shown in inciting the Texan rebellion, or his citation under fire at San Antonio in December. It was revealed when Bowie's health failed as the Mexicans approached, and Travis took command of the men, and held them. Bowie, collapsing with pneumonia on February 23, passed his authority publicly to Travis. The true measure of this man, with his soldier's cap, his sword, his exalted ideas of honor, and his florid rhetoric, was that he captured these violent frontiersmen and bent them to his purpose.

His message to Smith and the world, on February 24, revealed Travis' exaltation at commanding the Alamo, the values in his heart and mind, and the grimness with which he would hold to them. Throughout the 19th century, this message was regarded as one of the great statements of defiance and courage in the English language.

Commandancy of the Alamo
Bexar, Feby 24th, 1836

To the People of Texas and All Americans in the World—
Fellow Citizens and Compatriots:
I am besieged with a thousand or more of the Mexicans under Santa Anna. I have sustained a continual Bombardment and cannonade for 24 hours and have not lost a man. The enemy has demanded surrender at discretion, otherwise, the garrison is to be put to the sword, if the fort is taken. I have answered the demand with a cannon shot, and our flag still waves proudly from the wall. I shall never surrender or retreat. Then, I call on you in the name of Liberty, of patriotism, and everything dear to the American character, to come to our aid with all dispatch. The enemy is receiving reinforcements daily and will no doubt increase to three or four thousand in four or five days. If this call is neglected I am determined to sustain myself as long as possible and die like a soldier who never forgets what is due his honor and that of his country.
VICTORY OR DEATH.

William Barret Travis
LT. COL. COMD'T.

Buck Travis was one of those most fortunate of men; on the grim stone walls of the Alamo he had found his time and place. He was between twenty-five and twenty-seven years of age.

The characters of Travis, Bowie, and Davy Crockett, who arrived the day Neill left, seem to be increasingly puzzling to later Americans. They were widely disparate, but in some ways very similar men. All were tall—six feet or more—and all were fair. Bowie and Travis shared red hair. All had what the Mexicans came to call blue-gray killer's eyes. They were all highly intelligent men, and each was a creature of the American frontier.

Bowie, born somewhere in the South in the 1790's, was raised in a family that became wealthy in Louisiana early in the century. He roamed, running slaves with Jean Lafitte in contravention to what every Southerner felt was a stupid law, exploring Texas, fighting Indians. Bowie was remarkable in two respects. He fitted in easily with the best society of the Creole towns and vast plantations, and he had the enormous respect of the wildest and toughest men on the harshest of all American frontiers. He was a killer: he killed the son of Jean Lafitte, who crossed him, crippled "Bloody" Sturdivant, gutted Major Norris Wright and a verified number of others, in the most desperate "medleys" or duels. He made the great knife his brother Rezin forged for him a glittering legend; soon Bowie knives were manufactured in England for sale on the American frontier. Yet Bowie was simply not a killer in the modern, civilized sense. He lived in a violent society, and men of keen judgement and good breeding considered him quite sound. The respect tendered him far exceeded that of any duelist.

After a bloody feud in Louisiana, he drifted into Texas. At San Antonio, he entered Spanish society easily. He married the beautiful Ursula Veramendi, daughter of the Vice-Governor of Texas, and ended up owning leagues of Texas lands. Tragedy struck his life in 1833, when in the great cholera epidemic his wife, his infant son, and daughter died. Bowie had had no contact with the Texan colonists until this time. He was a wealthy, and honored, citizen of Mexico. But blood called to blood, and with his ties gone, Bowie drifted into the Revolution. He served with distinction before Houston dispatched him to the Alamo. Houston sent him because Bowie was one of the few men in Texas Houston knew and respected.

Crockett, the other living legend in the Alamo, was also a frontiersman, born in the State of Franklin before it became Tennessee. Like Bowie's, his father had fought against the British, and had arrived from Ireland. And like Bowie, he was one of the two most famous characters in the Old Southwest. But Crockett was never a planter or a businessman; he remained a hunter and a drifter all his days.

When the planters and farmers filled Tennessee in the normal pattern in the early years of the century, Crockett failed to prosper. Instead of moving on, he entered politics, as a representative of the hunter-trapper-squatter population. Eventually, he served in Congress, and here came into opposition to the powerful President of the United States, Andrew Jackson. Jackson, for all his outward democratic biases and prejudices and the propaganda of his being the first President "from the people," concealed a deep conservative nature. The frontiersman in Jackson never liked the gentry-born, despite his enormous holdings at the Hermitage and his hundreds of black slaves, and his Kitchen Cabinet and other peculiar manifestations of vulgarity in the White House were symbolic of this. But if Jackson, like all classes of Westerners, disliked tight money and the United States Bank, he also removed the "civilized tribes" from the territory of the United States and paid off the public debt. Crockett opposed all these things, and came into violent opposition to the Administration. Crockett seems to have been an early Populist, who wanted federal funds used for domestic spending in the states, something Jackson's Roman sense of values opposed. The mass of the public was with Jackson on both the Bank and Indian questions; the Bank was closed, and the Indians forcibly removed. Neither Davy Crockett nor the Supreme Court prevailed, whatever the constitutionality of their cause. Further, Jackson, who controlled the patronage of Tennessee, saw to it that Crockett was effectively purged at the polls.

David Crockett's national fame rested on his ability with a rifle, and his ability to tell about it as a raconteur. He made a short concession speech, in which he told his constituents to go to Hell, while he went to Texas.

Crockett had had a wife and children along the line, who somehow had gotten lost. He had had woman trouble, like almost every one of the Texas immortals: Houston, Bowie, Travis, and a hundred others. Houston and Travis separated from wives in the United States under circumstances of scandal, though no evidence attached blame to either. Bowie's life was blasted by tragedy. Crockett, like Houston and Bowie a man in middle years, drifted into the Texas Revolution in search of a cathartic, a new life, and a new career. Destiny, manifest or otherwise, worked in devious ways.

This fact is disturbing to some determinist historians, because destiny, in the Texas Revolution, hardly bears inspection. With these admitted and admired paladins were a thousand men, lesser probably in only minor ways. Twelve Tennesseans marched west with Crockett. Three dozen, more or less, each came to the Alamo with Bowie and Buck Travis. Here they found a hundred kindred souls, from every walk of the frontier. They had one thing in common. They were all instinctive warriors, bred to arms if not formal warfare. They rode to the scent of trouble. None of them consciously planned to die. In the Alamo, in the shadow of Santa Anna's blood-red flag, loyalty to Bowie, to Travis, and in some way few of them could define, to their land and people, and to themselves, held them fast. Travis, in his glory, distributed his paladins great and small across the walls. Crockett, who refused a command and asked to be a "high private" among his Tennessee boys, was allotted the most dangerous and exposed part of the wall. Travis tendered it, and Crockett accepted it, as an honor.

Some measure of the grim, not heady, determination and exaltation that pervaded this group can be glimpsed in James Butler Bonham, courier and honorary colonel, who made dangerous trip after trip to the outside, carrying requests for help, begging Fannin at Goliad to move his army west. There was no help, except thirty-two Texans who gathered at Gonzales. They rode to the Alamo and fought their way inside, when they knew no other help would come. In these men Travis' words struck home; they came to fight, and die. At the very end, the weary Bonham, a lawyer, a Carolinian of exalted family and a friend of Travis, turned his mount around and rode back toward San Antonio. He was told it was useless to throw away his life. He answered that Buck Travis deserved to know the answer to his appeals, spat upon the ground, and galloped west into his own immortality.

On March 3, 1836, after days of siege and bombardment, Travis addressed his last letter to the Council at Washington-on-the-Brazos. He knew a new consultation was now being held, but he did not know that Texas had declared its independence. His battered walls still flew the Mexican colors; his men, on duty and in combat day and night, were reeling with exhaustion. Travis no longer expected rescue. He wrote, apparently, to stir his countrymen into action, that the country might be saved:

> . . . I shall have to fight the enemy on his own terms. I will . . . do the best I can . . . the victory will cost the enemy so dear, that it will be worse for him than defeat. I hope your honorable body will hasten reinforcements. . . . Our supply of ammunition is limited. . . . God and Texas. Victory or Death.

As the struggle for the continent recedes, Travis has become less and less an acceptable, understandable hero. But from the Alamo, from his first message before the arrival of the Mexicans to his last, his words had the ring of prophecy. The Texas historian who stated publicly that few people would want to have a son serve under William Barret Travis had forgotten, in the comforts of long security, the reasons men make war.

After ten days of siege, of cannon battery and counterbattery, which the Texans lacked powder to pursue effectively, and of numerous sallies by the defenders at night, and after some dozens of Mexican gunners had been picked off by rifle fire, the besieging army worked its guns in close. On March 5 a breach was battered in the Alamo east wall.

Santa Anna was now impatient. His intelligence told him that the Texans were meeting again on the Brazos, but he knew no other resistance lay between the Alamo and the Sabine. The fortnight he had lost, hammering at the mission walls, had delayed him by that long from the destruction of Anglo-Texas. He called a commanders' conference on March 4, and talked with his generals of brigade. They were divided; some were prepared to attack now, with a decisive assault; others preferred to wait until after the 7th, when two twelve-pound siege guns were due to arrive. With these guns the Mexicans could completely breach the defending walls. Those officers, like Cós, who had seen Texan rifle fire at close range were cautious; Santa Anna, his mind on the campaign's delay, was not. When Colonel Almonte warned him the cost would be high, Santa Anna re-

marked he did not care; the nut must be cracked. Orders for the assault
were issued on the afternoon of March 5.

Five battalions, about 4,000 men, were committed to the action. Only
trained soldiers were used; others, whose training was not considered sufficient, were confined to barracks. The attack order was efficiently written
and issued, and ended, since this was a professional, more than a patriot
army, as follows:

> The honor of the nation being concerned in this engagement against the
> lawless foreigners who oppose us, His Excellency expects every man to do
> his duty and exert to allow the country a day of glory, and gratification to
> the Supreme Government, who will know how to reward distinguished
> deeds by the brave soldiers of the Army of Operations.

The brigades that assembled in the chilly pre-dawn darkness on the open
fields beyond the Alamo on March 6 were veteran, and good. They were
well-fed, smartly uniformed, and armed with flintlock muskets, which were
still the standard weapon of every army of the day. Each man carried a long
bayonet in good order; the Chief of Staff's instructions emphasized this.
Despite some weaknesses in the top commands, where matters devolved on
politics, the officer corps was professional, and competent. Throughout the
officers were sprinkled numerous Europeans, most of whom were veterans
of the Napoleonic or other respectable wars.

The tactics used were the standard Napoleonic techniques; attack in
columns, cavalry on the flanks and in reserve, batteries to soften the enemy
before the charge. Two weaknesses here, however, glared: Santa Anna
lacked sufficient guns to give the enemy a sufficient Napoleonic blasting,
and his heavy cuirassiers could not hurl their shock action against thick
limestone walls. The assault had to be infantry in column, bearing bayonets
and scaling ladders. Probably, no marshal of France would have faulted
the organization or the charge. But neither Napoleonic marshals, nor Santa
Anna, had ever assaulted American riflemen ensconced behind high
walls.

Nor could they know that British army instructions of the time warned
that American riflemen, behind breastworks, could be attacked frontally
only at unacceptable cost. British officers had seen the Sutherland High-
landers shot to a standstill, and battalions chopped to pieces, before the
massed cotton bales at New Orleans in 1815. There, Jackson, and men like
these men in the Alamo, had commenced firing at the unheard-of range of
three hundred yards. At one hundred yards, a British, or a Mexican,
musket could not hit a man-sized target one time in ten.

Both history and legend record that Travis gave only one coherent order
to his awakened, stumbling men: "The Mexicans are upon us—give 'em
Hell!"

The Alamo cannon smashed some columns, then the flat crack of small-
bore rifles swelled. Flame and lead sleeted and sleeted again from the

sprawling walls. Marksmanship was hardly an American, rather a Western, tradition. The Tennesseeans, Kentuckians, and all the others shot and seldom missed. On the frontier men got guns at about the age of seven; and a boy or man who missed with a single-shot weapon usually went hungry, or lost his hair.

The smartly columned army, marching with its regimentals, bayonets flashing in the dawn, its bands blaring the "Degüello," a blood-tune that reached back to Moorish days, stumbled into a swarm of lead. The first ranks went down, then the ranks behind them. Everywhere, colonels and majors and captains cried out and fell. It was an American tradition to shoot at braid.

The first assault never reached the walls. The defenders sent up a ragged cheer; they were still fighting for their lives.

The bands roared, and the Mexican bugles sent the columns forward again. Now, the ladders went up the walls—but they could not stay. *Fire, ram, put powder, patch, shot, ram, splash the flash pan, aim, fire*—this was weapons-handling the Mexican officers had never seen. Some felt there must be a hundred men inside the fortress merely loading guns. At the wall the ladders wavered, then collapsed. A scattered trail of uniformed corpses marked the Mexican retreat.

But massed musketry had knocked many Texans off the walls, this time; the great fortress had always been thinly held with less than two hundred men. There were now some sections with few defenders, and several Mexican officers had spotted weak points, from where the fire was less.

These brigades were brave men, and as disciplined, if not so stolid, as any British grenadiers. After several hours, in which the battalions were regrouped and the reserve called, the Mexicans came back, at about eight in the morning. Santa Anna remained across the river in San Antonio. If he sensed what was happening to his army—the deeper wounds beyond the dead and groaning wounded he could see—he gave no sign. One of his column commanders was already dead, but the others beat the battalions back into line. Now, from all four sides of the Alamo, a new general assault began. This time, the ladders went up against the north wall and stayed. Mexican soldiers sprayed into the fortress like scuttling ants. Men fell all over the walls. Only flaming courage, and the determined leadership of a number of Mexican junior officers took the charge into the heart of the Alamo.

Now, the defenders no longer fought to win. They charged into the Mexican soldiery to kill as many as they could. These troops had seen much cruelty and understood it; but they had never seen the savagery of the Trans-Appalachian American at close range. The Texans had no bayonets, but by Mexican standards they were enormous men, towering a head higher or more. They smashed, butted, used tomahawks and knives. They had fought as paladins, each touchy of his rights and his own section of the wall. Now, they died as paladins, each with his ring of surrounding dead.

A terrible and understandable fury and hatred suffused the Mexicans who broke into the courtyard. They had been punished in the assault as they had never been punished before. Inside, at last they could employ their bayonets. They had crushing numbers. They killed, and after they had killed, mutilated the bleeding corpses with a hundred wounds. At the end, as the defenders were at last exterminated, Mexican officers admitted they lost control. The one woman in the Alamo, the wife of a Texan lieutenant, who with a Negro slave was spared expressly at Santa Anna's orders, saw Bowie's body tossed aloft on a dozen bayonets. He had been taken on his deathbed. Mexican accounts say, probably accurately, that a few defenders vainly attempted to surrender. These, who may have included Crockett, were shot.

No white defender survived; as the inscription on a later monument stated, Thermopylae had its messenger, the Alamo had none. Mrs. Dickenson, the Negro, and several Mexican women and children were the only ones to tell the story. These Santa Anna released, not so much in gallantry as in the trust that their tale would spread terror throughout Texas.

At nine o'clock, March 6, 1836, five hours after it began, the assault was over. The Alamo had fallen.

Gallantry of itself in battle is worthless, until its results may be assessed. Travis to begin with had given Anglo-Texas twelve precious days. The five-hour engagement on March 6 extended his country several weeks. These were weeks without which Anglo-Texas could not have survived.

When the fury of the assault passed, the tolling bells of San Fernando rang out over a shattered army. The Battalion of Toluca, the assault shock force of 800 men, had lost 670 killed. The other battalions had lost in each case approximately 25 percent. In all, there were nearly 1,600 Mexican dead. These figures are reliable; they were made by *Alcalde* Francisco Ruíz of San Antonio, who also indicated Santa Anna left 500 wounded when at last he was able again to march. This Santa Anna's secretary again confirmed.

These were casualties to shatter the morale of any army. They came from the permanent, best-trained battalions, the flower of the Mexican force. A thousand Mexican settlers now flocked to Santa Anna's cause, but these could hardly fill the ranks. The Mexican army, like the Roman, was organized and disciplined; new recruits under the Mexican system could not be trained in weeks. Nor did Mexican civilians, unlike North Americans, learn to use firearms as youths.

The damage to the soul of Santa Anna's army was not to be revealed for another forty-six days. At the Alamo, only the Mexican loss in blood and bone could be assessed. But this was enough to sate even Travis' and Bowie's bloody-minded ghosts—here, for the first time, the legend of the *diablos tejanos,* the Devil Texans, was spawned, a shuddery legend that would go into Mexican folklore.

The casualty figures were to be disputed over the years, mainly by

Mexican historians. Santa Anna's official report to the Supreme Government stated 600 Americans had been killed, and minimized his own losses to 70 dead. Other Mexicans later claimed at least 1,500 defenders had been behind the walls of the Alamo. But *Alcalde* Ruíz stated positively that the number of Texan bodies burned under his supervision was exactly 182. Ruíz also found no room to bury all the Mexican dead in the San Fernando churchyard; he ordered many corpses put into the San Antonio River.

The charred remains of the Alamo dead were dumped into a common grave. Its location went unrecorded and was never found.

Whatever the numbers engaged on each side, whether 1,600 Mexican soldiers out of 5,000 were killed, or 600 out of 1,800, the historic result of the battle remains the same, and is indisputable.

While the funeral pyres and campfires of the groaning Mexican army were lit on the night of Sunday, March 6, Santa Anna penned a report of a glorious victory for the Mexican nation. But Colonel Juan Nepomuceno Almonte, who had something of a classical education, was heard to repeat King Pyrrhus' despairing remark. Whatever mystical title to the soil of Texas Travis' stand had won, Santa Anna had paid too great a price to gain this ground.

Part III

STAR LIGHT,
STAR BRIGHT

13

AT THE
SAN JACINTO

When a government has ceased to protect the lives, liberty and property of the people, from whom its legitimate powers are derived, and for the advancement of whose happiness it was instituted, and, so far from being a guarantee for the enjoyment of those inestimable and inalienable rights, becomes an instrument in the hands of evil rulers for their oppression: . . .

THE BEGINNING OF THE TEXAS DECLARATION
OF INDEPENDENCE, MARCH 2, 1836

I have travelled near five hundred miles across Texas, and am now enabled to judge pretty near correctly of the soil, and the resources of the Country, and I have no hesitancy in pronouncing it the finest country to its extent upon the globe. For the greater portion of it is richer and more healthy, in my opinion, than West Tennessee. There can be no doubt the country east of the Rio Grand of the north would sustain a population of ten millions of souls. . . . It is probable that I shall make Texas my abiding place. In adopting this course, I will never forget the country of my birth. . . .

SAM HOUSTON'S REPORT TO THE PRESIDENT
OF THE UNITED STATES, 1832

Remember the Alamo!

COLONEL SIDNEY SHERMAN, COMMANDING THE
2D TEXAS REGIMENT, AT THE SAN JACINTO

GㅌNㅌRAL Don José Urrea, with approximately a thousand men, crossed the Bravo at Matamoros February 17, 1836. In his vanguard rode a light brigade of 301 heavy cavalry, cuirasses and lance heads glittering in the sun. Urrea's orders were clear: protect Santa Anna's eastern flank from Texan action and destroy the foreign army at Goliad. With his cavalry, Don José Urrea was superbly equipped to operate on the Gulf crescent coastal plain. Urrea was an honorable man, who handled his troops splendidly in the field. He could not know he was marching into infamy.

The two Anglo-American bodies of troops, at San Patricio and Goliad, were anything but equipped to march or fight in this wide-spread country. Two hundred miles separated them from their goal of Matamoros. The Georgia and New Orleans volunteers had arrived on foot. They, and their commanders, were accustomed to the forested country of the east. Both Grant and Fannin were effectively halted on the edge of the southern savannah; neither knew quite how to move his men across this arid, riverless plain, where waterholes were few and trees grew only in scattered clumps. Fannin waited in vain for ships to sail south. Grant and Johnson took to catching the mustangs that ran wild around San Patricio.

Neither Frank Johnson nor Dr. Grant was in complete command of their approximately 150 troops. Major Morris, of the Grays, was independent, and most of the volunteers were their own men. Due to a quarrel over horse hunting, Grant and Morris split off, while Johnson remained in San Patricio. Each group contained only about 50 men.

Urrea's cavalry swept into the dusty, straggling settlement of San Patricio after nightfall on February 27. The Americans were taken completely by surprise. There was a shout, a spatter of shots, and a few screams; the entire force was cut down. Johnson, and Grant's business partner in Mexico, Dan Toler, by sheer luck escaped in the night and fled northward to Goliad.

The Mexican lancers spread out to locate Grant and Morris, who were known to be nearby. The horse hunters were run down March 2, 20 miles to the west at a place called Agua Dulce, or Sweet Water. The Mexican cavalry surrounded Grant in a neat action, and attacked. Grant, Morris, and Placido Benavides died on the end of Mexican lances. Only three Americans survived; one, who was roped and taken prisoner, later escaped, and said he had seen Grant mutilated with a dozen sword cuts. Grant was well known, and particularly disliked, in northern Mexico.

Fannin, at Goliad, now knew from Grant's survivors that Urrea was in the country. He drew back into the presidio at Goliad. His supplies, especially of powder and provisions, were pitifully low, and Fannin hesitated in an agony of indecision.

Colonel Fannin's actions at Goliad, beginning February 16, 1836, do not bear inspection. On that date he received a message from Travis in the Alamo, requesting aid; Fannin refused this in writing. Bonham arrived with this refusal February 23, the day the Mexicans under Ramírez y Sesma marched into Béxar. With Mexicans actually at San Antonio, Travis confidently again requested help. Fannin commanded the largest force, in fact, the only real army Texas had, with his 500 men.

He was reluctant to march westward to San Antonio, although then he had no knowledge of Urrea's presence. Both Bonham, who tried again to obtain support, and Captain Juan Seguín, sent as a Spanish-speaking courier from the Alamo, were unable to get any effective response. After Seguín's appeal, a few days before the final assault on the Alamo, Fannin ordered the army to march west. Four miles out of town, an army supply wagon broke down. Fannin, according to his own word, took this mishap as a sign the relief of the Alamo was "not feasible." He called a conference of his officers; all agreed to turn back. There was no enthusiasm among the Volunteers to march—only determined leadership could have held them to such a purpose, and this Fannin simply did not have.

Fannin's troops could not have met Santa Anna and defeated him. But an extra few hundred men in the Alamo, with the sally force of cavalry Fannin had, would have made that fortress the rallying point that Travis hoped for—it could have held until Texas mustered. Actually, when Fannin commenced his abortive march, Santa Anna, with superb intelligence from the Mexican countryside, detached a brigade to try to meet him. This force was allowed to turn back and be in at the finish of the Alamo. Fannin, apparently, though he is treated gently in most Texan accounts, was in that coma of indecision that strikes doomed commanders.

It was the knowledge that Fannin would not move that led the gallant 32 settlers at Gonzales under Kimball to make their lonely effort, and march alone, to sure death at San Antonio. When they fought their way into the fortress on March 1, it was meant to be a symbol that Texas heard, and someone cared.

Travis' calls from the commandancy of the Alamo were not entirely in vain. A few men began to move toward Gonzales, the southernmost Anglo settlement. But more important at the moment, the imminent danger brought an end to the worst of the colonists' governmental folly. A new convention assembled at Washington-on-the-Brazos, 150 miles northeast of San Antonio, on March 1, 1836. This convention probably took the wisest course by simply ignoring both Governor Smith and the impotent Council.

By this time, the delegates knew that Travis was invested and in mortal danger, and that Urrea was slashing his way north from San Patricio. Santa Anna's intentions were widely known as well. This was no longer—and this should be remembered in the light of history—a limited war, to decide the form of government under which Anglo-Texans should live. This fight had become one of survival or extermination. The imminent peril was clear enough to prompt quick action, so far as action was within the convention's power. Texas had to have a government. It had to rouse its people. It had to delineate and enforce the government's powers.

Sam Houston, still on furlough from the army, attended the convention as a delegate from Refugio. He was instrumental in beating down one wild motion that the convention adjourn and hasten, gun in hand, to the Alamo. Houston denounced this seemingly patriotic move as folly and treason to the people. He shouted that the Alamo was in its present straits because Texans had not made a government. He was heard.

Immediately, a commission was appointed to draft a statement on what was now in every colonist's mind: independence. Santa Anna's invasion had broken whatever ties that still bound some to Mexico. The commission worked all night, and on March 2 reported a declaration, which was adopted. If this was quick work, it must be remembered that George Childress, who wrote the document, had a model ready-made, one that Thomas Jefferson had penned sixty years before. He followed it assiduously, changing words and details to fit the time and place.

Among the 59 delegates on the Brazos were several men of good education and vast experience, such as Robert Potter, Samuel Carson, Richard Ellis, Martin 'Parmer, Thomas Rusk, James Collinsworth, and George Childress. They had served in the Congress of the United States, or they had helped draft the constitutions of other Southern states. Lorenzo de Zavala, the eminent Republican, brought his mind to bear. Of all these men, most historians are agreed the most important man at the convention was Sam Houston. He was not an intellectual, but he kept the convention's mind to its business, which was to get something quickly done.

Texas was declared an independent Republic on March 2, 1836.

Now, the next step was to make a constitution. This was done again at breakneck speed; again, the delegates had a model they knew and loved. Zavala, who had a broad education and the knowledge of the centuries, at one point tried to begin a speech: *"Mr. President, an eminent Roman statesman once said—"* But he was cut off abruptly by Tom Rusk, one of whose descendants would one day be the American Secretary of State. Less diplomatic than his descendant, Rusk snapped that the problem was not dead Romans but live Mexicans. Spurred by such directness, the Constitutional Convention adopted a document on March 16.

The Texas Constitution was a composite of the constitutions of both the Union and several Southern states. It had only a few distinctly non-American features. One was that Texas was a unitary, not a federal, Republic; there was no provision for it to be divided into several states. The others derived from the Spanish-Mexican experience: the President served three years and could not succeed himself; nor could he, without the consent of Congress, lead an army in the field; no clergyman, of any faith, might hold an office; and each family head in Texas was entitled to a league and one *labor* of land. Slavery was legalized, but slave-running was equated with piracy, as a sop to minority sentiment.

An interim government was elected in convention: David G. Burnet, President; Zavala, Vice-President; and Thomas Rusk, Secretary of War. Sam Houston, earlier, had been appointed Commander in Chief, this time with a commission that spelled out complete power to command all armed men in Texas, regular and/or volunteer. He received these powers on March 3, and immediately departed south. He had what he had come for.

The convention closed March 17, and shortly afterward, the government prudently moved its seat to Galveston Island, since the problem of live Mexicans was becoming dangerously acute. When Andrew Jackson, in April, was apprised of these actions, he stated the moves were rash and premature. Actually, all but one of them came too late; only Houston's reappointment as Commander in Chief helped save Texas and win the war.

Houston was the most remarkable figure, and most unusual agent of destiny, that ever appeared on the old frontier. He was a man of his times, like Travis and Andrew Jackson, but something more. He was one of those Americans of power, vigor, and determination, who in the early decades of the century seem to come primarily from the border country of Tennessee. He was an Anglo-Celt of the old tradition. He despised Europe, all its works, and its so-called cultured men who willingly seemed to bow to tyrants and aristocracy. He had a limited but adequate education; his favorite author was Alexander Pope. He was born in Virginia, then taken across the mountains; he refused to learn a trade, and spent much time among the Cherokees. He served as a regular officer with distinction against the Creeks, when the British government incited them to war in 1812. He became Andrew Jackson's protégé, eventually a militia major general, a Congressman, and Governor of Tennessee.

At the apex of this career, which might have led to the White House, his personal life destroyed him. A young bride left his bed and board, under circumstances never told. Most historians, but not his numerous enemies of the time, believe this girl neurotic, and Houston entirely blameless. Still, the event, and Houston's determined silence toward it, destroyed his political career. Like David Crockett, another well-known but far lesser man, he drifted West, to Texas. He lived for some years among the Cherokees, known to them simply as Big Drunk.

The disturbances in Texas revived him, and he joined the colonists' revolt of 1832. There is evidence that he never lost Jackson's confidence or friendship, or ceased to work at a grand design the President had already stated, to explode the United States from sea to sea. Like Jackson, he was more than a Southerner, and a Unionist to the end. In one drunken letter, Houston wrote he intended to conquer Mexico, or Texas, and be worth two millions in two years. He had his dreams, but they were big ones, and the measure of the man was that he fulfilled them. To history, motives are less important than results, and Houston served his nation well.

He was another man moderns find difficult to understand. His mother once gave him a small gold ring, in which inscribed was the single word *Honor;* his most determined enemies rarely accused him of lacking it. He was a great man, with the passions of a great man, but in the crucial moments, he could exert the iron restraint and discipline of heart and mind all great men must have.

These qualities, his former fame, and the certain knowledge he had the ear of the powerful President of the United States brought Houston to prominence in Texas. The delegates who appointed him military commander had no real prescience of destiny, but they appointed better than they knew.

He was six feet three, two hundred forty pounds of muscle in early middle age, a giant. He was never "six foot six," as the border legends ran, but when he put his iron-hard eyes on men, they gave him extra stature. In Texas in the spring of 1836, Sam Houston needed every inch.

After the battle of the Alamo, Santa Anna found himself unable to proceed until the army could recoup. He sent Ramírez y Sesma's cavalry brigade east on harrying missions, but these did not reach the Brazos. Thus he was inactive when Houston hurried southward to Gonzales, still the Texan's marshaling point. Houston's army consisted of exactly four men, not a general's escort but more a corporal's guard. At Gonzales Houston planned to take charge of the assembling militia and lead it to the Alamo. He came into the anxious town on March 11.

Here he found a total of 374 "effective men," with no food, and some without arms and ammunition. These were men who had assembled on their own, without leadership, to help Travis at the Alamo. The best of these, in arms and appearance, was the company of 50 Kentucky rifles Sidney Sherman had brought, at his own expense, from the United States. Houston organized this group into a "regiment," with Edward Burleson as colonel, Sherman as lieutenant colonel, and a man named Somervell as major.

Gonzales was in a state of fear and horror. On March 11 a Mexican came into town, and stated that the Alamo had fallen. Houston sent three of his invaluable scouts, "Deaf" Smith, Henry Karnes, and R. E. Handy, riding west for news. These scouts found Mrs. Dickenson and the pitiful female survivors of the Alamo stumbling down the road and brought them back to town. Now, twenty widows and a hundred children heard of the death of Gonzales' gallant men, amid "almost indescribable scenes in the

streets." Houston also learned from Mrs. Dickenson that General Sesma
was close behind.

Now, Houston did the hardest thing any general could be called upon to
do; in the face of disaster he ordered a general retreat. He had his reasons,
some of which in Texas were never understood. His regiment was small
and undisciplined and untrained; it could never meet Santa Anna in a war
of maneuver in the field. Also, this was the edge of Mexican country;
Houston preferred to pull the enemy into Anglo-Texas, with its numerous
defensive rivers. He counted, too, upon accumulating some thousands of
Texas men on the way.

He wrote Fannin at Goliad unequivocal orders to blow up the fortress
and retreat; he needed Fannin's 500 men. Then Houston took charge of his
hungry, grousing regiment; set fire to Gonzales, and marched northeast. He
reached Burnam's Crossing on the Colorado on March 17. He now had
600 men. Houston, whom Bowie's father-in-law Veramendi had once described as a deep, inscrutable, and dangerous man, kept his own counsel,
and the army in iron order. He halted nine days at the Colorado, to teach
the men to drill. On March 28, he marched further north, to San Felipe on
the Brazos. He came to Groce's plantation, where he camped and trained
ten days. His army swelled to approximately 1,400.

At Goliad, Colonel Fannin's Greek tragedy continued. He sent one third
of his force to Refugio, a nearby town, to assist the evacuation of Anglo
settlers, whom he advised to flee. This force, under King and Ward, was
snapped up by the main body of Urrea's army. Captain King and some 20-
odd men were caught in the open and cut down; Ward retreated into the
crumbling, two-thirds-destroyed Refugio mission. Here his riflemen
knocked several lancers out of the saddle, and later repulsed a determined
assault. But Ward ran out of ammunition, and with dark on March 14
ordered his men to scatter and filter through the nearby woods and
swamps. Urrea took Refugio, and turned toward Goliad.

Here, Fannin refused to move until he had word from Ward and King. A
scout, Frazier, returned with news of the defeat at Refugio on March 16.
Fannin called a council of war, and now everyone decided it was time to go
north, to Guadalupe Victoria.

But now Urrea was in contact; a skirmish was fought on the 18th. Still,
Fannin decided to abandon the walls of La Bahía fortress and take his
chances on the plains. The army, shielded by a ground fog, moved out
March 19.

The sun burned, the fog disappeared, and after a few miles Fannin's
transport animals, burdened by too many heavy guns, weakened. Fannin
demanded a halt, though some officers insisted on reaching a nearby
creek.

Now, Urrea had him fixed, in a small depression in the open prairie,
away from water, away from the sheltering woods. In the timber of the
close-by Coleta, or Encinal del Perdido, the Georgians and others could

have fought well. As it was, they performed creditably, under a sweltering sun, in a hollow square, until the sun went down. The big guns that delayed the column fatally were of little use. There was no water to cool the pieces after firing, and the one man who knew how to handle artillery in the field was wounded.

Fannin, enveloped by Urrea's vastly superior force, was unnerved all night by the cries of his suffering wounded, begging for water. At daylight, Urrea's field guns began to spray the Americans with grape and canister. In the end, Fannin took out a flag for parley, and capitulated.

For years Texans insisted Fannin got honorable terms. The evidence is otherwise; Mexican army archives hold a document with Fannin's signature, in which he surrendered at discretion, meaning, unconditionally, and put himself and his men at the Supreme Government's mercy. But it is absolutely certain, from the survivors' statements and those of some of the Mexican army, that Fannin's men believed they would be permitted the honors of war. Urrea knew Santa Anna's and the Supreme Government's standing orders, but he promised to intercede with the *Presidente*.

One reason, probably, that the Americans were confident of being disarmed and exiled back to the United States was that the foreign professionals with Urrea's army—the only officers who could speak English—cheerfully told them so. These men, Captain Dusague, who interpreted at the surrender, Lieutenant Colonel Holzinger, and Colonel Guerrier (sometimes spelled Garay), unquestionably believed this themselves. Holzinger actually stated, "Gentlemen, in ten days liberty and home!" The "Georgia Battalion," the "Red Rovers," and the others, now heartily sick of war and Texas, marched willingly back to Goliad and jail.

Urrea personally mentioned to Fannin that the Mexican government did not execute prisoners, even pirates, who appealed for clemency. But Urrea reckoned without General Santa Anna, who was forging a new Mexican state of affairs. Urrea did write the President. The President wrote back a rather rambling letter, the force of which was to state he had no power to remit the Supreme Government's instructions pertaining to such criminals as these. In the meantime, on March 24 and 25, Ward's survivors, who had been rounded up, and some Nashville volunteers who had just landed unknowingly at Cópano Bay, were brought into the crowded brick *cuarteles*.

On Palm Sunday, March 27, Colonel Guerrier came into the room where the American surgeons, who had volunteered to care for Mexican wounded, were kept. White-faced, he said, "Keep still, gentlemen, you are safe; these are not my orders, nor do I execute them." Several other Americans, not knowing what was afoot, were hidden and kept out of barracks by the wife of a Mexican officer named Álvarez. The rest were divided into three columns and marched out on three roads under heavy guard, believing they were going home. A little way from Goliad they were shot. Only a handful, in the confusion, broke away.

The wounded prisoners were dragged into the streets and shot there. The officers were shot last, after they had learned what happened to their men. There are accounts that Fannin took the news calmly, and that he did not, that he asked merely not to be shot in the head and given decent burial, and that he begged for mercy. At any rate, he was shot in the head and dropped into the common grave. Three hundred and ninety Americans died. Twenty-seven, saved in various ways, escaped. When the army left, Guerrier saw to it that the men he had hidden got away.

Urrea himself refused to be on hand for the executions. He professed that he "and every soldier in his division was confounded, amazed, and thrown into consternation" by the order. He wrote later that Fannin had "certainly surrendered in the belief that Mexican generosity would not make their sacrifice sterile," otherwise, they would have fought to the last. The professional officers were particularly outraged; naturally, no class of men clung more strenuously to the notion of the "honors of war." But Urrea obeyed orders. He would not, like Colonel Guerrier, who risked being shot himself, have escaped judgment at Nuremberg a century later.

This execution of pirates was not a crime under international law. Fannin's men were foreigners, not part of any recognized or proper army, in arms on Mexican soil. It was a blunder; as Talleyrand described one of Napoleon's executions, it was worse than a crime. As the Texas historian Davenport wrote, if Fannin's motley starvelings had been shipped to New Orleans, they would have spread tales of folly, mismanagement, and disaster; "Texas' standing with the American people would have fallen to a new low." Instead, Santa Anna made 400 martyrs, and even immortalized James Fannin. Here, he lost, forever, the propaganda war in the civilized world. Years later, rather pathetically, he was still writing letters trying to absolve himself from responsibility.

At the end of March, 1836, Santa Anna felt supremely confident that at Béxar and Goliad Texan resistance had been broken. He believed the entire "Texian" army was destroyed, and he decided to return to Mexico. Only the advice of his officers, who argued the Presidential presence was needed with the troops, dissuaded him. Now, Santa Anna divided his thousands of soldiers into five divisions or columns. In retrospect, this was to seem sheer folly. At the time, Santa Anna saw no further mission than to pursue and destroy. Columns under Santa Anna, Ramírez y Sesma, Filisola, Amat, and Urrea began a massive sweep toward the Sabine.

Their orders were to burn every town, plantation, farm, and dwelling in their path. The Anglo-Saxon presence was not to be conquered or cowed; it was to be erased.

Santa Anna intended to start a panic, to drive the colonists across the U.S. frontier. He was successful. The next few weeks in Texas were to be known, half-ashamedly, as the "Runaway Scrape." The entire population of Anglo-Texas, frightened and horrified by the tales of Mexican atrocities, deserted the countryside ahead of the Mexican army. Most able-bodied

Texas men, including many boys, had joined Sam Houston's army; the women, children, and old men on the land were left to fend for themselves. In a space of days, the colony that Austin built crumbled away. With wagons pulled by straining oxen, on horseback, or pitifully on foot, carrying what treasured possessions they could, the Texas women herded their families east. Soon, a pathetic litter lay along the trails.

This was the rainy season in east Texas. The rivers were up, and soon the ferries were jammed. One refugee, Dilue Rose Harris, wrote afterward that when she and her family reached the San Jacinto River at Lynch's Ferry on April 10, 5,000 frantic people were swarming at that point. Any flight of refugees from war is attended by misery, tragedy, and terror. There were hundreds of tales of heroism and self-reliance, as the women struggled over the muddy roads toward the Sabine, without their men, abandoning their homes and the labor of years, with the smoke of the Mexican swath of destruction rising behind them. Soon, there was hunger; fever and sickness spread, babies began to die. There was worse: looters began to appear. There were men who galloped into settlements far ahead of the invading army, shouting, "The Mexicans are coming!"—then stole horses, silver, anything, when the panicking inhabitants fled.

Sam Houston's retreat to the Brazos, and the movement of the government east, spurred the flight as much as rumors of Santanista terror. Desperately, the columns of women and children clogging the frightful roads tried to keep up, behind the Texas army. The struggling, sodden stream of pitiful humanity poured past Houston's encampment at San Felipe on the Brazos; watching it, one of Houston's captains, Moseley Baker, broke down and cried.

The government moved east of the Brazos, to Harrisburg on Buffalo Bayou, near Galveston Bay. President Burnet was in agony over Houston's apparent dalliance. He wrote: "The enemy are laughing you to scorn. You must fight them. You must retreat no farther. The country expects you to fight. The salvation of the country depends on you doing so."

General Houston wrote back laconically to Rusk, the Secretary of War, that he was holding no councils and consulting no one. If he erred, the blame was his. At Groce's, Houston was desperately trying to instill some discipline into his motley forces, which had grown to more than 1,400 men. No one, except Houston and a few officers, had ever fought in formal warfare before. The Texas men knew nothing of forming columns, or fighting in line, or even obeying the commands of their company officers. During these weeks, it was not Major General Houston of the Tennessee Militia but a former junior officer of the 39th United States Infantry whose mind ruled the army. Houston did not make the mistake of despising the enemy too much. He knew what disciplined troops, on open ground, could do to his ragged horde. But his drilling became increasingly impossible. The vast majority of his army were now Texas men, whose homes were being put to the torch, and whose women and children were fleeing forlorn

and hungry to the east. Houston was faced by a hostile army that demanded to fight.

When Houston retreated down the Brazos past San Felipe and ordered
the town burned, Captains Moseley Baker and Martin of the Texans refused a further retreat. Houston left them to hold the crossings over the
Brazos, while he and the bulk of the army went across the river on the
steamboat *Yellowstone*.

Houston had no real battle plan. He was faced with superior numbers
and a superior force. His only hope was to bring Santa Anna to battle on
his own terms. He fell back, and back, waiting for the enemy to make a
mistake.

Santa Anna, who joined with Sesma's troops, reached the Brazos at San
Felipe. Here he found the fords covered by Moseley Baker's sharpshooters.
He shunted south, and seized the ferry at Fort Bend. He heard the Texas
government was at Harrisburg, about 30 miles away, and he marched to
capture it. Burnet, Zavala, and the others barely got away; the Mexicans
pursued them to Morgan's Point, overlooking Galveston Bay.

In this column Santa Anna had 700 to 800 troops. The other Mexican
columns were many miles away, except for Cós, who had been absolved of
his pledge and was again leading troops in Texas. Santa Anna burned
Harrisburg to the ground. He proceeded to the town of New Washington,
on the bay, then swung back northwest to the San Jacinto River. Here, he
trapped Sam Houston, who had marched from the Brazos to Harrisburg,
left his sick and disabled in the ruins, then coiled into a position between
the San Jacinto and Buffalo Bayou.

Houston deliberately let himself run out of territory, because he was
running out of time. Hundreds of his men had left, gone to find and help
their fleeing families, disgusted with this strange commander who would
not fight. But it was the Napoleon of the West, not the ex-U.S. lieutenant,
who made the crucial mistake. Santa Anna had at last placed an inferior
force in front of Houston, on terrain where neither army could easily
retreat. The hard-riding Deaf Smith had taken a Mexican courier on April
18. The dispatches revealed Santa Anna's planned movements. Houston let
himself be "trapped."

He turned toward the Mexican column and took a position with his back
to the river and bayou. The evidence is that if he had turned away from the
enemy at this time, the army would have revolted. The Texans were at
perfect pitch. They were tired but not exhausted, angry, and murderous.
Their enthusiasm was worn away, but so was any nervousness or fear.
Houston had marched and drilled his army just enough. Now, Houston
placed his cannon (the Twin Sisters, which were a gift of the city of
Cincinnati, Ohio) and threw his small cavalry force on the open prairie to
his right. He was ready to fight.

On April 20 Santa Anna found and fixed him, with a light skirmish that neither side tried to press home. Santa Anna did not want to attack, since he was waiting reinforcement. Why Houston did not attack on the morning of the 21st has never been explained. He allowed Cós to march into Santa Anna's camp with an additional 400 men; now, the Mexican forces outnumbered him. Houston had reached the San Jacinto with only 918.

Santa Anna had indeed grown contemptuous of Sam Houston, as Burnet had charged. The Mexican President felt there was no hurry. He camped about three-quarters of a mile from Houston's army, behind hasty fortifications made of saddlebags and brush breastworks. A swell in the ground in front of this camp protected the Mexicans from Houston's field pieces. It also hid the Texas army from Mexican view.

Houston held his war council at noon on April 21. He had planned to attack on the morning of the 22nd, and to this the majority of his officers agreed. But the rank and file were impatient and rebellious; they voted, company by company, to fight immediately. Houston shrewdly acquiesced.

The problem with a proper army was that it was usually predictable. Santa Anna's veteran were getting all the rest they could, for the morrow's battle. The afternoon, in the humid April warmth along the bayou, was devoted to *siesta*. Santa Anna himself had retired; most of the officers dozed under trees.

Certain details, such as the exact size of the Mexican army of approximately 1,200, are still unclear; and it is unclear how the Texas army of almost 1,000 at midafternoon of a bright, sunny day could walk across almost a mile of open grassland and take a veteran force by complete surprise. It happened. Santa Anna had made his last, and fatal, mistake in Texas.

Houston sent Deaf Smith and a few trusted men to demolish Vince's Bridge across the Brazos, some miles away. This had a double purpose. It cut off the Mexican retreat—but also trapped the Texans, if they should lose. Houston was not the first commander to burn his bridges behind him; now, like Cortés' men in Mexico when their ships were burned, the Texans could only conquer or die.

In this army were men and leaders whose loyalty Houston had held by a thread: Sherman, Somervell, Lamar, and Wharton. Wiley Martin and the colonist lawyer, Moseley Baker, would follow him if he fought. There were also his backers, who included Millard, Wells, Burleson, and Tom Rusk. But now, for the first time since it began, the Texas army was united.

Houston formed them at three in the afternoon. Sixty horsemen mounted on the right, under the courtly Georgian fire-eater, Mirabeau Buonaparte Lamar. Lamar's orders: keep the Mexicans from breaking across the prairie. Next came the two small companies of the Texas "Regular" Army, paced by Lieutenant Colonel Henry Millard. Beside the regular infantry stood the Twin Sisters, ready to roll under Hockley (Neill, the senior artillery officer, was injured). One gun would support each wing.

Then, Burleson's First Regiment, the Texas backbone of the army, took its place in line, then Moseley Baker's riflemen, and Sidney Sherman's Second, with its Kentucky core. On each flank was water, the deep and black bayous.

Houston formed a line of infantry, one man deep, that spread a thousand yards. Columns were for armies that attacked with the bayonet. The Texans had only rifles, tomahawks, and bowie knives. In the center floated the Republic's flag: plain white silk, with five-point azure star, and the motto *Ubi Libertas Habitat Ibi Nostra Patria Est*—"where liberty lives, there is our homeland." Beside the flag, Houston rode his huge white stallion, Saracen. A thousand men were in this army, and this afternoon a thousand separate legends were being made. Posterity could take its choice of them. Only the bodies and blood on the field of San Jacinto remained ever afterward undisputed.

Field music was found, a German who could play the fife, and a Negro freedman who could beat a drum. Two other musicians volunteered, But this combo of four did not know "Yankee Doodle" or any other martial air. They knew only popular music of the day. Grinning, General Houston told the field band to strike up "Come to the Bower," a tune regarded as quite risqué. Houston made no speech; he had none of Travis' impassioned rhetoric. He had not liked Travis, but on this day he missed the cold-eyed, deadly competent Bowie. He said something like, Hold your fire until you make it count. Forward—Texas! Only a part of the line could hear him. All saw him draw his sword, and all heard the field music screech into the air:

> *Will you come to the bow'r I have shaded for you?*
> *Our bed shall be roses all spangled with dew.*
> *There under the bow'r on roses you'll lie*
> *With a blush on your cheek but a smile in your eye!*

Tired, dirty, bearded, hungry, angry—terrible—the army leveled its long rifles and went forward across the open plain. A Georgian Huguenot on the right, a Kentucky colonel on the left, at the head a Scotch-Irish agent of destiny from Tennessee, paced by a German fifer and a Negro beating on a drum, the Texans marched across the grass, up the swell, and down upon a dozing Mexican camp.

They were seen. Sentries' muskets thudded, but incredibly, Santa Anna had had no pickets, nor any scouts watching the Texan camp. The line of the army, beginning to wave and break now, was in rifle range of the Mexican barricade before the shrieking, discordant notes of the *"Centinela Alerto"* went up. The bugles were too late. So was the Mexican cannon— the big Golden Standard was fired too quickly, too high. Its grape screamed uselessly over the Texans' heads.

Incredibly, using the muscles of thirty men, Hockley had the Twin Sisters poised in front of the piled saddles and brush. He blew a tremendous hole, Cincinnati's gift to Texas, at a most proper time. The line kept walking forward, under fire now, but the main body of Mexicans was trying to assemble into disciplined order under shout and bugle call. Without that order, it was as doomed as Hessians on the Delaware. Mexicans, like Europeans of the time, were not trained to fight as individuals, without commands.

In the Texan line, it was inevitable that the shout arose. Colonel Sidney Sherman, on the left, apparently yelled it first: "Remember the Alamo! Remember Goliad! Remember the Alamo!" The line dissolved, but it was running screaming at the enemy. Moseley Baker, who wept at the Brazos, took a bullet. Dr. William Mottley stumbled and went down. Texans later could name them individually, because on this day they were so few. Saracen, Houston's great horse, shrieked and crashed to earth. The General seized another mount from his aides. Houston, trotting ahead of the line, pointing ahead with his sword, his heart thudding in a tremendous passion, coolly, coolly, with his soldier's brain knowing no power on earth was going to stop this headlong charge.

At something like twenty yards the Texas rifles began to blaze, a tremendous staccato roar. The barricades were swept clear. Burleson's regiment went into the position headlong and tore the fragile fortification apart. Sherman's line came leaping at it from the flank. Eight hundred rifles had left gray-uniformed dead and dying scattered all across the trampled ground. The Mexicans could not reload, could not form, could not wield the bayonet. The Texans went into them with rifle butt and long-bladed knife. They died.

The battle lasted only a few minutes. The slaughter took longer. Santa Anna, General of Brigade Castrillón, and a dozen colonels of various degrees ran about, shouting conflicting orders: fire, form up, lie down to avoid the enemy fire. Some of the confused soldiery stopped fighting and threw down their arms, begging for mercy. The rest fled. Houston had his second horse shot from under him at the barricade, and this time his ankle caught a copper musket ball. Reeling, giddy, Houston bellowed for his men to Parade, and get back in order. He went unheard.

The Mexicans who dropped their weapons and tried to surrender as individuals were clubbed and stabbed, some on their knees. Deaf Smith, plunging over the barricade on his horse, urged the Texans to "take prisoners like the Meskins do!" The terrible, high-pitched shout was everywhere: "Remember the Alamo!" It drowned out the cries of Santa Anna's broken and fleeing ranks.

The great part of the Mexican army was never able to form or fight at all. Retreating in a panic, hundreds of soldiers found their retreat blocked by a deep ravine, or bayou. A few fled to the open prairie, where they were chopped down by Lamar's horsemen. But a great mass of struggling, screaming men pressed up against the banks of the bayou. Some rushed into the water and were drowned. The slaughter at this point became methodical: the Texan riflemen knelt and poured a steady fire into the packed, jostling ranks. Here, not on the barricade but several hundred yards behind the Mexican camp, the greatest carnage took place.

Rank had no privileges in this screaming death trap. General of Brigade Castrillón, four colonels, two lieutenant colonels, five captains, and twelve lieutenants were killed in the press; five colonels, three lieutenant colonels, two majors, seven captains and a cadet were down, wounded. The Mexican army disintegrated. Only the gallant Juan Almonte was able to gather some hundreds and withdraw them in a semblance of order, too late to save the battle, but in an attempt to save Mexican lives. Colonel Almonte realized he could never get these broken men back in battle order, and toward sundown, when the Texans' bloodlust had been sated, he surrendered them. Almonte used his own judgment; the President and his brother-in-law Cós had disappeared.

At nightfall, Houston sat under a tree with his boot full of blood, hearing the reports. Six hundred thirty Mexican corpses were scattered in clumps across the field. Almonte surrendered about the same number more, 200 of whom were wounded. These men sat on the ground, under guard, like dispirited cattle, still dazed by the horror that had overtaken them.

The Texans lost two killed in action. There were about thirty wounded, of whom seven more would die. The figures cannot be precise; Houston's official report of two killed, twenty-four wounded, six mortally, was made after a hasty survey. Likewise, his report of more than 700 Mexican prisoners of war, when added to the 630 Mexican dead, exceeds the total figures on the Mexican army rolls. These were errors only in slight degree, however; what was clear was the army that was demoralized and routed suffered immense casualties, while the victors emerged almost unscathed.

To this toll at San Jacinto must be added the 800 American dead who fell at the Alamo and Goliad. In the twilight at San Jacinto, however, this cost was small. Although no one quite knew it when the red sun went down on April 21, 1836, the balance of power in Texas had turned.

The American West was won.

14

AFTERMATH

Army of Operations,
The Camp at San Jacinto, April 22, 1836.

His Excellency, Don Vicente Filisola, General of Division:

Excellent Sir — Having yesterday evening, with the small division under my immediate command, had an encounter with the enemy which, notwithstanding I had previously observed all possible precautions, proved unfortunate, I am, in consequence, a prisoner of the enemy. Under these circumstances your Excellency will order General Guano, with his division, to countermarch to Béxar and wait for orders. Your Excellency will also, with the division under your command, march to the same place. The division under the command of General Urrea will retire to Guadalupe Victoria. I have agreed with General Houston for an armistice, until matters can be so regulated that the war will cease forever. . . .

EXTRACT OF THE LETTER FROM ANTONIO LÓPEZ DE SANTA ANNA
TO THE MEXICAN FORCES IN TEXAS

Towards sunset, a woman on the outskirts of the camp began to clap her hands and shout "Hallelujah! Hallelujah!" Those about her thought her mad, but following her wild gestures, they saw one of the Hardings, of Liberty, riding for life towards the camp, his horse covered with foam, and he was waving his hat and shouting, "San Jacinto! San Jacinto! The Mexicans are whipped and Santa Anna a prisoner!" The scene that followed beggars description. People embraced, laughed and wept and prayed, all in one breath. As the moon rose over the vast, flower-decked prairie, the soft southern wind carried peace to tired hearts and grateful slumber.

FROM THE ACCOUNT OF MRS. TERRELL, ONE OF THE RUNAWAYS
TRAPPED UP AGAINST BUFFALO BAYOU NEAR HARRISBURG
ON APRIL 21, 1836

I N the days and weeks before the battle at San Jacinto, Stephen F. Austin, William H. Wharton, Branch T. Archer, and a number of other Texas agents were working night and day in the United States. Most Texans, after the fall of the Alamo, believed that only American intervention could save Anglo-Texas. Austin and Wharton traveled up the Mississippi and Ohio Valley to New York, where they tried to negotiate a loan. They found the New York bankers cautious and cool. Interest in Texas receded in direct proportion to the distance eastward from the middle border.

Austin, Archer, and Wharton secured $100,000 in institutional loans and some $25,000 in private donations in the United States. One group in New Orleans gave $7,000, and two wealthy families each donated $5,000. There were many pledges of land, slaves, and personal property, but these were virtually worthless, as they could not be translated into ready cash. Thomas McKinney and William Bryan, who were Texas agents and Texas merchants in New Orleans, got local merchants to supply powder, lead, flour, rifles, and clothing on faith for the most part, and for the rest used their own funds. The suppliers of the Texas Revolution, like those of 1776, expended their own fortunes out of patriotism. Small as these stores were, without them Houston could not have remained in the field at all.

The Texas agents had better luck recruiting men than finding money. Travis' letter of February 24th, 1836, was read to audiences all through the southwestern states. It produced violent emotional reactions in the border country. All through the Mississippi Valley friends of Texas held mass meetings to send volunteers or "armed emigrants," as Austin called them, to the war. The largest recruiting centers were New Orleans, Louisville, and Cincinnati. Many small companies were raised and outfitted, among them the New Orleans Grays, the Mobile Grays, the Alabama Red Rovers, and the Kentucky Mustangs. Most of these men died with Fannin at Goliad.

Almost every Southern and border state sent men or weapons. Cincinnati sent the Twin Sisters down the Mississippi; Alabama stripped its state arsenal of muskets for Texas. Thomas Chambers, who was authorized by the Texas Council to raise an "Army of the Reserve" in the United States, successfully propagandized Ohio, Kentucky, and Tennessee. He raised and equipped almost 2,000 volunteers and sent them on their way.

The three official commissioners, however, were most interested in getting the United States government to move. On April 15, 1836, Austin sent a letter to the President of the United States, his Cabinet, and most of the

Congress. He made the letter public at the same time, having it printed by friendly newspapers. The letter was propagandistic, but it summed up the attitudes that were being privately expressed by many prominent Americans of the time:

> Pardon me for this intrusion upon your valued time. I address you as individuals, as men, as Americans, as my countrymen. I obey an honest though excited impulse. We have recent dates from Mexico by packet. It appears that Santa Anna has succeeded in uniting the whole Mexican nation against Texas by making it a national war against heretics; that an additional army of eight thousand men is organizing in Mexico under Gen. Cotazar to march to Texas and exterminate the heretic Americans. Santa Anna is now in Texas, as we all know, with about seven thousand men fighting under the bloody flag of a pirate—he is exciting the Comanches and other Indians, who know nothing of lines or political divisions of territory, and massacres have been committed on Red River within the United States. This is a war of barbarism against civilization, of despotism against liberty, of Mexicans against Americans. O my countrymen! the warm-hearted, chivalrous, impulsive West and South are up and moving in favor of Texas. The calculating and more prudent, though not less noble-minded, North are aroused. The sympathies of the whole American people en masse are with the Texans. . . . Will you, can you, turn a deaf ear to the appeals of your fellow citizens in favor of their and your countrymen and friends who are massacred, butchered, outraged, in Texas at your very doors? Are not we, the Texans, obeying the dictates of an education received here, from you, the American people, from our fathers, from the patriots of '76—the Republicans of 1836? . . .
>
> Well, you reply, what can we do? In answer, I say, let the President and the Cabinet and Congress come out openly and at once and proclaim to the public their opinions—let Texas have some of the thirty-seven million dollars now in the national treasury—let the war in Texas become a national war, above board. . . . Who can deny that it is a national war in reality—a war in which every American who is not a fanatic, abolitionist, or cold-hearted recreant to the interests and honor and principles of his country . . . is deeply, warmly, and ardently interested. In short, it is now a national war sub rosa. Let the Administration . . . take this position at once . . . and the Government of the United States will then occupy that open and elevated stand which is due to the American people and worthy of Andrew Jackson—for it will occupy above board the position which this nation as a people now occupy in heart.

Austin's words also pointed up certain ominous flags flying in the wind for the nation as a whole, whether Texas survived or sank. The eastern seaboard did tend to be cool and cautious toward a war with Mexico, and many Northerners already strongly opposed any liaison with Texas because it was slave territory. The South and West was much more impulsive and belligerent and ready to accept what came naturally to American hearts. The West and South regarded the Eastern doubts as legalistic nonsense at best, cowardice at worst.

The evidence is plain that the American nation as a whole was strongly in favor of Texas, though only the South and Southwest were in favor of becoming involved. The Administration, however, was truly caught up in doubts and legal difficulties, which was already the normal situation for the United States government to occupy. Austin's letter irritated Andrew Jackson. He scribbled on the margin of his copy:

> The writer does not reflect that we have a treaty with Mexico, and our national faith is pledged to support it. The Texans before they took the step to declare themselves independent, which has aroused and united all Mexico against them, ought to have pondered well—it was a rash and premature act; our neutrality must be faithfully maintained.

Here an interesting dichotomy between the government and the American public was raised. From the beginning of the trouble in Texas, in 1835, the U.S. State Department had advised prominent Texans not to declare independence, since such a move would play into the hands of those foreign observers who claimed the whole Revolution was part of an American plot to acquire Texas. But one reason the Texans did declare independence in March, 1836, was that by then it was clear that the U.S. public was totally uninterested in supplying arms or aid for an internal Mexican revolution. Americans had never heard of, and cared nothing for, the Constitution of 1824. The Southwesterners who marched to Texas, or sent guns, did so in the full hope and belief that Texas would become American soil. What the State Department, its eyes on legality and the world scene, was advising the Texas leaders to do was to cut their own throats. A renewed pledge of loyalty to Mexico in 1836 would have halted tons of supplies and armaments on the docks, while the United States, for all its advice and irritation at the "premature move" promised nothing in the way of immediate aid.

The private feelings of Andrew Jackson are clear enough. Jackson had already made a remark that Texas was the key to the nation reaching the Pacific. Jackson wanted Texas; he was a Westerner and a man of long vision, he was already looking beyond the Rio Grande. But Jackson was trapped by the treaty that renounced Texas "forever." This was more important to him, obviously, than antiwar and anti-Texas sentiment in the Northeast; he was prepared to move, if he could find any legal excuse to intervene in Texas. Jackson was the most powerful President up to this time, but the powers of the Presidency were not construed in the 1830's so as to allow him to engage the nation in war by executive action.

The evidence indicates that he might very well have been moving in this direction. The War Department issued orders to General Edmund Gaines, the U.S. military commander in the Southwest, to march to the Sabine to prevent violation of U.S. territory by either belligerent, and if necessary, "to cross the Sabine to insure the neutrality of the Indians." The treaty with Mexico required that both parties prevent Indian depredations from originating on its side of the border. Texas agents had already spread the word that the Mexicans were in alliance with the Indians, planning a war of extermination against the whites that would not end at the river border.

The President had already decided to press a claim for the land between the Sabine and the Neches. This was based on an argument originated by Anthony Butler, who was Jackson's minister to Mexico, that in 1819 the Spaniards had mistakenly written "Sabine" into the treaty when they really meant "Neches." Jackson was cocking the United States for some kind of action in the Southwest—but his devout attention to appearances and legalisms merely infuriated the Texans, whose own inclination was to do what came naturally, and damn the hypocrisy.

If there was one crime the Mexicans were not guilty of, it was allying with or instigating the Comanches or other dangerous Indians. But the accusation opened a door quite a few Americans, including the President, seemed willing to pass through. From Baton Rouge, on his way to Natchitoches, General Gaines informed the Secretary of War that he "should deem it his duty to anticipate the lawless movements of the Mexicans and their red allies." If it appeared American soil was menaced in any way, Gaines was prepared to cross "our supposed or imaginary national boundary and meet the savage marauders wherever to be found in their approach to our frontiers."

General Gaines' instructions allowed him sufficient latitude to start a war, and he showed no signs of being afraid of one. In the Congress, John Quincy Adams and other Easterners attacked Gaines' orders in the most violent terms; these men wanted no part of a Mexican war, and above all, no extension of American slave territory. Both the old North and old South were adopting an increasingly parochial viewpoint, often masked by hypocritical ideologies. The West, with men like Houston and Jackson, still clung to Unionism and the notion of one nation, expanding, right or wrong. In the West, men could see far horizons, and more rivers to cross, and they had a thirst to cross them.

In Natchitoches General Gaines was bombarded by Texan alarums, Mexican atrocities, and tales of Indian uprisings across the border. The streams of pitiful refugees pouring through Natchitoches heightened the tension. Companies of volunteers were also passing west, and Gaines maintained close liaison with these. He had good intelligence of the state of affairs in east Texas. He was also contemptuous of certain large numbers of armed men who now began passing through to the east, from Texas—apparently American volunteers who changed their minds when they ran into the headlong Texan retreat toward the Sabine.

Gaines felt the situation was dangerous enough to call out the militia or national guards of Louisiana, Alabama, Mississippi, and Tennessee. His orders did not include this. If Jackson had cocked the nation for trouble, Gaines was now splashing powder in the priming pan. However, the trigger was never pulled. Gaines reached Natchitoches in early April, 1836, and the news of San Jacinto reached him three weeks later. What might have occurred had Gaines marched over the Sabine earlier will never be known.

The word of the victory on the San Jacinto raced up the muddy trails and quagmire roads by horse courier, overtaking thousands of women and children still trying to get out of Texas. It passed across into Louisiana, reaching company after company of approaching "armed emigrants." The news cheered these Americans immensely; they hastened onward into Texas, and more ships set out from New Orleans, carrying men and arms to Houston.

The word rolled slowly through the South, and up the Mississippi Valley. It was greeted everywhere with cheers, prayers, bonfires, and rejoicing. It was a remarkable reaction to an event in a "foreign" war. On May 16, 1836, Gaines' dispatch rider pounded into Washington and rode up to the White House. This officer had a report from General Gaines, and a personal message for the President from west of the Sabine.

Jackson, in great excitement, seized the letter from Texas. He said, "Yes, that's his writing! I know it well! That's Houston's hand—there can be no doubt of what he states!" The contents of this letter were never revealed. Houston had written it immediately after finishing his official report for the Texas government. The President demanded a map. He wanted to find the San Jacinto, but the tiny river was not marked. Jackson's finger moved across the map enthusiastically: "It must be there! No, it must be over there!"

Cabinet officers and dignitaries high and low gave parties or held celebrations. Even John Quincy Adams, Texas' principal enemy in the United States, seems to have forgotten himself. In his diary for this day he wrote: "Glorious news from Texas that Santa Anna has been defeated and taken by Houston, and shot, with all his officers." The public celebrations dismayed the Mexican minister. He delivered a note expressing "shock and astonishment at this intemperate joy."

But, whatever the joy of private Americans and official Washington, for sixty terrible days Anglo-Texas had fought alone. None of the money and none of the volunteers raised in 1836 reached Sam Houston before San Jacinto. His supplies were mainly those bought by Texans' credit in New Orleans. The American volunteers who had come in 1835 were mostly slaughtered at Goliad and San Patricio, because they refused to obey orders or accept a Texan command. Houston's army, by the time he reached the Brazos, was overwhelmingly composed of colonists.

These facts were not completely lost on the true Texans, and they had their historic effect.

Santa Anna and many of his officers had been taken, but by the grace of Sam Houston's vision, he had not been shot. On April 22, the day after the battle, the Mexican dictator and his brother-in-law, General Cós, were both rounded up by Texan patrols. Santa Anna was not recognized at first, because he had escaped the battlefield only in his silk shirt and drawers, and had somewhere dressed himself in a private soldier's rough gray trousers. The Texans smelled him out only because of his own men's immediate deference when he was marched into the prisoner compound.

When word reached him of Santa Anna's capture, Andrew Jackson wrote Houston immediately that he must not be executed, for political and propaganda reasons. But Houston never had any intention of shooting Santa Anna, although he utterly despised the Mexican ruler, and was under no illusions as to the kind of man he had taken. Santa Anna gave Houston immediate leverage to follow up his field victory with a total political triumph in the war. Houston had that common Southwestern American trait: a man of firm honor himself, he possessed no idealism about the honor of others, or scruples about using them to political advantage. In 1832, he had written Jackson that the Mexican government was "essentially despotic and must be so for years to come. The rulers have not honesty and the people have not intelligence." Houston saw the true situation and did not mince words. Now, on April 22, his grasp of the Mexican situation allowed him to play the splendid fish he had caught with considerable cleverness.

Santa Anna and Houston seemed to have understood each other well enough, though Houston did improve his case with a sort of war of nerves against the President. He refused to talk directly with Santa Anna about a treaty, but insisted, as he was legally bound to do, on going through the Texas government. Meanwhile, the captive was exposed to Texan hostility and threats—the majority of Houston's army were eager to hang him to the nearest oak. Santa Anna quickly realized Houston wanted to buy a peace for Texas, and that Houston had the price—Santa Anna's neck. With mounting hope, each man realized they could make a deal.

Houston was in agony, and in danger, from his bullet-smashed foot. He had to sail to New Orleans for treatment, but before he left, he got the Mexican President to cooperate in everything he asked. Santa Anna immediately penned orders to his commanders in Texas to retire to Béxar pending a total cessation of the war, and agreed to negotiate a treaty of peace with the Republic of Texas. Houston then turned Santa Anna over to President Burnet, who had the same goals and same understanding as the General, and left Texas.

Burnet now entered into negotiations with Santa Anna, much against the will of the Texas army and public opinion generally. The colonists were now streaming home to ruined farms and burned-out plantations; the widows, the farmers, and the soldiers were all athirst for personal vengeance. Santa Anna was denounced in the Texas congress as a murderer, who should be shot out of hand. Burnet treated these complaints with cool contempt, reminding his critics that there was no law, national or international, and no legal usage anywhere, by which the commander of an enemy army could be tried or punished for his official acts. If Texas intended to behave as a responsible nation, then Santa Anna was immune. This public uproar, however, unquestionably had its effect on the dictator's mind.

On May 14, 1836, at Velasco, Santa Anna signed a public and a secret treaty with the Republic of Texas. By the public treaty he agreed to the following points:

He swore personally never to take up arms again against Texas.

All hostilities between the two nations would cease immediately.

The Mexican army in Texas would withdraw below the Rio Grande.

All American prisoners still held would be released.

The treaty would immediately govern General Filisola, now in command of the Mexican army.

Santa Anna would be shipped to Vera Cruz as soon as "deemed proper."

By the secret treaty, Santa Anna pledged himself to work within Mexico to achieve four things: diplomatic recognition of Texas; Texan independence; a treaty of commerce; the Rio Grande acknowledged as the Texas-Mexico boundary.

The Texas campaign of 1836 laid the foundations for a deep sense of national humiliation in Mexicans, which the events of the coming decade only made immensely worse. Mexicans found it psychologically unbearable to accept the fact that a few thousand colonists had inflicted hideous losses on their best soldiers and captured the greatest Mexican general of the time fleeing in his shirt and drawers. Understandably, it became almost articles of faith that United States intervention won the war (and American numbers were greatly exaggerated) and that the whole debacle was the result of an American conspiracy. While there is no doubt of a continuing United States "conspiracy" against Mexican soil in Texas, and Sam Houston in the historic sense was an American agent, the victory, and whatever glory might ensue, belonged to the men who had emigrated from the United States. Yet Mexican propaganda, completely submerged during the war by Texan, in later years almost won the point: the world came to believe that even in 1836 the "powerful" United States wrenched Texas from "poor, bleeding Mexico."

The Mexican effort in Texas should not be considered despicable. The Mexican army was effective; the rot was hardly at its roots but near the top. The attacking columns at the Alamo—ordered into an unfavorable tactical situation—displayed great discipline and courage, and initiative by junior officers. Urrea's lancers swept every American they found in arms from the field, and did it neatly—with the single exception of the time they tried to assault riflemen behind Refugio's walls. Shooting Fannin's men after their surrender reflected no credit on that commander—but it was done by Santa Anna's express order. The crime of Urrea and his soldiers, which other men before and afterward had to face, was that they marched under a dictator's command.

Santa Anna had planned a bold sweep into Texas; he had moved with almost incredible speed. He came within an ace of succeeding. He would have succeeded, but for Travis at the Alamo. But he had paid a price for speed. His columns in Texas in the spring of 1836 found themselves without sufficient guns, and worse, desperately short of supplies. It is taking nothing from Houston's glory at the San Jacinto to read the Mexican orders of the day and discover that General Filisola, even before he received Santa Anna's orders written on April 22, was in retreat. Filisola, following Santa Anna into East Texas with a powerful column, was logistically in trouble.

The Mexican army, like the British army in the American Revolution, was an effective instrument, but its leaders met a kind of opposition and field circumstances they had never seen and did not understand. They failed to credit frontier marksmanship. Equally important, the Mexican Army of Operations in Texas entered a country without towns, without a countryside it could live off, and without roads. The Texan flight, and Houston's scorched-earth policy, greeted Filisola, after marching across a veritable desert of several hundred miles, with desolation of another kind. The Italian-born General Filisola's description of Texas is significant. The Americans who called it the best and richest country in the world were farmers, or land-hungry men with an eye for fertile soil; the professional soldier Filisola described Texas as endless and everlasting mud.

He had tried to march through the coastal plains during the rainy season, and he pushed his men not through hell but a ghastly quagmire. He found himself mired down hundreds of miles from the nearest magazine. By April, many of Filisola's columns were ragged, and thousands of Mexican soldiers were going hungry.

An enormous, often overlooked factor in the Mexican debacle was the control of the Gulf by the tiny Texas navy. Since the Mexican army was separated from its bases by the "Desert of Dead Horses" along the Rio Bravo, resupply by sea, even along the treacherous Texas coast, was necessary. Mexico was not a maritime nation, but it did have a navy, and sufficient merchant sail under its flag to support Santa Anna's army.

One of the first acts of the Texas Council in November, 1835, had been to authorized letters of marque and a regular navy of four ships. The privateer *William Robbins,* a ship bought by private Texas citizens, put to sea and took the Mexican warship *Bravo* and other vessels. However, Jean Lafitte had destroyed the favorable image of the privateer. Opinion in the United States strongly disapproved this form of enterprise; the government of Texas therefore purchased the *William Robbins,* rechristened her the *Liberty,* and sent her to sea again with the same captain and crew. The commissioners in the United States also bought three other armed vessels: the former American revenue cutter *Independence* and the schooners *Brutus* and *Invincible*. These sleek, swift men of war terrorized the Mexican merchant marine and paralyzed its operations off the Texas coast. All of them took valuable prizes, filled with cargo consigned to the Mexican Army of Operations.

The Mexican government took to shipping supplies under fraudulent manifests, indicating the cargoes were bound for New Orleans. This did not save them; the Texans attacked every Mexican flag on the Gulf. However, some Mexican supplies did get through by sea to the army at Goliad. One Mexican ship was captured while lying in Cópano Bay by Isaac Burton and some twenty mounted Texans on June 2, 1836. Burton's men, unable to attack across water on horseback, seized a ship's boat, and rowed out to the ship and boarded her. Burton and his men went into Texas song and story as "The Horse Marines."

All in all, General Filisola in late April was very much in the position of Napoleon in Moscow in 1812. He was mired in mud, and angry Texans were now buzzing south to harass him. The dozen cavalrymen who had escaped from the San Jacinto helped destroy the morale of his army with their exaggerated tales of defeat and massacre in the north. Filisola was under orders to do nothing that might endanger Santa Anna's life. Although the Supreme Government repudiated the treaties Santa Anna made with Texas, the Italian general had no real choice but to withdraw to Mexico. He was on half-rations when the march began.

Most military historians, and Filisola himself, felt he was lucky to arrive south of the Rio Grande in good order by June 18. His men were half-naked, starving, and exhausted from the terrible march across the burning savannah from Goliad.

One final Mexican humiliation was that their President considered his life coequal with the cause of the Mexican nation, and he bartered on that basis. This was of course inherent in the monarchical form of government Santa Anna had installed. Although the Mexican Supreme Government— the Cabinet and Congress—invalidated his treaties on the grounds they were signed under duress, the executive authority was paralyzed. There was no leadership in Mexico to prosecute the war. By June, 1836, Texas had won *de facto* independence, although Texas' position with Mexico was analogous to that of Israel vis-à-vis the Arab states between 1948-1968. Mexico would not recognize Texas, or even admit officially its Republic existed, while it was powerless to change the fact of its existence.

Mexico suffered from overcentralization and the unwillingness of various leaders to act on their own initiative. The problem of the interim government in the Republic of Texas was the exact opposite. The convention at Washington-on-the-Brazos had not created a nation merely by declaring one.

The red sun over San Jacinto had hardly set before the Texas farmers in Sam Houston's army began to drift away. They were seeking their families and going home. They were warriors, but never soldiers; they were unpaid, they were raised only for the current emergency, and they had crops to get in. As had happened before, and would happen again, a citizen army had won battles, but it could not be used by its government as an instrument of policy during the peace. Within a few weeks, virtually every Texan private soldier, both volunteer and regular army man, had departed for his home.

The people themselves reestablished a sense of order and purpose quickly. The vast majority of fleeing refugees immediately turned around, before it was even certain the Mexicans were beaten. The real problem in Texas, ironically, now became one of controlling the "Texan" army, upon which the ultimate security of the country still rested. Houston fought the battle of San Jacinto with less than 1,000 men, but a month after Houston passed the command to Secretary of War Rusk and sailed to New Orleans, the army had grown to more than 2,000, despite the departure of the veterans. This army was wholly composed of American volunteers, all of whom had been promised land in return for service—as much as 320 acres for three months.

The government, now at Velasco, had no hard money, and almost no way of supplying this army. The Texans could no more live off the devastated land than the invading Mexicans. All provisions had to come in by water from New Orleans, and lack of credit, and some unfortunate bungling, delayed the arrival of food. What did arrive was not enough; the size of the army grew faster than army commissioners could anticipate. The news of San Jacinto caused a veritable rush into Texas by Americans.

By May, 1836, the army was going hungry, and its temper was growing short. The argument of patriotism was futile. These men were not Texas citizens, and· many of their officers or leaders were ambitious and disgruntled that they had lost an opportunity for glory on the Texas frontier. Tom Rusk did not really want the command, but took it as a favor to Sam Houston. He followed the retreating Filisola south to Victoria with a force that, in time-honored American fashion, was already holding mass meetings, denouncing him, and writing its grievances in insolent terms to President Burnet of Texas. Oddly, the matter that seemed to infuriate the volunteers most was that Santa Anna was going to be released, according to the treaties of May 14.

Burnet, on June 1, allowed Santa Anna to board the Texas warship *Invincible* at Velasco, with his secretary Caro and the faithful Colonel Almonte. Lorenzo de Zavala and Bailey Hardeman, Texas commissioners, were to sail with him. But Burnet held the ship until June 3, to give the commissioners final instructions. This delay was fatal. Indignation against the Mexican leader was high, and the arrival of two hundred American volunteers under one General Thomas Green on the steamship *Ocean* destroyed Burnet's initiative. Tom Green and some of his officers were determined to play at statecraft. They demanded that Santa Anna be taken back ashore, and, in the argument, actually threatened Burnet's life.

Burnet "stuck by his guns," as he said, with coolness and courage, reiterating that for Texas to violate its own treaty with Santa Anna would make the Republic contemptible before the world. He again stated the advantages Texas had gained by the treaty, but he was talking mainly to men who really wanted a continuation of the war. Finally, fearing riot and insurrection inspired by the armed Americans thronging Velasco, Burnet ordered Santa Anna removed from the *Invincible* for his own protection. Santa Anna, thinking he was to be shot at last, created a great scene, and had to be removed by force. He was taken ashore under heavy guard.

Burnet's position was worsened by the news that the Mexican upper house had repudiated Santa Anna's agreements, and because General Urrea, who was already in Matamoros, imprisoned three Texans sent under a Filisola passport and flag of truce. On June 17, Rusk wrote from Goliad that Urrea had crossed the Rio Grande with his army. This was untrue, but it caused great excitement and resentment against the distinguished prisoner at Velasco.

Rusk found himself unable to quell or control the army. President Burnet, feeling the resentment might be against the commander personally, replaced him with a genuine hero of San Jacinto, Mirabeau B. Lamar. But the army, in a mass meeting, refused to accept Lamar as its leader, and further, a plan was discussed to arrest Burnet and have him tried before an army tribunal. This last, however, was too much even for this motley array, and the notion died. President Burnet, pardonably hoping to get rid of his principal problem, wrote a letter encouraging the army to adopt Fannin's old plan: a march to Matamoros. The army failed to move and continued to clamor for its pay and rights.

In July, 1836, President Burnet called for a general election to be held the first Monday in September, to create a new Texas government. The Treasury notes issued by his administration were already as worthless as Continentals; by August 31, the Government of Texas was $1,250,000 in debt. Burnet planned to pass these problems on to his successor. In the meantime, he wrote to the Texas commissioners in New Orleans for God's sake to send him no more U. S. volunteers.

Santa Anna's captivity continued. In August, some loyal Mexicans tried to effect his release, but this attempt was thwarted, and Santa Anna suffered for it. He was moved frequently from place to place, and kept in leg-irons. He was frequently subjected to humiliations, and at times not even fed. His officers and men were treated similarly. The treatment of these soldiers was shameful by any standards, and has generally been ignored by American historians. Whatever indignities Santa Anna had earned, these were not due Almonte, his staff, or the common soldiers under the President's command. Many died in captivity, and all were eventually repatriated in poor condition.

In Texas, after a long, dusty summer of discontent, the man of the hour had become the man on horseback from San Jacinto. While Houston was convalescing in the United States, it had become more and more apparent that Texas had been saved in the spring by his splendid leadership, and nothing was more needed with the first cool winds of fall. Sam

Houston—major general, visionary, politician, President's friend—only Houston could control the army, the arising Texas politicos, and influence events in the United States. To the unhappiness of the old planter group, Houston was proposed for President of Texas.

Many of the oldtime Texans preferred Stephen Austin. But Austin was sick; he had spent almost all the past few years either in a Mexican prison or in the United States; he had worked wisely and well for Texas, but he had not been with the army when the final shots were fired. He was also badly tarred, in the newest immigrants' minds, with the most damaging of all words: pro-Mexican.

Burnet's proclamation of July 23, 1836, called on Texas to choose a President, Vice-President, fourteen senators, twenty-nine representatives, ratify the Constitution, and answer the question: should Texas seek annexation by the United States? The new government, with its mandate, was to assemble at the town of Columbia, on October 3.

Out of a total of 6,640 qualified votes, Austin received 587. The two men in the van at San Jacinto carried the day. Sam Houston was elected President with 5,119 votes, more than three-quarters of the whole. Mirabeau Buonaparte Lamar became Vice-President. The Constitution was ratified almost unanimously. The vote on the proposition to seek annexation was significant: it carried, 3,277 to 91.

The clamor for Houston to take the reins was so great that Burnet, gratefully, moved the appointed date for the inauguration ahead almost two months. As soon as the Congress met, it voted to make Houston President, "at four o'clock, this day," again moving ahead the ceremony. Thus Houston was called on to make an impromptu inaugural speech.

Houston spoke in a dignified manner, reciting recent history, referring strongly to the hope of union with the United States. Then, he unhooked his sword and passed it to the Speaker of the Texas House—the "emblem of his past office"—in a scene of tremendous emotion and to roaring applause. It was more than a mere symbolic act. Sam Houston was no more a militarist than Wellington; the army and armed conflict, in which he had twice almost lost his life, were to him nothing more than means, or tools, to win his dream. He rode in front of his army to extend America, just as Wellington fought at Waterloo to "preserve the England that produced such gentlemen as these."

There was a time and place for all great men, and Stephen Austin knew it. He accepted his eclipse with grace. Austin, in fact, much better understood the heart and mind of Sam Houston than the roaring crowds that cheered him now. Houston pursued no wild and aberrant star; like Austin, he wanted most of all the Americanization of the piece of earth that had seized his soul, the State of Texas.

Between them, the warrior and the diplomat, they had almost achieved it. A modified American flag waved over Columbia and the twenty-three counties that formed the enclave of Anglo-Texas, now the Republic of Texas—red, white, and blue, emblazoned with a single five-pointed star.

15

THE REPUBLIC

The final act in this great drama is now performed; the Republic of Texas is no more.
DR. ANSON JONES, PRESIDENT OF TEXAS, FEBRUARY 19, 1846

THE Republic of Texas was supposed to be ephemeral. The people of Texas voted overwhelming approval of union with the United States on the same ballot by which they elected the Republic's officers. The people of Texas had cultural, economic, political, and military reasons for seeking annexation, and obviously the United States had a tremendous strategic stake in Texas. Texas blocked American expansion to the Pacific, and a weak, unstable nation on American borders invited penetration by still-ambitious European powers. The Monroe Doctrine could not by any stretch of the imagination keep British influence out, if Britain chose to fish in Texas waters.

Sam Houston's republic was a straggling frontier community of less than forty thousand people; it was a series of plantations and farms carved out of the Southern forests along the river bottoms extending up from the Gulf, with an utterly colonial economy. Most Texans were subsistence farmers, with a little barter on the side. The planters exported their cotton against imported goods; the balance of trade was yet adverse. The largest towns were frontier outposts with mud streets and at most a few thousand assorted people. There was no money economy, nor any money. There were no banks or improved roads or organized schools. There was no industry—everything from pins to powder had to be imported from the United States. Over this sprawling community the government was only loosely organized. The Texans replaced the old *ayuntamientos* with governmental units they considered more comfortable, counties, but real government consisted primarily of sheriffs and justices of the peace. Texas barely approached the

247

basic requirements for statehood. It would take more than the accumulated political experience of a handful of capable men, and the traditions of the English-speaking peoples, to make it a viable sovereign nation.

The Lone Star flag flew proudly and perilously over Texas for ten years, but not through Texans' choice. The problem was the political situation that had developed within the past half-dozen years inside the United States.

President Adams had been prepared to buy Texas in the 1820's, and Jackson sent his first Minister to Mexico, Anthony Butler, with an obvious interest in obtaining the region. But by the middle 1830's Monroe's old worry, that further expansion of the nation westward might threaten its very existence, was proving ominously true. Suddenly, the question of annexation of Texas became inseparably linked with the whole question of Negro slavery in the United States.

On May 25, 1836, shortly after the news of San Jacinto was celebrated in Washington, and when petitions and resolutions to recognize Texan independence were pouring into Congress, John Quincy Adams suddenly denounced the Texas Revolution on the floor of the House. He stated the whole purpose of the revolution and ensuing war was "the reestablishment of slavery in territory where it had already been abolished through Mexican law" and attacked the President bitterly for sending General Gaines to the border "in defense of slavery." It was quite true that the Southern states wanted the entry of Texas to strengthen their minority in Congress vis-à-vis national affairs, and the Northern states desired to prevent any such reinforcement. But to let the whole question of the acquisition of an immense western territory turn on such a matter was, in restrospect, a very parochial view. It was one that Westerners like Houston and Jackson could hardly comprehend. They had very little ideology; they tended to see slavery as an economic problem, but above all, they believed in the expansion of the territory and power of their own race, and trusted it to find its moral solutions in good time. Houston and Jackson almost equally despised Northern abolitionists and Southern nullifiers; both threatened the greater Union. From the language they used, it appears that in 1836 Westerners, Southerners, and Northerners all had different concepts of what the American Union was all about. The problem transcended slavery, but slavery became the common emotional tool. The old South, where in 1820 the only antislavery societies in the country existed, began to defend what was a moral liability no one liked very much with incredible intransigence. The Northern abolitionists gradually began to mount an attack on the institution of slavery that could not be supported under the existing framework of the Union.

Adams' speech attacking Texas showed everyone, including the President, that annexation had become political dynamite. It was uproariously supported by most of the Northern press, and by Northern opinion generally. In the North, not only the Missouri Compromise but the idea of compromise itself was almost dead. One hope in the old South, and great fear in the North, was that Texas would open a great band of slave expansion through the Southwest. This opinion revealed an utter ignorance of geography: climate itself, and the Great Plains, made any such expansion of the cotton kingdom impossible. With Anglo-Texas along the Brazos, chattel slavery had reached its natural geographic limits in the United States.

While Texan agents lobbied for recognition and continued to press their resolution for annexation, the matter was deferred for the elections of 1836. Van Buren was Jackson's man, but he was elected by such a small majority that the lame-duck President was hamstrung. Jackson still wanted to recognize Texas, but Van Buren's friends argued now that any such move would damage Van Buren's administration before it began. The hope of immediate annexation of Texas was completely gone, after Adams' stand; the distinguished Massachusetts Congressman spoke against Texas almost every day of the summer of 1836, and even the question of recognition of Texas' independence was very much in doubt.

Jackson's agent in Texas, Henry Morfit, sounded the local situation out in August and September, 1836. Morfit reported back that Texas' best hope of continued independence lay in the "stupidity of the rulers of Mexico and the financial embarrassment of the Mexican government." Morfit was not impressed with Texas' prospects otherwise and advised the President to go slow. Jackson's Secretary of State, John Forsyth, was disturbed because Texas' referendum for annexation seemed to put the United States in a bad light. The quick vote for annexation seemed to show the whole revolution had been part of an expansionist plot. Forsyth advised Jackson not to recognize Texas, until Great Britain or some other major power did so first.

Under these circumstances, Jackson's message to Congress in December, 1836, was cool toward Texas and proposed a delay in recognition. This dismayed the Texas government, just as it must have puzzled the Mexicans, who did not understand the terrible split in opinion within the United States. Relations with Mexico were badly strained. The Mexican minister, Eduardo de Gorostiza, circulated a paper condemning Jackson for dispatching General Gaines to the Sabine. This pamphlet both broke diplomatic courtesy and angered Jackson. Gorostiza picked up his credentials and went home, but the Mexican government supported his stand. However, there was no danger of a real war with Mexico at this time; the government was in collapse, the treasury was bankrupt, and the nation was impotent. The United States had nothing to fear from Mexican anger, but this was not clearly seen in some Washington quarters.

Hoping to break the diplomatic impasse, Houston and Stephen Austin decided to send Santa Anna to Washington. The Mexican dictator himself had come up with a long-visioned plan, by which the United States and Mexico would establish a new border, on the Rio Grande. In return for a cash payment, the United States would be free to annex Texas. This plan, which was denounced both in Mexico and the United States, had enormous merit, for both countries. It might have avoided another war. But Santa Anna had no real powers now to negotiate, which Jackson knew, and further, Jackson was in no position politically to absorb Texas. The capitals of both nations, in 1836–1837, singularly lacked historical vision.

Santa Anna arrived in Washington on January 17, 1837. He was received courteously, spent six fruitless days in discussions, and then sailed from Norfolk for Vera Cruz. Jackson offered to entertain the Mexican's offer to sell Texas provided it came through regular diplomatic channels, which was impossible, and he also tried to include California in the deal. Santa Anna departed owing some $2,000 in expenses, which the Texas government eventually reimbursed.

On April 19, 1837, Anastasio Bustamante again became President of Mexico, assuring a new hard line. Any hope of continued negotiations died here. Santa Anna, discredited by his defeat in Texas, retired to Jalapa to await a better day.

The Texans in Washington swallowed their frustration and tried to keep in Jackson's favor. Jackson refused to put direct pressure on Congress to recognize Texas. His term was running out, and he had little real power. But from the sidelines Jackson kept up a devious game. Earlier Stephen Austin wrote to a Washington correspondent that if the United States was not prepared to extend aid and recognition, Texas might have to look elsewhere, Jackson turned this letter over to the Congress, with a notation that further stalling might alienate Texas forever. Austin and Sam Houston were to find this argument the most effective one they had, both in securing recognition and eventual annexation. Neither Austin nor Houston had any desire to become involved with Britain, quite the opposite, but only the threat of concessions to Great Britain, and the specter of a new British colony in the middle of America, seemed to have any effect on the antiexpansionist Northeast. Houston continued the policy after Austin's death.

A resolution to recognize Texas floundered in both the Senate and the House for months. Representative Waddy Thompson of South Carolina and Senator Robert J. Walker of Mississippi labored to pass the measure, which had been tabled as late as February 26, 1837, by a House vote of 98 to 86. The resolution was watered down, in the House version. It now merely provided money for the sending of "a diplomatic agent to Texas whenever the President of the United States may receive satisfactory evidence that Texas is an independent power and shall deem it expedient to appoint such a minister." The original words "the independent Republic of Texas" were stricken out. The measure was a wonderful example of American euphemism and political compromise, to say nothing of passing the buck.

Even then, it passed the House only because most members either thought it would die in the Senate, or be implemented at the discretion of Martin Van Buren, who was neutral and would do nothing. Pacifying the Texas lobby with what was considered a "cheap vote," many House members lukewarm to Texas voted for it. It carried 121 to 76.

Through some dazzling political footwork, Walker added the Texas resolution to a general civil appropriation bill before the Senate on March 2. This rider survived an attempt to knock it out, 24-24. This Senate action sent the bill to the President for signature on Friday, March 3, less than twenty-four hours before he left office. Jackson signed it.

Then, he drafted a message to the Senate. He wrote he now deemed it proper and expedient to acknowledge the independence of Texas, and he nominated Alcée La Branche of Louisiana to be chargé d'affaires to Texas. Jackson finished this message late on the evening of March 3. Thus, not with a flourish but with neat footwork, was history made.

Jackson requested the Texan agents to come to the White House, for "the pleasure of a glass of wine." At midnight, the President of the United States raised his glass: "Gentlemen, the Republic of Texas." The Texans, William Wharton and Memucan Hunt, drank to that. Jackson had another toast: "The President of the Republic of Texas."

Jackson was a frontiersman; he never forgot a friend. It is perhaps significant and revealing that President Jackson, "King Andrew," spent his last hours in office talking about Texas, and reminiscing about one of "his boys, who had beaten it back and made good." Jackson capped his career in the White House by recognizing Texas. Banks and gentry and current ideology might come and go, nullifiers and abolitionists and all their accursed quarreling kind fade into dust—the land was wide and went on forever, and Jackson's America was still pointed toward the western sea.

The news of U.S. recognition caused celebrations throughout Texas, but it left Sam Houston with all his enormous problems intact. The first, and most pressing, was not the still-existent state of war with Mexico but the Texas standing army, now completely composed of a horde of ill-fed and intractable American volunteers. The army had rejected Mirabeau Lamar; when Lamar resigned his commission to become Vice-President, the army chose Felix Huston as its chief. Huston was a military adventurer of the old filibuster stripe. To get rid of him, Sam Houston appointed a capable new officer, Albert Sidney Johnston, to the supreme command. Felix Huston not only refused to go, but he seriously wounded Johnston in a trumped-up duel. Then, Huston went to Columbia to lobby in the Texas Congress for his bright new plan: a march on Matamoros, Mexico.

Now, Sam Houston was aided by American experience and tradition. He solved his army problem the same way George Washington did, two generations before. While Huston was away, the President furloughed the army with the exception of some 600 men. He could not discharge it, because he could not meet the arrears in pay. But he gave all the men a furlough, and never bothered to call them back. This may have exposed Texas to Mexican danger, but it effectively got rid of the threat of military dictatorship, as Huston's clamoring army faded away.

The Lone Star State was sovereign, but Houston found it $1,250,000 in debt. The financial figures for the revolution may have seemed more those of a corporate business than an emerging nation, but the money trouble was serious. Houston was able to feed his rump army now only by personally signing government notes. Henry Smith, the Texas Secretary of the Treasury, was in an incredible position: he could not perform his duties because he had no official stationery, and there was no money in the Treasury to buy any. Most local officials were being paid in kind, and the proliferation of offices required now by a new national government strained the resources of twenty-three counties beyond endurance. The fact that many officers served out of patriotism, without pay, has sometimes been overlooked.

Houston, with the vote for annexation of September, 1836, considered his mandate called for him to damp the war with Mexico, avoid Indian trouble on the frontier, and try to get Texas into the United States. These aims, and his finances, required him to follow a quiet, conservative policy.

Texas formally claimed the Rio Grande as its southern boundary in 1836, and this meant no hope of a settlement with Mexico. Historically, the Mexican counterclaim of the Nueces as the Texas boundary was correct; the Nueces, not the Rio Grande, had been the boundary between the province of Texas and the Mexican state of Tamaulipas, formerly Nuevo Santander. No Anglo-Texans lived south of the Nueces, but for that matter, only a few Mexicans lived north of the Rio Grande. The land was empty. The only real merit to the Texans' claim was that the Rio Grande was a much better defined boundary than the tiny Nueces, which looped up into Comanche country northwest of Béxar and dribbled out, but despite that, they held it vehemently and were not likely to give it up. Many intelligent Mexicans saw that Anglo-Texas was now an undigestible nut, and gone forever, but the claim for the Rio Bravo put national honor to new strains.

Mexico refused to recognize Texan independence, and a formal state of war went on, although for some years there was no fighting. This state of war held back Texan settlement at Goliad and Refugio, and even San Antonio remained outside the normal Anglo-Texan sphere. Texas ruled the settlement at San Antonio, but few Anglo-Texans lived there. There was only a tiny garrison, and now and then a Texas magistrate arrived.

White settlers, after 1836, were rapidly spreading up the Brazos and Colorado, and a steady stream of immigration was demolishing the wilderness across the northern part of the country. This movement was impinging on the settled Texas Indians: the remnants of the Caddoans, now a border tribe, the Wichitas, Tonkawas, and the Cherokees, Kickapoos, and others who had been pushed into Texas by being driven out of the United States.

The Cherokees, a powerful tribe, were particularly restless and frightened. They had been pushed all the way from the mountains of Carolina and Tennessee, and now they, a forest and mountain people, were up against the Great Plains with nowhere to go. Whites were chopping the woods down and building cabins on the edges of their last refuge; Mexican agents went among them, talking war against the hated Americans. Houston was worried about this imminent Indian war. He submitted a bill that would have guaranteed the Cherokees title to their Texas lands. The Texas Congress angrily rejected it, but Houston, keeping state forces out of Indian country, was able to avert a serious war. The Kickapoos, aided by some Mexicans, took the warpath in the summer of 1838 under a Mexican agent, Vicente Córdova. Tom Rusk stamped this rebellion out with a force of hastily raised volunteers, while the Cherokees held aloof. The Cherokees' self-restraint did them no good; although they were a remarkably peaceful and civilized tribe of Amerinds, in Texans' minds they were merely marauding red men, standing in the way of rightful, Anglo-American progress. Houston, who had lived among Cherokees, wanted to protect them, but rather sadly, he knew the Indians' days were numbered. All he could do was hold off bloodshed so long as he was President.

Despite Houston's innate conservatism, the government went further and further in debt. Houston was forced to spend some $2,000,000, and revenues in no way matched this. Texas' only productive tax was a tariff, ranging from 1 percent on bread and flour to 50 percent luxuries like silk. Such levies as tonnage fees, the poll tax, business taxes, and license or land fees raised only small amounts; the direct property tax was virtually uncollectable. Texans did not like taxes. Even much of the taxes or fees collected were returned as audited drafts or canceled claims against the government, so Henry Smith's Treasury stayed bare. The only substantial money that arrived was a loan of $457,380 from the Bank of the United States in Pennsylvania; efforts to borrow the $5,000,000 Houston needed were fruitless. In the end, Houston did what every government in such a situation did, although everyone knew the solution's inherent folly. The Government of Texas in 1837 started printing paper money, in the form of promissory notes. At first, these notes held their value very well, but with the second issue, in 1838, they depreciated to about seventy cents on the dollar.

Besides keeping the war with Mexico damped and the Indians quiet, Houston's foreign policy was to continue to seek annexation by the United States. Memucan Hunt, Minister to Washington, was ordered to press the matter, and on August 4, 1837, Hunt formally approached the government of the United States. Forsyth, still Secretary of State, made it clear he felt treaty obligations with Mexico, by which Texas had been forever renounced, prevented any such act. Still, a bill was introduced in Congress in early 1838. The matter was brought to a boil, while Van Buren, lacking both Jackson's powers and skills, seemed to hope it would go away. John

Quincy Adams made himself Texas' foremost villain, by speaking against annexation every morning session of Congress from June 16 to July 7, 1838. Congress finally adjourned without action. Houston, now realizing that the honor of Texas as a sovereign nation was at stake, ordered Dr. Anson Jones, Hunt's successor, formally to withdraw the petitition of annexation. This was done, ratified by the Texas Congress, and the matter died. This rejection meanwhile built an increasingly powerful anti-American party in Texas, now headed by Mirabeau B. Lamar.

Lamar began to talk of Texas building its own empire in the West, if need be, in enmity and opposition to the United States. There were discussions among ambitious, burning-eyed men along the Brazos. If the United States was going to let the slavery question halt it at the Sabine, then the far Pacific might fall to another, more vigorous American Republic rising in the West. Sam Houston despised this talk. But under the constitution he could not succeed himself, nor could he find any Texas politician of sufficient stature to oppose Lamar. Houston's choice to succeed himself in the election of 1838 was Peter Grayson, but Grayson committed suicide before election day. Lamar ran on a platform of Texan greatness and future glory. He was elected President almost unanimously and carried the Congress along with him.

There were no true political parties in Texas, but the old division between the conservative planters, the Peace party, and the more warlike radicals, the War party, continued. Houston had selected his cabinet to bridge the split, with Austin, a conservative, as Secretary of State, and Smith, a radical, his Secretary of the Treasury. But Austin died in December, 1836, worn out at the age of forty-three. This left Houston supported by almost no one of stature. The planter group in Texas was far less interested in national politics, on the whole, than the adventurous lawyers pouring in from the United States. The radical, or expansionist group, increased daily.

Mirabeau Buonaparte Lamar was inaugurated as President of Texas in December, 1838. In his first speech, he revealed a new policy: no more of Houston's pennypinching and conservative caution, no more of Houston's wheedling after the United States. Lamar inherited a basically unstable situation: increasingly restive Indians on the edges of Anglo-Texas, a smolderingly hostile Mexico that refused to end hostilities to the south. Houston had let these problems hang fire, trying to avoid further bloodshed with Mexico and making promises to the Indians he could not keep. His assumption and hope was that when Texas fulfilled its destiny as he saw it and became part of the United States, Washington, not the straggling, bankrupt Republic between the Brazos and the Colorado, would deal with the Indians and Mexico.

In contrast, Lamar considered his own programs much more realistic. They were, in simplest terms, based on the idea that Texas had to fend for itself. He felt that the Mexican government should be given a full chance to negotiate a boundary and a peace with Texas, and if it did not, then the Mexicans should be brought to their senses by knocking them to their knees. The Indians Lamar considered merely trespassing vermin on Texas soil. Because of his outright hostility to Indians, Lamar has been often harshly regarded by American historians. But Lamar invented nothing—the notion that Indians were tenants at will, without inherent title to American soil, and that white men might dispossess them without formal legal action was already imbedded in American thought and practice. They were policies that already had acquired the legitimacy of two hundred years. Lamar, with the full agreement of his Secretary of War, Albert Sidney Johnston, and Indian commissioner, Bonnell, merely enunciated them without hypocrisy.

It had been established again and again in American history that the government had no powers to prevent white encroachment on Indian lands, and if the Indians resisted, the government owed the settlers protection. Sam Houston was one of the few great Americans who tried, not to give the Amerinds a reservation or treaty lands, but a legal title to their soil under Anglo-Saxon common law.

The attitudes of the majority of Texans, who violently opposed this, were essentially no different from the attitudes of the men who earlier conquered Massachusetts. Many of the people who denounced Mirabeau Lamar stood on ground where the bones of their forefathers' Indian victims had long moldered; only time had given that conquest its legitimacy.

"If peace can be obtained only by the sword, let the sword do its work," Lamar stated in his inaugural address, to thunderous applause. It was an American philosophy that neither began nor ended with Texas' President Lamar.

Lamar advocated pressure against the Mexicans, war against the Indians, and, sometimes overlooked because it was not implemented, a policy of education and development within the state. Lamar did not look to Washington, and if his programs were impossibly ambitious, he caught a part of every Texan's heart.

Here, in the third year of the Republic, Texas history took its essential 19th-century pattern, and it also began to fragment. It could no longer be followed as a steady stream. The pattern of immigration into and consolidation of Anglo-Texas continued, but meanwhile, Anglo-Texas began to expand along a genuine frontier of war, against the Indian west and against the Mexican south. Virtually all Texan historians have seen Texas history in terms of a long, three-cornered conflict. The folkloric historians, such as Walter Prescott Webb, have seen this most clearly of all: Anglo-Texas, marching out of its mild, rich-soil Brazos bottoms and southern, watered forests, was at continual war with a hostile civilization in the savannahs of the south; in savage conflict with the most formidable Amerinds Americans had yet faced; finally, though not least, locked in an endless struggle against a rough and arid and blazing land such as no Anglo-American had tried to settle before. Each mile toward the Rio Grande, each step up the endless rocky plateaus, Texans left their blood, bones, and blasted dreams.

Similar dramas were enacted in other parts of America. But nowhere else was the fight so vicious, nor did it last so long. In every other state, the true frontier was ephemeral. In most, there were water and wood, and the dangerous Amerinds were removed before real settlement began. Even the brutal Kentucky frontier was of short duration, though it put a lasting mark on the men who continued westward. The savage years lasted hardly a decade; what was called the "frontier years" was really a period of settlement and development—cutting the country down to size, implanting American law and civilization.

In Texas the slow, steady advance of the farmer and the homesteader struck up against a land where the Amerinds rode horseback and the rain ran out. Here, for two full generations, the frontier wavered, now forward, now back, locked in bitter battle. Equally dangerous Amerinds were engaged in distant areas, such as the Dakotas and Arizona, but there was one enormous difference. No Americans farmed, or took their families by the thousands into those territories until the army had pacified or driven the Indians out. In Texas, solely, was there a clash of cultures between the English- and Spanish-speaking peoples, which in Texas enhanced the consciousness of race. In Texas, in the 1830's and 1840's, when the great bulk of the American people were still east of the Mississippi, the Anglo-American Far West began. Here, Americans first adapted to a new land, and eventually carried newly learned values, whether toward Mexicans or toward cattle, to New Mexico and other states. Here, the Anglo-Celt vanguard fought some of its greatest battles and formed its last great enclave, with its value system adapted to a broader frontier but otherwise intact.

The human hallmarks of most true frontiers, the armed society with its almost theatrical codes and courtesies, its incipient feudalism, its touchy independence and determined self-reliance, its—exaggerated as it seemed to more crowded cultures—individual self-importance, and its tribal territoriality, not only flourished but became a way of life. The Texans came closest to creating, in America, not a society but a people, like the peoples who had come before them.

It was always a mistake to ascribe the notorious Texas chauvinism, so misunderstood and laughed at in other parts of America, to the brief ten-year flying of the Lone Star flag. Neither the Republic nor the Confederacy nor even the Union totally captured the 19th-century Texas mind. Governments came and went; some hindered, some helped. But Texan patriotism was never based on concepts of government or on ideas. It grew out of the terrible struggle for the land. Significantly, Hispanic and European observers have continually called the true Texan—the descendant and inheritor of the frontier experience—the most "European," or territorial, of

Americans. The Texan's attitudes, his inherent chauvinism and the seeds of his belligerence, sprouted from his conscious effort to take and hold his land. It was the reaction of essentially civilized men and women thrown into new and harsh conditions, beset by enemies they despised. The closest 20th-century counterpart is the State of Israel, born in blood in another primordial land.

The territoriality of Texans—the feeling for place and tribe—and the attitudes this engendered have sometimes been misinterpreted by other Americans, probably for psychological reasons. The Texans in the 19th century did not create a "usable past," or one that buttressed 20th-century American mainstream thought. The Texans emerged with a "blood memory," in the Texan writer Katherine Anne Porter's memorable phrase.

The ceremonial flying of six flags—Spanish, French, Mexican, Texan, Confederate, and American—over modern Texas, so puzzling to visitors, is an almost conscious symbolism: flags change, the land remains. If the American Manhattanite has almost forgotten he lives on soil, has shed his history, and is shaped more by social pressures than a sense of territory, the Texan can never, even in his cities, forget or be free of the brooding immensity of his land. His national myths were more influenced by the Alamo and the burden of a century of a wild frontier than concepts conceived at Philadelphia. Tragically, next to memories of the struggle for freedom from Mexico are the smoldering memories of a long and losing struggle against the encroachments of cultures from other regions of the United States. If the Texan became the most "European" of Americans, it was because in his history he has been both a conscious conqueror, and a member of a vanquished race.

Under President Lamar, a series of wars or campaigns began against the Indians. Militia, regular Texas army forces, and local bands called "ranging companies" were employed; in one campaign in east Texas, more than 1,000 soldiers were mobilized.

Texas put heavy pressure upon the Penatekas, or southern Comanches, in the San Antonio region, but the main blow fell against the border Indians who still occupied large fringes of territory between the Comanches and the whites. These were broken, dominated, and forced back. Above all, the Cherokees and several other "immigrant" tribes, who had moved into east Texas after being dispossessed in the United States, were attacked and driven either into Oklahoma or Arkansas.

The campaigns against the Comanches were justifiable, for Comanches had begun raiding Anglo-Texan settlements. The moves against the inoffensive Cherokees, however, were more in the nature of a land-grab. The mass evictions of the remaining agricultural Indians in east Texas were carried out for the same reasons, and with the same injustice, as they had been done under the Jackson Administration to the east.

In these operations, a large number of whites, and many more Indians were killed; the warfare was bitter, bloody, and brutal all along the borders of Anglo-Texas.

However, these wars expelled virtually all the immigrant Indians from the United States and opened up all east Texas to white settlement. They pushed the Comanches back in the area north of Bexar, and bought a period of peace along the frontier. As the historian Richardson wrote, the justice of Lamar's campaigns "may be questioned, but their effectiveness is beyond dispute."

These Indian wars cost the Texas treasury $2,500,000, however, and Lamar, like Houston, was unable to negotiate any respectable loan. Lamar proposed to found a Bank of Texas, but there was no money to fund it. More and more paper money was printed, more than $3,000,000 in "red back" notes, which soon fell to around a dime on the dollar.

Lamar did try to make peace with Mexico. At this time France was blockading Mexican ports in an attempt to collect the claims of French citizens, and the old Federalist-Centralist quarrel caused civil strife in several Mexican states. But Lamar's offer of $5,000,000 for recognition and acceptance of the Rio Grande boundary was not accepted. Mexico, however, kept negotiations alive during 1839 and 1840 for one reason: the small Texas navy, under Edwin Moore, was now at sea, and a threat to Mexican commerce. Great Britain then agreed to mediate between the two powers, and signed a treaty with Texas to that effect. But despite British pressure on Mexico, Mexico refused to negotiate seriously. James Webb, the Texas emissary, was not even received. At this point, in 1841, Lamar resolved to reopen the war.

Lamar signed an alliance with the Mexican state of Yucatán, which was for some months engaged in a civil war with the Supreme Government. This conflict dribbled away as Yucatán rejoined Mexico, but now hostilities had been taken up again. Lamar, who talked openly of a Republic of Texas that reached to the Pacific Ocean, dispatched an expedition to the Upper Rio Grande, to take possession of Sante Fe. There was a considerable belief in Texas that the Mexican inhabitants of New Mexico would welcome it.

Instead, this expedition, after marching across 1,300 miles of burning plains, suffering Indian attacks, hunger, thirst, and exhaustion, was easily captured by the Mexican army when it reached New Mexico. The survivors of the 300-odd soldiers who left Texas were brutally chained and marched deep into Mexico. They were held in the Mexican fortress of Perote until April, 1842. The Spanish had learned some centuries earlier that troops could not march at will across the High Plains; now, the Texans, who had never explored the region, had to learn their own lessons, painfully. The province of New Mexico was weak enough; the Texas government had claimed everything east of the Rio Grande—but the territory was effectively beyond reach.

It was also easier, in the south, to declared the war reopened with

Mexico than to carry the war to it.

Lamar's influence defeated a plan to settle 8,000 French colonists along the Rio Grande in the south. These people were to be imported to form a buffer, much as Mexicans had imported Americans to place a wall between themselves and the Indians. The scheme, however, would have created a semiautonomous French state within lands claimed by Texas. Sam Houston favored it; but Lamar, perhaps clearer-sighted, felt the all-important unity of Anglo-Texas would be breached. Meanwhile, the declared hostilities languished, since there were no Texans in contact with, or within 300 miles of, the southern Rio Grande.

Lamar's second great success, besides quelling the Indians, was that his exercise of Texan sovereignty secured some foreign recognition. During Houston's administration, Great Britain failed to acknowledge Texas, for three reasons: Texas was proclaimed Negro slave territory, and sentiment in Britain was opposed to slavery; British interests had heavy investments in Mexico, which Lord Palmerston hesitated to alienate; and finally, the British government supposed Texas would soon enter the United States. Ironically, Lamar's aggressions and the simultaneous withdrawal of the annexation petition quickened European interest and strengthened the acceptance of Texan sovereignty. Lamar was acting like the ruler of an Anglo-Saxon republic, as both the French and British governments understood one. In 1839, assisted by French exasperation with Mexican debts, Texas signed a treaty of recognition with France. In 1840, a treaty with The Netherlands followed. Late the same year, Palmerston became convinced Texas might be here to stay. Three British-Texas treaties were signed: recognition, commerce and navigation, and, as a Texas concession, a convention permitting the Royal Navy to suppress slave-running on the Texas coast. This last was a sop to British antislavery opinion. Very few blacks were being brought in by sea; they were being purchased or imported from the United States.

At the close of Lamar's presidency, Britain, France, Belgium, and The Netherlands had recognized, or had commercial treaties, with the Republic of Texas. None of these nations, however, was willing to grant a loan to Mirabeau Lamar.

The capital of Texas had been moved to the town of Houston, then just being laid out, in the last days of 1836. But Houston provided no better site than the old Columbia. In 1839, a commission appointed to study the question of a new site selected a location on the Colorado, almost in the center of the claimed territory of the country. Lamar moved his government to this place, which was named Austin. By 1840 this new capital held almost nine hundred people, but the location, whatever the long-term political implications, had great disadvantages. Austin lay far beyond the frontier of Anglo settlement, 70-odd miles north of San Antonio, and it was on the edge of Comanche country. The combination of being remote from Anglo-Texas and near the Indians made many members of the Texas government unwilling even to travel there; they lacked the President's compulsion to look and go West.

As Lamar neared the end of his term, in 1841, his expenditures and wars had revived the old Peace party, the conservative planter class. Their candidate was Sam Houston, who was now remarried, a member of the Baptist Church, and a firm advocate of governmental economy in all things. The campaign, in Texas style, however, was fought not on ideology but on the issues of which candidate was the greatest coward, drunkard, or public thief. On these terms, the War party candidate, the former President David G. Burnet, was defeated easily by the hero of San Jacinto, who, after an interim, could legally be President again. Edward Burleson, another war hero, was elected Vice-President, on an independent ticket.

President Houston brought a planter congress in with him, and this 6th Texas Congress turned off the public tap. In a series of acts dozens of offices were abolished, salaries of officials were reduced to mere honoraria, the army was reduced to a few companies of Rangers, and the Texas navy, an expensive proposition, was ordered sold. Commodore Moore, who protested the ignominious auction of the four ships that had served Texas so well, both in war and diplomacy, was first declared a pirate and then dishonorably discharged by President Houston. However, the navy was never sold. The citizens of Galveston, who had fallen in love with the Lone Star flag on the high seas, held mass meetings. When the ships put into port, citizens threw armed guards around them, and the orders of the Republic could only have been carried out with bloodshed. For three years this impasse remained. When Texas, in 1845, became a state, the Lone Star ensign was replaced by the Stars and Stripes; the navy was transferred intact to the service of the United States.

Houston's congress repealed all Lamar's currency and banking laws. The issuance of new money was tightly controlled; only about $200,000 was printed, in "exchequer bills." In his second three-year term, Houston spent less than $600,000, and government accounts began to resemble those of a retail store. Thus, in some measure, passed the glory of Lamar's Republic.

Houston, if he had not been the undeniable hero of San Jacinto, would have been branded as an Indian-lover. He had tried to save the Cherokees, and he had a generic sympathy with all Indians. In return, most tribes respected Houston. He was able to sign treaties with the Wacos, Tawakonis, and southern Comanches. These tribes now continued to provide a buffer between the settlers and the more warlike bands on the Great Plains, and for some years Indian warfare ceased. Houston's success here, however, was caused more by the fact that white settlement had not yet filled the vacuum Lamar's campaigns had made than by any Texan acceptance of Indian rights.

Houston's most serious war was a feud that broke out in east Texas between newcomers and early squatters near the old Neutral Ground. This region dissolved in lawlessness and anarchy. After several notorious public shootings and murders, between the "Regulators" and "Moderators"—names carried all the way from Appalachia—Houston turned out the militia and put the Republic back in control. Many private feuds, growing out of these times, went on. Lasting feuds, by 1844, had become a feature of Texas life; they were to mar the politics of the state throughout the century.

However, Mirabeau Lamar had succeeded at last in arousing Mexico, and Houston inherited the minor whirlwind the Buonaparte of Texas had stirred up. Santa Anna had bided his time and was again President of Mexico. Fired by the belief that Mexico, to keep any international belief in its sovereignity over Texas and to prevent further raids like the one on Santa Fe, had to do something, Santa Anna sent an expedition north across the Rio Grande, in the spring of 1842. This was not an attempt to reconquer Texas; it was a show of force. The Mexican army easily captured San Antonio, Refugio, and Goliad—this time unopposed.

The new invasion re-created the scenes of the Runaway Scrape in these outermost parts of what was then called West Texas. Houston moved the government from Austin to his namesake, Houston, but citizens of Austin prevented removal of the archives, in a farce that came to be called the Archive War. The Mexicans retired south after only a few days; no damage was done; but the Texas militia swarmed again toward San Antonio. However, Sam Houston had no intention of reliving the grim and deadly days of '36. He did send agents to the United States to seek assistance—this fitted with his long-range plans—but he vigorously vetoed his Congress' declaration of war, on the grounds that the financial measures provided to support it were inadequate.

Santa Anna refused to let the war die. Again, in September, 1842, General Adrian Woll with a thousand men reentered San Antonio. Woll caught the Texas district court in session, and this time he took 67 Texans prisoners. These included all male Anglo citizens in the town. Again, however, the Mexicans only remained a few days, then retreated with their captives. Two brushes were fought with Texas militia. In one fight, at the Salado, Matthew Caldwell and John C. Hays shot up the Mexicans badly in a brushy bottom, forcing Woll to back off with about one hundred dead. Woll's force caught another group of Texans, about fifty men under Captain Dawson, in the open. In this battle the Mexicans prudently remained beyond rifle range and killed all but 15 of Dawson's force with artillery fire. The survivors were added to the bag taken at San Antonio.

Houston was now forced to call for volunteers; he ordered a descent upon the Rio Grande. Houston still did not intend to make war, but he had to do something to allay public opinion. By November, 1842, 750 men were assembled in San Antonio. This army marched to Laredo, north of the Rio Grande but a Mexican town, and captured it on December 8. Here, some of the men left the army and went home. Somervell, the Texan general, marched south along the river for a few miles as a demonstration, then ordered the army back to Gonzales. He was working under Houston's orders, and even the army suspected he did not intend to make war.

Some 300 men were infuriated by this retreat and refused to go. They elected a new colonel, Fisher, and crossed the border, taking the town of Mier. Here, after a desperate battle, the force was rounded up by the Mexican General Ampudia, on December 26. The captives were started for Mexico City; they tried a break, and in retaliation, after the typical lottery, they were decimated—one man in ten was shot. Those left were incarcerated in Perote prison, with the survivors of the expedition to Santa Fe. After some months, they were released, largely due to the efforts of Waddy Thompson, Texas' old friend in the U.S. Congress, who was now U.S. Minister to Mexico.

Another expedition, authorized by Houston, under Snively attempted to raid the commerce passing between Missouri and Santa Fe. This march provoked a serious incident with the United States. The Mexican mule trains were guarded by United States troops, on soil claimed both by the Republic of Texas and the United States. Although the attack did take place on Texas soil, Snively's men were captured and disarmed by the United States Army, and sent ingloriously home. On Houston's protest, reimbursement for the arms was made.

During these months Houston consistently attempted to damp the war; he refused to respond to public demands to attack Mexico. There was no doubt that world opinion, everywhere except in South America and the United States northeast, favored Texas, but Houston used this favorable opinion primarily for propaganda purposes. He asked Britain and France to "require of Mexico either the recognition of the Independence of Texas, or to make war upon her according to the rules established and universally recognized by civilized nations." Santa Anna's decimation of Texas "pirates" backfired, like his executions at Goliad. Under some pressure from abroad, Santa Anna offered Texas a peace treaty, in return for the recognition of inherent Mexican sovereignty. Houston might have taken this, had his goal been anything less than union with the United States. Houston realized that this would block annexation for years, if not forever. Santa Anna, of course, was seeking two things: a way to satisfy Mexican notions of national honor, and at the same time, without recovering Texas, to keep the United States from arriving on the Rio Grande.

Houston, wisely, did not reject the overture, but used it to proclaim a truce, on June 14, 1843. Mexico and Texas negotiated, with British mediation. These talks solved nothing, but they did give an excuse for a general armistice—not recognition or peace—which went into effect in early 1844. Houston was stalling, because the annexation question had risen again.

The great irony of these years was that while Houston never wanted anything but annexation and worked both directly and deviously for it, it was actually Mirabeau Lamar who knocked open the door. The Texas Congress had claimed not only the Rio Grande but passed a resolution claiming the Californias as Texas soil. This was not so ridiculous as it sounded, since the western boundaries of Texas were as yet undefined by international or any other kind of law. The Republic, on fighting free of Mexico, was in a position to claim anything outside of U.S. territory in the West it could take or hold. Houston vetoed the Californias bill, but it was repassed over his veto.

Lamar's unsuccessful Santa Fe expedition, not Houston's moderation, had aroused new interest in the United States. The public was titillated by the journal of an American newspaperman who joined it for a "vacation." The sufferings of the expedition and the brutalities of the Mexicans were recounted in heroic terms. In Washington, where there was already growing interest in the Pacific coast, and which was involved in a dispute with Great Britain over Oregon, the government was chilled by the concept of an aggressive Texas, expanding west. It was one thing to write off the Brazos slave country; it was something else to relinquish the entire Southwest, from sea to sea. Jackson and many other far-seeing men already felt the United States must acquire California and Oregon and thus be forever strategically secure in the hemisphere.

Further, Lamar's vigorous assertion of sovereignty, carrying the flag west and showing it with the Texas Navy on the high seas, gained him the great-power recognition of Britain and France. This roused new American fears: if Texas lacked the power to dominate the American West, its commercial treaties with Great Britain seemed to allow British influence its return. Captain Charles Elliot, the British chargé d'affaires, did not trust Sam Houston and suspected he was being used as a cat's-paw, but still the British worked to gain influence where they could.

This fear of British penetration—a Texas allied with Great Britain, disputing possession of the Far West, created certain nightmares—caused President Tyler to swallow legality and open negotiations for annexation, on October 16, 1843. Mexico had still not surrendered Texas, and the United States was still bound by treaty obligations, but it simply could not afford to leave a vacuum for British power to fill. Houston cannily now played coy. He refused to let negotiations proceed until he had the assurance of American protection. He got this. There was a growing feeling in many Washington quarters that strategic considerations overrode domestic politics or even the danger of war with Mexico.

On April 12, 1844, the Texans Isaac Van Zandt and J. Pinckney Henderson signed a treaty of annexation with John C. Calhoun, by which Texas would become a Territory of the United States.

The U.S. Senate, however, lacked the Secretary of State's concern for dominant strategy. On June 8, the Senate rejected the treaty, through a strange alliance of antislavery men and Southerners who demanded full statehood for Texas now. Another factor in this defeat was the imminence of the national elections. Few Senators were sure of public opinion on Texas.

This put the question squarely into the Presidential campaign, where two of the leading contenders, Henry Clay and Martin Van Buren, hoped it would never appear. Clay, the Whig, could not support annexation; he would lose too many Whig votes in the North. Van Buren, trying for a comeback in the Presidency, chose wrong, and cut his political throat. The leading Democrat contender for the nomination, he tried to make a deal with Clay on Texas, to keep it out of the campaign. This lost him Jacksonian support; Andrew Jackson, who was still a power, and the Western expansionists threw their support to a virtual unknown, James Knox Polk, of Tennessee.

Polk was a friend of Sam Houston; in fact, he had succeeded to Houston's old seat in the House. He was a Jacksonian through and through, and "King Andrew," now rapidly failing, managed his whole campaign. Polk won the Democratic nomination. He went on to assail the quibbling Clay, who probably wanted the Presidency far too much. Polk, who never wanted it at all but took it as part of a plan of dominant Jacksonian policy, attacked on two issues: Texas and Oregon ("Fifty-Four Forty or Fight"). His running mate, George Dallas of Pennsylvania, backed annexation.

There is some evidence the American Anti-Slavery Society overplayed its hand. William Lloyd Garrison roared that "All who would sympathise with that pseudo-republic hate liberty and would dethrone God!" But 90 percent of Texans were neither slaves nor slavers, and Houston himself was no friend of that peculiar institution. The coupling of Oregon—into which New Englanders were moving—with Texas made thousands see the true territorial issue, which was, as Sam Houston said, whether the glory of the United States would culminate too soon.

Men such as Jackson and Sam Houston, certainly, were seeing a distant, almost impossible dream: the future world preeminence of the United States. It is almost certain, in retrospect, that Houston's motives were different from Mirabeau Lamar's only in degree. Sam Houston, as he had promised, never forgot the land of his birth when he made Texas his abiding-place.

In the campaign of 1844 opinion changed. Even Northern newspapers, which had attacked annexation in the past, now editorialized that annexation was inevitable and that it should be done with grace. Polk won, by a narrow popular vote. It was enough, however, to assure that Polk would acquire more territory for the United States than any President, including Jefferson, had ever done before.

Tyler read this mandate, and placed the annexation issue before the Congress once again.

Houston, meanwhile, came to the end of his second administration. This time, he had the satisfaction of seeing his policy vindicated at the polls. The "Houston" candidate won the Presidency in 1844, defeating the "war" or "Lamar" man, Burleson, 7,037 to 5,668. Dr. Anson Jones, Houston's successor, in general was pledged to Houston's goals. His victory was attributed, even by him, to Houston's popularity. Houston had galled Texans mainly on four things: higher tariffs, the movement of the working government from Austin to Houston, the "coddling" of the Indians, and his failure to secure the release of Texan captives in Mexico. Against these faults he could claim two accomplishments: he had not involved the Texas planters in a major war—in fact, he had gone out of his way to avoid one—and he had allowed eastern Texas to develop without governmental interference. Lamar's dreams of glory caught the Texas mind, but they also strained the economy beyond endurance. The vote for Dr. Anson Jones and Burleson, who favored Lamar's policies, split dramatically between east and western Texas. The old cotton counties, particularly the country east of the Trinity, went for Jones. The newer, western regions of the Republic preferred Burleson.

Now, in early 1845, the pendulum shifted. The United States, which had coolly put Texas off for almost a decade, was now almost desperate to annex the Republic. The government was committed to it; a majority of the people were in favor. But, with Polk's election, it was Texas' turn to delay and play for the greatest advantage. After consultations among Tyler, President-elect Polk, and Polk's new Congress, a much more liberal annexation bill was presented to Congress.

The new terms called for the admission of Texas as a full state, provided it passed its own ordinance before January 1, 1846; the ownership of all public lands in Texas by the state, not the federal government, upon annexation; the permission to divide Texas into four more states, with slavery banned north of 36° 30'. A provision was also made that if Texas refused these terms, the President was empowered to adjust them. This bill passed February 26, 1845.

Andrew Jackson Donelson, the U.S. representative in Houston, presented these terms to Jones. A few days later, Polk was inaugurated and he wrote to Donelson urging no delay. But Jones and his cabinet were now holding high cards and playing for tantalizing stakes.

There were important men in Texas who saw not only a chance for a Texan empire stretching to the Pacific but, with gloomy prophecy, the possibility of other Southern states seceding from the Union and joining Texas. The British, who had at last tried to move strongly into the Republic, and the French minister, Comte de Saligny, used all their diplomatic skills now to prevent annexation. President Jones, and his very able Secretary of State, Dr. Ashbel Smith—the man who had written the Texan white paper that had brought so much French and British pressure on Santa Anna in 1843—were not much inclined toward a Texan empire. But they did want to avoid offending the two European powers; there had been some promises made that, with annexation, would be impossible to keep.

Captain Elliot and Saligny jointly proposed to Jones that nothing be done for ninety days, while France and Britain pressured Mexico into signing a treaty of recognition and peace. Santa Anna had been replaced with General Herrera, and now, at the eleventh hour, Herrera was convinced that Mexican intransigence was producing the worst of all worlds: the final loss of Texas and the planting of the U.S. flag on the Rio Grande. He gave Captain Elliot a signed treaty that recognized Texas' full independence, provided the Republic did not join the United States, in May, 1845. But it was far too late; the American government had acted first.

Smith and Jones proposed to place this treaty before the Texas Congress, which was now called to meet on June 16, along with the U.S. treaty of annexation. But Jones quickly realized that Texan sentiment for annexation was too strong now; the people had overwhelmingly shown acceptance of the liberal American offer. Virtually all the propertied people in Texas favored union: annexation offered military protection from both Mexico and the Indians, U.S. postal and other services, and a sound currency and financial system. The retention of public lands by the state, and the American acceptance of the Rio Grande boundary, pacified the land-hungry, belligerent western counties. Texans were, as the Union was then construed, surrendering nothing and gaining much. They already paid high customs fees and tariffs; this was the only real source of income for the Republic; and in those days the federal government collected no taxes and left virtually all internal regulation to the states. Jones did not wait for his Congress to convene; he called for a general convention to be elected at once, to meet July 4.

When the Texas Congress met at Washington-on-the-Brazos, it rejected the Mexican treaty and recommended the American treaty be approved. The convention that assembled a few days later adopted the U.S. offer with only one dissenting vote and began immediate work on a state constitution. This constitution embodied most of the forms of the old Republic and also borrowed heavily from the state constitution of Louisiana. The constituent assembly that wrote it included an unusual number of able men: T. J. Rusk, J. Pinckney Henderson, Isaac Van Zandt, R. E. B. Baylor, N. H. Darnell, Hiram Runnels, and José Antonio Navarro of San Antonio. Navarro was the only member born in Texas. Eighteen writers came from Tennessee, eight from Virginia; Georgia furnished seven, Kentucky six, and North Carolina five. Among these men were scions of several distinguished American families, several former members of Congress, a chief justice of Alabama, and a former Mississippi governor.

The constitution provided for a popularly elected governor, with a term of two years. Other high officials were to be appointed, though five years later this was changed, and the attorney general, comptroller, and treasurer were to be elected. The legislature met biennially.

Specific Texas provisions, which became fundamental Texas law, were continued: the anticlerical provision that no minister of the gospel could serve in the legislature; the guarantee of separate property rights for married women; exemption from foreclosure of private homesteads; an anti-corporation law. The planters of Texas already hated "soulless corporations." Only a two-thirds vote of the Texas House could create a private corporation, and no bank under any circumstances might incorporate.

The constitution was approved, along with annexation, by a vote of approximately 4,000 to 200 on October 13, 1845. It was immediately accepted as adequate by the Congress of the United States. On December 29, 1845, Polk signed the act that merged the Lone Star into many, and in a brief ceremony, on February 19, 1846, the Texas flag fluttered down. The last President of the Republic handed over his authority to the new governor, Pinckney Henderson. Sam Houston and Tom Rusk were new United States Senators, and a United States army already stood on Texas soil.

As Anson Jones concluded his farewell address: The Republic of Texas was no more.

16

THE LONE STAR
STATE

*It is doubtful whether ten years' trading would give Texas a
better bargain than she can now make.*

THE LA GRANGE *Monument,* ON THE
NEW MEXICO BOUNDARY BILL, 1850

THE Mexican War is now generally seen by American and other historians for what it was: a Presidential war of dominant Administration policy, carried out for strategic reasons against the wishes of a considerable
body of public opinion. The war was tremendously successful for two
reasons: American arms were surprisingly and quickly victorious, and the
goals, immense though they might seem, were limited to the acquisition of
territory either useless to, or only under the nominal control of, Mexico.
The American armies secured a treaty and evacuated Mexico before a
popular uprising against occupation could commence, as the Spanish rose
against Napoleon or the Mexicans would later rise against Maximilian, and
the folly of annexing the millions of Mexico was avoided. The United
States never wanted to own or control Mexico, but to assure its subordination: Mexico was removed permanently as a rival for the continent. The
year 1848 marked the first time the American Republic was at last strategically secure.

The historic distaste for the war inside America rose mainly from the
internal politics of the time, and the fact that Americans had a penchant
for a crusade. The Mexican War was not a plot merely to extend slavery,
but neither did it have a soul-satisfying ideological base.

The years between 1844 and 1848 marked the last great surge of the

268

Jacksonian Democrats. Soon afterward, the Democratic Party was destroyed by sectionalism, and its stalwarts, from Sam Houston to Thomas Hart Benton, were destroyed with it.

Texas and the South fell into the very trap Sam Houston repeatedly warned against: the answering of Northern sectionalism with a responding parochialism. Andrew Jackson, Houston, Benton, and the whole group loosely known as "Jacksonians" and Jacksonian Democrats, of course had their own political views; they were Westerners, suspicious of Eastern ways. But above all they had a mystical view of the growth of the United States—a country grown so great that even fools could not completely destroy it. Their concept of national greatness had more to do with land and people than specific programs or forms of government. The Jacksonians as a group had no particular love for Negro slavery; many of them saw it as a national curse. The charge that the acquisition of Texas and California was part of a plot to extend slavery, apparently believed in the North, was specious. The Jacksonian view of the United States could accept that institution, or accept its disappearance. It was a concept that saw the nation itself as greater than its passing economic or political phases, which had to be worked out internally from time to time.

The Jacksonians succeeded before they disappeared. It was left to James Polk to cap the dream. Oddly, though Polk gained the United States more territory than any President before or since and made the nation finally strategically secure, he has never been given rank in the American pantheon of heroes. Apparently, there were several reasons: Polk, an able man, was always overshadowed by Jackson, whose man in the truest sense he always was. In the White House he carried out concepts and plans already conceived. And Polk seems to have had no real interest in the presidency, beyond the winning of the American West; he was not likely to catch the imagination of later generations who increasingly saw the White House in different terms.

There is no evidence that Polk wanted a war with Mexico for its own sake. He did want Texas and California and was willing to fight, if necessary, to get them. Part of this dream grew out of a natural desire for more territory, but the strategical vision must never be overlooked. The Rio Grande was, especially in those years, a formidable river, and it gave the United States a clearly defined southern boundary, which the Nueces could not do. The expansion to the western ocean prevented any other powerful nation from securing an enclave there, and it left the United States as the dominant power upon the North American continent. The frequently discussed "manifest destiny"—no nation ever had a true "manifest destiny"—was merely a popularization of these logical strategic goals.

Polk honestly tried to buy the Mexican claims to Texas and California. But a power struggle was at this late date inevitable; the Mexican government, weak as it was, was not prepared to accede to American predominance. The Mexicans were not just stubborn; they were intransigent. With the renewed discussion of annexation in 1844, Mexico immediately voided the truce with Texas. Perhaps with the mistaken notion that this would deter the United States, Mexico emphasized that it was still at war with the separated province. Mexico also began preparations for a larger war. Polk's emissary, John Slidell, was not even received in Mexico; the Mexican minister to the United States was recalled. The evidence is that President Polk, faced with these two events, decided upon a declaration of war.

But Polk as President had to play his cards carefully. The South and Southwest, as always, were ready for war; these regions had become almost belligerent in their attitudes. But the rest of the nation was not, and a majority in Congress stood opposed to a war with Mexico, over Texas or anything else.

There was nothing dishonorable about a war with Mexico at this time. In fact, Mexico had almost assured conflict by making it clear that the United States was inheriting the Texan struggle with the Mexican nation. If the United States, in its own interests, annexed Texas, a part of the dowry, unfortunately, had to be the Texas-Mexican quarrel. The more unfortunate Whig propaganda in the United States, that the conflict grew out of a Southern plot to extend slavery to the Pacific, not only tended to reinforce Mexican innocence but convinced millions of Americans as well. The American South, of course, happily viewed any extension of slave states westward: the more slave-state Senators, the better. But Polk and his dominant group saw this as only a side issue. And, finding Mexico unwilling to negotiate or even talk, Polk's Administration coolly and rather brilliantly outmaneuvered Mexico at the power-politics game.

When it was apparent Texas would ratify annexation, but before the treaty was ratified, Polk sent General Zachary Taylor with a small U.S. army into Texas. This move was part of the negotiations, to protect Texas during the discussions, as agreed. Taylor, who was himself a Whig, arrived on the Nueces River at Corpus Christi in July, 1845. Here he was supplied by sea and drilled for some nine months. Only when Polk clearly understood that the Mexican government would not negotiate, and his ambassador was rebuffed, did he send Taylor orders to march to the Rio Grande. Taylor moved south in April, 1846.

This country north of the river was seething with Mexican cavalry. The Nueces-Rio Grande region was claimed by both nations, and both under these terms had the right to send armed forces into it. Taylor fixed a base at Point Isabel, where the Brazos de Santiago pass permitted deep-water entry to the Texas coast. This was only a few miles above the Rio Grande. Then, he established a detachment under Major Jacob Brown in a bend of the river directly across from the Mexican city of Matamoros, ostensibly to keep the large Mexican forces there under surveillance. Each morning and evening, in full view of General Arista, Brown raised and lowered the Stars and Stripes to the fife and drum. His presence inflamed the landowners who lived in Matamoros, many of whom held grants north of the Bravo. Arista was pressured into action. He ordered some fifteen hundred cavalry across the river, then followed his lances with his main force. In this way, Polk used Zachary Taylor to precipitate the gathering crisis, and Taylor, Whig or not, was obviously ready and willing.

The chaparral was filled with blue and gray coats; something was bound to strike fire. On April 24, sixty of Taylor's heavy dragoons, out on patrol, blundered into a Mexican cavalry trap and were snapped up by a full brigade. Then, the Mexican force opened fire on Fort Brown, as the barricade in the bend of the river came to be called, and laid siege to the breastworks. Arista did not attempt to smash Major Brown with his full force; he was playing strategy and laying a trap. Arista placed his main body in wait at the edge of the river brush, where it opened on the Sacahuiste Prairie facing Point Isabel some twenty miles away.

Arista expected Taylor to move west from Laguna Madre, where he was camped on the edge of the bay.

Move Taylor did. He notified Washington by packet that "hostilities may now be considered as commenced." Texas Ranger scouts kept him informed of Mexican movements. Taylor's position was that Mexican troops had entered U.S. territory and fired first; Arista seems to have acted almost as if he were following Polk's plan. Taylor now called upon the Governor of Texas for four regiments, two of foot and two of horse. He had already, rather to his disgust, found the half-wild Ranger companies he had accepted earlier for political reasons invaluable. They could ride country where his own heavy mounted infantry, or dragoons, maneuvered only with difficulty. Now, Taylor marched toward Fort Brown with 2,300 men, and his guns and wagons, at three on the afternoon of May 7. He was heavily outnumbered, but stated that if Arista opposed his route of march, "in whatever force, I shall fight him."

The American vanguard struck the emplaced Mexicans at Palo Alto, a small rise on the coastal plain just beyond the chaparral. After a touch-and-go battle, Arista retreated. The two armies engaged again on May 9, at Resaca de la Palma, an oxbow lake a few miles from the Rio Grande. This time Arista was badly mauled by the superior American infantry, and he fell back across the river in disorder and with shattered morale. Both battles were American victories over great odds.

Taylor then marched into Fort Brown. The flag still waved over the American breastworks, though Major Brown had been fatally wounded. (On this spot the future city of Brownsville would be built.)

Now President Polk, armed with Taylor's dispatches, had what he wanted. He went before the Congress with the message that American blood had been shed on American soil. The Congress, North and South, dared not do anything but declare war.

Polk had handled the situation shrewdly, confidently, and coolly—the mark of a man of the old frontier. Like Austin, Houston, and Andrew Jackson, he left his visible results on the land, a lasting heritage of soil; ironically, the admitted intellectual leaders of the day, Webster, Clay, and Calhoun, left mostly rhetoric behind.

The rest of the war, in which American armies marched into Mexico across the Rio Grande, and from Vera Cruz, and other forces swept the far West, was fought outside Texas. The American historian Lynn Montross perhaps put this war in its truest perspective:

> Of all American conflicts the one with Mexico has been most often condemned as dishonorable. This tradition may be traced to the rabid politics of the day, for the Whigs and Abolitionists came dangerously near to treason in their opposition. Such leaders as Clay and Webster denounced the struggle as a conspiracy to bring more slave-holding states into the Union; and a Whig newspaper declared it would be "a joy to hear that the hordes under Scott and Taylor were every man of them swept into the next world."
>
> That such strictures are not to be taken seriously is shown by the fact that both the victorious generals became Whig candidates for the Presidency. Nor is there any reason for accepting at face value the denunciations of American motives by Whig orators . . . the actual causes of the Mexican strife were obscured by the causes which would soon lead to Secession.
>
> An understanding of the background is necessary to dispel a commonly held belief that the United States crushed a weak and unprepared neighbor by overwhelming bulk. On the contrary, the actual odds in the field weighed heavily against the Americans. The northern army faced four times its own numbers in the principal battle; and as a triumph of skill over obstacles, Scott's campaign has no equal in the world during the half century after Waterloo. . . .
>
> Nor could it be said that the Mexicans were unworthy opponents. A generation of civil war had trained a hardy native soldiery which defended a formidable terrain with ability as well as courage. In the critical campaign the Americans found the enemy particularly strong in engineering and artillery—two arms which are not the resources of a military rabble.

Significantly, European observers praised American military feats as prodigious. Ironically, it was Americans themselves, in a war fought for the long-term interests of the American nation, who robbed themselves of glory. But, probably most significant of all, even the harshest critics of the war never proposed that the spoils be given back.

By the Treaty of Guadalupe Hidalgo, ratified in July, 1848, the United States purchased California, New Mexico, Arizona, Utah, Nevada, Wyoming, and a part of Colorado, making a territory four times the size of France, from Mexico for $15,000,000 and the assumption of Mexican debts. Mexico relinquished all claims to Texas, and the boundary was set at the Rio Grande. All of this territory, except California and New

Mexico, was only nominally Mexican, and in the last two regions the writ of the Mexican Supreme Government had already ceased to run. The Mexican Empire was not only static in the early 19th century; it had already fallen apart due to internal disorder.

Fortunately for the American nation, internal disorder enveloped the Hispanic southland first. Had the American internal conflict developed earlier, the Jacksonian dream—that the nation and its people were mightier than their ideology or passing internal quarrels, and that the nation could be glorious either with slavery or without it, as it had been in the past— might have had a very different end. The Republic of Texas, not the United States, might have battled Mexico in a long and mutually disastrous war for the West, while the former nation split the continent into three separate, weak, and hostile English-speaking states.

If the Mexican War was eventually recognized by both the North and South as a national war, the issue of slavery had already poisoned the peace. The Wilmot Proviso, repeatedly put before Congress, tried to prohibit slavery in any territory gained through the war. This was construed by some to mean not only California but also the disputed lands in south Texas and New Mexico east of the Rio Grande. In all this sound and fury, North and South, there was no real understanding that slavery, based on cotton agriculture, had reached its natural limits. It had no future west of the 98th meridian; where the Balcones Scarp began in Texas, the rainfall, and the plantation system of the 19th-century South, abruptly ended. From the middle of the state, on a line almost even with Austin, the rainfall dribbled away from 30 inches annually to 15 or less across the vast plateaus. The farm line halted in crippled agony roughly along the San Antonio and Nueces rivers toward the south. The Spaniards had failed to plant vast *haciendas* here, not because they were fools but because the country was suited under the technology of the times mainly for wild Indians. The land of the numberless buffalo, and the arid mesas of the far West, was a Comanche paradise, but a nightmare vista to men who earned a living with the hoe, and whose whole history had never had to cope with a lack of wood and water.

The sincerity of the men who battled each other in the Senate of the United States, arguing whether the Southwest should be slave or free, cannot be doubted. Their intelligence concerning the land itself was extremely faulty.

The slave territory question, which was to tear the nation apart, immediately embroiled the State of Texas in a new boundary dispute—this time with the United States. Texas had claimed the Rio Grande not only as its border in the south, but westward as far as Colorado. This included half of New Mexico, with the capital, Santa Fe, in Texan territory. The claim was just as specious, but no more so, than the claim for the land south of the Nueces. Neither in the far south nor the far west was it supported by

Spanish or Mexican history. Polk, however, and his Secretary of State, James Buchanan, supported the Texan rights to both areas.

But if Polk could involve the United States in war by executive action, he could not define internal boundaries except by action of Congress, and this was a subject on which the Congress would not be stampeded. The land south of the Nueces was never in serious dispute, but New Mexico had Spanish-speaking settlers, Northern American traders, and a history of its own.

It was separated by many hundreds of miles from the populated portions of Texas, across Indian country. There were geographic, economic, and social reasons why New Mexico should not be part of Texas, but the territory was separated more for emotional than logical reasons by what seems to have been a genuine conspiracy against Texan sovereignty by certain Americans.

When General Stephen Kearny's Army of the West occupied Santa Fe in 1846, Kearny helped organize an interim local government, which paid no attention to Texan pretensions. This infuriated the Texas Legislature and Governor, who were assured, however, by Polk and Buchanan that Texas' claim would not be prejudiced. But the argument of whether slavery was to be allowed in this territory, which it would be automatically if it became part of Texas, paralyzed all official action in Washington. Buchanan was unable to deliver.

Meanwhile, two events occurred. In New Mexico, sentiment against the *Tejanos* was stirred up by American interests, mostly traders who had come in from the north. It was not hard to alienate the thoroughly Mexican population against Texas, and this was done both by speeches and by newspaper. United States Army officers abetted and assisted in this work. Then, again with the cooperation of the Army, a political convention assembled at Santa Fe in November, 1848. This convention sent a petition to the United States government, requesting territorial status, and asking that slavery be kept out of New Mexico. New Mexico had its own labor institution, peonage, but this was not understood or acted upon by Congress until ten years later. Meanwhile, the State of Texas took the bull by the horns in early 1848, even before the Treaty of Guadalupe Hidalgo was ratified. The legislature created "Santa Fe County," which conveniently included all of New Mexico east of the Rio Grande. A Texas magistrate, Spruce Baird, was dispatched to New Mexico to take control.

Judge Baird made the hazardous journey to Santa Fe only to be informed coldly by the commander of U.S. forces there that the local regime would be sustained against Texas by the army "at every peril," unless ordered otherwise by Washington. The army was on safe ground. Polk's Administration was ending; the new President, Zachary Taylor, was a Whig and favored statehood for the "conquered" territories. Taylor died in office, but he was succeeded by Millard Fillmore, who was even more adamant, and who was prepared to use force against Texas if it pressed its claim. Slavery and free soil advocates were again stalemated in Congress. Frustrated, Baird had to return to Texas—significantly, by way of Missouri. There was no safe passage to Santa Fe, except through Mexico or U.S. territory.

When Baird reported this federal interference, there was great indignation in Texas government circles. Governor Wood, and his immediate successor, Hansborough Bell, proposed to send state troops to Santa Fe. Other politicians demanded secession from the Union. On the record, this was a betrayal of faith, because Texas had been specifically promised the disputed territory, first by Major Donelson in 1845, and the map attached to the Treaty of Guadalupe Hidalgo showed the Texas boundary following the Rio Grande to its source. Mirabeau Lamar's old argument against annexation—that Texas would be made subject to the interminable conflicts and irreconcilable prejudices of other Americans in other states—had come true.

Now, starting in 1849, there began several lasting trends in Texan-Washington relations. These were to continue in some degree for a century, and for the first thirty years of statehood, the crisis was acute. Texans tended to resent all national interference, even when there was a national consensus, in their own affairs, whether the matter was a question of boundaries, finances, or internal politics. The dominant Texan view of the American Union was that it was composed of sovereign states. The federal apparatus was seen primarily as a convenient tool to do those difficult or expensive things the people of the state could not, or would not do for themselves: frontier defense, postal and diplomatic services, harbors and roads. The problem of frontier defense, in fact, had been paramount in the decision for annexation; Texas could never be secure so long as it had a border quarrel with ten million hostile Mexicans to the south. Texans expected the state and federal governments to remain approximately co-equal, each in its own sphere. If this was a simplistic view of national government, it was not specious: it was almost exactly the dominant view of Americans in 1789. The people who had marched southwest from Appalachia had not left the 18th century; they still held to "strict construction of the Constitution," with no erosion of state powers in favor of the central government. The mystique of the "nation," a 19th-century notion, had not replaced their own mystique of race, blood, and soil, based on the battle for the ground on which they stood.

Intensely touchy about national interference in local matters, Texans were equally certain that the national government was niggardly toward them, and never did enough. There was one genuine basis for this growing belief: in 1845 Texas disbanded its army and turned the problem of its frontiers over to the federal authorities, who were constitutionally bound to protect national borders. The federal authorities handled the frontier problem, which at most times men in Washington only dimly understood, quite poorly. In the 1840's and 1850's, neither the War Department or the U.S. Army had much understanding of the Plains Indian frontier. No state had ever come into the Union with more than half its territory unsettled, and with at least 20,000 extremely warlike Amerinds living within its borders. And these were Indians of a type the army had not fought before.

For long periods, between 1845 and 1875, and even later, the federal government tried to make peace with Indians and Mexicans, or failed to act, along a frontier where warfare and bloodshed was already endemic, a way of life. Some two hundred Texans were killed by Indians or carried off into captivity in the year 1849 alone. The U.S. Army kept only a few thousand soldiers in the state, and these were heavy infantry—mounted only occasionally on mules. They provided no defense against the wide-ranging Comanches, while Washington refused to push a war with the Comanches home. People were still being killed on the outskirts of Austin, where the state capital was fixed again in 1850. The Texas people grew increasingly bitter, and the Governor, over the objections of the local army commanders, again and again ordered state troops, the Rangers, into the field.

The Army disliked the Ranger operations. The Rangers grew to hold the army in increasing contempt. The reasons were simple enough; the two forces, state and federal, operated under conflicting orders and sets of rules. The army tried to police the frontier primarily by keeping the peace. The Texans rode to punish the Indians and to push them back. The state again and again demanded that Texas be rid of hostile Indians, while Washington remained reluctant to act. All this created understandable tension.

Two other trends that were strongly established at this time were the habit of securing federal monies through political action and the policy of the state government to seek windfalls to shore up its inadequate financial structure. Two such windfalls—provided no other state—came with annexation and were the result of President Jones' coy politics with the now eager President Polk. The Republic's finances had always been chaotic. Even Houston's strict financial discipline could not prevent continuing deficits, and these came on top of the revolution and Lamar's expensive wars. In Texas the only commodity of value was the endless land. This already had great symbolic, even mystic value, but very little of the Republic's lands could be translated into ready cash. In fact, because the problem of more people was primary, the Republic continued to give its lands away.

On annexation, the Federal Congress appropriated $5,000,000 to defray some of the Republic's debts, which the United States assumed; and to satisfy the remainder, the state was permitted to retain title to all its public lands. Thus, there were no federal or national public lands whatsoever in Texas; the state owned all undistributed lands within its borders. But in the 1840's and 1850's, this land was of little use to settle the continuing debts.

One reason was that the Comanches still held possession, even if they had no recognition under the law.

The Republic's debt was of two kinds: revenue and nonrevenue. The nonrevenue debt was that owed to individuals, mostly Texans who had contributed goods or services during the revolution or Lamar's Indian wars. Most claims were small. The revenue debt was that owed to holders of Republic of Texas bonds, for which the customs receipts of the country had been pledged.

After 1845, the Texas state government used its $5,000,000 to settle the nonrevenue claims, for obvious political reasons. The Federal Treasury, saddled with the revenue debt, protested strongly, but in vain, while millions in claims, many by foreigners, went unpaid. The state government, after exhausting the initial grant, continued bankrupt; the claims were pressing, while millions of dollars in new state services were still required.

It must be understood that Texas had never had a true money economy during the colonial and Republican years, and there was no source of wealth except land within the state. Texans had vast respect for acres, but none for paper money. Further, they had fought a revolution to escape oppressive regulation. No local government was inclined to impose a direct tax of any kind; no planter was inclined willingly to accept one.

This background gave both the central government and the state leverage to settle the New Mexico boundary dispute. As part of the last great national compromise over the slavery question, the series of acts called the Compromise of 1850, Texas was offered $10,000,000 for its claims to the Upper Rio Grande. In this national compromise, Henry Clay, Daniel Webster, and John C. Calhoun met in debate for the last time, and very nearly saved the Union, over Calhoun's obstruction. During the Congressional action, Sam Houston and the Texas delegation in Washington, working through the Maryland delegation, were able to secure the Boundary Act, by which Texas sold the United States its rights to Colorado and New Mexico.

The act was strongly attacked in Texas by demagogues who argued that one provision—the retention of $5,000,000 in escrow to make sure the revenue debt was paid—impugned state honor, and that Texans should never surrender a foot of "sacred" soil. Against this cooler heads prevailed. Houston and many responsible conservatives ignored the question of "federal interference" and fought the issue out on the grounds that Texas had more desert lands already than it could use and that the old debts, sooner or later, had to be paid. The deal was actually a tremendous bargain for Texas; sentiment swung, and the Boundary Act was ratified by a special state election in which the planter vote was decisive. These men controlled the state government, and they needed money.

But even this $10,000,000 was not enough; debts had piled up and interest had accrued. The revenue debt, which the Federal Treasury held ultimate responsibility for, was cannily left for Washington to deal with ultimately; however, again over protest, it was scaled down. There were two justifications for this: the old bonds had in many cases been bought up by speculators for as low as ten cents on the dollar, and in others the Government of Texas had never received full value for its bonds. They were scaled out to average a return of seventy-seven cents on the dollar.

Meanwhile, the Texans pressed a mounting claim for state expenses for frontier defense. Each time the Rangers were called out, the bill was delivered to Washington, via Congress. Finally, in 1855, the Congress passed a new appropriation act: $7,750,000 more was given Texas, to settle both the old debts and frontier claims, once and for all. The details of this settlement are not important, nor is the fancy footwork that its passage entailed. What was important, then and for future history, was that the state emerged with almost $4,000,000 free and clear.

This new windfall permitted the state to live officially "high on the hog." It began a vast building program of state structures. The federal monies allowed Austin, for six years, to remit nine-tenths of locally collected revenues back to the counties; one-tenth was constitutionally remanded to the state education fund. The money returned to the counties was splurged on new county courthouses and other local projects, few of which had been built before. These were, for local politicos, flush times in Texas.

Two millions of the Federal windfall were put aside to endow the public school fund. Lamar had put an education act upon the books, but like most of the Republic's ambitious legislation, public education had not been implemented due to lack of funds. The actual credits were immediately loaned by the educational fund to railroad corporations, to finance construction. As with public buildings, Texans tended to prefer to spend for visible, practical signs of progress.

The net result of the boundary bill bargain was that Texas during the 1850's was financed publicly almost entirely by federal money, and this had a more immediate effect than the setting of a theoretical boundary out in Indian country. Schools were endowed, public structures built, and the transportation system enhanced, all without a dollar being raised in domestic taxes. Manifest destiny, even above the costs of the Mexican War, proved expensive to Uncle Sam.

But as Rupert Richardson observed, "The advantages of such a condition are obvious, but the system may have worked injury as well as benefit. The people learned to look to outside sources rather than to taxation as the means of supporting their government and were not prepared for the day when windfalls would cease."

It is recorded that by 1860, the state government was once again almost $1,000,000 in debt.

17

STAR LIGHT,
STAR BRIGHT

*During the decade and a half between the annexation of Texas
and its union with the Confederacy, Texas experienced the most
rapid growth in its history. Its population increased more than
fourfold and its assessed property more than eightfold. That its
cultural progress did not keep pace with its material development
was the result of frontier conditions rather than the lack of fine
innate qualities in its people.*

RUPERT N. RICHARDSON, *Texas, the Lone Star State*

*A great country for men and dogs, but hell on women and
horses.* OLD TEXAS PROVERB

THE attitudes and institutions of Texas civilization were firmly established in the years between 1835 and 1861. This era was the great formative period of the heartland of the state.

The pattern of American civilization in Texas was already widely diver-
gent from the society then undergoing rapid change in the North and
Northeast. Ninety percent of the immigration into Texas was composed of
native-born people from the old South. About one-half came from the
upper South, with its forested hills and frontier attitudes that lingered still;
the rest came from the plantation economies and the black belts of the
deep Gulf bend. Therefore, Texas was basically Southern in its cultural
patterns; it was entirely agricultural, and it was a slave state. But it had one
major difference from the Southern states: Texas still possessed a long and
savage internal Indian frontier.

279

In fact, by 1860, no other American state still faced a true frontier, where a line of fixed settlement was exposed to continual threats of violence.

California and the Oregon Territory, which were becoming states at the same time, and the regions of the upper Midwest—Iowa, Wisconsin, and other states—experienced pioneer conditions, but in reality almost none of their populations were ever exposed to a real frontier. There were either no truly recalcitrant, warlike Indians in these regions, or else all Indians were removed before large-scale settlement began. In Oregon there was only one brief Indian uprising. In Texas, between 1836 and 1860, an average of about two hundred men, women, and children were killed or carried off each year. The reverberations of this warfare spread far beyond the actual limits of the Indian frontier, affecting both attitudes and organization.

In other emerging states, the problems were those of clearing and settling virgin lands, forming local governments, and establishing law and order. Oregon had no difficulty in re-creating, on the Pacific coast, a prim and prosperous new New England. Oregon's inhabitants were earth-breakers. They were frontiersmen only briefly, during their passage west in covered wagons.

The original Anglo enclave in Texas resembled the settlement of other states: Austin had chosen a region remote from dangerous Indians, and behind an Indian buffer. One quick, decisive campaign by his "ranging companies" convinced the sedentary eastern and central Texas tribes, such as Wacos and Tawakonis, that the Americans were better left alone. The Karankawas, already reduced to pitiful skulkers by the Spanish, European disease, and Jean Lafitte, were exterminated or scattered.

The next step in a long tradition was that when the whites grew more numerous and needed more lands, the government was pressured to push the Indians out. This Lamar's administration did. Lamar cleared millions of acres of northeast Texas of Cherokees and allied Indians, and Lamar's wars in the southwest drove the Penateka Comanches higher up on the limestone scarp. After 1845, the Texans forced the U.S. government to move all the sedentary or semicivilized Indians out of Texas into Oklahoma. In this way one-half of the lands within the boundaries of the state were opened up for settlement; these included all the lands that were readily exploitable by the agriculture of the time. Settlement advanced into the vacuum across northeast Texas until it reached approximately the 98th parallel of longitude. Here, white civilization clashed abruptly with two factors it had not encountered before: the Great Plains, alive with mounted Indians, and a harsh climatic frontier.

But the major expansion of Texas in the antebellum years was into and across the watered pine woods of the east, through the post-oak belts beyond, and finally, to the end of the rich, dark north-central prairie soils. At the same time, the old enclaves along the rivers expanded, filling up the interfluves. This was a huge area, and in spite of the massive influx of

Southern people, it was still thinly held in 1860. While Oregon was re-creating a distant farming colony, settled by New Englanders, Texas re-sembled most closely the old 18th-century Southern frontier.

Life, culture, and agriculture had changed very little from the conditions of the previous century. Attitudes do not seem to have changed at all. Texas between 1836 and 1861 developed a new Cohee and Tuckahoe split, with cotton planters and Negroes in the eastern regions, a surly, sturdy horde of small corn farmers in the west. Thus, except for the fact that the state was newer and rawer, Texas was essentially no different from the South. Politically, and economically, it was part of the cotton kingdom—in fact, in these years, Texas was becoming the cotton kingdom itself. Until 1860, it was the fastest growing Southern state, and one of the fastest growing in the Union.

The news of San Jacinto sent thousands of Americans heading west. Statehood, which promised even greater stability, increased the flow. In 1836, 5,000 immigrants crossed over one ferry on the Sabine. The panic of 1837, bad crop years, and the continuing depression in the United States pushed thousands more into Texas. The years 1840–1841 saw the greatest immigration in Texas history. The Mexican invasions of the south in 1842 only briefly halted the flow; the news of the annexation treaty started more wagons rolling into the Southwest. Men painted "Polk & Texas" on their wagon tops, and passed through town after town, to cheers. All along the way, other families joined the trek. In some cases, whole communities in the older regions moved.

Some of the migrants, restless, went on to California, especially after the word of gold arrived. Most carved out farms in Texas.

The restless, continuing migration of the Anglo-Celtic upper South was now channeled across the Sabine. Iowa and Wisconsin had no Indians, but the climate repelled the Southern-born. The hardscrabble hills of western Arkansas were uninviting; the delta was already filled up. The new Indian border along Oklahoma was protected by the United States government, and it was considered permanent. The thousands of families who had worn-out, eroded lands, who had experienced bad luck, or who faced rising land prices in the States were pulled to Texas. Many left debts, but only a few, contrary to popular tradition, left crimes behind.

The various governments in Texas, both Republican and state, used every possible means to lure more people in. This was not all caused by dreams of expansion of the race or a vision of Texas spreading from sea to sea. Texas was always a nearly moneyless region, living year to year on a credit economy based on the future values of land. Credit economies, and debtor regions, must expand in order to survive. The merchant, the land owner, and the state government not only profited from immigration—they had to have it merely to keep going. From the time of Stephen Austin, Texans equated growth with progress, and this became a fixation that never died.

Texas' great bait was open lands. The Republic gave its land away freely; and the state, under the peculiar terms of annexation, owned all the public lands and continued the same policy. Legislation in Texas founded the right of every family to own land, with the exception, it must be recorded, of Indians and Negroes. The Constitution of 1836 guaranteed every family head already in the Republic access to a league and a *labor* of public land, more than 4,000 acres. Of course, these figures were more glittering than real: few families could work more than a few acres, unless they were rich in slaves. The land thus granted, if preempted, was rapidly sold off.

The law provided any family man moving into Texas between March, 1836, and October, 1837, with 1,280 acres of free land. This acreage was later reduced to 640, but this was still more than any ordinary farmer could cultivate. For years, there was no requirement that a grantee had to live on, or improve, his acres. Later, a residence of three years in the state was required in order for final title to pass.

The aim of the state was to create a country of freeholders, every white family owning land. This was considered the soundest possible democratic basis for the state. The system of Negro slavery was not thought inconsistent with this dream. Chattel slavery was restricted to Negroes, and Negroes, like Indians, were not classed as part of the American nation. Historically, such institutions were hardly unusual: Athens' famed democracy was restricted to some twenty thousand citizens, though the Athenian state encompassed many times that number of people.

The land grant system was simple. A board of local commissioners in each county reviewed applications, and if valid, issued certificates for land to be taken out of the public domain. The grantee then engaged a locator or surveyor, who marked off a plot. Since the public domain in these years was enormous, the surveyor had no difficulty in finding lands within the average county. For his service the locator usually received one-third the grant. The survey field notes were certified and sent to the state land commissioner, who issued a patent. This system was a combination of Spanish-Mexican and American Southern practice. Its great benefit was that it passed title to individuals, yet cost the public nothing.

Texas also enacted the first homestead legislation in America, in 1838. Among other things, this act provided that genuine homesteads could not be seized for debt—a radical, but lasting, innovation. Land was Texas' great, and only, resource; it was assuming sacred proportions at law. Against the rights of private property, in Texas, even the public rights of eminent domain often were in doubt.

Another feature of this trend was the institution of preemptive, or squatter's, rights. Men who owned no land could claim public lands they happened to settle on, at fifty cents an acre, up to 320 acres. Land continued to be preempted until 1889, when there was no more public domain in the state. Even afterward, the codes provided for squatter's rights: if a man actually lived on a piece of ground long enough, he could not be moved off, even by the person who held legal title.

These laws had nothing to do with land reform. They were passed to ensure the small holder's rights, in a time of confusion of surveys, when land speculation was rife and when most of the state was unexplored.

Laws also granted large portions of public land to any and all the veterans of Texas wars, from the heirs of the Alamo dead to later American volunteers. Thus it was virtually impossible, theoretically, for a Texas family to be landless.

However, the laws did not prevent speculation, frauds, resale, and other unsound practices. Land speculation was already an American curse; it was carried intact into Texas. Speculators continually worked to secure title to lands ahead of the actual wave of white settlement. Using their own, or purchased, or fraudulent claims, sharp operators established legal claims to choice properties far west of the current farm line. Locators and surveyors sneaked into Indian country, staked out river bottoms, river crossings, and other selected sites. The state then certified title to these lands, which were legally "public domain"; during the Republic it was established that Indians held no property rights. The federal government, in these years, could not negotiate even a treaty with the Texas Indians, because in Texas the American nation owned no soil. The federal courts, of course, determined eventual equity at law. But during the 19th century American constitutional practice held that the function of the federal judiciary was to uphold state law.

An interesting fact of the Texas frontier is that the land maps of virtually every central Texas county show that the best lands, with their precious water rights, passed into private ownership between ten and thirty years before these counties were settled by whites, even before county governments were organized. The true farmer-pioneer in Texas often found the lands he wanted alienated before he had reached them. This, and other land practices, caused continual litigation and turbulence on the western line. Millions of acres continued with "unquiet" titles. There was horrendous litigation, lasting for years in many parts of Texas. In the Southwest, Spanish land grants, grants of the Republic or state, homestead rights, and simple purchase might all conflict, since all might cover a portion of the same acreage. Some titles were not quieted at law until the next century. All this produced, among many true frontiersmen, a ferocious hatred of "Eastern" law and a vast dislike of lawyers, who usually emerged with choice plots, whoever won in court.

The Republic confused an already chaotic situation in the early 1840's by reopening empresario contracts. Several important new empresario commissions were authorized, very much on the terms of the old Spanish practice. Thousands of square miles beyond the fringe of settlement were marked off for an empresario colony; the empresario was to receive ten premium sections for each hundred families settled onto the land. He also had other direct means of income, from surveying, selling cabins, necessities, and charging for transportation costs to colonists he recruited. The Republic took this step primarily to raise money. The government reserved alternate sections of 640 acres within the empresario grants, and it was felt that rapid settlement would allow the Republic to sell these off and make a profit from immigration at last.

The program was at once ferociously unpopular with the public. Many Texans felt empresarios were now anachronisms, and the removal of millions of acres of public domain for such purposes was bitterly opposed. These sentiments prevailed, and in 1844 the program was voided; further, the Republic and state began a process of harassment and legal action to take back what had been granted. This was a breach of faith, but it was taken with overwhelming public approbation. Several important empresario contracts had been let: to W. S. Peters and Associates in the region of the future city of Dallas, to Charles F. Mercer south of Peters, to Fisher and Miller further west, and to Count Henri de Castro of France, southwest of San Antonio.

Peters, operating as the Texas Emigration and Land Company, introduced two thousand families, mostly from Kentucky, but he was soon involved in insurmountable difficulties brought on by public hostility. In 1845 the attorney general filed suit to cancel his contract. The court battles continued for years. Mercer faced the same problems. In 1848, a Texas magistrate rather arbitrarily voided his contract, although the legislature passed a relief act in favor of his settlers. The state never dispossessed families who moved onto the new empresario grants, but it did work to dispossess the empresarios. Generally, the state succeeded, and one by one the new proprietors were put out of business. However, claims and litigation clouded the issues for decades: Mercer's claim against Texas was not finally disallowed by the Supreme Court until 1882, on a split decision.

The Fisher-Miller grant proved to be entirely inside Comanche hunting grounds, and the proprietors were not able to settle anyone on it. The empresarios unloaded their rights to a German emigration society, actually after they had been forfeited for noncompliance with the terms of contract.

The empresario Castro was not dispossessed legally, and he founded the first successful town south of San Antonio in September, 1844.

Despite the admitted legal troubles and occasional chaotic situation with unquieted land titles, millions of acres of Texas soil were still transferred successfully. This land pulled hundreds of thousands of Americans across the Sabine. In 1835, the settlement of Texas was confined to the Guadalupe, Colorado, Brazos, and Trinity rivers, with the region surrounding Nacogdoches and several deep-woods enclaves on the Red. Nowhere on the settled streams did the frontier line run inland more than 200 miles, and the interfluves were empty and unpreempted. This unsettled land in the old Austin colony allowed room for development, and President Lamar's campaigns of 1839 cleared the Indians out of all of east and northeast Texas. While thousands of families settled in the older, river-bottom regions, the major push of Texas expansion after 1835 went across the northeast from the Sabine, and followed the Trinity and Brazos rivers inland from the coast, far beyond the coastal plains into the oak belt and beyond it, to the black-soiled prairie. By 1860 both the black waxy prairie and the adjoining "Grand Prairie" were settled, and the frontier line had reached the Cross Timbers—where the rain and wood ran out. This frontier ran roughly north to south along the 98th meridian, from the Fort Worth-Dallas region to just west of Austin, looped a few miles southwest of San Antonio, and swung into the coast along the Nueces. There was no Anglo settlement south of the Nueces except for some towns and ranches hugging the north bank of the Rio Grande. These towns, like Brownsville, had grown up as a result of the Mexican War, and the stationing of the army on the new border. The population of the border area was heavily ethnic Mexican, but the towns were developing an American dominant class. The land between the border and the Nueces remained as unsettled and as sunbleached as it had been fifty years before; in fact, it was less settled, because when Mexican General Woll retreated in 1842, he ordered the Mexican population to evacuate the country with him, and many ranchers did.

San Antonio itself, in 1860, still had very few Anglo citizens. The vast mass of the population was European and Mexican. One little-known fact is that by 1850, and for many years afterward, European, mostly German, immigrants in San Antonio outnumbered both Mexicans and Anglos.

The slave plantation economy had a large expansion between 1835 and 1860, with the greatest increase coming in the first years of statehood. The older regions near the Gulf developed rapidly, as the existing planters spread out and took in more land, and new farmer-capitalists deserted already worn-out regions of the old South for Texas. The river bottoms of the entire coastal plains were devoted to cotton plantations. The new area of expansion was in the deep northeast, along the Red. Not gradually but explosively, like all American settlement of the past decades, the pine woods region was filled up with new plantations, and thousands more acres broken to the plow by black men.

The farming, society, and outlook of this region, although it was rougher and had the earmarks of a newer frontier, were identical with the old South. Planters moved out of Mississippi and Georgia into east Texas without crossing any real frontier.

However, in those years it was not understood that the soils of the prairies that opened up beyond the tree belts in Texas would grow cotton. Also, this far inland the rivers shallowed and became unreliable for navigation, and the plantation economy of the South had always been river-bound. In the antebellum period, the plantation economy and Negro slavery generally halted about halfway through the Texas geographical prairies province, even before it reached its "natural" limits with the dropping rainfall and rising stony plateaus that began almost in the center of the state. The rich lands of the Waxy Black Prairie and the Grand Prairie that bordered on the pine and post-oak woods were first broken by Tennesseeans and Alabamans who migrated from the hill regions of those states, and owned few slaves.

Almost half the settled regions of Texas, extending beyond the river-bottom plantation belts, were populated by yeoman farmers, hill and forest men from the South. This area built a frontier farm economy and a frontier crop system very similar to that of the Midwest. The people who staked out their small farms along this great semicircle, reaching from Sherman-Denison in the north down to the vicinity of Austin, were alien, even hostile, to black servitude. The society was a rough, scattered one of distant small farms dotting the broad horizons. It was puritan, hardy, hard-working, and intolerant, in the way the Anglo-Celtic frontier of America had always been. The people had a passion for the land and an everlasting bias against social organism.

Thus this region between the Sabine and the Gulf and the inland, rising plateau line, where antebellum settlement stopped, which was to become the heartland of the state, was already divided economically and socially between the two great divisions of the old South, the old plantation and the old frontier. The coastal nucleus of Texas consisted of great plantations laid out among the moss-hung oaks along the broad, muddy rivers, where cotton grew splendidly in the mucky alluvial soils. Inland, where gently rolling post-oak belts and rich, blackland prairies began, the country was a series of log cabins and rough-hewed farm fences, enclosing fields of straggling corn. Beyond the oak and prairie belt, where the horizons broadened into rising plateaus of low, flat, stony-soiled hills, and the enormous seas of grass began, the settlement dribbled out. The cabins became more distant, separated by miles and miles, and the settlements significantly were no longer called towns, but forts. If the lights in the Texas forest by the middle of the 19th century were still few, in the middle of the state, on a north-south line that extended only a few miles south of San Antonio, the lights on the edge of the Plains were swallowed in vastness.

Within the confines of this prairies province, between the deep pine woods and the semidesert on the west, in a broad band running southeast from Dallas-Fort Worth to the fringes of Austin, excluding San Antonio, and curving inward toward the coast along the Guadalupe River—an expanded Colorado-Trinity enclave—most of the migrants settled, and a hundred years afterward, in these regions most Texans still lived. This must be called the Anglo heartland. It was completely agricultural in occupation, rural in outlook, ethnically divided between white Southern Americans and Negro slaves. There were almost no other influences beyond those of the old South and the old Southern frontier.

The origins of immigration into this heartland provide the key to Texan institutions and history as a whole. In 1836 the total population consisted of approximately 30,000 Anglo whites, 4,000 Mexicans, and 5,000 Negro slaves. By 1847, there were 100,000 Anglo whites, who owned 40,000 slaves. An enormous part of the early influx was made up of Southern planters, who came to acquire cheap or free lands, and brought their capital in the form of Negroes. For some years, the greatest inflow came from the upper regions of the South, hill men and small farmers, who took up the outer fringes of the heartland. In fact, immigration into Texas was almost equally divided between the upper and the deep South, but the percentage of Negroes, with the steady expansion of the cotton kingdom, rose. In 1850, Texas had 154,034 whites, 397 black freemen, and 58,161 slaves. But ten years later, in 1860, in a total population of 604,215, there were 182,000 slaves. These blacks were not spread evenly throughout the settled portions of the state. They were confined almost entirely to the eastern plantations; on the western frontier, and south of the Guadalupe River, slaves existed only rarely, and then as house or body servants.

This immigration into Texas was part of the expansion of the South itself; it was not an expansion out of the adjacent states of Louisiana or Arkansas, but by families who leapfrogged from Alabama or Tennessee. One-half the white population came from these two states, Alabama and Tennessee. These settlers largely came from the hill and forest sections, not from the plantation South; they were "red-necks" or yeoman farmers who went entirely into the prairie and post-oak regions far up the Texas rivers. They wanted to get away from the slave plantations, with which they could not compete; they could most easily acquire land on the far edge of settlement, and there was, noticeably, in these people an urge toward the far frontier. They took their cabin lights to the edge of Indian country.

Beyond even the Alabamans and men from Tennessee, there was a fringe of Missourians—these were borderers who pushed early across the Mississippi from Kentucky, and then moved southwest.

Georgia and Mississippi supplied large contingents, especially to the plantation regions near the coast. Georgians went heavily into the pine woods in the northeast and were also responsible for the growth of plantations along the Red. Only a small minority of Texas immigrants came from Louisiana and Arkansas in the years before 1860.

Because of climate, occupation, familiarity, and associations, immigrants congregated remarkably in certain regions. The Louisianans were mainly sugar planters or merchants. They rarely ventured beyond sight or smell of the Gulf of Mexico. They formed an actual majority of settlers from the Sabine to Galveston Bay; they made small enclaves at the mouths of the Nueces and even the distant Rio Grande.

Georgians and Mississippians stayed in the vicinity of Nacogdoches, expanding the slave society northward to the Red. One large group of Mississippi people gathered far south on the Guadalupe, however, and brought Negroes further south than they had been before. Other planters from these states helped fill the prairies between the river bottoms near the coast.

The Alabamans almost always went west of the coastal plains, up to where the rolling hills and oak trees began. They staked out their farms in rolling, grassy, tree-studded country, where once the Tawakonis and Wacos of the Wichita tribes had made a buffer between the Comanches and the coast. The Tennesseeans went even further west, across the two large prairie bands of north-central Texas, and to the edge of the cross timbers that stopped abruptly near Fort Worth. Here, there were also enclaves of Alabamans and Missourians, but the great outer frontier was populated primarily from Tennessee.

A phenomenon of this settlement was that pioneers from different distant areas did not usually congregate or mix. For hundreds of miles along a certain band, settlers from one region, such as Alabama or Tennessee, would be a hundred to a hundred fifty times more numerous than settlers from all other states combined. Mississippians and Georgians likewise peopled entire counties, and built them in a familiar image. The Missourians on the rimlands retained a Western, rather than a Southern, flavor. Ninety percent of all Texas immigration arrived out of the Southern states, but this did not mean it was entirely cohesive: west and east Texas re-created something similar to the old division between Appalachia and the tidewater.

One real variation in Texas, compared to the South, was the percentage of European immigration. In 1860, 43,422 Texans were foreign-born. Of these, 12,000 were Mexicans; "foreign," although most had been born in Texas, since they had not been born citizens of the United States. This Mexican population was almost entirely south of the Colorado River, and outside the heartland of Anglo-Texas.

In the early 1840's the Mavericks and a few others were the only Anglos in San Antonio, and there was only a handful of non-Mexicans in the settlements north of the Rio Grande.

One striking feature of the southwestern regions of Texas is that the border settlements were organized and dominated by people the Mexicans called Anglos, but who were primarily European immigrants. Germans, French, Austrians, and other assorted nationalities drifted to the frontier of Texas in those years in large numbers. They joined with a few Americans, almost all of whom came out of the Northern states, such as Pennsylvania or New York. These men were traders or merchants, following professions largely outside the Southern ethos; just as Pennsylvania Presbyterians had become the merchant class of the Ohio and Mississippi valleys, they cropped up surprisingly often on the dusty border, where the economy was entirely based on the Mexico trade and supplying Army garrisons. Conspicuous examples of these mercantilists were Captains Kenedy and King, who first arrived in South Texas as steamboat men serving the U.S. forces holding the Rio Grande. There were ephemeral fortunes to be made freighting and trading along the Rio Grande, and these men filled a vacuum the native Spanish-speaking ranchers could not fill. They hauled goods, loaned money, and acquired lands.

The tenor of Mexican life remained almost unchanged at the bottom, but at the top political control passed completely into the hands of the new arrivals. American and European immigrants organized the new counties, assumed the offices, and ran the country. This was not part of any ethnic plot to dispossess the Mexicans, who by the Treaty of Guadalupe Hidalgo were U.S. citizens. But few Mexicans were literate; they refused to learn English, and even the upper class was entirely ignorant of Anglo-Saxon institutions and politics and tended to be contemptuous of both. Under these circumstances political as well as economic control passed into the hands of recent American or European arrivals, from Brownsville to San Antonio. The Mexicans, whose vote was all-important, were "voted," as the saying went. They elected Anglo sheriffs and judges as they were told by Anglo merchants and bankers. In these first years, however, there was much social mixture and intermarriage between American newcomers—the merchant adventurers, unlike farmers out of Tennessee, rarely brought wives—and members of the Spanish upper castes.

In the 1850's, the border towns of El Paso and Brownsville, and San Antonio itself, were dominated by a handful of leading merchants or financial men, none of whom were born in Texas or the South. This peculiar politico-social system, in which ethnic Mexicans usually possessed numerical superiority but remained politically inert as individuals, became a lasting feature of south-Texas life. It was a logical outcome to centuries of Hispanic-Mexican tradition, in which the Indian and *mestizo* base were allowed no function in politics, and in which even the Spanish landed elite possessed no initiative beyond being permitted to sit on local municipal councils. Another feature of this developing society was that the American or Americanized newcomers acquired extensive lands; the early entrepreneur, if he stayed, became a rancher. In this way Richard King and Mifflin Kenedy, who with a few others at one time dominated all Texas south of the Nueces from Brownsville, became two of the largest landowners in the South. In the 1850's the nucleus of the immense King Ranch was formed.

In this way, also, much of the old caste and class structure of Mexico was perpetuated in south Texas. An Anglo-Saxon, or mixed Anglo-European-Spanish caste replaced the old Spanish land grantees at the apex of society. Although the new structure was American-oriented, English-speaking, and politically aware, it unconsciously adopted much of the patronizing attitude of the *rancheros,* whose ignorance of and impatience with the vagaries of American law and political practice completed their decline. Many Spanish landowners could never adapt to the American practice of taxation, where lands were taxed on assessed values, rather than merely on what they happened to produce from year to year. Each party—American and Spanish—considered the other system immoral, but the older owners' failure to exploit their lands cost them many titles through public sales. Further, the vast majority of Mexican inhabitants of the border regions could never make up their minds as to citizenship—American or Mexican —for almost one hundred years. This left them able to enter Mexico any time they chose, and many Texas-born Mexicans became prominent in Mexican government over the years, but it left them at a disadvantage at home.

Just as the Mexican presence that clung stubbornly to the fringe areas of Texas was outside or beyond the Anglo heartland, the great part of the European immigration avoided the Anglo regions. In 1860, there were slightly more than 30,000 European-born citizens in Texas. The vast majority were settled in the south-southwest, somewhere west and south of the Colorado. Unlike much of the foreign immigration that was now pouring into the northern United States, these migrants were almost entirely rurally oriented and agricultural.

During the 1820's and 1830's a number of French and Germans (Austrians and Swiss were among these, but usually called themselves Germans) entered Texas, but these men or families came individually. They either took up farming or sought employment as mechanics or artisans in the settlements, almost always founding their own businesses, since none existed before they came. The early immigrants joined in with the people of Anglo-Texas and almost invariably lost their European cultural identity quickly. The people who arrived in the 1840's and later did not, because they came en masse and formed enclaves. Meanwhile, the Irish colonies in south Texas had thrown in their lot with the Anglos politically in 1835, and except for a lasting Catholicism in some families, were hardly distinguishable from the Anglo mass. In Texas, no potato-famine Irish ever arrived.

The first successful non-English-speaking enclave was founded by Henri de Castro, on the Medina River fifty miles southwest of San Antonio in September, 1844. Castro's empresario grant, which included lands far south and west to the border, was in the path of the Comanche raiding trail to Mexico. He placed his town of Castroville in its safest, far northeastern corner. This was beautiful, rolling country, on the fringes of the Balcones Scarp, with a band of tall cypresses rising along the clear Medina. The region had stretches of fertile, river-valley soils, much like the area immediately surrounding San Antonio, though the general tenor of the landscape was rock and brush. Castro began with 300 colonists, most of whom were French citizens of Alsatian origin.

Though Henri de Castro himself went bankrupt in the process, he advertised widely in France and the regions of the Upper Rhine in Germany. He acquired many colonists. Medina County, which grew from this settlement of Castroville, spread for some miles along the river on either side of the town, which retained a certain Old World charm, blended with the starkness of the New World frontier. In three years, Castro brought a total of 2,134 settlers in through the Gulf of Mexico. The majority of these were listed in old censuses as French, but this tended to be confusing. They were primarily ethnic Alsatians; they spoke a Germanic tongue, and in Texas they generally described themselves as "Germans." A number of the Castroville people were also Swabians, Württembergers, and Swiss. They were heavily Catholic, and built one of the first non-Hispanic Roman churches in Texas. This colony clung, grew, and spread north and east until it merged, almost imperceptibly, with spreading German settlement coming down from the Balcones Scarp. The Castroites, however, kept their own historic and sentimental identity; in the 20th century thousands of south-central Texans, who could no longer speak a foreign language, referred to themselves as "Alsatians." They held annual mass reunions, but more from historic sentiment than cultural aloofness, for they had become indistinguishable from most Anglo-Texans.

There was a French colony, founded on the socialist principles of Fourier, established not far from Dallas in 1855. Here, 500 people gathered, cooperated briefly, quarreled, and drifted away. This colony, La Reunion, failed, but many of its educated French zealots stayed within the state. Small Scandinavian and Czech groups arrived in the 1840's. The Czechs (listed under Austrian nationality) were mainly intellectuals, fleeing the turmoil and repressions of 1848. They achieved, because of their level of culture, a remarkable influence in the skimpy intellectual landscape, though they merged quickly with the frontier population. Bedicheks and Nowaks soon sat comfortably in the pews of the Baptist Church.

English and Scots entered Texas. Forty-odd men born in the British Isles died in the Alamo, but since none of these came in bunches, and merged rapidly, they left no lasting mark, except Scots names on many of the places along the frontier. Cameron County, where both Palo Alto and Resaca de la Palma were fought, was named for a Scot in the Texas service.

In Texas, however, the German people planted what was to be their only successful colony overseas. Other Americans, and Germans touring Texas, are often startled to hear German speech, and to find wholly-German townships scattered through the scenic plateau on a diagonal stretching northwest above San Antonio from Cibolo-New Braunfels to the town of Fredericksburg, and to find almost a dozen counties in this hill country, so typical of the American Western frontier, where Germanic surnames predominate. Germans in Texas, not Indian-fighting pioneers, made the first permanent settlements above the Balcones fault.

This came about because of a tragicomic-romantic dream of a group of German noblemen, whose princedoms for the most part had been mediatized by Prussia. The vision and idealism of these princes is hard to fault, but the manner in which their ideas were implemented almost produced tragedy. It did result in one of the enduring legends of the Texas frontier, and in the end, sank German seed in Texas soil.

In 1842, these Prussian nobles formed the Society for the Protection of German Immigrants in Texas, called *Adelsverein* in German for short. The purposes of the *Adelsverein* were several: to create a new German father-land in America, where the German working classes and peasantry might emigrate and prosper, thus opening new markets for the industry at home, also developing German maritime commerce. The concept was thus the usual mixture of paternalistic idealism and mercantile colonialism that permeated many European circles. It is certain that some of the men involved genuinely wanted to offer the crowded and oppressed peasantry in the industrializing Germanies a better life; others were seeking an oppor-tunity to plant German influence, if not the flag, overseas. The Republic of Texas was chosen as the colonial base, for three reasons. It had the reputa-tion in Europe of having a healthful climate and good soils; it lacked the tariff and other barriers erected by the United States and other American republics; and last, Texas was small and emerging, and the princes hoped the German immigrants would be able to take and hold an influential, if not dominant, place in the Republic.

The Society sent one of its most energetic members, Prince Carl of Solms-Braunfels, to Texas in 1844, while thousands of emigrants were recruited in the north-central German states. The Society offered the fol-lowing bargain to each willing head of household for $240 and a promise to cultivate at least 15 acres for three years: free transportation to Texas, free land (320 acres per family), a log house, financing through his first crop, and a system of public services, such as mills, gins, hospitals, churches, asylums, and the like built at *Adelsverein* expense in the com-munity. Only some $80,000 was raised by the noble members to finance these services. This was extremely optimistic, but the Society was mistak-enly convinced that huge profits would be made soon by the sale of Texas lands. The *Adelsverein* had acquired the old Fisher-Miller empresario grant and proposed to settle half and sell the other.

This was one of the great and unheralded land swindles of the century, because Fisher and Miller not only had no right to sell the land, as the Germans thought, but when the transaction took place, they had already forfeited their empresario contract through failure to implement it in time. The fact that the entire grant lay inside Indian country, was far removed from all Texas civilization, and possessed only thin and stony soils without much rainfall were not understood by the *Adelsverein* until 1847—when 7,000 or more German settlers had already arrived in Texas. The two noble agents who investigated Texas in 1844 naïvely assumed that the geographical characteristics of the state were similar throughout. They never set foot on, or went near, the 3,000,000 acres the *Adelsverein* be-lieved it had acquired.

Prince Carl of Solms-Braunfels was thirty-three, handsome, and a first cousin to Queen Victoria. He was also something of a monumental fool, though he undoubtedly meant well. In Texas, he rode up the Colorado bottoms, displaying both aristocratic snobbery toward the rather rough-cut planters and intolerance toward the system of Negro slavery. This, his appearance in full uniform with sword and decorations, and his retinue of servants, valet, architect, cook, secretary, and someone hired as a "professional hunter," strained even the famous Texas hospitality.

Solms-Braunfels realized that the Fisher-Miller lands were too far from the coast to be reached at once by the emigrants who had already set sail behind him. Therefore, he set out to acquire nearer tracts, to be used as staging areas. After some difficulty, twice making deals with men who didn't own what they sold, he did secure some broad lands just above the sharp rise of the Balcones fault. The Prince was delighted with this country, which lay partway on the route to the Fisher-Miller grant. The fraying limestone had spectacular scenic beauty; the creeks and rivers ran clear, their beds green with watercress; the giant cypresses growing incongruously this far west along the waters and the pecan trees sprinkling the valleys made it seem fertile and rich. The Prince ignored miles of unpreempted black, rich soils below the scarp, and chose a site near a waterfall on the Guadalupe. He called this townsite New Braunfels. A large log house was thrown up and named *Die Sophienburg,* in honor of a light o'love.

But now crisis was crowding the Prince of Solms-Braunfels. Several thousand German peasants, recruited mostly from the Hesses, Hannover, Brunswick, and other central German states, were piling up on the docks at Galveston. They were transshipped to the *Adelsverein* base at Indianola, a landing point on the Gulf. These people were arriving with stars in their eyes; Texas was described in German newspapers as the land of milk and honey, full of Biblical promise. In crowded Germany, where farmers were used to working their lives out on fractional plots, the concept of 320 acres was almost too much to bear. *Geh mit ins Texas* (Go with us to Texas) they told each other, and the *Adelsverein* had almost 10,000 recruits.

It was also almost bankrupt. The Fisher-Miller lands could not be exploited, at least for years, and many promises were not to be kept.

The *Einwanderer* or immigrants were left camping on the fever coast, while plans were changed. Miserable, hungry, wan after weeks on shipboard, these stolid families sickened; infants died, and the great exodus quickly turned into a nightmare. Typhus broke out, and Texas was becoming a German grave.

At about this point Prince Carl of Solms-Braunfels resigned his commission and went home. He turned over the project of settling these countrymen to his deputy, Otfried Hans, Freiherr von Meusebach. Fortunately, Von Meusebach possessed the most important requisite of the true pioneer: he was adaptable. With great good sense, he began to call himself

"John O. Meusebach" among the Texans; he took Texan citizenship, and to the people of Texas he was always known as John Meusebach, a good man to do business with all around.

He tried desperately to get the Germans off the unhealthy coast, but due to war conditions in Texas it was impossible to hire enough freightwagons. The immigrants set out on foot, for a journey of some 300 miles. It was again a time of unusual storms and rains in east Texas. The ragged stream of humanity had to cross swollen rivers and toil day after day through endless mud. Then, the sun burned out, as they crawled westward. Along this march from Indianola to New Braunfels, many immigrants peeled off; exhausted or sick, they stayed behind and settled where they stopped. But the main body toiled on; soon, the Germans were leaving a trail of dead in their wake. The pitiful letters sent back to Germany reveal that the most fervent wish of many on this trek was that they be buried if they fell. A pillar of circling vultures followed the column for many days.

They came into the New Braunfels region and founded their town in 1845. Here, at least the climate was healthful and the country fair, though the farmers looked with some dismay at the hardscrabble rocks and flinty soils. Prince Solms-Braunfels had chosen lovely country, but not one in which pioneers could easily make a living. But the Germans spread through the valleys, and here and there they discovered sufficient meadow plots and plowable fields.

Meusebach realized that the New Braunfels community could not support all the thousands on the road. He needed more lands further west, toward the grant. He sought out the Penateka Comanches, who owned this country, and began to parley. His great point was that his people were neither Texan nor Mexican, two tribes the Comanches hated. The Penateka councils agreed to share their hunting grounds with *los Alemanes,* whom they recognized as a separate tribe. Meusebach offered the Indians about $3,000 worth of gifts, and in March, 1847, a deal was made. Meanwhile, during the parleying, the town of Fredericksburg, some eighty miles northwest of New Braunfels, had already been founded.

This Comanche-German treaty was never broken, but there was bloodshed when the Indians became embittered by other white aggressions in later years. Indians could not easily distinguish one Caucasian from another, and after 1860 much German hair adorned Comanche lodge poles.

The Germans founded a series of communities, in a long, fragmented stream reaching west from New Braunfels. Sisterdale, Boerne, Comfort, and several other small towns were planted through the hills. A handful of Germans even reached the Fisher-Miller lands, in the future Mason County, but the rainfall and the Indian attitude was too uncertain for the main body. During 1844–1846 the *Adelsverein* brought 7,380 Germans into Texas, and most of these, and the thousands who followed later, settled along the Balcones Scarp just above San Antonio. Though the Society went bankrupt in 1847, Meusebach stayed in Texas, working for the cause. The Germans underwent terrible hardships, but they were peasant-tough; they had avoided trouble with the Comanches, and they survived.

After 1848, a number of German intellectuals fled to Texas. There was one German utopian colony in the Fisher-Miller grant, called the "Latin Colony" because, although none of these people had ever farmed before, they were well educated. Although all the Germans were confirmed by the state in their lands, this colony went the way of most utopian communities on the frontier.

The Germans farmed intensively, on small plots, and they created a lasting impression of being better agriculturists than Anglos. But their influence on Texas farming has been overestimated. They settled in poor soils, compared to the heartland regions, and they adapted to the Texas frontier, rather than attempting to create a transplanted European way of life.

Along the Pedernales and other central Texas streams, the Germans farmed and ranched next to the Alabamans and Tennesseans filtering down the same valleys, and the two soon became almost indistinguishable. Although the Germans clung to their language in these hills, they adopted Texas agriculture. They abandoned wheat and rye for corn, and they soon let their stock run wild as the Southerners did, although such a custom was unheard of in Europe. The first German log cabins looked like Anglo cabins, and the small, limestone houses that followed them and soon weathered to a rich beige were Southwestern in style. This architecture, like the Victorian mansions along the San Antonio River the German patricians were soon building to the south, was not German; rather, it followed the dominant style of its place and time. Only the early churches looked European; they were transplanted cultural influences, like the Lutheran and Catholic creeds themselves.

Outside of the German tongue, which remained primary for about one hundred years, the other cultural differences, such as women working peasantlike in the fields, soon passed away. The one big difference between the Anglo and the German farmer was that the latter was less mobile. When the German put down roots, he did not leave. This trait later was praised extensively, but the 19th century Germans who stubbornly clung to their small rocky farms in the Hill Country fell into a kind of trap. They farmed intensively, in a day when land was open and could be acquired extensively by men of enterprise or vision. Those Germans who left the enclaves and entered the plantation economy did remarkably well, and those, like the Kleberg family, which intermarried with the Kings and eventually came to own the vast King Ranch, showed ability equal or superior to the Anglos at empire-building.

With their dominant peasant ethos, most Germans put enormous labor into their farms, but it took a century for most of them to prosper. They remained an isolated, ingrown community, healthy enough in themselves, stubbornly self-reliant, but adding few influences to the whole state.

The Europeans who struck out for the towns and settlements did vastly better. By 1860, there were more than 5,000 German-born citizens in San Antonio; these outnumbered the native Mexicans. More important, these immigrants, many of whom were middle class in origin, gave south Texas its first large mercantile and financial patriciate. They originated and founded most of the business enterprises in San Antonio, from banks to lumberyards, and with the Alsatian-French refugees from Castroville, soon gave San Antonio, with its Casino Club, a cosmopolitan air utterly unlike Anglo-Texas.

Noticeably, also, the Texas Europeans who settled in the towns quickly lost their foreign languages and cultures; these towns were small, and had no foreign quarters like those found in the North. The San Antonio Germans lost their German language at least two generations before the hill people did, and this same pattern held true with other groups, such as Czechs or Poles.

The heaviest European immigration, proportionally, arrived in these years, but compared to that in other parts of America, it was small. There were some 32,000 Western Europeans in Texas in 1860, but there were more than 400,000 native whites, and the European influences, although apparent and important in certain enclaves, never had any appreciable political or cultural influence on the State.

The advance to the 98th meridian from the old colony of Texas differed in no important way from the march out of Appalachia. The first men up the long rivers, the Brazos and Colorado, were Indian traders, who built blockhouses or forts, usually at forks or fords. A few families, living mainly by hunting, filtered in. Then, the remorseless push of the earth-breaking pioneer ruined both the good hunting and the Indian trade. Between 1836 and 1860 this advance into Indian country was similar to what it had been in the United States. First, Lamar's Texas militia drove the settled Indians out of the lands the whites coveted. Later, after 1845, the U.S. Army took over this function, first herding the remaining Indians further up the rivers, then, finally, unable to restrain the public clamor or protect the now pitiful remnants of the agricultural tribes, the whole conquered Indian population was marched north into Oklahoma.

By the middle decade of the century, Texas had carved a thousand-mile-long frontier into the center of the state. Counties were organized up to, and beyond, the actual settlement frontier. In the far south, Cameron County, with its seat at Brownsville, reached upward from the Rio Grande to Corpus Christi on the Nueces. Like the limits of the old Spanish land grants, legal boundaries proceeded many leagues ahead of the people themselves. Maps of the time could be misleading.

The most important factor in this development was that politically, socially, and economically the American frontier in Texas did not differ radically from the conditions of the 18th century. There were three great classes of people, excluding Indians and slaves: subsistence farmers, cotton planters, and the inhabitants of the towns. The towns were few and far between. The vast landscape was overwhelmingly rural.

The pattern of society was the same: hunter-trader-trapper on the far frontier; hunter-farmer behind him through a large yeoman belt; then the planters, forging their own kind of civilized existence in the rear. The towns, most of which were minor ports or river stations or mere crossroads settlements, supported this settlement when and where they could. Cities were not needed; none arose in the Texas heartland, in the antebellum years.

The vast majority of people lived no better, and most of them lived considerably worse, than the colonial inhabitants of British America. This was not due to any regression, but to the almost fantastic explosion of the settlement frontier. People continually outran their civilization when they passed beyond the reach of roads and rivers, and the countryside did not yet have rails.

Texas conditions were everywhere rougher and more primitive than in other states; many travelers noted this. During the whole antebellum era Texas was still a log cabin frontier. Although in the southwest Mexican inhabitants clung sensibly to adobe, or sun-dried clay bricks, and in the hill country the new German immigrants began building sturdy houses of native beige limestone, the vast majority of Anglo-Texans made dwellings out of hand-cut logs. Even in 1860, when sawmills had become more common in the state, most Texas farmers lived in homemade log cabins. The quality of cut lumber, and the shanties made out of it, tended to be wretched, and no improvement over hand-hewed timbers.

The home of the ordinary Texas settler was called a "dog-run." It consisted of two separate rooms or cabins connected under a continuous roof, but with an open corridor or "dog-run" left in between. This double cabin was usually built in segments, one room at a time. A porch was commonly extended in front of the dog-run house; this provided storage space for harness, tools, kegs, and saddles and a place for men and hounds to rest out of the hot sun. The cabin walls were roughly hewn logs, with dovetailed corners. The inevitably large chinks were daubed with mud. Chimneys were put together from mud-plastered sticks. The cabin roof was made of clapboard, anchored by weighted poles. The usual flooring was hard-packed mud.

To extend the dog-run, a lean-to shelter could be attached to the back side. This made extra storage space, or room for guests or a growing family. The older, more elaborate Texas farm cabins had outside kitchens and log smokehouses nearby. Cabins were located near a stream or spring; otherwise, a well was dug in the vicinity.

The common dog-run house was the result of social and economic necessity. In these years there were few settlements in Texas that could supply such things as lumber. The majority of pioneers who settled near the frontier could not afford the prices of imported materials or goods, and there were no carpenters or skilled craftsmen in the backwoods for hire, even if money could be found. Exactly like their forefathers along the Appalachian frontier, the early Texans made almost everything they needed or used, except salt, weapons, and metal tools. The Texas freeholder could erect a dog-run with his axe and saw, and almost without the use of a single nail. Even nails, like other artifacts, had to be floated down rivers from the industrial North, an incredible distance away. The pioneer was self-sufficient not through choice but through bitter necessity.

The families who went far up the Brazos, the Trinity, or the Colorado, left 19th-century civilization far behind. That they were, and had to be, self-reliant needs no elaboration. Just as the advance from Appalachia had no historic parallel, this march into the deep interior of Texas by thousands of individual families, supported by no government or other agency, against tremendous hazard, was almost without precedent. These people went west, each farmer yearning for his own small kingdom, willing to suffer hardship beyond counting while he carved it out with his own hands.

But if the dog-run house became the Texan's castle, it could hardly be called his pride. The frontier ethos of the Anglo-Celt rarely saw beauty in nature; it even more seldom created beauty out of man's domination of Nature. The usual cabin sat in a fire-blackened clearing; sometimes it was years before all the nearby stumps were removed.

Houses were surrounded by litter: farm implements, tools, beaten earth —there were no gardens or improved yards—and hungry hounds. The porches were stacked high with an accumulation of various junk; everything had its use, but no set place, on the frontier. The dog-run acquired its name from its most popular use, and the corridor was hardly the most sanitary of spots. Travelers who stayed overnight in the Texas countryside complained of holes in the cabin walls that let in moonlight and cold wind. Rutherford Hayes, passing through Texas, wrote that he slept in one dog-run through whose sides a cat could be hurled "at random." Sanitary facilities consisted of two kinds: crude outhouses or the nearest woods.

The people who inhabited these dog-runs were farmers of one kind or another, whether they were Tennesseans or Missourians living partly by their rifles, or Alabamans planting corn and yams in the post-oak belt. The small farmers did grow cotton when they could, for cash, but the ubiquitous crop was corn. All farmers, and even large planters, grew some corn. Corn, not wheat, was the Texas staff of life. It fed the pigs; it was sold or traded; and it made the daily bread. The average farmer harvested between forty and eighty bushels of corn per acre, although some, in richer lands, grew as much as one hundred. The next most common crop was sweet potatoes or yams, on which the Alabamans doted.

There were various kinds of livestock on these rough-cleared farms. Swine were the most common, although cattle were found, too. The idea that Anglo-Texans did not bring cattle with them is erroneous; the Southern farmers took oxen as well as pigs and chickens west. All this stock was permitted, as it always had been, to run wild in the surrounding woods. A few improved breeds had been imported into Texas from England, but animal husbandry was not yet a business, let alone a science. There was no market on the frontier. Horses were immensely more valuable than any other kind of stock, particularly good breeds. The reason was that horses provided the only available transportation, and horse racing was by far the most popular sport and pastime in Texas. There is a record of one fine piece of horseflesh being valued at $6,000 in the 1850's—three times the price of the hardest-working Negro. A good horse could earn money for its owner, and there existed also a phenomenon that could only be compared to Americans' passion for automobiles in later times: some farmers had, or acquired, horses they really could not afford. This love of horseflesh probably arrived out of Kentucky, but in Texas it seemed to spread to all citizens, wherever they were from.

Certainly, cultural traditions kept most Texans from enjoying a better life, particularly in the matter of diet. Texas soil and climate could support an enormous variety of cereals, vegetables, and fruits. Bees made superb brush honey, and cattle were beginning to roam widely, in large numbers. But almost all Texas pioneers lived on miserably restricted fare: salt pork, usually fried, corn bread, normally served hot, sweet potatoes, and molasses. Fresh meats, except game, were rare, and so was wheat bread. Although the Germans in the hill country planted fruit trees and made cheese and sausage, the pioneer American kept no milch cows and churned no butter. Texans stubbornly clung to the ways of the 18th-century mountain frontier, on which they had been raised. Children sometimes got pellagra—later the mark of the class known as "white trash."

Foreigners entering the great frontier band of Texas often could not help considering all the pioneer stock in the "trash" classification. The dog-runs were crude; the scars on the soil and forest were still raw. Thousands of Texans had been born in log cabins farther east, and they had always eaten corn pone and some kind of sweet syrup; no backwoodsman ever kept a garden. Many Texans who eventually became rich in the west kept on eating corn bread and fatback until they died, and considered milk barely fit for babies. But although there were thousands of genuine "white trash" who lived on as hopelessly and shiftlessly as they had wherever they had come from before moving to Texas, evidences of thrift, hard work, and resourcefulness abounded. For every family that brought up its dirty children to urinate against the dog-run, or let the half-wild cattle or pigs uproot their straggling fields, thousands more instilled the old Protestant, later called the American ethic: work as an absolute virtue, thrift as holiness, and visible success the outward evidence of both. Like almost all Americans, North or South, the Texans were puritans who were taught to equate cause with effect, and to look on life as a sort of battleground, in which the best man won and the weak were despicable failures. Since those who were weak failed conspicuously on the harsh frontier, this ethic was not without its logic.

Ironically, it was again not laziness but custom that made the Germans in the flinty escarpment northwest of San Antonio appear more diligent than the average Texan. The Europeans were brought up to intensive agriculture; they worked their small plots to perfection. But the American-born had never known, and could hardly conceive, of crowding, or an end to resources or land. They used land, then moved on. They thought in terms of leagues, while Germans treasured acres. In the 19th century, the native American concept was perhaps more valid than the rooted, European attitude toward intensive improvement of the land. The record is clear that the vast majority of great successes, and men who became large proprietors in Texas, were Anglo-American. The *Einwanderer* made decent, endurable small communities, but became trapped in them. Few Germans succeeded hugely—but then few of the European communities from Fredericksburg to Castroville suffered from the terrible residue of human detritus that littered the Anglo-American frontier. The tremendous strength of the American frontier was that many men thought big. Its seamy underside was that not every man had the strength, tenacity, or energy to fulfil his dreams, and the land broke him and his.

The family head who worked hard in these years, and who suffered no ill health or ill luck, showed steady, visible improvement. He put up fences of rails or stone with backbreaking labor; he spent twelve- to fourteen-hour days in the fields. He replaced his log dog-run with a house of neater frame. He began to be able to afford a few luxuries. He acquired a few Negroes, or to the south, some Mexicans for the dirtiest work. The first marks of affluence, which were still few in 1860, were the appearance of factory clothing or other "made goods" on the farm line frontier. But for many decades shoes, soap, candles, wheels, harness, shirts, and even coffins, were painstakingly homemade. The frontier man and woman had to be jacks and jennies of many trades, while gradually the fields began to take on the look of older, longer-settled areas, and rocks and stumps disappeared.

This life was hard, dirty, terribly monotonous, lonely, and damagingly narrow during the brutal years. Few of the Americans who later eulogized it would care to relive it. But it was also possible to despise the frontier farm, and the people who lived on it, too much. Tocqueville was one cultured man who saw or sensed that the American was living an ephemeral frontier phase. For every man, woman, and child trapped in a stultifying existence, thousands more were building the roots of an economic civilization, if not a new culture, on the land. As Tocqueville marveled, every frontiersman seemed to live with both an axe and a local newspaper in hand, and when there were a dozen pioneers within a few square miles, they pooled their small resources and began a school. These people lived worse than many European peasants, but they did not think as peasants. Their ethic did not permit it.

The great and lasting impression of this ephemeral time was the independence of the Texan in the west. The man who took his family out to the fringe of 19th-century civilization was beholden to no man. His land, in Texas, came free, or almost free, not in labor but in original money price. If he had no bank, or agency to assist him with cash or seed, he had no instrumentality to put him in debt. He had no landlord to sap his ambition or his fruits. The American pioneer, historically, was almost unique, because he did not have to go west, and though he went to improve his lot, he from the first intended to stay. If he suffered terrible failures, he made greater successes, because the country grew.

The enormous strength of this breed lay in their complete rejection of the organism of human society. The Texan, like all Westerners, was not antisocial, but asocial. He congregated or cooperated only for education, or defense, and then with some reluctance. No other breed, probably, could have lived contently for years on a far-flung frontier, where the distances between houses or farms was measured in miles. No Hispanic race, psychologically, could have endured it; the very notion chilled most Latin peoples to the core. They were gregarious; the Anglo-American, comparatively, was not.

Despite his terrible responsibility and the never-ending work, this was a tremendously exhilarating time for a strong man. Texas was open country. Although the Anglo settler could not much admire Nature, regarding it as an obstacle rather than a force to which he should attune, Nature provided a sense of freedom and exuberance. There were thickets to explore and prairies to ride. Here, where there were still deer, bear, big cats, and other game in every county, man's natural instinct as a hunter had full play. Almost every Texan hunted and killed game.

Beyond the pine woods, where Texans hardly changed much from the Southern stock from which they came, a man could see far and smell winds that coursed down from Canada across a thousand miles of plains. There was an apparently endless, rolling vista north and west and south. The small woodchopper, with an axe and a couple of brawny sons, could catch a scent of landed empire or dream of possibilities to come. Less than half a million Texans scattered across a land as large as Britain, and the land itself had to remain dominant. The new Texans tore down trees, built cabins, threw up fences, and scratched furrows in widely separated small fields, but there was too much raw land for the countryside to take on a settled, civilized look. And the tremendous vagaries of weather in this part of the world—the Texas land mass was subject to blazing droughts, followed by torrential rains, the mild winters were stabbed by sudden, chilling, arctic cold fronts, called "northers"—made all settlers uneasily aware of forces beyond human control. The average Texan was still just a speck on a vast land; he could not forget that land.

A feature of this frontier was that only a few men could create empires, or even riches, in the new west. Most families were unable to clear and plant even the generous initial grants of the Republic and state. The pioneer farmer had only his own, or his sons', labor, and sons left home early. The average family scratched out a limited living from their subsistence farm. But the dream of personal empire, which had somehow become permanently attached to the name of Texas, never died. Big country, even terrible country as Texas could be in the western counties, fed big dreams, and even the outright failures never quite lost them. Almost every man in Texas, walking over his broad acres, seeing the far horizons, fell in love with his dreams and the land. The changeable weather, the distances, the soil, and the loneliness were merely hardships or obstacles to be overcome. But if men loved Texas, women, even the Anglo pioneer women, hated it. Women had different values and different dreams. In diaries and letters a thousand separate farm wives left a record of fear that this country would drive them mad.

In their lonely clearings and isolated dog-run houses, women went for days and weeks without seeing a neighbor, and without the security and comforts of the civilization they had left.

The agriculture and land-breaking of the Texas heartland impressed few foreign travelers. Techniques were hardly improved, except for steel plows, from biblical times. Europe was far ahead in the practice of intensive farming, and the American Midwest was already forging ahead of Europe in mass agriculture based on broad fields and new machinery. Only a few of the most far-seeing visitors noted that Texas above the cotton belt had few social handicaps, such as absentee land tenure or a settled peasantry. Most noted instead that the European peasant lived better than the average Anglo pioneer.

The one remarkable aspect of this frontier, however, was its literacy and general political awareness. In 1860 there were seventy-one newspapers in Texas, with a total circulation of about 100,000. Ninety-five percent of the white population could read and write and some publication reached virtually every family. No European nation of the time could boast a better average, certainly not among its poorest, rural population. In this sense, Texas was truly an extension of Anglo-America. If it lacked the seeds of culture, it had already put down the roots of civilization: literacy and schools.

The newspapers, daily and weekly, were devoted more to political comment than the dissemination of factual news. Ordinary events, such as disasters or personal news, were rarely printed. There was no telegraph south of New Orleans; also, taste prohibited the mentioning of women's names in public print. But papers devoted themselves to the public issues of the hour, from the local to the national scene. Editorial writing in the backwoods was an art before newspapers became mere advertising media.

This writing was often irate, biased, and misinformed—but much of it was clear and sound. It kept the freeholders of Texas fully aware of events; many farmers could quote Senator Stephen Douglas or Sam Houston at length. Texans were already keen political animals.

Like the newspaper publishers and printing presses, the schoolmasters and curriculum were imported from the older states. Although there had been no official provisions for public schools until 1854, when the windfall from the New Mexico boundary settlement was made available, the frontier counties as well as the older regions already had an adequate educational system. The settlers worried much about the education of their children, both boys and girls. As soon as a dozen or more families were located in any region or new-made county, the farmers tried to organize a school. A building was thrown up or made available; a schoolmaster was imported from the East. Every family shared the costs of the teacher's salary, which as often as not was paid in land or kind. No schoolteacher in Texas went hungry or failed to find a place of honor at any table.

In the antebellum period the courts held that the creation of county school districts, and the assessment of general taxes for education, was unconstitutional. It was not, however, considered illegal for the state to reimburse parents for each child enrolled in a recognized school. The government paid out, beginning in 1854, sixty-two cents per year per student, without regard to the nature of the school: private, parochial, or "field." This amount was raised to $1.50 in 1855. Most Texans in the rural areas attended "field schools"—a school which families in a community or region had established by providing a building and hiring a teacher, on their own. Thus there were no direct taxes, and the state monies went a long way toward paying the cost of instructors. Books were not a great problem, because only a few—primers, readers, and simple arithmetic texts—were used. The system was both public and private, but it created no constitutional or social problems. The population was remarkably homogeneous, almost tribal in its culture, and the education provided was sufficient for the time and place.

Those small groups outside the Anglo mass, Roman Catholics or Mexicans, either had their own schools organized the same way or were indifferent to education. No true public school system was established prior to the War Between the States. And since there was so little foreign immigration, the notion of the public school as an "Americanizing agency" simply never arose. Boys and girls went to school to learn certain essentials to fit them for their future life, not as part of any planned social process. The graduate of a field school, with a grade school education, was completely fitted to extend American civilization as he knew it further west. Culture and philosophy were not Anglo-American concerns. Neither had any real function on a frontier where everyone had to work. Yet an enormous amount of both was transmitted through the Holy Scriptures, which were used as a text in most schools. And the Protestant or "American" ethic was preserved and enhanced also by these local schools, quite unconsciously, because it was the ethic and culture of the land; teachers and pupils shared it and had learned it before they even went to school. It was this last that eventually made Roman Catholic immigrants increasingly concerned about "public" education, and led the clergy to establish its own schools in a long and in the end futile attempt to isolate Catholic children from Anglo culture.

The historical role of the English Bible in this Texas has increasingly been overlooked. But the King James Version afforded this stultified civilization on the fringes of the 19th-century Western world with a great part of the basic culture it required. It gave the frontier farmer what later Soviet poets tried to transmit and preserve in Russia under Communism: a basic folklore, philosophy, and literature. It was, in fact, almost the only literature most families possessed.

The Old Testament fitted easily into the 19th-century Texas world. Its revelations of the human condition were held, even by the nonreligious, to be entirely valid and timelessly true. The young Texan read of evil that was ancient and ever-present, requiring eternal discipline of man; he learned of false prophets and lying sycophants, of licentious Jezebels and foolish kings, of mighty warriors and wise men. He absorbed an unflattering impression of such intellectual tribes as Scribes and Pharisees. And although few could articulate it or explain it, Texans gained a timeless portrait of man's world, of the rise and fall of peoples, of bondage and deliverance, of God's patience and wrath, and man's enduring inhumanity to man. Visitors were often surprised to find Texans, who had no apparent cultivation, able to strip vanities and euphoric philosophies from better-educated men. As a cultural, folkloric instrument the Holy Bible played its part, in a way no official history or intellectually fabricated philosophy ever could.

There was a developing higher education, too. In 1859, Baylor University, a Baptist institution, awarded twenty-two bachelor degrees. There were forty academies, thirty-seven colleges, twenty-seven institutes, seven universities, two seminaries, and one medical college. These terms were then loosely used, but this was an impressive total. All these schools were private, and the great majority were denominational. They were established and supported initially by the more highly developed society in the older states. Both through its schools and its continuing stream of Eastern-educated lawyers moving west, the frontier was chained inescapably to the region behind; the last frontier was an extension of American society already made. The farmers supported themselves, but the literacy and the outlook of the region could not have been supported without the steady flow of young teachers, professors, clergymen, lawyers, and academicians arriving daily in the West. Thus all the "Western" cultures that derived from, or arose on, the frontier were and had to be abortive.

The hundreds of thousands of independent subsistence farmers staking out lands in Texas were the mass of its people and the salt of its earth, but the distinguishing ethics, ideals, and social customs of the state were not transmitted by dour Missourians on the frontier or red-necked farmers from Alabama or Tennessee. The yeoman farmers of Texas were not much different from their colleagues in Kansas or Illinois; all initially came from the same frontier stock. But the great difference between Texas and the other regions of the West was that Texas had a planter class. The cotton planters, not the farming middle class, stamped the lasting standards of conduct upon the Lone Star State.

Planters came with the first Anglo-Texans; in fact, Stephen Austin's immigrants were heavily composed of this class. The true frontier farming element did not begin to arrive until twenty years later. Understandably, both because of early settlement and social and financial prominence, the planters formed the apex of society in Texas. They were not a ruling class, but they exerted a profound influence on government, manners, and thought, out of all proportion to their numbers, which were always small.

Southern capitalism took a different turn from that developed in the North. The Texas capitalist had two ingredients to work with, fresh lands and Negro slaves. Out of this land and forced labor he created new capital, which almost universally was reinvested in more land and more slaves. The system was vitally different from the incipient industry in the North in two respects: the surplus produced, cotton or sugar, was sold overseas or to the industrial North, and thus the economy remained colonial. And Negro slavery, introduced by the English in the 17th century as a purely economic expedient—there never was, and never would be, sufficient white agricultural labor in America—was institutionalized as a way of life.

Both developments, historically, were enormous social errors. Yet in 1800, or even several decades later, as Toynbee speculated, this was not apparent. The plantation system of the South produced more wealth, and a greater surplus of capital, than the rocky soils of New England or the forests of the Middle Atlantic States. There were rich merchants in Boston, New York, and Philadelphia, but none of these compared in grandeur to Harrisons, Carters, Rutledges, or Middletons, baronial planters not only with vast estates, but with impressive educations and law degrees. It appeared that the Southern concept of America would prevail, particularly after the invention of the cotton gin and the explosion of the plantation economy west. But this explosion and expansion was remarkably static; like the advance of the Roman Empire after the time of Caesar, it spread the old culture and created nothing new.

The South, from Virginia to Texas, remained agricultural, because its leading men were agriculturists, and because soils, climate, and the existence of a growing slave population were superbly fitted to the accretion of *latifundia*. A noticeable trend in colonial America was the movement south of many New Englanders in search of opportunity; North Carolina and Georgia were brought into the American Revolution by transplanted Yankees. Few, if any, of these 18th-century migrants who succeeded—as lawyers, doctors, merchants, or overseers—failed to acquire Negroes and set themselves up as Southern gentlemen. This indicates that geography more than morality permitted the American North and West to escape the incubus of Negro slavery. The fact that Northern shipmasters furnished Virginia and the Carolinas with their original slave stock indicates the same.

It is also very clear that the Southern concept of America failed because the plantation system failed to make any impression on the American West above the Ohio. The vast Middle West and Far West were economically and socially allied with the North and Northeast. Without the millions of freeholders in this West, the abolitionists of Boston and the industrialists of the Middle Atlantic could never have politically or militarily dominated the American South. Just as geography turned the North in other ways, geography finally assured that the glittering cotton kingdom would never be more than an American enclave. In 1860, the plantation system was within a hundred miles, roughly, of its farthest natural limits at the edge of the Texas Plains.

Very few of the Founding Fathers of the United States, from ethical reasons, favored human slavery. Even the conservative George Washington, probably from association with Lafayette and Jefferson, experienced qualms. Just as the Englishman was poorly fitted by his law, ethic, and experience to "make a slave of any man," Americans were similarly badly suited to hold Negroes in bondage. Yet, in 1776, the problem was seen as economic. Slavery had to be accepted by the Union, or else there would have been no Union. Carolina would not ally with or enter into a confederation that did not respect its domestic property. It is also clear that at least until the 1820's, the principal opposition to slavery on moral or ethical grounds centered in Virginia and the South. Ironically, abolitionism collapsed in the South just as it began to become virulent in the North. There was a strong infusion of regional politics, economic differences, and political ideology in each case.

The Southern states' view of the Union as a confederacy of sovereign entities was constitutionally more valid than the North's growing concept of a common market, with common economic and social regulation, and the Southern defense of low tariffs was a completely logical argument based on self-interest. There was no more reason for a Southern cotton grower to sacrifice anything to build an American industrial machine than for a Northern industrialist to be tied to an agricultural national policy. In the course of human events, sooner or later, one region or the other had to be subordinated or the Union dissolved. Even the English-speaking genius for political pragmatism and compromise could not paper over the split forever. But the terrible weakness of the Southern economy was not its colonial vulnerability but its dependence upon Negroes. By the middle of the 19th century slavery was no longer in tune with the times. The mere existence of slavery gave the North an enormous moral weapon to make the average man, who was somewhat indifferent to the constitutional question of whether the Union was a confederacy or unitary state or whether industrialism should be helped or hampered by law, fanatic enough to be willing to fight. At the same time, the aroused fear of enforced Negro equality among Southern freeholders produced a similar fanaticism below the Ohio. One reason the Northern states could be sanguine about emancipation, then and later, was because almost all the Negroes were in the South.

Aside from the emotional questions of right or wrong, or subordination and equality, emancipation by 1860 had become economically unreasonable. In Texas, the assessed value of all slaves was $106,688,920—20 percent more than the assessed value of all cultivated lands. Whatever its moral capital, the South had invested its economic capital in blacks. Like many another capitalist or dominant group before and since, the Southern gentry, in coping with a labor problem, had fallen into a terrible cultural and racial trap. It was more vulnerable to criticism than either the Northern industrialist paying out slave wages or a government using forced labor, because the cotton planter was creating no fruits for the descendants of his workers to enjoy. The great mass of Negroes were never expected to rise out of bondage. And the profits of the plantation economy were rapidly creating a new leisure class that, however admirable in many respects, was already an anachronism in the 19th-century Western world.

Seen in perspective, the Texas cotton planter was of all Americans closest to the old gentry or squirearchy of the Atlantic slopes. There was not much difference, in education, outlook, ethic, or manners, between a Texas cotton grower in 1860 and one of Long Island's landed gentry a hundred years before. Both held vast estates, both hunted and rode their fields, both believed in lavish hospitality, both were intimately engaged in public affairs. Neither considered their kind an aristocracy on the European order, but rather the natural leaders of a society of freemen. Nothing is clearer than that the "deferential society" of colonial America, with its ethical liberalism, economic conservatism, and somewhat organic outlook, survived all the way to Texas, while concurrently it dissolved in the North. There was no real regression—but there was little change. More than any other group in the 19th century, the planters tended to perpetuate the manners, ideals, traditions, politics, and codes of the gentry that founded the United States. But where Washington, the Adamses, the Morrisses, Livingstons, Monroes, and others once led an agricultural American society, the Texas planter now existed in an American nation where 92 percent of the productive power and two-thirds of the people had abandoned deferential ways. He was still powerful and respected in his region, but he was beginning to be despised nationally, for reasons that went far beyond slavery.

As both its politics and literature show, the American North meanwhile had gone through a process of vulgarization, immigration, economic growth, and political change. The Northern gentry never extended beyond the valley of the Hudson or the center of Pennsylvania, and where they stood, they were submerged.

While the puritan, egalitarian society of the frontier developed unhindered through Ohio westward, a combination of European immigration, rising industrial wealth, decline of the old rational ethic, and the increasing turbulence, violence, and economic fanaticism of America itself sapped the original gentry. As lethal as anything was the growing power and concept of money, which seemed to have a deadly effect on the public spirit and instincts of the squirearchy. And in its way, the westward movement destroyed the old liberal, ethical America: the nation exploded across the continent, killing Indians and Mexicans, building a vast economy and a dynamic industrial machine. All of this seemed to happen without rational decision or control; the governments of America merely kept adjusting or reacting or rationalizing to events already in full swing. The Eastern gentry were generally in favor of none of these things; they could not prevent them. The election of Andrew Jackson was not a blow against the gentry, but merely a symptom of its decline and of the rise of a new necessity for America: the political party, and the political boss, and the alliance between groups and regions rather than compromises worked out by a few men. The gentry had always been regional in outlook, fighting for a strong Federalism only to assure credit and good order. But the rise of the first political boss, Martin Van Buren, without whom Jackson could not have reached the White House, indicated a new kind of Federalism was in the wind. At the same time, the precipitation of a financial panic by the gentry opposed to the first President "from the people" indicated starkly the bankruptcy of what had once been America's most ethical group or class, and showed that the American people, perhaps, needed a new type of tribune. By the 1830's, it had become increasingly difficult to distinguish a genuine American gentry. The old families had increasingly declined into a mere financial or industrial upper class, whose rational ethos was already operating on a kind of Darwinism before Charles Darwin popularized his limited studies of what was then thought to be the way of all life.

This was logical, a reasonable outgrowth, because apparently America had been operating under a form of social Darwinism for some time. It no longer seemed either feasible or reasonable for a handful of intelligent, highly motivated men to shape, or even direct, public affairs. At any rate, there was a mass desertion of public service by the old-new rich. If three out of four of the new financial or industrial elite came from old colonial families, all disappeared into the economic whirlpool. The age of the coal or steel senator, manipulated by money interests, was at hand. The power of northern America was increasing by quantum leaps, while the loss of social values was equally profound, long before the existing situation was rationalized into the new Republican Party.

The changes in the North were also erasing state boundaries. There was a tendency among immigrants from Europe, whether Irish or German, to insist on being Americans, not citizens of Illinois or New York, and this had its influence. But industrialism and the tying-in of the Midwest with the North economically was a greater factor in changing the view of sovereign states to one of a unitary nation. The emerging, classless, amorphous, silk-stockinged new elite in the North was largely without ethic, and thus without responsibility, but it did have clear economic vision: they looked upon the United States not as an alliance of regions but as a potential market. The industrial leadership's role in forging national laws and destroying state powers over business and industry was to be immensely greater in the 19th century than the efforts of all the reformers and advocates of Presidential power combined.

The life, and the role, of the Texas planter was light-years removed from that of the Northern businessman and from the existence of the subsistence farmer who lived beside him. The planters had gone a long way to forging Texas in the old, or 18th-century, American image.

By the time Texas became a state, "planting" was becoming less and less a business enterprise and a road to wealth, and more and more a genuine way of life. Cotton planting, despite falling prices in the 1850's, was still profitable. But the evidence indicates that many successful men in other lines, such as law or medicine, deliberately bought plantations and slaves at an outlay that could hardly be remunerative for years. Even in bad years, the prices paid for field Negroes constantly rose. Most successful men aspired to be planters, for the same reasons that English merchants of the 18th century purchased landed estates at prohibitive prices—eighteen or more times annual rents. The ownership of Negroes, with its implied and actual removal from trade or labor, imparted status. It was impossible for a man to pose as a landed gentleman without slaves.

Contrary to popular opinion, even a large number of European immigrants who settled in or bordering the Anglo heartland by 1860 had purchased blacks.

Owning slaves, however, did not make a man a planter. The title belonged only to families who had enough black capital to justify the expense of a white overseer—usually considered to be twenty or more Negroes. The planter, who never called himself a farmer, was thus completely removed from direct participation in his enterprise; he was a member of an owning, directing, semi-leisure class. He gave orders to his overseer, or rode past his fields; he rarely entered them except for inspections.

The vast majority of Texans owned no slaves, although they were farmers. More than half of the actual slaveholders owned five or less. These men supervised their own slaves, and frequently worked in the fields beside them. Although some thousands of yeoman farmers owned between one and twenty Negroes, the true planting class was extremely small. It numbered about two thousand families. Of these, only fifty-four held one hundred or more slaves. Since a good field hand could be rented out for

$200 to $300 per year, or was expected to produce eight bales of cotton, these families were relatively quite rich. And since a healthy field hand cost as much as $2,000 in Texas, and a "plow boy" almost as much, the larger planters held an enormous money investment in their way of life. In these years the greatest Texas planters were very rich, even by Northern money standards. This was not unnoticed, or unresented, in the North and West.

During this period, there was a continual importation of Negroes from the older states, particularly those of the upper South, where the plantation economy was phasing out. Importation from Africa or the Indies was illegal. However, dealers in Galveston and Houston, on the coast, were always able to have slaves of all ages and both sexes in stock. The mayor of Galveston himself supervised a slave auction at least once a week. The supply never quite caught up with the demand. The common supposition that Texas, or the Gulf South, was or would soon have abandoned slavery for economic reasons does not bear out. Between 1850 and 1860, the census years, the slave population of Texas increased 213.8 percent. The white population, in these same years, rose at a rate of approximately 177 percent.

In the old Brazos-Colorado colony and in much of east Texas, the black people greatly outnumbered the white. Only at the plateau line, in central Texas, did the countryside become completely white. And slavery was encroaching westward; it would have reached the Dallas-Sherman line in a few years, as soon as it was realized the black prairie soils would grow cotton as efficiently as coastal muck.

Freed from work, if not from worry, by his slaves, the planter had both the time and inclination to be influential in the state. As an obviously wealthy and successful man, he was given at least a grudging due and deference. Almost every true planter enjoyed considerable influence in his own area or county. Lesser men consulted him on political or business affairs; his choice for sheriff or commissioner was closely watched. He performed the only true social life in the county, and he set the dominant social standards other families looked up to. The greatest planters were known throughout the state, and some had influence in Washington.

In his own society, the Texas planter was neither passé nor phasing out; if he had suffered the general loss of ethic and rationalism the whole century was heir to, he was still vigorous and possessed of high morale. He had not succumbed to the funks of the Northern landed class, who were increasingly taking refuge in pure money power. Significantly, the planters had little true money power; their influence was based on deference and the fact they filled a social vacuum at the top. Many planters dabbled in mercantile enterprises and investments on the side, and they were completely allied with the practitioners of the law. Most judges were planters; and many planters, with no intention of serving at the bar, read law. Lawyer, clergyman, doctor, and—a tradition that never saw birth in the North—soldier were the genteel occupations; at the base of all these, around which they revolved, was the landed slave estate.

The mark of the planter class was not its wealth as such but its removal from labor and economic activities. This was a tradition carried unbroken from the English squirearchy of the past, as was the tradition of concern with public affairs. Also, a significant number of planter families were Episcopalian, in a Trans-Appalachian West where the mass of farmers had deserted the Reformation churches for fundamentalism.

Although there was ample evidence of class conflict in the South, particularly in the mountain states, it is difficult to uncover this in Texas. The biggest reason was that Texas was new country, with millions of acres of undeveloped lands. A family that found itself stifled or encroached upon by burgeoning planters in the east could move easily up the rivers toward the west. The small farmers thus congregated in their own belts beyond the planter coast; they did not yet really impinge upon each other. The dirt farmer could and did resent the planters' prosperity and social arrogance. But although the planters strongly influenced state politics, they did not, in this era, deny the poorer whites anything to which they considered themselves entitled. The small farmer was as violently opposed to direct taxation on his acres, for any social purpose, as was the conservative, constitutionalist planter on his estate.

Nothing like a landlord-tenant, noble-serf, or employer-employe relationship existed. The aristo-democracy of Texas worked well, because every citizen was, or had the potentiality to be, a freeholder. This system, however, confused not only some later Americans, but contemporary European immigrants of socialistic views. Some Germans in San Antonio went about nailing up placards condemning the "oppressor class" while Anglos read these with bewilderment. It was, of course, impossible for any Texas white to identify with "niggers"; many Europeans, however, were too recently removed from serfdom. It was very easy for newcomers, unfamiliar with American society, to equate cotton planters with cotton barons.

The sweat of his Negro chattels allowed the planter to live better than anyone in Texas; the life of plantation whites was a different world from the disorder and labor of the average dog-run. Although a feature of early Anglo-Texas was that all classes, planter with slaves and free farmer alike, lived in hastily thrown-up log cabins, many of the planters were making incomes of $5,000 or more while the yeoman had a surplus of only a few bags of corn. Immediately after San Jacinto, some of Austin's Old Three Hundred began erecting impressive houses. These dwellings were built of walnut, pine, cedar, or cypress planks, and in a few cases out of brick. Texas plantation houses were similar to, but did not follow exactly, the Greek revival architecture of the Mississippi delta. They were generally less large and imposing, and had simpler lines; this was probably due to the influence of the ever-present frontier. But they were sturdy and well built, with large and airy rooms, set into broad lawns or natural shrubbery. Most plantation houses had extended porches, or galleries, some surrounding the house. Many were fully carpeted, with decorated ceilings. Mirrors and chandeliers were shipped in from Europe, and marble for fireplaces was brought from Italy. Furniture, of walnut or other woods, was usually locally made, or imported from the United States; it was simply and beautifully made. Very few Texas country houses showed evidences of florid, baroque, or rococo styles; they did have lines that later builders often sought to imitate. The Varner Plantation House, built on the Brazos in 1836, Wyalucing, erected by Beverly Holcomb at Marshall in 1850, and the McNeel House, in Brazoria County, were outstanding examples of important family seats.

From these houses planters looked after their operations, almost always from a room called the "office." Here business agents were consulted, and overseers were given their orders. The "office" much more resembled a library or study than a modern business room; in fact, those Texans who possessed libraries invariably called them offices.

Not far from the main or Big House were the overseer's little house, and the slave cabins, usually in a row. There were no bars on the cabins, but occasionally bars on the kitchen of the big house, to prevent food filching by hungry blacks. The overseer sometimes ate with the planter, but never slept in the big house. House slaves worked in the kitchens and in the plantation house, but an unwritten protocol required them never to sit down while inside. Intricate codes of conduct, between slave and master, overseer and owner, and even slave and poor white, were already far advanced. Since there were codes, there was none of the social unease that frequently attended the relationship between servant and master in the North.

The traveler William Bollaert, who was familiar with the homes of the English aristocracy, left this impression of a day in the life of the leisure class at Galveston during the Republic:

> About sunrise prudent and judicious people will arise, prepare their toilette, clad themselves lightly, walk or work in the gardens, then ride or bathe on the seashore. . . .
>
> A small bell is now rung when all take their places at the breakfast table—the ladies at the top. We all appear to suffer a little langor, the air is sultry . . . we get this meal, which is a most excellent dejuener [sic] a la fourchette—retire, light the gentle Havana, discuss the politics of the day . . . then those who have business attend to it. Idlers may return to their rooms, read—and these idlers and visitors read a great deal—Bulwer's last novel of Zanona is here, this is a great favorite—then, before dinner, billiards or ninepins may be played. . . .
>
> We congregate on the Verandah—impart to each other news etc— probably take an iced mint-julep—the ice comes from U. States—a glass of Madera [sic] and bitters etc. etc. . . .
>
> Towards 4 or 5 o'clock pairties [sic] are made to go fishing on the beach . . . or a gallop on the prairie till dark . . . it is generally a tea supper—a quiet smoke on the Verandah—long chats—then each one off to some evening party or other—but it does not require much pursuasion

[sic] to sit for an hour or two in the cool of the evening, sup a mint-julep—touch a guitar and sing the song most loved.

The description fits the life of almost any landed leisure class, from the country houses of England to the *haciendas* of Mexico or Peru. Some historians have claimed that this manner of life was well on its way to giving birth to a genuine indigenous culture. This is doubtful, even though the links to the dominant American puritanism were fast eroding away; the English gentry, with centuries-longer existence, failed to produce a genuine culture. The American planter was a recognizable reflection of his British cousin, in a completely rural atmosphere without the civilizing effect of London. In another generation or two the Texas planter might have become a patron of the arts, but this would not have replaced his preoccupation with his hounds. It was not incumbent upon a leisure class to create art, and the planter had visible business-capitalist origins, despite his movement in search of aristocracy.

Yet this life of Grecian symmetry, or monumental idleness, was producing intimations of an American culture quite different from the dominant puritanism of both the North and the South. A studied languor replaced the furious display of energy the middle class considered proper. Many planters worked at their businesses, and worked quite hard, but the trick was to pretend not to. Gentlemen did not sweat. Planters were not frugal or thrifty. Their tables carried enormous varieties of meats, fish, vegetables, fruits, hot breads, cakes, preserves, and jellies, as a facet of the code of hospitality. It was not unusual for a planter to seat forty people at lunch. He imported excellent boots and fine firearms from London, and wines and liquors from the Continent.

The planters, as a class, were not "moral" in the puritanical sense, as the farmer and tradesman tried to be. Planters drank, smoked, gambled, cursed, loved a horse race; they brooked no insults, either direct or subtly implied. There were dark corners in their sex lives that did not meet the Victorian codes. But the planter lived by a stern ethic, or was supposed to: he was gracious, hospitable, and courageous, decent rather than frigidly moral. He did not lie, cheat, or steal; he was considerate to "inferiors," and his womenfolk were always "ladies." On all these recognizable aristocratic manifestations the planters built an imposing image, both public and personal. It permeated the entire Texas frontier by 1861, because, as one historian rather sourly noted, enough of it was true.

Hundreds of miles from the lower Brazos where the plantation houses stood, mothers in dog-runs and sod shanties begged their frontiersmen sons to "act like Southern gentlemen." On the edge of nowhere, the Anglo-Celt farmer who had neither the inclination nor wherewithal to be hospitable to strangers felt called upon to ask passersby in for meals. On the frontier that eventually stretched from Brownsville to Calgary, many men learned unhappily that pistol-hung Texans of non-gentry background had somehow acquired a sense of honor that was better not scoffed at or impugned. In Texas, the influences of the planter class penetrated far beyond the falls of the Colorado. They sank into the far frontier and created a certain, lasting confusion in the Texas frontiersman's social patterns. He emerged part surly borderer, part puritan democrat, part normal Westerner, but with the traditions of the Southern gentleman seeded ineradicably in some corner of his soul. He could slip from one role to the other unconsciously, confusing everyone but himself. If the wheat farmers of Kansas evolved with certain differences from the corn hoers of Texas, it was because Kansas never had a planter class.

The inherent liberalism of the planter was not transmitted because it was the liberalism of social confidence, never that of conformity or popular prejudice. The old saying—anyone could enter through the planter's door, while the middle classes made inferiors and "niggers" go round back—had a biting truth. The planter, like the early Presidents from the same class, never cared what worse-disposed men wanted or believed; he deliberately gave each man his due, according to his worth or attainments. Negroes were slaves, and were treated like slaves—but the planter was more disposed to regard blacks as human beings than poor whites. He could value a good Negro above a poor white man, something the more tribal breeds of Americans never dared do. He demonstrably, in this era, took Jews and European Catholics on their personal merits; the only Jewish United States Senators in the 19th century were elected from the South. This liberalism, however, was regarded both by Northern businessmen and Southern poor whites as arrogance. The American concept of democracy, in the 19th century, was moving rapidly in the direction of mass conformity and the enforcement of popular prejudices.

In the same way, while many of the Southern universities and colleges were first rate and gave the planter a superb education to fulfill his role, they won no later praise. The antebellum universities were not organized to create an elite or permit the rise of some sort of new mandarin class from the soil. They were designed to train the existing elite, precisely like the universities of England. Politics and business, in Texas, were still amateur affairs, in an America that elsewhere was beginning to succumb to professionalism. The planter attitude toward education would not be dominant, because the farming mass looked upon it as a tool toward immediate, practical goals.

The entire existence of this glittering cotton empire was based on the subordination and labor of the Negro slaves. There were 182,000 blacks in bondage in Texas, approximately one-third the entire population. Slavery was not completely popular. It was disliked by most free farmers, on racial, social, and competitive grounds. The planters themselves never successfully rationalized the institution in moral terms. They recognized it as "peculiar," and justified it from the fact that it had "always" existed, and that the

Negro was "racially inferior" and could fill no other social role. The whole slave society had gradually built itself, and the American nation with it, into a serious social trap; it was one that the 18th-century rational democracy of the Founding Fathers could find no escape from, for economic reasons.

But the problem of slavery was insoluble in Texas and the South for social reasons, too; the economic interests of the planters by no means provided its sole political cement. The private views of Abraham Lincoln, who hated the peculiar institution as much as any man, illustrate the terrible quandary Lincoln himself did not live to face. Lincoln, like almost all white Americans, did not consider the Negro an ethnic or social equal. The people who lived where there were no concentrations of Negroes could demand emancipation on moral grounds, without really thinking through the problems of citizenship, adjustment, and social role. The whites of Texas, and the South, could not. Negroes, in dozens of counties, outnumbered them, rich and poor alike.

To ignore ethnic attitudes and consciousness was simply to ignore or try to set aside all human history.

The lives of this slave class were utterly submerged. At a time when slavery had become the dominant popular issue of American politics, the slave himself had no role in it. Anglo-American law was forced by its own inherently liberal logic to dehumanize the Negro, because it could not accept the concept of subordination of one people to another, or inequality at law. This had created, and continued to create, a terrible moral confusion and definite hypocrisy in the American mind, toward both Indians and Negroes. Law, the organic cement that held American civilization together, never recognized the inherent tendency of a more powerful people to dispossess or take advantage of any weaker race upon whom they impinged. Law therefore adopted the concept that Negroes were not subordinated human beings, but mere chattels—property like swine or cattle—just as law also looked upon Amerinds as vermin. That this rationalization permitted and even justified far more damaging human crimes than a rationalization of inequality or conquest was desperately slow in reaching the American consciousness.

Both North and South and West did what came naturally to all peoples, but the 18th century ideals and manifestos continued to lash and confuse the American conscience. The American response was to submerge a problem that could not be rationalized.

Under the Napoleonic Code, which governed other 19th-century areas where slavery existed in Western civilization, the slavemaster controlled the labor, but did not own the body, of his bondsman. This was more than a subtle difference; it was a recognition at law that the slave was human, and thus possessed certain human rights. He was entitled to some sort of family life. Significantly, the slave population of the Indies, while fully and cruelly exploited, never suffered the hideous scars of dehumanization inflicted upon American chattels. It was no accident that, in the 20th century, an enormous proportion of Negro leadership in America arrived out of other lands.

Under American law, the Negro slave could be sold at will, bred at will, and be separated from his mate and/or offspring at the whim of his owner. The utterly disastrous human results of generations of this treatment need hardly be explored. Another difference of American law was that children of slave mothers were slaves unto any generation; there was no provision for gradual emancipation as under other codes. Finally, under American law, one drop of African blood classified its possessor as a Negro, while Hispanic code and custom recognized interbreeding and accepted the concept of "dominant blood." In Hispanic America, in a process never fully understood in the United States, slaves or former slaves could breed themselves out of negritude, though it remained socially disastrous everywhere to be *wholly* black.

For some years there was a myth, created by Southern historians and widely accepted elsewhere, that Negroes were amenable to, and even happy with, slavery. Newspapers and private correspondence in Texas between 1850 and 1860 indicate that this view was entirely euphoric. The slaves were crushed psychologically, because they had all been born in bondage, and they were socially powerless. The African had a strong survival instinct, which led him to smile, sing, and endure. But in the Texas background there was always a foreboding threat of violence.

The fear of a slave rebellion lay endemic over the black areas of Texas. There was one uprising in Colorado County in 1856; apparently a number of Negroes secured and hid arms. They planned to rebel, kill the local whites, then fight their way to Mexico and legal freedom. This plot was discovered and crushed with terrible severity. A number of Negroes were killed in various ways, and about two hundred "severely punished," as current accounts read. It was widely believed that Mexicans in the area had instigated this abortive revolt, which was a normal mechanism of psychological defense. The planters of Colorado and Matagorda counties forced all Mexicans out, and passed resolutions never again to hire or employ a Mexican. By the late '50's, the discussion and miasmic fear of a slave revolt had reached almost hysteric proportions in some regions of Texas. Rumors—always false—of massacres in adjoining counties arose. No planter was willing to believe his own chattels were at the point of revolt, but most held an underlying fear that his neighbors' Negroes were lusting for white blood.

This incipient hysteria was strengthened, if not entirely caused, by abolitionist agitation in the North, which at this time, with almost lip-smacking satisfaction, was prophesying chaos and murder in the South. It did not affect just the planters; in fact, it seemed to affect them least. All whites, particularly the non-slavers, were antagonized and terrorized by the thought of Negroes being instigated or set loose upon the countryside.

"Vigilance committees" and posses were formed in most counties, to bring back runaways or put down any sign of slave resistance.

That many slaves were not entirely happy on the plantation is revealed by the fact that many ran away, desperately forging into Indian country, more often trying to reach the Rio Grande. Geography defeated them. It was very easy for a Negro to escape his master in far-flung Texas, but it was quite another for him to get away. The records show that most runaways, after a fearful sojourn in the wilds, crept back home.

Because of the mass white attitudes, these runaways were in far more danger of being lynched or flogged by non-slave-owning posses than of being punished by their legal masters. Sam Houston, as Senator, complained wryly about the hatred of simple blacks by agitators who possessed none. Several Texas papers editorialized bitterly about the failure of the planters to "discipline their niggers" properly.

The evidence is that most owners treated their chattels with dehumanizing indifference coupled with genuine interest for their material welfare. Because it was so easy for a slave to escape south of the Guadalupe or Colorado, planters tried to keep them as contented as possible. Another reason, apparently, that slaves generally fared better in Texas than in some Southern states was that in Texas they were more valuable; they brought a greater price. These years saw a great "sale South" of surplus blacks from the Upper South, Virginia, Kentucky, and Missouri. The older slaves along the Colorado, however, were spared the great Negro horror of being sold South, with separation of parents and children, because Texas was the end of the line. The history of slavery in the Western Hemisphere shows a definite pattern: where slaves were scarce, or in demand, they were treated with greater consideration. North America never recorded the disgusting tortures perpetrated on Negroes in Haiti and the Indies—crucifixion and burning alive on some islands where they were a dangerous surplus. In Texas, where a good buck was worth up to $2,000 in gold, the whipping post was sparingly used. The Brazos planter would no more have whipped a stubborn Negro than he would have ordered his overseer to torment a recalcitrant race horse or prize Berkshire pig. Ethics were also involved; gentlemen did not beat slaves.

However, the Southern pretension that a system of complete legal, moral, and physical domination of one race by another produced few abuses must be described as nonsense. It was the nature of power to be abused, and the slaveowner was restrained only by his ethic, not by custom or law. There were thousands of slaves who were treated like prized pets, or even lesser members of the family. There were others who were bred callously for their increase, and worked to death under a broiling sun generally considered too hot for white men to endure. Either way, destruction was visited upon the whole slave race.

But there is no question that on the better plantations slaves lived a better life, materially, than the poorer whites. Negro diet was similar to that of the western farmers, but in many cases it was better: the planter gave them garden plots and insisted that they raise and eat greens. The hands were usually fed from a common kitchen, which the planter supervised with some degree of pride. Hands were furnished two sets of clothes per year, and women two cotton dresses. The planters had already discovered it was cheaper to buy these in the industrial North than to have them locally made. Many slaves were permitted to earn money for special services, such as making shoes. A future Texas millionaire, as a slave, accumulated $600 in silver as a cobbler, at 10 cents per shoe. In 1865, he possessed more capital than his former master, who cheerfully helped him to invest it in choice lands.

In one important item, medical care, slaves fared much better than the people of the frontier. No planter could afford a sick slave, and he could afford doctors.

The basic weaknesses of such a colonial, nonindustrial, one-crop economy, in which all the true surplus was produced by servile labor, were recognized even then. No one saw any workable means of change. Criticism out of Boston was rejected as furiously as criticism out of Paris or Madrid would have been; the Texan was truly regional in attitude in a way northern Americans failed to comprehend. Although Texas was among the fastest-growing of all states in terms of settlement and new population, its growth was merely the spread of a static empire. Texas was painfully making a new Virginia or Georgia, and those regions were already anachronisms in the swirl of population and power of the 19th century. The planter's greatest crime was that he was already, nationally, out of date.

The Texas countryside, from the great semicircle of the frontier to the banks of the Sabine, was overwhelmingly rural. Distances, the lack of roads, the subsistence freehold, and the plantation economy all combined to keep it so. There was no industry, very little commerce, and therefore no real need for towns.

The lack or inadequacy of improved roads, ports, and rails, the backbone of commerce, was striking. The Texas Gulf coast was composed of bars, reefs, and shallow bays. It had always been hazardous for ocean-going vessels. There were almost no deep, natural harbors. The Colorado mouth was obstructed by a bar, and closed to shipping. The Brazos and Trinity were navigable, and Houston could be reached up Buffalo Bayou. Cópano and Corpus Christi bays, and the Laguna Madre at Point Isabel in the south, provided landing places. But these were not true harbors, only shallow, semisheltered bays. Ships had to be unloaded by lighter; there were no channels, docks, or improved facilities.

Steamboats provided transportation on the long, narrow, rapidly shallowing rivers, from the Trinity to the Rio Grande. These were adequate to move cotton out of, and a few trade goods into, the river bottom plantations. But as in 18th-century Virginia, the plantation system provided no spur to the growth of settlements.

The largest ports were Galveston and Matagorda, high on the coast. These served east Texas. Indianola, which was later destroyed entirely by a hurricane, was the main port of entry for the western regions.

It was difficult enough to get goods ashore in Texas, but it became a nightmare to move freight overland. Only a few miles of roadway in the entire state in 1860 were graded; exactly twenty miles in all was planked or similarly improved.

The arteries called "roads" were actually only well-defined main routes of travel between various points. The Camino Real between San Antonio and Nacogdoches was a prime example. In use since the early 18th century, in some places it was only a mass of wagon ruts cutting through the forest or across the prairie. Lesser roads throughout the state were more like cow trails. They were easy to follow, terrible to traverse.

Most travel over these roads was by horseback. Goods were hauled in giant-sized wagons—some carried 7,000 pounds—drawn by mules or oxen. In good weather, freight rates averaged 1 cent per mile per hundred pounds. In wet weather, the trails turned into quagmires. Freight did not move, because the charges in these periods were prohibitive. Even in dry seasons, the movement of freight or goods was painfully slow. There were continual complaints of mail arriving damaged or disastrously late.

Railroads, which had already linked most of the northern United States, were almost nonexistent in Texas. The first track was laid in 1852. This road ran only from Harrisburg on Buffalo Bayou to Richmond on the Brazos, or thirty-two miles. Houston tapped into this line with a road built through a civic tax, and several lines radiated out of Houston for short distances into the plantation country. There was a track from Marshall to Shreveport, Louisiana, and another from Indianola to Victoria. These track layings were all small, local efforts, and in no way connected the major areas of the state. The rails had to be supplemented in all directions by steamboat, wagon, or stage. Thus there were neither telegraphs nor post offices in most areas. San Antonio got its first post office in 1850, with a postmaster serving out of his own home without pay.

In the 1850's, a few excellent stage coaches began to appear on Texas roads. Stage became the principal carrier of passenger traffic, though stage line operators made their money from government contracts hauling mail. The superior stage coach service that began just before the Civil War, however, did not connect the principal Texas towns, and was never intended to. The Southern Overland Mail, the Butterfield, and another line ran stages regularly between San Antonio and San Diego, California, over new trails scouted by the army to the West. None of these could be considered part of the Texas transportation system, though they made it possible to ride from Missouri to West Texas.

Settlements were laid out in the Texas heartland, but they failed to grow. The largest settlements, significantly, were on the edges of Texas: Galveston, on the upper coast, the principal port, and San Antonio, in the far southwest, the jumping-off place for Mexico and California. Galveston, in

1850, had not quite 5,000 permanent residents. San Antonio, Houston, New Braunfels, and Marshall—widely scattered, and in no way connected or doing business with each other—followed in order of size. These were the only settlements that contained 1,000 or more people. Austin, the state capital, lay on the edge of the Indian frontier up the Colorado. Its population, including the government, was 600.

By 1860, German and other European immigration had raised San Antonio to 8,000, making it the first city in Texas. Galveston slipped to second place, among a total of twenty communities that counted 1,000 souls. The noticeable thing about the great corn- and cotton-growing belt of Texas was that it germinated few towns. In Texas, these grew up as centers of outside trade or distribution, and a wholly agricultural society just did not create cities. Brownsville, just across from Matamoros on the Rio Grande, was more of a city in these years than Dallas in the rich country of the north. Brownsville, and its merchants, lived off the border garrisons of the army. It had erected some dozen brick buildings, and established Catholic, Presbyterian, and Episcopal churches. Its pattern of life was mercantile, like San Antonio's.

Many of the small settlements and communities of the original Anglo-Texas, in fact, in these years quite faded away. They had no function, and disappeared.

These towns of Texas varied greatly, due to different climatic conditions and different kinds of inhabitants. Apparently San Antonio, again the metropolis, had not much improved from the previous century. A German traveler, who wrote down his reactions, was as little impressed as the Spanish grandees who visited it earlier. The streets were unpaved, and impassable in rain; there were a few good limestone structures, nothing more. In the 1850's, however, this rapidly changed. European immigrants began to put up solid buildings, with what later were called typical Southwestern lines.

San Antonio supported itself almost entirely through California travel, and supplying the army garrisons that in the 1850's were scattered along the border river and the Comanche West. The Mexico trade, through the straggling adobe town of Laredo, was also important. San Antonio was a center for stage lines and freighting companies.

Galveston, on its island, was a center of deep-South architecture; it was putting up a number of stately frame mansions as men grew rich from seafaring and the cotton trade. Marshall, connected with Shreveport in the deep pine plantation country, already had handsome houses and public buildings of red brick. Galveston, Marshall, San Antonio, and Brownsville, all separated by hundreds of miles, also represented quite different worlds, inhabited by rather different kinds of people. In this age, there was no dominant standard of American architecture; each community, out of the traditions of its settlers, threw up its own.

There were no paved town streets anywhere, and aside from a few mansions such as Wyalucing in Marshall, the most imposing buildings in any town consisted of the courthouse and the public hotel.

The average hotel of the day was typical of the fringe of civilization: dirty, without services or courtesy, with guests assigned to common rooms and lucky to get them. Food was indifferent, mainly consisting of fried pork. The opening of the Menger, in San Antonio, was the beginning of a new era, connecting Texas with the Golden West. The Menger Hotel was built beside the crumbling walls of the chapel of the Alamo, whose outer walls had already been taken away for fence and building stones. The Menger was finely made, by European artisans, out of stone, two-and-a-half stories high. The furnishings were hauled in from the coast at enormous expense; they cost $16,000, when the U.S. dollar was worth fifteen to twenty times its later value. Here army officers, California travelers, or *hacendados* up from Mexico could bathe, dine, and drink in solid Victorian splendor. A graying lieutenant colonel of the U.S. Army, Robert E. Lee, had a favorite room in this hotel. The Menger, and most hotels, however, were too rich for the average transient, who bunked down in wagon yards.

Almost anything, useful or luxurious, could be bought in San Antonio, Galveston, or other major towns. Everything arrived out of Europe or the North, usually via New Orleans, and with heavy mark-ups. Anyone with good money could purchase ice, jewelry, finely made guns, drugs, clothing, cosmetics, and good liquors. This trade was limited to a tiny, affluent class. The farmer families bought salt, powder, and lead, and sometimes a few yard goods on the side. Texas, except for a few, still did not represent a money economy.

The laws against incorporation of banks kept banks out of the state. Banking services, therefore, were carried on by freighting or mercantile firms, such as McKinney and Williams in Galveston, Groos in San Antonio and on the border, and a commission firm in Austin. These businesses and others like them held money on deposit, and made occasional loans. McKinney and Williams at last opened the first and only bank in Texas prior to 1861, through the use of an old State of Texas-Coahuila charter issued under Mexican rule in 1835 and a loophole in the law. The utter lack of banks and banking facilities, naturally, had a deadening effect on potential financial or industrial growth, but this was precisely the way the farmer-planter-dominated legislatures preferred it.

What money there was took three forms. Depreciated banknotes from the United States circulated widely. These were not federal notes, because no paper money was issued by the United States until the Civil War; some of this paper was issued by wildcat, or even nonexistent, banks in other states. Passers and accepters had sometimes to guess its worth. Promissory notes were traded between businessmen and merchants like cash. When hard money was essential, the major medium of exchange was old Spanish or Mexican silver pesos or dollars and their fractions. Very little gold or silver U.S. coinage had penetrated Texas.

Until 1857, these foreign coins were legal tender in the United States, and they continued to circulate in Texas freely until the end of the century. It was customary to smash the image of the King of Spain on the older coins with a hammer, or to deface the Mexican eagle. Such mutilation in no way damaged bullion value and did assuage national pride.

The census of 1860 listed over one hundred different occupations in Texas. Since far more than half of the people were farmers, the other occupations were centered in settlements and towns. There were 2,000 merchants, big and small, and the same number who claimed to be carpenters. There seem to have been enough wheelwrights, blacksmiths, masons, saddle makers, and foundrymen to satisfy the demand. A very high percentage of merchants and skilled artisans in Texas were foreign, or Northern born. The ordinary Anglo clung to farming.

There were only two factories in the state. One made hats, and the other, clothing. Both employed slave labor. There was almost no such thing as hired labor, except for a few Mexicans. Mechanics worked for themselves, and the permanent residents of towns were almost entirely professional men, merchants, or artisans.

If the supply of entrepreneurs was limited, there was almost a plague of lawyers. Marshall, with only 1,000 people in all, had twenty-eight members of the bar. There were a thousand licensed barristers in Texas in 1860, and this was a continuing trend. There were two reasons. Law was the most honored profession in nonindustrial America, and the principal career open to educated men. Further, the frontier pulled lawyers in droves from older states, just as it attracted medical doctors in large numbers.

In these years there were even more doctors of medicine than lawyers scattered across the breadth of Texas. Then the situation was almost exactly the reverse of later times; economic and social opportunity was far greater on the frontier for professionally educated men than in the older sections of America. Young doctors or lawyers had to compete with established practices in the East; on the edge of civilization all men started equal. One good case, and a lawyer or doctor could be made. Lawyers could quickly build large landed estates and become planters; doctors could do the same. Professional fees were relatively steep. British travelers, for example, complained bitterly of the exorbitant costs of medical care compared to England.

Texas lawyers and doctors and dentists (who enjoyed much lower status) were sketchily trained by later standards, and most were trained in other states. They were not nearly so professional or restricted in their careers as later. A horde of both lawyers and doctors accompanied every Texas filibustering or military expedition; it was not unusual to find doctors commanding armed parties rather than acting strictly as medical men. Doctors, in the South, slipped in and out of the military role as easily as lawyers or planters.

Before the War Between the States, there were only three actors, no writers, and two Negro businessmen in Texas.

There is a certain futility to exploring true cultural activities on the frontier, because in general they did not exist. The discussion of these by Texas historians is a defensive measure, like the sometime attempt of Catholic historians to establish a Catholic presence in the American Revolution. The few examples stand out, because they were exceptional.

San Antonio, with its European influences, had its Casino Club, where at times there were both distinguished guests and entertainment. Elsewhere, there were occasional road tours by traveling troupes. Culture, like the cotton kingdom, remained colonial; it had to be brought in. This frontier, unlike the Iranic and Hellenic frontiers of ancient times, did not spawn any kind of cultural vigor. Such activity was not part of the genius or the ethic of the English-speaking race.

Because the society, and social leaders, were rural, social activities were private and centered more around prominent homes than in the towns. This was to be a lasting tradition; no public place could ever compete with planter hospitality. Genteel people in Texas retreated to their country places. This had a permanent, damaging effect on the growth of cities and towns.

The planters, and generally the more affluent townspeople, possessed the usual culture of all squirearchies, especially those of short tradition. They read imported books, sent their children away to school, conversed about public affairs, enjoyed relaxed, enormous meals; they hunted and rode. Languor in polite company was matched by furious activity in the saddle. All such atmospheres, of course, tend to be unintellectual, though hardly unintelligent.

The artisans were not very influential toward cultural attitudes, but the slaves had already formed a sort of culture of their own, which naturally was separate from that of the dominant whites.

The culture of the most numerous white farming population was still centered around biblical influences and the backwoods churches. The church meetings had become almost as much social as religious activities, and because there were no offsetting influences in the farmers' lives, the churches began to exert a dominant influence that colored Texas and has not always been recognized. The pressure was not so much religious or spiritual—though this was strong—as social. It generated strong drives toward temperance, fundamentalism, tribalism, and social democracy. The Baptist and Methodist persuasions, which were by far the largest in the state, were brotherhoods under lay control rather than organic, hierarchical churches which preached catholicity while recognizing social distinctions. The influences of the Baptist Church, and similar organizations, all strongly puritanical, seeped through all the people who were to form the emerging frontier middle class. This was no fundamental change from the regions farther east below the Ohio, but in Texas, because of lasting frontier conditions, the frontier denominations had a more lasting effect upon society.

Thus the codes, patterns, practices, outlook, and beginnings of virtually all Texan institutions were in being by 1860, if not in all cases fully developed. Most of these would prove too strong to be swept away with the wind that was already rising in the North.

Part IV

THE CONFEDERACY
AND THE CONQUERED

18

SECESSION

The North has gone overwhelmingly for Negro Equality and Southern Vassalage! Southern Men, will you submit to the degradation? EDITORIAL, NAVARRO, TEXAS, NEWSPAPER, 1860

In the 1850's, concurrent with the growth of the cotton kingdom and expansion of the western frontier, a smoldering atmosphere of political crisis was brewing in Texas. This was part of the larger social and economic crisis that was enveloping the United States, separating the North and South. The real enemy of the North was Southern political power, insisting upon the strictest construction of the Constitution in a defense of states' rights that hindered and hamstrung industrialism and infuriated Eastern bankers, railroad magnates, and manufacturers. The true enemy of the South was industrialism itself, which threatened its agriculture with a worse colonialism and the destruction of its Constitutional rights in a flood of money and material goods. The two sections, doing what came naturally, had built two quite different societies; as Toynbee wrote, and few Americans have ever been willing to accept, the Valley of the Ohio marked at least as great a cultural line as the gates of the Danube below Vienna. If "Europe" ended at Vienna, one kind of America stopped at the Ohio.

With genuine economic and political grievances against each other, the Northern states and the South found their flashpoint in the question of Negro slavery. The Negro question made the states' rights question so crucial and violent. The South insisted upon states' rights to maintain the status quo, which the North was increasingly determined to alter. If a balance of viewpoint could have been maintained, some eventual, bloodless solution might possibly have been worked out. The essence of English-speaking politics, as more than one foreign observer has noted, depends upon no side or faction taking stands that may not, or cannot, be compromised by rational men.

The British Empire ended Negro slavery in the nineteenth century by both abolition and reimbursement. Other nations went through a process of gradual emancipation. None of these solutions was perfect; starting with the incubus of human servitude, no social solution could be perfect. But even this hopeful approach was torpedoed by two American developments: Southern intransigence that amounted to belligerency, and a Northern equation of slavery with sin.

Calhoun's premise that the South could defend its peculiar interests and institutions only by going on the attack and controlling the federal apparatus, and a growing Northern refusal to treat slavery as a political and social, but not a moral problem, led the whole American body politic into a vast morass. The South, always with a growing insecurity and terrible problem of rationale, went into a psychosis mentality, while the North deteriorated from a reasonable moral stance into crusade.

Most reasonable men in the South were aware that slavery was condemned by the entire civilized world. The trouble was that the South, having fallen into the trap, had compelling social and economic reasons for continuing Negro bondage. The fear that a larger, richer, and more populous North would eventually control the national political machinery, and enforce its own concepts of morality and society upon the South, was hardly unfounded; it was a natural trend. The extreme stand against change —wrapped, as always in America, in a Constitutional cloak—was clearly the mark of a badly insecure and intellectually tortured society.

But on the other hand, much of the North did not comprehend the social and status implications inherent in the presence of a large, subordinate, and racially differentiated mass of people with the boundaries of certain states. Slavery pricked the Northern conscience, but the slaves themselves did not impinge upon Northern society.

If the farmer class in Texas had absorbed different ideas and ideals of society from the planters, they also differed from Middle Western farmers in another striking way. The slave system created a terrible sense of insecurity in Texas and the South. The institution of Negro slavery was not really popular with the more than 400,000 white Texans—95 percent of the population—who owned none, although they had grown up with it and considered it normal. What was sometimes not understood fully in the North was that the average white Texan feared a Negro insurrection as much as the slavemaster, because a slave revolt threw all whites in danger. Also, the white farmers supported the institution of slavery vehemently, because virtually all of them were adamantly opposed to Negro equality. Tirades against black "equality" speckled the Texas newspapers of the 1850's; these editorials were written by members of the professional middle classes. The evidence is strong that no Western farm states had much regard for the Negro as a man—even after the conclusion of the Civil War many Northern states denied the franchise to freedmen. But the Wisconsin farmer did not feel insecure toward the Negro, because he did not live up against the slave horde.

This fear of Negro disorder and fear of Negro competition inevitably kept a flame of hatred for the Negro alive in the heart of the average Texan. This was not unusual in any historical sense. It was a characteristic of all societies based on the subordination of one differentiated group to another, from Norman Sicily in the Middle Ages to Hispanic America. The Negro lived in another country from the white farmer; he was a faceless mass; he was hardly thought of as human. The men who owned, and even abused, slaves tended to think of them in more personal terms, as human beings, than those who watched and feared them from a short distance.

The interesting thing is that these recognizable social manifestations of fear of encirclement and social change, producing a predictable belligerence, affected the people most immediately endangered the least. The slowly gathering drive toward secession sentiment—if the South could not control the Union, then it should get out—was a mass, popular movement, led by professional politicians and lawyers and supported hugely by the voting middle class. The great slaveowners seem to have been as appalled by gathering radicalism as Lincoln was horrified by the supporters of John Brown. There were simple, logical reasons: the substantial men were as always conservative toward continuity and law and order. Most large planters were oldtime Whigs; Constitutionalism to them meant support of the American Constitution by carrying on the battle by legal means, not "upholding" it by rupture. The evidence shows that in Texas, and in some other states, the planters were willing to follow John C. Calhoun in an effort to capture the Democratic Party, but when this effort waned and the strict "Constitutionalists" veered toward secession, the great landowners remained Unionist. Men of property, they did not relish casting adrift on uncharted, radical-tossed seas.

The states' rights movement was one more of hysteria than logic, because ironically, the Constitution was the planter-slaveowners' greatest prop. While Lincoln's statement that the nation could not continue forever as a house divided—that either the slave states or the free states would enforce their concept of legality on the other—was essentially true, the Constitution still gave the slaveowners enormous room to fight. The Dred Scott decision stands as a case in point. It was impossible for the organic, 19th-century American law to ignore property rights; the law had been building an intricate maze of support for property rights for more than a generation. The planters were actually in a position in which, with enough senators in Washington to block significant political change for years to come, they could sit back and watch the Abolitionists become psychotic.

Abolition, then, was impractical both from economic and psychological reasons in Texas. But the great dilemma of the nation was that black subordination was not morally supportable, and both North and South grew increasingly psychotic over the issue. The South defended slavery as coequal with the American law and way of life, while the North stubbornly refused to reward "sin." This infusion of moral stands and principles into national politics was hardly invigorating; it was disastrous. It made political compromise, the cement of the nation, impossible, and it destroyed the single, necessary unifying force, the national political parties. Two newer, aggressive political groups sprouted from the mouldering remains of the two former national parties, the Constitutional or Calhoun Democrats of the South, and the Republicans of the North. Both split off significant groups from the older Whigs, who disappeared. The influential planter class in the South, which had been largely Whig, deserted to the Democrats and briefly captured that Party. The Whig Eastern financial and business interests swelled Republicanism. Because of the spread of railroads above the Ohio, linking the Western farmers with the industrial East, and the slavery question, the Democrats increasingly lost the Middle West. And the Democrats, with the rise of the Constitutional Party in the South, finally splintered into not two, but three groups.

In terms of national government, all this was catastrophic, because each of the alignments was purely regional. There were no Republicans in the South. There were almost no pro-slavery Democrats in the North. Workable, equitable government demanded sectional alliances and regional compromises, and these became impossible. The angry statement of the Southern delegate, "We are for principles, damn the party!" showed that effective American politics had disappeared. The preachings of Seward and others about "irreconcilable conflict" and "higher laws" showed that the North was not entirely free of guilt. The Civil War was hardly spawned in innocence, because neither morality nor the American Constitution could ever be a substitute for practical politics.

The propaganda that eventually made the American internal conflict seem a struggle between an aristocratic tradition and a burgeoning social democracy throughout the English-speaking world obscured the fact that Texas, at least, was a complete political democracy. The planters' influence was more social than political; the planters could not vote or control the volatile 400,000 whites. Insecurity and radicalism pervaded the white farmers far more than it touched the men in plantation houses; in one sense, the "poor whites" betrayed the very system they now gathered noisily to defend. When the South rose, two thousand Texan planters were submerged by the genuine Southern version of democracy.

In Texas, as everywhere, approaching disaster was heralded by the collapse of the old political parties. Texas had naturally been fervently Democratic, since annexation was a Jacksonian policy. However, the Party as such had never been efficiently organized. In the early 1850's it still revolved around a pro-Houston and an anti-Houston group, as in the Republic years. Sam Houston, meanwhile, was returned regularly to the U.S. Senate. The top men of the state, Governor Elisha Pease and Senator Thomas Jefferson Rusk, were basically Unionist; the old Carolina poison of nullification had never reached this far west.

The political issues of the day centered around such matters as public schools and, above all, the defense of the Indian frontier. Every governor was criticized for not doing enough; and the Congressional delegations' battle with the Union was in securing garrison troops. The Democratic Party was more a party of personalities than issues; state-wide conventions had never been held. In the absence of any real dissent on major issues, small caucuses could decide on candidates or make decisions affecting government.

But the Southern complex, fueled by Calhoun and carried by steady immigration, spread rapidly throughout the state. The old families along the Brazos, who had once deserted American citizenship, were oddly enough completely American-oriented; Southernism as a creed or mystique had not yet arisen in the 1830's. Because of geography, these people, like Houston, had been and stayed Jacksonian Democrats, though their instincts might be more readily termed Whiggish. In a normal progression, however, the one-time "radical" Jacksonians gradually became the conservative structure in the state.

Meanwhile Sam Houston, the loyal old Jacksonian, had outlived his old national Party. Like Tom Benton of Missouri, he was falling out of date. Houston kept the viewpoint of the 1830's and 1840's: the mystique of a great American nation, based more on the concept of blood and soil than transcendental ideas, which would expand the English-speaking race from sea to sea and be in a position to defy the world. He did not hate the Europe of culture and tyranny from which the American race had sprung; he rather despised it and feared its material power. All Westerners born in the 18th century, and who had fought Indians in the 1812 war, detested the British nation, with reasonable grounds. Houston also mistrusted the French, who threw out brilliant concepts of democracy but could not seem to found a stable democratic regime at home. Like Andrew Jackson, Houston had been born in humble circumstances but reached the political heights; he was conservative, but he never liked the arrogance of the Atlantic seaboard, North or South. He did think of Northerners as nothing but Americans, bred to the same language, laws, and concepts of government as the American South; he never considered the North, as a whole, bent on destroying either the South or the Constitution. He seems never to have fallen into the pit that swallowed his own people: the equation of Negro slavery with the American way of life. Like Jackson again, he seems to have privately regarded the importation of Africans into America as the greatest potential curse that ever befell his country—not so much on moral grounds, but because the intrusion threatened his whole dream of a great American Republic.

Houston was a craggy, piercing-eyed old warrior, westward-looking, true to his friends, hard on his enemies, but with a large streak of purposeful pragmatism and magnanimity. He had seen to it that Santa Anna was protected and gotten safely back to Mexico via the United States, when a lesser and shorter-visioned man would have punished him, as the public clamor demanded. Houston had hated Henry Clay as much as any Jacksonian during the partisan wars, but he lived to praise Clay when he understood the Kentuckian was a loyal American and sincere. Indians, at the Horseshoe Bend, had put an arrow in Houston's leg, and bullets in his arm and shoulder, almost killing him and invaliding him out of the regular service. Yet no western political figure in America fought harder to preserve to the Indians some legal rights. He had won the Presidency of Texas on horseback at San Jacinto, yet no Texas leader tried more sincerely to end the war with Mexico. Hard, brave, stubborn, proud, and canny, Houston was an intensely ethical and honorable man.

Now, in the Senate Houston was as valiant as when he had led the forlorn hope against the Mexican army. And because of his deepseated Unionist bias, his words and stands were to be prophetic. Tragically, this was prophecy his own constituents could never understand. Houston, fighting for what he believed, cut his own political throat, in the politicians' phrase.

In 1848, he voted for the entrance of Oregon as free territory, standing against the senators from the South. He refused to sign Calhoun's manifesto on "aggression by the free states," exciting irate comment throughout Texas. He debated vehemently against the Kansas-Nebraska bill of 1853, which in effect abrogated the old Missouri Compromise. Stephen Douglas' political plan to allay his own Democrats in the South through the concept of "territorial sovereignty" on the question of slavery was enthusiastically supported by the Calhoun Democrats; it was belatedly backed by the Democratic Administration. It opened Kansas, where slavery had been forever barred, as slave territory if the inhabitants so agreed. Although it was instigated by an Illinoisan, as part of a political move to re-create a national Democratic consensus, it devolved into a Southern attack upon the status quo, and as such Houston fought it. It was the first of a series of hideous Southern political errors.

Houston felt that the 1820 Compromise held the nation together, and that even if Kansas opted for slavery, which he considered unlikely, the South would be damaged. Houston, who was born in Virginia, matured in Tennessee, and risen to glory in Texas, again and again attacked the concept of a narrow sectionalism in politics. The South did not have the power to mount its own party, and Houston argued that Southern sectionalism must beget an answering Northern response. He was correct. The Kansas-Nebraska bill, pushed through Congress, resulted in "bleeding Kansas," excited the Abolitionists, who had been declining, to new frenzies, and in the end, the concept of "territorial, or squatter sovereignty" did not unite but split the Democrats, costing Douglas the White House.

As Lincoln shrewdly saw, the Douglas policy of live and let live toward the South could not include an approval of slavery. But the Calhoun partisans would settle for nothing less. The repeal of the Missouri Compromise was symbolic; compromise was dead.

When Sam Houston, loyal to the end, voted against the bill, the Texas legislature let it be known he would not be returned to the Senate. Houston was openly described as a "traitor to the South."

Houston also split the Democrats of his home state. Two factions emerged, pro-Houston men, or "Jacksonians," and a newer, radical faction, the "Calhoun Democrats," who soon styled themselves the Constitutional Democrats.

It soon became evident that the Jacksonians were in the great minority, and Unionist sentiment in Texas was losing its political base. The Whigs were gone.

Houston flirted with the American, or Know-Nothing, Party, which entered Texas explosively in 1854. Some historians criticized this, but the move had an obvious base. His own Democrats were purging him. The whole party structure in the United States was in confusion and flux. And the Know-Nothings, though they were an antiforeign, anti-Catholic movement originating in the East, were essentially Unionist. They wanted to keep political America "Anglo-Saxon," but they also wanted to keep it whole.

An air of unreality surrounds the entire Know-Nothing phenomenon in Texas. The group undoubtedly fed on the destruction of the Whigs and on the underlying unease gripping the country as a whole. There were almost no Catholics in Texas, and the foreign, heavily Catholic elements that existed, Germans and Mexicans, were politically inert. There never were any potato-famine Irish, such as triggered the Know-Nothings in the East. The Party really had little to sink its teeth in, in Texas. Yet it aroused great excitement and attracted a considerable number of prominent men.

The Know-Nothings resembled a cross between a secret society and a fraternal order more than a mass political party. They had a "Grand President," were run in an authoritarian manner, and formed "committees of vigilance" in many communities. They did not hold conventions, but secret conclaves. Houston expressed sympathy and approval with all this, and the Party elected the mayor of Galveston, twenty-five state legislators, including five state senators, and swept in a whole city slate, in of all places, predominantly foreign and Catholic San Antonio.

This last probably signified that contact with an alien group made more for estrangement than understanding.

Then, as quickly as they formed, the Know-Nothings faded. Afterward, many supporters admitted they were not quite sure why they joined, attributing it to the uneasiness of the times.

But the phenomenon had one visible result: it frightened the Democrats into organization. In 1856 and 1857 the Party held state-wide conventions for the first time, in which almost every county was represented. And at the 1857 convention, the Calhoun Democrats emerged in complete control. Sam Houston was purged, although the term was not then used.

With no hope of being reelected to the Senate by the Calhoun legislature, Houston appealed to the people; he ran for governor against the Democratic nominee, a wealthy, states' rightist planter named Hardin Runnels. He lost, badly, the first time Texans had repudiated Sam Houston at the polls.

Now, though matters had been slow in coming to a boil, they began to fulminate. The Democrats took up the "Calhoun" attack. The legislature authorized the governor to send delegates to a "Southern convention" if one were held. The state Democratic chairman, Marshall, lobbied for resumption of the importation of African slaves. The party convention resolved that Cuba should be annexed, as a slave state. There was a great deal of radical demagogery on all sides.

In 1859, Houston, now past his sixty-fifth year, determined to appeal to the people once again. His platform was clear: he supported slavery, he supported the Constitution, but he pledged allegiance to the Union, come what may. It was not a popular platform, but Houston could not believe that the Texans were prepared to forsake the greater nation he had done so much to build.

Houston was hardly ignorant either of sentiment or conditions. He had been governor of an important state, and President of an independent country. He had spent years in Washington, mixing with Americans of all kinds. He was certain the continued sectionalism of the South, and what he considered Calhoun's treasonous activities, would arouse their own Frankenstein in the North, because Northerners were basically the same kind of people; they could neither be threatened successfully nor overawed. But he possessed a perspective few Texans saw. And his contention that a Southern secession could not be successful, nor alliances made with European powers against the North, was simply not believed. Houston knew, and said, that before Britain would help the South, the South would first have to make some pledges toward ending slavery. Parochial in knowledge as well as vision, the radical lawyers he argued with did not believe it; the South did not realize how isolated it had become.

Houston was determined to build a Unionist base Texans could rally around. He felt that secession, already openly proposed by radical politicians, was rebellion against the nation—precisely as did Robert E. Lee. But Houston, like Lee, was one of a small group of men, holding to their own concepts of honor, helpless against a tide they deplored. In the summer of 1859, however, the cause did not yet seem hopeless.

Running as an independent against the organized majority party—in fact, the only party—Houston got significant support. This contest had unusual facets. Houston was opposed by the entire political structure, but not by the older power structure of the state. He had a majority of the planters on his side. He had former Governor Pease and many former Whigs, such as J. W. Throckmorton and B. H. Epperson. A significantly high percentage of substantial men agreed with his stand, but these were men of property, rarely politicians or professionals of the kind increasingly noticeable in the South.

Houston staged a famous, rip-roaring campaign. Knowing he could never win on his platform alone, he traveled Texas in a buggy. He wore an old linen duster; on hot days, when he worked up a sweat, he orated without his shirt. He slept in great plantation houses and farmers' dog-run shacks. Everywhere he went, his dust raised cheers. But they were for Houston the hero, Houston the man.

Runnels, running for reelection, had handicaps. He had nothing of Houston's mystique or personal popularity. He had neglected the Indian frontier, or so the western farmers believed. And his states' rights position had alienated most of the influential planter class; they felt he was moving much too fast. Still, it was something of a miracle when Houston won, by 9,000 votes. But it was a mandate for the hero, not for his Union precepts.

What now happened to Houston in office was part of a deepening national tragedy, which no man could any longer control. John Brown raided Harper's Ferry on October 16, 1859. Brown was most probably insane; his act was irrational by any test. With thirteen white men and five Negroes, he launched a movement to lead a mass insurrection and arm the Southern slaves, and to create an Abolitionist republic on the ruins of the plantation South.

The first step was to capture the U.S. Arsenal and rifle works at Harper's Ferry, in Virginia. Brown set out from Maryland, where he had been for some months, gathering funds and creating a base of operations. Harper's Ferry fell; the mayor was killed, and one Negro freedman. But as Lincoln said, "It was so absurd that the slaves, with all their ignorance, saw plainly enough it could not succeed." No one, white or black, joined Brown, although he forcibly enlisted a few blacks. He was put down easily, his men killed or driven off, and captured by a detachment of Marines, under Army Lieutenant Colonel Robert E. Lee. Brown was given a public trial in Virginia, and duly hanged for murder and other assorted crimes.

This was a small event. But it seems to have created a terrible crisis of ends and means in the North, particularly among an articulate, intellectual group in the East. John Brown, at his trial, threw up a facile, self-serving line of argument that was accepted at face value by some, because if they could not quite condone Brown's murders, they hated slavery more. While generally political figures of all parties considered Brown criminally insane, if not legally insane, and there were massive anti-Brown rallies in Boston and New York, there was an amazing reaction from what could only be considered the moral and cultural elite of the North of that time. This took the line that Brown might have been "insane," but his acts and intentions should be excused on the grounds that the compelling motive was "divine." Horace Greeley wrote the Harper's Ferry raid was "the work of a madman," but he had not "one reproachful word." Ralph Waldo Emerson described Brown as a "saint." Henry Thoreau, Theodore Parker, Longfellow, Bryant, and Lowell, the whole Northern pantheon, with the exception of Walt Whitman and Nathaniel Hawthorne, took the position Brown was an "angel of light," and not Brown, but the society that hanged him was mad. The late, falling-leaf intellectuality of New England in the 19th century seems to have become infused with a newer, strikingly intolerant puritanism. Thoreau bitterly condemned both the public and the greater folk wisdom of Whitman for not agreeing. Thoreau as much as anyone pointed up one difference that had emerged between the American East and the American Southwest. Thoreau was willing to go to jail rather than support a war against Mexico for the ultimate control of the continent, in the long-term interests of the United States. But he was not pacifist: he was also willing to shed American blood in furtherance of his own ideology. Never far from the moral question of slavery was a deep and growing hatred of the American planter class in the industrial North, probably based in a revived puritanism, an almost Roundhead fervor. Garrison said bluntly, "Every slaveholder has forfeited his right to live." The planter had become an enemy class; although slavery was indefensible intellectually and morally, still something new and vicious had been injected into American public attitudes. The imperishable greatness of Abraham Lincoln, in this period and afterward, rests partly on the fact that he never succumbed to this malaise. He recognized slavery as a dangerous problem no amount of moral frenzy would solve; he was prepared to damage slavery if he could, but not if he had to damage the nation in the process. He considered slavery morally wrong, but that it could not "excuse violence, bloodshed, and treason." Lincoln was prepared to stand by the law, either as a private citizen or President, even when he thought the law in error; he made this very plain privately, in his 1860 campaign and afterward. It was a distinction the South understood too late.

The misunderstanding was understandable, however, because Lincoln, for whatever reason, made no real attempt to refute Seward and the other Republican fanatics who preached irreconcilable conflict. All Black Republicans were linked with their loudest spokesmen; Lincoln took on the same radical image.

On the day Brown died, church bells tolled from New England to Chicago; Albany fired off one hundred guns in salute, and a governor of a large Northern state wrote in his diary that men were ready to march to Virginia.

Further, a terrible suspicion of a widespread conspiracy in the North to foment a hideous slave insurrection in the South grew out of the investigation by Congress into the Brown affair.

The revelation that Brown had been able to collect $23,000 in four months in Boston in 1858, for an admitted guerrilla war against slavery, and that many intellectuals refused to pronounce him guilty after it was proven that he had engaged in bloody executions in Kansas, because it was "decreed by God, ordained from Eternity," had a blood-chilling effect south of the Ohio. Above all, the identity of the "Secret Six" who had financed Brown's raid came as a horrifying shock. These were out of the cream of Northern society: minister of religion, capitalist, philosopher, surgeon, professor, and philanthropist, four of them with Harvard degrees. They had knowingly diverted arms and money raised to be used in "bleeding Kansas" to Brown in Maryland. As one admitted many years later, "It is still a little difficult to explain." It could be explained only in the sense that fanaticism was clouding American decency, confusing ends and means. This acceptance of civil violence by intellectuals still throws a somber light over American history.

The conspiracy was neither widespread nor well-organized, although papers found on Brown seemed to prove so, and the puritan intellectuals who hated the South along with its peculiar institutions were a small minority. Although as some Southern historians like Woodward have pointed out, their view eventually became the dominant view, and the whole nation ceased to see the inherent blasphemy in the words of the "Battle Hymn of the Republic," this probably could not have happened had not their sound and fury ignited a corresponding psychosis in Texas and other states. The notion that the entire North was determined to bring about bloody revolution not only paralyzed the planters, who were half convinced against their better judgment, but inflamed the average white. A Negro insurrection would not just affect the gentry; it would kill and burn out all white people in the counties.

Again, because Southerners had been defensive too long over slavery and had cut most of their bridges of communication with the North, they lived in a sort of self-imposed intellectual exile. This, and the eroding effects of a continual physical and psychological insecurity, now fired hysteria. Ready to believe the worst, Texans reacted with characteristic violence.

An inferiority and insecurity complex gripped almost the entire white frontier farming middle class. An old American practice, the "witch hunt," was revived. In such an atmosphere any irresponsible evidence was easily swallowed; everyone who had ever spoken against slavery, upheld Negroes or the North, was suspect. The countryside, from the evidence of letters to authorities and private correspondence, in the year 1860 was in panic. It was thought the South was honeycombed with traitors, and that every Negro was bloody-minded and ready to rise and kill.

The panic took all its recognizable forms. A sixty-year-old preacher, a Democrat born in Kentucky who believed the Bible sanctioned slavery, criticized the flogging of Negroes in a sermon. His Texas congregation tied him to a post and almost killed the old man with seventy lashes on the back. In Palestine, Texas, a self-appointed committee collected all "dangerous books for destruction by public burning." People also burned possessions of Northern manufacture. Northern-born schoolteachers were hounded out; Yankee seamen were mobbed in the port towns. Guilt by association, if a man had Yankee friends, was accepted without question. Vigilance committees, the vigilantes, were formed everywhere. A secret organization known as the Knights of the Golden Circle sprang up across the state. The Knights' aims were to make the South safe for slavery and to conquer Mexico as a side order. Two filibusters were actually armed and organized, but before they reached Mexico, they were diverted to another, bigger war.

During the summer of 1860, a series of mysterious fires blazed along the North Texas frontier. Barns and buildings went up in flames in Dallas, Denton, Waxahachie, and several other towns. Newspapers reported "abolitionists" were trying to burn out the South; horrible atrocity tales of slave risings, poisonings, and political murder—for which there was no basis in truth—pervaded the western counties of the heartland. At Dallas a large mob hanged three unfortunate Negroes, for no known cause. Three white men were lynched in Fort Worth, on the suspicion they had "tampered" with slaves. A spirit of paranoia and intolerance seems to have been everywhere, but noticeably, the wildest rumors and violence were confined to the white regions, west of the "black belt." In the old counties along the Colorado and Brazos the slaves continued to hoe and pick cotton peacefully, while the great planters agonized with Governor Sam Houston about the state of local and national politics.

Similar violence and panic was occurring in some degree across the whole South; the wildest rumors seem to have begun in Texas, but they rapidly spread northward as far as the Potomac. In Virginia and Mississippi, many people believed Texas was in a state of chaos, induced by Northern conspiracies. One historian compared this mass delusion and mass fear with the "Great Fear" that seized France in 1789; in any event it precipitated political crisis.

The great American tragedy was that in both Texas and in Northern states otherwise decent men had come to believe in diabolism and depravity on the other side. There were ugly aspects on each side. The repellent slavering by intellectuals over John Brown's body was matched by editorials in Texas advocating the restoration of the slave trade and violence against anyone who disagreed. Abolitionists ranted that the South must be "cleansed by fire" while Southerners grimly determined that the "higher law of self-preservation" was the only defense against the higher law defying their institutions and property rights preached by the Abolitionists. The failure of the North to condemn John Brown unequivocally produced a psychology of lynch law. While Garrison, in the North, asked the North how much outrage it would continue to take from the slavers, Albert Gallatin Brown, in the South, demanded "to what depth of infamy" his people were sinking if they took the provocations heaped on them. The Northern papers printed diatribes against slaveowners and "waved the bloody shirt." Texas editors told their readers if they permitted the North's conception of Negro equality, they were not men. Thus paranoia fed on paranoia, and in this poisonous atmosphere the ruling Democratic Party in the South convened at Charleston, South Carolina, in April, 1860.

In Texas, the Calhoun Democrats had already gained complete control; now, they "abandoned restraint." In the state convention, the leadership resolved that Texas had the sovereign right to secede and resume its place as an independent nation. The party platform attacked the "unnatural" efforts of a "sectional party" in the North, the Republicans, to fight slavery. The men sent to the national convention at Charleston were radicals: Runnels, Lubbock, Bryan, Hubbard, and Ochiltree.

Events at Charleston grew completely out of the crisis atmosphere. Douglas of Illinois, leader of the Northern wing of the Democratic Party, insisted, and had to insist upon his concept of "squatter sovereignty" in the western territories. The Northern Democrats, predominantly conservative, were willing to compromise with the South but not to follow the Constitutionalist lead. Although it was recognized the Republicans had gathered strength, and it would require a united national effort to retain the Presidency, the Texan and seven other delegations refused to accept Douglas as a candidate or to make any concession to Northern Democratic sentiment. They walked out of the convention. They knew they were destroying the national Party; they were sanguine about it because the vast majority of these men had already made up their minds to secede.

The Northern Democrats reacted to the Southern threats of secession much as Sam Houston had predicted: they told the Texans and the others to go to Hell. The delegates from these states nominated Douglas and Herschel Johnson for their ticket. The eight Southern states that bolted the convention gathered in a rump session at Baltimore and nominated John C. Breckinridge of Kentucky, a strong states' rights man, for President, and Senator Joseph Lane of Oregon for Vice President. The single unifying national party in the United States was now hopelessly sundered, but this was not enough; the conservative Southerners split off from the dominant radicals. The conservatives organized their own Constitutional Union party at Baltimore.

This last group contained and represented most of the men of property, including the largest slaveowners, in the South. Secession frightened these men. They declared it would be ruinous to the South. They represented the calmest and best-educated elements in their states, with the least parochial view, and their platform was that the property-holders of the South must fight encroaching industrialism and abolition within the framework of the Constitution. If the South had been a genuine "aristocracy," they might have prevailed.

Sam Houston of Texas received fifty-seven votes as the Constitutional Union standard bearer on the first ballot, but John Bell, of Tennessee, got sixty-eight. Bell carried the second ballot, and Edward Everett was selected for Vice President.

A further split came when the Houstonians put their man up as a "People's candidate," but Houston, who toyed with running, soon withdrew and threw all his support to Bell.

In this state of public hysteria in the countryside, which intensified, and this condition of political chaos, the nation approached the election of 1860. It was apparent to most people that the Republican Lincoln-Hamlin ticket might get an overwhelming electoral vote.

As a Texas newspaper declared: "The great question that is agitating the public mind . . . is, 'What shall be done if Lincoln is elected?' The general sentiment in Texas . . . is against submission to the black Republican administration. . . . Such a submission . . . involves the loss of everything, and if consummated, will end in the prostration of the Southern states."

This attitude can only be traced to mass hysteria, and a rising interest on the part of basically ignorant people in public affairs. The "black Republican" platform did insist that slavery was illegal in the territories, and that even Congress and the courts had no authority to enforce it there. But it did not, and could not, attack slavery in the established slave states without attacking the Constitution itself. Lincoln made clear his antipathy toward slavery, but also declared that he had no legal right, nor any intention, to try to destroy chattel slavery in the South. The planters were strongly for John Bell. They knew he could not win, but they hoped to salvage a Unionist sentiment. The great mass of voters, however, were overwhelmingly for Breckinridge in Texas.

It was soon clear to political figures that neither Bell nor Breckinridge could win nationally, and the prospect set before the people was essentially this: a new Southern Confederacy, composed only of slave states, was preferable to continuance in a Union under Republican rule.

Sam Houston was now sixty-seven years of age, and ill. But on September 22, 1860, at a mass Unionist rally he called at Austin, he got up from his sickbed to make what was probably his most eloquent speech, and also his worst-received. It was to be many years before Texans could read these words with anything like understanding of the true motives of this dying man.

Houston spoke ringingly against disunion, come what may:

> I could point to the land of Washington, Jefferson, and Jackson . . . where freedom would be eternal and the Union unbroken. I have seen it extend from the wilds of Tennessee, then a wilderness, across the Missis-

sippi, achieve the annexation of Texas, scaling the Rocky Mountains. . . .
I have seen this mighty progress, and it still remains free and independent. Power, wealth, expansion, victory, have followed in its path, and yet
the aegis of the Union has been broad enough to encompass all. . . .

What is there that is free that we have not got? Are our rights invaded
and no government ready to protect us? No! Are our institutions wrested
from us and others foreign to our taste forced upon us? No! Is the right
of free speech, a free press, or free suffrage taken from us? . . . Has our
property been taken from us and the government failed to interpose . . . ?

No, none of these! Whence, then, this clamor about disunion . . . are we
to sell reality for a phantom?

There is no longer a holy ground upon which the footsteps of the
demagogue may not fall. . . .

I come not here to speak in behalf of a United South against Lincoln. I
appeal to the nation. I ask not the defeat of sectionalism by sectionalism,
but by nationality. These men who talk of a united South know well it
begets a united North. Talk of frightening the North by threats? American blood, North or South, has not yet become so ignoble as to be chilled
by threats. . . . The Union is worth more than Mr. Lincoln, and if the
battle is to be fought for the Constitution, let us fight it in the Union and
for the sake of the Union. . . .

Who are the men . . . taking the lead in throwing the country into
confusion? Are they the strong slaveholders of the country? No; examine
the matter and it will be found that by far the large majority of them never
owned a negro, and will never own one. I know some of them who are
making the most fuss, who would not make good negroes if they were
blacked. And these are the men who are carrying on practical abolitionism, by taking up the planters' negroes and hanging them. . . . Texas
cannot afford to be ruined by such men. Even the fact that they belong to
the Simon Pure Constitutional Democracy will not save them!

Treaties with Great Britain! Alliance with foreign powers! Have these
men forgotten history? Look at Spanish America! Look at the condition
of every petty state, which by alliance with Great Britain, is still subject to
continual aggression!

We hear of secession—"peaceable secession." We are to believe that
this people, whose progressive civilization has known no obstacles, but
has driven back one race and is fast Americanizing another, who have
conquered armies and navies, whose career has been onward and never
receded, be the step right or wrong, is at last quietly and calmly to be
denationalized . . . !

The error has been that the South has met sectionalism by sectionalism.
We want a Union basis, one broad enough to comprehend the good and
true friends of the Union in the North. To hear Southern disunionists
talk, you would think the majority of the Northern people were in the
black Republican party, but it is not so. They are in a minority, and it but
needs a patriotic movement like that supported by the conservatives of
Texas, to unite the divided opposition to that party there and overthrow
it. Why, in New York, Pennsylvania, and New Jersey alone, the conservatives had a majority of over 250,000 at the last presidential election . . .

because a minority in the North are inimical to us, shall we cut loose from the majority . . . ?

If Mr. Lincoln administers the government in accordance with the constitution, our rights must be respected. If he does not, the constitution has provided a remedy. . . . I have been taught to believe that plotting the destruction of the government is treason; but these gentlemen call a man a traitor because he desires . . . to uphold the constitution.

Who are the people who call me a traitor? Are they those who march under the national flag and are ready to defend it? . . . They are the 'Keepers of the constitution'. . . . They have studied it so profoundly that they claim to know it better than the men who made it . . . here is a constitutional party that intends to violate the constitution because a man is constitutionally elected president. If the people constitutionally elect a president, is the minority to resist him? Do they intend to carry that principle into their new Southern Confederacy? If they do, we can readily perceive how long it will last. They deem it patriotism now to overturn the government. Let them succeed, and in that class of patriots they will be able to outrival Mexico.

Houston spoke as long as his strength lasted, clearly, pragmatically, destroying the arguments of the radicals one by one, pointing out their peculiar frame of mind, that of threatening secession every time something went against them. If it were not the election of Lincoln now, it would be because the slave trade were not restored, or slavers were hanged as pirates tomorrow. But he was talking to a mass of people who were not interested in anything but their own fears, hatreds, and emotions.

I can speak but little longer; but let my last words be remembered by you. . . . In the far distant future the generations that spring from our loins are to venture in the path of glory and honor. If untrammeled, who can tell the mighty progress they will make? If cast adrift—if the calamitous curse of disunion is inflicted upon them, who can picture their misfortunes and shame?

This was Sam Houston's valedictory, a vision of a nation of honorable men, dedicated to certain basic laws, shunning all who would disrupt it, for any "convenient" reason, a mighty country bigger and more eternal than its passing frenzies or ideas, right or wrong.

Houston tended to be an ethical, rather than a moral, man. This marred his image in some eyes. In the last months before calamity, Houston was actively exploring the chances of fomenting a war with Mexico. He moved Rangers toward the border, and tried to secure financing for the greatest filibuster of all. In this work, Houston's forty-seven years of advancing the cause of the United States westward must be taken into account. Houston never wanted a battle except when it served a greater purpose; his plans in 1860 were not a sign of senility but a desperate scheme to prevent the destruction of the American nation through secession. Houston briefly dreamed of a great, patriotic campaign to conquer all Mexico, which might make him President of the United States and allow him to save the Union short of civil war. Looking backward, a completely courageous Jacksonian in the White House might well have prevented the coming national tragedy. A man who could have again put down both Abolitionists and Secessionists with impartial severity might have retained an American balance. But Houston was too old, and the hour too late. As one writer described the Jacksonian years, *There were giants in those days,* and Houston was the last of them.

On November 8, 1860, the event dreaded in Texas happened; Lincoln secured sufficient electoral votes to win the Presidency. It was, as Houston predicted, a triumph of sectionalism over sectionalism, rather than a national victory. Lincoln was a minority President, by almost one million popular votes. He received 1,857,000; Douglas 1,365,976; Breckinridge 847,953; and Bell, the planters' choice, only 590,631. But Lincoln's victories were confined to only a few big states, all in the North. He would have carried all but two of them, Oregon and California, even if all his opponents' votes had been pooled. The startling, and dangerous, quality of this victory was that Lincoln got less than 100,000 votes outside the states he carried. He got none at all in Texas and in several other Southern states.

The American people, as such, elected no one in 1860; they had been divided into states versus states, and the big states won.

Breckinridge carried Texas, as expected, on the farmer vote: 47,548 to 15,463 for Bell. Bell represented the conservative Southern Unionist vote. He won only Kentucky, Virginia, and Tennessee.

Lincoln's party, because of the regional nature of his victory, failed to carry either house of Congress. The Republican President lacked eight of having a majority in the Senate, and twenty-one seats in the House. The evidence is that Mr. Lincoln was to be another futile, even tragic Tyler, Pierce, or Fillmore in the White House if the South merely kept its head. Lincoln was in no way responsible for the rupture that followed, though some blame must attach to him for not silencing or refuting the spokesmen like Seward, who attacked slavery and the South. Lincoln himself affirmed the Constitution, stated he had no powers or intentions to abolish slavery although he opposed it. But he was a Black Republican, a bogeyman, and the politicians of the South had already promised to secede, if he won, long before. Now, it was the "simon pure" Constitutionalist Democrats who scrapped the Constitution, raised rebellion, and forced Lincoln into a historic greatness he would have preferred to avoid.

Events went fast. South Carolina put secession in motion a week after the election. The nursery of nullification was the sire of secession. On December 20, 1860, South Carolina formally seceded from the United States. Other states of the old Gulf South followed. In Texas, enormous pressure was put on Houston to call a convention to discuss secession. He

refused to act. However, the Party acted without him, and unconstitution-
ally, by calling a state convention. Houston at last agreed to call a special
session of the legislature, which authorized a public election for convention
delegates. By now five Southern states had seceded. Houston argued eloquently that the situation did not call for Texas to follow suit.

Houston, with supporters David Burnet, E. M. Pease, James W. Throckmorton, the Hancocks, Edmund J. Davis, and A. J. Hamilton, took the
position that they deprecated Lincoln's success, but that the state must
yield to the American Constitution. This position was eroded rapidly by
attacks by both a majority of the political figures and the press. Unionism
in Texas revolved around a number of prominent men, most of whom were
not in public life; it simply had no mass base. Another problem was that
Unionist sentiment was simply that neither the North nor its philosophy
nor developing social ideas had an iota of planter support. This must be
understood in the light of the immense turn, in the ensuing months, of the
followers of Bell to reluctant support for the Confederacy, from Texas to
Virginia. It became unthinkable for a Texan to side against his own people
once Lincoln began to put down the rebellion, and the secessionist majority
was at war.

The special convention to vote on secession was assembled at Austin
during the last days of January, 1861. It was apparent from preliminary
maneuvers that secession was ascendant. Sam Houston attended the sessions, as an observer recognized by the chair; he attempted neither to
support nor obstruct. Houston's tactic was to delay. The convention was
chaired by Oran M. Roberts, a justice of the state supreme court and an
ardent secessionist.

The actual balloting on passage of a secession ordinance came at high
noon, February 1, 1861. There was an atmosphere of tension and drama,
and the galleries of the convention hall were packed. One hundred seventy-
four delegates, from the Red River to the Rio Grande, shouted "aye" or
"no" as their names were polled.

Seventy delegates voted for secession before a single "no" was registered. The first negative vote brought down jeers and catcalls from the
gallery.

Oldtime Whig James W. Throckmorton, of Collin County, rose and addressed the chair as his turn came. Throckmorton was a known Unionist.
"Mr. President, in view of the responsibility, in the presence of God and
my country—and unawed by the wild spirit of revolution around me, I vote
'no!' "

This brought a feeble cheer from the Unionist minority, which was
drowned out in a wave of hissing. Throckmorton, a tall, immensely courageous politician wearing a short beard, said in a voice that could be heard
in the farthest corner: "Mr. President, when the rabble hiss, well may
patriots tremble!" Throckmorton sat down.

The convention almost dissolved in disorder; the galleries screamed abuse; the chair and the delegates themselves shouted the mob down. Very few people in the hall agreed with Throckmorton, but he was known as an honorable man. The balloting continued. At its end, only seven men from all Texas joined Throckmorton.

When the result was officially announced, thunderous cheers rocked the hall. A procession immediately started down the aisle, led by arch-secessionist George Flournoy; in its van, carried by several ladies, was a magnificent handmade Lone Star flag. This emblem was ceremonially raised to the place of honor over the platform, where the national flag was normally displayed. Outside the hall, Austin went wild as the news was carried about. Couriers rode at the gallop north, east, and south. In a burst of wild, popular enthusiasm, most Texans believed the day of deliverance from Northern evil had arrived. Everywhere militia companies gathered, shots were fired in the air, and bonfires lit.

Quietly, almost unnoticed, the handful who had voted against secession left the hall and had themselves photographed standing together for posterity. Sixty-six years were to pass before this photograph was to be printed or shown in Texas.

Sam Houston, who sat quietly, saying little, during this drama, now threw his whole weight into an attempt to have the ordinance voted down by the people. Its terms provided that Texas would become sovereign on March 2, 1861—twenty-five years after the first Texas declaration of independence—unless an open referendum turned the ordinance down.

The ordinance, together with a declaration of causes, was printed in 20,000 copies and distributed throughout the state. The six causes for Texas' secession are historically important; they revealed the dominant Texas mind. Even those men who opposed secession agreed with all, or some, of these statements. The "causes" were as follows:

The general government of the United States had administered the common territory so as to exclude Southern people from it (meaning, Congress had consistently barred or tried to bar slavery in the Western territories).

The disloyalty of the people of the North and the "imbecility" of their leadership had created incendiarism and outlawry in Kansas.

The Union had failed to defend Texas against both Mexican bandits and Indians.

The Northern people had become inimical to the South and to "their beneficent and patriarchical system of African slavery, preaching the debasing doctrine of the equality of all men, irrespective of race or color."

The slaveholding states had become a minority, unable to defend themselves against northern aggression against slavery.

The extremists of the North had elected as President and Vice-President "two men whose chief claims to such high positions" were the approval of all the above wrongs, and these men were pledged to the final ruin of the slaveholding South.

In these weeks, there was a noticeable trend among the more conservative newspapers to support secession. The principal motive was emotional: submission to a Black Republican President, whose party had come to symbolize racial equality in the South, galled the Southern soul. The almost universal confusion of questions of domination and subordination with manhood in such situations arose. Southern manhood would be degraded by enforced equality; true men would never submit. This feeling was not, historically, confined to the American South. It tended to exist everywhere, before and later, a master-inferior social complex arose, from South America to South Africa. The American North, opposing what was a basic human instinct with concepts of morality, never fully understood this, because the North did not live in the daily presence of a conquered, enforcedly servile race.

All evidence shows that then (and afterward) much Southern educated opinion felt that the Union was designed originally as a confederacy, in which sovereign states possessed an inherent right to come and go. Many of the men who opposed secession did not disbelieve in this right, considering it a basic freedom the people enjoyed. This feeling must be understood in order to understand the reason that the vast majority of the Texans who voted against secession, and believed the destruction of the Union was a mistake, eventually fought loyally for their native soil. Many of the great planters remained opposed to secession to the end; then, when it was inevitable, like ordinary citizens across Texas, they offered their services to the state.

Sam Houston, Throckmorton, and the small band of prominent Unionists mounted a "noble effort" to win the popular vote. This was hopeless. Ten predominantly German counties around Austin were carried for the Union, though Europeans in the more eastern regions of the state supported secession. Throckmorton seems to have been instrumental in getting eight north Texas counties to vote no; these counties contained many Upper South, or border state immigrants, as well as a few Yankees. But the heartland and the black belts of the coast and pine woods went overwhelmingly for secession, with only a few exceptions. The state-wide vote was 46,129 to 14,697, closely duplicating the Breckinridge-Bell vote.

Again, many landowners did not favor secession but could not influence the popular democracy in full tide. Arguments that secession was a strategic error were pallid against the emotionalism that gripped two-thirds of the people.

The special convention, which had been legalized by the legislature, was already acting to accept the surrender of federal forces in Texas before the vote was in. There were over 2,000 border garrison troops in the state; the surrender of these was eased by the fact that General Twiggs, in command, was a Georgian Southern sympathizer. Everywhere, over forts and government posts and agencies, the Stars and Stripes were torn down and the Lone Star emblem raised. Many federal officers, both civil and military, were Southern, and joined the movement.

With its popular mandate, independence was official March 2. The convention now authorized a Texas delegation to apply to the Confederacy, now organizing at Montgomery, Alabama, for admission to the new nation of Southern states. This was unnecessary. The Confederacy had already taken the step of admitting Texas, before the state applied.

There was some sentiment in Texas to stay aloof from the rest of the South, to go it alone as an independent state. But two things made this impossible for the old-time Texas settlers: the great influx from the Southern states in recent years, which carried ties of blood, and the fact that it was common knowledge that the Northern states were not going to permit the Union to dissolve peaceably, although this last notion had been much expounded by politicians. The Confederacy was from the first a defensive measure, and all deeply committed slave states felt compelled to join. Houston refused to try to obstruct the entrance into the Confederate States, on the grounds this would provoke civil conflict within the state.

Houston now faced his last two great decisions in public life: whether to take the oath of allegiance to the Confederacy, as all state officers were now required to do, and whether to fight to retain his office under the U.S. Constitution. He did neither. He declined the oath to the Confederacy on the simple grounds it violated his oath to the United States. This caused the convention to remove him, on March 16, 1861, by declaring his office vacant and appointing Clark, the lieutenant governor, in his place.

President Lincoln, through a federal military officer, offered Houston the use of the U.S. Army to retain his office. Houston declined this firmly. Fort Sumter had not yet been fired on, and Houston was determined not to be the first to precipitate civil war. Houston now satisfied his own concepts of honor. He remained true to the Union; he sent a message protesting the illegality of his removal, and he retired to his home in Huntsville.

Houston faced the same dilemma thousands of Southerners who had taken an oath of allegiance to the United States faced. All were torn painfully between personal and professional honor, beliefs of right and wrong, and their deep sense of blood and soil. The agony of Robert E. Lee in these weeks is illuminating. Lee, a lieutenant colonel of the 2d Cavalry, met with Edmund J. Davis of Brownsville, a district court judge, in a small hotel off Main Plaza in San Antonio. Davis, a transplanted Floridian, told Lee that he was the ablest man in federal service, and begged him to stand by the Union, on both legal and emotional grounds. Davis was a Southerner who believed secession was suicidal. Colonel Lee, "superb, perfect, handsome, bronzed, and compact," as a Union-sympathizing observer wrote in his diary, showed visible anguish. He began to pace the room. Finally, he told the judge that his arguments were "correct and unanswerable." Secession was suicidal and meant certain disaster for the Southern people. But Lee said quietly that his higher loyalty must be to his own people, and to the state his family had served so long. He would go with Virginia.

Lee's demeanor and decision profoundly affected the Unionists in the room, who never forgot the scene.

Sam Houston chose both the American nation and Texas. He refused to violate his oath or to serve the Confederacy; he also refused to do anything to shed Texan blood. He reluctantly approved the decision of his eldest son to enlist in the Southern army, recognizing young Houston's own right of choice.

James W. Throckmorton, politically the bravest of the brave, fought secession to the last. Then, his own sense of duty compelled him to don Confederate gray. He eventually became a brigadier.

A great factor in this coming war was that it was not a true "civil" war in the ideological or social sense. America was still an imperfect nation, made up of strikingly different regions, with tremendously different outlooks. The war at bottom was regional, an outgrowth of the regional configuration of the Presidential election. Only in limited areas, mainly border states, was it a brother-against-brother conflict. What began as a rebellion against the federal apparatus turned into a war between two States. Significantly, men from Northern states without feelings either about slavery or the Union fought in the federal forces; the early resort of the Confederated States to conscription made the Southern effort "national" rather than ideological.

Thousands of Southerners had to choose between abstract principle and people; and to the Texan and Southern mind, soil and people were paramount. It was extremely difficult for Union-thinking Texans to stand for principle, because there was no real Unionist base in the South to make such a stand respectable. Inevitably, although only three out of four Texans voted for disunion, nine out of ten refused to support a cause carried on by "foreigners" in the North.

In retirement and isolation at Huntsville, Houston was a tragic figure. He did not live out the war. In these last years of his life, the mixed emotions all Texans felt toward their greatest hero tended to color his long career. He was a giant of the early American nineteenth century, who had outlived his time, and the full understanding of his countrymen.

Trying to assess Houston, the Texas historian Webb wrote he was "fully conscious of the possession of superior talents . . . bold and intelligent." But Walter Prescott Webb found it hard to like Houston. He was "a finished master of guile and deception."

Houston confused men; he had the politician's knack of listening attentively to everything brought before him, saying little, and always giving the impression he might go along with every argument. He had so little ideology, other than a profound belief in the American nation and its destiny, that many people never knew where he stood on lesser issues. But in crisis, as Webb said, he was "a statesman, and never a scoundrel."

When Santa Anna was brought before him, and a blood-thirsty mob clamored for the Mexican's blood, Houston never thought of anything except to use the captive President for his country's advantage. When he dreamed huge dreams and plotted the explosion of the United States westward with Andrew Jackson, he found it expedient "not to let his right hand know what his left hand was about," and to "keep his own counsel." Let others believe what they wanted to believe; Sam Houston did what he thought was required.

He had no great faith in lesser men, and time and time again they justified him fully. Yet, Houston held his own word and honor sacrosanct. No Texan ever inspired more confidence to men around him. He had monstrous ambitions; even as late as 1860, he had never given up hope of becoming President of the United States. Yet, he sacrificed ambition to honor many times, from the governorship of Tennessee to his nomination for President.

He was hard—rocklike on the battlefield—and he had in one way or another killed many men. But he had a streak of magnanimity broader than most Americans of his time. Few men ever showed less rancor for his former enemies, above all when they were at his feet.

He was a difficult man for even his own age to understand; genius always is. During the grim months of 1860, he posed as a new American Alexander, preparing to bring American civilization to Mexico at the point of a Texan sword. Houston was surely sincere in thinking Anglo-Saxon conquest would have been good for Mexico, and here he was by no means alone. But his actions in 1860 must be measured against his acts as President of Texas, when he almost singlehandedly damped a Texas-Mexican war. And when he tried to gather guns, ammunition, and Rangers to invade the south, Houston was scrupulous every step of the way to compromise neither the honor of his subordinates nor of the United States. Houston was the kind of man who could evision an appalling conflict between the states, and coldly choose to avert it by shedding Mexican blood instead. He was a patriot in the oldest, Roman, sense.

In his last years Houston compromised his future image as a Texan hero. But then he had never been a "Texas" hero, anymore than Jackson was a "Southern" President. He was an American patriot, soldier, and statesman, first and last. In the Jacksonian age, he was better understood. He died at Huntsville in July, 1863, at the age of seventy-one, a generation past his time.

Three months after he was buried, the Confederate legislature of the State of Texas passed a resolution that stands, like the state itself, as his epitaph: "His public services though a long and eventful life, his unblemished patriotism, his great private and moral worth, and his untiring, devoted, and zealous regard for the interests of the state of Texas command our highest admiration, and should be held in perpetual remembrance by the people of this state."

The historian Webb said it better, when he wrote: "Whether we like him or not . . . the fact remains that Sam Houston was no ordinary man."

19

THE BONNY
BLUE FLAG

> Texas has furnished to the Confederate military service thirty-
> three regiments, thirteen battalions, two squadrons, six detached
> companies, and one legion of twelve companies of cavalry . . .
> making 62,000 men, which with the state troops in actual serv-
> ice, 6,500 men, form an aggregate of 68,500 Texans in military
> service . . . an excess of 4,773 more than her highest popular
> vote, which was 63,727. From the best information within reach
> . . . of the men now remaining in the state between the ages of
> sixteen and sixty years . . . the number will not exceed 27,000.
>
> GOVERNOR FRANCIS R. LUBBOCK, FEBRUARY 5, 1863

ON April 12, 1861, Confederates in South Carolina fired upon the
United States garrison at Fort Sumter. Blood was shed, and three days later
President Lincoln called for volunteers to preserve the Union. This precipitated war. Each state and each individual American now had to choose
sides, and only a few were able successfully to remain neutral.

In Texas, a vast surge of popular patriotism replaced the "Great Fear"
of the year before. With the issue defined, almost all prominent men loyally
supported the state. J. W. Throckmorton was commissioned a Confederate
brigadier. The people who still remained Unionist, or neutral, the more
common reaction among the dissidents, were noticeably of Northern or
foreign birth. Pockets of Northern immigrants in north Texas resisted allegiance to the Confederacy, and the Germans spread through the hill country above the Balcones Scarp did not rally to the Stars and Bars. Yet this
reaction was hardly universal. A large number of merchants and planters

born in New York, Pennsylvania, and other far-off states were now strong Confederates, choosing their neighbors over broken or forgotten ties. The switching of political allegiances to conform with immediate environments was already an American phenomenon; ideology itself was weaker in America than social pressures. A majority of the German and other European immigrants, though little publicized, supported their new state. Those Europeans who were most integrated and not living in separated communities with their own kind were the staunchest Confederates; in communities like Fredericksburg and San Antonio, social pressure worked in the opposite way, because here a majority tended toward neutrality. Recent immigrants provided a number of distinguished leaders to Texas: Colonel Augustus Buchel, born in Germany; Colonel John C. Border and Generals Walter Lane and Thomas Waul, all from the British Isles, and General Xavier Debray, of Epinal in France. The dissent of the foreign-born, out of loyalty to the Union and opposition to slavery, has always been exaggerated.

Ninety percent of the population eventually stood by the state.

The Mexican minority, located almost entirely south of San Antonio, was politically inert. A few prominent families, such as the Benavides of Laredo, came out for the Confederacy. The majority, who took no part in Anglo-American politics, regarded the war as a gringo affair and opted out. Efforts of Union officers to stir up rebellion along the Rio Grande failed. Because of the remoteness of the areas of Mexican population from the rest of the state, Mexicans were largely left to themselves.

Several thousand men who could not or would not support the Confederacy did leave the state. Most of these congregated across the border in Mexico, where U.S. consuls helped some return to the United States, and recruiting officers enlisted others in the U.S. Army. Other men simply hid out or "laid low." Both slackers and those who joined the Union armies were generally thought of as traitors throughout Texas.

On Confederacy Day, March 16, 1861, most Texans believed that the mere declaration of the new nation made it so. They expected the North to fight, but no one thought it would be a serious war. The Confederacy would be sustained. There were, of course, three fatal flaws in this belief: The relative power of the older Southern states vis-à-vis the industrial North—the South contained only one-third the people and 8 percent of the North's productive capacity—was not understood. Foreign alliances, above all with Britain and France, were expected; Texans had played that game before. The last great error was mistaking, as Houston warned, the will and determination of the American North.

In the spring of 1861 the Union was already destroyed, and the loyal states gave every evidence of indecision and confusion. Abraham Lincoln's superb ability to raise the concept of the Union to the "sublimity of religious mysticism" in the North was not anticipated, nor was the President's determination to prosecute the preservation of the nation ruthlessly, regardless of ultimate cost. The great majority of Southern lawyers believed their own rhetoric.

The first months of 1861 were an unbroken chain of triumphs for the rebellious state. The Convention aggressively applied itself to reducing the Federal power in Texas, and to seizing Federal property. Committees of safety were formed, militia units raised under veteran state officers. The Convention resolved that all U.S. property was "renationalized" upon secession, and thus became the property of the state. The militia, under old Rangers John S. Ford and Ber and Henry McCulloch, marched to enforce the order. State units headed for north Texas, San Antonio, and the Rio Grande, where there were concentrations of Federal troops.

Ten percent of the U.S. Army, 2,700 soldiers under Major General D. E. Twiggs, was stationed in the state. Twiggs himself was a Georgian and not disposed to fight Texans. From his headquarters at San Antonio, he queried Washington for orders. He got none, and this must be credited to his reputation, because in February, 1861, no one in Washington knew what to do. Twiggs found himself surrounded by a hostile militia force in San Antonio, demanding his surrender, while none of his superiors would take responsibility for what he was supposed to do.

Twiggs at San Antonio had only 160 men, headquarters troops. The regular army was scattered at small garrisons and Indian-watching forts along a thousand miles of Mexican and Comanche frontier. Feeling his position was impossible, General Twiggs chose to resign his post. But this did not provide him with a solution. The Texans demanded that he make a protocol before he left. He was forced to turn over all Federal property and munitions, while his troops were to be permitted to march to the coast with their personal arms. This compact was extended to include all Federal military units in Texas.

The Federals were not evacuated, however, by the Navy as planned. Before the scattered garrisons could march to the coast, the news of Sumter reached Texas. Considering the state now at war with the United States, the Convention voided the protocol and made the Federal troops prisoners of war. This action was sustained by the Confederate government in Alabama. Without firing a shot, Texans disposed of a large part of the Federal army and seized $3,000,000 in military stores.

Many regulars, particularly officers, were Southerners. A high proportion resigned their commissions and joined the Confederate forces.

Then, in May, 2,000 Texans under Young pushed north over the Red River and captured three Federal forts in the Indian Territory of Oklahoma. The remaining Union forces retreated all the way to Kansas. Texas was freed from any immediate invasion danger.

As a border state of the Confederacy, Texas was removed from the centers of action in Virginia and along the Mississippi. The desert and Indian-infested areas north and west of settled Texas counties made Union invasion from that direction almost impossible. The greatest peril lay along the Gulf coast, where Texas was exposed to the operations of the superior United States Navy. Another peril, not at first realized, was the hostile Indian frontier, from which the cavalry was now withdrawn. Somewhat ironically, the Texan defense of the seacoast was to be one of the Confederate States' most brilliant feats between 1861 and 1865; but the defense of the interior frontier was to prove a disaster for the state.

In the general euphoria of early 1861, the secessionists believed it would never be necessary to send Texans across the Mississippi to sustain the Southern Confederacy. As in the ominous days of the Revolution, Texas farmers thought mainly about getting their crops planted. Most of the militia disbanded. The new government took only certain defensive measures. Governor Clark and the legislature created 32 militia districts, each commanded by a local brigadier, and a few state troops were dispatched to take over the abandoned Federal forts in the west and on the Rio Grande. The western counties up against the Indian danger were instructed to organize companies of minutemen. Clark further ordered that all arms and ammunition in the hands of private merchants be surrendered to the state, but very little was ever turned in. A canvass of firearms in private hands was also ordered, but this proved something of a fiasco. Only 40,000 weapons, mostly obsolete, were reported. Few Texans were willing to list their firearms, fearing eventual confiscation.

The surveys, however, still revealed a dangerous situation. Despite the windfall provided by General Twiggs, Texas was poorly supplied to fight any kind of sustained war. As a frontier community, Texas depended upon the industrial resources of Europe and the North for firearms. Guns had always been one thing the self-sufficient frontiersmen could not make themselves.

Meanwhile, all partisan political activity ceased. The majority Democratic Party did not bother to make endorsements in the summer elections of 1861. The various contests for state and Confederate posts—Texas was reorganized almost as before, the Federal capital merely being moved to Richmond—devolved into personal popularity contests, and revolved around which candidate would do most to support the war. On this platform Francis R. Lubbock, a sometime lieutenant governor under Hardin Runnels, won the governorship by 124 votes.

Lubbock was energetic, and a deep believer in the South. He traveled up to Richmond while still governor-elect. He arrived in the post-Manassas hour of truth, when both Richmond and Washington were realizing what had been wrought. This was going to be a long, bitter, costly war. Lubbock saw President Jefferson Davis and his Cabinet, and asked them what Texas might do to support the war.

Francis Lubbock was one of the few Southern governors who ever asked this question sincerely, and he was one of the few who won Jefferson Davis' undying gratitude and friendship. The parochialism of the South had not ended with secession, as Davis and his government were already discovering.

Lubbock, even more strongly than many men in Richmond, was convinced that the fate of the Confederacy depended upon quick and decisive military action. Lubbock said that the North must be defeated before it could bring superior manpower and resources to bear. His viewpoint was radical to many Texans, who neither saw their state in danger nor accepted the fact that the fate of Texas would be decided eventually along the Potomac. But Lubbock rode home determined to throw Texas into the War Between the States, to the hilt.

In Texas, Frank Lubbock beat the drums of patriotism and alarm. He issued a proclamation urging "every able-bodied Texan" to enlist. He had received official calls for only 8,000 men from the Confederacy, but he recruited many thousands more. He anticipated the call for companies to serve in the East, and was more than prepared for it when it inevitably arrived.

There was a tremendous "tradition" in Texas, as Rupert Richardson observed, that young men should join the colors in any crisis. When the flag was raised and rallies held in every scattered, dusty town, the response, by any historical standard, was phenomenal. Richmond asked for twenty companies of infantry in the late summer of 1861, "for service in Virginia, the enlistment to be for the period of the war." Thirty-two companies answered the call. These men, drawn from dozens of distant counties, marched to Virginia, and into shot, shell, and legend, as Hood's Brigade. This was the Texan Brigade that broke the Federal lines at Gaines' Mill and was given the glorious, if dangerous, honor of first place in Longstreet's Corps. Some members survived to witness Appomattox.

The figures of the troops Texas gave the Confederacy cannot be completely reconciled; records of the time were poorly kept. The 1860 census showed there were 92,145 white men between the ages of eighteen and forty-five in the state. Between 60,000 and 70,000 men saw service—two-thirds of the military-age population. Even though these figures, basically correct, include frontier service and many reenlistments, they can be reconciled in one way. Thousands of boys below eighteen, and thousands of men up to sixty and beyond, joined the Stars and Bars.

The one great contribution of Texas to the Southern cause was men.

Tradition was both made and fulfilled, but at appalling human damage.

The leadership class in Texas was composed of planters and professional men; traditionally, these were more responsive to the bugle call than men from the countinghouse or factory. The great planters had feared secession, but they sustained the Southern army to the end. In each county, landowners raised unit after unit, many armed and equipped at their own expense. They filled most of the posts from captain to colonel, while the ranks were filled with tough farmboys thronging in. The rock of both armies, Blue and Gray, was this horde of small farmers. But evidence is incontrovertible that a higher percentage of the social and capitalist elite joined the colors in the South, while professional graduates of West Point commanded in every major battle on both sides.

Texas supplied 135 general officers and colonels to the South, including two professionals of superior talent, John B. Hood and Albert Sidney Johnston. Hood became a temporary full general in 1864, while Johnston's tragic death at Shiloh is believed by some historians to have markedly affected the outcome of the war. Only one native-born Texan became a Confederate general: Felix Huston Robertson. He was the last Confederate general officer to die.

Hundreds of medical doctors and lawyers enlisted or secured commissions. Doctors who drew the sword rather than the scalpel included Generals Richard Gano and Jerome Robertson, and Colonels John S. Ford and Ashbel Smith. Generals W. R. Scurry and A. W. Terrell and Colonels Hugh McLeod, John Marshall, and Roger Mills were fighting lawyers. Two high officers, Wilburn King and William Rogers, held degrees in both medicine and law. These men lent a certain blaze of glory to the Southern legions under the Bonny Blue Flag. Their blood, and the loss of this high-minded elite put a somber, lasting pall over the future of the land.

Scurry bled to death cheering his men on at Jenkin's Ferry in 1864. John Marshall, at the head of the 4th Texas, died from a minié ball at Gaines' Mill. Doctor William Rogers—"the bravest man who ever wore the gray" —fell riddled as he planted the St. Andrew's Cross on the Union parapet at Corinth, Mississippi, in 1862. The graves of the Texan educated elite lay scattered in a grim procession across six states.

Whatever their motivation, and whatever their faults, no group of men ever more bravely sustained a forlorn cause. They gave it a certain haunted holiness few Texans ever completely forgot.

Two-thirds of the Texan companies fought west of the Mississippi, in bitter, bloody battles that rarely gained recognition or national fame. Terry's Rangers were never excelled, in Union eyes, for reckless mobility and heroic dash. Two-thirds of Terry's men were killed, their bones scattered in a hundred sites. Ross' Brigade fought valiantly on both sides of the Mississippi. Here again the war took a hideous toll, not only of landowners but of ordinary men. Texas' loss in blood and bone was proportionally higher than that of any Northern state.

By 1864 the old units were ragged remnants. Companies of infantry could hardly muster a corporal's guard; battalions could barely surround their tattered battle flags. Proud of their tradition and honors, many older units refused new blood; no replacements were accepted. This was military idiocy, but as an example of cavalier magnificence it still stands.

Many of these units were still fighting, in 1865, when the population of the South, as a whole, had forsaken the war. As military historians know, and many Americans have overlooked, Lee at Petersburg was with an army sustaining a broken nation, and not the other way around.

The sustaining of the War Between the States in Texas was a magnificent achievement over-all, by a completely agricultural, frontier society totally unequipped to fight a total war against an industrial power. Southerners, between 1861 and 1865, sacrificed more to a general war than any body of Americans before or since. The losses were enormous: 200,000 soldiers died, and a quarter of Texas' most vigorous manpower was killed or incapacitated. The entire economy gradually became paralyzed, due to the Federal naval blockade that tightened by the middle of 1861. And in the areas where the armies marched the destruction of property was total. Texas was spared this last, not by chance but by a vigorous defense of its soil in the latter months of the war.

The lack of manufactures and resources and industrial skills was more fatal in the long run than the disparity in numbers between North and South. Without a navy, the Confederacy fought from isolation against impossible odds. Even so, however, the South made the cost of restoring the Union almost too great for the Northern states to bear. Confederate determination, gallantry, and military brilliance on the battlefield forced the North to fight a war of attrition. This bled the Confederacy to death, as both Grant and Lincoln knew it would, but in the summer of 1864, while General Grant was presiding over the "unbroken Union funeral train" in the Wilderness, Union morale nearly crumbled. The peace party in the North was active, calling for negotiations or arbitration by outside nations —which would have meant tacitly giving up the South. Even in November, when the disintegration of the Confederacy was obvious, Lincoln won reelection by only 200,000 votes. Millions of Northerners did not think the war was worth the price: 300,000 Union dead. The American Civil War was the bloodiest conflict in modern history, in terms of populations and forces engaged.

With sufficient munitions and any kind of industrial machine, the South would have made Union victory unfeasible.

The Federal blockade forced an immediate economic revolution in Texas. Cotton continued to be grown, but it could be exported only with great difficulty. More acreage went to corn and other food crops. The departure of the men threw the burden of supplying food and clothing on women and slaves, and it also threw the plantations back on their own resources. The Texas cotton plantation was never a self-sufficient estate, like the Mexican *hacienda*. It was a capitalistic enterprise. The most progressive planters had long bought even their tools and slave clothing from the Northern factories.

Plantation families worked to spin cloth for uniforms; it was remarked that travelers could not approach any house without hearing the sound of wheels or looms. The big plantations and isolated settlements established shops to try to make such necessities as hoes, knives, and shirts, from scratch. Surprising progress was made in some areas. Through the efforts of a state board, 40,000 pairs of wool and cotton cards were secured from Europe and imported through Mexico. Texas was able to sell some $2,000,000 in cotton by hauling it to the Rio Grande during the war. This exchange was invaluable.

Wives and daughters could make uniforms at home, but other military needs proved more difficult. A cap and gun factory was built at Austin, the first in the state. A region where almost the entire population went armed had never thought of making its own weapons; the North could do it better. The Austin arsenal forged only a handful of cannon, all of doubtful quality. Meanwhile, though dozens of ambitious charters for various industrial projects were issued, all of these dreams fell through. Grandiose plans were discussed for all sorts of manufactures, but in Texas there was no infrastructure for industry. Skills, tools, and transportation were all lacking. Lawyers drew up charters; the legislature approved them; the factories were never built.

The penitentiary at Huntsville produced 1,500,000 yards of cloth each year with convict labor. Salt works were established in several parts of the state, since military stores required huge amounts of salt. New ironworks were erected near Jefferson, Rusk, and Austin, while officials struggled with the realization that dishes, cups, candles, knives, and spoons, which had always been so conveniently bought abroad, now had to be made at home. Actually, Texas publicly and privately made an impressive total of uniforms, hats, shoes, and produced an enormous amount of bacon and flour. Tragically, little of this total ever reached the hungry and ragged Confederate armies, because there were few roads and no rails.

The crops were fortunately good during the war years. No community really suffered from lack of food. Families lived on yams, used pipe ashes for soda, and drank burnt okra for a coffee substitute. No substitute for sugar—also cut off—was found. But a great pride was taken in this austerity, because it supported the war. A thousand irritations and minor disasters, such as the breakage or loss of irreplaceable items, were borne cheerfully. Clothing wore out, but now there were patriotic songs about "homespun dresses, like the Southern ladies wear."

One horror of the war years was the disappearance of medicines. The Union placed medical supplies, including all anesthetics, on the war contraband list. This was a hardheaded act of modern war, but few things caused more suffering and resentment in the South. Confederate hospitals, military and civilian, were tragic and hideous places late in the war.

The greatest burdens fell on the frontier women, who had to go into the fields with hoe and plow to raise food for their families. Farm work by women was not an American tradition. Women were used to grinding, endless labor, but field work often exceeded their strength and skill. That so much food was grown, and few families actually went hungry, can only be laid to the wartime burst of patriotic cooperation that suffused the majority. Thousands of soldiers left wives or children without adequate means of support. But as Oran R. Roberts observed, "An almost universal humane feeling inspired people of wealth as well as those in moderate circumstances to help the indigent families of soldiers in the field and the women who had lost husbands and sons by sickness or in battle."

The large plantations opened their granaries freely. Citizens surrendered their specie, and women donated jewelry to provide foreign exchange for blockade runners. Years of accumulated wealth, of all kinds, was willingly given up to the needs of war. Relief committees were active, collecting food, clothing, and money. In Houston alone, $3,000 per week was raised by private subscription by the start of 1863.

The government exacted tithes of produce, hogs, and various goods to supply the army. But by the third year of war there was a general realization of the widespread destitution of soldier families. In 1863, Texas appropriated $600,000 for direct relief of soldier families. By 1864, 74,000 women and minor children were on the state war relief rolls, showing again the enormous drain of manpower from the state. An agrarian society, committed beyond its powers, was beginning to exhibit unbearable strains.

An agricultural economy could put a large army in the field for a season or two. It was utterly incapable of sustaining a war of attrition that went on for years. The heroism with which it tried, and the valiant struggles that took place on a hundred thousand scattered Texas farms, must always remain a source of American pride.

One remarkable aspect of the war years was the behavior of the Negro slaves. Thousands of able-bodied men were left in charge of women, old men, and boys on the river bottoms. A region that had long been haunted by the specter of slave revolt—it was only months since the hysteria of 1859—did not record a single incident. As the chief justice of Texas stated: "It was a subject of general remark that the negroes were more docile and manageable during the war than at any other period, and for this they deserve the lasting gratitude of their owners in the army." The fact that the slaves labored mightily and peaceably through the war has never adequately been explained. But certainly more humane treatment helped, and many slaves seemed to have been genuinely caught up in a feeling for a plantation, land, and society in which they had no stake. There were innumerable cases where a white mistress directed the efforts of dozens of slaves, in isolated places. No white woman or child was ever molested, and even more remarkably, fewer slaves tried to run away than in the previous years.

While Governor Francis Lubbock worked devotedly to support the Confederate nation, certain significant strains and tensions between government and people, and between the state and Confederate regimes, soon developed. Although Lubbock urged every man into uniform, saw that laws were passed suspending debts for the duration, pushed through bonds and special local taxes, and authorized the receipt of Confederate paper to pay state obligations—all revolutionary acts in 19th-century America—there was still enormous ineptitude in certain places.

One source of trouble was General Paul Octave Hébert, the commander of the Military Department of Texas. The appointment of Hébert to this post was unfortunate. The General was a West Pointer, but he had spent much time in Europe, and he affected continental military styles. He was arrogant, arbitrary, and cavalier; he also lacked common sense. Thomas North, in his *Five Years in Texas: Or What You Did Not Hear During the War,* described Hébert as a "constitutional ape." He "preferred red-top boots, a rat-tail moustache, fine equipage, and a suite of waiters. . . . He was too much of a military coxcomb to suit the ideas and ways of a pioneer country; besides, he was suspected of cowardice." Texans could have put up with his costumes and airs, probably, had Hébert spent less time meddling in state affairs and more time seeking the sound of the guns.

In November, 1862, Hébert issued an order barring the export of cotton except under government control. On the surface this order made sense, except that the Confederate authorities were not equipped to implement it efficiently.

Since July, 1861, the Texas coast had been under naval blockade. No cotton, the state's only resource, could be shipped to hungry European markets. But Mexico provided a loophole. Baled cotton was hauled south to the Rio Grande, delivered in Matamoros, and shipped from the Mexican side of the river in the thousands of British and French sail that congregated in the Gulf. Treaties had been negotiated with Mexican authorities in Matamoros to expedite this by the Confederate commander at Brownsville. A vast trade quickly built up; foreign ships by the hundreds lay off the mouth of the Rio Grande, while their captains clamored for cargoes and bid the price of cotton to enormous sums. The American war had caught British mills by surprise.

To protect this trade against a possible Yankee breach of the doctrine of freedom of the seas, the French and British governments sent strong squadrons to the Gulf. It was said in Texas that Admiral de Villeneuve's ships, not respect for legality, kept Federal patrol vessels far north of the Rio Grande.

The haul from the Colorado to the border was long, arduous, and expensive; there were only trails through the chaparral. But the brush country was white with falling cotton lint, because the fiber sold for a dollar, gold, per pound.

Although Texas received $2,000,000 from this export, and got back vital guns, medicines, and tools that could be gotten nowhere else, two things about this enterprise disturbed the Confederate authorities. One was that a great amount of this cotton ended up in Yankee mills—Northern manufacturers were just as desperate as the British, and sometimes, through agents, outbid them. The trade was all in the South's favor even so, but in some governmental minds it became contaminated.

The other objection was more valid. The trade was in private hands. While the wagons returned from the Rio Grande with nails, medicines, Napoleon muskets, and Enfield rifles and Kerr revolvers, they also brought back sugar, coffee, wax candles, and a few French gowns. Merchants were merchants, and the profits on luxury items were immense. By 1862, even near-luxuries and things formerly considered necessities brought fabulous prices in Texas. Every civilized amenity had been cut off, but there were people in Texas who would pay any price for certain things, war or no war. Whenever a merchant arrived back from the Rio Grande actual riots were sometimes set off, with housewives clamoring for goods.

The pioneer Mary Maverick of San Antonio wrote in her journal that after a tiring battle, "wedged up and swaying for hours," she finally fought her way to a counter and purchased one bolt of domestic cloth, one pair of shoes, and one dozen wax candles for $180. The broker in question paid $60,000 in specie for this shipment, and he sold everything out in less than a week.

This diversion of resources to "nonessentials" understandably concerned the military. But Hébert's orders did not improve matters; it merely threw impossible bureaucratic bottlenecks into the process. The whole trade was halted, and here Hébert got himself into serious disfavor with important men.

Hébert was already hated because of other policies, especially his implementation of the Confederate conscription laws. He was relieved because of these pressures and replaced with General John Bankhead Magruder, fresh from the Peninsula campaign. Magruder was a "dashing and festive" soldier; he took personal command of certain military operations then proceeding at Galveston, and he was a leader better suited to Texas styles.

But Bankhead Magruder was equally unequipped to command the vital export trade. He issued supposedly helpful instructions that only made things worse. In April, 1863, he disgustedly withdrew all controls, to see if this would help; but this move was intolerable to the Confederate commissioners and Congress. A law was enacted to regulate the trade, but which was again unworkable, and soon even the most patriotic merchants and agents were conspiring to get around the government.

The Confederacy thus never fully exploited the Mexican loophole. Too little cotton would have reached the border in any case without roads or rails, but soldiers and bureaucrats without logistic or business experience either stopped the trade or let more and more foreign exchange be lost to speculators and profiteers.

This logistical ineptitude colored the whole war and shadowed the genuine Southern battle gallantry. The lawyers and landed gentry who formed the Richmond government could write florid ballads to the valor of Southern manhood, while Southern manhood bled futilely away. They moved perceptibly away from the American federal system toward an aristocratic parliamentary regime, on the British model, but this did not face the Southern problem. The traditions and reality of a colonial-economy South did not prepare men to run a railroad, much less understand and manage a logistical complex.

Hood's Brigade charged cheering across wheat stubble in bare feet, while thousands of good leather shoes gathered dust in Confederate North Carolina. Ross' veterans fought with empty bellies, with five million range cattle roaming Texas. The premier soldiers of the South, such as Hood and Johnston, were splendid tacticians, with a greater gusto for their trade than their often-amateur counterparts from the North. But the industrially trained managers behind the Union far better understood the strategic shape of modern war. They raised, equipped, and prodigally maintained 2,000,000 bluecoats in the field; they outdid Napoleon, which few Continental observers—even with their hearts in the South—failed to see.

The South raised less than a million men, and could not feed these.

The basic loyalty of the bulk of Texans did not waver during the war. But patriotic rallies and real efforts could not hide the fact that after 1862 the conflict began to take an inevitable toll. The early euphoria vanished, as the Southwestern states were increasingly thrown on their own. The strategic brilliance of the Federal seizure of the Mississippi split Texas, Louisiana, and Arkansas from the South; it not only stopped Texan food and clothing from reaching the fronts, but it caused consternation in the West. In June, 1862, the governor of Arkansas stated that if the western states were to be left to their fate, the sooner they knew it the better. Although Lubbock cooperated fully with the Confederate authorities, held several meetings, and helped get a high-level Trans-Mississippi command, under General Edmund Kirby-Smith, approved, bitterness increased. A move grew in Texas, not to make peace with the Yankees but to secede from the Confederate States.

In early 1863, Governor Lubbock referred to "signs of a latent dissatisfaction . . . if not a positive disloyalty to the Confederacy." He worked to halt this. He called a special legislative session. He doubled taxes and began the first statewide soldiers' relief. These measures were more apparent than real. By this time, the internal and external credit of Texas was collapsing. The old recourse to unsecured currency went its usual way: Confederate scrip was only good so long as confidence in the Confederate government lasted. Now, Texas notes and warrants, backed by nothing but a promise to pay at some future date, depreciated into worthlessness. The state government maintained elaborate accounts, but stayed heavily in debt even in paper money terms. The accounts actually became meaningless: taxes were levied, and paid, in worthless bills. This financial and fiscal collapse did nothing to assist business and industry.

Inevitably, there was great speculation in real goods against soaring inflation. Few things caused more bitter complaint from the people at large, but the government was powerless to find a solution. The final misery was that war relief paid to widows and orphans was now paid in currency that could buy nothing.

The real cancer of internal disaffection, however, did not center around money but on the Confederate draft. By 1862, an incredible number of Texas men had volunteered for service; but Lee, in Virginia, faced a constant deficit in numbers. Lee's personal influence was instrumental in securing the passage of a Confederate conscription law. The concept, though this has been obscured by the enormous Southern war effort, was no more popular in Texas than it was to prove later in the North.

For one thing, all the men who wanted to fight, or felt they could leave their families, had already gone. For another, there was very little available manpower left on the western frontier. It was not possible to take all men from an agrarian society without grave damage.

The first law, passed in April, 1862, applied to all white males between eighteen and thirty-five. Soon after, the limits were raised to fifty and dropped to seventeen. While this early draft is frequently praised as military realism, it had a definitely seamy side.

This draft law was poorly drawn and executed. It was discriminatory and unevenly applied. Officeholders, even petty ones, were exempt, as were men "considered indispensable." Exemptions in medicine and frontier defense made sense, but substitution was permitted. As in the North, a wealthy man could hire a poor one to go in his place. Finally, in Texas, the law was interpreted to exempt almost any substantial man of property and affairs. It was regarded bitterly, both by the civilian population and a large proportion of the soldiers, including those who had volunteered.

Resistance to the law was immediate. Thousands of citizens protested it on principle. General Hébert's reaction, in May 1862, was to put all Texas under martial law. Hébert appointed provost marshals to administer conscription. These officers were responsible only to himself. From this time forward, large parts of Texas were regularly placed under military rule; the powers of the provosts were virtually unlimited. Both Lubbock and the state supreme court reluctantly upheld these acts. This meant there could be no appeal against a Confederate provost marshal's decision.

The ruthless prosecution of the draft and property confiscation codes was actually unnecessary, and the too vigorous enforcement of both drove some parts of the state into actual resistance. As various testaments show, protests were common. "Men who ought to be under the care of a doctor" were pushed into the army. In a country where birth certificates did not exist and records were rare, provosts, often young second lieutenants, decided which boys "were old enough." In some pitiful scenes, men were taken from large families by arbitrary action, leaving them to live on charity, and young boys were hunted down despite their parents' tears. There were heated protests against these acts by prominent men who had given sons to the army, and who were the staunchest Confederates in the state.

The confiscation of property also aroused Texan hackles. The property of "disloyal" persons, as adjudged by local officers, was sequestered. There were cases where the lands of men unavoidably detained—by internment in the North—were taken, as well as those of Texans who happened to be fighting for the South in some other state. Unionists suffered greatly, even if they had committed no overt disloyal act.

One of the characteristics of this program was that more attention was paid to the 10 percent trying to avoid commitment to the war than to the 90 percent supporting the state. At the least sign of resistance, military officers were prone to declare whole counties or regions in "rebellion" and dispatch troops. Frequently a peculiarly intolerant and arrogant type of officer sought out this domestic occupation duty; the state troops were noticeably despised by those who had volunteered for service in the East. Incidents became common by 1863.

Martial law interfered with legitimate business, and it humiliated important men traveling legitimately from their residences to other counties. A doctor, lawyer, merchant, or planter could not leave his county of residence, on any business, except with a passport signed by a military officer, who sometimes insulted him in the process. The provosts brooked no protests. An editor was threatened with arrest "for treason" because he wrote that the passport system was a violation of basic right.

Only some 2,000 Texas residents had left to serve with the Union army, but other thousands were really neutral toward the war. Trouble came when the draft was enforced against these. There was violence in pockets of north Texas, where many immigrants from Northern or border states had farms, and among the Germanic element surrounding Fredericksburg and San Antonio. To these protests the Confederate military authorities reacted viciously.

Fredericksburg, a purely German town on the Pedernales, was occupied by troops under Captain James Duff. Duff stated that "the God damn Dutchmen are Unionists to a man," and "I will hang all I suspect of being anti-Confederates." The largely European counties—Gillespie, Kerr, Kendall, Medina, Comal, and San Antonio's Bexar—were immediately in turmoil. General H. P. Bee, commanding in south Texas, virtually declared war on these areas. This persecution drove literally hundreds of men out of the area, and some even into the Union service.

In the summer of 1862, one group of Germans, who were actually neutralists in sentiment, fled this region for Mexico. They armed themselves, under the command of a Major Tegener, but their purpose was to flee the state rather than fight the Confederacy. Tegener rode south with some 65 men and boys. When Duff learned he had gone, he dispatched a force under a Lieutenant McRae in pursuit.

The refugees camped on the Nueces River, about two hundred miles from where they started. They did not expect close pursuit. On the night of

August 9, under a full moon, Tegener and the group held a lively discussion about the meaning of "Fatherland," "citizenship," "Civil War," and Mexico. According to the statements of John William Sansom, who was there, most of the German farmers were deeply confused as to what the war was all about.

McRae rode down upon the camp while the Germans lay sleeping. He surrounded it and opened fire indiscriminately. The result was massacre. Nineteen Germans were killed by gunfire, and six more trampled to death by McRae's cavalry. Nine surrendered. McRae ordered them shot, and they were executed on the spot. In his report to Duff, the Lieutenant stated he met "determined resistance, hence I have no prisoners to report."

News of the Nueces massacre touched off rioting and violence in San Antonio and the towns above the Balcones Scarp. It was bloodily put down, and a number of men were hanged, despite General James W. Throckmorton's biting comment that the greatest number of traitors seemed more remarkable for "ignorance about the war" than overt disloyalty.

Many years afterward, a monument to the German dead was raised in Central Texas. Under the inscription *Treu Der Union* (True to the Union) it listed, as "murdered," the names of the men killed on the Nueces. Many of the men who later honored them, such as Maury Maverick, Jr., were descendants of men who had helped put the Unionists in jail. But throughout the 19th century a certain bitterness, on both sides, did not entirely die.

Although, because of a number of literate European immigrants, the incidents in the San Antonio area received more publicity, the persecution of Unionists was more violent in the north. A so-called Peace Party sprang up in far north Texas; this again was basically a neutralist group, whose main concern was to avoid the draft. It was, however, suspect at once, and accused of murderous plots and treason against the state. Confederate agents infiltrated this group, and troops were sent from farm to farm arresting anyone who openly had denounced the war, including one family which merely suggested it might move to Kansas.

The arrested persons were haled before "People's Courts." These seem to have been constituted under neither Texas civil nor military law; apparently they were community drumhead tribunals, set up on the spur of the moment. One such People's Court convicted forty men at Gainesville, in Cooke County, on wholly hearsay testimony that they had talked against the South. All were promptly hanged.

Five more men were executed in Wise County, and in Grayson, another forty were sentenced to death. Fortunately for these people, Brigadier General Throckmorton heard about the case and rode for Grayson County. In uniform, he intervened with a ringing plea for Anglo-Saxon justice under the law. Throckmorton's courage and decency shamed the People's Court, and the cases were remanded to a special civil court. After a hearing, all but one of the condemned were set free.

Since habeas corpus had been suspended, there could be no real defense of civil right at this time, except where military officers themselves were disgusted and turned accused men loose. This happened. But at the same time, the ignorant, the immigrant, and the lowly were not the only ones to suffer. At Hempstead, Dr. Richard Peebles and four leading citizens protested the current hangings as "lynch law." Peebles and two others were exiled to Mexico by legal action.

Understandably, since many men were unreasonably drafted, desertion in the Southern army reached serious proportions. This was not confined to Texas; desertion was commonplace during the war in both the North and South. By 1863, some thousands of deserters were living on the western fringes of Texas, staying as near to their homes as they could, but escaping into Indian country or into the northern thickets when hunted. Henry McCulloch, the local commander, complained he lacked enough troops to search deserters out or to capture them if he found them. Regular Confederate troops were rarely used for this unpleasant job, and state troops were never effective.

In the Denton area, north of Dallas, so many deserters congregated that they dominated the countryside and were able to control both the authorities and the populace. Significantly, however, while these men would fight if pursued, they rarely abused either the people or private property. By early 1865, bush soldiers, as they were called, actually from both armies, had turned parts of north Texas over to anarchy.

Lubbock, faced with increasing problems in 1863, chose not to stand for reelection. Jefferson Davis immediately appointed him to a post on the Presidential staff. Pendleton Murrah, a strict Constitutionalist Democrat, defeated T. J. Chambers on a platform of stronger support for the war. But Murrah, in office, immediately became embroiled with the Richmond government.

The Confederacy was structured with strong powers reserved to the states, and Murrah intended that these should not be usurped, war or not. Murrah charged that both the rights of the people and the rights of the state were being infringed in the name of the war effort. The Governor was correct; at this time both the Union and the Confederacy were tending to ride roughshod over Constitutional states' rights. Lincoln was putting unconstitutional pressures on the neutral border states and justifying this in the overriding cause of the Union. The Confederacy, desperately staving off defeat and oblivion, showed an equal disregard for legality. Murrah's frequent messages to his legislature reveal an increasing dismay at "national encroachment" upon Texas. He felt it availed Texans little to be free from Washington City, if they were to be ruled from Richmond.

The two real disagreements centered around life and property, the draft and the cotton trade.

The Confederacy was now trying to incorporate the Texas militia and state frontier troops into its armies. The Confederate Constitution, following the U.S. model, made frontier defense a federal responsibility—but it was one the C.S.A. never tried to fulfill. Late in the war, the Comanches and Kiowas were savagely harassing the western regions of Texas. The minutemen were not effective against this kind of guerrilla campaign, and the state had sent its own state troops to the frontier to assist these local posses. Theoretically, these state forces were supposed to be reserved for the use of the Confederacy on call, through the Military District commander. By 1863, none were available.

Further, in 1863, Texas enacted a frontier defense act, which exempted all men serving in western local defense units from regular conscription.

This was a classic case of state-federal juxtaposition; Texas interposed its own military laws between its citizens and Confederate law. Murrah defended the Texas position stubbornly. His case was simple: Richmond could not require Texas to enforce laws at variance with its own needs or the desires of its own citizens. Murrah was a strict constitutionalist and never wavered. He caused vast annoyance in Richmond, where Davis, beset with problems, had no brief for constitutional niceties.

In 1864, General Kirby-Smith was in desperate need of men to fight Union movements in Louisiana. Kirby-Smith demanded the dispatch of Texas state forces. Murrah ordered the state units not to cross the Sabine. He quibbled on technicalities until the crisis passed; the Texas forces never did reach the front. A bitter showdown, and possible Confederate military action against the government of the state of Texas, were averted only by a shift in Northern strategy. General U. S. Grant, who had been pounding Kirby-Smith unmercifully in the Southwest, was suddenly transferred to command on the Potomac in March. With Grant, the principal theater of the war moved East. For the rest of the war, the Southwestern Confederacy was a sort of backwash area; bloody actions were fought, but Kirby-Smith's Department was able to stave off disaster.

The second great irritant was still the cotton trade. While the motives of the various officers who tried to regulate this under Confederate laws stand inspection, their results do not. What happened after 1863 was simple: Confederate edicts played into the hands of speculators. Honest and patriotic merchants and cotton agents, trying to fulfill the law, were hamstrung. The trade was carried on by men perfectly willing to profit exorbitantly and to break the law doing it. The Confederacy received even less benefit.

The tightening of the Federal blockade—runners were unable to get through by late 1863—led to renewed interest in the Texas border. A new law was enacted by the Confederate Congress, organizing a Cotton Bureau at Shreveport, Louisiana. The Bureau was empowered to impress cotton. Bales were to be hauled to Mexico under government supervision, and there sold only for war matériel. The planters objected to impressment; a compromise was made by which they were paid in worthless certificates or bonds for one-half their cotton, while the remainder was certified from impressment.

The flaws of this system were obvious, even if the Texas Military Board, an agency responsible for war procurement for the state government, had not begun a devastating form of competition. Texas also bought up one-half the production of individual planters for state bonds—but under the "state plan" invented by Pendleton Murrah, the Board transported all of the contracting planter's cotton to Matamoros. Here the planter, or other holder, could do with his half as he pleased, selling it for gold or for trade goods. The planter or speculator could make enormous profits, at no risk. The "state plan" soon virtually drove the Confederate Cotton Bureau out of business.

Unable to control Murrah in any other way, the Confederate Congress on February 6, 1864, prohibited the export of all cotton and tobacco except under the express direction of Jefferson Davis. Needless to state, Pendleton Murrah and most Texas cotton men were scandalized at this new invasion of states' rights. The Texas governor held a conference with Kirby-Smith in July, and apparently the General finally impressed upon Murrah that the Congress was determined upon state control. From July, 1864, until the end of the war the Texas government cooperated fully with General Kirby-Smith in most things, but it was now far too late for the export of cotton materially to affect the war.

Texans were intransigent in defending states' rights against the Confederacy; they were strikingly not a problem-oriented breed, who would willingly sacrifice individual freedoms in furtherance of a common goal. This was perhaps the most dominant frontier characteristic in America. But Texas was even more stubborn in defending its own soil. No Federal forces ever penetrated deeply into the state. In fact, Texans carried their own war to the West.

In 1861, Col. John R. Baylor was entrusted with the defense of the frontier that ran roughly from Fort Worth to the Nueces south of San Antonio and faced Mexico along the Rio Grande. Baylor's soldiers occupied the old U.S. Army posts west of the 98th meridian, the Comanche frontier, and manned the other posts that guarded the route of communications from San Antonio to El Paso. But Baylor was not content to sit out the war fighting Indians. He planned to march west.

On August 1, 1861, Colonel Baylor issued a proclamation establishing the Confederate Territory of Arizona, comprising the former U.S. Territory of New Mexico south of the 43rd parallel. He was declared governor.

To make the proclamation stick, Baylor's regiment rode west. They reached Tucson; the Federal forces were in disorder and fell back. Baylor established a constitutional government in which all posts were held by

Texans. There is no evidence that the native Mexican and Indian residents of Arizona paid much attention.

The East-West Butterfield stage route was now firmly in Texan hands from San Antonio to Arizona, but there were strong Federal forces in northern New Mexico. Three regiments of Texas troops, under General H. H. Sibley, moved against these. Sibley scored an early victory at Valverde on February 2, 1862. Now, the Stars and Bars fluttered over Albuquerque and Sante Fe.

The old dream of expanding Texas westward to the limits of the Rio Grande had come true at last.

But Sibley faced the same problems the Texas expedition of 1841 had faced; he was separated from his Texas bases by more than a thousand miles of desert and Indian country. His troops were low on supply. Meanwhile, the Federals mounted a strong effort out of California. Sibley gallantly now presided over a series of Texan disasters, in which the Confederate forces were seriously mauled. Sibley was pushed south, until in the spring of 1862 he had vacated the Confederate Territory of Arizona. As he fell back, the officers of the provisional government packed and departed with him.

The long march back to San Antonio was a horror. Only remnants of the three regiments arrived. In this way died the last Texan dream of driving to the western sea.

The Baylor-Sibley expedition had long-term disastrous results. The Federal forces, now firmly gripping Arizona and New Mexico, made no attempt to invade Texas from the west. But the regiments originally planned to hold the Indian frontier were uselessly dissipated. McCord's State Frontier Regiment was neither disciplined nor effective, and the local county militia or posses were almost useless in the far west.

In the next two years, the Anglo-American frontier recoiled eastward two hundred miles. In 1864, Comanche-Kiowa raiding bands rode as far east as Young County, driving settlers back by the thousands from the 1860 frontier.

Where the settlement line hung on, Texans spent the war in or close to stockades—"forted up," as the saying went. These years were hardly different from the days of Daniel Boone. Texas could not fight a great war in the east, and at the same time hold its own frontier. At least three regiments of regular cavalry were required to police the west, and nothing approaching that force was ever sent.

A little-known battle was fought between the Texas state troops and Indians in January, 1865. The Texans encountered a large camp of Indians on Dove Creek, a branch of the South Concho River. They mistook this band for Comanches and attacked, thus making two errors.

The Indians were well-armed Kickapoos, who were moving south out of Oklahoma seeking refuge in Mexico. They had done no raiding. But the band, several hundred strong, repulsed the state troops with heavy losses.

Dove Creek was the largest battle fought against Indians during the war, and one of the bloodiest in all the Indian wars, as well as one of the best forgotten.

By the spring of 1865, the Texas frontier was marked by chaos. The westward advance was in general retreat.

Against the Yankees, however, the Texan record was outstanding. In 1862, Federal forces began a drive to capture all Confederate Gulf ports. New Orleans fell, with lasting damage to the South. In October, 1862, the Federals seized Galveston Island.

When General Bankhead Magruder replaced General Hébert, who was more occupied with enforcing martial law than fighting Yankees, Magruder decided to retake Galveston. Careful, secret preparations were begun. Two steamboats plying Buffalo Bayou, *Neptune* and *Bayou City,* were converted into Confederate "cottonclads," by emplacing breastworks of cotton bales around their gunwales and decks. On these two vessels Magruder embarked the remnants of Sibley's brigade of New Mexico veterans, about 300 men. Supporting these "cottonclads" as tenders were two smaller ships, also filled with riflemen. Then, Magruder concentrated a land force at Virginia Point, on the mainland just opposite the island. He took personal command on December 29, 1862, for a joint assault by land and sea.

During the hours of darkness on December 31, Magruder's troops waded across into Galveston town. At dawn, the Confederates attacked and drove the Federal garrison to the extreme north end of the island. Meanwhile, the cottonclads steamed in against the flotilla of four Union ships in the harbor—a steamer, brig, gunboat, and transport.

Federal gunfire sank *Neptune* in shallow water as she steamed in, but *Bayou City* ran in close, while Sibley's converted "marines" raked the Federal vessels with deadly fire. The U.S. steamship *Harriet Lane* struck her colors, after a vicious, close-in firefight in which all her officers were killed. The brig *Westfield* trying to maneuver out of the way, ran aground, and was scuttled by her crew. The gunboat and transport fled the behemoth cotton-armored *Bayou City* and were able to escape to the open Gulf. When this happened, the Federal garrison on the island surrendered. Magruder took 300 prisoners of war, and was commended by the President of the Confederacy.

The Union held complete initiative off the coast, however, with command of the sea. There had been some skirmishing around Sabine Pass, where the Sabine and the Neches rivers both flowed into the Gulf. Recognizing this as a weak point, where the Federal naval supremacy could bear, Admiral David Farragut and Major General N. P. Banks drew up plans for a major campaign in 1863. Sabine Pass was to be seized, and 5,000 veteran troops put ashore. Farragut and Banks hoped to repeat earlier Union successes at New Orleans and Mobile.

On September 8, 1863, four U.S. gunboats, leading a flotilla of 20 transports proceeded against Sabine Pass. This was a carefully planned assault, whose ultimate objective was the capture of Houston, Beaumont, and in turn, Galveston. At the very least, it was expected to open up a sustained campaign near vital areas of Texas. Major General William B. Franklin of the U.S. Army was in over-all command.

A small Confederate post, Fort Griffin, defended the Texas side of the Pass. Here Odlum's Company F (Davis Guards) of the 1st Texas Heavy Artillery stood on watch. Neither Odlum nor his lieutenant, Smith, was present; the company, two old 24-pounder smoothbores, two 32-pounders, and two howitzers, and forty-two men, was commanded by the junior lieutenant, Richard (Dick) Dowling. In the vicinity, also, was the Confederate steamer *Uncle Ben* and a detachment of infantry from Company B, Speight's Battalion.

While the landing force of 5,000 stood offshore with its escort warships, the four Union gunboats moved up the channel and bombarded Dowling's command. The shelling continued for an hour and a half. The Federal boats then withdrew, let the meaning of the bombardment sink in, and came back again. In similar situations outnumbered and outgunned Confederate posts had withdrawn.

With great coolness Dowling ordered his battery to withhold its fire. He let the Federal warships come within 1,200 yards. Then, under heavy fire himself, Dowling poured fire from his old smoothbores into each Federal vessel in turn. The result was spectacular. U.S.S. *Sachem* was holed in the steam drum and fell out of action. *Clifton's* tiller rope was carried away, and the gunboat drifted helplessly aground under Dowling's battery. *Clifton* struck, running up a white flag.

Shocked and battered, the remaining flotilla raced back out to sea. The armada and its 5,000 invasion troops eventually sailed back to New Orleans.

U.S. naval forces lost two ships, 100 killed and injured, and 350 prisoners. Dowling's battery was untouched. In a few minutes, Lieutenant Dick Dowling had fought the most brilliant and decisive small action of the Civil War. No Federal effort was ever made in this area again.

The outcome of Sabine Pass raised a great outcry abut the efficiency of the Navy in the North; coming with Bragg's victory at Chicamauga, it gave the Union a severe psychological shock. U.S. credit declined abroad; the dollar lost 5 percent of its value against gold.

By order of Jefferson Davis, one of the two war decorations officially awarded by the Confederacy was specially struck for the Davis Guards.

The Union forces, however, were not to be completely denied. Banks landed forces in the far south, over the beaches at Brazos de Santiago, just north of the mouth of the Rio Grande. A war base was set up at Point Isabel. In November, 1863, Union General Dana moved into Brownsville with 6,000 men.

Other descents were made further north on the Laguna Madre; the tiny ports of Corpus Christi and Aransas Pass were seized, also. At the end of 1863 Sabine Pass and Galveston were the only ports on the Texas coast still in Confederate hands.

These Union operations actually had little effect on the state. The points on the Gulf were then remote from the populated centers of eastern Texas, and since the blockade was in force, their loss changed nothing. General Banks' mission was not to try to subjugate Texas. The Union sought control of the coast to prevent possible collusion and cooperation between the Confederate states and the French, who had moved into Mexico in force.

The fear of French-Confederate cooperation was real in 1863. But it soon was apparent that the invaders of Mexico had too much to occupy them in that country to become entangled in the American Civil War. As the fear subsided, Banks gradually withdrew all his garrisons from the coast except the one at Brownsville. This controlled the lower border, and disrupted the Confederate cotton trade.

N. P. Banks, who had scarcely more success in the Southwest than he had earlier enjoyed in Virginia, made one last great effort to carry the war into Texas. In the early weeks of 1864 Banks concentrated 25,000 splendidly equipped and supplied combat troops at Alexandria, Louisiana. This force was supported by a flotilla of gunboats. The Union strategy was to make a vast sweep through the richer regions of the Southwestern states, to cut a swath of destruction similar to the one Sherman planned for the Southeast. Union General Frederick Steele was to march south from Little Rock, Arkansas, with an additional 15,000 men and to join Banks' force along the Red River. The combined Union armies would then strike deep into Texas; the Confederate marshaling points and shops at Henderson and Marshall were strategic objectives.

Kirby-Smith, commanding the Confederate Trans-Mississippi Department, worked desperately to avert this disaster. Magruder stripped Texas of all the regular troops under his command, but these barely offset Kirby-Smith's own losses due to disease and desertion. The Texas units in the Confederate service marched east to Louisiana. In this crisis, however, Governor Murrah of Texas refused to release the state militia because of his quarrel with Richmond over states' rights.

With a crumbling, ill-fed, and desperate army, the Confederate generals completely frustrated the Union plan. Sterling Price stopped Steele at Camden, Arkansas. Badly mauled by the Confederate cavalry, Steele, although he outnumbered Price by two-to-one, failed to join Banks' main force.

General Richard Taylor, immediately facing Banks' 25,000, was reinforced with a conglomerate body of Louisianans, Missourians, and Arkansas units. Even with Walker's division of Texans and Tom Green's Texas cavalry brigade, he mustered only 11,000. His position appeared hopeless. However, he chose to attack.

On April 8, 1864, Taylor smashed Banks at Mansfield, Louisiana, just forty miles from the Texas line. Although Banks repulsed a second attack at Pleasant Hill on April 9, both his nerve and the Union drive collapsed. The invading army retreated back to the Mississippi. There was never to be a Union song called "Marching Through Texas."

Historians generally regard the defense of the Texas coast and borders as one of the greatest military feats of the Confederacy.

In the late spring of 1864, the war in the Southwest degenerated into a sort of stalemate. But the fighting was not entirely over. There was yet to be fought one more bitter, little-known campaign, which included the last pitched battle of the War Between the States.

20

THE CAVALRY
OF THE WEST

Headquarters Cavalry of the West
San Antonio, December 27, 1863

Persons desiring to go into service will report to me at San Antonio without delay, where they will be subsisted and their horses foraged. . . .

The people of the West are invited to turn out. They will be defending their own homes. Shall it be said that a mongrel force of Abolitionists, negroes, plundering Mexicans, and perfidious renegades have been allowed to murder and rob us with impunity? Shall the pages of history record the disgraceful fact, that Texians have tamely and basely submitted to these outrages and suffered the brand of dishonor . . . ? For the honor of the State, for the sake of the glorious memories of the past, the hopes of the future, you are called upon to rally to the standard and to wash out the stains of invasion by the blood of your ruthless enemies.

JOHN S. FORD
Col. Comdg.

I N the fall of 1863, the United States Army began to consolidate its command of the Lower Rio Grande. General Banks' major purpose was to seal off the border between the Confederates and the French-dominated Empire of Mexico; it was not to use Brownsville for a marshaling point to invade Texas. But the appearance of thousands of bluecoats on the Rio Grande set off a chain of events not foreseen by the strategists either in Washington or Richmond.

373

The flow of cotton out of the Confederacy was cut off, as Union General Dana sent 4,000 men westward along the Rio Grande. Neutral brokers in Matamoros held chests of medical supplies, new Enfield rifles, and gold for Texas; thousands of European ships lay waiting off the river mouth. Now, the trade route had to be moved far northwest through Eagle Pass, adding three hundred miles. The new trail also lay through desolate and dangerous country, swarming with Mexican bandits, Apaches, and Kickapoos. The cost, as well as time, of delivery doubled.

The situation was intolerable to Texans living along the Rio Grande, as well as to cotton interests further north. Great pressure was put on "Prince John," General Bankhead Magruder, to act. But Nathaniel Banks had fixed Magruder by a clever feint in Louisiana in late 1863. Prince John did not dare open a war on the Rio Grande and leave the heartland exposed.

Some of the greatest pressures were put on the Confederate government by prominent Brownsville citizens and other south Texas merchants. They wanted an expeditionary force raised, and they wanted it to be commanded by an old Texas Ranger they knew well—Rip Ford. There is considerable evidence that the said Ford not only abetted these efforts but probably instigated them.

On December 22, 1863, the Texas Department commander wrote a confidential letter, addressed to "Colonel" John S. Ford. The letter requested that officer to raise a regiment of cavalry—a purely auxiliary force —to undertake a campaign on the Rio Grande. Thus began one of the most fantastic episodes in the War Between the States. Its central figure was one of the most colorful—and, perhaps, most typical—Texan leaders of all time.

In 1863 John Salmon Ford was almost fifty. He had already lived through a fantastic career—medical doctor, lawyer, prominent journalist, state senator for two terms, mayor of Austin, and captain of Rangers. Born in South Carolina, educated in cabin schools in Tennessee, he arrived in Texas as a doctor of medicine in 1836. Ford was an old "Texian." He had a failed marriage behind him, and he was just twenty-one.

Over the next five decades, he was to be the only man in Texas history who was involved in a major way in every action or controversy of his time. He was to be one of the fantastic, but forgotten, figures of the old frontier. Ford was star-following, pragmatic, restless, and apparently without an ideology of any kind. He was impatient, brilliant, and erratic—and yet compulsively self-disciplined when he had to be. He had prejudices but no philosophy. Above all, he instinctively went where the action was.

He was a staunch Houston supporter for years, then a Know-Nothing leader, a Knight of the Golden Circle, and a Secessionist delegate to the Texas 1861 convention in turn. He shed roles easily, as popular ideas changed. Yet this leaves his image unclear, because Ford was a man of major strengths. Profane to the point of ingenuity, an inveterate gambler, free with both "his money and his pistol," Ford was a great captain, a leader of men, and a diplomat of considerable skill. He lived great times; he was the last of his line, and he died poor. Most of the great frontier captains did the same.

Ford dropped a brilliant professional and political career in 1846 to serve with the Texas Rangers in the Mexican War. He loved a horse, the wide brush country, and the smell of danger. In Mexico with Jack Hays, he contracted the malaria that was to haunt him all his life. He also acquired a nickname that delighted him. He was the Ranger adjutant, and it was his duty to record the names of the dead. At the end of each casualty list, Ford wrote *Rest in Peace*. As the war and the reports lengthened, he shortened this to R. I. P. The sardonic Rangers named him Old Rip Ford.

After the Mexican War, Ford saw more frontier service than any other officer of the state. He rode to El Paso in the distant west; he fought Comanches from the Canadian River in Oklahoma territory to Laredo. He played a major role in running the rebel Cortinas into Mexico in 1859. Through all this service, Ford was explosively energetic, capable, ruthless, and shrewd. He was tough enough to rule wild men. He showed a thirst for intrigue and a drive for power. Again and again, he employed reason to obtain his objectives, and chose to bargain rather than fight. But, rubbed the wrong way, he would fight—the bloody-minded battle-to-the-end of the frontier Anglo-Celt.

As a Ranger captain, he showed he would desert his own concept of justice if this happened to conflict with the majority's frontier prejudices. Nor would he sacrifice his notion of right to administer merely legal justice. Ford also did things that seemed quixotic; they damaged his career. He had that blend of Presbyterian piety—R. I. P.—and blue-eyed brutality that Mexicans found it impossible to understand. He was not cruel; few Texians of the old school were cruel. But they would pistol a man for knocking off their hat. Ford posed the bluff, simple outward front and border vulgarity that pleased common men. But Oates, who edited his papers, came closer to the real mark: here was a man capable of inhuman drive and endurance, and of forcing it from others; "even more complex and profound than the polygonal public servant" he pretended to be. Ford's character and drives were significant, because he was a true Texian, a leader-type of the old frontier.

In 1861, the Secession convention appointed Ford a colonel of state cavalry and sent him south to the Rio Grande. Here he performed two signal services, which Oran Roberts, the Old Alcalde, always held went unrewarded and overlooked. Fitz-John Porter held Fort Brown with a strong garrison. Instead of precipitating the Civil War, Ford chose to reason with Porter, and he reasoned him into departing Texas. Thus it fell to the state of Ford's birth to start the conflict.

The first blood of the war was shed in Texas, however. On April 1, 1861, a Mexican named Ochoa declared against the county officers of the border area of Zapata, between Brownsville and Laredo on the Rio

Grande, who had come out for the Confederate states. Ochoa gathered a band of men and hanged the country judge. He issued a *pronunciamento* against the Confederacy, thus dignifying a stand that probably had more of banditry to it than ideology. Ford sent his cavalry after Ochoa and killed twenty of his followers. The rest fled into Mexico. Technically, this little action could be rated as the first battle in the War Between the States.

Ford commanded at Fort Brown through 1861. Again, he played the diplomat and probably set a pattern that prevented the Confederacy from becoming involved in Mexico. Ford understood the importance of the Matamoros gateway. Through the services of the British and Prussian consuls, he arranged a commercial treaty by which Mexico permitted Texan cotton to pass through. This was a tremendous accomplishment, done by playing on European hopes for the Confederacy and Mexican fears of invasion.

He also advised Richard King and Mifflin Kenedy, the transplanted Yankees who dominated commerce in south Texas, to transfer their steamboats to the Mexican flag. This stratagem would free them from Union interference while serving the Confederacy on the river, and off Brazos de Santiago. Both men, who were loyal Confederates throughout the war, did so, with much benefit all around.

Ironically, Ford's diplomacy was better appreciated by neutrals and the enemy than his own people. Ford could be devious, especially in dealing secretly with Mexican officers, and he was too devious by far to suit many of the Southern people in his command. It was protested that his advice to King and Kenedy removed valuable property from Confederate control. Ford grew in bad odor with many powers in the state. In late 1861, his command was dispersed to Colonel Earl Van Dorn's troops, and he was replaced at Fort Brown by Colonel Thorkelin de Lovenskiold, whose military reputation rested mainly on the fact that his brother was a Danish field marshal. The border was pacified; Ford was furloughed.

When the Secretary of War of the Confederacy ordered a regularization of forces, with election of new officers in April, 1862, Ford could easily have been elected colonel of the 2d Texas Cavalry. He chose not to stand, for reasons of his own. General Paul O. Hébert then offered him a regular commission as major, which Ford refused. Finally, Ford was appointed by the state as Superintendent of the Bureau of Conscription, a job which consisted mainly of running down draft dodgers and which he despised. Ford did not like the draft laws. He believed all good men had volunteered, and that the laws deferring petty office holders were unjust.

In this post Ford's true military status was most unclear. His state appointment as a colonel was no longer valid, and he held no Confederate rank. Hébert, however, addressed him as "Colonel," and he saw that Ford was paid as a full colonel. Bankhead Magruder continued the practice in 1863.

When Magruder wrote Ford confidentially about fighting on the Rio Grande, he then and later tried to secure Ford a commission. For reasons of its own, the Confederacy refused. The man who was to become Texas' best-known soldier in the Civil War—in his own time, that is, not later—was never carried on Confederate rolls.

Magruder could not suspend the conscription laws, nor divert men from the state or Confederate service to Ford officially. Exemptions were not granted for service in auxiliaries. This meant Ford had to recruit a sizable force in a thinly populated, manpower-drained west Texas from draft-exempts—men too old or too young. The nucleus of his force, however, was to be the inclusion of several state, militia, and paramilitary units on the southwestern frontier. Magruder and Ford conspired on this.

Ford could not give his new regiment an official name, so he called it the Cavalry of the West. He wore a battered black cavalry fedora, emblazoned with the CSA emblem. He called himself Colonel, and made it stick.

He raised the Lone Star flag and the Stars and Bars at San Antonio, nailed up placards, and sent couriers north, south, and west. His call reached from Burnet County to the Nueces. Men began to come in.

The many small militia and Indian-fighting units in the area would have marched under his orders. But only a few could be withdrawn. In Blanco and other counties above San Antonio, the Comanche danger was so acute that the frontier hung by a thread; as Ford wrote Magruder: "The withdrawal would result in an immediate abandonment of that part of the frontier."

Only units from Karnes and Guadalupe counties, to the southeast below San Antonio, were taken, along with Captain Tom Cater's company of men from Burnet, Williamson, and Travis counties. Walthersdorff's battalion and Dorbant's and Heermann's companies were left on the Balcones Scarp. Major Albert Walthersdorff himself, however, was detached to San Antonio to act as Ford's "tactician." The German officer was a huge man, who could lift a recruit and shake him with one hand.

Three things made west Texans pour into San Antonio. The seizure of Brownsville and the Rio Grande Valley by the Federal XIII Army Corps under Major General Dana had aroused the state. When the 19th Iowa unfurled its colors on Brazos Island and splashed across the shallow arm to Texas soil, the fear of invasion, with all the horrors Northern armies were bringing to the South, became acute.

Colonel James Duff's 33rd Texas Cavalry fell back from Brownsville. Some of Duff's state troops, including one whole company, deserted into Mexico. The "butcher of Fredericksburg" moved back across the Nueces. Colonel Santos Benavides, a prominent Laredoan who had declared for the South, defended above Rio Grande City with a small force. Generals H. P. Bee and James E. Slaughter, the ranking Confederate officers in south Texas, had neither forces nor inclination to engage the battle-hardened Iowa and Illinois regiments. Meanwhile, Union cavalry—Colonel E. J.

Davis' 1st Texas—rode reconnaissances in force. They pushed Benavides back upon Laredo, and galloped a hundred miles north, raiding the King ranch headquarters and running off beef cattle. The appearance of these bluebellies in a region remote from the war caused understandable alarm across the underpopulated frontier.

But two other factors ignited the spirit of resistance. Davis' force was composed of Mexicans and traitors to the state, as Unionists were called. The U.S. XIII Army Corps also contained two Negro regiments. Thus Ford cannily called for volunteers to fight "mongrel abolitionists and perfidious renegades." Resentful Texans poured in. Dozens of European immigrants, remote in region and feeling from the Southern heart of Anglo-Texas, arrived. Young boys stole horses and guns and made for San Antonio. Confederate cavalry had to provide its own horses; Ford could only supply his men with corn. He got this, at times rather brutally, by sequestration if farmers refused his copious supplies of paper money.

One of Ford's officers, scandalized, said, "Fifty-seven children have joined my battalion." Ford merely stated he would enlist any man he could without violating "law and propriety." His view of both was broad. He set the lower age of enlistment at fifteen, but did not question good-sized youngsters about their age. In some thirty days, the Cavalry of the West recruited 1,300 boys and men.

Major Walthersdorff faced a brigade of baldheads and troopers who had not learned to shave. He did the best he could.

Ford asked for two field guns; these were never sent. He needed tether-ropes, but had no hard money to buy any. His official plan of supply was horrifyingly complicated: baled cotton was being stored along his route to the Nueces; he was to pick it up and haul it to the Rio Grande. The cotton would then be sold for cash, and cash would buy the Cavalry of the West whatever it might need in Mexico.

On the march to the river, Ford was also to assimilate and take command of certain Confederate forces in the region—Major Matt Nolan's riders at Corpus Christi, Ware's battalion at San Patricio, Giddings' battalion at Eagle Pass, and Benavides' regiment at Laredo. The titles of these units should not be misconstrued—some "battalions" consisted of two tiny companies, and companies rarely exceeded the strength of a modern platoon. A full company of horse was 50 men.

If Ford gathered in every unit, he could muster perhaps 1,800 men. Against this force, the new commander at Brownsville, General J. F. Herron, deployed some 6,479, supported by twelve field pieces and sixteen heavy guns.

Ford was delayed at San Antonio until mid-March. He explained his problems in a letter to an officer of Magruder's staff: "I regret not having been able to take the field. . . . I had serious obstacles to surmount. Exhausted resources, a population almost drained of men subject to military duty, oppositions from rivalry, and the nameless disagreeable retardations incident to an undertaking of this character . . ." The oppositions came from one Lieutenant Colonel S. B. Baird, commanding the remnants of the 4th Arizona Cavalry, which despite its name was made up of Texans. The Arizona outfit was assigned to Ford's command. Baird held a regular commission in the Confederate army, and refused to serve under a rankless officer. Magruder supported Ford, and Baird was transferred. Command of the unit fell to Lieutenant Colonel Daniel Showalter, who, "when not under the influence of liquor was as chivalrous a man as ever drew a sword." Dan Showalter agreed to obey Rip Ford.

The Colonel did assemble a remarkable staff. Captain C. H. Merritt was quartermaster; he was a cotton man released by the Cotton Bureau. Captain W. G. M. Samuels rode down from north Texas to be ordnance officer—if and when the Cavalry of the West got ordnance. Major Walthersdorff was tactical officer. Major Felix Blücher, grandnephew of the Prussian co-victor at Waterloo, was made chief of staff. Blücher was a skilled surveyor and geographer and knew Texas south of the Nueces as only a German geographer could. He had command of five languages and no command of an alcohol problem. He was later cashiered.

Officers of all grades of ability and every social background were sprinkled through the regiment, from elegant Captain Granville Ouray and the adventurous Charles de Montel to hardbitten Indian-fighting captains like Cater and Dunn. Matt Nolan was an ex-U.S. Army enlisted man, with long service on the border. John Littleton was invaluable because he knew the location of almost every ranch or farm. Captain Littleton procured most of the expedition's corn.

There were some old Army camels in San Antonio, but Ford left these behind when it was discovered they did not thrive on corn.

On March 17, 1864, the Cavalry of the West stood to horse; it mounted and rode through the sun-baked plaza in front of the Alamo, a long, strung-out column in various shades of gray. Ford was at the head, wearing his black hat, a sword sash, and well-worn boots. Behind him came men born in, or with ancestry from, a score of nations and states. They sang "The Yellow Rose of Texas."

They were more dangerous than they looked.

Ford drove the column fast. It was a terrible march. South of San Antonio the singing stopped; the cavalry choked in dust. The winter of 1863–1864 was one of those terrible times of extended drouth in south Texas. The brush country burned dry; water holes and streams had disappeared. The column passed skeletons of cattle and other animals. Fortunately, Major Blücher was also dry and found the remaining grass and water with remarkable skill.

Within a week the Cavalry camped at Banquete. Here Ford received a courier from Santos Benavides. Benavides—supported mostly by his own numerous clan—was fighting off Yankees behind cotton bales in the streets of Laredo; he begged for ammunition. Ford now marched west, toward

Laredo. He put Nolan's "riders" out to cover his flank to the east and south, and to reconnoiter a Union party that had landed at Corpus Christi. His main force pushed southwest, reaching Laredo on April 15.

At Brownsville, Herron knew Ford was in the field, but he had faulty intelligence of Texan numbers. Ford's strength was put at about 650.

Rip Ford, however, was more worried about events in Mexico than what Herron might do. Mexico was in political and military chaos, and this situation immediately affected his own. There was more than a Yankee-Confederate war going on along the Rio Grande; the conflict was actually four-cornered. There was civil war in Mexico, and interference in each conflict from both sides of the river. This embroglio of Confederate-Union-Imperialist-French-Republican policies and forces along the Rio Grande was incredibly complex.

After the war with the United States, Mexico continued in civil turmoil. The country was bitterly divided between the liberal, federalist, anticlerical faction and the conservative, centralist, ecclesiastic element—a controversy that in the 19th century at some time or other engaged the entire Hispanic world. In Mexico, as in other Spanish-speaking nations, the struggle continued for generations. In the 1850's, the liberals gained the upper hand, and in 1856 and 1857 a liberal Congress and constitutional convention separated Church and State. Under the new laws, civil or religious corporations were no longer permitted to hold real estate, and tenants of such property were to purchase it on easy terms. To understand the importance of, and the controversy caused by, this reform, it is necessary to understand that the Church, in Mexico, was immensely wealthy, owning more land than almost all smallholders combined. The measure was bitterly fought by the clergy. Some friars and high churchmen were exiled in reprisal.

The constitution of 1857 had a characteristically short life. It was suspended on December 1. President Ygnacio Comonfort fled to the United States. The liberal party installed the chief justice of Mexico, Benito Pablo Juárez, as President. At the same time, General Felix Zuloaga assumed leadership of the conservatives, declared himself President in honored *caudillo* fashion, and with the army drove Juárez and the liberals into Vera Cruz.

Zuloaga proceeded to annul all obnoxious liberal legislation. The liberals fought back with a revolution in the countryside. In eighteen months, seventy battles were fought. Conservatives won most of them, but they could not end the war. Mexico was again bankrupted, and both factions sought foreign aid. Juárez tried to secure a small loan from the United States in 1859 in return for concessions. This failed to go through, primarily because it drew ferocious Mexican, British, and French opposition.

The conservatives were, unfortunately for Mexico, more successful.

Fifteen million dollars were acquired, on most unfavorable terms, from Britain and France.

However, by 1859, Juárez seemed to have again put the liberals in control. The United States recognized him as the legitimate President. On July 12, Juárez issued a church confiscation decree, giving the following rationale: the Church had been Royalist in the revolution against Spain; it opposed all liberal ideas; and the clergy were determined to hold not only religious but civil supremacy. The order nationalized all church property, reduced priests to voluntary fees, and dissolved all religious orders. This was so radical that it threw more Mexicans on the side of the Church, and Juárez was not able to reenter the City of Mexico until 1861.

Whatever the value of the religious decrees, Juárez made a dangerous error. He suspended all payments to foreign creditors and also confiscated property belonging to foreign nationals. France, Britain, and Spain jointly seized the port of Vera Cruz. Juárez was able to pay the Spanish and British, and these nations withdrew. The French government, meanwhile, under Louis Napoleon Bonaparte, had succumbed to a new vision of Gallic grandeur. Napoleon III proceeded to attempt the conquest of Mexico, taking advantage of the civil war and the immobilization of the United States in its own domestic conflict.

The French proclaimed a Mexican monarchy. This caused the Conservative Party to ally with the French; Conservatives became Imperialists. The great majority of wealthy and well-born in Mexico supported the Imperial cause; the official Church did likewise.

The French had planned an easy conquest, but the protectorate was harder to establish than they hoped. On May 5, 1862, an obscure Mexican general named Porfirio Díaz routed the French general Lorencez at Puebla. The *Cinco de Mayo* provoked French escalation. Napoleon III dispatched a much larger army of French, seized the capital, and through a *Junta* appointed by General Forey, offered the Archduke Ferdinand Maximilian Joseph of Austria the throne.

Maximilian, who had to drop his hated first name in Mexico, was a descendant of Charles V, and thus had a strong appeal to traditionalist aristocrats. He arrived in Mexico on May 28, 1864, accompanied by his wife, the daughter of the King of the Belgians and Louise of Orléans, and contingents of Austrian and Belgian troops. The British approved his elevation. Now began a terrible, bloody civil war, that because of the tragic aspects of the unstable Empress Charlotte's futile efforts to save her husband, took on romantic colorations in the United States.

This war arrived on the Rio Grande. It was preceded by much purely local fighting in 1861. In Matamoros, Cipriano Guerrero and Jesus de la Serna, flying yellow and red flags, battled for the control of Tamaulipas. The *Crinolinos* took Matamoros in September, driving hundreds of Serna *Rojos* into refuge in Brownsville. A standard pattern now began—combatants crossed back and forth across the river, either for refuge or to secure a base to launch a new campaign.

When the Union recaptured Brownsville, most Confederates immediately crossed to Mexico, and plotted against the invasion from the neutral side.

The Reds crossed back to Matamoros late in 1861. Now was fought the bloodiest battle in Tamaulipas history; beautiful buildings were gutted and destroyed; dozens of men on both sides were stood against the arsenal wall. Hundreds of Mexican-Americans and some Anglo-Americans participated in this warfare, which was a continual menace to Brownsville, not only from firing but from deserters prowling the riverbanks.

The person in power in Matamoros changed rapidly, from the conservative Santiago Vidaurri, to liberal General Manuel Ruíz to Maximilianist General José Cobos. Cobos' rule was short. Three days after crossing from Brownsville he was shot by his own second-in-command, Juan Nepomuceño Cortinas, who declared for the liberal Juárez government. Cortinas released Ruíz from prison, but Ruíz sensibly fled to Brownsville, not waiting to see what further vagaries politics held.

General Cortinas was now somewhat reluctantly accepted by the beleaguered Juárez government as their governor in Tamaulipas. A far better than average politico, Don Juan still held this post in 1864, though he was growing apprehensive as the French moved into northern Mexico, and he was thinking of turning Imperialist. One immense complication here was that Cortinas was a former resident of the Texas side, and he had been driven into Mexico by Rip Ford and the Rangers in 1859.

All through the 19th century, prominent Mexican families on the Texas side took their U.S. citizenship lightly or not at all. They were Mexican citizens also, by Mexican law. They entered vigorously into Mexican politics. Quite frequently, a Texas "Mexican bandit" or "notorious cattle thief" was a prominent general or patriot on the southern shore.

Addie Ford, the Colonel's third wife, meanwhile entered Mexico, down from San Antonio to Matamoros via the stage from Eagle Pass. Addie Ford's mother was in Brownsville, and she hoped to visit. Her sister Lu, however, got word to her that the Federals were watching for her. Now, General Cortinas, who was a professional *gringo*-hater but gentlemanly in private life, and his half-brother, Don Sabas Cavazos, called on Mrs. Ford and offered her money and aid.

As Governor of Tamaulipas Cortinas also secured her a safe conduct into Brownsville through friends in the Union forces. In this weird four-sided war, there were certain general patterns. United States troops favored the Juáristas, unless they happened to be Irish Catholics. Washington still recognized the Juárez regime. Confederates of all persuasions preferred the Imperialists. This was an alliance of convenience purely; many Texans, like Ford himself, detested foreigners and kings. There was to be much mutual assistance across the Rio Grande among all four armies.

Cortinas did not follow any pattern. He had a general bias against all *gringos* for running him out of Texas. He rather scrupulously avoided offending whatever power was ascendant on the northern bank at any time.

Certain, through his wife, that he would not be attacked or harassed from the Mexican shore, Ford now launched the Cavalry of the West into the southern triangle that formed the delta of the Rio Grande. Tall, hard, ruddy-faced, and handsome, wearing a short gray beard beneath his dark hat, he led his odd force into a classic guerrilla campaign. There is an enormous amount of fragmentary material, but few real known facts concerning this border warfare. Ford's memoirs were written after twenty years; other accounts, like so much Texas history, rested on old men's tales. As Ford himself said, "Texians proved themselves good soldiers, but they were not willing writers." It is almost impossible to find two matching accounts or to separate legend from history, while an enormous amount of fascinating data was allowed to disappear. But the over-all picture is clear.

The terrible drouth had made pasture scarce along the river. Ford had a horde of horsemen, but he could not assemble them in one place at any time. At the start, he had almost no supply. He was forced to scatter his command over hundreds of miles, and depend on the countryside, above all Mexico, for his military and forage needs. He gathered a small force, not more than 400 horse, and with this began to roll up the Yankee garrisons.

The Indian-fighting captains ranged through the thick border *monte,* or brush. They laid ambushes in the *ebonal.* They popped in and out of the chaparral; they cut Union communications and supplies. Ford had the advantage of position, and greater mobility. Too much of the Union army was sweating, bluecoat infantry, fighting in a burning, almost tropical country. The Union cavalry—Davis' small force, and Vidal's partisans, the last deserters from the gray—fought well, but were both outnumbered and outclassed.

In April, torrential rains fell. This did not at once improve the grass, but it turned the Rio Grande Valley into a steaming hell. Wet and hungry, tired and sodden, Ford's cavalry lived in the brush; for ten solid days of rain they pushed their way toward Ringgold Barracks. They took Los Angeles, Los Ojuelos, and Comitos. The Federals evacuated Rio Grande City without a fight.

Now, Ford consolidated, while a cavalry screen protected his front and eastern flank. He rode into Mexico to make sure his other flank was secure. He seized cotton he found and sold it for coin. The silver bought food. He established working relations with Mexican commandants around Camargo, and thus closed the border to Vidal's raiders, who used the river as a shield. He put liaison officers with Cortinas, including a man who had served as a lieutenant colonel in Juárez' army. He employed another officer to purchase guns from Union deserters south of the border. With Granville Ouray, he visited Matamoros personally and dickered with Cortinas for cannon.

During this time, he got no support from the Confederacy. A thread of discord is visible even after a hundred years. The Confederate establishment had arms, men, and supply in south Texas; Waul's Legion, under Steele, ran an encampment at Gonzales. But Ford got nothing from Duff, or Bee, or Slaughter, except trouble.

The establishment issued orders taking some of his troops away. He had Magruder's sanction, but Magruder could not make his own brigadiers like Ford, or help him. The brigadiers detested Rip Ford and his whole ragtag army.

Troubles in consolidation and supply immobilized the Cavalry of the West for six weeks. Ford took the field again in June. He was burning with fever and reeling in the saddle. At Ringgold Barracks his old malaria returned.

The next weeks required a superhuman will. Ford held on; he not only held on, but he won the hearts of all the common soldiers in his command. Carrington, a captain in his service, wrote that the troops respected their colonel, and would follow him to Hell. Many of Ford's officers, educated men, seem to have been less enthusiastic.

By June 21, Ford was about thirty miles west northwest of Brownsville. He had rolled the Federals back almost two hundred miles. But he had to clear Brownsville and Fort Brown, the principal port of entry, the key prize. Then, on a red-dawn morning, the Cavalry of the West struck Davis' 1st Texas at Las Rucias ranch house. Captain James Dunn, leading the vanguard, was enveloped by the 1st Texas' Companies A and C. Under heavy fire, Dunn led a charge directly into the enemy. Showalter's men, with Cater and Refugio Benavides, went in with him. The engagement became general, in a sodden downpour.

The Union cavalry fought desperately. They believed that the Texans, considering them renegades, would show no mercy. They were outnumbered by the approximately 250 Confederates engaged, and bent back across the adobe brick ranch headquarters. Just before Giddings' battalion came up, they broke and ran. Many were cut down, about thirty captured. Others dashed to the border and swam to safety in Mexico. The victory was complete; only eight Union cavalrymen escaped to report to General Herron. Ford took horses, saddles, wagons, guns, food. He lost three dead, including the gallant old Ranger, Dunn.

Ford waited for Herron to retaliate, but nothing happened. Apparently, the enemy infantry was not going to sally into the brush.

Ford now pulled in his whole command, assembling about 1,500 men. He had new supplies and guns, and bullet pouches filled with shiny lead.

On July 19, the Cavalry of the West moved toward Brownsville again. Ford could not make it to his saddle without help, but once astride, he stayed. He led a grim, gray, ragged, but now thoroughly dangerous army east.

His ranks were full of fifteen-year-olds and old men. But this was a frontier-raised generation; its boys were lean and tough, with muscles developed early. Some of them were sick, but if Old Rip Ford could sit in his goddam saddle, so could any man. On July 22, they struck the Yankees again, this time at Ebonal. They went into the enemy with a shrieking, rebel roar.

They drove the Union screening forces precipitously back into the Brownsville city limits.

Now, Ford had outrun his supply line again; it was upriver. Cortinas, playing his own scrupulous game, refused to do business within reach of Federal guns. But he did do business some miles northwest. Ford waited, throwing out a cavalry screen. He had no intention of charging into Union trenches and big guns.

On July 25, he advanced again, this time with Showalter's Arizonans leading the way on foot. Contact was made, but little damage was done on either side. A sort of impasse arose. Ford had no intention of charging into the deadly Union cannon, while the Federal officers refused to sally beyond the protection of their own guns.

At this time, civilians began to cross the river to fight with Ford. One old man was a veteran of San Jacinto.

Then, on July 30, Dan Showalter made a reconnaissance and found Brownsville strangely quiet. The Cavalry mounted and rode in. They found the town in possession of a group of armed Confederate civilians; the Federals had gone. A trail of scattered equipment led toward the coast from Fort Brown.

Ford detached a force to pursue and harass; these horsemen drove the Union rearguard in upon the retreating main body before breaking off. The Union army reached the Gulf and splashed across Boca Chica to Brazos Island, a sand strip some four miles long. Without fighting a mass engagement, with only one pitched battle and with few casualties, John Ford had driven a superior force from the Rio Grande. The Union army embarked, leaving only about 1,000 soldiers under Colonel H. M. Day to hold Brazos Island.

Ford saw the Stars and Bars lofted over Brownsville on July 30. That night he collapsed in a dead faint. He was to be so sick he could not even sign his name to orders for many days. Ill as he was, he ran the Cavalry of the West from his bed. He had to—his senior lieutenant colonel, Dan Showalter, was dead drunk, along with his chief of staff.

The Cavalry had to be dispersed again, for forage. A force was thrown out to watch the enemy; several companies were stationed north for courier service to Gertrudis and the King Ranch. Benavides and most of his clan rode westward to Laredo. The 4th Arizona was placed under an officer named Fisher until Showalter recovered, because it was dispatched to screen Day at the coast.

The first official communication Ford received from his superiors was a complaint from General Thomas Drayton, district commander. Drayton was angry because many of Colonel Duff's state troops were deserting, saying they were going to the border to fight with Old Rip Ford. A few such leave-takers did show up, but most kept going until they were on the far side of the Rio Grande. When the Confederate government offered full pardons to deserters in Mexico—there were large numbers from both sides —who returned, and allowed returners to join any unit, many who came back chose Ford. The Cavalry was not only colorful, it was not going to leave the West. This hardly improved Rip Ford's popularity with the Confederate brigadiers.

Meanwhile, the Mexican situation was volatile and more dangerous to Ford than the remaining Yankee threat. A powerful French squadron arrived at the mouth of the river and seized Bagdad, or Boca del Rio, the mushroom port city that the cotton trade had made on the marshy flats on the Mexican side. A strong Imperialist army moved north under General Tomás Mejía, a devout Mexican Indian who was Maximilian's most able officer. Ford worried much about a change in power to the south. Cortinas was now cooperating fully with the Confederates, but neither Cortinas nor Ford could trust the other. The Imperialists were an unknown quantity. In August, Ford sent Colonel Fisher and Major Waldemar Hyllested to confer with naval Captain A. Véron, the French commander at Bagdad.

Véron not only received the Confederate officers with respect, he stated that "all persons and property covered by the flag of their nation" would be protected by the French. This was tantamount to recognition of the Confederacy and meant that the cotton trade would go on. Ford was jubilant.

But as French and Cortinistas began skirmishing between Matamoros and the Bagdad enclave, Showalter's troops could not be restrained from sniping at the Mexicans. Showalter held Palmito Hill, a rise in the Palo Alto coastal plain, about a dozen miles southeast of Brownsville and overlooking the river. This small rise dominated the approach to Brownsville from Brazos de Santiago.

At this same time, Leonard Pierce, the U.S. Consul at Matamoros, entered into a conspiracy with Cortinas, who was casting about for plans to escape the Imperialist net. Cortinas was offered a brigadier's commission in the U.S. Army if he would seize Brownsville from the Confederates. Apparently he agreed, or seemed to agree. A troop of about 600 Mexican soldiers moved west, to cross the river above the city, while Cortinas wheeled his artillery into position facing Brownsville, and closed the Rio Grande to all Confederate traffic. Colonel Day, commanding the 91st Illinois at Brazos Island, was supposed to support with an assault overland. This Day did, moving strongly against Showalter at Palmito.

Ford was worried about Colonel Showalter's performance; on one occasion, due to his "illness" he had allowed a whole Union wagon train to escape. Ford therefore sent Giddings' Battalion to reinforce Palmito Hill.

Day struck Showalter on September 6, 1864. As the Federal attack developed, Cortinas' artillery suddenly hurled shells into the Confederate ranks. This surprise fire from Mexico caused the 4th Arizona to panic, primarily because Showalter, as the subsequent courts-martial revealed, was in no condition to command. Once too often he had tried to wash away unpleasant memories in alcohol.

George Giddings came up behind Palmito to find the Confederates "flying in confusion." He relieved Showalter on the spot, and finally stabilized a defense several miles to the rear. Major F. E. Kavanaugh assumed command of Showalter's battalion. Heavy rains immobilized Day before he could exploit his capture of Palmito.

Cortinas did not move on Brownsville. Servando Canales, his ranking colonel, bitterly opposed the attack and refused to allow his regiment to go against Ford. This allowed Giddings, now a colonel, to counterattack Day and roll him back to the sea. Ford estimated Union casualties at 550, which was certainly too high, but the Rio Grande was once again free.

Giddings found that some of his Union prisoners were Mexicans— members of Colonel Echarzetta's Corps of Cortinas' army. Day sent word that these men were regularly enlisted U.S. volunteers. Despite much Texan sentiment for hanging them as brigands or pirates, Ford accepted them as legitimate prisoners of war.

Cortinas surrendered Matamoros to the Imperialists on September 29, 1864. He also temporarily renounced Juárez. Some of his officers rebelled at this and crossed over to Brownsville with their men. They sold their arms to Colonel Ford and were granted political sanctuary.

Now, the Confederate authorities decided to regularize the peculiar situation on the Rio Grande. Ford was still only an auxiliary officer, with no rank. His successes, military and diplomatic, were ignored. Lieutenant Colonel Matt Nolan was authorized by the District of Texas to muster Giddings' unit, now a regiment, into Confederate service, and take enough troops from the Cavalry to raise Santos Benavides' regiment to a brigade. Benavides had been offered a generalcy in the Union Army earlier because of his influence with Mexicans along the border; now the Confederacy, for similar reasons, wanted to do the same.

Ford, who quarreled with Benavides, was caustic with Nolan. He told Nolan that any attempt to do these things would destroy the Confederate military stance at Brownsville and reopen the region to invasion. Nolan then rode with Ford to Giddings' camp, when the ranks volubly refused to serve under any commander except Rip Ford. Nolan forgot his orders at this point.

However, Brigadier James E. Slaughter arrived in Brownsville and established his Western Sub-District Headquarters in November, 1864. Slaughter divided the border area into three divisions, letting Ford command the one at Brownsville. The relationship with Slaughter was complex and uneasy. The general was no warrior, and Ford retained the loyalty of his men.

With Mejía's entry in to Matamoros, actual warfare on both sides of the river waned. Ford admired the loyal Mejía personally, although he despised his cause. Cotton was flowing again. The border enjoyed its greatest boom.

Brownsville swelled to about 25,000, and Matamoros to 40,000. Bagdad on the Rio exploded to 15,000. The population was polyglot, with peddlers, merchants, deserters, gamblers, swindlers, undercover agents, and whores from a dozen nations. Times were flush; a number of merchants made immense fortunes from the cotton trade. Common laborers earned $5 to $10 daily, paid in good silver, when hourly rates were then an unprecedented 20 cents in St. Louis. Lightermen could make $40 a day. There is no record of how much prostitution and swindling paid. But millions in gold passed through all three towns.

Belgian, Austrian, and French troops visited Brownsville; half the Confederate population preferred to remain in Matamoros. Both cities thrived in flush times. Citizens in Matamoros began construction of an opera house, to welcome an expected visit from Maximilian and his Empress. Ten stages ran daily from Brownsville to Matamoros, then down to Bagdad on the Mexican side. Through all this prosperity the Cavalry of the West rode threadbare on picket duty; Ford and his men went unpaid; they had never been paid since they left San Antonio.

On March 6, 1865, the Union soldier-politician Lew Wallace, the later author of *Ben-Hur,* appeared at Brazos de Santiago. General Wallace came to try to make a truce on the Rio Grande, with Lincoln's approval. Wallace had concocted a fantastic scheme of getting the Confederates to surrender and reenter the Union, and then joining their army with Juárez in Mexico. Together, this force would drive the French and Imperialists out. The Rio Grande still inspired wild dreams.

On March 11, Wallace met Slaughter and Ford under a flag at Point Isabel. The $600 worth of "refreshments" Wallace brought to the truce tent seem to have contributed to "amity and concord," as a biographer of Rip Ford said. But after extended negotiations, nothing happened. Actually, both Ford and Slaughter understood the Confederacy was tottering and were willing to talk terms. Ford, particularly, found certain aspects of the deal fascinating. Everything collapsed, however, because dispatches on the discussions fell into the hands of Confederate Major General J. G. Walker, an officer of the "last ditch school." Walker reprimanded Slaughter and Ford, and the project fell through. Afterward, Ford mentioned this was a mistake. Lew Wallace, for all his schemes and hope of personal fame, offered Texas an honorable peace and reentry with honor. The Texas forces were to be permitted to keep their arms, for use in Mexico against the French. As Ford said, all this might have been treason to the Confederacy, but it was preferable to what actually occurred, in Reconstruction.

Although the talks fell through, Wallace and the Confederates agreed to a truce on the Rio Grande. Nothing that happened there would decide the war. For two months, then, as Lee endured his final agony in Virginia, a gentleman's agreement kept peace on the Palo Alto.

At this time, a new officer, Colonel Theodore H. Barrett of the 62d Infantry (Negro) commanded at Brazos de Santiago. Barrett had his own regiment, plus the 34th Indiana; the Morton Rifles, a New York regiment; and some Texas cavalry, commanded now by a Brownsville man, Jack Haynes. He was well supported with artillery. Barrett was a politically appointed officer, who had so far seen no combat service. As one of his officers wrote, and was published later in the New York *Times,* Barrett, like hundreds of other Northern officers, was looking forward to a political career. He felt he had "to establish for himself some notoriety before the war closed." He asked his immediate commander, General E. B. Brown, for permission to demonstrate against the Confederates. The Union department headquarters, where this request went, told him to stay quietly on his sand hills. Despite his orders, and the vehement protests of Lieutenant Colonel Branson of the 34th Indiana, Barrett decided to do great things.

At sunup, May 12, 1865, he ordered his Negro regiment to march to Palmito Hill. About dusk, they were halted by Giddings' rifle fire. Giddings sent riders to Ford in Brownsville, and within the hour, Ford had couriers galloping through the brush. The Cavalry of the West was called in; Ford was angry at this breach of the truce, and determined to fight.

But in Brownsville, General Slaughter was demoralized. He ordered the wagons loaded; he had confiscated a carriage from a civilian and packed his personal gear. Slaughter was going to order a general retreat. At supper that night, Ford's blue eyes were deadly cold. He told Slaughter something that he obviously had been holding back a long time: "You can retreat and go to Hell if you wish. These are my men and I am going to fight!"

By eleven on May 13, Ford's horsemen were thundering in. He marshaled them on the parade ground at Fort Brown. He now had artillery— some fine French guns "loaned" him by Commandant Véron. Ford mounted, and the Cavalry of the West rode southeast, to the sound of Giddings' guns.

Four hours brought the column to Palmito Hill, now wreathed in powder smoke. Giddings was fighting steadily against a strong Federal skirmish line; Barrett threw his whole strength into a general advance. The Indiana and New York regiments, however, had been marched inland during the night at a forced pace; these men were already deadly tired in the humid heat.

Ford took his cavalry into a clump of thick brush that curved along the edge of the Palo Alto plain. He sent some infantry to annoy the Federals on the other flank, while his field pieces, under Lieutenant O. G. Jones, were unlimbered on Palmito Hill. Jones opened fire, with demoralizing effect.

Ford, on a nervous, prancing horse, shouted at his Texans: "Men, we have whipped the enemy in all previous fights. We can do it again." The troops cheered, and this drew Yankee fire into the thicket. Ford yelled, "Charge!"

He led three hundred horsemen galloping into the Federal flank. According to Carrington, the yell the Cavalry sent up could be heard above the guns over three miles of prairie. Shrieking, shooting, they struck the Union skirmish line and broke it into a hundred fleeing parts. There was nothing more frightening to scattered men on foot than to be overtaken by a thundering cavalry charge. The veteran New Yorkers and Hoosiers never had a chance. Barrett ordered a general retreat, but in his fear and confusion forgot to call in his extended picket line. The Cavalry rode these men, who stood and tried to fight, down to the last man.

Three times during a seven-mile retreat toward the Brazos de Santiago, Barrett tried to halt and fight. But nothing was harder to turn around than a general retreat. Ford kept his horse artillery close behind. It threw shells into the Federal stands. The Cavalry rode around them and broke them up. At dusk, with the rearguard stumbling with exhaustion, firing wildly against the circling pursuit, the broken Union command reached the salt waters of Boca Chica. They splashed across in bits and bunches. The color sergeant of the 34th Indiana wrapped the regimental flag about his body and tried to swim to Brazos Island. A Texan bullet killed him, and Ford's horsemen seized the flag from the water.

The last event of this weird day, which took place over a month after Lee surrendered at Appomattox, was the ride of General Slaughter. Slaughter had not ridden to Palmito Hill, but had stayed in Brownsville to watch the Mexicans. Now, at the head of Carrington's battalion, he dashed up to Ford and demanded that Ford continue to punish the Yankees. Ford refused; he was not going to send his men against Brazos Island in the dark. Slaughter then rode furiously to Boca Chica, pushed his horse withers-deep in the tide, and emptied his revolver at the stumbling Yankees—three hundred yards away. The battalion behind him watched in amazement and no little disgust.

Ford that night drew back above Palmito and took count. The victory was staggering: no Confederates were dead, although there were a number of wounded men. By comparison, the 34th Indiana had lost 220 out of the 300 soldiers on its rolls. Union dead lay all over the battlefield, and strung over the seven miles to the sea. Other bodies floated in the Rio Grande; they were drowned Union infantry who had tried to swim the river to escape the terrible charging horse. Ford had also taken 111 men and 4 officers as prisoners of war. He released these men, and later, in his memoirs, stated that no distinction was made between genuine Yankees from New York and the Negro soldiers and Southern renegades—all were "agreeably surprised" at being released.

This was not the whole truth. The prisoners who made it back to Brazos Island told a different tale. They had seen many of Haynes's Texas Unionists shot down after they had surrendered, though Jack Haynes himself was spared. Most of these Southern deserters had died fighting rather than surrender.

The survivors also told Barrett something that must have grated on his soul. Several of Ford's men said they knew the "war was played out," and they would have surrendered if Barrett had come forward and demanded it with white troops. But they would never surrender "to niggers." A bitter pride prevailed.

Palmito Hill was the last pitched battle of the Civil War. There were reasons on both sides that made it preferable to forget, and so it was.

A few days after the battle, General E. B. Brown of the Union Army sent Colonel Ford a flag of truce and a message. Ford was informed that General Lee had surrendered at Appomattox more than a month before. Ford cursed violently for a spell, then began to laugh. He agreed, not to surrender but to an exchange of courtesies.

Federal officers rode into Brownsville. Ford entertained them at his house. One Union major remarked that if his wife knew what he was doing, she would not speak to him. In these last days, there was more than a little understanding among the soldiers, North and South, and a shared weariness that transcended bitterness. But the major's remark, and similar things General Lew Wallace had said about his conviviality with Confederates at Point Isabel, prophesied that bad times would come, from civilians, after the war.

Rip Ford hugely enjoyed taking a party of Federal officers across to Matamoros, where they attended an Imperialist military revue as his guests. The French were badly startled. Although French officers held lively discussions in those days about defeating the U.S. Army in battle, an end to the American war boded ill for the French presence in Mexico. Ford, who cordially detested the French, delighted in keeping them mystified as to real events.

General Sheridan had embarked from City Point, Virginia, with 25,000 Federal troops, bound for the Rio Grande. Ford knew the war was over, but Slaughter, in command, was intransigent. Slaughter refused to surrender; he wanted to take the command south and formally join the Mexican Imperialists, in the hope that the Confederacy would rise again under the French aegis. Ford and the majority of the Cavalry of the West were not interested. Ford turned down General Mejía's offer to send lancers disguised in civilian clothes to help him hold Brownsville.

Over Ford's objection, Slaughter sold the Confederate artillery to Mejía for 20,000 silver pesos. Apparently, Slaughter planned to keep this money, or at least keep control of it, in the name of the South. Ford insisted that the Confederacy was dead and that former Confederate property rightfully belonged to the troops. In this, the entire Texan army agreed with him.

Ford now arrested General Slaughter at pistol-point. The silver was confiscated and distributed among the Cavalry for back pay. Only a small number of the troops, still in Brownsville, received money. Ford took $4,000 for himself; this was, however, less than his arrears. Slaughter then signed over his command to Ford on May 26, 1865.

Ford dismissed the Cavalry the same day, and took his family south of the border with Mejía's consent. The Federals marched into Brownsville unopposed.

Kirby-Smith surrendered the Trans-Mississippi Department on June 2. For the next month, prominent Confederates passed over the Rio Grande. Officers thronged Maximilian's capital; a grandiose colonization project was begun on the Mexican Gulf coast. These plans fell through; Maximilian, soon to be deserted by the French, had no help to give, nor were the Southerners comfortable in a foreign land. When the Union offered paroles and declared an amnesty in July, most soon returned. Fever, clericalism, autocracy, racial antipathy, and homesickness brought them north. Rip Ford came back to Brownsville on July 18. He was courteously received by General Sheridan, and helped other Confederates return.

There were some diehard souls in the Cavalry of the West. They joined with other groups, some from far Missouri. They mounted for the last time on Texas soil, then rode south to join Maximilian's army. At the Rio Grande, they wrapped their faded Southern battle standards in canvas and buried them in the silty sand.

These men left their bones in many lands, from Mexico to France. The flags of the Cavalry of the West, unresurrected, rotted away.

21

THE CONQUERED

Yankees went to war animated by the highest ideals of the nineteenth-century middle classes. . . . But what the Yankees achieved . . . was not a triumph of middle-class ideals but of middle-class vices. The most striking products of their crusade were the shoddy aristocracy of the North and the ragged children of the South. Among the masses of Americans there were no victors, only the vanquished.

KENNETH STAMPP, NORTHERN HISTORIAN

THERE was no formal surrender in Texas after Palmito Hill. The Confederate army and state government simply melted away.

Generals Kirby-Smith, Magruder, Slaughter, and Governor Murrah all took refuge in Mexico. The soldiers disbanded and went home. Human detritus from the war filled the roads and clustered in the dusty towns. The blaze of courage had burned out; the Southern sun had long passed high noon; everywhere there was a stunned feeling of despair. The people had put too much into the war, and were sapped.

The returning soldiers were scarred by bitterness, not only at defeat but by a gnawing feeling that their sacrifices had not been shared. Inept and unscrupulous politicians had wasted the South's resources, while the home front had let them down during the war. In mass meetings at La Grange and in Fayette County, soldiers seized and distributed Confederate and state property to indigent military families. Stores in San Antonio were pillaged; the state treasury was robbed. All government had collapsed. However, property in private hands was not molested by the veterans, bitter as they were.

The great mass of poor farmers in the corn belt were sullen about the present and frightened for the future. In 1865 almost every farmer in

Texas could be classified as "poor white." All progress had ceased for a
total of four years. The farmers had borne the brunt of the bloodshed and
sweat during the war; they now tended to blame their troubles on the
slaves. The hatred of Negroes above the falls of the Brazos and Colorado
was a flaming thing.

The planter class was demoralized. Its entire capital, moral and financial, had been shot away. The Southern way of life had received a stunning
defeat, not quickly, not cleanly, but through a degrading conflict of attrition. All money, deposits, and bank stocks of this class were gone, as well
as their prime source of wealth, their Negro slaves. The loss of illusions
and ideals was profound.

The economy and future of Texas lay in ruins. Fully one-fourth of the
productive white male population was dead, disabled, or dispersed. Almost
every form of real wealth, except the land itself, was dissipated or destroyed. The world was not to see such wholesale ruin again until the wars
of the next century.

On June 19, 1865, General Gordon Granger of the Union Army landed
in Texas. At Galveston he proclaimed, in the name of President Johnson,
that the authority of the United States over Texas was restored, that all
acts of the Confederacy were null and void, and that the slaves were free.
This was the historic "Juneteenth," afterward celebrated by Texas Negroes
as Emancipation Day.

Thousands of bluecoats arrived in Texas; 52,000 were sent to the border
areas alone. This force was meant to overawe the French. The other thousands congregating along the coast were sent as a show of force to keep
order in the state. None of these troops proceeded to the old Indian forts;
few marched to the interior. They camped in the centers of population in
the east. There was no opposition. All Texans conceded that the main war
issue—secession—was dead, killed by the force of arms. Nor was there
any real opposition to the end of slavery, which had become a driving force
behind the Union crusade.

Thousands of Texans watched Union soldiers march through the state
with fife and drum; men, women, and small children saw miles of bayonets
go by. A certain sense of history, which is more the remembrance of
humiliations and defeats than recollected glories, entered the Texan soul, in
a way non-Southern Americans never understood. Few Texans saw the fact
that the big battalions had won as "right." They had fought valiantly for
the right as they saw it, for the Constitution as their people construed it,
and for liberty as Texans felt it. The Texas saying, "If Goliath had been a
Yankee, little David would have lost," expressed more than a thousand
words.

The Texans were stubborn and prideful people; they consciously thought
of themselves as a powerful, conquering race. Their ancestors had beaten
the British and defied the world. They had conquered Mexicans and driven
out Indians. Now, they were the conquered. Few Texans then living saw
things any other way; the Northern enthusiasm that the war had been a war

for democracy had no currency. In 1861, Texas had been an Anglo-Saxon democracy, too.

The knowledge of defeat was bitter, but the coming humiliations were worse. The state was placed under military rule. Army tribunals replaced the civil courts—not without some justice, since no Union man or Negro could hope for fairness from a Texas jury. Army officers were able to act as they saw fit. The great majority of commanders acted reasonably and kept their troops within bounds. A significant number did not. More galling than the actual atrocities, however, was the fact that many Northerners took an almost sadistic pleasure in demeaning or ridiculing the pretensions and folkways of the Southern race.

The great majority of the high-minded young men from Massachusetts or Illinois who had saved the Union went home; few idealists, in any age, seek occupation duty.

This was one of the great tragedies of the era. The North was superbly equipped to win the conflict; it was poorly prepared to usher in the peace. Thousands of the occupation troops in Texas were composed of Negro regiments. In every locality where Negroes were stationed, there was trouble, without exception. The public could not bar them, but it refused to accept them. Texans took the other side of the street to avoid passing them; women spat on the ground they trod. Men who made gestures of resistance, or who appeared in public in remnants of gray uniforms, were arrested.

Union officers were pariahs, and some reacted bitterly to this. At Victoria, the Negro garrison terrorized the town. Its white officers refused to let any professed Union man or Negro be jailed by local citizens for any offense. At Brenham, Negro troops burned down the town. No soldier or officer was ever brought to trial or admonished for this act. Other Union soldiers raided Brownsville. Men who were, or posed, as Union sympathizers could get almost any favor from the occupation forces. Men who were known Confederates, which included 90 percent of the population and all its local leadership, were frequently humiliated publicly, if they came hat in hand to beg some favor of the occupying army.

None of this was historically unusual in the aftermath of war; in all fairness, few occupying armies ever stayed within such bounds. There was almost no looting of private property, and few executions for any reason. But this kind of thing had not happened to Americans before, and few people in the North ever understood its full effect. The great American misfortune was not that it happened so much as that it was to go on so long. In Texas, outside rule was to last not a few months, but for nine long years. These years seeded for a century certain hatreds, fears, distrusts, and suspicions along with psychic damage in the native Texan soul.

With Granger's Juneteenth proclamation the slaves were free. The total slave population of the state had increased by 35 percent during the war; thousands of blacks had been sent south by worried owners in Louisiana and Arkansas. Now, more than 200,000 Negroes were cast adrift in one of the greatest social revolutions of all time. The first instinct of the plantation slave was to pick up and go. But he had nowhere to go. Thousands jammed the roads and trails, wandering from county to county, finally thronging into the settlements where the Freedmen's Bureau offices were being set up. This Bureau, created by the Federal Congress in March, 1865, was given control of all Negro affairs. It set up its own tribunals and courts, and even attempted a system of Negro schools. In the first months the Bureau was honest; it tried to assist and protect the freedmen. However, since it interfered between former slaves and former masters, it was fiercely resented by whites.

Slaves were eager to test the limits of their new freedom. They were naturally euphoric, and expected to be led into some new Promised Land. But nothing like a red dawn appeared in the state, or in the South. The slaves made no attempt at reprisal for past wrongs, but they did refuse to work under new terms or to obey orders. They left the land, and thousands of plantation acres fell into disrepair and disuse. Somewhere, a joyful but tragic rumor started that every freedman was to get forty acres and a mule. Bureau officers tried to dispel this notion, but for many months with limited success.

In July, 1865, A. J. Hamilton, a former Texas Congressman who had stood with the Union, returned with a Presidential appointment as Provisional Governor. Jack Hamilton was an honest, deeply conservative man. He had no rancor or hatred for his state, and his entire purpose was to bring it back peacefully into the Union.

Hamilton appointed Unionists to office so far as he was able. James H. Bell, a former supreme court justice, was made Secretary of State, William Alexander appointed Attorney General. But Hamilton could not find enough qualified Unionists to go around, and he hesitated to appoint hacks for purely ideological or political reasons. He declared a general amnesty for any Texan who would take a new oath of allegiance to the United States, and he began to appoint men he personally knew to be honorable and capable as local officials. Hamilton had little power, however, to interfere with the military, which was a law unto itself; and he did not try to set aside the military courts.

At this time, Texas was under Presidential Reconstruction. Andrew Johnson had set only three conditions for the reentry of the state into the Union with full self-government. These were the abolition of slavery by law, the repudiation of the secession ordinance of 1861, and the repudiation of all Confederate debts and obligations. This was a wise and farsighted policy, containing nothing of vengeance in it. Nor was there anything in it that Texans could not immediately accept. It would have restored the Union as it had been in 1861, with two essential changes: the discrediting of the right of secession and of chattel slavery for all time.

This was essentially the Lincolnian policy toward the South. Abraham

Lincoln had gradually assumed tribunician powers to preserve the Union after 1861. He expanded the powers of the Presidency, which in reality meant he had prevented the Congress from participating in policy-making during the war. Whatever damage this did to traditional American representative democracy, few things better stood the inspection of history. Lincoln did not succumb to the current Northern malaise of crusade. He saw his mission as that of restoring the American people, not further dividing them. He did not see the war as holy, or himself as an avenging angel. At his last Cabinet meeting, he "thought it provident that this great rebellion was crushed just as Congress had adjourned and there were none of the disturbing elements of that body to hinder and embarrass us. If we were wise and discreet we should reanimate the states and get their governments in successful operation with order prevailing and the union recreated before Congress came together in December." Lincoln was not Caesar, nor was he hostile to the Republican Congress. But he knew that radicalism and a punitive spirit were rising in the North, and he feared them.

Abraham Lincoln's profession of malice toward none appalled the majority of his political associates. To eschew the winy fruits of total victory after a crusade that left 300,000 Union dead required more humanity and folk wisdom than most Americans possessed. Probably, had he lived, Lincoln would have prevailed. His advisers disagreed with his live-and-let-live policy toward the South, but they had disagreed with almost every decision he had made during the war. It was certainly a relief to many in the government when fate presented them with a dead martyr rather than a live, folk-hero President, whose people might not really understand his pragmatism but loved him all the same. Booth's bullet was more disastrous to Texas than Brutus' dagger had been for Rome.

Andrew Johnson, the poor-boy Tennessean who became an accidental President in 1865, was a national disaster of another kind. Johnson, a Southerner and a Democrat—the usual compromise candidate for the Vice-Presidency—understood and completely sympathized with Lincoln's views. But Johnson, holding the powers his chief had made enormous, lacked support in the dominant Republican Party and thus any real political base. Nor was he a hero to the Northern masses; Lincoln's lost magic could not be transferred. Finally, Johnson was well-meaning but tactless, stubborn, and inept. In this first address to a Congress still smarting from its chivvying by Lincoln he said: "Your President is now the Tribune of the people, and thank God I am, and intend to assert the power which the people have placed in me."

Johnson not only was tactless and espoused an unpopular policy toward the late Confederacy, but he opposed the bulk of the domestic legislation of the Republican Party, on taxes, railroads, monetary policy, and states' rights. President and Congress were on a collision course.

Very little of this was seen by the native leaders in the paralyzed South, not even by Jack Hamilton, who worked to put things back together on Johnson's terms. The first step was to hold elections for a constitutional convention, which assembled on February 7, 1866. In this group were both old Unionists, such as John Hancock and Edward Degener, and one-time Secessionists, H. R. Runnels and Oran Roberts. The Blue faced the Gray. The majority of delegates, however, were conservatives of both factions. They chose as their leader General James Throckmorton, C.S.A. The old Whig, who had spent his political life fighting for what he believed best for Texas at the time, was now respected in both camps.

The convention quickly proposed several amendments to the state constitution of 1845, abolishing slavery, nullifying the secession ordinance, renouncing the future right of secession, and repudiating not only Confederate, but actually all state wartime debts. Civil laws unconnected with the war or Confederacy were approved. No real controversy arose in these fields.

A more troubling problem was the question of the new civil status of the former slaves. This was a problem the North, for all its commitment to freedom and pressure toward equality, never really understood or faced in the 19th century. Its own Negro population was miniscule. There was complete agreement in Texas that slavery was dead. But it was politically impossible for Texans to consider giving the freedmen full citizen rights. The remembrance of slavery was one factor, but the actual class status of the blacks was equally, or more, important. The horde of Negroes, through no fault of their own, were impoverished, illiterate, and unskilled. They were a bottom group, the lowest of the low, who had never participated in society or government. If Dr. W. E. B. DuBois later wrote that in 1861 not one white American in a hundred believed that Negroes could ever become an integral part of American democracy, the percentage in Texas was probably just as high in 1866.

The men sitting at Austin would have been dubious of giving rights to an equivalent horde of poor whites. However, there was another factor, which tended to be deprecated, denied, ignored, or obscured. This was the prevalent and entirely characteristic feeling of racial superiority common to all Northern European peoples. The educated and higher social classes in Texas took it for granted that the Negro was inherently inferior to the white; they could justify it by the Negro present and Negro past if forced to articulate. To whites lower in the social scale, it was not only a matter of truth but an article of faith.

In the retrospect of history it is not easy to offer simplistic criticism of Throckmorton, Pease, Hancock, Hamilton, and other capable men who struggled with the problem of Negro status. The Negroes were thoroughly differentiated both by color and by culture. It had taken the bloodiest conflict in modern times to make the Negroes free; it would have taken a social cataclysm of the most immense proportions to give the Negroes equality. In all times and in all places there were only three ways by which greatly differentiated peoples had lived together: as slave or serf and master; by miscegenation; or by some system of caste. The first and the last solutions, historically, were commonest; they had been employed from the New World to India. The Spanish, in America, had imposed a combination of the two, with considerable miscegenation on the side.

The new Texas constitution ignored the Thirteenth Amendment, which freed the slaves but also carried definite connotations of Negro equality. Freedmen were recognized as having status at law, with the right to hold private property. They had rights before a jury, with one exception: no Negro could testify in court in cases involving whites. They were specifically denied the right to vote.

John Reagan, who had been Postmaster General of the Confederacy and who had recently returned from detention in the North, repeatedly warned the convention that the state should make some token step toward Negro suffrage, such as giving the ballot to freedmen who could read and write. Reagan wrote that the North was in an ugly mood, and there was much sentiment for Negro equality; a little compromise could turn away much wrath. Texans treated this view with derision.

They had reason to. In 1866 Negro equality was by no means a Northern commitment. The evidence that it was not abounded. The Union army had included 200,000 Negro soldiers, who received unequal pay, allowances, and promotion. The Yankee army displayed continual overt evidences of discrimination and even hatred for the Negro throughout the war, as letters and diaries attest. In the occupation forces, Texans had seen ample evidence of a sneering, patronizing attitude toward former slaves. Lincoln himself had told a delegation of black leaders in the White House: "There is an unwillingness on the part of our people, harsh as it may be, for your free colored people to remain with us. . . . When you cease to be slaves, you are yet far removed from being placed on an equality with the white race. . . . I cannot alter it if I would. It is a fact. . . . It is better for us both, therefore, to be separated."

More concrete, throughout the war there had been riots directed against Negroes in Chicago, Cleveland, Detroit, and New York. The majority of Western states had passed laws prohibiting Negroes from settling, or attending white schools. Only five states permitted Negro suffrage. In 1865 Minnesota, Wisconsin, and Connecticut voted down referenda giving Negroes the ballot; the Nebraska constitution of 1866 limited voting to whites. Four major Northern states were to pass similar legislation within two years. On February 5, 1866, Senator Charles Sumner stated in Congress that educational qualifications should be imposed on Negro voting. Horace Greeley, in the New York *Tribune,* wrote that colored voting must be limited to those who could read and write, paid taxes, and were established in a craft or trade. Sumner and Greeley were known as Negro champions. The Presidential recommendation to the South requested that, at the least, any franchise be limited by literacy qualifications.

Few Texans, other than John H. Reagan, realized that the North was rapidly moving toward a double standard of enforcing Negro equality both as a political and a punitive measure. Nowhere, probably, was this to be better expressed than in Thaddeus Stevens' equation of slave-owning with sin, with a required expiation by the humiliation of Negro equality, not ignoring the "Party purpose."

The proposals of the Texas convention were submitted to the public in June, 1866, as amendments to the state constitution along with the general election of state officers.

The governor's race narrowed to Throckmorton and E. M. Pease. Both men were Unionists and moderate conservatives, although Pease was a little more radical. Under military government, only a Unionist of some stripe could take full part in political affairs. The two men did not differ essentially on issues. Throckmorton was opposed to any form of Negro suffrage, but upheld the Presidential Reconstruction program in all respects. Pease agreed personally on the issue, but thought expediency required literate Negro voting.

In this campaign, however, an explosive cleavage split the Unionist, or Republican, Party in two. It did not center so much around ways and means but was a conflict in basic goals. The Republican-Unionist camp now began breaking visibly apart in two soon-to-be-hostile groups.

The first faction was the largest. These were the Throckmorton-Hamilton men, called the Conservatives. The Conservatives had opposed secession, but they were now dead-set against further fighting of the Civil War. They wanted no punitive measures to be employed against former Confederates. Their avowed purpose was to return Texas to the Union as a free state as quickly as possible. They included a strong dash of Whiggery from old times, and had the support of many planters. The Conservatives had no quarrel with the old social order, and they did not greatly worry if local Democrats returned to power.

The second, minority faction of Republicans were the Radicals. They consisted basically of two kinds of men: turncoat Texans and extreme Unionists. The Radicals advocated a number of drastic measures: disenfranchisement of all ex-Confederates, Negro suffrage, and the splitting of Texas into several states. Among the turncoats there was a high percentage of ne'er-do-wells and misfits, as well as a great many people from the lower levels of the social structure divided between genuine radicals and men out for gain. The extreme Unionists included many Northerners who had arrived in the state. As the Texas historian Nunn wrote, there were few idealists among them; some wanted to change the South, but most came to see what fortune held. All Radicals were scandalized at the prospect of Texas being returned to the hands of the old regime. What they proposed, in the name of union and patriotism, was a complete overturn and the imposition of Negro rule. They, of course, in alliance with the Republican powers in the North, would control the rulers.

Both wings were almost unanimously regarded by Texans as traitors to the state.

Throckmorton won in a free election, 49,277 to 12,168. The amendments to the state constitution were approved by a much lesser margin.

In August, James Throckmorton was inaugurated in the governorship, and the eleventh state legislature convened. The legislature was dominated by Conservative Republicans and Democrats, who were allied on almost everything except past history. On August 20, 1866, President Johnson declared the rebellion in Texas at an end. Ostensibly, the state was now prepared to reenter the Union.

It was completely logical that the new legislature and administration wanted to reconstruct Texas in its old image; they had no valid internal reason for doing otherwise. They began to do so, certainly with the approval of the vast majority of voters in the state. Texans generally believed that their house was cleansed, and readmittance could not be far behind.

The old South began to emerge at Austin in impoverished but still regal form. The legislature, in a gracious gesture, elected David G. Burnet, past President but also past Unionist, to the U.S. Senate; like Throckmorton, Burnet had Union views but had remained to serve his state. The other Senator, however, was Oran Roberts, who sparked the 1861 Secession convention.

All of the three Congressmen sent to Washington were ex-Confederates.

All of them, with the two senators, were rejected. None could take the "ironclad oath" now required by the Radical Republican–dominated Congress—that they had never voluntarily borne arms against the United States or supported any "pretended" government hostile or inimical thereto. This oath, of course, barred virtually all of the leadership of Texas from ever serving in Washington. Its purpose was "patriotic" but the skeletal fingers of political policy were beginning to show through. The Congress wanted no representative Southerners seated and voting.

This was a grim warning, but Throckmorton proceeded onward, with that keen sense of legality that had sustained him all his life. He had survived Secession, the war, and Presidential Reconstruction, but now his adherence to the United States Constitution was finally his undoing.

Throckmorton advised the legislature not to act on the Thirteenth Amendment, because it aroused antipathies in Texas better left buried, and it was totally unnecessary anyway. Enough states had already ratified it to make it the law of the land; there was no Constitutional requirement that an amendment had to be made unanimous.

With his approval, the legislature overwhelmingly rejected the Fourteenth Amendment, which guaranteed freedmen extended civil rights. This amendment had first appeared in the Civil Rights Act of 1866, which passed over Johnson's veto, then had been questioned on constitutional grounds. Not to be denied, the Congressional majority submitted it as an Amendment to the states. It did not include the right of franchise, and gained important support, above all in states where no Negroes were found. In the South, only Tennessee ever accepted it.

Then, the eleventh legislature passed a series of so-called black codes. These regulated Negro affairs, and in Texas they were never so stringent as similar laws erected concurrently in other states of the old Confederacy. They were not planned to punish the Negro, but to put him back to work. All through east Texas plantations were being overgrown with weeds, while thousands of Negroes still congregated around Freedmen's Bureau offices hoping for acreage and mules. The attempted system of hiring Negroes by the day, or by contract, as labor was often hired in the North, had not worked. There were two immense problems. The former slaves delighted in taking no orders, a perfectly human reaction after years of forced labor; and the planters were bankrupt in money terms. They had no U.S. greenbacks with which to pay.

The new labor laws, which were never termed Negro legislation, covered vagrancy, apprenticeship, labor contracts, and enticement of workers. They required "vagrants" to be usefully employed, and forbad them to leave employment through enticement to another job. Provisions included a prohibition of leaving the place of work without permission or having visitors during working hours; one clause required workers to be "obedient and respectful." The effect of such codes was obvious: they put the former slave back on the plantation, under a form of peonage. Some such, though probably less offensive, strictures were absolutely required; the Congress, which was in these years subsidizing railroads with millions and giving them millions more acres in land, refused to accept any responsibility for freedmen welfare. This led more than one member of the old slaveholding class to suspect the Northern goal was more to destroy the power of the obstructionist Southern planters than to raise the Negro in American life.

The passage of such laws, however, waved a red flag before Northern champions of black rights. The slavocracy was rising again; today it regulated Texas; tomorrow there would be a solid phalanx of "Southern gentlemen" in Washington, arrogantly obstructing the Industrial Revolution once more. Both idealistic and humanitarian feelings for the freedmen and political fright seethed through many parts of the North.

Throckmorton, meanwhile, tried both to have the Federal occupation incubus moved into the Western forts and out of the state. But the Army did not go; Congress did not want it to go. The military officers, despite the reestablishment of civil law and the fact that the President had declared the rebellion ended, still held to their courts-martial. Civil supremacy at law was still denied, nor could any soldier be tried before local courts. Throckmorton now had the Federal Constitution on his side and felt secure. But in the weird morass of post-Civil War politics into which America was sinking, the Constitution was a badly tattered banner. More important was the fact that in Washington the President and Radical Congress were staging a war. Each day Johnson lost power and prestige. No Army officer with an ounce of brains obeyed a Presidential order. Meanwhile, Governor Throckmorton made himself an enormous nuisance by standing righteously before the occupation authority. Sometimes he had to appeal to the head of the Freedman's Bureau to get some editor who criticized the Yankee presence in print out of jail.

General Charles Griffin, commanding in Texas, was deeply offended by the Governor on one occasion. On a recommendation by the Freedmen's Bureau, he requested Throckmorton to release 227 Negro convicts from the penitentiary at Huntsville. A Bureau official, passing through, had interviewed this group and decided their offenses were all trivial. He did not investigate. Throckmorton gave this unprecedented request the reply it deserved. Griffin never forgave the 'Reb General."

Under these circumstances the Texas governor found it almost impossible to restore law and order to the state. Through 1866, more and more areas were beginning to succumb to a sort of anarchy. Local sheriffs had little power; the Austin government had almost none at all.

Meanwhile, a Radical press and Radical leaders in Texas kept the governor under continuous fire. Throckmorton was accused of disloyalty, treason, and plotting to run all good Union men out of the state. Radicals filled letters to Washington about Unionists being insulted on the streets. The "bloody shirt" of the Negro—and in these months more than a few blacks were beaten or murdered by Texas mobs—was energetically waved.

The Radical faction had no hope of ever coming to power in Texas through popular election, and they knew it. Their only hope was to precipitate an avalanche from the North, and they failed to pull strings to do so. The acts of lawlessness in Texas were exaggerated beyond reasonable belief, but there were people who believed these accounts, just as Southerners in 1859 had believed the worst about the North. A generation that cried over *Uncle Tom's Cabin* was demagogue meat.

Without the potent poison of political expediency being added, however, Texas would probably have been left alone. The final act of the American tragedy might have been avoided.

The Civil War ennobled no one, except perhaps its central figure, but it brought enormous and probably inevitable changes in the North. The Unionist states actually gained wealth, population, and power between 1861 and 1865, during the concurrent destruction of the Confederacy. War manufactures exploded industrial production, made agriculture prosper, and a flood of immigration from Europe more than replaced the blood and bone buried in the South. Until 1861, the full effect of the Industrial Revolution had been held in check by the powerful agronomists from

Virginia to Texas. With this check removed, the industrial states consolidated their gains swiftly.

While the war itself was moving political power irresistibly toward the Federal capital in Washington, money power was centralized in New York through the wartime Currency Acts. And an enormous centralization, through economic expansion, was going on. Businesses and enterprises were being formed that soon transcended the states themselves. All these currents moved together. The removal of real power to a national capital was the first necessity for an expanded transportation and industrial complex that lay across many states. The concentration of fiscal power in New York broke the monetary freedom of state legislatures. As business enterprise became more and more national and spread on rails, old boundaries were, and had to be, meaningless. All this would, in quick time, forge a new society. The old America of a huge farming, small-holder class with a tiny mercantile and professional elite was not gone; vast islands of it remained. But it was submerged in flooding money and roaring steam.

If the men and interests behind the rise of the new industrial America did not realize fully where they were going, they understood their basic imperatives well enough. They needed certain things from government: high tariffs on industrial products; business subsidies and the diversion of public finances to railroads; centralized money control; continued massive immigration to curb native workers and create a labor pool; and a hard money policy, without which a solid financial-industrial complex was difficult to build.

The political instrument of this new force was the new Republican Party, which inherited the financial and railroad interests by default. Here other refugees from Whiggery found a home. The alliance with Western farmers, first over slavery and then because of the shared patriotic experience of the war, made this coalescing Party national, or at least, spread across the most populous and dominant states. Though some Eastern financial interests remained Democratic, and here and there pockets of small-town gentry did the same, with immigrant workers whose natural instinct was to vote against employers, Republicans absorbed the burgeoning energies and talents of the great northern tier of America as no political party had done before. The men who led it were not only capable and shrewd; they were prepared to battle strenuously for what they wanted. As virtually all foreign observers have seen, the erection of the immense American politico-industrial-financial machine after 1861 was not pure destiny; it took a certain kind of genius.

The goals of the emerging society were hardly universal, or even a majority view. The oldtime, or Conservative-leaning, Democrats still had a majority of all Americans in 1860. This did not depend wholly on Southern reaction. Things were not all that good in the new industrial empire.

The new wealth was more monstrously maldistributed than it had ever been. Millions of Northern workers were little better off, in grimy tenements and working long tedious days, than Texas slaves; many, in fact, were cared for worse. Native-born workers, who had enjoyed decades of scarcity and demand, begged for a limit to flooding immigration as they were drowned. In the 19th century they were hardly sustained by the 20th-century illusion that they rose on each succeeding wave. Hard money policy pinched farmers, particularly those in the West with mortgaged lands. It made things stable for industrialists but depressed the entire debtor class.

The disparate distribution of wealth between rich and poor, which had been notably lacking in early America compared to Europe; the beginning of real urban poverty on the English scale; the denigration of labor into a working class; and the enormous power achieved by swollen corporate enterprise were some ironic results of the great crusade for middle-class democracy that the Republicans presided over between 1861 and 1865. There was more real, if less merely apparent, equality in 1859. If the war released the energies of the American industrial middle class, it also freed their vices. Shrewd, capable, immensely hard-working, and merciless, a new dominant group emerged. Adamses, Cabots, Stocktons, and Lees were not to set the standards for a new America.

The new breed was described by a French historian:

> . . . An unprincipled, amoral ruling class of fabulous wealth and power, of feudal barons who sliced out the new world of productive wealth . . . They no longer ruled territories and vassals but natural resources and means of communications. They were steel kings, coal kings, oil kings, industrial magnates who ruled over entirely new realms—razor blades, plumbing and fixtures, newspaper chains. There were banking empires and railroad empires whose clerks were often respectable Senators. . . . Many of these industrial corporations and trusts had become more powerful than the individual states . . . dwarfing local governments, manipulating political machines, accentuating the centralizing trend that placed every major economic problem on the national scale. The result was the cultural monstrosity known as the Gilded Age, in which a luxurious style of living was marked by the worst taste ever displayed, a lack of true distinction and refinement. . . .

Against this grimy, soon-to-be gilded age there was an enduring wail of protest, while a few Adamses, Cabots, and Roosevelts, bypassed in time and place, husbanded a pale form of aristocracy and survived. Lincoln was barely reelected in 1864, by only 200,000 votes. The Republican-industrial alliance had gained two priceless assets out of the war: the destruction of organized, ably led opposition from the South and the tremendous prestige of having saved the Union. The new Party could and quickly did wrap itself in patriotic, nationalistic garb. Slavery had divided Southern and Western farmers; the war itself split them irrevocably afterward. After Appomattox, it became almost impossible for a wheat grower from Kansas to break bread with a cotton chopper from Tennessee.

In the patriotic, punitive fervor of a dying crusade, the Radical Republicans won tremendous victories in the elections of 1866. Passion, more than any understanding of or admiration for Republican imperatives, returned a horde of Johnson-and-Southern haters into Congress. In this election, no Southern state could vote, so the Congress remained purely regional rather than national. The great increase in the Radical strain of Republican gave Thaddeus Stevens, the House leader, and Charles Sumner, the Radical Senate chief, full control of Congress, and, they thought, the nation.

They would hardly have been human had they not wanted to consolidate it. The new order in the nation could not be preserved if the Southern delegations returned in force and resumed their old alliance with Democratic elements in the North and West. The Southern representatives had always led the battle against railroad and business subsidies, corporations, hard money, and almost everything the new class held dear. It was far from certain, in 1866, that America had completely deserted the plantation economy and strict construction of the Constitution to keep the nation in the mold of 1789, or that it would now direct its dominant energies and policy into economic development for the next hundred years. Rhetts and Robertses were reentering the Senate, determined to halt the rush toward a mass economy and the middle-class ideal of a mass society, graduated only by wealth. Stevens and his cohorts writhed in hatred and anguish at the Presidential Reconstruction policy. As the House leader said, the readmitted Southern tier was sending a "solid rebel representation to Congress" where it would cast a "solid rebel vote." By "rebel" he meant it would oppose the new order of things. "They, with their kindred Copperheads [Northern Democrats] . . . would always elect the President and control Congress."

The fear of the industrial society seizing control had led the South to secession. Now, a fear of a return to 1856 drove the North into suppression.

Texas and the other states had played into Radical hands in many respects. They had elected aristocratic, ex-Confederate members of the old "slavocracy" governors and senators. There was a deep and lasting hatred for these people in the rest of the nation, more virulent than before the war. Millions in the North, who had lost kith and kin in the war, were antagonized at the election of a Confederate general as governor of the nation's largest state. Also, the early reemergence of Southern pride was fatal; it infuriated millions who still thought of the Civil War as some sort of moral crusade. The Texans did not come back to Washington humbly; they did not say *mea culpa;* they arrived demanding their Constitutional rights and generally raising hell about Yankee usurpation.

Most dangerous of all, men raised into a system of Negro bondage saw nothing wrong in putting the Negro back into some similar state. Slave codes, exact and detailed, had governed Negro life. All white Southerners believed that some sort of similar "workers' codes" were necessary for the reestablishment of orderly society. But here they allowed the Northern politicos to glorify sectional legislation by wrapping it in the hapless freedman's ragged, bloody shirt. In the very months that New Jersey, Ohio, Michigan, and Pennsylvania rejected Negro suffrage at home, their spokesmen demanded it come about in the South. Gideon Welles summed up the demands of Stevens, New York's Roscoe Conkling, and other Radicals in a damning entry in his diary: "It is evident that intense partisanship instead of philanthropy is the root of the movement."

After Emancipation, the fact that the United States was a voting democracy was one of the Negro's greatest handicaps and became his lasting tragedy. He became a pawn of people who never really personally wanted to admit him into American society; he was "voted" for a hundred years by Parties whose philanthropy was mainly political, whether Republican or Democrat. An autocracy might have oppressed him worse, but it also might have found a solution without the public hypocrisy that all mass democracies were heir to.

The only way the Congressional chieftains saw of suppressing the revived "rebellion" the Presidential Reconstruction had allowed was to destroy the Southern social order. Stevens was more blunt than most Yankees, then or afterward: he "intended to revolutionize their feelings and principles. This may startle feeble minds and shake weak nerves. So do all great improvements."

The first great improvement was passage of the First Reconstruction Act, over Johnson's inevitable veto, on March 2, 1867. It was an act of Congressional expediency, which had both support and opposition among the ordinary people in the North. There was both confusion, caused by Radical exaggerations and propaganda, and genuine idealism in some popular support. The Negro did desperately need guidance and protection, though hardly in the way in which it was being rendered. Hardest to evaluate, but always present, was the now established Northern middle-class philosophy that a little humiliation was good for the Southern soul.

The Reconstruction Act did five things. It declared the new regimes in Texas and the old Confederacy illegal and unsatisfactory and abolished them. It divided the South into a conquered region of five military occupation districts. It required the former rebellious states to write new constitutions that guaranteed Negro suffrage and to elect brand-new governments on the basis of Negro voting. It made mandatory the ratification of the Fourteenth Amendment before any state could be readmitted to the Union. It was also, by any then or later standard, unconstitutional. It was upheld.

To the protestations in the North that this imposition of military government, which was obviously designed to turn the South over to its Negro-Radical minorities, would humiliate the Southern social order, Stevens snapped: "Why not? Do they not deserve humiliation? If they do not, who does? What criminal, what felon deserves it more?"

The Southern states had long humiliated their slave class and denied it human status. On the other hand, only two states—Mississippi and South Carolina—had Negro majorities. Caucasians, whatever their biases, were the dominant race in every respect, and their dominance could only be set aside by outside force. From substituting concepts of morality and law for politics, some Americans were now prepared to replace politics with bayonets. Union bayonets were all-powerful, but the one thing they could not wreak was democracy.

The military commanders in the South were given power to remove or replace the civil authorities as they saw fit. Charles Griffin, still smoldering against Governor Throckmorton, conferred with General Phil Sheridan in New Orleans. Sheridan issued an order in the summer of 1867, branding the Texan as an "impediment to reconstruction." Throckmorton was summarily removed.

Neither the Mexican invasion of 1836 nor the bloody days of the Civil War marked the most disastrous period in Texas history: it began now.

22

THE CARPETBAGGERS

> There is no Andy Johnson "policy," no Throckmorton "Con-
> federate record," no Jack Hamilton "rebel coalition," in the
> present programme. Let the people of Texas rejoice. "Come thou
> with us and we will do thee good."
>
> HOUSTON Tri-Weekly Union, A RADICAL PAPER

> We had hoped, and we believe the Republican party of the
> nation hoped, that with the completion of reconstruction the
> rights, interests, and wishes of the people would everywhere be
> respected. There were so many wicked and foolish things con-
> nected with the reconstruction of the Southern states, that the
> Republican party is already seriously injured thereby.
>
> AUSTIN Daily Republican, A CONSERVATIVE ORGAN

THE events of 1867 in Texas convinced the vast majority of Texans that whatever face had been put on it, the real drive of the North in the War Between the States was for domination of the South. The evidence is overwhelming that most Texans had accepted the indivisibility of the Union and the fact of legal emancipation of the slaves, which were the primary and secondary issues of the war. Texans, with other Southerners, did not accept the idea of Negro equality, but that had never been a Union commitment. The fact that, in the same year that a majority of Northern states prohibited Negro voting by law, it was thrust by Federal fiat on the South was not lost on them. It was felt by virtually the whole population that the policy of the United States was to continue the prostration of the conquered states through easily manipulated Negro suffrage.

With the stubborn and honorable J. W. Throckmorton out of the way, General Charles Griffin proceeded to cleanse the state. Armed by continuing

Reconstruction Acts from Congress, the U.S. Army carried out a purge of all state officials, which reached deep down to the county level. Everywhere, officeholders, even petty ones, with a Confederate past were dismissed. They were replaced with Union men. There were not nearly enough capable Unionists to go around, and many exceedingly dubious appointments were made.

In this period, there seemed to be an intensification of hatred toward former Confederates on the part of Northern officers. The entire military hierarchy—Grant, Sheridan, and Griffin—took views that can only be called tyrannical. The test or "ironclad" oath was extended to civil juries. Prospective jurors who could not swear that they had never voluntarily served or supported the Confederacy were barred. This act removed nine-tenths of the white population from jury duty, and its real effect was to destroy the civil courts.

Congress on March 23, 1867, extended the disenfranchisement of Southerners to include all persons who had ever held a state or Federal office *before* the Rebellion and later supported the Confederacy. The U.S. Attorney General ruled liberally on this, presuming it applied only to major offices. Generals Griffin and Sheridan interpreted the edict much more strictly, with Grant's express approval. In Texas, any man who had ever been a mayor, school trustee, clerk, public weigher, or even a cemetery sexton was disenfranchised. The Grant-Sheridan view was later written into Congressional law.

Another military edict, which Congress validated in July, was to give registration boards complete authority to accept or reject applicants on the grounds of "loyalty," as each board saw fit. The boards were in the hands of Army officers or Union men. In a state which was only about one-quarter Negro, they registered 49,779 Negroes to 59,633 whites. A strong effort was made to place every freedman on the rolls. The most surprising aspect of this operation was that most Federal officials pretended to view it as essentially moral. The enormous social gulf between the auction block and the voting booth was ignored, or demolished with the argument that in no other way could past sins be rectified. Whatever truth or morality this argument had was utterly lost on Texans, because the process was so self-serving to the Republican hierarchy. The Army and the Freedmen's Bureau not only registered the Negro vote; both agencies also told the registrants incessantly who had freed the slaves and who now had presented them with the ballot. Understandably, despite an ineffective flowering of the Ku Klux Klan in Texas, they garnered the Negro vote.

During this period the President opposed the Congressional Reconstruction every step of the way. His vetos were overridden. He was growing more lame-duck each day; the Southerner in the White House was without influence. The Congress deprived him of his Constitutional command of the Army by completely detailing, through law, the Army's operations in the South. The Senate prevented him from appointing any pro-Johnson men to his Administration. Finally, when Johnson tried to fight back, it moved to impeach him. No President was ever quite so thoroughly mauled.

The impeachment failed to carry by one vote, and only because certain cooler Republican heads in business and finance, outside the Congress, prevailed. The form of Presidential government thus survived, and the concept of a tribunate of the people, which Jackson began and Lincoln fostered, could await a stronger man.

The consensus of most historians, North and South, is that this Congressional uprising was a national disaster.

Delegates to a state constitutional convention, to rewrite the Texas instrument in accord with Northern prejudices, were elected in early 1868. This convention met at Austin in June. So complete was the political revolution that only six men who had sat in the convention of 1866 came to Austin in 1868.

The Republican slates of delegates won, 44,689 to 11,440. A Democratically inspired campaign to invalidate the elections by sitting them out —a majority of registered voters had to cast ballots—barely failed. The Democratic slogan was "Better Yankee than Nigger Rule," but just enough whites voted to legalize the result.

The new constitution emerged in conformance with prevailing Republican thought: it strongly reflected centralization and the aspirations of the national, if not the Texas, middle classes. The governor was given a four-year term, and the power of appointing all top state officials, including the justices of the state courts. County courts were abolished. Political offices were thus made stronger, and power largely removed from local influences, especially the influence of the planter class. Another important innovation was a centralized state public school system, funded by public land sales, a poll tax, and from the general revenue. Until this time, Texas had not had statewide public schools.

Unrestricted Negro suffrage was guaranteed by a clause prohibiting disenfranchisement by "race, color, or former condition of servitude." But only those whites already barred from voting by the Fourteenth Amendment were disenfranchised.

Over-all, the new constitution was a Conservative Republican, rather than a Radical, document. Because of this, there was a violent split in the Republican ranks. Although the Conservatives, under A. J. Hamilton and E. M. Pease, prevailed, only 45 members of the convention signed the finished instrument in February, 1869.

The Radicals, under E. J. Davis and Morgan Hamilton (A. J. Hamilton's brother), bolted the convention toward the end. Their policies were strikingly different. Radicals wanted to disenfranchise all Confederates and to divide Texas into three new states, permitted under the original terms of annexation.

Both factions carried their positions to Washington, the seat of all real power. General J. J. Reynolds, the new military chief who replaced Griffin when that officer succumbed to yellow fever on the coast, sided strongly with Jack Hamilton. He expressed strong Conservative Republican views, arguing that only white men should serve as registrars, and opposed division of the state. He chided the Radicals for acting like children in bolting, and Radical chieftains were able to prevent their rump convention from asking for his removal by only a single vote.

History, however, is a series of accidents. Reynolds had a secret wish to cap his career by entering the United States Senate. Preferring the mild Texas climate and seeing a chance of preferment in his grasp, he had his "secret" desire carried to Conservative leader A. J. Hamilton. Hamilton officially let it be known that the Republicans could find a stronger man. What he said privately about this proposition threw the General into a white-faced fury.

Jack Hamilton was understandably reluctant to promise one of the most hated men in Texas a Senate seat. But his refusal set the stage for tragedy.

Elections now were scheduled to select the new state government that would bring Texas back into the Union for the third time. E. M. Pease had been appointed provisional civil governor by General Sheridan in New Orleans, but Pease was to hold office only until the end of Reconstruction. Elisha Pease was a moderate, a former Texas governor who was more Whig than either Democrat or Republican, and so far as he could, served the state well. He had very little real power, as events soon showed.

At the start of 1869, it appeared that the Conservative Republicans would win the elections and organize the state. The majority of these men were longtime residents; they were Southerners with basic Unionist, rather than Secessionist, views. In fact, both the Conservatives and the Democrats considered fusion with each other, but the idea failed. The scars on the Blue and the Gray were still too new for full cooperation, though little real hatred separated the two.

The Conservatives had the support of most prominent men, and the backing of every important newspaper in Texas.

The Radical faction, meanwhile, was a minority within a minority, and were detested not only by A. J. Hamilton's group but by almost every white person in the state. When they organized early in 1869, and presented their own candidates for office—E. J. Davis for governor; J. W. Flanagan, lieutenant governor; Jacob Kuechler, land commissioner; and George Honey, treasurer—it seemed they had no chance. They did not even put up their own ticket by choice, but because the Conservatives would no longer tolerate them within the regular Republican Party.

The Radical leaders were Texas residents, though they were supported by people arrived out of the North, such as Freedmen's Bureau officials, Army officers, and the like. However, the whole faction began to get a new name, Carpetbaggers, a cynical allusion to the fact that many Yankees came South with their entire worldy possessions in a traveling case. The term, unfair in Texas as compared with other Southern states, clung.

The Radicals, both native Scalawags and Carpetbaggers, were a remarkable band of political buccaneers. Their ideology, beyond Unionism, was primarily a dislike for the old Southern order and a general desire to remake Texas more in the order of a Northern state. In this they were "moderns," but their main cement was a hunger for political office. They had no real uniformity. E. J. Davis, discharged as a Union brigadier, was impeccably honest in money matters; most of his closest cronies were not. The genuine idealists among the Radicals were few—Morgan Hamilton, A. J.'s brother, was a Southern gentleman among thieves.

These potential pirates always realized their best friends were in the Northern Congress. That men such as Charles Sumner tolerated them and even supported them can be laid only to the fact that the Radical program lay nearer than the Conservative one to the hearts of Northern politicos. Jack Hamilton was as appalled as Throckmorton at the social revolution Reconstruction intended, and equally determined to restore the society of the state.

This Northern bias in their favor was a tremendous asset. Political history turned upon it, and upon the fact that J. J. Reynolds, an Army general, had the ear and confidence of U. S. Grant, who had just been elected overwhelmingly as President of the United States.

Reynolds switched sides. In a state still under military occupation, this was decisive. During the summer of 1869, the Army systematically stripped all Hamilton men of political offices, patronage, and favors. The vacant offices were filled with Davis men. With the connivance of the Army, Davis made an alliance with G. T. Ruby, state president of the Union League, a secret society whose members had come South to educate the Negroes to vote Radical Republican. Between the Union League and the Army, the freedmen were dragooned and told that A. J. Hamilton intended to reinslave them. In this way, the Davis Radicals began to gain control of the powerful black vote.

Jack Hamilton, who considered himself a loyal Republican, protested vigorously to Washington. General Reynolds, however, had the final word. He wrote President Grant on September 4, 1869 that the election of A. J. Hamilton meant a "restoration of Confederate government in Texas" and that the only "real Republican" party in the state was led by Davis. Grant, who seems to have been a basically honest man presiding over a world he did not understand, listened to the General and to his Party Radicals in the North. He turned the full power of the Federal government behind Davis.

Pease, the puppet provisional governor, was so nauseated he immediately resigned. He wrote Grant bitterly in his letter of resignation that "eight-tenths of all educated [a euphemism for "white"] Republicans" favored Hamilton, and that Davis represented a "carpetbagger and Negro Supremacy party."

Davis retorted that the Conservatives had "sold out to the rebels." Grant's advisers lined up even more strongly behind him.

The real tragedy of the Texas election of 1869 was not the imposition of Carpetbagger rule, but the fact that to impose it the entire democratic political process was perverted. Less damage would have been done had the Army simply continued martial rule. There had been no organized opposition when the Reconstruction Acts were forced upon the South. Despite great bitterness, Southern leaders everywhere counseled meekness. Former Confederate generals from Beauregard to Throckmorton indicated that Southerners were "a conquered people"—the actual words most commonly used—and must submit. There was a belief that the American political process would eventually be restored.

The problem was that Radical rule in Texas could only be imposed by bayonets or wholesale chicanery and fraud. United States authorities, unable to countenance the first, chose the second. Such was the feeling of the day.

Reynolds appointed only Davis men as voting registrars on October 1, 1869. These officials were given almost limitless powers. Their abuses—if this were to be any kind of representative election—were also without limit. Although it was prohibited in the constitution, men who had volunteered for Confederate service were rejected. Further, Texans who were known Unionists and had suffered for it were also rejected and forbidden to register—if it was known that they were Hamilton men. This included thousands of men who had registered freely the previous year. Then, after registration ended, some thousands of names were arbitrarily stricken from the rolls. In some cases there seems to have been no political reason, merely personal prejudice.

The election, held between November 30 and December 3, 1869, was supervised by Davis Radicals, backed fully by the Army. Military detachments stood at every polling place; at each an Army officer acted as election official. The polling was a farce, conducted in an air of white resignation and gloom.

Negroes, some in slave rags, were herded to the polls. Led by Radical white men, they came singing, "As He died to make men holy, let us die to make men free." They were voted—no Negro was refused the right, on any grounds.

Democrats had put up Hamilton Stuart, editor of the Galveston *Civilian*. They knew he could not win; also, most Democrats feared that if he did, the North would impose full martial law. Few Democrats even attempted to vote. Most whites tried to vote for Jack Hamilton, the Conservative Republican.

The Army had been ordered to close the polls in any place where trouble occurred. Significantly, this occurred only in heavily white counties, where Army officers apparently were hoping for reasons to stop the voting on any pretext. If a voter found his name stricken and argued the fact, the polls were immediately closed down. This cut the Hamilton vote.

In Navarro County, the registrar realized a heavy Hamilton majority was certain to be cast. This man took the registration lists and departed before the election; no votes from Navarro were ever counted. In Milam County, the polls opened, but the results were never reported in; they were not even counted. In Hill County, the ballots were removed to another jurisdiction, and counted by a single official, a Davis man. He reported a huge Davis majority, despite the fact that the vote certainly went the other way.

Less than one-half the registered white voters in Texas, in these circumstances, were able to cast a ballot.

There was no canvass, nor were the ballots ever made public. General Reynolds certified to President Grant that Davis had been elected, by a vote of 39,901 to 39,092. Despite the fact that affidavits charging fraud were sworn before magistrates all over the state, and even a number of U.S. Army officers protested to Reynolds about this farce, Reynolds certified the entire Radical ticket, and Grant refused to investigate.

Hamilton was counted out. Despite all handicaps, the evidence is overwhelming that he got almost the entire white vote. The returns on the ratification of the new state constitution were perhaps an indication. This was a Conservative document, which the Radicals detested. It carried, 72,466 to 4,928.

Led by E. M. Pease, a dozen Republicans of known integrity petitioned Washington. Documented cases of serious fraud, presented to Congress and the President, were ignored.

In an atmosphere reeking of Spanish cigars and sour Bourbon whiskey, the Radicals congregated in the capitol at Austin. General Reynolds eased the new regime on its way. On January 8, 1870, by general order, he appointed the officials-elect to office before their constitutional terms began. He convened the new twelfth legislature on February 8. Before convening it, he took the unusual step of appointing Major B. Rush Plumley speaker of the Texas House.

The twelfth legislature contained a Radical majority. Seventeen Radicals, seven Conservative Republicans, and six Democrats sat in the Senate; two of them were Negro. There were fifty Radicals, nineteen Conservatives, and twenty-one Democrats in the House. Eleven state representatives were black.

Four Texas Congressmen had been elected. Three were Radicals; the fourth, who claimed to be a Democrat, was a discharged Union Army officer and Carpetbagger.

The legislature routinely ratified the Fourteenth and Fifteenth Amendments to the Federal Constitution without serious debate. J. W. Flanagan and Morgan Hamilton were elected to the U.S. Senate. On March 30,

1870, the President signed an act of Congress admitting the Texas delegation to sit in Washington. General Reynolds relinquished military authority to the Davis regime on April 16.

The Davis crew, flamboyant and energetic, was not without ability and a certain political genius. They had smelled the wind's direction and correctly trimmed their sails. Now, they showed a remarkable amount of political inventiveness.

Davis, who was born in Florida in 1827 and arrived in obscure circumstances in Texas in 1848 with his widowed mother, typified the rise of a new type of American officeholder. At some time he apparently reau law, but no details are known. His main thrust in life was seeking office. In 1850 he gained the position of deputy customs collector of the Rio Grande. In 1853 he became a district attorney, and the year afterward, district court judge at Brownsville. He married the daughter of an army officer, and while in this post opted for the Union in 1861.

He spent the war either in exile in Mexico, or fighting Rip Ford's cavalry along the Rio Grande. He was commissioned a colonel of cavalry, and discharged at San Antonio in 1865 as a U.S. brigadier. He had no reason to love Texans, nor they him. By 1866, he was a leader of the faction demanding disenfranchisement of ex-Confederates, division of the state, and Negro suffrage. Now, in 1870, E. J. Davis was governor of Texas.

He was personally honest, and there were far worse Reconstruction governors in the Southern states. But Davis had some notions that bespoke a native ingenuity, and afterward, as a reaction, were to have long-lasting effects on his adopted state.

The first considered action of the Davis administration was to extend its term of office. Under the 1869 constitution, elections for Congress were to be held again in 1870 and for state officers in 1871. Davis' legislature by majority vote postponed both till November, 1872. The official excuse was to make local and Federal elections coincide; Davis privately mentioned that the people would not be sufficiently "reconstructed" before 1872.

Morgan Hamilton, when he heard of this in Washington, choked on it. Probably, Hamilton had been sent to the capital to get him out of the way.

Davis next proposed a number of bills, each of which was most unusual in the American 19th century. The first was called the Militia Bill. The title was innocent; all states had militia regulations. But the Texas law put all male citizens between eighteen and forty-five subject to military duty, under the personal command of the governor. Its startling provisions, beyond this, were: the governor was permitted to declare martial law in any Texas county, suspend the laws, and maintain this until the legislature convened; the governor could assess the districts put under martial law for all costs of such operation, and also assess punishment of "offenders."

Another radical bill was a provision for a State Police. This would consist of 200 men, under the command of the governor through the state adjutant general. The State Police would have the authority to operate anywhere—hitherto, law enforcement was limited to sheriffs and local constables, who could not cross county lines. The State Police was to have extraordinary powers, including an unconstitutional privilege of taking offenders from one county to another for trial, and of operating undercover, as secret agents. At this time, there was no such force in any American state.

The Enabling Act enabled the governor to control patronage on a truly kingly scale. Under it he could appoint mayors, district attorneys, public weighers, and even city aldermen. It centralized power and patronage in the executive's hands as no American legislation ever had. Davis could and did appoint 8,538 state officials, earning $1,842,685 in salaries, and another 1,386 officers who were paid by fees.

The Printing Bill provided an official public printer, a state journal, and provided that regional newspapers be designated to print the various required official notices. This in effect instantly created an "official" state press, subject to government control and influence.

The terms "police state" and "propaganda machine" had not yet come into American English. The Davis Administration, in power in a state where nine-tenths of the white population detested it, was instinctively and logically doing what came naturally. It had not arrived in power through the democratic process; it could not be expected to behave democratically.

These Radical bills passed the Texas House easily, where the Radical majority was absolute. But a deadlock over the Militia and Police Bills developed in the Senate. The thirteen Conservative Republican and Democratic state senators formed a solid opposition bloc; a tie vote emerged. The governor handled this first legislative crisis firmly.

All thirteen opposition party senators were arrested and detained. This broke the tie—but someone noticed the state senate now lacked a quorum. Four of the detained men were released and hustled to the capitol to solve the problem. One of these officers was expelled shortly afterward for "resisting arrest."

The remaining Conservative and Democratic officeholders were kept under house arrest for three weeks. During this time, the entire package of Radical legislation was rushed through.

A. J. Hamilton, E. M. Pease, and James W. Throckmorton joined in a joint appeal to the Congress to restore Texans the civil rights guaranteed under the Federal Constitution. Discredit was thrown upon their loyalty to the nation, and the appeal was not acted upon.

The years of Carpetbagger rule were gaudy, violent, sometimes comic in retrospect, but always tragic at the time. The national view towards the era wavers with whatever view toward the American Negro minority happens to be fashionable at any given time. The regime was founded on Union bayonets and Negro votes, but evidence is small that it did either the Union or the unfortunate minority any good. Negroes put the Carpetbaggers in the state house, but with rare exceptions the ragged horde did not share the wealth.

A large number of men who were indisputably honorable actively supported this sort of rule in Texas and other states. Probably, wrapped in their own drives and biases, honorable men in the U.S. Government simply failed to see the folly of permitting the domestic wreckage in Texas. Charles Sumner of Massachusetts in most respects was as blind to the cruelty, injustice, and folly committed in the name of the Reconstruction of the South as contemporary English governments were blind to the cruelties and follies of the Anglo-Irish Ascendancy.

The period was a weird melange of corruption and genuine social reform. Negro suffrage—combined with white disenfranchisement and wholesale fraud—produced a political revolution. Meanwhile, social and economic revolutions went on. A few years after the war, the "bottom rail was on the top," as Texans said.

Corruption was most evident in the printing and railroad bills. Davis appointed some 10,000 men to valuable offices and made the fortunes of many, but this was essentially legitimate patronage. So were the enormous increases in salary the legislators voted officeholders, and their own increase in per diem. The new governing class were poor men, without a touch of aristocratic ideal or ethic. They possessed an enormous middle-class grasp for money, and they voted themselves a raise. This was characteristic and inevitable; it would happen again. The real corruption, however, came with the $200,000 the printing bill gave the administration to spend. Radical newsheets sprouted in the state like noxious weeds.

Railroad legislation provided similar windfalls. The legislature voted the International Railroad Company twenty sections of land for each mile of track and tax exemption for twenty-five years. Similar grants were provided the Southern Transcontinental and Southern Pacific. In credit to Edmund Davis, these acts were passed over his veto, and his veto stopped several other similar bills. At the same time the state gave away its lands, enabling acts of the legislature allowed cities to vote large railroad and other bonds, totaling more than $1,000,000. These acts were in contradiction to the constitution of 1869.

In their defense, proponents of railroad legislation could point to more than 1,000 miles of new track.

Opponents saw resources of the state—more than required to subsidize the tracks—handed to corporate interests, which profited enormously. They saw a huge increase in taxes and bonded debt, which went to pay for the liberality the Radicals bestowed. Most of all, they saw legislators who had never had a dime sprouting gold watches and gold-headed canes, building or buying fine mansion houses, and driving English carriages behind blooded horses. The railroad boys and other lobbyists did spread a bit of their windfalls around.

Much Radical legislation could stand the inspection of time. The Carpetbaggers tried to build a state road system, though they never progressed beyond levying taxes to support it. They passed a homestead exemption law by which no homestead of 200 acres or less could be seized for debt, except a direct mortgage. The state school acts of 1870 and 1871 created a genuine free public school system for the first time, adequately supported by taxation. In requiring compulsory attendance of children between six and eighteen, without regard to race, the legislature was fifty years ahead of the age. In its centralization, with a state superintendant, state board of education, and 35 district supervisors, who appointed local school boards and thus removed control of education completely from the public, the Radicals were more than a century in advance of America.

Even the good things were intensely unpopular, because the regime itself was universally held in contempt.

The corruption and extravagances of the Carpetbaggers, which reflected the worst of Anglo-American politics, have been easily seen. The rise of a new mercantile and landowning class with them in Texas has not been so clearly marked. The almost complete destruction of the old planter gentry, not by the war but in its aftermath, escaped attention. But it is a truism, if not universally true, that few families that had wealth or station prior to 1860 survived the following two decades with either.

The war bankrupted the planter class by destroying its capital in money and slaves. The principal assets of the planters had always been invested in Negroes; they vanished on Juneteenth. The planters still held land, but they were unable to hold it long. Without labor, they could not put it back in production. And for several critical years the labor situation in Texas—and the whole South—remained in turmoil. The stabilization of 1866 could have saved many planters, but it was overturned. The freedmen once again came to believe they would be cared for by the Government; the Radicals made promises, though they were not kept. Millions of acres were freely granted for the development of rail lines; hardly a dollar and not an acre went to former slaves.

By even the most optimistic evidence, neither Negro nor plantation owner ever adjusted adequately to day or contract labor. Even allowing for white prejudices, historians have shown that this kind of freedman labor was inefficient. It did not work, and proud plantations grew up in weeds.

Another disaster, quite beyond control, was that the price of cotton—the only possible cash crop—fell. Cotton sold for thirty cents a pound in 1866; it had dropped to seventeen in 1870, and thirteen five years later. This savaged the small farmer in the uplands. It put the planter out of business.

Under these pressures, land values collapsed. Land fell to a tenth of the 1860 price in some regions; throughout the state there was a general loss averaging *80 percent*. The planters' acres became worthless. If they were mortgaged, they became a genuine liability. Mortgage sales were universal. East Texas records in these years show an almost complete turnover in ownership of land.

This pressure came in an era of relatively high taxes, imposed by a prodigal state government. Planters, in agonizing case after case, simply could not raise the cash. Taxes had to be paid in hard money; everything else could be paid in kind. They lost their estates.

Much harder to measure than the effects of falling cotton and land prices and the scarcity of money in east Texas was the immense psychic damage done the planters. They had been vigorous enough, but by 1860 too many of them had climbed part way up the ladder of aristocratic illusion. They had removed themselves, and above all, their children, from the idea of economic competition. In the terrible debacle of 1865, planters, like most aristocrats, lacked the resilience to withstand humiliation; they did not know how to go back to making money, and most disdained such grubbing. They could no longer swim in the dirty stream that most Americans and all Southerners had to breast. They sank out of sight.

Here ended that abortive culture in Texas, the cotton kingdom.

The lands and houses of the former gentry did not disappear. In logical fashion, new families arose, but with several immense differences. The new men came from mercantile, middle-class origins; they were shrewd, tough, energetic, cynical, and generally lacking in public spirit. They despised both the languor and the airs of the planter class. This class grew up out of increasing business in the towns from the Sabine to Dallas in the West as tracks and roads went in. It was better fitted to a sweaty, gaudy, gaslight America, and looked back on the Grecian era with contempt. It built cotton gins and warehouses, and bought up bottomlands at two dollars per acre; in central Texas some lands sold for sixty cents. These new Texans were mercantile rather than industrial, but they strongly resembled the rising Yankee industrial upper class. Their entire orientation was economic. They began to produce the same alienation toward culture that industrialism produced in the North.

These new owners discovered the sharecrop solution to Negro labor and stabilized the South. They lived with most of the old trappings of Southern gentry, surrounded by Negro servants. But they developed no real ethic, nor did they attempt to become aristocrats. They were sometimes called Bourbons, and they were flamboyant and tasteless as planters never were. They peopled Faulkner's novels.

The term "planter" survived in other states, but in Texas the name almost entirely disappeared.

During the breakup of the plantation system, the corn farmers in the interior were little disturbed by these changing social conditions. For some years their own condition did not much change. In central-west Texas the Indian problem was paramount, because the Army rendered almost no protection at this time. In fact, when it was discovered that cotton would grow well beyond the mucky alluvial soils, the new cash crop exploded westward to the Dallas-Sherman line, and farmer prosperity temporarily increased. There was a large increase in new small farms.

Noticeably, there was more resistance to the new regime in the western-central counties than in the east. Too much of the morale of plantation Texas had been shot away. But the western borderlands were armed, accustomed to violence, and surly. Cultural diffusion made these Texans as Yankee-hating, and more Negro-despising than, those of the bottomlands and piney woods.

The first opposition to the Davis crowd was carried almost entirely by Conservative Republicans; Democrats were still too cowed. Conservative papers protested the new acts of the legislature, while Conservative legislators, when not under house arrest, orated violently on the floor. Editorial after editorial was hurled against the horrendous corruption of officials, the open sale of votes to railroad and bond lobbies, and the repressive police acts.

Significantly, Morgan Hamilton, Radical U.S. Senator, was scandalized by his own colleagues. Morgan Hamilton was an idealist; he believed in Radical social and governmental reforms, and the habilitation of the Negro. But he attacked the unconstitutional extension of terms of office, the Militia Bill, and the State Police law. He said openly these were violations of the Party's pledges; he also said the Radicals were honor-bound to support the same liberal principles advocated by his Conservative brother, Jack.

Davis and company soon got a bellyful of Morgan Hamilton, as one Carpetbagger put it. On a manufactured technicality, the legislature declared his election as U.S. Senator invalid; it then chose General J. J. Reynolds in his place, although it was brought out on the floor of the state senate that Reynolds was not a Texas citizen or even a legal resident of the state. At this time Reynolds, a brevet major general, held the rank of colonel in the regular U.S. Cavalry at San Antonio. Governor Davis wired the General congratulations, and Reynolds graciously accepted.

Ironically, all twelve votes cast for Hamilton in the Texas legislature were by Democrats. This honor to Reynolds, a man almost all Texans believed had injured and humiliated them, caused general outrage. More important, it seems to have at last turned Senator Charles Sumner's stomach.

It was widely expected that President Grant would use his influence to have Reynolds seated. Reynolds did proceed to Washington on the President's order. The Senate refused to seat him; the judiciary committee determined that Hamilton was entitled to his full term. It was a sign in the wind that the Civil War was ending in the North.

But the war was entering its most bitter phase in Texas. At the heart of the conflict were the Militia Bill and the State Police. An odor clung to Davis' implementation of both, and on this all historians, North and South, Democrat and Republican, have agreed.

The first mass resistance to the Carpetbaggers began in the summer of 1871. It was spurred by the unprecedented taxation that was now being imposed. The moves were orderly and constitutional. E. M. Pease, George Hancock, and Morgan Hamilton, all Republicans, sponsored taxpayers' meetings across the state. A mass gathering of Texas taxpayers was finally held in Austin in September; it was attended by united Republicans and Democrats from 94 counties. Major George B. Erath, an early Austrian immigrant who had become prominent in Texas, held the chair.

E. M. Pease addressed the convention. He attacked the disastrous financial and fiscal policies of the Carpetbaggers, as the state administration was now called, and pointed out that when Davis took office there had been a healthy surplus in the treasury. But by 1871 the state was not only bankrupt and borrowing heavily, "the warrants of the State are hawked about the streets of Austin at six bits on the dollar, and sold with difficulty." Six million dollars were to be levied in state taxes, against an estimated $800,000 actually needed to run the state.

Seven members of the taxpayers committed tried to meet with the governor to discuss cutting expenditures. Davis refused to see them. Balked, the committee prepared a series of honest and authoritative reports, signed by both Democrats and Republicans. These reports to the people were factual —and appalling.

The tax rate had risen in two years from fifteen cents on $100 property valuation to $2.175, not including occupation taxes, city taxes, the $2 annual poll tax, or the levies to retire railroad bonds voted by the legislature. The railroad levies alone amounted to another sixty cents per $100.

Approximately 21 percent of Texans' total income went for taxes. This would have been extraordinary in the 19th century, but supportable if the taxes were evenly applied. But they were not. They fell almost completely on property holders, and even then were levied with great injustice. Planters and farmers were being ruined; businessmen generally escaped. There was no income tax.

The reports indicated also that $695,000, rather than $6,000,000, would adequately if austerely support the state government. The convention was angry over the uses for which the money was being spent. Even the school taxes were attacked, because the school system created a bureaucratic hierarchy and denied local taxpayers all voice in its administration.

The convention then demanded that elections be held in 1871, as required by the constitution of 1869, despite the legislature's setting this aside. If elections were not held, Pease and the others suggested a "taxpayers' revolt." They did not advocate mob action, but suggested that injunctions and court action be instituted and fought in every county, while payments were held up.

Davis reacted characteristically to the orderly meeting in Austin. He had

Radical leaders assemble a huge crowd of singing, turbulent Negroes in Austin; he marched at their head through the streets to the Capitol. At the Capitol steps, Davis addressed the throng.

"The temple of freedom is being defiled by taxpayers!" he roared to the assembled Negroes. "It is up to you, my colored brethren, to purify the place!" At the Governor's command, the mob formed in double ranks. "March around the building singing those glorious hymns of freedom, with which you all are so familiar."

An Austin newspaper printed these remarks, and also the events of the next few hours: "Thereupon, this squad . . . the most ignorant, superstitious, and servile representatives of the race . . . marched around the building, at the hour of midnight, singing 'John Brown's Soul is Marching On,' and 'Rally Round the Flag, Boys.' "

A number of papers were "aghast that such rabble was countenanced by the Governor of the State of Texas."

The capitol was thus purified, but the taxpayers' revolt prevailed. It forced Davis to call for elections in 1871, rather than wait a year as scheduled by the Davis law of 1870.

It was apparent that Conservative Republicans and Democrats were ceasing to fight the war and were fuzing against the Carpetbaggers. At Seguin, east of San Antonio, a great fusion rally was held. Ex-Confederate officers and staunch Unionists who had not spoken to each other for years now solemnly shook hands. Radical leaders rode to Austin, expressing fright. Davis himself was worried. He now issued an election order to the state Adjutant General: all peace officers, militia, and State Guard personnel were to conduct the polls, and police the "conduct of the people." He threatened to declare martial law, under the Militia Bill, in any county where disorder prevailed. In effect, Union soldiers were to be replaced in this election by Davis police.

The effect of this order was explosive. Conservative Republican newspapers printed denunciations: "It is impossible for us to express the indignation which it has aroused. . . . Governor Davis and his satraps may learn to their cost, that the People of Texas cannot and will not always submit to their arbitrary usurpations and tyrannical acts!"

Ex-Governor A. J. Hamilton openly campaigned for the Democrats. Almost all the moderate and conservative native Unionists deserted with him. Two enormously influential newspapers, which suddenly found plenty of funds, began to print Democratic news and doctrines. The San Antonio *Herald* and Austin *Democratic Statesman* overcame the advantage Davis had enjoyed through the Printing Act and his controlled press.

Meanwhile, the Carpetbagger group—"Davis' plunderers and office-holders, the Morgan Hamilton honest faction, and the railroad-bought boys"—were angry and quarreling among themselves. Democrats and Conservative Republicans had only one real fear, that they would be defrauded again.

The San Antonio *Herald* reported that in Harris County (Houston) ". . . Colored voters never die nor remove. Of 1,500 white voters registered in 1868, which was half the real number, 250 had died or removed, including a prominent merchant now living in the city. Of 2,400 Negroes registered in 1868, of whom not more than 1,000 ever lived in the county, one had died, one removed."

In these years, there had been a crying need for a genuine state police force. The frontier, the aftermath of the Civil War, the crumbling of old society and standards, and hordes of bitter and unemployed soldiers from both armies, all created conditions approaching anarchy in some parts of Texas. In many counties, armed mobs of desperadoes held local citizens and sheriffs in virtual submission, as at Lampasas in west Texas. Davis' State Police had moved courageously against criminals in certain cases, and it had done some good work. Thousands of arrests had been made, and eight police officers killed in the line of duty. But two things destroyed the effectiveness of the State Police: Davis gave the badge to Negroes and paranoids and to a considerable number of criminal men; he also used the State Police as a political tool of repression.

As the *Democratic Statesman* reported: "The Adjutant General picks out some poor devil in the street who has not a dime in the world and tells him he would like to make a policeman out of him." The police were poorly paid, often unpaid, and they were overcharged and bilked as well. They had to pay for all their equipment—a $30 carbine was sold to them at $40. Three dollars deposit was withheld for their badge or shield. The treasury warrants with which they were paid depreciated to half their face value. Few reputable Texans would serve.

No institution in Texas ever aroused so much hostility and hatred as the Davis Police. The documented stories of oppressions and incidents are almost endless; the record of a few events tells the tale.

At Galveston in 1871, Governor Davis took personal command of the city police under the Militia Bill, and put this force under the orders of State Police Captain George Farrow. The reason was that a great political rally was being held, and the Governor wanted to keep "order." He did not consult Mayor Summerville, Judge Sabin, or Judge Dodge, the legally constituted local authorities. The local Conservatives were silenced and crushed.

In a scene described as "pandemonium" by a paper, two Radicals, both Negroes, were nominated by "acclamation" by the Party convention. A Conservative, Nelson, shouted that this was a "put-up job." The State Police, under a Negro sergeant, cut off the gaslights and drove the convention out on the streets before the nomination could be overturned or questioned.

When Conservatives tried to hold a rump convention and choose an opposition slate, they were rousted out again by the police. In other conventions, the police impounded or destroyed written ballots.

At another rally, when a Texas Negro tried to speak up for the Democratic Party in Austin, the city marshal strode to the platform and struck him with a whip. State Police stood by, laughing, ready to protect the marshal from the crowd. This meeting ended in a near-fatal shooting scrape between Radical Ratcliff Platt, chairman of the county executive committee, and editor John Caldwell of the *Democratic Statesman.*

At Dallas, a Negro orator also spoke up for Democrats. A mob of other Negroes descended on him, screaming, "Kill the damn dog! Shoot the ————hypocrite!" A deputy sheriff drew his pistol to protect the speaker and was arrested by the State Police for inciting violence. A few white men hustled the speaker away and protected him with guns against knives and razors.

At Paris, two policemen took a young man out of his home and shot him in the back, before witnesses.

At Marshall, two Negro officers killed another white man, an unarmed teen-ager, who ignored arrest. There were fourteen such murders in all.

A real calamity occurred in Limestone County in the fall of 1871. In the town of Groesbeck, a citizen named Applewhite was murdered on the street by four Negro State Police, who apparently were drunk. According to reliable witnesses, one killer shouted, "There is another white son of a bitch I want to kill! I will have the town flowing with white blood before morning!" Flourishing pistols, the police barricaded themselves in the mayor's office, shooting at random at people who came out into the street.

Mayor Zadek ordered all citizens to arm themselves, but despite flaring anger he was able to keep control. Zadek said there would be no mob action; the killers would be arrested according to the law. While a posse was organized, the four police escaped out of town and rode to a Negro settlement. Here they gathered a large body of their fellows.

However, two of the killers were taken by the sheriff and lodged in jail. Although there was some rumbling in the Negro community, Groesbeck was quiet.

In this atmosphere, Radical leaders wrote to Governor Davis that Negroes were not going to be allowed to vote in the crisis. Although the evidence was entirely otherwise—no white *wanted* the Negroes to vote, but no one had broached doing anything about it—Davis reacted violently.

He declared Limestone and neighboring Freestone counties in insurrection and under martial law. He issued a proclamation with inflammatory charges. He did not bother to notify the legislature of this act.

Habeas corpus was suspended in the affected counties, the State Police were sent in, and a fine of $50,000—3 percent on all taxable property—was levied. There was no resistance; the State Police spent their time riding about the counties collecting the fine. It was collected by a police captain and a few men, visiting each homestead in turn.

This was not an isolated case. Huntsville was put under martial law and cowed. So was Walker County. Martial law was declared frequently, and noticeably where anti-Davis elements were vocal or strong. The great bitterness was caused by the fact that in virtually every case, the proclamations were unnecessary. They were political.

L. H. McNelly, who was badly wounded and almost killed while acting against desperadoes as a State Police captain, in an unguarded moment gave a Galveston reporter a damaging view of Davis' declarations of martial law. When asked about conditions in Walker County, which the Governor described as far gone in armed rebellion, McNelly, one of the few honest police officers, suggested the real reason was "money." The Adjutant General was then riding through Walker county with "seven or eight men," collecting fifty cents on each assessed $100 valuation.

These fines were assessed on every resident of the county and collected at pistol point. McNelly drawled that if the county was really in rebellion, Adjutant General Davidson would need an army. When this report was printed, McNelly was forced to retract and claim he had been misquoted.

These practices and perversions of the police power were enormously destructive of law and order. There was hardly a prominent, respected citizen, editor, or minister of religion in Texas who had anything but contempt for the State Police. The statement of one Texas historian that this emboldened actual desperadoes everywhere is, if anything, an understatement of the case. Criminality, in most occupied or oppressed countries, tends to become respectable if it is combined with resistance to corrupt authority. This happened.

In September, 1871, John Wesley Hardin, who already had considerable reputation as a gunman and was a known desperado, was arrested by two Negro State Policemen at Gonzales. Although both officers "had the drop" on Hardin—their pistols were on him and his was in his belt—he easily drew and shot them both dead. When the news of this spread about town, a group of citizens gathered about Hardin, and together they "declared openly against negro or Yankee mob rule and misrule in general," as Hardin himself told the story. "We at once got about twenty-five men, good and true, sent for negroes to come along, that we would not leave enough of them to tell the tale . . . from that time on we had no negro police in Gonzales."

The use of black police was too much of a "setting of the bottom rail on the top." Any criminal who shot one turned into a sort of hero.

The elections of 1871 were for Congress. Although armed State Police stood around every polling place and broke up political rallies and demonstrations, this year thousands of white Democrats streamed to the polls.

Davis canvasses threw out thousands of votes, including the entire returns of Limestone, Brazos, Bowie, and Marion counties, on specious grounds. Despite this, the Democrats carried every Congressional seat. In a state-wide vote of 125,812, the Democratic candidates won by a majority of 24,279.

The Radicals disputed one seat, that of William T. Clark against D. C. Giddings.

Governor Davis issued a certificate of election to Clark, the Radical, over Giddings, the Democrat. The contest went on in courts and in Congress for some months, until, on the overwhelming evidence, Giddings was seated.

In the aftermath of this dispute, the United States District Court in Texas indicated Davis for vote fraud and for issuing fraudulent election certificates, both offenses under the Federal Enforcement Act. Garland, the Federal District Attorney, was a Republican, but he had no intention of quashing these indictments. Garland had expressly warned Davis against issuing the false certificate when Davis had "tried him out" after the election.

The Governor's confidence in going ahead was well founded. The Washington *Chronicle,* a Republican paper in the capital, printed that the indictment was "obviously meant as an insult to President Grant." In very similar circumstances in Arkansas, Grant had removed both a Federal district attorney and a U.S. marshal who had presented evidence against Governor Powell Clayton of that state. Now, Davis, Senator J. W. Flanagan, and Texas Secretary of State Newcomb, together with the deposed Congressman, Clark, wrote the President to dismiss Garland.

Morgan Hamilton heard the rumors, and went to the United States Attorney General. The honest Radical said bluntly that Garland's dismissal from office would be in fact telling all Federal officers to ignore dirty work where high Party politicians were concerned.

Hamilton then departed Washington on a brief trip. The day he left the capital the President dismissed Garland and appointed a replacement. The appointment was rushed through the Senate before the Texas Senator returned.

When the Davis election fraud case came up, the new Federal attorney presented a very strange case. No documentary evidence was presented to the jury; it had somehow been mislaid. Nor was the principal witness for the prosecution called to testify. Davis was acquitted.

Now, the Davis administration was beginning to show the strains of several years in office. Despite high tax collections, the treasury was bankrupt. This fact startled a number of Radicals in the Texas House. They formed an investigating committee, which reported "reckless disorder in the treasury" and the regular use of public funds for "private ends." Treasurer George Honey kept few books. An indictment was prepared for him, but Davis had this quashed.

The Radicals now had to face their second national election. They approached the fall of 1872 with anger and dread. One problem was that too many former supporters, even Radicals, were demanding honesty and cooperating with the enemy. It was still possible to surround polls with Negro police, but it was becoming impossible to pull the shenanigans of 1868 and 1869. There was even a certain coolness emanating toward the Texas statehouse from Washington.

Radicals ran on the "just and honest" administration of U. S. Grant, and on the "personal integrity and incorruptibility" of E. J. Davis, as their platform read. Swarming Democrats gathered at Corsicana, vowing to "remove the abuses under which our people labor."

Just before the election, Adjutant General James Davidson suddenly departed the state. A hasty check of the State Police chief's accounts revealed a shortage of $34,434.67. General Davidson turned up some time later in Belgium, whence he never returned. The State Police again surrounded the polls on election day, but there were visible signs of confusion and morale failure in their ranks.

The votes were counted with the usual problems, but Democrats threw the state to Horace Greeley over Grant, and elected a majority of the state legislature. They won a large edge in the House, and a majority of three in the state senate. The governorship was not at stake.

The thirteenth legislature approached Austin with more determination than rejoicing. There was deep sentiment to impeach Davis—the Democrats and Conservatives had both the evidence and the voting strength. But caution won out. A very real fear of Presidential intervention pervaded the state. Everywhere, men said that Washington would reimpose military rule if its friend in the governor's mansion were touched. All through these years there was a noticeable hesitation on the part of Democrats to assert their rights. Their former humiliations and the constant appellation of "rebels" hurled at them hurt—and few of them felt they had any hope of justice from the North. Only slowly did the term "reb" assume intimations of distinction, and the old "rebel" spirit break forth.

The "rebel legislature" contented itself with demolishing the Radical program. One by one, every Radical act was repealed. The School Act was revised—there was too much good in it for the destruction some wanted: to wipe out the educational bureaucracy and return the schools to local, county control.

In a scene of great emotion, the Police Act was overturned. The House went against it by 58-7, and the Senate by 18-7, thus passing the repeal over Davis' veto. Significantly, most Republicans joined the Democrats; only diehards dared to vote for the Davis Police.

John Henry Brown, who authored the repeal, wired his hometown newspaper: "The police law is abolished over the Governor's veto. Glory to God in the highest; on earth peace, good will towards men." One editor became almost incoherent over the news. He wrote: "The people of Texas are today delivered from as infernal an engine of oppression as ever crushed any people beneath the heel of God's sunlight. The damnable police bill is ground beneath the heel of a indignant legislature."

Word of the demise spread from town to town like wildfire. Bonfires were lit, saloons were packed, guns were shot off in some localities till dawn. Former State Policemen sensibly disappeared. As one wrote sourly in his letter of termination: "I find great rejoicing over the repeal of the Police law, by the Ku Klucks, murderers, and thieves." No doubt there was. But the whole population seems to have rejoiced as well.

Davis had to run for reelection in 1873. The hostile legislature redistricted the state, simplified the registration procedures, and called for polls to open on the first Tuesday in December.

James Throckmorton, John H. Reagan, and a number of prominent Democrats nominated a Confederate veteran, Richard Coke, for governor. By this time, the Conservative Republicans had disappeared; most shunned the term and joined the Democrats. E. J. Davis still possessed great power. He had thousands of appointed officeholders, the Negro vote, and Federal influence. But the Democrat Party approached the December election as a great crusade.

Rupert Richardson wrote of the election of 1873: "The genius of legality had forsaken the people; men practiced fraud unashamed." What seems to have happened is that the Carpetbaggers had taught the Texans how. Democrat politicos bluntly indicated that power would be won depending on who outfrauded whom. No practice was ignored.

Negroes who were being organized by Democrats were threatened with death by the Loyal League. Democrats rode into Negro settlements and gun on hip ordered blacks to stay away from the polls. There was terror, intimidation, and some murders on both sides. White men in some counties pulled guns on Davis officials conducting the polls. Unregistered whites and boys years under the legal age were voted. Desperadoes, thieves, planters, sweaty farmers, and ministers of the gospel damned black Republican rule and voted Democrat. Coke won, by more than two to one.

The great drama was not yet over. Davis, now claiming an irregularity in the election laws, tried to invalidate the result in the state supreme court.

This was a conspiracy to set aside the election. E. J. Davis himself had proposed the Texas election codes and signed them into law; the test case that the Radicals presented to the courts was planned before the election was held. The state supreme court was Davis-appointed. On January 5, 1874, the court declared the election law was unconstitutional, and that the results of the December balloting were invalid. This ruling would have prevented Democrats from assuming almost every office in the state, because the Democrats had won them all.

The supreme court's order was not resisted—it was ignored. In January, all over Texas the newly elected officials went to their offices and took them over. In some areas, ominous crowds gathered behind them. Although Davis issued a proclamation forbidding the new officials to act, or the new fourteenth legislature to sit, there was no one to enforce either order. Public offices changed hands. The people accepted the new officers and obeyed them.

Meanwhile, the new legislature and many prominent Texans moved on Austin. The San Antonio *Herald* expressed the dominant mood: "If Texas is a State, and if her citizens are men, Coke will be inaugurated, and the Fourteenth Legislature will sit."

Davis and his coterie were determined not to give up power. The governor played his trump card—he wired the President of the United States for military assistance to "apprehend violence and put down insurrection." In very similar circumstances in Louisiana, Grant had set aside a Democratic triumph, and Davis apparently had every confidence this would happen again.

A concurrent drama was acted out in Washington. The Texas Congressmen, Hancock and Giddings, saw the President. They showed him copies of the state constitution and the election law. Grant read these carefully, then remarked that the proper time to have disputed them in court was before, not after, the elections. Grant did not attempt to rule on the legal aspects, but he gave every indication he sniffed a rat. He told the Texans he would not send Federal troops.

Later on the same day, January 12, 1874, Senator J. W. Flanagan had an audience with the President. Flanagan made a strong effort to persuade Grant to go to Davis' aid. Grant said two things that were very significant: he did not want another Louisiana fiasco, where the Federal government had overturned an election with bayonets, and he had to think of the Congressional elections this year. The country as a whole was tired of the military occupation in the South. With some asperity, the President told Flanagan that Davis had been decisively beaten and the time had come "for him to get out of the way."

Flanagan then wired certain friends in Austin to "withdraw." The game was up.

Grant wired Davis also: ". . . The call [for troops] is not made in accordance with the Constitution of the United States . . . would it not be prudent, as well as right, to yield to the verdict of the people as expressed by their ballots?" As a Northern historian expressed it, Grant and the North were not prepared to refight the Civil War.

Davis did not accede. Now, in Texas, a dangerous situation was brewing. Richard Coke, the Confederate veteran, conferred with men he knew and trusted about taking over the state government peaceably. These men were Generals Henry McCulloch and Hardeman; the sheriff of Travis County, Zimpleman; and Colonel John S. Ford. Coke wanted these former officers, who were local heroes, to try to control the public. He intended to be inaugurated; he intended the new legislature to convene, and he expected Davis to use force to prevent this. All the Texans agreed that Davis would try to use an outbreak of fighting as an excuse for Yankee intervention. They agreed to move quietly and peacefully. At this time, they did not know of Grant's wire to Davis.

Acting quickly, armed citizens acting for Coke took possession of the legislative chambers in the Capitol building. They repelled an attempt of Radicals to enter by force. Police acting under Davis' orders and parties of armed Radicals gathered in the Capitol basement. Austin had divided into two armed camps, with the old and new governors, and both the fourteenth legislature and a rump of the old thirteenth claiming to be the legal regime.

On January 15, groups of Negroes from the country further down the Colorado River entered Austin. Davis' Adjutant General armed these newcomers with rifles from the state arsenal.

It appeared that bloodshed was inevitable.

One Major Russell, from the staff of General Augur, commander of the U.S. Army Department of Texas, arrived in the capital. A rumor spread among Coke's people that Russell had told Davis the general had instructions from the President to declare Federal martial law. All believed that Davis intended to provoke violence. But despite some very delicate incidents, Coke kept control. His officers, who more and more resembled a convention of Confederate survivors, kept the populace quiet. At one point some Radicals, under a Carpetbagger Union officer named De Gress, aimed a cannon at the Capitol. But Coke's men had spiked it earlier, and hugely enjoyed the frustration of Davis' men.

The Governor ordered out the local militia, called the Travis Rifles, only to see the company, surrounded by citizens led by Sheriff Zimpleman, go over to the other side. Davis apparently could not understand the changed temper of the North or realize that the great experiment in Texas was over. He telegraphed the President again, for troops.

Grant did not deign to reply personally. His answer came through the Attorney General of the United States: ". . . Your right to the office of the Governor at this time is at least so doubtful, that he does not feel warranted in furnishing United States troops to aid you in holding further possession of it."

Governor Davis now had the choice of starting a war to hold his office against impossible odds, with no help in prospect from his Northern friends, or of surrender. He felt that Grant had virtually ordered him to surrender. His organ, the *Daily State Journal,* expressed Radical feelings in a bitter sentence: "The courts are powerless; the government of the state has been forcibly usurped, and President Grant has backed the usurpation."

From his office he could see the stacked arms of Texas militia—stacked against him. Old Rip Ford, tall, grim, still ruddy-faced and handsome at sixty, was marching toward the Capitol at the head of an armed, angry, but disciplined body of men. They were singing "The Yellow Rose of Texas" in a mighty roar.

Davis surrendered. He vacated his offices on Monday, January 19, 1874. He did not present Coke with a key, but that did not stop the ebullient Texans. On the orders of a state senator from east Texas, the door was broken down, and Richard Coke went in. The secretary of state, a die-hard Unionist, was ousted from his desk.

The militia paraded with music to the Capitol, where a salute of 102 guns was fired. The legislature passed a resolution thanking President U. S. Grant for his decision. Coke and his lieutenant governor, Hubbard, addressed a deliriously happy throng from the Capitol steps.

The first phase of the Civil War in Texas was over. The next phase was to last at least a hundred years.

23

THE RESTORATION

> *He [President Grant] says he opposed the Fifteenth Amendment and thinks it was a mistake, that it had done the Negro no good, and had been a hindrance to the South, and by no means a political advantage to the North.*
>
> ENTRY IN THE DIARY OF SECRETARY OF STATE
> HAMILTON FISH, DATED JANUARY 17, 1877

IN January, 1874, Richard Coke and his band of joyous Democrats at last had control of the never-again-quite-so-sovereign state of Texas. Their euphoria was to be short. They had inherited not the whirlwind but what the long storm had left behind. The state was ruined economically; only now had cotton production reached what it had been in 1860—500,-000 bales. These losses could be restored. There was political, judicial, and social damage no one could repair.

The next few years must be interpreted not according to later views but in the light of the foregoing fifteen years. Texans now began a long, detailed, and exhaustive program that was nothing short of a rebellion against government itself. If between 1874 and 1876 Texas turned its back on much of the 19th century, the great majority of Texans had seen little in the postwar world to admire. They had acquired an abiding prejudice against centralized government of the state and against the powers of government at any level. Government had done them nothing good.

The state was disastrously in debt. The Carpetbaggers collected $4,000,000 in taxes, but borrowed $3,000,000 more. Coke found current receipts in 1874 would cover only half the programmed expense. To make things worse, the national panic of 1873 now hit Texas hard. Texas could take one of two courses: try to prop up the present system by finding new funds, in a country where industry and commerce hardly existed and land prices were falling, or simply call a halt to it all.

They chose to wield a radical knife.

State expenditures were slashed, without mercy. Salaries were cut, the school funds stopped, although both measures caused considerable anguish. However, history had shown that compromise in such a program was fatal; expenditures could only be reduced if the frame of mind that produced them was changed.

No way to reduce costs was ignored. The state prison system was made self-supporting, by leasing out convict labor to private employers. This caused hideous abuse, and doubled the convict death rate, and was finally abolished in 1883. But for some years money was saved. Pensions, to Revolution veterans, were no longer paid in money but in grants of public land. A hundred other economies were introduced. These economies not only began to balance the budget, they dismantled government as a side-effect. The state treasury was able to go on a cash basis in 1879. By this time, too, conditions had eased. Cotton production had grown rapidly, and cattle money was bringing gold and silver to the state.

Public parsimony, however, was popular over-all. The basic reason was simple: Texas was an agrarian state, and now the government was again in the hands of farmers. However much small farmers believed in education, pensions, or adequate public salaries, the taxes fell on them and their land.

While the legislature sliced away at costs, it took up other problems. Foremost was the restoration of law and order, followed by replacement of the constitution of 1869. The Texas Rangers were brought back; there would never again be any organization in Texas called a "state police." The Frontier Battalion was organized. Between 1874 and 1880, both on the Indian and Mexican borders, the Rangers had their great days and were a spectacular success. Both Indians and internal anarchy disappeared. Order was restored first, then law.

The judiciary had to be dismantled. The terms of the Davis-appointed courts were closed. Oran M. Roberts became Chief Justice, presiding over a new bench. Further, the legislature removed most of the Republican district judges around the state.

Delegates to a constitutional convention assembled in 1875. Not one man who had written the constitution of 1869 sat in this delegation. The convention was composed almost entirely of old Texans: John Henry Brown, Sterling C. Robertson, son of the empresario, Rip Ford, John H. Reagan (Ex-Postmaster General of the Confederacy), and a bevy of generals who had worn the gray. Of the ninety members, more than twenty had held high rank in the C.S.A. This was a restoration convention.

There were forty-one farmers, twenty-nine lawyers, seventy-five Democrats, and fifteen Republicans, six of whom were Negro. Congressman W. P. McLean sounded the keynote of the day: "If future State Governments prove burdensome and onerous, it ought not to be the fault of this Convention."

The document rewritten at this convention made it almost impossible for government in Texas to be burdensome or onerous in the future. It was a landowners' group, including forty members of the Grange. Its first act was to reduce its own per diem allowance to five dollars. Its second was to vote down a motion to have proceedings printed, because a public stenographer cost ten dollars a day. Then it proceeded to write what was to remain the fundamental law of Texas for the next one hundred years.

This was an antigovernment instrument; too many Texans had seen what government could do, not for them but to them. It tore up previous frameworks, and its essential aim was to try to bind all state government within very tight confines. The bicameral legislature was continued—thirty-one senators and not more than 150 representatives—but the term of senators was reduced, requiring election every four years. Biennial sessions replaced the annual assemblies under the instrument of 1869. This was done, as one Texan said, not only to save money, "But the more the damn legislature meets, the more Goddamned bills and taxes it passes!"

The dominant spirit was to allow the state government no real latitude to act. The powers of the legislature were much reduced. It could not incur a debt of more than $200,000, come what may. It could not impose taxes of more than fifty cents on the $100. Property could be taxed only in proportion to its value. The credit of the state was not to be lent, nor any appropriation made for private purpose—and "private" was interpreted in the Roman way. The legislature could appoint no office or commission lasting beyond two years. Finally, it had no powers to suspend habeas corpus, even under martial law.

The executive was equally, or even more, curtailed. The terms of all state officers were set at two years, though no prohibition was made against reelection. Almost all state offices were made elective; thus the power of a governor to appoint an administration was denied. The Texas governor was made one of the weakest in the United States. He was denied authority over both state and local officials; he was made, in fact, a peer among equals. The lieutenant governor, who could call up legislation in the Senate, was to be henceforth a far more powerful man. On top of this, the constitution slashed the governor's salary by 20 percent.

The governor was left awesome responsibilities but few powers, which ever afterward few of his constituents could really understand.

Judgeships, for similar reasons, were made elective, including the bench of the supreme court. No judge who had to run for reelection regularly was expected to decide cases against the popular feeling, on some new-fangled point of law.

None of these changes was controversial; they were what the people wanted. One popular provision failed. This would have required a poll tax payment for voting rights. Another amendment, female suffrage, was hooted down. The real controversy in 1875 concerned the public schools. The convention went on record supporting these, but what actually emerged from committee was a compromise.

Centralization of school supervision was abolished; the state system was destroyed in favor of local systems. Compulsory school attendance was also dropped. The revenues from a $1 poll tax, and some general revenue, was earmarked for public education—the amount was to be argued bitterly for years. The public school system and new university system, however, were endowed with a vast acreage of public lands, about 42,000,000 acres. The lands originally set aside for educational endowments, which had been in fertile north-central Texas, were now exchanged for sections in the arid, still unsettled west, which were still unappropriated domain. Here the school system suffered a great, immediate loss, but one which, ironically, was to be more than made right by future discoveries of petroleum. The tenor of this legislation also revealed what was to be a continuing pattern in Texas. Huge endowments were set aside for building funds, but very little was provided for annual maintenance of the system from tax monies.

The state road system begun by the Radicals was also abolished. Personal service was resubstituted in lieu of road taxes. This was a regression, but railroads were made common carriers, following an example in other states. For many years, however, no regulation of railroads was enforced.

The constitution of 1876 was in spirit and letter an instrument of the older, agrarian South, not that of an emerging industrial state. It was designed to protect the farmer and landowner, not Yankee-dominated banks and industries. Although nothing in the constitution was actually hostile to business or corporate enterprise—this came later, with the rise of Populism—in many ways it slowed and hampered industrialization and financial growth.

The emergence of Texas into the modern world was presided over by farmers, and not by businessmen. Texas was a completely agricultural region, and Texans determinedly held on to their heritage. As one Texas historian wrote:

> All in all the constitution complied with public opinion quite faithfully. Biennial sessions of the legislature, low salaries, no registration requirement for voters, precinct voting, abolition of the road tax . . . a homestead exemption clause, guarantees of a low tax rate, a more economical school system, with schools under local control, a less expensive court system, popular election of officers—all these were popular measures with Texans in 1876. The constitution was a logical product of its era.

Certain other things, which were included in, or grew out of this outlook, should be mentioned. The state immigration bureau, which brought new people west, and which all agreed did useful work, was abolished because of its operating expense. Farmers did not believe in tax-supported public works, if the taxes had to be levied directly on them. This was an attitude that was to last.

Other measures eventually incorporated into Texas law grew out of this restoration, though the most severe restrictions placed on finance and industry came as a result of the long Greenback and farmers' revolts of the coming years. The banking codes, which had always been restrictive in Texas, prevented the establishment of branch banks with the exception of subsidiaries on military posts. This rule, together with the fact that in Texas no horse or homestead could be attached for private debt, nor any wage or salary garnisheed, gave farmers immense protection. But it made the rise of any really significant financial institutions impossible. Corporations as well as people could plead usury in Texas, under low legal interest rates. No industrial state ever adopted such codes.

The constitution of 1876 was also a very imperfect instrument, which required amendment at the polls for almost every conceivable change. California had a similar constitution, but there was one enormous difference between the two states: in Texas, traditionally, the great majority of proposed significant changes were regularly voted down. A lasting philosophy that no legislature or governor was to be trusted kept Texas more a popular than a representative democracy, and it kept society itself, rather than laws or government, in control. The governor had no power over county sheriffs, who were subject, naturally, to local forces; and with the legislature the governor was merely another equal among peers. Most appointive offices were outside his control. A strong, charismatic governor could have influence on the voters, but no man on earth could really govern the state.

Ironically, the governor continued to be thought of as the leader and the focus of state politics, because most Texans failed to see the true state of affairs. The clearest indication, however, was that in Texas men who preferred power to local prestige went to Washington. Traditionally, Senators became more powerful, even within the state, that the incumbent in Austin, who more often than not was a symbol of forces beyond his control.

In the 19th century, and for the first three decades of the 20th, the national government of the United States impinged less on its citizens than any in the Western world, except the Swiss. The national government, and its industrial power structure, set important national policy, but it collected almost no taxes, nor did it interfere or try to influence the citizens' daily life. It left almost all decisions affecting society to local option.

Because of this, important changes in America in this era were made by the states themselves, or not at all. The constitution, outlook, and philosophies of 1876 brought Texas into the modern world with very much the viewpoints of 1836, because in Texas these did not substantially change.

Other products of the era were as pervasive and lasting, if not so easily discerned as law.

Although Texas elections had been rough and ready in the early days, they do not seem to have been violent, or attended by wholesale fraud. After Reconstruction, they were never entirely free of either. Some lessons were learned and habits acquired too thoroughly between 1867 and 1873. The trouble to the body politic spawned these years cannot be overestimated.

The great family and factional feuds, such as the Sutton-Taylor fight and the Mason County War in which men were shot in the 20th century, were born in Reconstruction politics. Virtual wars continued in many Texas counties for years between Democratic and Republican factions, usually under different names. Old Party, New Party, Jayhawks, Blues, all packed pistols to the polls. Fraud became a fact of political life; ballot stuffing and even the theft of ballot boxes were common. Both violence and cynicism was a part of local politics. A striking characteristic of Texas politicians and leaders, almost never articulated where it might be damaging, was an underlying lack of sympathy with democracy as it was interpreted in the North. The very concept of the rule of law—as opposed to the rule of order—was secretly held in considerable contempt. Texas politics, out of the Reconstruction period, became increasingly devoted to the seizure or retention of power, devoid of any definite ideology beyond the underlying feelings of the tribal mass. This led to bitter factionalism, but also to certain political strengths. There was little confusion over goals, or how to get them.

Texans developed political leadership untrammeled by any ideological unreality, though circumscribed by local prejudices. In an increasingly one-party state, they built personal, rather than party, machines. They continued in the traditional path of American politics, in which the emphasis was not upon programs, but personal power. This power, however, because of the constitution and the public feeling, was exercised within severe bounds. A Texas politico could be ruthless during elections, amiable and reasonable in office.

Following Reconstruction, there was a pervading hostility to the North, not so much against the Northern people personally as against their instrument, the Federal apparatus. The great fear of the Strict Constructionalist Democrats—that the institutions of the South would be dismantled if it ever lost Federal control—came true. After Reconstruction, it was difficult for old-line Texans to see the Congress, the Presidency, or the Judiciary as guarantors of constitutional rights. All had combined, in Texan eyes, to enforce regional prejudices and popular passions on the state. One result was that the Northern political party, the Republicans, was virtually destroyed. The party never built an infrastructure except on Negro votes. Since the national Republican Party remained in power for many years, what grew up in Texas slowly was a Federal patronage machine. Texas Republican leaders were more interested in holding such patronage control than in reviving the horse that Davis killed. The stigma, after the Davis regime, of the Republican name was so marked that while off and on thousands of Texans voted Republican, they invariably called themselves pure Democrats.

Almost the entire body of Conservative Republicans became official Democrats, without changing a single outlook or view. Nowhere was this more marked than in the Texas hill country, where local Republican officials invariably filed as Democrats, then and later. Pease, Hamilton, and Throckmorton led the way.

Texans returned to Washington with full respect for Northern, and Federal, power. They denied its right to regulate society except within broad parameters. But out of experience and racial memory, Texans picked up pragmatism. The clear-eyed understanding of the goal of politics, power, and the love of intrigue that Texas politics engendered from Reconstruction days, served Texas' representatives well. A long series of Democratic pragmatists, not so much orators as manipulators, gradually came to wield enormous power. Their skills were born of necessity, out of a minority position, self-protection, and a cynicism born of bitter experience. They expected that in the natural course of events Texas would get a dirty deal from the North; their common course was to see, so far as possible, that it did not. They were backroom men, because the real powers in Texas, after 1876, were always backroom men; the governor was usually something of a Judas goat.

From Colonel House to John Nance Garner, and from Majority Leader Sam Rayburn to Lyndon Johnson in the Senate, the state produced men who learned their lessons in a hard, pragmatic, unidealistic school. These men had genuine influence eventually on the national scene. They could not get Texas out of the Union, but they could and did get a lot out of the Union for it.

In all these men, and most of their constituents, there remained a basic distrust for the morality-spouting, consciously superior, pervasively powerful North. Texans had to play the Northern game, and they played it well. But they did not have to pretend it was their own, except in public.

Whenever the North renewed any kind of pressure on Texas, social or political, this hostility intensified, though it rarely provoked outright resistance.

In 1873, and lasting for many years, a natural reaction began. Far from proclaiming *mea culpa* over Secession, it became something of an honor to have been a Confederate. Sam Bell Maxey, running as an "ultra-simon-pure-secession-anti-reconstruction Democrat," was sent by the legislature to the U.S. Senate in 1874. Throckmorton, running as a former brigadier, was sent to the House. He might have been elected governor, but in Congress Throckmorton voted too much like the Whig he once had been. Oran Roberts, the 1861 radical secessionist, now known as "The Old Alcalde," became governor in 1879. It was next to impossible to be elected to anything, unless the candidate had worn the gray.

However, the old South in Texas was dead. Ex-Confederates could be sent to Congress, but the plantation system, and the planters, could not be restored. A new system of agriculture now dominated the eastern regions of Texas, though in the west the family farm still prevailed. The new system was called sharecropping.

Sharecropping was less efficient than plantation agriculture, but it was a logical compromise with Emancipation. It was technically a form of tenantry, by which the man who worked the soil, in small plots, received somewhere between one-half and one-third its yield. Landowners, now mostly new men, provided seed, implements, and even housing to their tenants. The system, widespread by 1870, worked, but it had its flaws. The "deducts" as they were called, ate up large chunks of the tenants' shares; employers kept the books. The tenants, who were predominately Negro but included many whites, were in no sense free farmers, but took on the coloration of a peon class.

Thousands of poor whites were pushed into tenantry in these years. The Negroes had no other choice. The Federal government freed them in 1865; but in the era when Congress supplied forty millions in railroad subsidies, it could not find ten to provide the freedmen land. The Negro could not compete in white society, even had the white middle classes been willing to let him. He had no money; he could not procure credit; he could not, in most cases, read or write. There was no way the freedmen could enter the American money economy. They passed back into the peculiarly Texas form of peonage, which spread across much of the South; it was that, or starve. Ironically, some fared worse than before, because the old paternalism of the planter class was gone. A savage, but not untrue, saying was that the former slaves had gone from the status of prized animals to that of range beeves, given a plot and allowed to forage for themselves.

The net effect of the Fourteenth and Fifteenth Amendments in Texas was to disenfranchise Negroes and impose caste.

The implementation of the Amendments in the state was disastrous. This indicated that American political wisdom stopped short of understanding problems of ethnic differentiation, status, and class. Both Amendments—giving the freedmen civil rights as citizens and the franchise—might have been accepted had they been implemented everywhere equally, and had they not been imposed as punishment on what was thought to be an "arrogant, rebel, slavacratic class." The Northern leaders—though the evidence was clear enough in their own backyards—did not understand that the opposition to Negro equality was not from former slaveowners but from the whole broad spectrum of the white farming mass. Men who worked with their hands instinctively feared Negroes more than aristocrats. To couple Negro suffrage with white disenfranchisement can only be described as blindness, unless military rule was to be imposed on the South for at least a generation. Reform was possible. But the North forced a too-visible revolution, then found it never believed in forcing the revolution in the first place.

Rather surprisingly, because they were human, the former slaves behaved with reasonable decorum and good sense in the Reconstruction years. The situations that became utterly intolerable to whites—the Negro police, the Negro senators, the Negro soldiery quartered on their towns—were all brought about not by Negroes but by Southern Scalawags and Northern Caucasians. The state senator with whip scars on his back, now in waistcoat and high silk hat, and with Radicals fawning in his ear, understandably showed a childlike vanity, insolence, and fiscal irresponsibility. The State Policeman who went berserk had an impossible job; no police force can uphold the law if it is completely devoid of public respect. What was overlooked was that the pistols, badges, and senatorial bribes and watchchains were all handed to Negroes by whites, not to help the race but for partisan gain. The moral pigsties in Texas between 1867 and 1874 were made entirely by whites, but the Negroes were made to pay for them.

Corruption was identified even in the North with Negro suffrage. The New York *Tribune,* a former Abolitionist organ, printed that while Negroes had been allowed "to develop their latent capacities," they proved that "as a race they are idle, ignorant, and vicious." A hundred Northern leaders, from Grant down, said the same.

There was no love for the Negro in Texas in 1860, but Davis' use of Negro State Police made hatred of the race not only popular but patriotic. A white man who publicly abused a Negro in 1860 was regarded by men of good taste as a sort of swine. A few years later, there were decent men and women who willingly closed their ears to Negro screams.

First the new-citizen Negro was forced back on the farm, then he had to be circumscribed by caste. Citizenship had been conferred by fiat, but it was not likely to work; it had no American currency in use and wont. Readjustment was ticklish and painful for both black and white. The slave had known the code; now the freedman had to learn the limits of his "place." It would have been far healthier for all Americans, including the blacks, if they had understood that the imposition of caste was an almost inevitable human reaction, which had taken place many times before. Americans were human; the 18th century manifestos and the 19th century amendments could not change basic instincts in the human race. The white Texan was neither sadistic nor cruel in the main, nor had he any intention of destroying the black race. He did want domination, whether he could logically rationalize this or not.

What happened to the Negro was inevitable, once the North muddied the waters, then beat a strategic retreat. Still, establishing the caste system took thirty years. It was not consolidated at once; Negroes in Texas continued for some years to vote. Not until the new "black codes" and signs went up in the 1890's and early 1900's was the transformation complete.

The Northern retreat was as much political as emotional. Northern Democrats, eager to renew old alliances after Emancipation, studiously never brought up the question of Negro rights for almost seventy years. The Republican business and political community lost interest, after the first full glimpse of their Southern monster child. By then, they no longer needed the South, anyway.

As always in America, the full retreat from the great crusade of 1861–1869 had to be rationalized by the courts. During the 1870's the Supreme Court, in a series of decisions, made the actual state of affairs constitutionally palatable by emasculating the Fourteenth and Fifteenth Amendments. The escape clause was simple: neither amendment put the rights granted by it under Federal protection or jurisdiction. The decisions were accepted with cynical amusement by educated Texans, and with righteous joy by others. The way was open for Texas and other states to bar the Negro from civil rights and suffrage by a number of devious, ingenious, and effective ways, ranging from economic pressures to the poll tax and grandfather clause.

The great irony of Reconstruction was that it was so unnecessary. It settled nothing that had not already been settled in 1865.

There was a great and not glorious alteration in the lighting of the United States's broad Southern tier after 1850. This is reflected by far more than the physical destruction and psychic damage visited upon the South. Books of fiction and nonfiction dealing with Texas, for example, have only sold widely when covering the events up to 1845. High noon, in this part of America, is instinctively understood to be long arrived and passed, though no one has ever quite dared say so. The towns, the rivers, and long-galleried houses remained, but even the ghost of a Greek-styled democracy in America was dead. The Thermopylae of the Alamo somehow became lost in the gunsmoke fogs of Palmito Hill.

In the last days of 1860 a Southern orator tried to picture Americans of the year 2000:

> Extending their empire across this continent to the Pacific, and down through Mexico to the other side of the great gulf, and over the isles of the sea, they established an empire and wrought a civilization which has never been equalled or surpassed—a civilization teeming with orators, poets, philosophers, statesmen, and historians equal to those of Greece or Rome—and presented to the world the glorious spectacle of a free, prosperous, and illlustrious people.

There was much that was brutal, unlovely, illusionary and even ridiculous to that dream. But against the actual reality of the next century, it might well stand. Most ages see themselves as perfect, or striving for perfection, and rarely see their real flaws in time.

Whatever dream had made Texas the fastest-growing state, whatever fascination pulled men to the silvery Rio Grande, ended. From a hundred dusty, brooding, straggling little towns in the woods and prairies of eastern Texas, some vital element disappeared. Cotton still piled high on the wharves; steamboats still hooted on the water. But the ghost of that dream was all that was left, preserved in iron or bronze, gazing gloomily down from a hundred courthouse statues of Lee's soldiers or gleaming frostily in moonlight on memorials to the Confederate dead.

Part V

UNTIL DAY BREAKS AND DARKNESS DISAPPEARS: THE LAST FRONTIER

24

RED NIGGERS,
RED VERMIN

We have set up our lodges in these groves and swung our children from these boughs from time immemorial. When the game beats away from us, we pull down our lodges and move away, leaving no trace to frighten it, and in a while it comes back. But the white man comes and cuts down the trees, building houses and fences and the buffaloes get frightened and leave and never come back, and the Indians are left to starve. . . .

MUGUARA, CHIEF OF THE PENATEKA COMANCHES, TO THE TEXANS

The same sequence of events has ocurred repeatedly in man's history; an invader with superior cultural equipment supplants and replaces a technologically inferior group. If the inferior culture survives it frequently does so in the marginal areas not coveted by the invader.

W. W. NEWCOMB, AMERICAN ANTHROPOLOGIST

FOLLOWING Pontiac's great rebellion in 1763, the British Ministry ruling North America tried to strike some kind of balance between the new colonists and the old, the white man and the red. There was a serious problem in America, bloodiest then in Pennsylvania, centered on the struggle between Amerind and advancing Scotch-Irish Protestants across the western hills. The British government attempted to form a line of demarcation between European settlement and Indian hunting grounds. Borders were drawn, boundaries surveyed, and treaties signed by 1768.

One year later Daniel Boone blazed his fateful Kentucky trail. Here began the last, great bloody collision between the aborigines and new invaders, a brutal and brutalizing contest that was to last more than a hundred years. The struggle was to reach its climax on the windswept Plains. More blood would be shed in Texas than in any other place.

The pattern of this conflict was locked in place in the 18th century. The British government drew a line of demarcation; it could not enforce it. The British recognized certain Indian rights; it begrudged the 12,000 pounds annual cost of honoring them. The British government pledged protection for both white settler and Indian tribe; it failed them both. Lord Shelburne, believing that English expansion across the Alleghenies must inevitably expand British trade, agreed to the Indian treaties arranged by Superintendents Sir William Johnson and John Stuart with hypocrisy in his heart. When Washington replaced Whitehall, nothing changed. Treaty followed treaty; the temporary absences of war between the races were mistakenly called peace; and each new treaty or line of demarcation between red and white was merely a deferred death warrant for the Amerind.

It was inevitably so. To confirm the Indians in possession would have required the vast continent to be set aside "as a game preserve for squalid savages," in Theodore Roosevelt's words. This was asking too much of human nature. There was some such sentiment in the older-settled, status-quo-minded East, which was more rational and less imperial. But the newer West was democratic and characteristically aggressive; it formed a pressure group that could not be denied.

The Westerners' view of Indians as natural obstacles to progress, vermin rather than human, became the dominant American one. The courts, as always, eventually upheld the dominant view, in making the Indian a tenant at the white man's will.

Because the North American Indians were aboriginal, the normal patterns of human conquest—slavery or serfdom, the imposition of caste, or miscegenation—could not be workably applied. The white's way of developing the land destroyed it for the hunting Indian's use. The tribesmen, whose culture was profoundly different from the European, would neither subordinate nor adapt. The refusal was psychological, willful, and valiant, but it destroyed the Indian with his habitat; in comparison, the subordinated and transplanted Negro actually grew in numbers and thrived.

The Amerind would have been eliminated in any case, but how to do this remained a fundamental American problem for generations. American governments did try to afford both the tribesmen and the frontiersmen some protection but invariably failed them both. Because the United States was democratic and ruled by pressure groups, its government was never able to dictate to the Western whites or stop their advance along certain lines. Because America was antimilitarist in spirit, it never provided a proper army to police its ragged, bleeding frontier. Because American statesmen were fundamental hypocrites toward the basic drives of war and conquest in their own people, they perpetually lit the conference fires and proposed useless treaties for both sides. In the end the Amerind was nearly exterminated, but national policy forced the frontier whites to become deeply brutalized in the process.

In both Kentucky and Texas, for long years national policy let the Indians and white settlers fight it out. A stronger government would have made efforts to tidy up the bloody mess, and avoided the double trauma that hypocrisy and violence caused in the North American soul.

Nowhere was the frontier violence in America so bloody, or so protracted, as on the soil of Texas. If Kentucky was the key, Texas was the culmination of the inner American experience. For forty years, frontier defense was Texas' most crucial problem, and frontier warfare continued for four decades.

The conflict with the differentiated civilization of Mexico continued for even longer. Blood was still shed in the second decade of the 20th century, and tensions in the middle of that century had far from disappeared.

The Mexican-Indian warfare, taken together, spawned an almost incredible amount of violence across west and southwest Texas. Almost every ranch, every water hole, and every family had its record of gunshots in the night and blood under the sun. Violence became commonplace. Every Texan historian is aware of whole chunks of Texas history moved in fiction to other states, simply because the reiteration of violence and conflict on the soil of Texas became boring to Americans.

Because of this history, the dominant Texan viewpoint was not that Texans settled Texas, but they conquered it. Many other Americans have never been able to rationalize this in terms of a mythical North American mission in the world. Texas was never a refuge for the lowly, or oppressed, or a beacon proclaiming human rights. It was a primordial land with a Pleistocene climate, inhabited by species inherently hostile to the Anglo-Celtic breed. Some North Americans chose to conquer it, and in the process unquestionably came to look upon themselves as a sort of chosen race.

This sense of being a chosen people, which was tribal and biblical, was an enormous Texan strength rather than a weakness. It gave Anglo-Texans immediate moral superiority, in action, over their enemies. It led to high nobility and at times a valor almost beyond belief. It also produced brutal prejudice, and ethnic self-satisfaction that amounted to chauvinism. The whole feeling was guileless, and therefore guiltless. Hypocrisy toward warfare was never part of the Texan ethos. The generations that moved across the Sabine were already bred to certain hatreds and war. Their mothers and fathers had endured Indians as they endured winters and the typhoid; the sons and daughters were entirely convinced that life would be better once both plagues were conquered. Mexicans were a new experience, but the quirks of Mexican warfare—the parleys, the guile, and the frequent treacheries—were quickly learned. To hold this land, Texans developed the pervasive beliefs that Indians must be eliminated and Mexicans must be dominated. These views were not palatable to many other Americans, but they cannot be fairly rejected or criticized by those who failed to share the Texan experience. Once the future Texans committed themselves to moving onto Mexican soil and Indian range, such attitudes were inevitable, and necessary, if they were to prevail. There *was* a great struggle for this soil; palatable or not, this fact cannot be ignored.

The struggle, the violence, the tribal instincts, and the feeling for place that these engendered may have separated Texans in some ways from other North Americans. But they tended to make Texans closer, in most ways, to the rest of mankind. Texas experience, in the 19th century, permitted few illusions. Texans had to be pragmatic to prosper and warlike to stay alive. They had to be as purposeful as Israelis in the next century, and as brutal as the Normans, who brought order and a new civilization to Saxon England with the sword.

The State of Texas stands as a historic reminder that Americans, on these shores, did not create something entirely new, nor emerge entirely innocent, into the brave new world.

Historically, no people voluntarily permitted wholesale immigration of foreign stock into their territory unless they expected the immigrants to perform some sort of dirty work.

The Mexicans were no exception to the rule. The biggest factor in their decision in favor of Austin's colony was their fervent hope that the Americans would become a buffer between Mexicans and the Plains Indians. In the 18th century the Spanish had failed to win their Indian wars. In the 19th century, the Mexicans had allowed the situation to deteriorate. Vast areas of northern Mexico were virtually under a state of siege. Villages were depopulated, and peasants cowered in the adobe-walled towns.

This was a role Stephen Austin deliberately eschewed. He understood the Comanche problem; he wanted no part in it. In 1822, on his journey to Mexico, Austin was actually captured by a band of Indians on the Nueces above Laredo. He was not killed because he convinced the Comanches he was no Mexican. Both Comanches and Apaches, like many primitive peoples, were not basically hostile to all strangers. In 1822, the Americans, unlike Mexicans and a whole tier of Amerind tribes, had no Comanche history. Austin was determined not to let one develop, particularly while his colony was weak.

Austin's Indian policy was one of classic diplomacy: he made treaties with the distant Comanches, whom he feared; he both made treaties with and demonstrations of force against the weaker, less numerous Tonkawas and associated Wichita tribes; he sent the despised and verminous Karankawas on their last short slide to extinction. As a result, the Brazos-Colorado colony enjoyed peace, much to the disgust of the Mexican political chiefs and even some of Austin's own people.

Austin pacified the Mexicans, while San Antonio and Goliad were raided by Comanches, by promising action when his colony was strong enough. This was a classic ploy of diplomacy, too.

This was a happy state that could not last. Gradually, inevitably, the American colonists that poured in during the 1830's moved up the Texas rivers beyond the coastal prairies into the post-oak belts, into Comanche range. The Comanches at times agreed to treaties, but the Comanche peoples lived for raiding. Nor did they have European social organization. No chief could bind the whole people, only his own small band. And warriors went from band to band at will, for Amerind society on the Plains was truly democratic. No Comanche followed a chief he failed to respect. If white treaties were worthless because treaties were a part of white diplomacy, which changed with changes in relative strength, Indian pacts were likewise technically unworkable. This fact, peculiarly, was apparently never fully understood by either side.

When the Texas Revolution began in 1835, falling timber, rail fences, and log cabin dog-runs had already begun to disrupt the game trails far up the Brazos. Isolated travelers on the western edges of the colony had been killed. Beset by a Mexican invasion, the government at Washington-on-the-Brazos immediately sent emissaries to the Indians, seeking out the newly arrived powerful Cherokee nation in east Texas and the Comanches on the Plains beyond. Debates in the Texas convention show a fear of Indian attacks on the vulnerable Texan flank. In addition to the promises of peace, the revolutionary regime authorized a "ranging force" to guard the western frontier.

The Cherokees, a civilized tribe now trying to adopt many white ways, agreed to peace. The Comanches who could be reached did not. However, during the brief 1836 campaign, the Comanches and their Kiowa allies did not interfere. Although at this time the Plains Indians outnumbered all Texan whites and could muster a greater fighting force, the distant tribes were ignorant. They understood neither the Anglo-Mexican war nor their own eventual danger. War was the Comanche way of life, but formal, organized warfare in the European manner they did not understand, nor could they wage it.

However, the long saga of death on the Plains and prairie was about to begin.

In the year 1834, Elder John Parker took his family, really a clan of 30 people, up the Brazos, into the later Limestone County. Parker was a "hardshell" Baptist preacher out of Virginia by way of Tennessee. The hardshells were what their name implied; stubborn, hardy frontier folk, who believed in closed communion and suspected that even other Baptists might be bound for Hell. The Parkers found open, beautiful, rich country, alive with wildfowl, bear, and deer. The land was oak-dotted and grassy, ephemerally splashed in spring with deep blue pools of the flowers called bluebonnets by Scots pioneers. John Parker built a stockade on the Navasota River and named it Parker's Fort. Here the clan lived, staking out corn fields in the vicinity. There were then only two or three other cabins in the entire region.

On the morning of May 19, 1836, most of the Parker men went as usual to work their fields, which were out of sight of the stockade. Six men and the women and children were left behind.

About midmorning, a large party of Indians rode up to the stockade walls. They were Comanche braves, with some Kiowa allies, and a few Caddoans. These horsemen showed a dirty white flag and asked for water and a beef.

Benjamin Parker parleyed with them outside the walls. He told his brother Silas that he felt these Indians were hostile, but it would be better to avoid a war. Silas and he went outside again, although the others begged them not to go.

Parker apparently told the visitors he had no beeves. They became angry, and suddenly several Comanches pierced him with their lances. Silas ran for the fort, but was cut down. Two more men, named Frost, were killed in a melee at the gates. Then, shrieking, the Indians poured inside Parker's Fort.

Elder John Parker, his wife Granny, and several of the women tried to run. The Indians overtook them all. They stabbed John Parker, scalped him, then cut off his private parts. Granny Parker was stripped, pinned to the ground with a lance, and raped. Other women were attacked.

In the midst of this scene, the Parker men came running from the fields with rifles. Whooping, the raiders leaped on their horses and galloped off. They left behind five dead men and several badly wounded women, two of whom would die. Granny Parker, however, pulled the spear from her flesh; she was of a tough breed, and lived.

The Indians also took five captives: Rachel Plummer and her small son; Elizabeth Kellogg; and John and Cynthia Ann Parker, aged six and nine.

The Comanches rode north-northeast, toward the Trinity River. They halted once far out on the prairie to hold a ritual victory dance. All of the captives were tied cruelly with rawhide thongs and thrown upon the ground. The two grown women were tortured, though not severely, and thoroughly raped. There was never to be a single case of a white woman being taken by Southern Plains Indians without rape. Then the raiding band split up, in Indian fashion.

Rachel Plummer lived as a Comanche slave for eighteen months. At last she was ransomed by an American named Donahue in Santa Fe, through the agency of Comancheros—the despised half-breeds who traded with the Comanches from New Mexico. The Comancheros found Mrs. Plummer in a camp high in the Rocky Mountains. During her captivity she bore a child, but the Indians killed it by dropping it on the ice. She was returned to Texas by way of Missouri, but soon died. She did not see her son James again.

Elizabeth Kellogg was slightly more fortunate. She fell to the Caddoan allies, who took her to the Red River and there sold her to a band of Delawares. The Delawares then sold her back to General Sam Houston in December, 1836, for $150.

John Parker and James Plummer were found and ransomed in 1842. Young Parker, raised for six years as a Comanche, was unable to readjust. He went back to the tribes, looking for his sister; finally, he married a Mexican girl who had been a Comanche slave and settled south of the Rio Grande.

Cynthia Ann Parker was in the hands of Quahadis, the most remote and most warlike Comanche tribe. They took her high into the Staked Plains. Though she was seen or heard of a number of times, all efforts to ransom her failed. In 1846, a U.S. Army colonel, at a council with the Indians, saw her briefly. He said she refused to speak, wept incessantly, and ran away. She was then seventeen. When the colonel tried to free her, he was threatened with death and had to desist. This was a frequent, bitter, frustrating experience of American officers on the Southern Plains frontier. The Indians here took female slaves among Mexicans and whites, and it was a common custom to carry off and adopt children. Although it was Indian practice to grant the adopted captives full tribal rights, the practice inflamed the American frontier mind as few other acts, even the hideous tortures, did.

Cynthia Ann Parker matured and became the wife of Peta Nocona, war chief of the Noconi band. The raid on Parker's Fort in 1836 thus began one of the great and tragic stories of the Texas frontier, because both Cynthia Ann and her half-Indian children would be heard from again, from this beginning of the Comanche wars until the bloody, bitter end.

The Parker raid was not unusual. It was to be repeated in various ways many hundreds of times. The Comanches had raided the Spanish-Mexicans for a hundred years; now the warfare became three-sided. But there was a difference to the Anglo frontier in Texas that colored the whole struggle, that embued it with virulent bitterness rare in any time or place. The Anglo frontier in Texas was not a frontier of traders, trappers, and soldiers, as in most other states. It was a frontier of farming families, with women and small children, encroaching and colliding with a long-ranging, barbaric, war-making race. For forty years, this bleeding ground was filled with men and boys, wives and sons, who had kinfolk carried off, never to be heard from again or to be ransomed and returned in shamed disgrace. Thousands of frontier families were to see the results of Comanche raids: men staked out naked to die under the blazing sun, eyelids and genitals removed; women and female children impaled on fence poles and burned; captives found still writhing, dying, with burned-out coals heaped on scrota and armpits; ransomed teen-age girls and women returned to their relatives with demented stares.

These were insults and injuries the Anglo-Celtic stock would not forgive or bear. This was racial war in its truest sense, and as in all true ethnic wars, there could be no parameters of right or wrong. The most moral of Indians lived by a code that nauseated whites. The most moral of whites, on this harsh ground, became savagely brutalized.

Noah Smithwick, a gentle, literate "Texian," wrote of another incident that occurred in 1836. He had enlisted in the new "ranging force" (soon called Rangers), under Captain Tumlinson. Tumlinson's force was patrolling along the Colorado, within ten miles of present-day Austin. One night, as the Rangers made camp, a young white woman stumbled upon them. She was wounded, bleeding and almost naked.

She could not talk coherently for some time. Finally, the Texans learned her name was Hibbons, and she had been traveling to her home on the Guadalupe with her husband, brother, and two small children. Comanches jumped them; the two men were killed, and Mrs. Hibbons and her children seized and tied to mules. The three-year-old took this well enough, but the other child, an infant, screamed so continuously that the Indians bashed its head against a tree.

That night a cold front or norther struck, forcing the Comanches to take shelter in a cedar brake near where the present city of Austin stands. The Indians took no especial pains to guard their captives, believing that in the cold and wild country they could not escape. But Mrs. Hibbons sneaked into the dark while the Comanches were snoring in their buffalo robes. She fled, leaving her small son behind. She walked for a long way in the icy river, to hide her tracks.

Now, she begged the Rangers to rescue the boy. Tumlinson and his men mounted and soon struck the Comanche trail. They followed it; the Indians seemed to be taking no precautions, as they were beyond the settlement line. They surprised the Comanche camp, shot down one Indian and rescued the Hibbons boy. Then, in Smithwick's words:

> The boys . . . awarded me the scalp. I modestly waved my claim in favor of [Conrad] Rohrer, but he, generous soul, declared that according to all the rules of the chase, the man who brought down the game was entitled to the pelt, and himself scalped the savage, tying the loathsome trophy to my saddle . . . thinking it might afford the poor woman whose family its owner had helped to murder, some satisfaction. . . .

To the frontier white, all Indians were vermin. Searching for the most damning epithet to dehumanize the race, Texans called them "red niggers." The frontier proverb, "The only good Indian is a dead Indian," did not originate in Texas, but it was probably used more there than in any other state.

The Texas Republic thus had inherited Indian wars at its birth. However, the first Texas President, Sam Houston, had no intention of waging this war, apparently for two reasons. Houston was a conservative, a planter-leaning President, who understood the weakness of the Texas economy and was determined to cut expenditures. Houston also was an enigma to his friends, because he loved Indians. He had lived with the Cherokees, and he recognized that the Indian and the European did not necessarily represent savagery and civilization respectively; the Amerind had an entirely different view of life. At this time, many of the red men living in the eastern half of Texas were peaceable remnants of once mighty tribes. The Caddoans and Tonkawas were natives; the Cherokees, Delawares, and Shawnees had been pushed westward when their lands had been usurped by the United States. Houston definitely wanted to stabilize the Indian situation, and uniquely among all Western leaders, he proposed a guarantee of Indian rights through the granting of legal title—not mere treaty rights—to Indian lands. Houston recognized a difference between the agrarian and Plains tribes; he believed a place could be made for the former within American civilization.

His Congress and his people did not. The Comanches were an admitted terror, but all Indians got the blame. It was true that even the lowly Caddoans were not above horse-stealing raids. They also occasionally joined the more warlike tribes, and parties of Caddoans had murdered whites they caught defenseless or alone. As for the Cherokees, Texans would not, and did not, distinguish between them and Comanches.

Houston's Indian policy, which was later much praised, actually was a tragic failure. He could not protect the Indians; he could merely defer their fate. In the meantime he made promises, especially to the Cherokees, he could not keep.

The temper of the Texas Congress was revealed in the bills it passed. In December, 1836, a battalion of mounted riflemen was authorized for the frontier, together with plans for a string of forts. In 1837, a corps of "600 mounted gun men" for use in the northwest was approved. Houston did not exert himself to implement any of these authorizations; he let local communities form ranging bands as they could. He did approve a bill, in 1838, to raise a regular cavalry corps for use in the border south.

On December 10, 1838, Houston's term expired. The new President, Mirabeau Buonaparte Lamar, abruptly brought the policy of hesitancy and diplomacy to an end. Lamar had two great hates: Indians and Sam Houston, not necessarily in that order. In his inaugural address to a cheering Congress, Lamar bluntly proposed that all Indians be expelled from eastern Texas:

> Nothing short of this will bring us peace or safety. . . . The white man and the red man cannot dwell in harmony together. Nature forbids it . . . knowing these things, I experience no difficulty in deciding on the proper policy to be pursued towards them. It is to push a rigorous war against them; pursuing them to their hiding places without mitigation or compassion, until they shall be made to feel that flight from our borders without hope of return, is preferable to the scourges of war.

In retrospect, Lamar was entirely correct. No permanent peace was possible on the white man's terms without a punishing war; the Indians could not live peaceably in the world the Texans were determined to make. Lamar's policy followed that of the United States in these same years; the United States was pushing all Indian tribes out of the South, into Oklahoma and the West. Seminoles, Cherokees, and many other tribes were officially being dispossessed. More significant, Lamar stated a policy that the United States government only adopted more than thirty years later: that the Indians must be pursued, and their sanctuaries destroyed, before the guerrilla warfare would end. If the Indians survived, it would have to be as powerless remnants, living on land no white man desired.

Lamar's policy was actually more merciful than the hypocrisy practiced by others, which continually failed to take white prejudices and dominant desires into account. It was proposed to end the Indian problem brutally but quickly.

But the fact that Mirabeau Lamar took obvious satisfaction in fighting Indians, and was so devoid of cant or hypocrisy in saying the Indians must go, has continued to haunt historians who realize he was right, but who would have preferred to write that the Texas tribes were exterminated in a fit of absentmindedness.

The coastal planters were in opposition to Lamar. They were exposed to no Indian danger, unlike the hardy types who were pushing up the rivers into the post-oak wilderness. Landowners and businessmen, they desired economy in government; they were not eager to pay for western wars. Here again there was the East-West tension that colored so much of American history. The Texas cotton growers were like the Philadelphia Quaker oligarchy of the 18th century, who saw neither profit nor reason in assisting the angry, bleeding, aggressive Scots-Irish frontiersmen.

Lamar knocked down the idea of budgetary problems with dashing rhetoric: war rarely succeeded according to the advice of "those who would value gold above liberty and life above honor." He also said history indicated warfare most commonly succeeded in proportion to money spent—in other words, niggardly efforts produced piddling victories. None of this was refutable; the western counties were belligerent, and Lamar had his war. He could not be accused of starting it; it had begun two hundred years before. There was no way to stop it. The men who built Parker's Fort and the Comanches who raided it were to themselves being true.

Albert Sidney Johnston, a very competent soldier, was in full agreement as Texas Secretary of War. So was Bonnell, Texas Commissioner of Indian Affairs. Between January 1, 1839, and the end of October approximately 2,000 men were enlisted for militia or ranging service. The general pattern of the war was to raise temporary companies of armed men and to seek out Indians. Another pattern followed was to engage Indian allies, usually Lipans or Tonkawas, to act as scouts or "spies." There was never any problem finding Indian allies; the warfare and hatred among the tribes long antedated the arrival of the Americans.

In January, 1839, Colonel John H. Moore led three companies of volunteers from the upper settlements along the Colorado against the Comanches. Moore had 63 white Rangers and 16 Indians under Castro, chief of the Lipan Apaches. He rode west on the Colorado, past the confluence of the Llano, high on the plateau homeland of the Penateka Comanches. The Apache scouts scoured the country and found a Comanche encampment on a small creek in the San Saba Valley.

Moore slipped down on the Indian camp and attacked. As was to happen again and again, the Indians, canny and careful warriors in the field, were easily surprised in their camp. Rangers and Indians attacked on foot and ran among the tepees, shooting some warriors in their robes. Finally, in a scene of pandemonium, Moore recalled his men. This so infuriated Castro that the Lipan allies deserted. The victory was a mixed one, although only one Texan was fatally wounded. In the course of the melee, the Comanches had found the Ranger horse herd, and escaped with 46. Most of Moore's men had to retreat back down the Colorado on foot.

Other parties of Texas gun men or Rangers were gathered all along the vast frontier. Captain John Bird led some 50 men from Austin and Fort Bend counties into Indian country on Little River. By accident, the company ran across Comanches hunting buffalo on May 26, 1839. The Rangers counted about 20 Indians on horseback, and they pursued these for several miles without catching them. By now Bird became nervous; he was far out on the Plains, and he ordered a retreat. The Indians immediately turned on him and filled the sky with arrows.

The Texans were forest men, armed with knives, single-shot pistols, and long Kentucky rifles. They were not able to meet the thundering Comanches horse to horse. Bird ran for a ravine, and soon found himself besieged by more than 200 howling foes. The Indians charged his position in the rocks repeatedly, but the long rifles knocked these rushes back with heavy loss. Finally, the Indians drew away.

Bird's "victory," as it was called, was Pyrrhic. The Rangers lost seven dead, including Captain Bird. The bloodied Rangers retreated back into Texas; they had stirred up more trouble than they had ended.

It was Mexican policy during all these years to foment trouble on the Anglo frontier; Mexico had not accepted Texan independence, and the two states were still, if informally, at war. Mexican agents continually worked among the Indians, especially in east Texas. Their great hope was in the Cherokees. Mexican representatives promised the Cherokees full title to their lands if Texas were reconquered; apparently there was a Mexican hope that an Indian nation might be erected along the Sabine as a buffer between them and the expanding United States.

The plans and plots were real; they formed a logical Mexican attempt to make trouble for an enemy. On May 18, 1839, a company of Texas Rangers attacked a party of Indians on the San Gabriel, about twenty-five miles from Austin. The attack was a success; the Texans captured 600 pounds of powder and lead, and more than a hundred horses. This material was being sent to the Indians from Mexico. More important, one of the dead men searched by the victors was Manuel Flores, a Mexican agent. Flores carried papers revealing a Mexican plan to unite all the Texas Indians for a great attack on the whites, to be launched with a Mexican invasion from the south. These plans were very detailed; they were written in Matamoros, and included tactical advice for the Indians. They were to wait until the Texas militia rode out, then strike and burn the settlements and towns. Also on Flores' body was a letter from another agent, Vicente Córdova, who was stirring up a rebellion among Mexican residents of Nacogdoches. Córdova wrote that the Cherokees had promised to join in the destruction of the Anglos.

There is no question that the Cherokees had talked with the Mexicans, but the evidence is almost definite that Bowles, the Cherokee chief, had no intention of joining in the war. The Cherokees had now been in east Texas for almost twenty years, and during this time they had lived in peace with the whites. They were agrarian, and civilizing rapidly. Houston was in close contact with them. But the Cherokee lands were extremely rich, and they were also now entirely enclosed by later settlement by whites. Their crime was that they had something the Texans wanted. But more than that, any red presence within Anglo-Texas had now become intolerable to the great majority of whites.

The Flores papers permitted Albert Sidney Johnston and President Lamar to declare a Cherokee war. The contents sent a thrill of horror and righteous indignation through the whole frontier, because the Mexicans made it clear that the Indians were free to exterminate the whites and keep their property as they chose. Johnston marshaled the entire Texas regular army in the north. Meanwhile, a commission was sent among the Cherokees to demand their voluntary removal from the state. This commission was composed of David Burnet, Johnston, Hugh McCloud, and Thomas Jefferson Rusk. These men told Bowles that Texas would pay for the improvements left on Cherokee land but could not pay for the land itself.

Bowles acquitted himself with grave dignity. He told the Texans that he could not agree with the Texan claim; the Cherokees owned, or ought to own, this land. He also said that he personally knew his people could not fight the more powerful whites and would be destroyed if they did. However, he also knew the temper of his people, and they would fight despite his counsel.

He asked the commissioners to allow the harvests to be gathered before the crisis began. The Texans refused. Generals Kelsey Douglas and Edward Burleson of the Texas militia and regular army advanced with large forces into the pine woods. Their orders were to drive the Indians out.

The Cherokees, who had tried to live like white men, tried to fight like white men. They met the Texans in a regular battle line, on July 15, 1839. Two days later they were in complete rout. Bowles was dead, killed brutally and unnecessarily.

Kelsey Douglas did not stop with the Cherokees. He recommended that the entire Indian rat's nest be burnt out, and all the villages and corn of the associated east Texas tribes be destroyed. By July 25, the Delawares, Shawnees, Caddoans, Kickapoos, Creeks, Muscogees, Biloxies, and Seminoles had all been harried across the Arkansas line. Only two tribes, the Coshatties and Alabamas, small and inoffensive, were allowed to remain, and these were removed to less fertile lands, on what was to be Texas' only permanent Indian reservation.

Some Cherokees under The Egg and Chief Bowles' son, John, tried to find refuge in Mexico. Burleson pursued this band to the Colorado with Tonkawa scouts. Here the band was attacked; its leaders were slain, and all the Indian equipage and livestock brought back.

This expulsion removed all Indians from the settled portions of the state, and opened up thousands of square miles for white settlement. At this time the Wacos and other Wichita tribes further west were beyond the colonization line; caught between Comanches and Texans, they seemed cowed.

Meanwhile, the war along the general line from present Belton to Austin to San Antonio was being waged brutally in the west. This was true "Indian" warfare, skirmish and raid, escape and attack. Companies of Rangers carried the fight to the Penateka Comanches with varying success. President Lamar had established the Texas capital at Austin, which was then fully within Comanche country; in fact, parties of mounted Indians on the surrounding hills above the valley of the Colorado watched the settlement being built. Lamar used the fact that Austin was in the geographical center of Texas as his excuse, but an underlying motive was to pull the settlers west. Lamar thought beyond Indians; he even had the far Pacific in mind.

The Penatekas were a formidable foe, as Bird's fate proved. But war, as Texans now waged it, became a trying sport. On January 9, 1840, three Penateka chieftains rode into San Antonio. They came boldly; San Antonio had long been "their" town, according to Comanche boast. Colonel Henry Karnes, a redheaded Ranger commander, met them for a parley.

The chiefs told Karnes that the tribes had agreed to ask the Texans for a peace. Karnes consented, but only on condition the Comanches returned all white prisoners, of which there were now about 200 in Indian hands. The Comanches promised to return again in twenty days.

Karnes wrote General Albert Sidney Johnston that he had no faith in Comanche promises, and he had not made prisoners of the three chiefs because they were too few to "guarantee the future." He recommended that commissioners be sent to San Antonio to meet with the Comanches, but that many troops also be sent, and that if the tribes did not return the promised white prisoners, those Indians who came to San Antonio should be held as hostages. Above all, Karnes urged that whoever was sent be able to act with decision and dispatch, with no dillydallying. Johnston accepted these recommendations in full, and sent three companies of the

1st Regiment under Lieutenant Colonel Fisher marching to Bexar. Fisher was ordered to seize the Indians if they did not fulfill their promise to return all whites.

The three commissioners appointed to treat with the Indians were all soldiers: Fisher himself, the Texas Adjutant General, and Acting Secretary of War. The terms to be given the Comanches were: they must stay within certain boundaries to the west; they must recognize that Texas had the right to occupy "vacant" land, and settlers were not to be interfered with; they must not henceforth enter any white settlement.

On March 19, 1840, sixty-five Indians rode in—men, women, and children, led by twelve chiefs and the great civil chieftain, Muguara, or Mukwah-rah, the Spirit Talker. The Comanches were brightly attired and painted for council. But they came with only two captives, a sixteen-year-old white girl and a Mexican boy, who did not count.

The appearance of the girl, Matilda Lockhart, was to turn this day, as the spectator Mrs. Samuel Maverick wrote, into a "day of horrors." Mrs. Maverick helped bathe and dress Matilda, who told the white women she was "utterly degraded, and could not hold up her head again." Mrs. Maverick described her:

> Her head, arms and face were full of bruises, and sores, and her nose actually burnt off to the bone—all the fleshy end gone, and a great scab formed on the end of the bone. Both nostrils were wide open and denuded of flesh. She told a piteous tale of how dreadfully the Indians had beaten her, and how they would wake her from sleep by sticking a chunk of fire to her flesh, especially to her nose . . . her body had many scars from the fire.

The Lockhart girl was extremely intelligent. She had been with the Comanches two years and understood some of their tongue. She said the Indians planned to bring in the captives one by one, and bargain for each, this way figuring to get a higher price. She knew of thirteen more in her own camp.

Now, in the courthouse (called the Council House) in San Antonio, on the corner of Main Plaza and Market Street, Chief Muguara began to demand high prices for the remaining captives: ammunition, vermilion, blankets, and bangles. Meanwhile, a file of Texan soldiers surrounded the small, one-story, limestone building, Indian boys played outside, and a crowd of curious onlookers stood around. The Texas commissioners grimly asked why the other prisoners had not been delivered as promised. Muguara, bald and wrinkled, said they were with other tribes but could be bought. Then he said arrogantly: "How do you like that answer?"

Lamar's mustached captains liked it not at all. Fisher ordered a group of soldiers into the room; all three men were pale with fury at the appearance and story of the Lockhart girl. Through the interpreter, Muguara was told all the Indians would be imprisoned until the rest of the white captives arrived. Then, ransom would be talked. The interpreter at first refused to repeat this, saying the Comanches would fight. When he did convey the message, he turned and fled from the room.

The Comanches responded with war screams. One went for the door and put his knife into the soldier who blocked his way. The Texas officers gave the order to open fire. Amid the crash of rifles, shrieks, and dense powder smoke, Comanches broke from the building and tried to flee to the river down the street. Indians, soldiers, and white onlookers were killed in a general melee and massacre. No Indian escaped; Muguara and all twelve chiefs died. Six Americans, including the Bexar sheriff and an officer, were killed and ten others wounded. Some of the Indian dead were women and children, but about 30 were caught and held.

A visiting judge was pierced and killed by an arrow as the young Indian boys outside the Council House joined the fight.

With the surviving Indians lodged in the *calabozo* or jail, a squaw was given a horse to ride to the Comanche camp. She was told that unless the Comanches brought in all white captives the prisoners in San Antonio would be killed. She was to have twelve days.

She never returned. A young white boy, who had been adopted into the tribe, told what occurred when this chief's wife reached the camp. The Penatekas went into a frenzy of despair—the losses were indeed hideous for any Comanche band. The women shrieked and howled and cut off fingers in mourning. The men gave the guttural moans for the dead. Horses were sacrificed for two days. Then, thirteen captives were roasted to death or killed in lingering, revolting ways.

From where the sun now stood, the Comanche nation was to observe no peace with Texas.

Three hundred Comanches rode near San Antonio. Chief Hears the Wolf (Isi-man-ica), with only one warrior, clattered into Main Plaza and circled it, screaming insults and challenges to battle. The plaza remained quiet; a voice from Black's Saloon, through an interpreter, informed the chief that the soldiers were at San José Mission—he could go there for a fight.

Hears the Wolf rode for San José. Here, Captain Read, in command during Fisher's illness, refused to fight, because the twelve-day truce still held. He invited Hears the Wolf to abide three days. But the Indians, too canny to charge riflemen behind walls and too mercurial to wait, thundered off. Read's sense of honor affronted Captain Lysander Wells and a considerable number of his command.

Wells used the term "coward"; the usual amenities were observed, and both officers perished in a pistol duel.

For some months the region around San Antonio lived in terror. The minutemen stood ready to ride at the sounding of the San Fernando Cathedral bell. Angry Comanches, who felt that they had been badly dealt with infested the roads; no traveler was safe. But no major blow fell, and by midsummer it appeared the Indians were gone.

The Penatekas, Tanimas, Tenawas and other Southern Comanches had retired deep into Comanchería, to hold council with the High Plains Indians and Kiowas. They told their grievances against the Texan tribe. Hot-bloods from the associated bands, and the Kiowas, joined them.

Under the Comanche moon of August, 1840, a huge band, numbering between 400 and 1,000 warriors, moved south. This array was led by Buffalo Hump, surviving war chief of the Penateka Comanches. They passed east of San Antonio, near Gonzales, and struck deep into Anglo-Texas above the Nueces. They cut a swath of destruction, and sent men who saw them riding in all directions. On August 6, Buffalo Hump surrounded the old town of Victoria. He did something few Indian war leaders had ever done: he not only "treed" Victoria, Texas, but took it. The settlers, hastily banded together, held only one part of the town on August 7. Some fifteen people, including seven Negro slaves, were killed in Victoria as the Comanches rode howling through the streets. When they left, they drove a herd of nearly 2,000 horses ahead of them.

These horses, the Indians' gold, were to prove Buffalo Hump's undoing.

The marauders poured down Peach Creek, moving toward the Gulf in a great half-moon crescent. Militia companies turned out but could only hover on the Indian's trail and flanks. These troops were kept busy burying the dead. One corpse, the body of Parson Joel Ponton, was found with the soles of the feet sliced off; the Indians had dragged him along on the exquisitely tender stumps for miles before they took his scalp. All along the route houses went up in smoke and Texans died.

On August 8, Buffalo Hump arrived in Linnville, a little town on Lavaca Bay, which served as a seaport for San Antonio. Most of Linnville's citizens escaped by taking to boats. One, Judge John Hays, became so angry at the idea of Indians ransacking the town that he waded back to shore and stood shouting at the swarming horsemen, waving an empty shotgun. The Comanches rode around him; whether they respected courage or considered Hays mad was never understood.

The Indians spent all day pillaging and burning Linnville. Among their loot was two years' supply of merchandise consigned to Samuel Maverick and James Robinson. John Linn's warehouse was despoiled. Three whites and two Negroes, including the collector of customs, were killed here.

The toll for the Council House in San Antonio fight was considered even by Buffalo Hump; Comanche blood was well avenged. Now, carrying dozens of mule-loads of loot, many prisoners, and driving between 2,000 and 3,000 stolen horses, the Comanches turned back. Sated, they rode for the high plateaus.

But dusty riders were pounding through the coastal prairie. Every male was turning out, from Lavaca, Gonzales, Victoria, and Cuero, and a hundred widely scattered farms. They were marshaled by the frontier captains, Tumlinson, Ben McCulloch, Matthew ("Old Paint") Caldwell, and Edward Burleson. A company pressed hard on the Indian trail, firing into them at times but lacking the strength to close and fight. Other riders ran for the Colorado settlements, seeking help. These reinforcements were to gather to intercept the Comanches at Plum Creek, approximately two miles from the later town of Lockhart.

At first, the retreating Comanches, with plenty of fresh horses, easily distanced their pursuit. But they bore too much loot. The mules slowed them, and the *caballado* or horse herd was unwieldy; it took many warriors to guard. If Buffalo Hump had cut back south of San Antonio he might have made it. Instead, arrogantly, he chose to ride northwest adjacent to the Colorado. Ahead of him, Ward, James Bird, John Moore and their companies gathered at Plum Creek. On August 11, General Felix Huston of the regular army arrived, and despite some protests by the frontiersmen, took command. On the 12th, Burleson and a hundred men under Jones, Wallace, and Hardeman rode in. The Bastrop militia arrived.

Tonakawa scouts, under Chief Placido, reported the Comanches were slowly moving north, raising a great dust trail. They would soon reach the Big Prairie, not far from Plum Creek, which was a branch of the San Marcos.

The Texans dismounted and waited for the Indians in the brush that screened the creek. When the great Comanche cavalcade moved out on the prairie adjoining the stream, Huston, Burleson, and Caldwell rode from the brush at a walk, two great lines of horsemen slowly coming together.

John Holland Jenkins, a Bastrop man, described the feints and challenges the Comanches displayed, as a prelude to combat: "arrayed in all the splendor of savage warriors, and finely mounted, [they] bounded over the space between the hostile lines, exhibiting feats of horsemanship and daring none but a Comanche . . . could perform." Jenkins, like many a gentle soul who found himself awaiting a fight to the death on the frontier, was awed by the barbaric unrealness of it all:

> It was a spectacle never to be forgotten, the wild, fantastic band as they stood in battle array. . . . Both horses and riders were decorated most profusely, with all the beauty and horror of their wild taste combined. Red ribbons streamed out from their horses's tails as they swept around us, riding fast. . . . There was a huge warrior, who wore a stovepipe hat, and another who wore a fine pigeon-tailed cloth coat, buttoned up behind. . . . Some wore on their heads immense buck and buffalo horns. One headdress struck me particularly. It consisted of a large white crane with red eyes.

But the experienced Indian-fighting captains were watching the Comanche antics with more sardonic eyes. Caldwell and Burleson realized that the Indians were trying to delay the real combat until they had pushed the horse herd ahead of them—loot was uppermost in their mind. The horses had made Buffalo Hump ride home on his downward trail, rather than splitting up and infiltrating west in the age-old Comanche manner.

The experienced men—Caldwell, Burleson, McCulloch—wanted to press the attack as the horse herd went by. Huston hesitated. Then, a Comanche in a magnificent feathered headdress rode out of ranks and began to caper in front of the Texans, challenging their chiefs to individual combat. He was a magnificent target, and a long Texan rifle knocked him down. A groan went up from the watching Comanches—bad medicine.

"Now, General!" Caldwell said. "Charge 'em!"

Huston gave the order. Screaming and shooting, the Texas cavalry spurred into the Comanche flank. They stampeded the great horse herd, and the Comanches, dispersed to control their animals rather than arrayed for battle, were stampeded with it. Horses and mules piled up in a boggy stretch. The Comanches were scattered, and those jammed in the *caballado* were picked off. Caldwell took his own men around on the left flank, methodically killing every Indian in his path.

A running fight went on for fifteen miles. The combat was close and cruel. Hardeman's horse was shafted; Burleson shot several Comanches; even John Holland Jenkins got his man. It was more a massacre than a battle; the heart was out of the Comanches. Eighty-odd Comanche bodies were strewn behind the stampede. Only one Texan was killed.

The captives of the Indians were not so lucky. Several were tied to trees and shot with arrows by Comanches during the chaotic retreat. One prisoner, the wife of the slain collector of customs at Linnville, a strikingly handsome woman, was wearing a whalebone corset. Her captors had not had time to figure out how to get her out of it. She was found fastened to a tree, with a blunted arrow lodged in her corseted breast. She was horribly sunburned on exposed limbs, but the whalebone had saved her life.

Jenkins saw one man leap on an abandoned, wounded squaw, stomp her, then pin her to the ground with a Comanche lance. However, a number of women and children prisoners were taken—it was the nature of Indians on extended war parties to take their families along. These captives later all escaped or were returned; Comanches made poor servants, as the Texans had found out by trial.

The Texans recovered a great pile of silver, cloth, whiskey, and tobacco, in addition to many horses. These liberated goods were divided among the victorious army. The Tonkawas, who had run on foot for thirty miles with Burleson to the battle, now had mounts. Huston wrote these fourteen "Tonks" a citation for bravery. When the moon came up over Plum Creek they held a victory dance, and ceremoniously roasted and ate several Comanche legs and arms.

Plum Creek punished the Penatekas severely. They had tried an unaccustomed form of warfare and failed. Afterward, no Comanche ever attacked a town again or raided down to the coast. They resumed the old guerrilla tactics, which were trouble enough.

The sequence of cause and effect in Lamar's Indian wars was not quite finished. The President and Johnston were determined the Comanches must be taught a lesson. In September, 1840, Colonel John Moore raised a force in Fayette County and rode up the Colorado. He had 12 Lipans, and about 90 white men. Moore rode farther west than any Texan, except perhaps James Bowie, had gone before.

Moore's Rangers passed the San Saba, the Concho, and came to the Red Fork of the Colorado. Moore found this country rich and beautiful, high, dry, covered with a sea of waving grass broken by occasional rivers and canyons, with tremendous vistas. On October 23, the Lipans smelled out a Comanche village. Moore guessed he was about halfway to Santa Fe.

Grimly and efficiently, Moore's riders mounted and moved down on the Comanche village at midnight, behind a wave of Lipan scouts. The Apaches estimated the number of the enemy at 60 families, possibly 125 warriors. Moore sent 15 picked riflemen under Lieutenant Owens across the Colorado to set up a killing zone behind the village. Then, at daybreak on October 24, he charged in.

The Comanches were caught by surprise. As the Texans dashed through the tepees on horseback, men, women, and squawling children ran about in terror and confusion. Moore's men dismounted and began to use their rifles and pistols with deadly effect. Most of the Indians ran for the river, and into the muzzles of Owens' sharpshooters. The killing lasted some thirty minutes. About 125 Indians died, 80 of them at or in the river. The Texans lost two wounded, one fatally.

Colonel Moore's report stated: "The river and its banks . . . presented every evidence of a total defeat of our savage foe. The bodies of men, women, and children were to be seen on every hand wounded, dying, and dead." This was a punitive raid; no attempt was made to spare Indians because of age or sex. The Comanches had spared neither in their raids. The government was satisfied with Moore's report.

With this raid, the Comanche war in southwest Texas ended. The power of the southern Comanche bands was broken. The Penatekas were still a nuisance but no longer a mortal danger. Significantly, however, the Texans and the northern Comanche tribes were not yet really in contact. One factor in the defeat of the Penatekas was that they had chosen territory only on the edge of the Plains. The encroaching white settlement pushed the buffalo west, but the other Comanche bands were not hospitable to the Penatekas following them. All through the Indian wars, red man against red man helped seal the race's doom.

No Texas historian has ever tried to justify the harsh treatment of the Cherokees. Chief Bowles behaved and died as a noble, tragic figure, a victim of hatred and greed. The Comanches and Kiowas, by their own nature, precipitated their final fate, but the fate of the Cherokee nation was more revealing of the true nature of human societies, and man. The Cherokees were weak, holding something valued by a stronger race. Whatever face was put on it, the result, as Walter Prescott Webb said, was inevitable.

Justifiable or not, President Lamar's Indian policy and wars were enormously successful. Lamar spent $2.5 million the Republic did not have, and many hundreds of lives were spent as well; but in vast areas of Texas the Indian problem ceased to exist. East Texas was finally rid of all its immigrant tribes. A vast tier of territory through central Texas was made relatively safe for survey, sale, and rapid settlement. Lamar opened hundreds of thousands of acres of rich soul.

More important, he had convinced thousands of frontiersmen that his was the only final solution. He was a popular, if not a lasting, hero because he left Texas with more "good" Indians than it had when he found it.

25

THE BORDER BREED

> *A Texas Ranger can ride like a Mexican, trail like an Indian, shoot like a Tennesseean, and fight like a very devil!*
>
> EDITORIAL BY JOHN SALMON FORD, IN THE
> *Texas Democrat,* SEPTEMBER 9, 1846

> *Of this far-famed corps—so much feared and hated by the Mexicans—I can add nothing to what has already been written. The character of the Texas Ranger is now well known by both friend and foe. As a mounted soldier he has had no counterpart in any age or country. Neither Cavalier nor Cossack, Mameluke nor Moss-trooper are like him; and yet, in some respects, he resembles them all. Chivalrous, bold and impetuous in action, he is yet wary and calculating, always impatient of restraint, and sometimes unscrupulous and unmerciful. He is ununiformed, and undrilled, and performs his active duties thoroughly, but with little regard to order or system. He is an excellent rider and a dead shot. His arms are a rifle, Colt's revolving pistol, and a knife.*
> LUTHER GIDDINGS, AN OFFICER OF THE 1ST OHIO
> VOLUNTEERS IN MEXICO

MOST Texan historians have depicted the essential story of Texas as one of enduring racial and cultural conflict and war. Other historians have been free to ignore this picture, but few have disputed it. The most striking aspect of this struggle is the adaptations the land and warfare forced on the Anglo-American vanguard. A significant element in American victory was the American ability to adapt and change.

Austin's Anglo enclave along the Brazos bottoms was nothing more than

465

an extension of the American cotton-planting South, with planter, merchant, lawyer, doctor, soldier, and Negro slave, with its fringe of rifle-toting free farmers nestled through its uplands. These riflemen and aristocrats, together, conquered the Mexicans at San Jacinto and drove the settled Indians from the east. There was nothing to distinguish Houston's army on the bayou, or Lamar's summer militia of 1839, from Trans-Appalachian Americans of their age.

Moving into east Texas, down the coast to the mouth of the Nueces, and inland through the post oaks and waxy black prairies, these Americans found nothing radically different from lands and soils they had known before. The pine woods along the Red reminded settlers of their Georgia homeland. Both Mississippi planters and their slaves felt comfortable beside the cypresses and moss-hung oaks of the middle Guadalupe. Louisianans saw nothing new in the coastline of Galveston Bay, nor did the sweaty humidity of the lower river bottoms oppress them. The Alabamans and men from Tennessee found that corn grew splendidly in the central woodlands. Through half of the accidently drawn boundaries of Texas, the social organization, agriculture, techniques, and warfare of southern America worked.

But the conquest of Texas in the 1830's was a conquest of only the extension of the Southern plain. The first abortive American culture, the cotton kingdom, took hold and flourished there; the years from 1836 to 1860 marked a consolidation of this empire, before its final downfall and enthrallment by the North.

Beyond this kingdom, Anglo-Americans confronted both a land and enemies totally unfamiliar to the English-speaking experience. From the middle of Texas, extending roughly on a north-south line connecting Sherman, Dallas, and San Antonio and curving along the Nueces below San Antonio to the sea, the entire nature of the country changed. Nowhere west or south of this line did annual rainfall exceed thirty inches; in most places it was much less. This was a wide, beautiful, but incredibly harsh land, which never quite left the Pleistocene age. It was subject to periodic, and violent change: blazing sun, ephemeral but chilling ice storms, rough winds, titanic floods, which preceded or ended decades-long droughts. There were months and years when the vistas burned with red and yellow flowers, and months and years when over large regions the grass shriveled and the limestone springs went dry. Extending for hundreds of leagues from north to south, this country was not all the same. It varied from the brushlands and chaparral-lined savannahs in the southern triangle to the cedar brakes above the Balcones Fault, and to the endless, butte-studded vistas of the far limestone plateaus. It ended, on the southwest and west, in arid greasebrush deserts overhung with blue-topped, treeless mountains. This was the southern extension of that geographical phenomenon known as the Great Plains.

The first English-speaking people to break out of the woodlands and

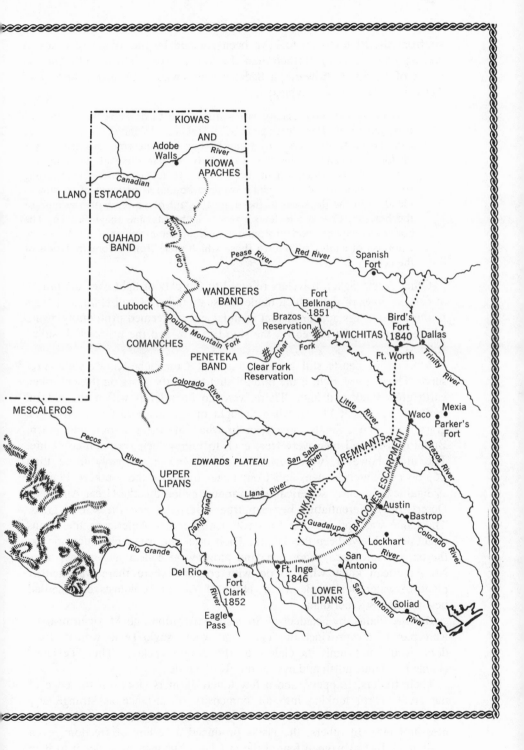

The Texas Plains in the 19th Century

confront the Plains seem to have been stunned by the aspect of a sea of
waving grass reaching farther than the human eye could follow. The account of David B. Edward, a Scots traveler who published a history of
Texas in 1836, is utterly typical:

> Now, reader, your relator is lost for words to describe the balance of
> this landscape, after crossing the river Trinidad [Trinity]; as no language
> can convey to the mind any thing adequate to the emotions felt by the
> visitor, in ascending this vast irregularly regular slope of immense un-
> dulated plains, which extend before the eye in graceful rolls, affording
> from the summits of their gentle swells, a boundless prospect of verdure—
> blending in the distance, to the utmost extent of vision, with the blue of
> the horizon. Few spectacles surpass it in beauty and magnificence. The
> boundless expanse and profound repose of these immense plains, excite
> emotions of sublimity akin to those which arise from a contemplation of
> the ocean. . . .

Other Anglo-Saxon travelers referred to the play of light over the prairie
at certain times of day, which made the scattered rises and clumps of trees
in this sea of grass appear distant islands, and all seemed profoundly aware
of the immensity of the earth, the sky, the sun, and the primordial, sullen
stillness.

Millions of beasts still roamed this vast Comanche-Kiowa game preserve. The soil was rich, if the rainfall slight, and the grass on the unbroken
earth grew thick and high. There were no boundaries within the natural
limits of the Great Plains; when drought or fire temporarily removed the
grass, men and animals moved on to where it was still rich and green.
Buffalo, deer, and men were free, each to follow their own source of life.
The men, however, were few. There were never probably more than
26,000 associated Kiowas and Comanches living on the southern Plains.

Significantly, early American geographers called this the Great American
Desert, not differentiating between true desertland and the sea of grass.
The name was apt, because for early 19th century Americans the Plains
might as well have been the Sahara. Their tried and true techniques, the ax,
the ox, the rail fence, seed corn, and plow, were collectively useless here.
No American knew what to do with country where there was neither
plentiful water nor ample wood. None of Austin's colonists ever settled
beyond the 98th meridian.

But the Plains, by accident of Spanish exploration and Mexican history,
were part of the province of Texas, and when Anglo-Texas won its freedom, it did not limit its claims to the Anglo enclave. The "Texians"
claimed all lands north and east of the Rio Grande.

Their traders, trappers, and a few lonely farmers stood on the edge of
the great scarp, looking into an immensity of distance as strange and
mysterious as the heart of Africa. To some men, the Plains meant loneliness and fear. In others, the vistas produced a feeling of freedom, even
exaltation. Just as women feared the cruel sea but men went down to it in

ships, there was an Anglo-American vanguard with bordering in its blood. This vanguard would pay its price for inland admiralty: the last great American frontier was to cost seventeen lives per mile of advance.

The land was not only harsh and strange to an essentially island, woodland race, but the enemies it presented were more so. Plains Indians in the north, Mexican *vaqueros* in the south, were outside the experience of Americans, who did not understand the ways or the mind of either. Yet they had to encounter both in a long, bloody, running war on their own ground for mastery of it. This was a war that never engaged more than a handful of the American nation, but it was to engage the American consciousness and create images and legends that would never die. The Plains frontier was ephemeral but influential. Upon the already bifurcated soul of Anglo-Texas, split between cotton empire and farming frontier, there was thrust a new experience. Here was where the West began.

San Jacinto and Lamar's Indian wars had delivered the old enclave of Anglo-Texas, but neither brought lasting peace. Mexico never acquiesced to the Texan surgery, though internal troubles prevented the Mexicans from serious action. The decimation of the Penateka Comanches did not affect the powerful northern bands, toward whose hunting grounds a swarm of Texas pioneers was inexorably moving.

Thus the return of Sam Houston to the Texas Presidency could only forge a precarious breathing spell rather than genuine peace. Historically, Houston's considered peace policy toward Mexico was well taken; Texas had more to gain at this stage by internal development than by foreign war.

Houston's Indian policy, however, stemmed more from goodwill toward Indians and hopeful thinking than the cold logic of which he was usually capable. He had no power to stem the steady encroachment of white settlers on Indian hunting grounds. As he once remarked with some bitterness, even if he built a high wall between whites and Indians, his countrymen would scheme night and day for a way to get around it.

Houston also failed to recognize that the nature of the Plains Indians made peace on white terms impossible. So long as a Comanche or Kiowa was free, he would raid and kill. This was imbedded in Plains culture; the Indian "couldn't help it," as General William Tecumseh Sherman later wrote. The Comanche economy was also attuned to raiding; since the days they left the Rocky Mountains, Comanches had depended on European settlements for their horseherds. In the face of culture and necessity, the agreements of Comanche chiefs to end raiding were as hypocritical and useless as the treaties ratified by the white government. While Anglo-American encroachment on the Plains precipitated war, it should be remembered that the Comanches were accustomed to raid deeply into Mexico, a region that did not threaten or impinge on them. They began to descend upon the Texan settlements as soon as Americans moved within

range, long before the actual buffalo plains were breached by white
wagons. They would continue to do so so long as they enjoyed a privileged
sanctuary high on the Plains.

Significantly, while Houston was able to secure truces with Wacos,
Tonkawas, Anadarcos, and other tribes at a great council held at Bird's
Fort (near present Dallas) and force promises that all these Indians would
remain northwest of the Austin-San Antonio line, the Comanche tribes did
not attend.

Small, deadly, burn-kill-rob-and-run raiding parties descended regularly
off the high plateaus during the light of the summer moons. The Comanche
raid became a certainty, not a possibility, of the Texas northwest.

These horse Indians were incredibly mobile by white standards. They
rode enormous distances by night, then hid in brushy streambeds by day.
The great distances and the thinness of white settlement made any kind of
passive white defense ineffective, as ineffective as the earlier Spanish presidios. Yet, tragically, a passive defense was usually the dominant policy of,
first the Republic, and later, the United States government.

Here, in these western regions, was repeated a war between agricultural
communities and wandering nomads that had counterparts in earlier conflicts between the nomads and agrarian civilizations of Asia. And as in
those earlier wars, at first the mobile, warlike nomads seemed to have all
the advantage.

Americans suffered from three great deficiencies: they were not horsemen; they lacked an effective war organization; and they were ill-armed to
face Indians on the open plains.

The old militia system was too cumbersome. It reacted with fatal slowness on a widely scattered frontier; by the time American hoemen assembled, the Indians had struck and gone. The militia could provide no effective pursuit. Militia could not sustain the far-ranging punitive expedition.

Also, while American farmers in Texas rode horseback, they were hardly
cavalrymen or mounted warriors equal to Kiowa and Comanche braves.
The average Indian could ride rings around the average mounted white.
Worse yet, the American weapons were not designed for horse combat.
The Kentucky rifle and the tomahawk were woodland weapons. The long
flintlocks (percussion caps began to come into use about 1820) were
awkward tools in the saddle; they lost their accuracy, and could not be
recharged easily. In the time it took a frontiersman to reload, a Comanche
could charge three hundred yards and shoot twenty arrows. In a country
without trees to hide behind, the whites were outclassed.

When whites engaged Comanches, they had to dismount and make a
stand, firing some of their pieces to hold the Indians off, but always keeping some loaded rifles in reserve against a charge by what was the best light
cavalry in the 19th-century world. Many Americans were saved, not by the
stubbornness of their defense but by the fact that it was against Indian
sensibilities and tactics to push an attack home. The best the Americans

could achieve with their single-shot rifles was a standoff. If they ran, however, they were doomed, unless they quickly found timber or rock. Frontier manuals and books were emphatic, in detail, against trying to outrun Comanches; when the enemy fled, it brought out the hunting and killing instinct, and the Comanche was splendidly armed, with the bow, to kill fleeing horsemen during pursuit.

Colonel Dodge, who wrote as an authority, described the American regular soldier as superior to the Plains Indian in only two respects: discipline and the courage to make a sustained fight. Captain John Bird's "victory" in 1839 was typical of early Comanche-American combat. Pursuit of Indians out in the open was dangerous. If the whites fired their rifles, the Comanches charged behind a cloud of missiles, shooting as they rode. At ten feet, the long rifle made a poor club; the long Plains lance was supple and deadly. Bird's command lived only because it found a rocky ravine to fort up in.

In these same years, noticeably, the worst defeats the Texas forces suffered from the Mexicans came when they engaged Mexican cavalry out on open ground. Urrea's troopers wiped out every unit of Americans they caught, with the exception of one which took cover behind mission walls. The embattled farmers were not equipped to stand their ground on the wide prairie.

The Anglo-Celts who filtered out to the Indian-Mexican frontier in west and southwest Texas in the 1830's arrived with the basic necessities for conquest. They were aggressive, competitive, ambitious, and given to prejudice and hate—the last characteristics of a well-developed, rather than a primitive, society. They possessed the mental and moral equipment to wage a sustained campaign. But above all, they showed the two most important traits of a genuine dominant race: intelligence and the ability to adapt.

Both Indian and Mexican cultures were peculiarly static and frozen; they would repeat their strengths and failures to the end. Further, the Americans had one final, priceless asset. The Anglo-Celt frontiersmen were the far extension of a race with budding industrial skills. The adaption of these skills to the frontier marked the turning point in the long European failure to conquer the Plains.

The Anglos who collided, at about the same time, with the terrible Comanches and formidable Mexican horsemen, found they had to change the traditional Anglo-American system of war. The first great change involved the horse.

They had to learn to use the horse as a military implement, in other words, to ride like Mexicans. The distances of Texas were so vast, and the country so open beyond the Brazos-Colorado bottoms and the eastern pine woods, that this came quickly and instinctively. Young Texans grew up astride. A number of observers made the valid judgment that a man who could not ride well, or who detested the saddle or the horse, had no business on the Texas frontier. He could not prosper, or even survive.

Conversely, the men who loved the saddle were irresistibly pulled to the western frontier.

Another factor that came about was the deliberate improvement of the American horse breed. Farm plugs could take a wagon to town, but Americans had to have breeds that could race the Spanish mustang. They captured or developed them, out of Kentucky race horses, mustangs, and mounts with Arabian blood.

Thus was a new breed of fighting man prepared.

Texas was thinly populated everywhere, and it was an agrarian society; its only early assets were approximately equally valueless paper money and open lands. At its birth the Republic inherited two bloody frontiers in the south and west, but Texas did not have the means to garrison or police them. The reaction against Lamar's wars was not a psychological one against their aims or violence; it was a practical one, against the bankrupting of the state government. Farmer militia could not fight or even find Indian raiders, and Texas could not afford a large regular army. This forced a new adaptation on the frontier settlements, as Noah Smithwick wrote: "So, the government provided for their protection as best it could with the means at its disposal, graciously permitting the citizens to protect themselves by organizing . . . ranging companies."

Ranging companies dated from Austin's colony; they had been formed in 1823 and 1826. The term Ranger was already old in Anglo-America; it referred to Indian fighters, the kind of men who carried war to the enemy, beyond the frontier. And from 1836 onward, the history of Texas Rangers was, as the historian Webb indicated, only a little less than the history of Texas, while the history of all west Texas was only a little more than the story of the Ranger force.

The Rangers were unique. They were first a form of mounted militia, though from the first it was recognized that they needed a semipermanent form. Ranger companies guarding the frontier had more or less permanent duty, because the danger never ceased. Yet, there was never sufficient funds to pay or equip them, at any period of the long frontier. They could never become an established, regularized force, standing from year to year.

What took place, in effect, was that the government of Texas authorized Rangers as a paramilitary force and supported them when it could. Their recruitment was left to the frontier communities, as, to a great extent, was their support. The comment of one Ranger captain, that when he arrived in a certain locality all he heard about was Indian depredations, but after he drove the Indians off he heard only complaints about his Rangers killing local farmers' hogs, summed up a world of Texan, and human, experience.

The ranging companies, without uniforms, badges, or even government-supplied horses or arms, evolved slowly but in strikingly adaptive ways. At first, even the leaders were not appointed by the state, or honored with recognized commissions. The state, accidentally but fortunately, let an indigenous brand of frontier leadership arise. The Rangers were to be described many times, at first as state troops, later as a police force or constabulary. During most of the 19th century they were neither. They were apart from the regular army, the militia or national guard, and were never a true police force. They were instead one of the most colorful, efficient, and deadly band of irregular partisans on the side of law and order the world has seen. They were called into being by the needs of a war frontier, by a society that could not afford a regular army. Texans passed in and out of the Rangers regularly; in the early years a very high proportion of all west Texans served from time to time. If they bore certain similarities to Mamelukes and Cossacks, they were never quite the same.

Very soon, the Rangers had certain marked characteristics, which they did not soon lose. They were not typical Texas farmers—the man with a farm and family could not spend his time riding the wild frontier. They were for the most part extremely young. Most great Ranger leaders earned their fame long before the age of thirty. That they were adventurous and uniformly courageous needs no explanation; they were all volunteers. More significant was the repeated assertion by observers that the Ranger captains were unusual men—not merely brave, but officers who showed an utter absence of fear. This breed of captain was called forth both by the rough nature of the men he led, and the incredibly perilous situation of the tiny Ranger bands on the war frontier. Historians have made much of the fact that Anglo-Texans outnumbered the Indians and Mexicans with whom they were in contact; but the farming population was not on the frontier. Throughout his whole existence as a fighting man, the Texas Ranger was outnumbered by his foes. This produced not caution but canniness, and an almost incredible aggressiveness. The Ranger found his best defense was to attack, dominate, subdue.

The Ranger captains had to be not only field generals but superb psychologists, understanding the enemy and their own men. They found their greatest strength in a legend of superiority, which in the early years they genuinely won.

To fight Indians and Mexicans, Ranger leaders had to learn to think like both, or at least, to understand what Mexicans and Indians feared. The collision between the Anglo-American and the Mexican on the southern frontier was inevitable, but some aspects of this were unfortunate. Contact did not improve either race; it seemed to strengthen and enhance the vices of both. The Ranger arrived with instinctive Teutonic directness, preferring the honest smash of the bullet to the subtlety of the knife. But against the Mexican, bluntness turned into brutality, because it was almost impossible for the Protestant Anglo-Celt to understand the Hispanic mind. Impatient with Mexican deviousness, the Ranger reacted with straight force. But the Mexican, to keep the records straight, slipped from deviousness to outright treachery; history records that Mexicans killed more Texans by the result of parleys than on all the battlefields. Each side felt themselves justified because of the incomprehensible and despised cultural attributes of the foe. The Rangers seemed barbaric Nordics, devoid of all gentlemanly intrigue or guile; they saw the Mexicans as treacherous, lying people, who never wanted to do the obvious, which was to call their play and fight.

One factor in this conflict must not be ignored. The Texas border breed had no real taint of cruelty; human torture for its own or any sake was an abomination to the Anglo-Celt. But among other painful lessons the Texans learned was that they could not surrender with war honors to either foe. This attribute of Indian warfare was already known, but the fact that Mexicans, out of their revolutionary brutalizations, also abused, tortured, and shot a significant percentage of all their captives made a lasting impression on the Texan mind. Moving into enemy country, Texans not only adopted the horse, but adapted their warfare to reply in kind.

The morality of this opening border warfare was meaningless, because morality could only be defined within a culture, never across two cultures. The moral, upstanding Comanche who lived by the laws and gods of his tribe enjoyed heaping live coals on a staked-out white man's genitals; a moral Mexican, for a fancied insult, would slip his knife into an Anglo back. The moral Texan, who lived in peace and amity with his fellows, would bash an Indian infant's head against a tree, or gut-shoot a "greaser" if he blinked. Relations between disparate cultures were to be determined, as always, by the relative strength and weakness of each, and by the dynamic or regressive nature displayed by Anglos, Indians, and Mexicans. Relations could not be governed by individual, internal ethics or morals any more than history had been determined by such parameters in the past. The great change the frontier Texan made from the Anglo-American mainstream in these years was the real, if unarticulated, understanding that his enemies were "different."

This was unfortunately much more true than mere prejudice implied. It was a factor in the success of all the great frontier captains, who never made the fundamental, and possibly fatal, error of believing their enemies were, or thought like, Anglo-Americans in red or brown skins.

The emergence of ranging-company leaders was apparent in the latter stages of President Lamar's wars. Moore's successes in the far West came only because he fought like a Comanche; he sneaked up on Indian villages exactly as a Comanche war band stalked an unsuspecting farmhouse. "Old Paint," Matthew Caldwell, was thinking like an Indian, or ahead of the Indians, at Plum Creek. The Ranger learned to seek out the enemies' weakness, then strike it without mercy. They played their own strengths against such weakness of discipline or mind as successfully as William the Conqueror disposed of Saxon thanes.

Still, there was one final, decisive factor in the winning of the Texas West. This was the invention of the revolving pistol by Samuel Colt, and the manufacture of this revolver at Paterson, New Jersey, by 1838.

It is a fact of history that Colt could not market his revolvers in the

East. There was no civilian need, or market, nor could he interest the military in their use. The U.S. Army was still forest-bound and had no true cavalry arm. Colt's only outlet was in the West, and significantly enough, his first working model was called "The Texas." Somehow, almost immediately, while Colt's enterprise sank slowly into bankruptcy, some of these firearms arrived in the Republic.

The U.S. Army ordnance experts saw no need for them; but those experts had never seen a Comanche band. The Texas partisans riding the frontier between Austin and San Antonio saw the Colt's significance at once. Every Texan tried to beg, borrow, or steal a Texas model Colt's in any way he could. This early gun had many faults; it was too light, a civilian rather than a military arm, and to load it, it had to be broken down into three component parts—a maddeningly ticklish operation at the gallop by a man with only two hands. *But it shot six times.* It gave one Texan horseman the firepower of six.

Just when and how the first revolving pistols—they were never called revolvers in Texas, but six-shooters, six-guns, and a host of other names—arrived is not known. They were certainly in some use by 1839. Captain Jack Hays who first proved the six-shooter in Comanche combat was stationed at San Antonio, the junction of the Mexican and Indian frontier, in 1840.

Hays was twenty-three, a Tennesseean from the same region as Andrew Jackson, the Texas McCulloch family, and General Houston; Jackson bought his "Hermitage" estate from Hays' grandfather. He drifted into Texas as a surveyor; being a borderer, he logically ended up against the far frontier. He fought at Plum Creek, and that same year was appointed Captain of Rangers at San Antonio by Mirabeau Lamar. Hays, handsome, quiet, "a gentleman of purest character" as the citizens of San Antonio described him, was important to history and to his state. He set an indelible stamp upon the Texas Rangers, and by doing so, upon the whole Anglo-American southwestern frontier. For almost a century, every Texas Ranger wanted to be "like Jack Hays"—a monumental epitaph for a man who ended his service at the age of thirty-four. Three things stand out about John Coffee Hays above all others: he was no talker, but a born partisan who liked to ride the wild country by the North Star; he was not a great gunman, but a leader without fear who rose by sheer ability from among his peers; and he was a superb psychologist, who could bend both friend and foe to his will. In some way, Ben McCulloch, Sam Walker, L. H. McNelly, John B. Jones, John H. Rogers, and even Big Foot Wallace were similar, and McCulloch, Walker, and Wallace were Hays-trained.

Jack Hays was the first man to use Colt's six-shooter on Plains Indians. He was jumped on the Pedernales River, probably in Kendall County, by a party of seventy Comanches. Hays had fourteen men. He turned and fought a desperate, running battle on horseback, carrying the fight to the enemy. He lost several Rangers, but killed thirty Indians. Caperton, who wrote an account of this battle, said: "That was considered the best-contested fight that ever took place in Texas, and it showed that they could whip the Indians on horseback . . . the pistols gave them the advantage."

Hays, according to Mary Maverick, back at San Antonio gave full credit to his new firepower and to the total surprise of the Comanches. He now rode with confidence, convinced that six-shooting Texans could defeat any Comanche band alive. Shortly afterward, Hays' company encountered another heavily superior force of Comanches west of San Antonio, in the Nueces canyon.

The Indians, shrieking and shooting arrows, swept around and surrounded the mounted Rangers. At Hays' order, the Texans emptied their long rifles, then leaped into the saddle. Hays yelled "Charge!" in his high, clear voice. The Rangers were at close quarters before the startled Indians —who had rarely known white men to do anything but fort up or run— could turn their horses.

"Powder-burn them!" Hays screamed, as Rangers rode between the Comanche ranks, knocking down Indians to either side. Comanches were entirely brave; they turned to stand, only to see the Rangers coming on, fire spitting again and again from their fists, striking down milling horsemen on all sides.

The Indians fled, and Hays chased them three miles. At the end, the demoralized Comanches were throwing aside their useless shields, lances, and bows and leaning low over their horses in routed flight. The Comanche war chief stated later that he lost half his people, and that wounded warriors died on the trail for a hundred miles to the Devil's River. "I will never again fight Jack Hays, who has a shot for every finger on the hand," the Indian moaned.

Hays, and all the Rangers of his time, never tried to downplay the crucial role of the revolvers in mounted combat. "They are the only weapon which enabled the experienced frontiersmen to defeat the *mounted* Indian in his own peculiar mode of warfare. . . ." a testimonial read. The Rangers learned to love and handle their new pistols with all the reverence the Anglo-American had lavished on his long German rifle. Every culture or subculture has had its distinctive arm: the Macedonians their 18-foot phalanx pike, the Romans their Spanish short-sword. In the 1840's the name of Texas became indelibly linked with the Colt's revolver.

The six-shooter was important beyond the romanticism and enduring symbolism it produced. A superb horseman in open country, armed with one or more long-barreled Colts, represented the most effective weapons system known to the middle 19th century. At one step, the Texas borderers achieved at least parity with the Plains Indians, and a marked superiority over the Mexican cuirassier's lance and the *vaquero's* rope. They would hold both until the dispersion of an effective, *accurate* breechloading rifle, which did not appear until the 1870's.

The revolver, very simply, meant power in southwest Texas, and long after the power was no longer needed, its symbol remained, much as the gentleman's sword was retained into the 19th century in parts of France and Ireland.

Hays and his comrades did not of course destroy the Comanche danger. The history of the frontier was that, as the Rangers became better Comanche fighters, the Comanches took up better "Indian" tactics, avoiding open combat, resorting more and more to the hit-and-run murder and stock-stealing raid. This was not to be ended until Texas again resorted to striking at the source from which Indian depredations flowed.

The Ranger and his revolver were to win enduring fame in 19th century America, however, not against Indians, but in the long Mexican wars.

Hays had served with Henry Karnes' spy service on the Nueces in 1839; in 1841 he was sent to Laredo to check on the possibility of imminent Mexican invasion. Hays rode boldly into the town, which at this time was wholly Mexican and garrisoned with Mexican troops. He stared down the Mexican soldiery, calmly ran off a few horses, and camped on the edge of town. Then, he gave the horses back with a warning to the Mexican commandant that in case there were any robberies or raids north of the Nueces the Mexicans knew what to expect. Later, when a band of brigands attacked one of the wagon trains constantly plying between San Antonio and Laredo despite the international tension, Hays set out again for Laredo, with a dozen Texans and thirteen San Antonio Mexicans under Antonio Pérez, a noted Indian-fighter.

Ten miles from Laredo, a party of thirty-five Mexican cavalry charged Hays with the bugle. At the end of the battle, the Mexican force grounded arms and asked for quarter, with the exception, as Webb wrote, "of the captain and three wise men who remained on horseback." The mayor or *alcalde* of Laredo came to meet Hays with a white flag and asked the town be spared. Hays spared it, again demanding that raids be stopped. Then he marched the hapless prisoners he had taken back over the dusty miles to San Antonio.

In these same months, Jack Hays fought too many combats with the Penatekas and other southern bands to be related in detail. He learned to ride into Indian country and locate Indian camps by the circling flock of buzzards that always hung over them, no matter how well they might be concealed in canyons. He hit them in bed and brush, where the Comanche bow was a useless weapon. He mauled Indians from the Nueces to the Llano, and never with more than fifty men. The remark of the Lipan ally Chief Flacco, who scouted for Hays on some of these raids, still stands: "Me and Red Wing not afraid to go to hell together. Captain Jack heap brave; not afraid to go to hell by himself."

"You may depend," General Houston wrote, "on the gallant Hays and his companions." Lamar's papers indicate that much of the success against the southern Comanches circa 1840 was due to Hays' detachment of Rangers.

In June, 1841, Lamar sent what Andrew Jackson called "the wild-goose campaign to Santa Fe." Its survivors were surrounded, they surrendered to keep from starving, and some were shot, all mistreated, but due to United States' diplomats' efforts, most were eventually returned. This raid caused the Mexican government to retaliate with the expedition against San Antonio, in March, 1842.

Hays had to let Vásquez take the city, since he had only about 100 men. He followed Vásquez back to the Rio Grande, but could not attack. The Ranger captain was never foolhardy. He was not involved in the clash between several hundred Texas volunteers under Davis and Ewen Cameron at Lipantilicán with General Canales.

Despite the fact that war was not open on the Nueces frontier, the Republic disbanded Hays' troop, except for himself and a few "spies," as scouts were then officially called. The reason was Houston's bankruptcy. Hays was "authorized" to raise and equip 150 men; he never did so because he could not pay or arm them.

On September 11, 1842, General Adrian Woll and some 1,200 Mexican soldiers again captured San Antonio. Woll meant this to be merely a demonstration in force, with the triple purpose of asserting Mexican sovereignty, chastising the Texans, and giving U.S. annexationists and Texas' European allies pause. Woll remained only a short time, but did succeed in capturing the district court, which was in session, and a number of prominent Texans.

Hays carried the word to the eastern settlements beyond San Antonio, and soon "Old Paint" Caldwell had raised 225 militia volunteers. Caldwell, with this small force, actually brought Woll to battle along Salado Creek on September 17. From the brush and timber cover, Caldwell knocked back 200 horse and about 600 regular infantry. He sent out calls for more men: "The enemy are all around me on every side, but I fear them not. I will hold my position. . . . Come and help me. . . . There are eleven hundred of the enemy. I can whip them on my own ground without any help, but I cannot take prisoners. Why don't you come? Huzza! huzza for Texas."

Caldwell was doing splendidly, because he knew how to fight both Mexicans and Indians and knew better than to give either an even break. The Mexican heavy cavalry could not ride into his timbers, and no Mexican infantry force of only three-to-one could assault Texas rifles firing from a rest. Woll retreated, carrying away his dead. But Caldwell's appeal resulted in Texan disaster.

Captain Nicholas Dawson rushed from La Grange with 53 men. Woll's horsemen spotted him in open country, and surrounded him, keeping out of rifle range. Mexican field artillery pounded Dawson brutally, and he surrendered under the white flag. Dawson did not know how to fight Mexicans.

The cavalry refused to accept the white flag, and Yoakum detailed how Dawson's men were cut down after giving up. Only fifteen got away, but Woll's triumph was very mixed. The long rifles killed 60 Mexican regulars.

Hays, at the head of a Ranger force, harassed Woll all the way back to the Rio Grande. On one occasion, Hays actually led a cavalry charge into a Mexican artillery position, killing every gunner with pistols and the shotguns many Rangers had now begun to carry in place of rifles. Woll is said to have offered five hundred dollars in silver for the head of this twenty-five-year-old, which, as the Texans gleefully said, was a lot of coin for a five-feet-ten youth who weighed about 160 pounds.

Sam Houston, the President, agreed to a demonstration in force to the Rio Grande under General Somervell. This, called the Mier Expedition, suffered from a historic flaw so many previous expeditions had; it was recruited from a rabble more intent on plunder than defeating Mexican arms. Somervell left San Antonio with 750 men on November 8, 1842, but in this army the frontier militia and Hays' force of Rangers were only a tiny segment.

Somervell easily captured Laredo, and his army, without orders, engaged in a rape of the town. Somervell arrested some stragglers and returned the plunder he could find, though he was unable to restore any women to their former state. This provoked a rebellion in the ranks. Two hundred men deserted. The remaining five hundred soon refused to obey General Somervell's orders in all things.

Somervell declared the demonstration aborted, and marched home. Major Hays and Ben McCulloch went with him, but about 300 men, including the Ranger Captains Ewen Cameron, Samuel Walker, and Big Foot Wallace, stayed for the fun.

The ragtag army marched to Mier, an adobe town in the northern Mexican desert. Here the Texans were surrounded by a large Mexican force. They could have fought their way out, but Colonel Fisher, the commander, was wounded, and in this mutinous-minded force no one had control. An election was held, and the majority of American volunteers insisted on surrendering, especially since Mexican terms involved their being treated as prisoners of war, and being held near the border.

After laying down arms, they were marched rapidly into the interior of Mexico. Cameron and Walker led a successful escape from Saltillo; in this escape the Americans captured a number of Mexican soldiers, but released them after stipulating the wounded men left behind must be treated with the honors of war.

The escapees became lost in the desert above Saltillo, and wandered hopelessly under hideous conditions. Some men ate insects, other dug feverishly for wet earth to wet their swollen tongues. A few, mad, drank their own urine and died a ghastly death. The Mexicans followed with cavalry, and when the escapees had thrown away their arms, rode down and put them all in irons.

Santa Anna, again in power in Mexico, at first angrily demanded that all should be executed. The American and British ministers put up a fearful protest at this, and Santa Anna relented. The Mier Expedition would only be decimated, in the Latin fashion—one in ten would be shot. A pitcher with 159 white beans, 17 black ones, was set in front of the prisoners. Those who drew black were to be shot. Big Foot Wallace, who cannily noticed the black beans were poured in on top of the white, "dipped deep." He lived. Ewen Cameron drew a white bean, but General Antonio Canales, who hated the big Scot, ordered him shot anyway.

The remaining white-bean men, were "horribly mistreated," as Webb and others reported, but again American and British diplomats eventually got them out. They lived to return to Texas just before annexation.

Their experiences were to have a decided effect on the Mexican War of 1846–1848, because the Ranger detachment with the Mier Expedition saw Mexican soil again, as conquerors. In such ways cruelty begat cruelty, and bloodshed shed blood.

26

SOUTH OF THE BORDER

*Hays's Rangers have come, their appearance never to be for-
gotten. Not any sort of uniform, but well mounted and doubly
well armed: each man has one or two Colt's revolvers. . . . The
Mexicans are terribly afraid of them.*

ETHAN ALLEN HITCHCOCK, MÁJOR GENERAL, U.S. ARMY

*The commanding general took occasion to thank them for the
efficient service they had rendered, and we saw them turn their
faces toward the blood-bought State they represented, with many
good wishes and the hope that all honest Mexicans were at a safe
distance from their path.* LUTHER GIDDINGS, *Sketches*

AROUND the cold camps in cedar brakes along the Nueces and the Colorado, Hays' boys frequently discussed the invention of Samuel Colt. They
had adapted the six-shooter to their use, but these fighting men were concerned with its salient faults. The breakdown in three parts, the disappearing trigger, the small bore (caliber .34), and the balance were all wrong.
Colt's first six-gun was not a military or range weapon; it was more an
Easterner's toy.

Some time after 1840 Captain Samuel H. Walker went East, to the
United States. His was an official trip, to buy the latest Yankee arms.
Walker, who had served first with Hays, was born in Maryland, and arrived
in Texas after fighting in the Florida Seminole campaign. He was remarkable, like Hays, for a brilliant coolness; he was only a few years older.
Samuel Colt, Walker, and Hays were actually all of the same generation,
and their histories were to be inseparably linked across almost 2,000 miles.

Sam Walker looked up Sam Colt in New York City. The young Ranger told the young inventor that his pistols were the best seen yet, but the Texas Rangers had some improvements in mind. Delighted, the Connecticut-born Colt took Walker to his Paterson plant. Out of this visit came the world's first martial revolver, which was to become world-famous, and which was called the Walker Colt.

This pistol had a heavy, strong frame, able to withstand rough use and wear. The grip was natural, slipping easily into a large hand. It had a sturdy trigger guard, so it could be worn in a belt. The new caliber was .44, and the balance was beautiful in the palm. Captain Walker was delighted with two improvements above all: the pistol could be used profitably as a club, on someone "not worth shooting," and it could be reloaded by a lever rammer, solidly affixed beneath the newer, longer barrel, without breaking the gun apart. This was a horseman's weapon. It, and its series of modifications and improvements, was to kill more men than any other handgun ever made.

But its issue did not prevent Samuel Colt from bankruptcy in 1842. Texas was too poor to support mass production; not enough of the guns could be ordered or procured. These were the dark years in Sam Colt's life. He was a great man to certain quiet, cold-eyed, weatherbeaten men who occasionally came up from Texas, but he was a prophet with a prophet's usual honor on his native soil. For five years, no Colt's handguns were made. Sam Colt even gave away all the ones he owned.

Then, suddenly, there was war between the United States and Mexico, in early 1846. Texas was a state, and General Zachary Taylor, on the Rio Grande, had asked Texas for two regiments of horse. Jock Hays, barely thirty, raised one; his officers were Ben McCulloch, Sam Walker, Mike Chevaille, Big Foot Wallace, and John S. Ford. Hays and these men were clamoring for a thousand of something called a Colt.

Zachary Taylor gave in to their requests; he wanted none of the new-fangled arms for his own U.S. infantry and dragoons, but politics had forced on him the use of Texas Ranger scouts. Taylor requisitioned Washington for 1,000 revolving pistols.

There were none. The government contacted Colt, who at that moment did not even possess a single model of his own. But Sam Colt behaved with the coolness and judgment that was to make him a millionaire. He advertised in New York newspapers for a Colt's pistol, in the meantime designing a few improvements, and signed a contract with the government to make 1,000 weapons at $28.00 each. Then he farmed the contract out to Eli Whitney, of cotton gin fame. But Whitney was not allowed to reveal this fact; each pistol bore the hallmark, *Address Samuel Colt, New York*. Colt lost $3,000 dollars on this deal. But after Jack Hays had his thousand pistols, Sam Colt's fame was to become worldwide, and his name a household word throughout the United States.

United States military historians, in remarking about the inability of high commanders on both sides to use cavalry in the American Civil War, have often commented that these incipient leaders found that in the Mexican War they were able to win without a mounted arm. This does not entirely state the case.

The United States Army had no cavalry arm in 1846, but had mounted infantry, called dragoons. These troops were heavy and cumbrous; they rode horses to battle, but much preferred to fight on foot. The reason the United States possessed no horse arm in 1846 was not military blindness but the fact that the entire population, save for a few Texans, were still living in a country dominated by woodlands. East of the Plains, cavalry could never be anything but an auxiliary arm.

The idea that the United States won the Mexican War without cavalry is not quite true. Hays' regiment, composed of West Texans, was cavalry. It performed all the normal tasks of cavalry—scouting, flanking, harassing, trail-blazing, and keeping Mexican cavalry from doing the same. Ironically, Hays' Texans achieved worldwide, popular acclaim but very little credit in U.S. Army annals. Here the reason was probably twofold. Hays' regiment of Rangers were irregulars, hardly proper soldiers, who fought like devils, but behaved like wildmen; and this, along with the fact that the generals knew nothing about cavalry, undoubtedly influenced their memoirs and minds.

An incident at the very beginning of the Mexican War is highly significant. Taylor, on the Rio Grande, found he did not know the country or the Mexican mind. Nor could his heavy, blue-uniformed, sweating dragoons perform the tasks they were assigned. Taylor asked for Walker's Scouts to keep his communications open, particularly after Arista's cavalry snapped up sixty of his own dragoons without a fight. Walker, with a few men, carried the vital messages between Taylor at Point Isabel and Major Brown on the river that set up the victories at Palo Alto and Resaca de la Palma.

After these battles, company by company—they were raised by company on the Indian frontier—Hays' regiment filtered down into Mexico. Gillespie's company came by way of Laredo, Ben McCulloch's from the middle Guadalupe. The riders were all frontiersmen of the first tier, not farm boys following the colors. It was generally thought that McCulloch's company was the finest group that had ever assembled in the ranging service.

Ben McCulloch was blue-eyed and taciturn, with a strong face he kept under perfect control. No one ever knew what was in his mind until his words made it clear. He was cool—the word runs through all Ranger descriptions—and above all cool to the point of incredibility in combat. And, like all true partisans, McCulloch seemed to think best under fire. He gave few orders; those he gave were obeyed.

McCulloch's Rangers moved into camp near Fort Brown on May 22, 1846. General Taylor gave them a vitally important duty: to scout the ground between Matamoros and Monterrey, and to select the route for the American invasion. At this time Zachary Taylor was entirely without officers who knew the country or cavalry that could perform such a task. But the Texas Rangers had both.

Ben McCulloch rode into Mexico with forty picked men on June 12.

The third day of the scout the Rangers defeated a party of armed Mexicans under Blás Falcón, a leading *ranchero* of the district. The Mexican army had already withdrawn south. The Mexican *escopetas* were no match for Colts, and the *rancheros* fled, leaving guns, horses, everything.

McCulloch's way was characteristic of the pattern Hays had set; McCulloch now polished and perfected it. He rode carefully, not seeking trouble, but he attacked it boldly when it arose. The *Quién vive?* of the Mexican challenge was answered by the lightning charge. McCulloch rode on forced marches by night, to come up behind Mexican villages or ranches from the southern, supposedly safe, roads. He doubled and twisted, throwing off any possible pursuit. Above all else, he went boldly, seizing towns and *ranchos* he could not gracefully avoid, not by numbers but by an awesome display of utter confidence. McCulloch seized and held moral superiority; the Mexicans were afraid of him.

Sending his lieutenant, John McMullen, on a side scouting expedition, McCulloch quickly determined that General Arista had retreated all the way to Monterrey and that the Linares route to that city was unfeasible due to lack of watering places. He had found out what Taylor wanted to know.

Turning about, McCulloch rode northwest, rather than on the direct route to Matamoros. The Rangers were eager to find and fight General Antonio Canales, who had long waged a bloody warfare against the Texans above the Rio Grande. Canales, like Falcón, was one of those landowners whose family held title to vast grants north of the Bravo, and these families provided a continuing leadership for Mexican raids and Mexican resistance to Anglo expansion south. Canales personally had secured the execution of Ewen Cameron after he drew a white bean. The Rangers wanted Canales' blood.

But the summer solstice brought roaring rains, and McCulloch found Canales gone. Having been deep in enemy country for ten days, and ridden 250 miles in that time, McCulloch rode into Reynosa, upriver from Matamoros, which Taylor had just seized. The Rangers had not taken off their boots, coats, or spurs during the entire ride. Their information gave Taylor what he needed to plan his campaign.

The rangers made camp at Reynosa. But now, there was an ominous hint of things to come. The Mier Expedition survivors had been treated barbarously by the inhabitants of this town, starved, beaten, spat upon. Some of the same men were with McCulloch; all of his Rangers had had kinfolk or comrades killed by Mexicans since 1836. One of them, Sam Reid, later wrote: "Our orders were most strict not to molest any unarmed Mexican, and if some of the most notorious of these villains were found shot, or hung up in the chaparral . . . the government was charitably bound to suppose, that during a fit of remorse and desperation, tortured by conscience for the many evil deeds they had committed, they had recklessly laid violent hands upon their own lives! *Quién sabe?"*

Zachary Taylor *sabe*-ed well enough that the Texans were settling old scores, but he was helpless: "I have not the power to remedy it. . . . I fear they are a lawless set." He said that if they would only obey orders, the Texans unquestionably would be the best soldiers among all the U.S. volunteers. Meanwhile, the Rangers colorfully celebrated every American and Mexican holiday with races and riding contests, including some very rough games on horseback. The American troops were awed and fascinated by these, not realizing they were seeing the birth of something new, which would one day be called the rodeo.

The tricks, stunts, and very notion had been absorbed by the Rangers from the Mexicans and horse Indians.

The Rangers also attended a few Mexican *bailes* or dances; fandangos as the Texans persisted in calling them. The appearance of these huge, bearded, cold-eyed men caused women to scream and men to bolt, and usually dampened all Mexican enthusiasm for *fiesta*.

Then, on July 9, Taylor marched to Camargo, preparatory to driving on Monterrey. The Rangers were in the saddle again, scouting the U.S. invasion route. They made a few side trips, seeking Colonel Juan Seguín. Seguín, a Texas Spaniard, had sided with the Revolution in 1835. Then, during the great turmoil of 1842 and retirement of Mexicans from south Texas ordered by Woll, he had returned to his own people. The Rangers wanted him, too. But again, McCulloch checked and discarded unsuitable roads. As the Texas historian Wooten quoted an American general: "He and his officers and men were not only the eyes and ears of General Taylor's army, but its right and left arms as well."

The American army in Mexico definitely possessed a cavalry arm.

Captain Duncan, during McCulloch's illness, led the vanguard. He actually accepted the surrender of Cerralvo. Now, a pattern was clear. The frontier Rangers were the vanguard, and the army's eyes and ears, while the Rangers under Wood—all east Texans—did escort duty.

Meanwhile, Jack Hays had left Matamoros with the main body of the Ranger regiment. Taylor's quartermaster was trying to buy mules at $20 each, but he was not finding any. He wrote, "This call might have been ineffectual, had not a Texan mounted regiment been moving into the quarter whence we expected these mules." By methods never recorded, Hays got the army all the mules it needed.

Taylor moved on Monterrey in September, 1846, with McCulloch and Gillespie's companies going ahead of one column, Hays going before the other. At Ramos, McCulloch struck two hundred Mexican cavalry and knocked them out of the way. Now, the mountains over the old Spanish city of Monterrey were in sight of all of Taylor's 6,000 men. The General ordered the "Texas mounted troops" to "form the advance of the army tomorrow, and to move at sunrise."

Taylor kept a group of Rangers with his staff, and General Worth, commanding the 2d Division, took Rangers with him on every personal reconnaissance. Once, before Monterrey, they saved his life. But these were minor services, which generally went unrecorded.

Worth's column, with the Rangers in front, moved out at 6 A.M. McCulloch immediately found himself riding into a large squadron of Mexican lancers, supported by infantry. This was Najera's squadron, beautifully mounted, uniformed, carrying lanceheads that glittered in the sun. Najera rode in front and gave the command to set lances.

Dirty, smelly, unshaven, the Rangers watched McCulloch. McCulloch never got Worth's order to dismount and smell the situation out. He did not give Najera time to get set; he charged. There was a violent melee, as lancers and Rangers fought at close range with lances, swords, knives, and pistols. McCulloch rode down everything in his path. At the end, a hundred Mexican bodies in brilliant uniforms lay in the road; Colonel Najera was dead, and the body of his troops were in flight toward Saltillo.

The reducing of the hills above the city and the entry into the fortified capital were bloody work for the American infantry and artillery. But Rangers went with every party, and their markmanship, with rifles, assisted materially in clearing the houses and squares. The American regulars broke the main resistance in front of the palace, driving off the Mexican battalions of infantry, light horse lancers, and the heavy cavalry, which tried to charge with broadswords. All met a disastrous fire and a wall of bayonets. But while Worth was carrying everything before him, Taylor himself, to Worth's east, was rather badly mauled. Monterrey could still have turned into a Mexican catastrophe, but Taylor accepted Ampudia's offer to parley.

At the end of negotiations, the Mexican army was permitted to evacuate with the honors of war and an eight-week truce. Monterrey was not to be a decisive battle. Protests to this were extremely violent among Hays' men. But they had no say in the matter.

During this truce, Hays' regiment went home. It had been enlisted for six months; the time had expired, and the Texans were now disgusted with the war. Zachary Taylor, for his part, obviously wanted to be rid of them. The thought of a thousand Texans camping in Monterrey worried Taylor badly; he issued the Rangers a general discharge on October 1.

Giddings, an officer with the Ohio volunteers, wrote frankly that the Army would have been much more regretful to see the Rangers go, except for the "lawless and vindictive spirit some of them had displayed" after the capitulation of Monterrey. Atrocities there were many, because the Texas troops detested Mexicans with a cold, consuming hate.

This was an entirely different attitude than the one toward Comanches. Texas looked on Indians very much as Western Europeans had once looked on wolves. They were hated as dangerous animals; they were marked down for extermination. The detestation of Mexico was different. Mexico had a culture and a civilization, but it was one Anglo-Celts, on close contact, instinctively despised. The Mexican and the Texan, as so often happened in such contacts, felt the ways of each impugned the manhood of the other. The Texan reaction toward Mexico was not one of destruction so much as a determination to dominate. Unhappily, the Mexican-Hispanic urge to press an insult could not be suppressed, while the Texan refusal to accept any kind of slur or comment led to bloodshed.

This puzzled some of the other Americans, because while the Texas regiment was tattered, unwashed, and bearded—from living in the saddle —Hays' people were by no means crude or ignorant as a group. McCulloch commanded lawyers, doctors, poets, surveyors, and men whose education was equal to any American's. Giddings referred to the frequent quotation of Latin or Greek around Ranger campfires. But the Ranger force lived in a world where the consciousness of war and killing was ever-present; the other volunteers did not. The Rangers represented most of the splendid qualities of their English-speaking race, but they had adapted at least part of their ethos entirely to the brutal frontier. Thus, Hays himself, with perfect truth, could be called a "perfect gentleman" by the citizenry of San Antonio, and a feared and fearful killer by Mexicans and Indians.

Without some such adaptation, very likely American casualties on the far frontier would have been much higher, if not disastrous. But the adaptation left its mark.

A strong, if not the strongest, factor in the Texans' leaving Mexico was concern for the Indian frontier, which the withdrawal of the companies had left exposed. Texas always had to balance its concern, and forces, between the Mexican and Indian wars.

Afterward, events in northern Mexico continued as a tragicomedy of errors. Taylor's truce was disapproved by the government, and he so notified Santa Anna on November 13, 1846. But Polk's Administration did not want Taylor himself to fight. It had wanted the war, but not for a known Whig general to win it for the United States. Winfield Scott was sent to the Rio Grande to extract 9,000 of Taylor's best troops for the planned Vera Cruz expedition, and to order Taylor to withdraw all his forces to Monterrey and remain on the defensive.

On January 3, 1847, Scott sent Taylor dispatches with these orders. Now, the absence of the mounted Texans changed history. From the day they rode north, United States communications had collapsed; couriers were killed; the army had lost its eyes and ears. Lieutenant John Richey, carrying Scott's written orders, was roped from his horse by Mexican *vaqueros* near Linares. They killed Richey with considerable cruelty; more important historically, they delivered his dispatch case to General Santa Anna.

Santa Anna, seeing Taylor was to be abandoned at Monterrey with a skeleton force, smelled the victory the Mexican nation so badly needed at this time. He marched toward Monterrey from San Lusís Potosí with a little more than 15,000 men. This was the best army Mexico had in the field.

Now, in January 1847, Ben McCulloch arrived at Taylor's headquarters with 27 Rangers. He had heard the war was recommenced. This was true enough. Zachary Taylor decided not to obey his orders to fall back on Monterrey, because they made no military sense in his situation. He had already taken Victoria and Saltillo, and to obey such orders would have dispirited his whole force. McCulloch offered to serve again, but at his own pleasure—not for duration, nor even for a year. Taylor was so desperate for riders that he violated army regulations and enlisted the Rangers into the U.S. service on their own terms.

The first duty of these paladins was to find Santa Anna's army. General Taylor had already lost two fine officers and part of the regulars trying to do this; American infantry was helpless on the northern Mexican deserts. McCulloch took sixteen men, crossed a thirty-five-mile desert, and found Santa Anna at Encarnación. He rode through the advance guard of the Mexican cavalry to do it.

On February 20, Taylor sent McCulloch back to Encarnación to determine the size of Santa Anna's army. With seven men, the Ranger captain went into the Mexican lines at midnight, scouting Santa Anna's bivouac like a Comanche camp. McCulloch counted fires, and arrived at almost the exact number in the force. He sent this word back to Taylor, while he and one man stayed inside the Mexican picket line until daylight, just to make sure. Then, when the Mexican soldiers lit green-wood breakfast fires, the two Rangers mounted and rode deliberately through the smoke, confirming that Santa Anna had between 15,000 and 20,000 men.

This information caused Taylor to retreat back to the pass at Angostura, near a *hacienda* called Buena Vista. Here he had a position that could not be flanked or turned. He took McCulloch's personal report, and said only, "Very well, Major, that's all I wanted to know. I am glad they did not catch you."

Santa Anna mistook this retreat, and pressed onward rashly, expecting to overtake a demoralized army. Thus he ran into the American rifles, artillery, and massed bayonets at Buena Vista, and suffered what was for Mexico, a disastrous defeat. This man, who personally did so much to destroy his own nation, was forced to lead a broken rabble back across the desert. He had not only failed to win a victory for morale purposes in an unimportant theater, but he had dissipated the force that might have stopped Winfield Scott before Mexico. He had also awarded Zachary Taylor the U.S. Presidency, as a result of the great victory at Buena Vista.

Again, McCulloch and his men went home. Taylor, in writing, demanded that he be sent no more Rangers. He gave the reason: "The mounted men from Texas have scarcely made one expedition without unwarrantably killing a Mexican."

This, in many American minds, overrode their services to the cause.

General Winfield Scott, whose main thrust was designed to win the war, landed at Vera Cruz in March, 1847, and immediately advanced toward the Mexican capital. Cerro Gordo, Contreras, Churubusco, Molina del Rey, and Chapultepec rolled down on the Mexicans, a series of disasters. Scott went into the City of Mexico on September 14. In this campaign he did not use, nor apparently did he need, cavalry. The terrain was eminently suitable for foot soldiers, and for maps and route evaluation Scott relied on his West Pointer engineers.

No Texas Rangers arrived until Scott was almost at Mexico City.

In the capital, however, the American army was in an unenviable position. It had arrived intact because, after Santa Anna's fiasco at Buena Vista, there was no formidable Mexican army in the field. But Scott's route of communications to the coast was long and vulnerable. It lay across a succession of thickets and forests near the Gulf, rising through a series of narrow defiles, gorges, and passes on the upper plateaus. This was beautiful country, which had inspired every arriving conqueror with a certain amount of awe. It was also infested with a new Hispanic opposition to Nordic might—the *guerrilla* (literally, "little war").

Behind Scott, the Mexican population was aroused: *rancheros* and *hacendados* took irregular forces into the woods and hills. They began to bleed Scott's supply line. In April, 1847, Robelledo captured ten American wagons. McIntosh, marching to reinforce Scott, lost one quarter of his wagons and many men. Pierce suffered a hundred dead out of a thousand on the passage, without fighting a battle. Wells, coming up with two-hundred odd, lost forty to guerrillas. The situation rapidly turned serious.

The efforts of both American regulars and militia volunteers against these guerrillas was almost ludicrous. The records, and one soldier's diary reveal each punitive expedition merely lost more men: ". . . fell in with some rancheros or guerrillas . . . several of our men killed. On Friday the Illinois company went out after carne [meat] and guerrillas; they came back without dead guerrillas but with two dead soldiers . . . more . . . went out to avenge the death of their companions. Later in the afternoon they returned. Two of their men had been lassoed, dragged on the ground at full speed, and speared to death."

All records agree that only one American officer seemed to know what to do in this deteriorating situation. J. J. Oswandel, in his *Notes on the Mexican War,* wrote in an entry dated May 25, 1847: "This morning Gen. Twiggs' division and a large train . . . arrived in Perote city. Among them I noticed . . . Capt. Samuel H. Walker, the Texas Ranger, with two companies of mounted riflemen, mounted on fine spirited horses. They are all fine, strong, healthy, and good looking men, nearly every one measured over six feet. . . . I learn they are to remain with us to keep the National Road open between this castle and the city of Jalapa. So guerrillas, robadors, take warning . . . for the renowned Capt. Samuel H. Walker takes no prisoners."

The "renowned Capt. Samuel H. Walker" now held a commission as captain in the regular army, Polk's reward for his singular services on the Palo Alto. But neither his contemporaries nor Sam Walker ever made much of this. Walker was always called "the Texas Ranger," and few have bothered to set the record straight. Walker acted, thought, and fought like a Westerner, never a captain of United States dragoons.

Walker's troop was stationed at Perote through the summer. This great, grim fortress remained a bitter memory to him, and to all the Texans who had been incarcerated there with him in 1843. Walker had buried a dime within the prison walls as a symbolic hope of his return; now he went and dug it up. Then, he looked at the Stars and Stripes floating over Perote, and took to killing guerrillas. The records show that again and again Walker rode back into Perote from a scout with captured arms, horses, wagons, and other sundry loot. He never reported any live guerrillas. When he rode out of the fortress on one occasion, an American there wrote, "Should Capt. Walker come across the guerrillas God help them. . . ."

Walker ranged wide; while the Mexicans harassed the roads he popped through the brush and harassed them, from the rear. He pressed after them into the villages where they assembled before and after raids. He broke them at Las Vegas and La Hoya, and chased them as mercilessly as his limited forces could. He fought guerrillas the only way they could be fought, by making the country entirely dangerous for them. In no other way could it be made safe for Americans.

While Scott took the capital, things became even more serious on his flank. Childs, who held Puebla with about 2,000 men, was under virtual siege by Santa Anna and a guerrilla army. When Santa Anna's forces grew to some 5,000, General Joseph Lane was ordered to march to Puebla to his relief. With Joe Lane came a regiment of Texans, commanded by Colonel Jack Hays.

Behind Hays' reappearance in Mexico lay a story that reached all the way to Washington. When the acute problem of guerrilla warfare along Scott's line of communications became known in the capital, Polk, as the President's diary for July 17, 1847, makes clear, insisted that the job of guarding the road be given to Jack Hays. The President's wishes carried over the protests of the Army, and thus another thousand mounted Texans arrived via ship at Vera Cruz. Here, before they set out for the interior, another significant event occurred. Samuel Colt's 1,000 new "Army" model revolvers arrived, and were distributed joyfully by Captain John S. Ford and others among the troops.

This regiment was composed of real Rangers, not a conglomerate force of Americans such as Walker was commanding and training. On the road toward Mexico, this column excited great wonder. Hays' men wore every kind of coat—blue, black, long-tailed, and short. They wore leather caps, stained fedoras, and soiled panama hats. Most were bearded. They rode every color of horse. The most excitement was caused by their armament. Each man carried a rifle, a knife, and a rope; some had single-shot horse pistols—but all had two Colt six-shooters prominently displayed in his belt.

Hays himself aroused much interest, because he was so unlike his men. The officers of Lane's Brigade, to which he was joined, could hardly believe this was the "world-renowned" Jack Hays. "I shook hands with him," one wrote. "Jack was very modest . . . plainly dressed, and wore a blue roundabout, black leather cap, and black pants, and had nothing about him to denote . . . the army or . . . military rank. His face was sun-browned; his cheeks gaunt; and his dark hair and dark eyes gave a shade of melancholy to his features . . . —made him appear more like a boy than a man."

On October 4, 1847, Lane's Brigade reached Perote, held by Walker. Hays and his old lieutenant, now with different commands, in different services, took the field, screening the brigade's advance to Puebla. Walker took the vanguard, directly ahead of the infantry. He was described by an American who saw him ride past as "rather short, slender, spare, slouchy . . . with reddish hair, small reddish beard, mild blue eyes and a quiet kindly manner."

Walker rode into Santa Anna's army at Huamantla, on October 9. The ex-Ranger yelled the charge to his U.S. dragoon command the instant contact was made. Walker's men spilled into Huamantla, shooting and sabering. He was carrying the day, when Santa Anna came up with his full force. In heavy fighting, the dragoons were pushed back, until Lane's columns could arrive. When they did, they swept the town and captured all the Mexican guns, but not before Sam Walker was shot dead. Walker's men broke into tears over his body. General Lane gave him the highest praise: "Foremost in the advance, he had routed the enemy when he fell mortally wounded."

Hays' Rangers took Walker's place. Lane and Hays moved to Puebla, and broke the siege. Then, Hays cut a swath of destruction north to Matamoros in November, considerably lessening the taste of the *rancheros* for partisan work. The Mexicans could hardly mount effective guerrilla war, when a band of ravening Texans were waging guerrilla warfare in their own rear.

Hays rode back to Mexico City to join Scott. He brought in some prisoners. "This," Oswandel marveled, "is one of the seven wonders." Oswandel did not understand the cruelties and necessities of true partisan war.

Captain Ford, who was now universally called "Old Rip," described the entry of the Rangers into the Mexican capital: "Our entrance . . . produced a sensation . . . They thronged the streets along which we passed. The greatest curiosity prevailed to get a sight at "Los Diabolos Tejanos"—the Texas Devils."

To this generation of Mexicans the *diablos tejanos* (Ford's Spanish was border Tex-Mex, and not the best) were still a shuddery legend. The Alamo, San Jacinto, and a dozen skirmishes since were not looked upon in

Mexico as valiant stands as they were in the United States. *Los Tejanos sangrientes*—"the bloody Texans"—Mexicans said, and women crossed themselves at the name.

Ford's diary recorded the Rangers' propensity for an eye for an eye, a tooth for a tooth, with appalling clarity. Already, the first shock of defeat was passing in the capital, and resistance was smoldering in the alleys and back streets. American stragglers and the visitors to brothels were being knifed. The American command took the line that this was the victims' own fault for exposing themselves so. The Rangers immediately showed a different reaction.

When a pickpocket stole a Ranger kerchief and was detected, a bullet knocked the hapless thief kicking to the pavement. The owner calmly picked up his property and went on, not bothering to look at his victim. Another Mexican made the error of hurling a stone at passing Texans. Another shot, another Mexican dead. When Rangers entered the National Theater restaurant, one waiter dropped his trays with a crash and fled. He was not going to risk offending a *diablo sangriente*.

Then, some inhabitants of Mexico made the monumental mistake of murdering a Ranger named Adam Allsens in one of the less reputable quarters of the city. Roberts' Company rode into the quarter. Nothing of that night was ever described, but reports from the next morning exist: "At breakfast time they had brought in fifty-three corpses. . . . In the evening the captain reported more than eighty bodies lying in the morgue. . . . They had been shot in the streets and left lying."

General Scott called in Colonel Hays and protested. Hays said mildly that no one could "impose" on the Rangers. The quiet-eyed, slender Hays faced the General down; "Old Fuss and Feathers," as the Texans called Scott, dropped the matter. He did find employment for the Ranger regiment outside the capital as soon as possible, however.

After this incident, no Rangers, and few Americans, were killed on occupation duty in the City of Mexico. The Ranger captains' methods were brutal, but not without their rationale. *Rinche* (Ranger) was passing into the Mexican tongue as a term of dread. But the Rangers had established a lasting moral superiority in combat; they were almost always outnumbered, but their greatest asset was the fact that their enemies were almost always afraid of them. This growing reputation was worth almost as much as the Colt pistol to the Ranger force. It put enormous pressures on Ranger opponents—Mexican, Indian, or white.

Jack Hays could keep the regiment in check when he felt it necessary. When Santa Anna passed through the Ranger lines, on Scott's safe-conduct, in the last stages of the war, there was violent sentiment in the Ranger ranks to seize him. Santa Anna's invasion of Texas had left lasting scars and hatreds. Hays stopped this talk, not by bluster or threats or reference to discipline but simply by saying that any such move by the Rangers would dishonor Texas. The Mexican general was noticeably pale when his carriage passed through the Texas regiment, but he passed safely.

The Treaty of Guadalupe Hidalgo ended the war between Mexico and the United States in 1848, but it did not entirely end hostilities between Mexico and the State of Texas, as many Americans never fully understood. There was to be more bloodshed along the border river for almost a hundred years.

The exploits of the Rangers brought worldwide publicity to the force, and to the State of Texas itself. The reports of newspaper correspondents and the letters and diaries of American veterans were filled with admiring references to the Texans. Both Hays' men, and their heavy revolvers, impressed themselves indelibly on the American imagination. By 1848, "Texas Ranger" and "Colt revolver" were household American terms.

Americans, from Ohio to Georgia, sensed something new in these men. It appealed strongly to the American character, because, after all, the Texas Rangers were manifestations of the American character under certain conditions.

The Rangers were a completely masculine society, with a deep camaraderie born of open spaces and the camp fire. They were taciturn, devoted not to talk but to direct, violent action. Hays made a tremendous impression: a quiet, modest, essentially decent man, who never boasted but never backed down. He did not look for trouble, but minded his own business. If someone gave him trouble, he retaliated with quick, clean, brutal force. His bravery, and that of his men, was so striking that physical courage became an inseparable part of the legend, unremarkable, taken for granted. If some aspects of Hays' reactions to trouble seemed shockingly brutal to later Americans, it must be remembered that in the 1840's Americans were at war with both Mexicans and Indians, two races few Americans admired.

The Ranger image was that of a tall, quiet-spoken Westerner, who preferred his horse to female society, who wore a well-oiled pistol and knew how to use it, and who, when called upon, would destroy the forces of evil by killing them. The image was appealing rather than repellant. Records of the times show that virtually every volunteer in the American forces in Mexico wanted to acquire a Colt's revolver, and most eventually did. Here, certainly, both the revolver and the symbology of the revolver entered American life. Both would be lasting.

The Texas Ranger and his six-shooter would enter American consciousness, to be eulogized under different names, and in a hundred different places, in song, story, and on the screen. The man, the gun, and the action would be as attractive to millions of Americans a hundred years later as it was in 1848. A new prototype was born.

The Mexican term *charro* had not yet been translated into English; the *vaquero* had not yet become a buckaroo or cowboy. But as Jack Hays and his troop began the long, dusty ride back to Texas (and, it is hoped, all honest Mexicans kept out of their way) the ways and world views, and the world image, of the American Western hero had been formed.

27

THE BLOODY TRAIL

The Texans had very definite ideas as to how Indians should be treated. Their psychology was fixed, and they refused to yield their views to the more lenient policies of the federal government. Out of the maelstrom of the past and its many bitter experiences they had come with hard and relentless methods. Their independent existence for ten years had fostered self-reliance and created new institutions suited to the circumstances, and produced in them a spirit that could not be cast off lightly. Theoretically, they were quite willing to turn the task of protecting the frontier over to the federal government, but practically they were unwilling to accept the federal plan; they soon demanded that the work be done through their institutions and leadership—at federal expense. They easily convinced themselves, for example, that the Texas Rangers knew best how to whip Mexicans and exterminate Indians, and their impatience with the clumsy methods and humanitarian policy of the United States Army was colossal.

WALTER PRESCOTT WEBB, *The Texas Rangers:*
A Century of Frontier Defense

I T was always evident that Texas came into the Union never expecting to surrender the amount of sovereignty other Americans came to demand. From 1845 onward, and even after the state's efforts to solve its problems through secession failed, there tended to be a deep divergence between the Texan and the national view on many things.

The dominant view in Texas toward state-federal relations was that Texans should dictate basic policies within the state, while the federal apparatus should assist with the implementation, especially with money.

This attitude was not illogical, certainly no more than the eventual federal system that emerged in the next century, by which the national government dictated internal policy, reserved the major revenues, but left the really troublesome social problems to the states. Texas' major controversies with the national government during the 19th century arose over policies toward Mexicans, Negroes, and Indians. In perspective, if Anglo-Texans' attitudes were often brutal, the distant government's policies were often absurd because they failed to take local conditions into account.

The first great dissatisfaction with the Union in Texas was over the United States' protection of the Indian frontier. Texas and the United States in the years immediately preceding annexation had evolved different Indian policies. All of the states east of the Mississippi had either expelled their Indians or confined them on reservations, and the United States had reverted to something similar to the old British Indian policy. The edge of the Plains was considered a line of demarcation, and the Great American Desert was to be reserved as a sort of wild Indian game preserve. The Texan view was radically different: the Texans wanted all Indians run out of the state.

The Texas situation was unique. Other states went through a territorial stage before admittance to the Union, and it had become axiomatic that by the time a territory was ready for statehood its wild Indians were either conquered or removed. But Texas not only had a savage frontier, but more than half the state was unsettled, much of it even unexplored. This, and the fact that the terms of annexation reserved all lands within Texas' drawn boundaries to the state, created serious problems.

Protection of the frontier and handling of Indians were federal responsibilities. But on the other hand, both the Indians and the U.S. Army were on Texas soil. The Army had no authority over the white citizens of Texas, and Army commanders could not behave or operate as they could on a federal frontier. Meanwhile, they were bound by an Eastern-imposed Indian policy, which did not envision aggressive war. The Army accepted the task of protecting the frontier, but the federal government refused the job of removing the Indians. This excited great exasperation in Texas, especially when in 1846, and again in 1848, the government went through an elaborate farce of making treaties with the Plains Indians at Comanche Peak, having these ratified by the Senate, and signed by President Polk. These treaties were absurd. They did not guarantee the Comanches and Kiowas a reservation or line of demarcation in Texas, because the federal government had no powers to grant them state lands. They did not halt the white advance to the edge of Comanchería, because Washington had no powers to do this, either. Finally, the policy-makers utterly failed to take the nature of the Comanches and Kiowas into account. These were hunting Indians, who had never in tribal history planted a seed in the ground. They were war Indians, who had seized and held the richest buffalo grounds; stealing horses and ripping scalps was at the root of their value system.

They were strong Indians, too, who had avoided all contact with the white man, and therefore suffered none of the demoralization that affected tribal cultures that succumbed to white artifacts or had their sense of superiority shaken by dependence on European ways.

They were not humble before the treaty-makers; they were proud and arrogant, as they had a right to be. They took American gifts, but their promises were as worthless as Washington's over the years. The Kiowa-Comanches never accepted, though they may have understood, the fact that the *Tejanos* and the *Americanos* were not two separate peoples or nations. A significant but little-mentioned aspect of federal-Texas relations with these tribes was that the Indians did consider the Americans friends of a sort, and accepted their agents in the Indian Territory of Oklahoma, but they considered Texas another country, and one they had a right to raid until the end of their independent days.

As *every* Texas-born historian, with roots on the old frontier, has tried to point out, this peace policy with the Plains Indians was not humanitarian, but mistaken. It only deferred the destruction of the tribes, while it further brutalized the white population for another thirty years along the vast frontier.

The government placed a string of forts along the Comanche frontier: Fort Worth, Fort Belknap, Fort Inge, Fort Clark, Fort Duncan. These ran along a general north-south line just west of the 98th meridian and the San Antonio-Dallas line. Eventually, other forts—Lancaster, Davis, Stockton, and Bliss—protected the California trail through completely unpopulated west Texas. These forts never adequately served their purpose, which was protection of the white frontier to their east. They did not and could not separate Indians raiders from the white settlements. They were static, while they were faced with continuing guerrilla war. They were separated by hundreds of miles through which Indians could ride at will; their garrisons were too small to cope with the numbers of Plains tribes involved; and for many years the troops themselves were inadequate and unequipped for the task. When the federal government assumed the job of protecting the Texas frontier, its army had no formal cavalry branch. Some of the first troops sent out on the edge of the vast Plains were infantry, mounted on mules. As Texans remarked bitterly, the only way they could damage the hard-riding Comanches was possibly by causing the Indians to laugh themselves to death. One Texas editor likened infantry toiling over the immense distances of the Plains, in pursuit of Comanches, to a "sawmill on the ocean." They were generally about as useful. Yet the War Department, dominated by men who never saw the West, was painfully slow to organize an effective horse arm. No real improvement came in Texas until Jefferson Davis became Secretary of War. Davis believed in cavalry; he also had a consuming interest in the West. He sent a succession of outstanding officers to Texas. He was accused of training warriors for the South, but he did bring some relief to Texans.

Although they were always scorned by the Texans, the bluecoats did learn to fight Indians; but the constant irritant was that Washington did not want them to fight. Federal soldiers were not permitted to kill an Indian unless they were attacked; in fact, they were required to protect Indians from Texans at times. Above all, the passive stance was fatal against a foe who understood all the niceties of partisan war. What the Army did was to grant the Comanches their Plains sanctuary, but to afford no sanctuary to the white pioneers in their rear.

In 1849 alone, incomplete figures indicate that at least 149 white men, women, and children were killed on the northwest Texas frontier. The effect of this kind of warfare, in a region where homesteads were many miles apart and people were very few, is easily imagined.

The *Texas State Gazette,* in September, 1849, printed the views of a man with vast experience and knowledge of the Plains tribes gained on the Santa Fe trail:

> I see that the Comanches are still continuing their forays upon the Texas border, murdering and carrying off defenseless frontier setttlers who had been granted protection. . . . They must be pursued, hunted, run down, and killed—killed until they find we are in earnest. . . . If Harney can have his own way, I cannot but believe he will call in Hays, McCulloch, and all the frontier men, and pursue the Comanches to the heads of the Brazos, the Colorado, and even up under the spurs of the Rocky Mountains—they must be beaten up in all their covers and harassed until they are brought to the knowledge of . . . the strength and resources of the United States.

But Harney, the Army commander, and his successors were rarely to have their way; they were circumscribed by distant policy. Nor did Harney and other officers want any part of Rangers. They could not ask for them without admitting their own forces were not the best Indian-fighters in the world. Parties of state troops were called for brief periods of service, but for the ten years following the Mexican War there was no real Ranger organization. The good men had gone, and the Rangers who did take the field from time to time were badly led and did poorly. There was a need for something like the Rangers, but Austin would or could not pay for their upkeep; besides, border defense was a federal responsibility. Meanwhile, for long agonizing years, the government would not admit the bankruptcy of its Indian policies in Texas.

Considered of equal importance to the army by the government were its Indian agents. These were civil officers whose duty was to execute Indian laws and implement treaty terms and policy; over-all, their mission was to see that the Indians kept the peace. In Texas, the Indian agent had no authority over civilians or state officers, and his control over Indians was at best always theoretical. Whatever results an agent got he got with persuasion and the force of his personality; he specifically had no control over federal troops.

These limitations were not understood either by the Texas population or by Washington, both of whom apparently expected the Indian agents to keep the aborigines under control by reading them the white man's law. Some aspects of this law were ridiculous to Indians, such as the treaty the United States signed with Mexico by which Indians were not permitted to raid south of the Rio Grande.

The principal figure among Texas Indian agents was Major Robert S. Neighbors, a Texan who had worked with Indians for the Republic. Neighbors from the start had an impossible job, because he could not win and hold the confidence of the Indians without losing that of the whites. One of the worst problems Indian agents faced was the desire of whites to start trouble. Texas had no laws preventing its citizens from trading with Indians. One particularly bothersome trader, George Barnard, had a post high on the Brazos, from which he sold Indians liquor and firearms and stirred up trouble for all. The Army wanted to remove Barnard, but had no authority to take such action within the confines of a sovereign state. The Governor of Texas had no objection to getting rid of all gun-runners and traders, but could secure no law to do so; nor did any federal code apply. The position of these traders was actually impregnable for many years; all deplored them, no one did anything about them in the squabbling over state-federal jurisdiction.

The main work of the Indian agents, Neighbors, Rollins, Stem, and others, was not with the Plains tribes but with the border remnants in west central Texas, the Witchita bands, Tonkawas, Lipans, and similar small surviving groups. By 1850, the farm line had reached its natural limits along the 98th meridian, and these Indians were caught in limbo. The Anglos had pushed the game—in numbers Indians could live on—beyond their lands. None of these tribes dared venture out too far on the lordly Comanches' range. They wandered about on the fringes of the white man's world. They were hungry, and in some cases actually starving. They committed a number of small depredations, such as killing beeves and stealing horses.

Agent John Rollins' report made it clear that the choice of these tribes was between stealing and starving, and even some Texas newspapers admitted that the "tame" Indians presented a pitiable sight. The Penateka Comanches, who had lost most of their range, were equally destitute. There were winters when the Indians ate all their dogs, and then their horses, the Indian's most prized possession. All these tribes had had considerable contact with European civilization, had tasted the white man's wars, and had been debilitated by both. They lived in terrible psychological confusion, unable to shake old Amerind values, unable to fully adopt white ways, having no longer any real belief in either.

Nothing was done about this Indian detritus until Jefferson Davis became Secretary of War. Davis wrote Governor Bell of Texas in 1853, outlining certain problems of defense, among which was the fact that the Federal government could not give the Indians a defined territory in Texas.

Davis promised that if the state would set aside lands for an Indian reservation, the government would restrict the savages to it, and be able to take control of them if they strayed off it. In February, 1854, the state legislature set aside twelve leagues, or about 70,000 acres. Neighbors and Captain Randolph Marcy of the U.S. Army surveyed two separate reserves, one for the Anadarkos, Wacos and other semiagricultural tribes a few miles below Fort Belknap, called the Brazos Reservation, and another, on the Clear Fork of the Brazos about twenty miles to its southwest. This was to be the Penateka home. Both reserves had wood and water, and lay in beautiful, rolling country.

Neighbors had the exhausting task of drawing the Indians in. In doing this, he won the respect of every civil and military officer in this part of Texas, but the hatred of most of the white settlers, who wanted the Indians exterminated or driven entirely away. Neighbors, who was a big, strong, immensely courageous man, patient with savages but angrily impatient with white prejudices, had to deal with Indian irresponsibility, interference by the Army, and white intransigence all at the same time. He got the Indians to congregate, but the promised food did not arrive. Then, a party of soldiers attacked his peaceful Indians for no apparent cause. Citizens fired on a large group of Tonkawas who were on their way to the reserve, scattering them. The whites feared all Indians and considered any mounted or armed Indian fair game. Some of Neighbor's assistants were incompetent and caused serious trouble. But in the end, Neighbors won the Indian confidence completely. By what still seems superhuman efforts, he got virtually every tribesman in Texas into the Brazos Reserves. Even half the Penatekas, who were dying of hunger this winter, arrived at Clear Fork, though another 500 apparently joined the northern Comanche bands. Neighbors was forthright, religious, immensely ethical rather than pious, and even the Comanches trusted him. The Penatekas presented a peculiar problem on the reservation, because they had never farmed and refused to plant corn. But still, the policy, under Neighbors' direction, seemed on its way to success. Tragically, however, Robert Neighbors was more successful at winning friends and influencing people among the Indians than in getting the cooperation or sympathy of his own kind. Because he protected his charges and saw to their welfare against the wishes of his own people, he was universally known as an Indian-lover on the harsh frontier.

Conditions in Texas improved briefly in 1856. The gathering of the border tribes into the reserves helped end petty depredations. More important was the appearance of the best-mounted regiment that ever rode the American West: Albert Sidney Johnston's 2d U.S. Cavalry.

When Jefferson Davis became Secretary of War in 1853, he was the first national government officer to recognize that the utterly different terrain and conditions on the edge of the Great Plains required a different military approach. Davis reorganized the U.S. Army between 1853 and 1857. He laid the groundwork for the famous cavalry operations in the West. He was never given the credit he deserved for his vision and effort, because the gathering national storm obscured most of it. Davis, correctly, was accused of furthering the military stance of the South; in Texas, however, he seems only to have served a national interest and purpose. He left a series of papers, showing clearly he understood the enormous difference between the problems the United States faced east of the Mississippi and on the edge of the Plains. In the West, a scattered people could not hope to defend themselves under the old militia system, and while cavalry was more expensive than infantry (the government's main objection), it was ten times more effective. Davis thought the dividing line between East and West lay at the 100th meridian, along which the forts then lay. West of that line, the Army had to operate in new ways: in strong garrisons, not scattered, tiny forts that excited Indian contempt, and through mounting of effective punitive expeditions, "to pursue and punish the offenders," much as the French then operated in Algeria. Davis was greatly interested that the West should be won. Of course, he expected it to be added to the South upon conquest; his vision did not recognize the fact that the cotton kingdom had reached its ordained boundaries.

The same North-South cloud has obscured the tremendous work of the old 2d Cavalry. Its commanders and most of its officers were Southerners, and its legends became lost in later prejudices. For a variety of reasons the 2d became outstanding. The regiment, a fighting unit, naturally pulled the better soldiers, throughout the army; and Texas, with fighting, surveying, and road-building to be done, was a career soldier's paradise in the 1850's. Then, the regiment had style; Davis saw to it that many appointments went to gentlemen. He was charged with training Southerners for a coming war, perhaps with justice, for in addition to Albert Sidney Johnston, Robert E. Lee, John B. Hood, and five other future Confederate generals were on its rolls. But the 2d also had George H. Thomas and George Stoneman, and a dozen lesser lights of Union fame.

Johnston was effective, but he had too little time. In 1857 Davis left the War office, and the greater part of the 2d Cavalry was ordered off to Utah. The Comanches remained ignorant of many things out on the Plains, but they were never totally insensible or stupid. As soon as Johnston's pressure subsided, the pressure on the Texas frontier became severe. Again, hundreds of farmhouses went up in flames.

Hardin R. Runnels, who became governor of Texas in January, 1858, was to be known primarily for his Secessionist stand. But disatisfaction with frontier defense always lay close to the heart of Texas politics. Runnels was elected partly on account of this discontent, and Runnels was always a deep conservative, who believed the shortest distance between two points was a straight line. When the legislature, despairing of federal action, authorized state troops again, Runnels immediately appointed John S. (Rip) Ford Senior Captain and supreme commander of all Texas forces.

Ford at this time was the most experienced Ranger available to serve the state.

Ford got specific orders: call a hundred men, establish a camp somewhere on the frontier, cooperate with the Federals and Indian agents, "but to brook no interference with his plan of operation from any source." The Governor agreed his position would call for delicacy, but stated Ford had the judgment to carry on. Nor could Runnels have appointed a better man for the job.

Ford was under no misapprehension as to what he was supposed to do. He was to "follow any and all trails of hostile or suspected hostile Indians" and "inflict the most summary punishment" on them. He was to do this quickly, because the public was howling for action, and also because his appropriation was limited and he could not exceed it. He also had something no other Captain had so far had: the authority to dismiss officers now in state service, and to replace them with his own.

The Governor gave Ford a free hand; both men understood that both their reputations rested on "drastic action," as Webb said.

Ford moved into northwest Texas, to the Brazos Indian Reserve. He planned to enlist Indian allies and scouts. Here, he was entirely successful; the son of the agent, L. S. Ross, recruited and led 113 assorted Indians under Ford's command. On April 22, 1858, Ford left Camp Runnels, as he called his Brazos station, with 102 Rangers, a pack train, and more than 100 Indians. He had planned his campaign. Indian spies had ridden far ahead and located Comanches north of the Red River. This was beyond the Texas border, but as one Texan observer said, Ford was after Indians, not out to learn geography.

Now began the bloodiest two years in Texas history since 1835–1836.

Behind his screen of Indian scouts, Ford crossed the Red on April 29. On May 10, his column found Indian signs—a buffalo with two Comanche arrows sticking in it and the marks of meat-laden Comanche travois. On May 11, Ford carefully reconnoitered a large Comanche camp. He had not been discovered. He moved swiftly, quietly, without campfires, bugles, shouted orders, and similar nonsense of the Army in Indian country. Like many old Rangers, Rip Ford could out-ride, out-trail, out-sneak, and above all, out-think any Indian.

Then, on May 12, his Tonkawa scouts attacked and demolished a small camp of five tepees. Two mounted Comanches got away; the alarm was out. Ford did not hesitate; he pounded after the two braves for three miles, and they led him to a large encampment beside the Canadian River.

The Comanches came out in magnificent, savage array, resplendent in feather and horn headdresses, iron lance points glittering in the morning sun. Their faces were painted black for war. They capered and pranced and thundered past on their ponies. Ford estimated he faced 300 braves that day.

It was a scene that was to be repeated in this region of the world many times in coming years: a shrieking, splendidly barbaric horde of Plains Indians, circling and prancing across the prairie; across from them, a band of bearded, sweat-stained riders in old clothes, calm and spitting tobacco juice, among their own screeching, threatening allies. They cocked their rifles, checked the seating of the red copper nipples on their Colts. They watched Rip Ford, cold as new ice.

At the head of the Comanches rode Iron Jacket, whose name came from a cuirass of burnished Spanish armor, lost on these Plains centuries before. Iron Jacket glittered in overlapping plates of steel; he was a great chief, with a legend of invulnerability in tribal wars. He rode out and challenged, to commence the combat.

Spanish armor would turn arrows, but not a Sharps' rifle ball. Several guns crashed, and Iron Jacket and his horse collapsed. Then, Ford knew it was time to go among them. He charged, and the battle broke into a shrieking, shooting, galloping series of small combats, covering six miles.

This battle was to be described a dozen times in fact and legend, a hundred times in fiction. Ford broke two Comanche charges, fighting until two o'clock. At the end, the Ranger horses were staggering, and could pursue no more. In running fights lasting about seven hours, the Rangers killed 76 Indians. They captured 300 horses, and 18 women and children. Their own losses were minimal; two Rangers died.

Ford rode back into Texas, arriving on the Brazos May 21. He reported to Runnels that the campaign was of much importance, not simply because the Indians had been punished but because it demonstrated several things. The Indians could be profitably pursued, fixed, and defeated on their own buffalo grounds by the right sort of men. It must be remembered that the Spaniards had felt three full companies of horse inadequate to cross these plains, which were still viewed by most Americans with awe and dread. Ford wanted to pursue this campaign with a strong force, into the winter. This he was denied, because he had expended his allowed funds in thirty days, and because he had stirred the federal forces into belated action at last.

Colonel Twiggs, commanding the Department, wrote to his next superior that a drastic revision should be made in federal Indian policy in Texas. Twiggs castigated the passive peace policy, which had put the Army on the defensive for a decade. He argued that a full regiment of cavalry be sent into the Indian country, pursuing the Indians summer and winter, to give them so much trouble they would not think of raiding Texas. Concurrently, Twiggs wrote Runnels that he always knew the Federal force was too small for its job, and the best way to do it anywhere was to attack. "As long as there are wild Indians on the prairie, Texas cannot be free from depredations," Twiggs stated.

Twiggs' letter, accompanied by two blasts from the Governor of Texas and a warning from Neighbors that Texas was contemplating violent action, jolted Secretary of War Floyd and President Buchanan into a temporary change of policy. On August 9, 1858, Major Earl Van Dorn of the 2d Cavalry was ordered to march into the Wichita mountains of Oklahoma with four companies of cavalry and one of foot. From a base camp here, Van Dorn was to scour the country between the Canadian and the Red, beginning September 15.

Van Dorn also gathered up some friendly Indians under Lawrence Ross, who had assisted Ford. These scouts located Comanches for him on September 29. Van Dorn marched ninety miles in thirty-seven hours with his Indians and four companies of the 2d Cavalry. He attacked a sleeping village of 120 lodges, 500 Indians, on October 1. Within thirty minutes, the cavalry killed 56 Indians of various sizes and shapes, took three hundred horses, burned the lodges, and dispersed the survivors across the hills. Although Van Dorn suffered heavier losses than Ford—he and Ross were both wounded, and two commissioned officers were among the American dead—Twiggs described his victory as "more decisive and complete than any recorded in the history of our Indian warfare." This was a palpable exaggeration, but it showed how deeply the regular army had been stung by Rip Ford. The Comanche menace was damped, but hardly destroyed.

Again, the reservation Indians rendered splendid service, as both Ford and Van Dorn acknowledged. But these Indians, without whom there would have been no such quick victories, were to be rewarded by the American nation in a sorry and entirely too common way.

In the years between 1855 and 1858, the advancing Texas settlement line had flowed strongly around the Brazos and Clear Fork Reserves. These Indians were now living in close proximity to white farms. When the severe Comanche raids of 1857 began, these settled tribes were caught between two fires. The wild Indians despised them; the whites, harassed by other Indians, hated all the tribes.

Throughout 1858 there were numerous small, if ghastly depredations along the Brazos. These were certainly committed by the Penatekas and other Comanches who failed to come to the Reserves. Also, certainly, the wild Indians did not forgive the "white men's pets" for leading Ford and Van Dorn on their own killing raids. There was a curious phenomenon discovered in these months: Indian trails were always hard to follow, but after several murder raids a trail an Easterner could follow was blazed from mutilated white bodies to the Clear Fork Reserve. Texas newspapers fully record that white opinion believed the worst.

In retrospect, it was obvious that the reservations could not succeed while there were still savage Indians raiding into Texas. Major Neighbors wrote clear-cut letters explaining this, and stating that neither the Penatekas on the reservation nor the whites in the area could be protected while the war bands still roamed. He begged the government to bring all the Indians into reservations at once. He also stated that the many claims of atrocities by the reservation Indians were exaggerated, which they were. He pointed up the good service these people had done as auxiliaries under L. S. Ross. His reasoned arguments went unheard. The government shuddered at the cost of an extended Indian war; there were people in the East who violently protested such a war in principle. The Texans in this region were already blind with hate and prejudice; Neighbors' pets could not be good Indians, because they still lived.

One man, John R. Baylor, a former Indian agent who had been dismissed in disgrace from this service, was instrumental in stirring up such feelings. Baylor, whose past experience led many Texans to believe he knew Indians, addressed mass meetings and cleverly played upon the emotions of Texans who had lost kith and kin. It is evident that his main motive was a furious hatred of Neighbors, the man who had got him dismissed, but his campaign bore poisonous fruit. Baylor insisted that all Indians be driven from the state, and he soon gathered a roaring mob behind him.

Ford was at Camp Runnels during this time. He determined to investigate the charges of reserve Indians' complicity in Indian attacks. One of his own officers suggested that such evidence could easily be manufactured, assuming this was Ford's desire. Ford said, "No, sir, that will not do." No evidence convicting the reserve Indians was found by the Rangers, and Ford called upon Baylor and the citizens to present their charges in writing. None were submitted.

But among Ford's own men, Neighbors was hated; Rangers could not understand an Indian-lover who took his office seriously and stood up for Indian rights. One Ranger captain intercepted Ford's mail, and, against express orders, conspired with civilians to bring Neighbors down. Ford's own comment on Neighbors is clear and says something about both men: "The ordeal through which Major Neighbors has passed endorses him. He needs no commendation from any quarter."

Neighbors himself went to Washington to plead his case. He had given up hope that the reservations could succeed in Texas, and recommended that all the Indians be removed north of the Red River. His motive was entirely one of protecting his charges from white action.

Events that took place two days after Christmas, 1858, justified his view. Seven Indians, Caddoans and Anadarcos, were shot to death while sleeping in a camp along the Brazos. Four were men, three were squaws. A sub-agent of the Brazos Reserve investigated fully. He reported these were the most inoffensive Indians in his charge, and he named six white men who were known to have done the deed. The names included Captain Peter Garland and Dr. W. W. McNeill. McNeill wrote Ford a contrary version: the whites had been trailing horse thieves, and had defended themselves in a bitter fight. The evidence clearly indicated that all the Indians had been killed in their sleeping robes.

The judge of the Texas Nineteenth Judicial District of Texas ordered

Captain Ford to arrest the six accused men. Ford refused. His grounds were that he was a military officer, not a civil one, and could not legally carry out such orders. Neighbors' own comment on this, that the Captain pandered in a contemptible manner to the prejudices of lawless men against the very Indians who led him to victory a year before, was largely true. Ford knew that the arrest of the whites would probably result in civil disorder, that no jury would convict them, but also, he could not bring himself seemingly to "turn renegade." He faced the terrible dilemma most basically honorable men faced in such racial conflicts, but in his choice, he had the roaring assent of the whole frontier.

Baylor and other armed men were now "prowling around the reserve," as Agent Shapley Ross said. A company of U.S. Rifles was at the Brazos, but Baylor told its captain that he was going to destroy the Indians even if he had to kill every man in the command. On May 23, 1859, whites and Indians fought a skirmish inside the reservation. Work had been suspended, and the Indians were huddling around Neighbors in fear.

On June 11 word arrived of a joint federal-state agreement to move the reserve Indians north of the Red, into Oklahoma. Captain John Henry Brown of the Rangers arrived to assist the federal troops in keeping order. One of Brown's first decisions was that the Indians could not be allowed to scatter to round up their livestock. Neighbors, who quarreled bitterly with Brown, informed the Indians they would have to leave without their cattle, horses, and pigs.

Escorted by soldiers and Rangers, the thousand reserve Indians marched north, leaving gardens, corn, and cattle behind. Their few belongings were carried in Army wagons. It was a long, dry, terrible trek, and some of the U.S. troopers who guarded it described the passage in bitter terms. On September 1, Agent Neighbors—who had never backed down to any man, who was respected by every official in the state, not one of whom would publicly acknowledge it—forded the Red with his pitiable crew, and turned them over to another Indian agent in a strange land. There is no record of how he said goodbye to the people who had put their faith in him. But that same night he wrote his wife in Texas:

> I have this day crossed all the Indians out of the heathen land of Texas and am now out of the land of the Philistines.
>
> If you want to have a full description of our Exodus out of Texas— Read the "Bible" where the children of Israel crossed the Red Sea. We have had about the same show, only our enemies did not follow us. . . .

These were the last lines Robert Neighbors ever wrote. He rode back into the land of the Philistines to make his final report. At Fort Belknap, while he was talking to Pat Murphy, Murphy's brother-in-law, Ed Cornett, whom Neighbors had never met, shot the Indian agent in the back.

It was "not possible" to bring Cornett to trial. But on the other hand, it was not permissible on the frontier to shoot a white man, even an Indian-lover, in the back. John Cochran and Ben R. Milam got together some "Minute Men." This group convened a "court" in April, 1860, months after the murder, and went after Cornett. He "made fight" on Salt Creek, as one of the members of this posse said, and all accounts agree that Ed Cornett was brought to justice without benefit of judge or jury.

28

WAR ON THE RIO GRANDE

*Some [Americans], brimful of laws, promised us their protec-
tion from the attacks of the rest; others, assembled in shadowy
councils, attempted and excited the robbery and burning of our
relatives' houses on the other side of the River Bravo; while still
others, whom we entrusted with our land titles, refused to return
them under false and frivolous pretexts; all, in short, with a smile
on their faces, giving the lie to what their black entrails were
planning. Many of you have been robbed of your property,
jailed, chased, murdered, and hunted like wild beasts, because
your labor was fruitful, and excited vile avarice. . . . There are
criminals covered with frightful crimes, but these monsters are
indulged, because they are not of our race, which is, they say,
not fit to belong to the human species. . . .*

Mexicans! Is there no remedy?

*Mexicans! My stand is taken; the voice of Revelation tells me
that to me is entrusted the breaking of the chains of your slavery.*

FROM THE PROCLAMATION OF JUAN N. CORTINAS AT
RANCHO DEL CARMEN, CAMERON COUNTY, TEXAS,
NOVEMBER 23, 1859

BECAUSE, in the 18th century, the Crown of Spain seeded a series of
communities along the lower Bravo, and granted vast tracts of land, reaching a hundred miles and more north of the river, to prominent citizens, it
laid the groundwork for future conflict. In the waning days of Spain, and
under the new Republic of Mexico, the territory south of the Nueces was

not considered part of the Province of Texas, but rather Neuvo Santander, later the Estado de Tamaulipas. This great expanse, mostly brushland or chaparral, dotted with both mild savannahs and near-deserts, remained largely deserted. It lay on the northern fringes of the Mexican cattle culture, which emanated palely from the old Spanish towns on the south bank of the Rio Grande. It was no part of Anglo-Texas, nor had any Anglo-Texan settled there, but it was claimed, under old maps, by the Republic.

Between 1836 and 1846 this area was both a buffer and a battleground. Laredo and the scattered *rancherías* between this town and the mouth of the Bravo remained under Mexican control. In 1842, however, General Adrian Woll, on the orders of the Supreme Government, advised all Mexican nationals to evacuate south of the Rio Grande. Many did, abjuring Texas citizenship and abandoning their land, from Juan Seguín of San Antonio to the Ballí heirs on Padre Island. However, near the river, and from Matamoros, many Mexican families still claimed title to the soil.

By the Treaty of Guadalupe Hidalgo, after the Mexican War, this strip was attached to the United States. By the treaty, Mexican land titles were confirmed to their possessors, and their holders granted U.S. citizenship, if they chose. It was a fair treaty, but difficult of implementation. What many Americans failed to understand, was that a Mexico irredenta was created along the north banks of the Rio Grande.

Because of the enormous differences in culture, politics, and legal systems, the Mexican inhabitants of the lower Bravo valley of Texas did not easily adjust. The common people remained entirely Mexican. They came under Texas state and American national government, but they did not become Americans in the sense that German, Scandinavian, Irish, or Slavonic immigrants became American. In a very real sense, the approximately 8,000 inhabitants of the three lower Texas counties, Cameron, Starr, and Webb, in 1850 were under foreign rule.

The ordinary people, mostly part-Indian peasants, were politically quiescent, because they had had no part in government under Spanish-Mexican rule. Because the American immigration into this region, especially at Brownsville, was almost entirely composed of merchants opening up a profitable Mexican commerce, or supplying the U.S. Army, a peculiar, and colorful society developed. There were no Anglo-American farmers on this frontier; the farm line faltered at the Nueces. This was Mexican ranch country which had not left the former century; it had been dominated by a few aristocrats holding forth from the towns. Over the whole landscape, the new merchants, also operating from the towns, imposed their control, in the name of Texas and the United States. An interesting, but hardly significant, aspect of these American immigrants was that almost none of them were old "Texians," or even Southern. A high proportion arrived out of Pennsylvania and New York, and some from Europe. Much more significantly, they quickly became the most ardent "Texans" of all—an inescapable reaction of a cultural minority holding sway over a differentiated mass.

Historically, close contact between two varied cultures tends to produce a polarization of their values. What grew up in far south Texas was a very polarized society, or rather two separate polarized societies. There was in no sense a melting pot then, or for the following hundred years.

Many Texas historians have come to the conclusion that different races tend to transmit their vices, rather than their virtues, to each other, and in Texas this seems generally to have been borne out, among Anglos, Mexicans, and even Indians. White social values and whiskey destroyed the agricultural Amerinds; and on the border Americans adopted many of the outlooks and attitudes of the Mexican upper class, but completely without its sense of cultural values and social organism. Mexicans were strongly attracted by Anglo social and political democracy and material success, but rejected most of the individual, internal discipline the pursuit of both required.

John S. Ford and others have described the 1850's as the great days of Brownsville, then the gateway city to Mexico. At least six men made fortunes that added into millions of dollars, but very little of this trade affected the 2,000 inhabitants of the Mexican lower class. Meanwhile, the American newcomers jostled uncomfortably upon the old Spanish *hacendados,* most of whom were gradually dispossessed.

One phenomenon, inevitable where the facade of political democracy had to be observed among a population who had no understanding of it, was the birth of genuine machine politics. The Americans quickly organized the Mexican citizenry into "cross-mark patriots," as they laughingly were called. These "patriots," who had only the vaguest notions of the practices or principles of representative government but were American citizens, were dragooned into political factions, the Reds and the Blues, and expected to X the ballots of their party. The colored ribbons symbolized the two parties, and they were selected specifically for an illiterate electorate. Both the leaders of the Reds and Blues were Anglos, and usually prominent, wealthy men. The Blue leader, Stephen Powers, was a friend of Martin Van Buren; but the Reds, who included Charles Stillman (the financier and father of the New York banker, James Stillman, who was born at Brownsville), Samuel Belden, Richard King, and Mifflin Kenedy, usually won control.

At election time, extravagant promises were made to the Mexican voters, almost none of which were ever kept. Elections, as an observer wrote, were a "combination of force, fraud, and farce."

This would have been supportable, as it was supportable in other areas of the nation, except for the double standard imposed by race and caste. The evidence is that the new dominant classes were in no way improved by being approached by the humble in the Mexican fashion, hat in hand. Walter Prescott Webb, who cannot be accused of favoritism for Mexicans, put it bluntly: "One law applied to them [Mexicans], and another, far less rigorous, to the political leaders and to the prominent Americans." A Texas Mexican who injured an American faced hanging. The injury or even the death of a Mexican by a white man—in this part of Texas Mexicans of the ordinary class, with Indian blood, were never referred to as "white"—was usually discovered to be justifiable under the law.

The law added injury to insult, because it failed to protect the Mexicans and actually was the chief instrument of their dispossession. Americans who never understood the almost universal denigration of the law and lawyers on the old frontier never understood the enormous distance between "justice under the law" and justice as the frontiersmen saw it. When ethicality began to wane in the United States of the 1830's, lawyers were not and could not be immune. A horde of lawyers arrived in Texas, and in few regions did they find conditions so inviting. The dispossession of frontiersmen by tricks of law was hardly new—Daniel Boone and George Rogers Clark were both despoiled of land they had won with their blood— but in Texas, where there was a confusion of Spanish, Mexican, Republican, and Anglo-Saxon common law, and where land titles and surveys had always been rather vague and usually conflicting, the clever lawyer came into his own. There is some truth that many Mexican landowners, especially the small ones, were robbed in south Texas by force, intimidation, or chicanery. But what is usually ignored is the fact that the *hacendado* class, as a class, was stripped of property perfectly legally, according to the highest traditions of U.S. law.

There was certainly ignorance on one side, and chicanery on the other, but the real problem stemmed from a continual change in sovereignty in this region: Spain to Mexico, and Mexico to Texas and then, to the United States. The English common law and Hispanic law conflicted, particularly on such matters as taxation, use and wont, and holdings in common, or *ejidos.* Two cases, out of a horrendous total of litigation, stand out. One, concerning the Sal del Rey, or the King's Salt, in the San Salvador de Tule grant to Don Juan José Ballí, was in litigation for fifty years, before the property became part of the King Ranch. This case was particularly important because it led to the constitutional amendment in Texas that established the state's law on mineral rights. The other was *Shannon v. Cavazos,* which led to a border war.

In 1782, Don José Salvador de la Garza received the Espíritu Santo *merced* of 260,000 acres, along the north bank of the Rio Grande. Lands and titles passed, with some confusion, to children and heirs, with much splitting, according to the Spanish custom. The part including the area on which Major Brown built his fort in 1846 came into the hands of members of the Cavazos family. One of the principal heirs was Doña Estéfana Goseascochea, a granddaughter of the grantee, who first married Don Francisco Cavazos, then, widowed, married the *alcalde* of Camargo, Trinidad Cortinas.

In 1848, the Treaty of Guadalupe Hidalgo confirmed all Mexican land titles in principle but could not guarantee them in practice. A horde of American businessmen, squatters, and ex-soldiers arrived on Espíritu Santo lands; many bore headrights, bounty warrants, and Texas veterans' land certificates. There was a general claiming that the land around Brownsville was "vacant," or national land, and thus public land under Texas law by right of conquest. A swarm of claims were filed, and a swarm of lawyers found employment. As Texas historian Frank Cushman Pierce wrote, three square leagues were "exacted to straighten out the titles" from the old landowners by American lawyers: Doña Estéfana, again widowed, conveyed some 4,000 acres of her inheritance to a firm of lawyers in order to get them to secure her title to the rest.

Meanwhile, the merchant Charles Stillman laid out the Brownsville Town Company and founded the city of Brownsville on 1,500 acres of the de la Garza grant. Title *was* unclear, and Stillman apparently purchased his rights from Mexicans who claimed to own it. Litigation was carried to the Supreme Court, which dismissed the case for lack of jurisdiction. Finally, a ruling was secured in favor of the heirs; however, the 1,500 acres in question ended up in the hands of an American law firm, who sold it to Charles Stillman for a fraction of the appraised value. As Pierce mentioned, "The Mexican owners suspected foul play."

The imposition of American law infuriated most Mexican landowners. They had to defend their ancient titles in court, and they lost either way, either to their own lawyers or to the claimants. In these years the humbler classes of Mexicans were finding that they were treated with contempt, and that the American law would not protect their persons; now the upper class felt that American courts were not upholding their ancient rights. The soil of the lower Rio Grande Valley was becoming ripe for revolution.

One particularly angry member of the upper class was Juan Nepomuceno Cortinas who saw his mother surrender a square league of her patrimony in order to keep the rest. The elder Cortinas had been an undistinguished ranchero, probably illiterate, but his wife had the blood of both the Garzas and Falcóns, the bluest of the blue. Cheno Cortinas, born in 1824, however, failed to grow up with the gentility his half-brothers and his brothers and sister displayed. He was wild. He was of average size for Spanish stock, with brown hair, gray-green eyes, and a reddish beard. He had the manners of a gentleman, but he was uneducated by choice, and a *vaquero,* rather than a border aristocrat, by personal taste. Cortinas liked to ride with a roistering crowd of lowly cowmen.

As history proved, Cortinas had certain qualities his solid-citizen relatives lacked. He was intelligent, with a native cunning and deft political sense for the feelings of his own people; he was a fearless gambler, and certainly possessed a fearless manner. He was to be called the "Red Robber of the Rio Grande," and Richardson passed him off briefly as a bandit, but then all Mexican men of destiny, from Santa Anna to Zapata, have appeared to be bandits in North American eyes.

Cortinas apparently fought in Arista's command at Palo Alto and Resaca de la Palma, though without distinction. He did not enjoy the outcome of the war, naturally, and apparently was mistreated afterward by a wagon master in Taylor's army. He was involved in a cattle-stealing incident, and arrested by Adolphus Glavaecke, a neighboring rancher, but the record here is most unclear, because Glavaecke apparently was engaged in stock-stealing himself, and was so indicted. Above all, however, Cheno Cortinas carried a grudge against Americans, and was bitter about the American conquest of his native land. In 1859 he was living at his mother's ranch on the Texas side about nine miles northwest of Brownsville, and he was a fuse waiting to be lit.

Each morning Cortinas liked to canter into the town to sit at a café and sip coffee with his friends. On the morning of July 13, 1859, the city marshal, Robert Shears, whom Cortinas called "the squint-eyed sheriff," arrested a drunken Mexican on the streets. This man had once been a Cortinas servant. The marshal, all accounts agree, was unnecessarily brutal; he gave the drunken Mexican the standard treatment. Cortinas protested, apparently reasonably, and was rewarded with an insult no *caballero* could take. Guns were drawn; the marshal fell with a bullet in his shoulder, and Cheno Cortinas put his rescued servant up behind his saddle and galloped out of town.

In such ways revolutions are made. It was an irresistible act: the hated gringo law humbled; the humblest of an oppressed race saved on horseback by one of the old and exalted families. The *Americanos* now made an immense mistake. No one wanted to go after Cheno Cortinas, and he was allowed to stay among his *vaqueros* for some days, passing freely in and out of Mexico. It must be remembered that Cortinas was recognized as a Mexican citizen south of the river, just as his half-brother could serve both as a Cameron county official and a field officer in the Mexican army. Mexican officers, including one of his cousins, knew he was planning trouble, but could not persuade him to go on an extended trip elsewhere.

On September 28, at 3 A.M., Cortinas rode back into Brownsville with a hundred men. There had been a gala ball in Matamoros the night before, which most of the Brownsville society attended; drunken parties had been coming across the river all night, and at first few citizens noticed the shooting and the noise. Only gradually did awakening people understand what the mob outside was screaming: *"Viva Cortinas! Mueran los gringos! Viva México!"*

By daylight, Cortinas had treed the town. He stated he had come to kill his enemies, the "Pole" Adolphus Glavaecke and the "squinting sheriff." These got away, so he shot and killed three other Americans, "notorious for their misdeeds among the people." He shot a Mexican, for trying to shield a gringo friend. The jail was opened, and all the prisoners let out. The Mexican flag was hoisted over Fort Brown, which had recently been evacuated by the Army on orders from Washington; but Cortinas' *vaqueros* did not have the technical skill to keep it flying from its pole. The band roamed the town, shooting and shouting. During this time, apparently not a single citizen showed up on the streets. Brownsville was not a frontier but a mercantile town, and the leaders of neither the Reds nor Blues were warriors. "Thus," wrote Major S. P. Heintzelman of the U.S. Army to Colonel Robert E. Lee, "was a city of from two or three thousand inhabitants occupied by a band of armed bandits, a thing till now unheard of in the United States."

Ironically, two Mexican officers, Miguel Tijerina, who was Cortinas' cousin, and General Carvajal, who commanded in Matamoros, crossed over and liberated the town.

Cortinas rode back to his mother's place, the Rancho del Carmen. Here, he seems to have issued his first *pronunciamento,* attacking all American lawyers and politicos: "Our personal enemies shall not possess our lands until they have fattened it with their own gore. . . ." Suddenly, hundreds of Mexicans, from both sides of the river, were riding, cheering, to Cortinas' camp.

It can only be recorded that the citizenry of Brownsville were in a panic. They sent calls to San Antonio, to Governor Runnels in Austin, and to President Buchanan. They begged Carvajal for help, and, to quote Webb, "American citizens witnessed the sorry spectacle of seeing themselves protected on their own soil by Mexican soldiers quartered in a United States fort."

Twenty-five men were raised to protect the town and patrol the streets, because Carvajal soon withdrew. Meanwhile, one citizen wrote a letter to the New Orleans *Daily Picayune:* "For God's sake urge the government to send us relief. Let the great guns again watch over our dear sister Matamoros, and the soldiers of Uncle Samuel keep marauders here in check, or practically the boundary . . . must be moved back to the Nueces."

At this time, Cortinas does not seem to have decided on his course; he was riding the wind, trying to feel its direction. The lower Rio Grande Valley was remote from Texas; he had time to wait. During these weeks Cortinas passed back and forth from being lionized in Matamoros to haranguing his bravos at the ranch. Then, the citizenry of Brownsville made an effort to attack him.

About two score Americans formed the "Brownsville Tigers," under W. B. Thompson. They allowed about forty more Mexican-Americans to join as auxiliaries. The Tigers had two small cannon, one sent over from Matamoros, and in these this militia set great store.

Thompson moved cautiously on Rancho del Carmen, so cautiously that later a devastating description of the whole episode appeared in the *Evening Ranchero,* a Texas newspaper. The Brownsville Tigers took four days to reach Glavaecke's ranch, three miles out of town. When they finally encountered a few *vaqueros* in the brush at Santa Rita, and some firing began, the whole troop "made a desperate charge—for home." They left their two brass cannon behind and made far better time returning than in going out. The official report reads differently, but both agree on one thing: nothing whatever was accomplished. The official report, perhaps with unconscious humor, says the retreat became general, with all being anxious to reach Brownsville first, and that the Mexican-Americans brought up the rear. The merchants and citizens of Brownsville were not gunmen; most of them had never seen an Indian or killed a man, and they could not be compared to the borderers who lived further north along the Colorado-Brazos frontier.

Cortinas had won prestige at little cost. Now, he fired a salute each morning from the captured cannon to wake the town. He intercepted the mail, and held an American named Campbell prisoner to read it to him. But although his men were now raiding throughout the country, Cortinas acted with enormous restraint. Nobody was killed, and even the perused mail was returned, resealed. On one occasion, his men took beeves belonging to a professed friend, James Browne. Cortinas returned most of these, and penned Browne a due bill for the few he butchered.

Then, the war took a new turn. A company of Rangers under Captain W. G. Tobin of San Antonio arrived in the valley. Webb wrote that Tobin and his men were a sorry lot. The Brownsville historian Davenport went further: that Tobin had one good man, but that he unfortunately fell off a carriage and broke his neck on arrival.

These men again were the street sweepings that so often were the first to join an expedition to the Rio Grande. With good leadership, they might have been effective; they did not have it. Their first official act in Brownsville was to storm the jail and lynch a captured sixty-five-year-old Cortinista, Tomás Cabrera; Heintzelman hinted at this, but Ford stated it bluntly, in his later report.

In retaliation, Cortinas ambushed a squad of Tobin's Rangers on the Palo Alto and killed three men. Tobin then led the reorganized Brownsville Tigers and his own troops against Santa Rita, where Cortinas openly waited. Mifflin Kenedy now led the Brownsville contingent, which had acquired another 24-pound howitzer. The results of this expedition are better not examined, but Tobin's Rangers did prove to be superior artillerists, because in the general rout they did bring the cannon back. Tobin fell back on Brownsville on November 25, 1859, and U.S. Army reports state simply that his decision to run was wise—his Rangers were so demoralized they would have been slaughtered had they stood.

Now, as Heintzelman wrote, Cortinas was a great man. He had defeated the gringos twice; he made Mexicans wonder how the gringos had ever got to the Rio Bravo in the first place. Over his camp he now hoisted the flag of the Mexican Republic, the red, white, and green. When he crossed over into Mexico, great throngs assembled and cheered him, bugles blew and music thundered; he rode his horse into the city squares like a conquering hero. He was the champion of his people, who would right all wrongs. In

Matamoros there was open discussion of rolling the border back to the Nueces; some ardent spirits held out for the Sabine.

Cortinas does not seem to have entertained any such dreams. He issued inflammatory proclamations, calling upon Mexicans to fight for their rights against the American bloodsuckers and vampires, but nothing in his proclamations indicated a plan for a separate Mexican state, or a reversion to Mexico. He flew the Mexican flag, but this was to attract recruits from south of the river. Cortinas expressed great confidence in Sam Houston, the Texas governor-elect; he said Houston would see that Texas Mexicans were protected. Cortinas did not know that Houston was seriously planning the establishment of a protectorate over Mexico itself at this time. Probably, Cortinas had no plan at all; he had accidentally started a small revolution, and being a daring gambler, he rode with it to see where destiny might take him.

His uprising, however, had already failed, because the Texas Mexicans did not flock to his standard. Significantly, his own family did not support him. His mother and brothers remained loyal to the state, and none of the great families joined Cortinas. The vast majority of the humbler class remained inert. Beyond all question, the great majority of Cortinas' fighting men crossed the Rio Bravo from Mexico. If the Tobin Rangers were mostly border scum, a similar breed in Mexico smelled plunder. Santos Cadena brought forty thieves from Nuevo León. Sixty escaped convicts from Victoria in Tamaulipas showed their patriotism by joining Cortinas and plundering gringos. The charge of banditry was true, and it clung; but as most Texas histories deliberately ignore, there was more to the Cortinas uprising than that.

Finally, on December 5, 1859, Major S. P. Heintzelman arrived on the Rio Grande with 165 U.S. Army troops. Heintzelman immediately led his force, combined with Tobin's Rangers, on a sweep toward Cortinas. The Rangers showed a great reluctance to fight, but Heintzelman met Cortinas at a place called the Ebonal, and forced the rebel to retreat with a loss of eight men.

Meanwhile, a short time before, Governor Runnels of Texas received reports that all south Texas, to the Nueces, was aflame with a Mexican war. Runnels found Rip Ford walking the streets of Austin and seized him by the arm. "Ford, you must go!" Runnels exclaimed. Ford left the next day, with a commission as major in command of all state forces on the border.

Ford rode out of Austin with only eight men, some six-shooters, a bag of grub, and not a dollar in public money. The treasury was bare. But on the way south he recruited certain men he knew he could rely upon, found wagons, and even secured a little money. He finished the five-hundred-mile trip at the head of fifty-three hard men. In such ways did the captains of the Rangers operate; it was a rough and ready force.

Ford arrived at Brownsville in time to hear the firing at the Ebonal but not to join the battle. Heintzelman and Ford immediately began a joint campaign, and Cortinas retreated west along the Rio Grande. The Mexican did not fight, but continually stayed ahead of the advancing Rangers and U.S. regulars. In the retreat there was much looting and burning of settlements and ranches by the Mexicans. The Neale ranch was destroyed, and the customs house and post office at Edinburg plundered. Smoke hung over the lower valley as the Mexicans burned or wrecked the American settlements in their path.

By the end of December, Cortinas had retreated upriver to Rio Grande City, then a small village. Ford and Heintzelman closed rapidly on him, and here Cortinas chose to fight. Ford and the Rangers rode down on his camp; the Cortinas army opened fire with its two cannon and attempted a set battle.

The Mexicans advanced against the Rangers with flags and bugle calls, but the Texan fire was deadly. Dozens of *vaqueros* were knocked out of the saddle.

Ford charged the Mexican line, and the fight broke up into the swirling, galloping melee in which Texan marksmanship with the pistol was so effective. In this kind of fight, Mexican *vaqueros,* like Comanche braves, were outclassed; they were not so well armed, nor could they handle six-shooters with the serious deadliness of Texans when they were. The three-hundred-man Cortinista army fled, leaving sixty dead behind. Ford suffered sixteen wounded.

Heintzelman's report to the U.S. Adjutant General was brief: "Major Ford led the advance, and took both his [Cortinas'] guns, ammunition wagons, and baggage. He lost everything." Although the Major's report did not specifically state, the regulars never made contact.

Cortinas and his bodyguard dashed for safety south of the Rio Grande. This ended the real rebellion, but the sanctuary of the border gave Cortinas the opportunity to continue his banditry. The long, open border, stretching from Eagle Pass to the Gulf of Mexico had already become a serious problem for Texas. The Mexican government, through most of the century, was caught up in civil war, too weak to enforce order in its northern states. Nor could the Mexicans effectively stop Indian raids, despite the Treaty of Guadalupe Hidalgo. Bands of Kickapoos, Lipans, and Seminoles, allied with half-castes along the border, had found refuge south of the Rio Grande near Piedras Negras, across from Eagle Pass. These Indians caused serious depredations north of Laredo, and as far east as Nueces County (Corpus Christi) and Rio Grande City. Further, since the Mexican side of the border passed from the control of one petty *caudillo* to another, different regions were controlled by different warlords, in competition with each other. Mexican border commanders in the three major ports of entry—Mier, Camargo, and Matamoros—tried to lure American commerce away from each other through reductions in tariffs and bribes, and sometimes American merchants got caught up in their wars. As early as 1849, parties of Texas state troops had crossed the border to recover American merchandise seized by Mexican soldiers. This merchandise may have been smuggled in the first place. Rangers on temporary service were in constant, if rather inglorious action, along the river in the 1850's.

The case of J. H. Callahan's company of Rangers was not untypical. Callahan was supposed to operate in the area near San Antonio, but in pursuit of a band of Lipan Apache horse raiders he ranged all the way from Bandera to Eagle Pass, on the border. Callahan's men were unpaid, and not supplied by the state. They fell in with some adventurers under a man named Henry. In October, 1855, a combined group of Rangers and adventurers pursued the Indians across the border, on what was more a filibustering expedition than genuine hot pursuit. This force fought a brief skirmish with a band of Mexicans and Indians, then seized the Mexican town of Piedras Negras, ostensibly as a hostage for delivery of the hostile Indians by Mexican army forces. However, the town was looted, and the local Mexican military, their pride stung, preferred to march against the Tejanos rather than help them round up Indians. Callahan set fire to Piedras Negras and retreated into Texas. He was dismissed for this act, but it was indicative of the general lawlessness, disorder, distrust, and hatred that prevailed on both sides of the river.

The governments of each republic, Mexico and the United States, abetted the disorder by not providing adequate forces for policing. But if Mexico was guilty of failing to do anything about deliberate depredations from its side, the state of Texas, especially during the 1850's, out of haphazard military policy and the usual bankruptcy, enlisted and dismissed a series of extremely dubious and damaging so-called Rangers in its service. The quality of these irregulars was entirely dependent upon the quality of their leadership, and of the captains of this era, such as Robinson, Neill, Carmack, Connor, Callahan, Frost, and Tobin, the record shows much bad and little good. Robinson, Neill, and Carmack did nothing on the Indian frontier. Frost spent more time feuding with Indian Agent Neighbors than hunting hostiles; Callahan and Connor were dismissed, the last by Rip Ford. Only when Runnels made Ford Senior Captain, later Major, did matters improve, and then Ford was still handicapped by holdovers like Tobin on the Rio Grande.

Cheno Cortinas set up a headquarters in Mexico in January, 1860. He was able to do so because the local authorities were too weak to control him; further, few Mexicans believed that a man who was fighting Texas could be really bad. A crisis came on February 4, 1860, when a detachment of Ford's Rangers stopped a Cortinista band trying to move some plunder across the river. In the fight, one Ranger was fatally shot.

It was known that Cortinas had fortified a bend in the river some thirty-five miles above Brownsville and would attempt to capture the King-Kenedy steamboat *Ranchero* from the Mexican side. The *Ranchero* was carrying valuable cargo, including $60,000 in specie. Ford, Tobin, U.S. Army Lieutenant Loomis Langdon, who commanded the small army detachment aboard *Ranchero,* and Captain George Stoneman of the U.S. Cavalry, all gathered on the Texas side across from Cortinas' camp at La Bolsa.

When Langdon queried Ford if he intended to follow Ranger custom and cross into Mexico, Ford said, "Certainly, sir." Here again was a typical situation. No effective action could be taken against Cortinas without crossing the Rio Grande. It was difficult for the federal forces, who more often than not were spoiling to do so, to invade Mexico without approval from Washington; no matter how bad things were on the border, Washington was wary of international incidents. Washington, naturally enough from the national viewpoint, was usually willing to sacrifice a few Texas cows in lieu of starting a war, or even lacerating the touchy Mexican pride. The Texas troops regarded this not only as colossal cowardice but a mistaken policy. History does record that strong action, more often than not, produced results on the border, because American diplomacy never secured the return of a single bandit, horse, or cow. History does not record quite so clearly, but does indicate, that Rangers and U.S. Army units were often able to arrive at a tacit understanding. The Texans would ride into Mexico; the Army would remain at the river's edge, but provide enormous moral support.

Ford crossed the Rio Grande via the *Ranchero* with thirty-five of his own men, and about ten of Tobin's warriors. Immediately, he became engaged with Cortinas' emplaced troops, while Lieutenant Langdon, aboard *Ranchero,* supported him by fire from the steamboat's two small cannon. In this fire-fight, several of the Rangers became demoralized, and one raced back to the river. Ford, pistol in hand, loudly announced that the next man who tried to race would have to outrun a Texas bullet. As one Texas historian described the scene, he "restored morale."

Ford then flanked Cortinas' breastworks and led a six-shooter charge. The watching Americans on the *Ranchero* could hear the "Texan yell" shrill and clear above the other screams and shooting. This high-pitched battle-cry, which the Texas Rangers had already made famous, probably was adopted in response to the Indian warwhoop and Mexican *grito*. It was soon to be transmitted to history as the "Rebel yell." Southerners who had served in Mexico in 1846–1848, and later along the Rio Grande, picked it up.

Cortinas commanded at least two hundred men, perhaps four hundred, of which sixty were mounted. He himself fought bravely, but was utterly unable to contain his army when the screaming Texans burst into the Mexican perimeter. His cavalry fled. Cortinas emptied his own revolver, then spurred away. A Texas bullet struck his heavy Mexican saddle. Another clipped his hair, and one smashed his belt. But much to Ford's disgust—Ford had detailed three men to pick him off—the Mexican leader escaped. Ford had one man killed and four wounded. The Mexicans, as nearly as could be told, suffered about thirty dead and forty injured.

In the aftermath, a number of shacks, called *jacales,* in the area were fired. In his official report, Major Heintzelman stated that this was done contrary to Major Ford's orders, and not by his men, which put the onus squarely on the Tobin Rangers. But regardless of who did it, a number of hapless Mexican peasants were made homeless in the February chill. Immediately afterward, the Tobin men recrossed the river and returned to Brownsville, possibly on Ford's request.

The following morning, February 5, Ford went back into Mexico with forty-seven mounted Rangers. He rode down the south bank of the river abreast of the *Ranchero* as it steamed downstream. The whole Mexican countryside was in alarm; women and children ran screaming from their huts as the *Rinches* rode past. At Las Palmas, a large body of Mexican soldiery appeared, led by the Prefect of that place. The Prefect asked Ford for a parley and demanded to know what he was doing in Mexico. Ford told him that he had come to wage war on Cortinas, and that he had secured permission first. As they talked, Ford counted approximately eight hundred men—soldiers, *vaqueros,* police—drawn up against him. He also saw about two hundred whom he was certain were Cortinistas. To his blunt query about this, the Mexican leaders shrugged and said, "Who knows?"

Now, what the Rangers called a "Mexican stand-off" developed. Outnumbered about sixteen to one, Ford camped, and spent the night, while the Mexican authorities awaited instructions from Matamoros. The next morning he again parleyed and stated that his mission was to protect the *Ranchero* and its cargo; if it were molested by anyone from the Mexican side, or depredations of the Texas side continued, he promised disastrous consequences for the Mexicans. The Mexicans promised that neither would occur. With such assurances, and with some relief, Rip Ford coolly rode back down to the river and recrossed into Texas.

Cortinas now retreated back from the river, into some mountains in the interior. But the Mexican authorities made no move to arrest him. Ford and Stoneman continued to patrol the Texas side, hopeful of catching him. On the report of an informer that Cortinas was at a place called La Mesa, Ford's Rangers and Stoneman's cavalry charged into Mexico on March 17. Reaching La Mesa, the Americans were fired on, and in a short gun battle, they took the town. Cortinas was not there. From a captured Mexican major, Ford learned that he had fought the local national guard.

"Shit," Ford is reputed to have said to Stoneman. "Captain, we have played Old Scratch—whipped the *Guardia Nacional,* wounded a woman, and killed a mule." Actually, it was a bit worse than that, because the woman, and five other Mexicans, were dead.

Back on the Texas side, Ford and Stoneman heard that the town of Reynosa, in a fit of patriotic outrage and fervor, had offered to pay $30,000 if any foreign troops "entered their town as the gringos had entered La Mesa." The two officers, who understood that pacification of the Texas side required that the Mexicans be afraid to aid or abet Cortinas, rode to Edinburg, across from the Mexican town. Here Stoneman halted, with a promise to cross the border if Ford got into a fight.

Ford, with his officers Littleton, Nolan, and Dix, boldly rode into the town plaza. They were surrounded by armed Mexicans on every side, but the Mexican officials came to parley. Ford bitingly stated he had come to collect the offered reward, and demanded the surrender of any Cortinistas in the town. He noticed several of his own men dropping their Sharps rifles, apparently hoping for an accidental discharge that would start a war. But no gun fired, and upon the Mexican assurance that there were no Cortinistas in Reynosa, Ford clattered back to the Bravo, leaving a badly shaken town behind.

Ford's and Stoneman's brand of border diplomacy was halted by the arrival of the new U.S. Army commander in Texas, the Virginian Robert E. Lee. Lee had been sent specifically to the Rio Grande to halt the trouble, and he carried authority from the Secretary of War, if necessary, "to pursue Mexicans beyond the limits of the United States." He was commended to Governor Houston as an officer of "great discretion and ability." He proved it, quickly bringing the Cortinas war to a quiet end.

Ford, Heintzelman, and Stoneman had already done the dirty work, but their results had not been decisive; Cortinas was still at large. Lee met Ford just as he arrived back from Reynosa, on April 7, 1860. He did not approve of the demonstration, but worked in his own way. He sent firm, courteous, notes to every Mexican official on the border; he explained in clear detail his own instructions. If Cortinas were held in check, there would be peace. If Cortinas were allowed to raid, there would be war. This dignified, utterly superior, beautifully self-controlled lieutenant colonel of the U.S. Army made an enormous impression on both sides of the river. The local chieftains explained the facts of life to the red-bearded *hacendado* hero, who was soon involved in much more profitable politics-cum-banditry on the Mexican side. Cheno Cortinas became a brigadier in the Mexican army, and soon afterward, the governor of Tamaulipas.

He did not give up sponsoring raids into his old homeland, but he was to have no further opportunity until the aftermath of the American Civil War.

On May 6, 1860, Lieutenant Colonel Lee left the border for San Antonio. Two enormously significant details stand out in his report to the Adjutant General of the Army: first, that 20,000 regulars were necessary to police the frontier adequately from Brownsville to Eagle Pass; and second, that most of the *ranchos* from Brownsville to Rio Grande City had been abandoned or destroyed. "Those spared by Cortinas have been burned by the Texans," Lee wrote.

In the aftermath of Cortinas' raids, the American population of the border made their own counterraids; a vicious, little-reported racial war ensued. Between Cortinas' banditry and Texan suspicion of all Mexicans, the delta was laid waste. Many *ranchos* were burned to the ground, and many ethnic Mexicans in Texas were intimidated into leaving their land.

Cortinas' mother, Doña Estéfana, was never molested by the authorities; in fact, she was treated as a great lady, with exquisite courtesy, by Majors Ford and Heintzelman. Cortinas was forever grateful to Rip Ford for this. It was known that Cortinas' mother did not support her son's actions. In fact, the two became estranged, not over politics but because Cortinas conveniently deserted his first wife in Texas when he fled south of the border.

In the Cortinas war fifteen Americans, one hundred fifty Cortinistas, and eighty Texas Mexicans, loyal or neutral, died. This toll was bad enough. But the evil that was spawned lived on; there was to be even more bloodshed on the Rio Grande.

29

THE TERRIBLE YEARS

During the Civil War, the Indians, unrestrained by the United States Army, held carnival across the plains—north to south and east to west—looting, pillaging, and marauding over a wide area, especially to the west and south of the federal forces at Fort Leavenworth, burning out the stage stations and disrupting travel across the plains. Colonization receded; homes and fields were abandoned in north central Texas and settlers were withdrawn for over a hundred miles.

MILDRED P. MAYHALL, *Indian Wars of Texas*

For a long time have this people endured an almost uninterrupted war-fare bloody and savage at the hands . . . of Indians. But sir those depredations have been growing from bad to worse until they are perfectly alarming to our people. I might give your Excellency scores of instances of recent date of murder, rape, and robbery which they have committed alone in the counties composing my Judicial District. It has been but a few days since the whole Lee family consisting of six persons were inhumanly butchered, three of them being females were ravished, murdered and most terribly mutilated. Then Mr. Dobs, Justice of Peace of Palo Pinto County was but last week murdered and scalped, his ears and nose were cut off. Mr. Peoples and Mr. Crawford of said county met the same fate. Wm. McCluskey was but yesterday shot down by those same bloody Quaker Pets upon his own threshold. I write to your Excellency, as to one who from your Exalted Position in our nation can if you will protect us from this inhuman butchery. . . . Your humble correspondent believes your Excellency to be endowed with at least a moderate amount of human feeling and a mind that cannot be trammeled by this one dread insane Pseudo humanitarian Policy: called the "Quaker Indian Peace Policy." Am I mistaken?

CHARLES HOWARD, JUDGE OF THE THIRTEENTH JUDICIAL DISTRICT,
TO PRESIDENT U. S. GRANT, JULY, 1872

THE plight of the Texas frontier during and immediately after the War Between the States has tended to be obscured by the bigger guns, glamour, and gore of the greater war. The frontier was a secondary front while the bulk of the American people were deciding the course of their nation and the future shape of their dominant society. Several things occurred in the West. First, almost all regular troops, whether Union or Confederate, were withdrawn. In Texas—the only area where a large white population actually lay within reach of the horse Indians—the various expedients of minutemen and local militia were utter failures. Farmer militia could not fight Plains Indians on their own ground. Toward the end of the war, it was an axiom on the frontier that the state troops employed there were composed almost entirely of men who chose border service to escape the considerably greater dangers of death or dismemberment with Hood, Bragg, or Lee.

Second, the Kiowas and Comanches had been badly mauled by the campaigns of 1858–1859; they did not understand the great war in the East; and at first they were relatively quiescent. Then, finding no real opposition—they raided, and no terrible ranging companies pursued them —they became almost incredibly bold. By the end of the war, the Texas frontier was a shambles, and in full retreat.

Finally, and most incredible to the frontier people, the end of the Civil War brought no real relief. For nine terrible years the federal government pursued a "peace policy," by which the hostile tribes were to be Christianized and protected on reservations. (Probably, no policy-maker in Washington in these years had ever studied the fate of the Spanish missions or the failure of this form of ideology on the 18th century frontier.) However well-intentioned this policy, it was a form of idiocy, because it completely failed to halt Kiowa-Comanche depredations on the Texas plains. It only prolonged the agony of the Indians, while it brutalized the Anglo-Saxon frontier to an even greater degree.

During these years in Texas, the frontier folk lived forted up, in constant danger and terror. They fought a hundred unseen battles, and suffered some thousands dead. The Young County, or Elm Creek, raid of October, 1864, one incident of many, tells the story as well as any.

After the removal of the reserve Indians, the country around Fort Belknap, including Elm Creek and the Clear Fork of the Brazos, grew rapidly. Young County had been organized, but this country was on the edge of nowhere. As France (or Francis) Peveler, one of the first Texans to settle here, wrote: "We were right on the frontier—nothing north of us but the

North Star." This was not true. North of Young County rode and hunted the Kiowa and Comanche Indian nations, as free to roam as the cold winds that blew down from Canada.

When the war came, the men in charge of frontier defense, Buck Barry and Jim Bourland of the Texas state troops, tried to get the settlers to fort up. At Fort Belknap, abandoned now by the U.S. Army, Barry built houses in a hundred-yard-long square of logs erected endwise in the earth, with picket bastions. A similar stockade was thrown up at Camp or Fort Murrah, where Rip Ford had headquartered in 1858. Behind log stockades and blockhouses, the settlers lived almost exactly as their forebears had in Kentucky a hundred years before.

There were ten or twelve families at Fort Murrah: the Harmonsons, Duncans, Powells, Matthews, Mullins, and Pevelers. These families, as in Kentucky, were Anglo-Celtic clans, including several brothers, cousins, fathers and sons, each with their individual wives and children. Most of these people arrived out of Kentucky, via Missouri; in a way that they could not quite articulate or even understand, they were uncomfortable if anything lay before them besides the far North Star. There were, probably, between fifty and sixty white people along Elm Creek.

In the early fall of 1864, large parties of Kiowas moved south onto the Llano Estacado, camping near their Comanche allies at Red Bluff on the Canadian. Here the combined Indian camp seems to have come under the influence of Little Buffalo, an ambitious Comanche chief. Little Buffalo was hungry for horses, loot, and above all, war prestige. He had scouted the territory along the upper Brazos carefully, and he felt it was ripe for raiding.

Little Buffalo moved among the Comanches of the far-northern bands and the Kiowas and Kiowa-Apaches of Rainy Mountain in the Wichita range. He held council, talking of great victories: the horse soldiers were gone from Fort Belknap on the Brazos, and there was nothing to fear from the *Tejano* soldiers who replaced them, who were few. Hundreds of Comanches agreed to follow Little Buffalo, and many Kiowas, including the prominent Koitsenko, or Kiowa warrior society leader, Aperian Crow. The war parties gathered many extra horses for a hard ride, and streamed southwest into Texas. On October 13, 1864, Little Buffalo reached the Brazos where it joined Elm Creek, ten miles above Fort Belknap. He led seven hundred braves. It was a clear, beautiful, crisp fall day. Here, as one chronicler put it, "the butchery and looting began."

There are many different accounts of the Elm Creek raid, told by different survivors, few of whom knew the whole picture at the time. In a valley beset by a hostile swarm, every man and woman and child knew only his own story. A wealth of detail remains, but the bare bones of the events tell the tale well enough.

The Indians rode down both banks of Elm Creek at midday. They came across Joel Myers and his young son, who were out looking for strayed oxen. The Myerses never had a chance; they were killed and stripped, and the bands moved on; soon they were ringing the Fitzpatrick place. Here, a number of the men were away, gone to the trading post at Weatherford for supplies.

There were three women and a number of children at the Fitzpatrick house. The women were Elizabeth Fitzpatrick, her daughter Susan Durgan, and a Negress, Mary Johnson, the wife of Britt Johnson, who, although legally a slave, had been allowed to live as a freeman all his life. Johnson had been inherited by Allan Johnson, a settler who had no use for slavery. He was universally known as Nigger Britt to the people on the frontier, and he was in Weatherford with the other men this day.

As the howling Indians surrounded the Fitzpatrick place, Susan Durgan grabbed a gun and went outside. She fought valiantly, but the swarming Comanches cut her down, stripped her body and mutilated it in the yard. Then they poured into the house and seized the other people. Two braves quarreled over who had captured Nigger Britt's oldest boy; they settled the argument amicably by killing him. Then the Indians threw Mrs. Elizabeth Fitzpatrick, Mary Johnson, two Negro children, Joe Carter, about twelve, and the Durgan children, Lottie, three, and Millie, eighteen months, on horses and rode off.

A little way off was the Thomas Hamby place, where the Tom (Doc) Wilson family also lived. There were three men here, including Thornton Hamby, a wounded Confederate veteran home on recuperation furlough. These men rushed their women and children to hiding in a cave under the creek bank. Then, they mounted up to warn the other settlers; smoke was beginning to curl upward across the valley.

The William Bragg family, warned in time, hid out in the brush. Doc Wilson, riding hard while the two Hambys fought a rearguard action against a war party, reached the Judge Henry Williams ranch and gave the alarm.

Two women visitors and their children were with the Williamses, also a young man named Callan. Callan seems to have seized his horse and rode away. Mrs. Williams herded her five children and her guests across Elm Creek. They lay down in the screening brush while Sam Williams, fifteen, stood guard with a gun. The raiders did not find them, although they sacked the Williams house.

Thornton Hamby, the wounded veteran, and his father rejoined Doc Wilson at the Williams place, then rode for the George Bragg ranch, a short distance further on. This was a two-room picketed cabin, built for strength. Now, the Comanches were in full cry after the Hambys. They leaped from their horses in the George Bragg yard and dashed for the door of the cabin. Doc Wilson failed to make it; a Comanche arrow struck him in the heart. He staggered into the house, said, "Hamby, I am a dead man," jerked the misssile out, and died.

Old George Bragg was in the house with five white women, a Negro girl, and a great brood of children. The Hambys had thought to fort up here, since they expected to find more men. Now, they were surrounded by Indians, and committed; there was no escape. Thornton Hamby later said: "I might have jumped under the bed—had it not been occupied by three families of women and children who made their way to the ranch for protection." This was the statement of an entirely cool and courageous man, however; when the Indians, blowing on a bugle, advanced on the blockhouse, young Hamby took charge of the defense. The older men were "pretty excited," but Thornton had been under fire before.

He ordered the women to load all the rifles and pistols in the house. One woman, braver than the rest, emerged and gave him great assistance.

The Comanches rushed the house, trying to dig up the pickets. The elder Hamby killed one with his pistol, but was wounded four times. The fight devolved on Thornton, "whose cool heroism saved our lives," as a survivor later said. He stayed at the loopholes, knocking back Indians time and again, while the women pressed recharged pistols into his hand. He was struck by an Indian bullet, but kept up the fight.

He was lucky enough to bring down Little Buffalo himself with one quick shot. At nightfall, after a desperate afternoon, the Comanches retreated, mournfully tooting on their bugle and carrying off their wounded and dead.

After dark, Thornton Hamby, with another man, went to the Fitzpatrick ranch to "see what happened." They buried the bodies they found there.

Meanwhile, the Peveler-Harmonson clans had assembled at Fort Murrah. Chief Little Buffalo had not known that this blockhouse stockade existed; it had just been built. From the top of the fort, the defenders could scan the countryside through a spyglass, and found it alive with Indians. France Peveler and Perry Harmonson saw the Indians playing with something in the mesquite brush. Peveler told Harmonson, "They are killing old man McCoy and his son right now." The McCoy men, who lived about a mile away on Boggy Creek, had not made it to the fort.

Harmonson told Peveler to shut up; Mrs. McCoy was in the fort, and "will be mightily distressed."

The Comanche-Kiowas did not try to storm the fort; frontal assaults on Texan rifles were not the horse Indians' style.

Meanwhile, Lieutenant N. Carson of Bourland's border regiment (variously called state troops, militia, and, erroneously, Rangers) had been near Fort Belknap with about twenty men. The Indians avoided the fort; this also was their style. But when Carson, with fourteen riders, tried to ride toward Elm Creek, they struck some three hundred braves. Five of Carson's men were killed outright, and several more wounded. Carson's report tended to be self-serving ("My men . . . acted with unexampled bravery"), but the troops fired and then galloped away for their lives. A stand, at any rate, would have undoubtedly gotten them all killed.

On this retreat, Carson's troopers came by the Isaac McCoy house, and picked up the two McCoy women. Riding double, militia and women made

Fort Murrah. A number of horses had arrows sticking in them when they arrived.

Fort Murrah prepared for a siege, bringing in milk and water from the spring branch. As night fell, the defenders could see Indians on three sides of them, and a fire blazing to the north. The Pevelers, who had one man mortally wounded from a brush a few days before, and Harmonsons agreed that a dawn attack was likely and that someone should try to ride to Fort Belknap to round up more state troops. Carson's people absolutely refused to ride out, so France Peveler and a man named Fields, from Gainesville volunteered to go. On the way out, they passed a picket standing guard outside the fort. He was seventeen, and France Peveler said later that he was more afraid of him than of Indian marksmanship.

Staying off the high ground, so the Comanches could not "sky-light" them, the two settlers passed a white object on the ground—Joel Myers' body. They came across a horse, pinned to the ground with a lance but still alive and trembling. They could not stop to shoot the pitiful animal. They galloped six miles into Fort Belknap only to find all the border regiment men gone—on a scout looking for Indians, it was said.

Another youth, Chester Tackett, volunteered to ride to Veal's Station, the nearest settlement, some seventy-five miles away. Young Tackett, who was about nineteen, rode out at one the next morning. Changing horses at every white clearing he passed, he arrived at his destination at 9 A.M. But there was no help at the Station. The exhausted Tackett had to stop; another rider pounded on to Decatur, another thirty miles. At sundown, Major Quayle, who had a company of militia, heard that Fort Murrah was besieged. Quayle mounted and rode, ordering no stop until Fort Murrah was raised, although the distance was eighty miles. At dusk the following day, Quayle was within twenty miles of the fort when he met a rider who told him that the Indians were gone.

Some men followed the Indians north-northwest for about one hundred miles on a fruitless chase.

In all its details, this was a classic Texas Indian raid. It followed a pattern, being only larger in scope than most. Eleven Texans were killed; eleven houses were despoiled or destroyed; seven women and children were carried off. The frontierspeople defended themselves as best they could, either by heroism or flight. The cavalry, as usual, failed to arrive in time.

The winter of 1864–1865 was a hard one on Elm Creek. Only three farmhouses survived. Food, bedding, furniture, most of the horses— everything was lost. The Comanches ripped up mattresses to see the feather ticking fly; they emptied five-hundred-pound bags of flour on the ground just to get the sacks, which they prized. As Thornton Hamby said, the Indians ate or stole all the food they could, then "the dirty devils stirred sand in the rest."

There is one more part to the story of Elm Creek, or the Young County raid. Nigger Britt Johnson rode back from Weatherford with Judge Williams to find his son dead and buried, and his wife and two children, both under ten, gone. He waited through the winter, then he said he was going to bring his family back. In April, 1865, he rode out north-northwest from the Brazos country all alone. He took a pack-horse, a rifle, two six-shooters, and some food and blankets donated by the settlers; the Hambys were the first to contribute. He rode into the wilderness until he struck the Wichita, about sixty miles.

He came across a lone Indian guarding a horse herd. Nigger Britt could "talk Mexican," which most of the Kiowas and Comanches understood. He made peace and found the Indian talkative. He learned that the Comanches had "a white woman" captive, and that the Kiowas had some *negros,* or blacks. In a short time, a band of Indians rode up, bringing more horses from a recent raid. Johnson knew every one of these; they were Johnson and Peveler horses from the Brazos. Again, the Negro was able to make peace, and he continued on with this war band for several weeks. They agreed to try to help him ransom his family. Some of these Indians were Penateka Comanches, who had been at the Clear Fork Reservation. Several of them knew Johnson and were not unfriendly. This was not an isolated instance. On the Elm Creek raid, several Indians had spared an old white man named Wooten they surrounded in the open. They called out his name, then ran him for several miles, perhaps shortening his years, because he hemorrhaged, but sparing his scalp. Wooten had delivered beef to Clear Fork.

Nigger Britt knew Indian traveling companions would be a godsend, and he went with them to the Canadian, in the Indian Territory. Here, in a Comanche camp, he found Mrs. Elizabeth Fitzpatrick. He learned that about twenty Comanches had been killed at the Elm Creek fighting, and that little Joe Carter, a son of Elizabeth Fitzpatrick by a former marriage, had been killed by the Indians on the trail back. The twelve-year-old boy had taken sick, and could not keep up.

Elizabeth Fitzpatrick was relatively rich, in cattle and land. She begged Johnson to get her and all the captives back; she would pay whatever it cost. He agreed, and in all the courageous Negro made four trips into Comanchería.

He rescued his wife, Mary, and their two children. He paid "two dollars and a half to get his wife back," and in this he was helped by Comanches. The Penateka chief Milky Way told him how to bargain with the tricky Kiowas, and even sent two braves to travel with him in case the Kiowa allies developed a desire for woolly scalps. Finally, he got every Negro and white captive back, except little Millie Durgan. She had been adopted into the family of Aperian Crow, the Koitsenko, and was not for sale. It was not until sixty-six years afterward, at Lawton, Oklahoma, that a Kiowa woman named Saintohoodi Goombi was identified as Millie Durgan. Her life was not an unhappy one. She was too little to remember her white background and blood, and all her life she stood high in the tribe. She married happily. When, years later, after the discovery of her identity, the Governor of Texas asked what the state might do for her, she answered, "Nothing." She died in Oklahoma in 1934.

Fate was less kind to Nigger Britt. He had won respect on the frontier, and he and three Negro partners began a successful freighting business between Weatherford and the new Fort Griffin. But in 1871, ten miles east of old Fort Belknap, the Kiowas got them all.

Texas historians do not care to explore the Cortinas war. American historians have a similar blind spot toward the terrible years on the Comanche-Kiowa frontier. These two tribes killed more white people than any other Amerinds, a fact not generally known. The reasons for avoiding the Indian wars in Texas are probably complex, and grow out of certain American traumas. The whites were the original aggressors, in that they moved onto Indian range, and the Texan hatred for red vermin could not be made to harmonize with certain American rationales. The culmination of the Indian wars was a tragedy, with all the classic inevitability of tragedy, and against true tragedy the North American soul revolts. Finally, the violence dragged on because of a triumph of Eastern theory over Western experience for some years, which left a sour taste in both Eastern and Western mouths. Whatever the nation as a whole, the vast majority of which never saw a painted Plains Indian, felt about the last stand of these most warlike of tribes, a bitter, never-quite-forgiven animosity grew in Texan hearts toward a government and people indifferent to their suffering. Texas frontier folk, and their descendants, believed that the Indian menace was not quickly ended out of anti-Texan prejudice, or hatred against the South.

Richardson describes the west Texas situation at the close of the 1861–1865 war:

> Indian raids, severe during the war, continued with increased fury after the surrender of the Confederates. The frontier was scourged as never before in its history. In some places the line of settlements was driven back a hundred miles. The country west of a line drawn from Gainesville to Fredericksburg was abandoned save for a few courageous people who moved into stockades. The worst raids were made on moonlit nights, and the soft summer moon became a harbinger of death. Charred rock chimneys stood guard like weird sentries, symbolizing the blasted hopes of pioneers and often marking their graves. Incomplete reports from county judges covering the period from the close of the Civil War to August 5, 1867 showed that 163 persons had been killed by Indians, 43 carried away into captivity, and 24 wounded.

It was understandable that the federal soldiers who returned to Texas in 1865 came to occupy it rather than defend it. Also, the government was more concerned with rebellion than the Indian depredations on the frontier. When, in 1866, Governor Throckmorton and the legislature authorized the raising of 1,000 veteran Rangers, General Philip Sheridan quashed this act immediately. But Sheridan made only half-hearted efforts to end the Indian peril.

Fredericksburg was not reoccupied by federal cavalry until September 1866. Troops gradually moved out to the old forts, Inge, Duncan, and Camp Verde, primarily to guard against Kickapoo-Lipan-Mescalero incursions out of Mexico. Not until two years later was the old line of forts, with some modifications, reestablished from the Red River to Eagle Pass. In 1870, the fortified line of demarcation was almost exactly where it had been in 1850.

Despite the experiences of earlier history, the mistakes of the pre-Civil War period were repeated. Policy was still made by men with no personal knowledge of the Plains frontier, who insisted upon substituting theory for human history.

In 1867, the government of the United States held a convocation of southern Plains tribes at Medicine Lodge, in Kansas. Treaties were signed with the Comanches, Kiowas, Arapahoes, and Southern Cheyennes, all of whom were now in some degree allied. By this treaty, the southern Plains Indians were to accept open reservations in the Indian Territory (Oklahoma), where, under the supervision of agents, they were to learn agriculture and receive some American education. By Act of Congress, the tribes had also been apportioned for proselytization by the various American religious denominations. The administration of the Indian agencies was given largely to members of the Quaker sect, on the assumption that this would be conducive to forging peace.

Under this "peace policy" the Army was given an entirely passive role. The tribes were not under the jurisdiction of the Army, unless they were caught in *flagrante delicto,* in acts of "murder, plunder, or theft." If the Indians left the Indian Territory, the Army was merely to escort them back. It could not follow Indians onto the reservations, even in hot pursuit. It could not punish Indians without the permission of the agents, for any cause.

The policy seemed practical and humanitarian, but in reality it was absurd. There was a number of glaring flaws. First, it was impossible, with the Indian social structure, to make binding pacts with these warlike bands. The old men could give their words, but the warriors could and did ignore them. For many years after the council at Medicine Lodge, the majority of the Kiowas, and at least half the Comanches, failed to show up on the appointed reservations. One powerful Comanche band, the Quahadis, did not even sit at Medicine Lodge, and never considered themselves bound by other Comanches' promises.

Second, while the tribes were willing to make peace with the *Americanos,* who did not impinge upon them, they considered the *Tejanos* a separate people. Apparently, the United States negotiators fell into some semantic traps. The tribes agreed not to make war on the United States, but never extended this courtesy to Texas. Psychologically, this was impossible for these Indians to do voluntarily. They had lived by raiding for generations. Further, they had good reasons on their side. They had been pushed out of parts of Texas, but they did not surrender their claims to this old hunting range. Texas and the Plains tribes had long been at war.

The Indians asked, logically enough, for a treaty that gave them the Great Plains buffalo range, which included the Panhandle of Texas and most of the high plateaus. They still held this ground; there were as yet no white men on it. But this was a game preserve that the mighty United States could not grant them. Under the annexation treaty of 1845—valid despite the Secession, because of the ruling that the states had never been out of the Union—all land within the arbitrarily drawn boundaries of Texas belonged to Texas. It was not national soil, nor would Texas even consider granting it to them. Texas had its own, single-minded solution for the Indian problem, as an editorial comment of 1870 showed:

> The idea of making "treaties" with the Comanches is supremely absurd; just as well make treaties with rattlesnakes and Mexican tigers. Property will be stolen, men murdered, women ravished, and children carried into captivity on our frontier until the Indians are all killed off, or until they are all caught and caged. . . .

The Plains tribes would not soon or easily adopt peaceful agriculture, like Mohawks, who were far advanced over them culturally when the Europeans arrived. They would not voluntarily give up their ancient ways and ranges, nor would any people in similar circumstances. It should have been apparent that the Kiowas and Comanches had to be cordoned off on their reservations by overwhelming force, but this the government failed to provide. A few forts, separated by hundreds of miles of open, unsettled country, and a few companies of cavalry could not keep them behind their arbitrary borders. With the forces provided in the West, it was within the power of Washington to destroy the Indians, but not to contain them if they continued to wage guerrilla war.

The effect of the peace policy resumed in 1867 was to grant the Kiowas and Comanches a privileged sanctuary from which to stage their lightning raids. The years between 1867 and 1873 are filled with accounts of Indian agents who stated they could not keep their charges under control, and of army officers who humilated themselves to buy back Texan captives in various states of repair. These officers could not threaten the Indians once they had reached the "reservation."

In one memorable scene, General B. H. Grierson had blond scalps, including women and children's hair, waved in his face while the Indians demanded presents. Grierson, who had led a cavalry brigade deep in Confederate territory during the war, was no coward, nor was he ignorant of what lay behind these fresh, grisly trophies. But he was bound by policy; he gave the presents.

Indian agents regularly refused to surrender any raiders for punishment, both from fear of a general Indian war and also from the forlorn hope that a little more understanding would in time bring peace. These agents themselves—though some were fearless, upstanding men—aggravated the situation. They were peaceable but not always honest. Huge profits were made by some, cheating the tribes of allotted government rations.

The Indian situation was not static. The Indians, even with their sketchy social organization, understood that the bison range was being narrowed every year from about 1830 onward. If the white farm line did not advance across the 98th meridian, white hunters did. The slaughter of bisons for their hides, by 1870, had become a national phenomenon. The federal government could not prevent this economic enterprise even had it wanted to, but it was making the Indians—who lived off buffalo, and who rode past thousands upon thousands of bleaching bison bones while increasingly game was hard to find—frantic. By 1870, the southern Plains Indians themselves were stepping up a retaliatory war. They were not quite so static in tactics or understanding as some observers implied. They acquired breechloading rifles from eager white traders and their old friends, the Comancheros. Many bands were better armed than the U.S. Army, and entirely formidable in waging war against the poorly protected Texas settlements.

While the army was bound to a passive policy of trying to keep the Indians out of the settled areas by patrol, the Carpetbagger regime in Texas pursued its own idiocies. E. J. Davis restored the old "minuteman" system of frontier defense. This system had not worked under the Confederacy, nor did it work now. The minutemen were unpaid and usually unsupplied. They were a reaction force, not a policing or punitive instrument, and against Comanches and the even faster Kiowas, their reaction time was invariably too slow. They assembled, buried the dead, and followed the Indian trail a few miles out on the Plains, then waited for the Comanche moon to come again. The bravery and efforts of all these minutemen companies should not be impugned, but they were ineffective for ranging war.

By the end of the 1860's the worst depredations in Texas history were occurring along the Mexican border, from Mescaleros, Lipans, and the battered but still powerful Kickapoos. The Rio Grande gave these Indians, who were often allied with Mexican communities in loot disposal, their sanctuary, just as the Oklahoma line provided the Kiowa-Comanches with glorious opportunities. The country above Eagle Pass, and down past Laredo, was regressing toward depopulation. Meanwhile, in central Texas, counties that had been laid out twenty years earlier were more unsafe than during the administration of Mirabeau Lamar.

In August, 1870, the *Daily State Journal* reported: "The counties of Llano, Mason, and Gillespie swarm with savages. The farmers are shot down in their fields, and their stock is stolen before their eyes. . . . Not for twenty years back have the Indians been so bold, well armed and numerous as now. At Llano, the frontier is breaking up. . . ."

Lampasas County reported this same month: ". . . During the last moon our entire county, and as far as reports can be credited, other surrounding counties, have been infested by large bodies of hostile Indians. . . . The truth is, if something is not done soon for the relief of the frontier it will have to be abandoned."

These were all farming communities, far behind the U.S. Army line.

At San Saba, however, the Galveston *Weekly Civilian* reported the situation as relatively peaceful in August, 1870. The statement was meant as factual, not ironic: "The Indians are not worse than usual. Only one man killed, two children captured, and about seventy-five head of horses driven away during the past 'light moon' in this vicinity."

There were dozens of accounts of unwary travelers caught and scalped, of farmhouses entered at night and women raped and slaughtered, and deposition after deposition was made to U.S. commissioners of children carried away. There were also happier stories—from the Texan viewpoint—like that of Mrs. Buckmeyer of Mason County, who blew two marauders out of her windows with buckshot.

During all this time, the reports that arrived on Secretary of the Interior Delano's desk received no action. It was felt, in some quarters, that while some horse-stealing was going on, the reports from Texas were exaggerated.

No doubt, many were. But one of the repellent aspects of this frontier warfare, which has often kept it from being detailed by Americans from other than a frontier background, was the crawling hatred of the Texas people for their indigenous red vermin. Newspapers regularly described Indians as "red fiends of hell" and similar terms. The ordinary speech used terms unprintable in the Victorian Age. The Texans had discovered they could not surrender to Indians, and they took no prisoners.

Many of the young or female captives were eventually ransomed out of Oklahoma. One such returnee, who candidly admitted what all frontier folk knew but rarely discussed, that she had been raped all winter and in the process learned some Comanche talk, reported an overheard discussion between two squaws: "Didn't these damned fools, the Americanos, give us fine things for the few Texas rats we delivered to them?"

If the Amerind attitudes were almost incomprehensible to their Quaker supervisors, the Indians were equally puzzled by Quaker ideology. The agents and the U.S. Army ransomed many captives with presents and promises—it got to be a game with the tribes. Unfortunately, such returns were rarely happy ones. The position of a ransomee, especially a female one, was always anomalous in the light of 19th-century mores. Mrs. Elizabeth Fitzpatrick was able to marry again, but she was rich. Many other returnees left the frontier forever.

The United States policies caused outrage in Texas. The Speaker of the Texas House, in preparing a joint resolution asking Congressional help in 1870, snapped that while Great Britain, the greatest civilized power, went to war with Abyssinia because of the detention of a half-dozen of her subjects, the United States "has not even raised her voice in protest . . . for the murder of one hundred of her citizens." Congress did make an investigation of conditions along the Mexican border in 1872, but this was curtailed for lack of funds. It was noticeable that army officers were able to act with a slightly freer hand towards the Indians residing in Mexico than in the Indian Territory. Colonel R. S. Mackenzie went across the border on a punitive expedition against the Kickapoos, and finally, in 1873, the pressure of Texan Congressmen got the government to pressure Mexico—over some violent Mexican protests—to allow the army to gather up the Kickapoos at Santa Rosa, south of the border, and to remove them to the Indian Territory. This ameliorated, but did not end, the frightful chaos in postwar south Texas, amounting to some $48,000,000 in claims for property losses.

Relief was not at hand from Washington. It seemed that the federal government was prepared to accept a few casualties in Texas as the price of the absence of a general Indian war. Ironically, the succor of the frontier lay in the hands of men who were still hated in Texas: the commanders in Union blue, officers like General Sherman and Colonel Mackenzie. They were to become heroes in Texas, and to force the final Indian solution, almost, if not quite, against the goverment's will.

30

UNTIL DAY BREAKS
AND DARKNESS
DISAPPEARS

*Briefly, the obliteration of Texas Indians was but a small part,
a footnote really, to the nineteenth-century development and
emergence of a new, and in technological terms, a tremendously
powerful nation-state.* W. W. NEWCOMB, JR., *The Indians of Texas*

*Their arrows are broken and their springs are dried up. . . .
Their council fires have long since gone out on the shores and
their war cry is fast dying away. . . .*
*They will live only in the songs and chronicles of their ex-
terminators. Let these be true to their rude virtues as men, and
pay tribute to their unhappy fate as a people.*
SAM HOUSTON ON THE FLOOR OF THE SENATE,
QUOTING CHARLES SPRAGUE

I N 1870, the Comanches and Kiowas, with some assistance from Kiowa-
Apaches, Cheyennes, and Arapahoes, still barred white men from almost
half of Texas. The farm line had failed along the 98th meridian for
ecological reasons; beyond it, ranging from thirty to one hundred fifty
miles in places lay a cattle frontier, where not more than one white person
lived per square mile. The whites, like the former Wichitas, dared live only
on the fringes of the great southern bison range, and here they were in
constant warfare.

The other tribes of Texas had disappeared. A combination of imparted white disease, war, and exile had removed all other Indians. In the middle of the century, the Wichita bands were struck by a lethal wave of smallpox, as were the Lipans. A few Tonkawas had returned to Texas, and lived in miserable circumstances along the white frontier. During the Civil War, the Tonkawas were set upon by the other tribes in the Indian Territory and almost exterminated. The Shawnees and others gave the reason as Tonkawa cannibalism, but a strong suspicion remains that the real reason was the fact that the Tonkawas, even after expulsion remained Texan allies. The tribe declared for the Confederacy, and after their virtual extermination, the survivors crept back to Texas. Here, they performed signal services as scouts for the U.S. Army and Ranger forces, and received the Amerind's usual reward.

The line of cavalry forts delineated the final frontier. Fort Richardson, at Jacksboro; Fort Griffin, near Albany; Fort Concho, at San Angelo; Fort McKavett, on the San Saba; and Fort Clark, near Brackettville, marked the edge of the Anglo-Saxon world. Beyond it were vast plains and plateaus, and only a handful of nomadic Stone Age savages, who ostensibly lived on the Indian Territory reservations, but actually roamed the high Texas bison range at will. These few bands were adequate to stall the white advance.

This was the Amerind last stand, in the struggle for North America. The eleven Plains tribes, from the Rio Grande to Canada, had remained the strongest, because their warlike spirit and way of life had kept them from the fatal contact with whites. The Kiowas and Comanches never let white men come among them. According to their historic codes and customs, they fought bravely to the end. And in the end, no white man could honestly say that they had been beaten fairly on the field of battle. To destroy them, white civilization had first to destroy their habitat, through one of the cruelest and bloodiest of logistic wars.

By 1870, the hunting of buffalo for hides had become a widespread, lucrative business. Every Easterner wanted a buffalo robe, as once every gentleman had desired a beaver hat. Also, an important leather business grew up, using bison hides. From Fort Worth, a burgeoning trading post near the final frontier, the hunters spread out into the plains. They congregated near the cavalry forts, especially at Fort Griffin. Here the hide hunters, a rough, bearded, dirty, violent band of men, waited for the annual migrations of the bison onto the southern range. These men, who worked in groups of about twelve, arrived with wagons, tons of ammunition, and heavy-caliber Sharps rifles. They set up camps in the shadows of the army posts, and they brought certain forms of European civilization with them.

Outside the walls of Griffin, The Flat arose. Originally a saloon, it grew into a typical hell-town of the Western frontier. Dance-hall girls and gunmen, prostitutes and professional poker players poured in, to prey on the men who preyed on the buffalo. At The Flat, red-haired Lottie Deno, the legendary Texas poker queen, ran her game, her cold-eyed gunmen all around. The Flat grew rapidly and raucously, a jangling and roaring boomtown on the edge of nowhere. There was no civil law, and the Army, austere behind its walls, professed no interest in what went on. With the coming of the buffalo, prosperity rocked the frontier, and freighters' wagons rumbled to and from the vicinity of the forts, carrying supplies for the cavalry and the rest of the army.

In the early seventies, there were still countless thousands of bison on the plains. An efficient hunter could kill between twenty-five and forty head per day. Buffalo were sighted, carefully stalked, then a "stand" was made. The nature of the beast was such that men with high-powered rifles could bring down a whole herd from afar, without a buffalo stampede. One hunter, Wylie Poe of Fort McKavett, was known to kill ninety beasts without moving from a single stand. When the singled-out herd was dead, the hunters moved on. Behind them came the hide wagons, with a dozen lowly skinners. These helpers stripped off the bloody hides, and left the carcasses to rot.

For miles and miles the high plateaus swarmed with circling vultures and were strewn with whitening animal bones. This was not sport but massacre for money. There were men who came out to join the trade and were sickened in a single season. But there was no shortage of hunters to carry on.

The buffalo were literally being exterminated. Everyone knew this; it was not done guilelessly or haphazardly. The Army, and the vast majority of whites along the cattle frontier approved, because the buffalo was the free Indian's staff of life. Without them, he was bound to the reservation and the government dole, and he would have to leave the land or starve.

The Treaty of Medicine Lodge, 1867, specifically pledged the Indians that there would be no bison hunting south of the Arkansas River. This would have preserved to them the richest grounds in all North America, the Staked Plains, the region along the Cimarron in Oklahoma, and the Texas Panhandle. There were two things wrong with this promise. The government had no authority to order citizens of Texas off legally recognized Texas soil, and while the government never openly abrogated the treaty, the U.S. Army changed its mind. General Phil Sheridan, commanding the Military Department of the Southwest, and General William T. Sherman, commanding the Army of the Missouri, agreed that there could be no solution to the Indian problem so long as the Plains tribes could support themselves outside the reservations. The "vexed Indian question," Sheridan stated, would be solved nicely by buffalo hunters' destruction of "the Indians' commissary." Sheridan and Sherman knew. They were modern generals, who had waged against the South, from the burned-out Valley of Virginia to the swath of destruction across Georgia, the most modern forms of war. The two generals were vehement spokesmen for this policy. Under them, the Army gave tacit approval to the buffalo hunters' operations against the last great herds of American bison in the United States.

It was dangerous to go onto Kiowa-Comanche ranges. But buffalo hunters were as hardy as they were greedy; they were heavily armed; and they went onto the Southern Plains in winter, when both climate and the shortage of grass kept most Indians comfortable in their lodges. Only when the Indians were panicked by the sight of mountains of whitening bones, and they saw that their own game was disappearing, did they react strongly against buffalo hunters. By then it was too late.

W. T. Hornaday, of the Smithsonian Institution, wrote the North American bison's bitter epitaph a few years later:

> The men who killed buffaloes for their tongues and those who shot them from the railway trains for sport were murderers . . . finding exquisite delight in bloodshed, slaughter, and death, if not for gain, then solely for the joy and happiness of it. There is no kind of warfare against game animals too unfair, too disreputable, or too mean for white men to engage in if they can only do so with safety to their own precious carcasses. . . . Perhaps the most gigantic task ever undertaken on this continent in the line of game-slaughter was the extermination of the bison in the great pasturage region by the hide-hunters. Probably the brilliant rapidity and success with which that lofty undertaking was accomplished was a matter of surprise even to those who participated in it.

There was a movement in Texas to protect the buffalo, to halt what some men called an insane killing of God's creatures. A bill to stop the slaughter was introduced in the state legislature, and despite opposition by economic interests and cattlemen, who coveted the bison pasture, it would have passed, if General Sheridan had not made a special trip to speak before a House-State Senate session. Sheridan was vehement. He said the white hunters were assisting the advance of civilization by

> . . . destroying the Indians' commissary; and it is a well-known fact that an army losing its base of supplies is placed at a great disadvantage. Send them powder and lead, if you will, but for the sake of a lasting peace, let them kill, skin, and sell until the buffaloes are exterminated. Then your prairies can be covered with speckled cattle, and the festive cowboy, who follows the hunter as a second forerunner of advanced civilization.

The bill was killed.

The cavalry had been sent West to protect the white frontier; under the peace and reservation policy in the Southwest it was not doing it; and whatever Army officers had thought of the policy in the beginning, they turned violently against it. The Army was in the cordon of death and destruction; it helped bury settlers; it ransomed demented captives, and again and again, futilely, cavalry pursued Indian marauders to the Oklahoma line, then had to turn back.

The definable turning point came in the summer of 1871. The reservation Indians made no secret of their coming and going. In May, some 150 braves, mostly Kiowas, set out under Satanta, Big Tree, and Satank, ostensibly to fight Tonkawas who were known to be camping near Fort Griffin.

On May 18, these Indians came across a large wagon train on Salt Creek, between Jacksboro and Fort Griffin, on the edge of Young County. They attacked it, killed the wagon master and five teamsters. The sixth, whom they took alive, they chained to a wagon tongue and roasted to death. Five freighters escaped; one, called Brazeal, though badly hurt dragged himself to Jacksboro and raised the alarm.

This raid was no different, or any worse, than a series that had occurred. On January 24, 1871, Kiowas killed Britt Johnson and three Negro partners near Salt Creek. They scalped all four, but threw the hair away in disgust on their homeward trail because it was too kinky and short to make good trophies. Soldiers from Fort Richardson buried the Negroes and pursued, only to be driven back with one trooper wounded.

On April 19, another white man was scalped alive on Salt Creek prairie. A day later, and again on the 21st, other attacks on whites occurred. At least fourteen frontierspeople were slain this spring in Young County. Jacksboro and the surrounding country was almost hysterical with fear and rage. It was incontrovertible that these raids were the work of reservation Indians. Back in Oklahoma these Indians boasted to the agents of their exploits in Texas.

However, on the day the May 19 wagon train massacre occurred, both General William T. Sherman and Major General Randolph Marcy, the Army Inspector General, were in the vicinity. Sherman and Marcy were among those who believed the stories from the Texas frontier were exaggerated. They rode north from San Antonio with a 15-trooper escort, on an inspection tour.

All along the frontier, the commanding general left the impression he thought the Indians were hardly so bad as they were being painted. At Fort Belknap, which now contained only a corporal's guard, and Fort Griffin, Sherman gave irate citizen delegations little encouragement. But he was at Fort Richardson when Thomas Brazeal was carried in from Jacksboro for treatment by army doctors.

Sherman questioned Brazeal, then ordered Colonel (Brevet Major General) Ranald S. Mackenzie to take the field with four companies of the Fourth Cavalry. Mackenzie was to investigate and pursue the hostiles, meeting Sherman later at Fort Sill in the Indian Territory. He rode out with his command in a blinding rainstorm.

General Marcy on May 17, 1871, had written in his journal, "This rich and beautiful section does not contain as many white people today as it did when I visited it eighteen years ago, and, if the Indian marauders are not punished, the whole country seems to be in a fair way to become totally depopulated." But he had not been able to convince Sherman that things were worse than before the Civil War, until the events of May 19.

The horribly bloody, mutilated, fly-covered bodies of the teamsters, and above all, the body of Sam Elliott, who the official army report described as found hung face-down over a burnt-out fire, his tongue cut out and his body crisped, changed Sherman's mind. The general gave evidence of being disturbed.

That night, quietly, Sherman gave his word to citizens of Parker and Jack Counties who came in a delegation to see him, that he would do everything within his power to reform the national military policy. Then, he rode on to Fort Sill and asked the agent, Laurie Tatum, if any Indians were off the reservation. Tatum believed that Satanta and some others were gone, but he expected them to be back, since it was time for issue of rations.

Tatum, who was known to the Indians as Bald Head, was a Quaker, but he told Sherman that for some time he had been trying to convince his superiors that military force would have to be used against the Kiowas, but they insisted that a policy of kindness would eventually succeed. He strenuously denied that he had sold any rifles or carbines to the tribes.

When Satanta appeared, Tatum questioned him in his office. Satanta, with some arrogance, admitted he had led the Salt Creek raid. He gave his reasons: he had asked for arms and ammunition, and they had not been given. None of the Indian requests had been granted; "You do not listen to my talk." Satanta said he had no intention of raiding "around here," but would raid in Texas when he felt like it. He wanted no more talk about it.

Tatum repeated this to Sherman, and the resident Army officer, Colonel (Brevet Major General) B. H. Grierson. With a file of soldiers, in a scuffle, the two officers arrested Satanta, Satank, and Big Tree, identified as the war party chiefs. When Mackenzie, who had had trouble following the war trail in the rain, but had finally traced it into Sill, arrived, Sherman ordered him to take the three Kiowas back to Texas for public trial.

This was the first time an Indian agent had ever allowed a reservation Indian to be arrested; by law, one could only be arrested on a reservation with the agent's consent. The Sill Indians fled in some consternation. The news caused wild jubilation in Texas.

An escort of soldiers, with a wagon, took the three accused Indians south into Texas; they were to be tried in the civil courts for murder. Satank, who was very old, boasted about his greatness as a chief, and complained that he should not be humiliated in this way. He was fastened in hand irons, wrapped in a blanket, and ignored. A few miles out of Fort Sill, the old Indian began to wail his death song:

> *O Sun, you remain forever, but we Koitsenko must die.*
> *O Earth, you remain forever, but we Koitsenko must die.*

The soldiers guarding him were recruits detailed for this kind of duty; they were new to the frontier. They ignored the warnings of Caddo George, a scout, and did not see that the other two prisoners remained frozen, watching Satank.

Beneath the concealing blanket, the old chief gnawed at the flesh of his hand and wrist until he was able to slip off his chain. Suddenly he leaped upon his guards. He badly wounded one, before another put a bullet through his lungs. Thus he died fighting, a *Koitsenko,* one of the ten greatest warriors of the Kiowas.

For the other two Indians a great farce began at Jacksboro. The murder trial was a national sensation, for precedent, for lurid testimony, and for the crawling hatred that lay in the courtroom behind red man and white. The trial could not establish true justice, because the accused were not guilty of crimes under the codes of their own people. Both Kiowas expected to be killed; neither begged for mercy. Satanta, who was about fifty, denied nothing, and said that if he were killed by the Texans, his tribe would take revenge. The younger warrior, Big Tree, said little.

At this trial, Prosecutor W. T. Lanham began the career that was eventually to make him governor of Texas. The two white defense lawyers went through the motions, defending the Indians at the risk of their careers, even, on this gun-slung frontier, their own lives. Due process was served; the jury found the prisoners guilty, and the judge condemned them to death by hanging.

But the great farce had just begun. Back in the East, a number of people were influenced by sentimentalism, or—in some government circles—by fear of an Indian war in retaliation. Enoch Hoag, Superintendent of Indian Affairs, begged President Grant to set the sentences aside. Grant could not do this; murder was not a federal offense; and Grant had no jurisdiction over a Texas court. But he did wire Governor E. J. Davis of Texas, asking that the sentences be commuted to life imprisonment. Davis, knowing that Grant was under much Eastern pressure, did this. Both Indians were sent to the state prison at Huntsville—actually, for a Plains Indian, a fate worse than death.

From Fort Sill agent Tatum reported that the Kiowas were agitated and uncontrollable, and that the warning that the future fate of their chiefs depended on peace was unheeded. By 1872, there was much evidence that all the Southern Plains tribes were planning for war. Worried, President Grant ordered a great conference of tribes to be held at St. Louis. Representatives from all the restive tribes were sent to hear the federal Commissioner of Indian Affairs; at Presidential request, the two Kiowas at Huntsville were sent to St. Louis under guard. At this conference, incredibly, federal agents promised the tribes that Satanta and Big Tree would be released in return for peace. This, whether judicious or not, was absolutely beyond the powers of the President. When the promise was made public, reaction in Texas was violent. The commutation of the death sentences had been widely disapproved; now, the state legislature overwhelmingly passed a resolution stating that under no conditions whatever would the two Indians ever be freed.

General Sherman was furious at the actions of the Indian agency. He penned Secretary Delano a strong letter, prophesying that if released, both

Indians would kill again. Despite this, Delano began to put pressure on Governor Davis, both through official and Party circles. Davis, now approaching his own political crisis in Texas, hoped for favors from the federal government. On October 8, 1873, he paroled both Kiowas and let them leave the state. When General Sherman heard this, he wrote Davis an absolutely vitriolic letter, stating that the parolees would raid again, and that "if they are to have scalps, yours is the first that should be taken."

Sherman was only half right. Satanta did take the warpath again; he was an old warrior and could not learn new ways. It was proved that he attacked a party of buffalo hunters; the fact that the hunters were on ground barred to them by treaty was ruled irrelevant. Satanta was arrested and returned to Texas in 1874. In prison, the Kiowa was like an animal caged. He cut his wrists, but a white doctor kept him from dying. Then, he leaped from the second-story prison hospital window, head-first into the prison courtyard. This time he prevailed, and died.

Big Tree, however, was an Indian cowed in spirit. Big Tree did not fight again. He took up Christianity, taught a Baptist Sunday-school class among the Indians, and lived to be eighty.

But meanwhile, total Indian policy was changing. Agent Laurie Tatum found his Quaker beliefs strained beyond endurance. He began to deny rations to Indians who left the reservation, only to find this forced his charges to raid all the more. He reported that: They have taken one young woman and two children captives and murdered in Texas twenty-one persons that I have heard of . . . They brought in two of the captives, Susanna and Milly F. Lee . . . They promised to bring in [the girls'] brother in two weeks. . . ." He stated that, unless directly ordered, he intended never to issue food to these particular Indians again.

Meanwhile, other records show that 1872 was a bad year. The Indian Commissioner admitted to 100 murders, and the theft of 1,000 horses by reservation Indians; this was a remarkable report to come out of Washington, since Tatum alone reported that the Fort Sill reservation Indians alone took 16,500 horses and mules out of Texas. In April, another wagon train was attacked in Crockett County, this time with the killing of sixteen white men. These raiders held off two companies of cavalry, finally escaping north across the Red River onto the reservation.

But something was happening, without as yet an official change of policy. Generals Sherman and Sheridan had agreed privately that the army must take the initiative. They quietly gave Colonel Ranald MacKenzie freedom of action to do something about the situation in Texas.

Mackenzie was an experienced officer, probably the best Indian-fighter at that time in the West. He was not flamboyant or headline-seeking, like Custer, nor did he have the sympathy for Indians attributed to Miles. He was a hard, thoroughly professional soldier. He knew how to select officers and men for particular jobs. He would use his own judgment without fear of consequences, whether to send his command into Mexico in hot pursuit of raiding Mescaleros, or to spread an enlisted slacker against a wagon wheel and have him flogged. He was no book soldier, and Sherman could not have had a better agent on the frontier.

In 1871, Mackenzie had raided far up into the Llano Estacado, far beyond the country where his Tonkawa scouts had been. He knew more about the Texas Panhandle than any other officer in service. From one expedition into this *terra incognita,* he was carried back on a litter, a Comanche arrow embedded in him. In 1872, Sherman could not give Mackenzie instructions to cross over into Oklahoma, but he could and did order the Colonel to hunt, hound, and harass every Indian on the High Plains of Texas.

Mackenzie took the field, now hunting the recalcitrant Quahadis, who had never gone on the reservation, and whose war chief, Quanah, was beginning to win a great name. Mackenzies' troopers did not defeat the Comanches, but they hurt them. Mackenzie gave the Quahadis summer and winter war, patrolling so vigorously that for some months the frontier was almost quiet.

This was the beginning of brutal times for the proud Quahadis, the fiercest of Texan tribes, and the beginning of the end. If the Comanches went to the reservation, they would be fed—but never enough. One of the minor corruptions of the Grant Administration was the starving of Indians; Indian agents who were against violence and capital punishment were not above graft. If the Comanches remained on the bison plains, their last great game preserve, they were in danger from Mackenzie, who hunted them, man, women, and child, implacably.

Worst of all, the game, the vital buffalo, the Indians' staff of life, was fast disappearing. The hide hunters' war against the vast herds was reaching its climax. The buffalo were being exterminated at a fearful rate; for days, at times, Indian hunting parties rode for miles, seeing no live buffalo, only swarms of vultures and rotting flesh. These Indians of the Plains knew what was happening to them.

The Comanches and the Kiowas were already declining and disintegrating as hopeful societies when Isa-Tai, a prophet, appeared among them. Isa-Tai, the messiah, was a recognizable phenomenon of social decay on these vast, lonely plains; his like was appearing in other places throughout the Amerind West.

Isa-Tai the medicine man prophesied that the Real Human Beings were doomed if they submitted to the white man. But if they fought, and drove all whites from the Plains, then the buffalo would come back. Amerind leaders were ignorant of many things, but they were not stupid. The chiefs of the five remaining Southern Plains tribes heard Isa-Tai.

The Quahadi Comanches, the Kiowas, the Kiowa-Apaches, the Southern Cheyennes, and the Arapahoes held a common council. Quanah of the Comanches, Lone Wolf and Woman's Heart of the Kiowas, and Stone Calf and White Shield of the Cheyenne, many of them former enemies, met and made a fragile alliance. Two things were agreed. The tribes would unite, as Isa-Tai urged, to destroy all the buffalo hunters in Texas. The Quahadi chief, Quanah, would be paramount leader.

This coalition could raise 700 warriors, no more. Of all the Comanches, only the Quahadis or Antelopes were still powerful; the zenith of Comanche power had passed. The other tribes were really already remnants. The 1870's, to be forever marked in the white American mind as the time of maximum Indian power because in these years there was so much war, did not mark high noon in Comanchería. For the Amerinds, it was nearly sunset.

Behind Quanah (Fragrance), the greatest war chief of the Quahadis, lay a significant and moving story. Quanah was half white; his mother had been Cynthia Ann Parker of Parker's Fort. The Texans took a bitter pride in this, even while Quanah scourged the frontier. He was never called anything but Quanah Parker in Texas.

Quanah was born in 1847, eleven years after the abduction of the nine-year-old Cynthia Ann. Tragedy seemed to dog the Parker blood. Cynthia Ann became a true Comanche, but she was not allowed to live out her destiny in peace.

The father of Quanah was Peta Nacona, a respected warrior, chief of his own band. Quanah had a brother, Pecos, and a sister, Flower. They formed a strong, and happy, Comanche family.

In the fall of 1860, however, Peta Nacona led a war party back into Parker County, near the old fort. As the Indians withdrew, Sul Ross, a competent Ranger captain, raised 60 riders and pursued them. Ross had Tonkawa scouts, 20 troopers from the 2d Cavalry under a sergeant, and 70 citizen volunteers. He decided to stay in the field, and strike a punitive blow to teach these particular raiders a lesson. He pressed on into Comanche country, persisting in the hunt into December.

On December 17, Sul Ross' "Tonk" scouts found an Indian camp on the Pease River, near the later town of Quanah. In this camp were only women and children, and some Mexican slaves. It was the camp of Peta Nacona, but Peta and the men were off hunting.

Ross rode down on the camp behind the dust clouds and noise kicked up by a howling norther, or cold front. The usual killing that marked a Texan punitive expedition took place. Accounts vary; however, Sul Ross believed that he killed Peta Nacona and several Comanche women. It is certain that the man Ross thought to be Peta was a Mexican slave named Joe, who tried to protect the women.

In the melee, while the Rangers fired at fleeing Indian forms, Charles Goodnight saw the wind blow back the blanket from one face. He saw dirty yellow hair and blue eyes. "Don't shoot her!" Goodnight yelled. "She's white!"

The blue-eyed woman was taken prisoner. Captain Ross agreed that she was undoubtedly Caucasian, although her skin was sun-darkened and her light hair was greased with buffalo dung. She carried an eighteen-month-old baby girl. She could speak no English; her name was Naduah, and her daughter's name was Topsanah, or Flower. Ross carried her back to civilization by force. Here she was positively identified as Cynthia Ann Parker —she recognized the name.

The Parker family had become prominent and respected in Texas. The family took her back, and did everything they could for her. The state of Texas voted her a pension of $100 a year, and granted her a league of land. But Cynthia Ann had lived as a Comanche for twenty-five years. Her husband and children were Comanche. She tried to escape, and had to be put under guard.

Topsanah died from civilization four years after she was taken; the little girl never adjusted. Naduah, to the horror of her relatives, behaved like an Indian mother. She scarified her breast in self-mutilation, prayed to the Amerind spirits, and starved herself to death.

Out on the plains, Peta Nacona took no other wife. He died from an infected wound. His younger son, Pecos or Peanut, succumbed to disease; Comanche lives were always apt to be short. Quanah, however, grew tall and strong. He showed great intelligence and force of character. In his twenties, he was the acknowledged leader of the tribe. Blood, the Texans said, would tell.

In 1874, while the remnants of the Southern tribes were holding council, hide hunters descended into the Panhandle from Dodge City, Kansas. Dodge was the nearest railhead, and the starting point for most hunters at this time. To find bison, however, the hunters were having to range further and further south, out onto the Staked Plains, the last great buffalo grounds. By the Treaty of Medicine Lodge this area was forbidden to white hunters, but the hunters had tacit army approval. They erected a base camp called Adobe Walls, because it was the site of an old trading post built by William Bent in 1844, when Americans and Comanches were still at peace. Adobe Walls grew into a small fortified town, while the hide hunters based there made a shambles of the richest game area left in North America.

They precipitated the last great Indian war in Texas.

On the night of June 27, 1874, Quanah led the five tribes against Adobe Walls. There were twenty-eight hunters and one white woman in the camp. Quanah struck in the early hours of morning, but, quite by accident, a hunter saw them coming and gave the warning. Failing to achieve surprise, the Indians still pressed the attack. Here they made a great mistake. The white men were superb shots, who made their living handling .50-caliber Sharps. From behind cover, the heavy rifles smashed back the Indian assault. One brave was knocked from his horse by a spent ball at a range of more than 1,500 yards.

Quanah and many of the most prominent warriors were shot from their horses in the charge. Quanah lived only because he crawled behind a mouldering bison carcass outside the walls. For three days, unable to ride the camp down, the assembled bands laid siege. They were well armed with carbines, but they were no match for buffalo hunters in this kind of war. The tribes lost heart; the alliance came apart. One Cheyenne struck the disgraced prophet, Isa-Tai, with his quirt, when the medicine man claimed the attack had failed because a Cheyenne, the day before, had destroyed the Indian medicine by killing a skunk.

The Indians departed, carrying fifteen dead and many more wounded by the terrible buffalo guns.

However, the hide hunters suffered. The battle at Adobe Walls marked the beginning of a widespread war. The bands split up, but they carried death and destruction across five territories and states. Parties of hunters were caught in the open and butchered; all of them fled into Texas or back to Dodge. The hunting season closed abruptly. From Texas to Colorado and from New Mexico to Kansas, this last great uprising killed 190 whites.

Large numbers of Plains Indians left the Territory reservations. One chief of the Comanches, Tabananica, stated he would live on the Plains even if he had to eat dung.

This uprising, and the attack on the buffalo hunters, broke the dam of official opposition to removing all Indians from the Plains. The "Quaker Peace Policy," as it was always called in Texas, came to an end. The new policy was to drive the Indians onto the reservations, and to keep them there by force. The freedom of *all* Indians was to be ended, and the Plains culture destroyed. After thirty years of contact, the leaders of the army convinced the government that President Lamar of Texas had been right. Nature forbade the Amerind from living in peace with the white man, and future peace was to be wholly on Anglo-American terms.

Mackenzie was at Fort Clark in August, 1874. He was ordered to move against the Indians, intercept them wherever he found them on the Plains, and to "break up their camps." The Army was now allowed to pursue and fight on the allotted reservations. There was to be no sanctuary—something the army had demanded for years. Mackenzie received orders to command the "Southern column" and march from Fort Concho, in conjunction with Miles, moving from Leavenworth, and Davidson and Buell, operating out of Sill. Price was to attack east from New Mexico. The Panhandle Indians were to be encircled and ground down from all sides.

Not the Texans, nor the Rangers, nor even the pressure of population was to bring a final end to the Indian wars. It was to be done by the regular army, a fact not always clearly understood in later years. But until the 1870's, the U.S. government failed to take the steps that the State of Texas had been demanding for decades. The new policy was essentially the same that had been carried out in the Jacksonian years: a removal of the Indians. It was the culmination of a conflict that had begun three hundred years before.

In the next few years, there were to be campaigns and conflicts all over the West, reaching to the Dakotas and Montana. But Mackenzie opened the last great struggle. He moved out onto the Plains with powerful forces, well mounted, well supplied, well armed. This was no longer a mere punitive expedition, but a well-planned, coordinated, and sustained campaign.

Finding the Kiowas and Comanches, however, was like finding a few ships on the vast sea. At first the Indians more often found Mackenzie. They circled his columns by moonlight—a "wonderful spectacle . . . in gaudy paint and feathers" as one of his officers wrote. There were brushes and light contact battles. The volatile Comanches struck, and "disappeared as if by magic." They harassed the infantry, which the army still stubbornly insisted on dispatching along with the cavalry, until the foot troops were mounted in wagons pulled by mules. The wagons could not pursue, but they made excellent forts.

Ranald Mackenzie had had long and frustrating experience on the Comanche frontier. He knew there was only one solution to this kind of war, which was to press the Indians without mercy, find their camps, and destroy them. The Indians were vulnerable in one way; they carried their women, children, and all their own supplies with them on campaign. Mackenzie knew it was almost impossible to defeat all the bands in open battle, because the Indians did not fight that way. Somewhere, he already knew, in the unmapped stretches of the Panhandle, the Indians had a great camp.

The official records of the Southern Column do not tell the whole story of how Mackenzie found Quanah Parker and Lone Wolf. The true tale had to come from the civilian and Tonkawa scouts. The only "civilized" men who knew the Comanche country, and had contact with the hostiles, were the despised half-breed Comancheros, who had traded out of New Mexico with the tribes for generations. These Comancheros, who were partly Mexican, with the blood of several tribes, took the horses, loot, and sometimes captives of the Comanches, in exchange for ammunition and guns. The sale of Texas horses, and sometimes Texas cattle, was a large business in the New Mexico settlements in these years. The army had come to look on the Comancheros much as the Texans did—as renegades beyond all civilized law. Mackenzie caught a Comanchero, José Tafoya, who knew Quanah well. He had Tafoya spread against a wagon wheel, and finally, the Comanchero talked. None of the soldiers mentioned this; no horse soldier in Texas would make trouble for Ranald Mackenzie. But Quanah Parker, later, said grimly "if he ever laid eyes on Tafoya, he would broil him in the fire." Tafoya told the scouts, led by Lieutenant Thompson and Sergeant John Charlton, where Quanah and the main body of the Comanches were hidden.

On September 27, 1874, Charlton rode out with Johnson and Job, two Tonkawa scouts from the thirty-five Texan plainsmen and Indians Mackenzie had hired. They moved some twenty-five miles from the column, seeing nothing but leagues of wavi ʾg, rich grass. The Staked Plains were an almost perfectly level, high plateau, mile after endless mile—but they were cut with awe-inspiring canyons, fissured by centuries of stream erosion through the Tertiary soils down into the limestone.

Charlton and the two Indians reached the Palo Duro, a tremendous ditch cut below the surface of the Plains by a small stream. The three men crawled on hands and knees to the lip of this vast crevasse and peered over. Far below, on the canyon meadows, they ould see hundreds of horses grazing, and Indian teepees strung out along the stream bed for three miles. "Heap Injun," Johnson, the Tonkawa, told Charlton. Charlton agreed. The scouts carefully slipped back to their horses and rode as fast as they could to tell Mackenzie.

Mackenzie had six hundred soldiers. He left one company of cavalry to protect his supply train at Tule Canyon, and mounted all the rest at dark. He marched all night, and at dawn on September 28 reached the edge of the Palo Duro.

The scouts were in advance of the main column, as always. The Colonel rode up to the point, and told Lieutenant William Thompson, his chief of scouts; "Mr. Thompson, take your men down and open the fight." There was a single trail leading down the canyon, which could only be traversed by men on foot, leading their horses. Mackenzie, wisely, wanted the scouts to reach the valley first.

The scouts went down, knocking off the sentries, but before they reached bottom, the Indian camp was aroused. Behind the scouts, in single file, passed company after company of cavalry, forming into line as quickly as they could on the valley floor. Mackenzie sent the first company formed, A, to stampede the Indian horse herd. Mackenzie himself attacked with L and H.

The Comanches, peerless on horseback, were caught in their teepees, away from the horseherd. Beaumont, with A Company, reached the *caballado* first. He drove it before him, while many of the screaming braves fruitlessly pursued the horses on foot. The Comanches then followed their usual tactics. The warriors set up a heavy covering fire along the stream, delaying the cavalry until the women and children could flee. The Comanches executed this well; all of the women were able to escape down the canyon. Then, the warriors, a huge swarm, followed. Mackenzie was not able to pursue, nor did he venture.

Thus, at dawn on September 28, 1874, the battle on the surface seemed an indecisive action. Only four Indians were killed, and several cavalrymen wounded. Mackenzie, however, had struck the death blow of the Comanche nation. He gave orders to burn all the teepees and Comanche supplies. Although the Tonkawas did much looting, huge stocks of food and provisions were set afire. Mackenzie burned flour, sugar, blankets, meat, and many new repeating rifles, which the startled Indians had abandoned.

Charlton and the scouts drove the captured remuda, 1,400 horses, back up the canyon trail, and across the plains to Tule Canyon. Charlton had been in the saddle now for forty-eight hours, and once Mackenzie snarled at him to wake up. He had fallen asleep, and was dozing as he rode.

"Shoot the Indian horses," Mackenzie said. There was no other way; the Army could not manage them, and it was imperative, as Mackenzie wrote, for the Indians not to get them. The shrieking animals were shot down in a thunderous roar of firing, more shooting than had been done in Palo Duro. For years afterward, thousands of horse bones lay whitening here, a stark monument on the Plains.

Ironically, few people appreciated Ranald Mackenzie's victory. He had not destroyed Quanah Parker with blaring bugles and flashing sabers, and all the things the Eastern papers loved to print. As Sergeant Charlton wrote much later: "My thoughts . . . go back to the grey dawn . . . when a column of blue-clad, tired, hungry men drew rein on the brow of Palo Duro Cañon, went down into the jaws of death; fought a winning fight and rode back unheralded. . . ."

Mackenzie, who was probably the single most effective Indian fighter on the Plains, never became an American hero like Custer. He did not fight like a Civil War hero; he fought Indians their own way, until they sickened of it.

At the Palo Duro, the Indians got away; women scrambled up the canyon walls, warriors helped each other climb the bluffs. But out on the Plains, although Mackenzie's troopers were too used up to pursue, the Indian plight was desperate. A dehorsed Plains Indian was a pitiable thing; he could not fight or find food; a part of his manhood was taken away. The Cheyennes and Kiowas who had been with Quanah Parker went their separate ways; the last fragile alliance of the southern tribes ended here. On the Plains, the Indians could not even carry the few supplies and goods they had salvaged from the canyon. Their trails were strewn with abandoned possessions.

Some took the long trek back to the reservation, hoping to be fed.

On the others, Mackenzie waged winter war, without mercy or surcease. He pushed strong columns through the Llano Estacado; his scouts cut every Indian trail. The Tonkawa remnants took their last scalps, and held their last, pale victory dances.

The Army officers who presided over the final destruction of the Plains culture were not all Indian-haters. Mackenzie was a professional soldier, who did his job in the most efficient way. He did not kill Indians who surrendered or went back across the line. Miles, who was destroying the Cheyennes further north, was one of the best friends the Plains Indians ever had. These men knew the inevitability of the end; they made it come as quickly and as painlessly as possible.

Twenty-five engagements were fought in the Texas Panhandle or its environs before Mackenzie rode into Fort Richardson on January 13, 1875, after four months in the field.

The Plains remnants, from north and south, fled through the *Llano Estacado* for some months. But the white men knew this country now; it would never again hold the old, primordial terror of the unknown. The Palo Duro could never again be a refuge. The buffalo were almost gone; here and there roamed scattered herds, but without horses the Quahadis could not hunt. They froze and starved. Lone Wolf and his Kiowas showed up at Fort Sill in February, 1875, where the army agreed not to attack them. One by one the bands came in. General Pope's report, in part, read: "In March, the Cheyenne Indians . . . nearly starved to death, and in a deplorable condition . . . under Stone Calf . . . surrendered."

Bands of Quahadis tried to find refuge in the Rocky Mountains; some retreated down the Pecos River into the arid wastes of the Big Bend country. They could not venture on the bison range because of Mackenzie's operations. The roots of their culture, the buffalo and the horse, were gone. Despite warriors' boasts, their women and children could not eat dung. Quanah's, and the other bands, lived through a hideous winter.

Sergeant Charlton sought them out through some of the reservation Indians. He gave the government's terms: the Indian Territory reservations, or extermination. Mackenzie would wage war to the knife if he had to hunt them down.

In June, 1875, Quanah Parker led all of the Comanche remnants to Fort Sill. He was the last Comanche, and the last of the southern Plains Indians, to surrender. Quanah was not treated harshly, although Lone Wolf, Woman's Heart, and many of the Kiowas were imprisoned, or exiled for a time to Florida.

The Comanches, Kiowas, and Kiowa Apaches were promised 3,000,000 acres between the Washita and the Red at Medicine Lodge. A few years after surrender, this reservation was much reduced. Despite vigorous Indian protests, the reservation lands were apportioned to individuals, 160 prairie acres each, and the surplus opened to white settlement. The Indian was to be forced to live according to the Anglo-American way; his reduction was complete.

Quanah served his people more ably in humiliation, perhaps, than in war. He and his descendants became valued citizens in both worlds. Quanah had won something of the whites' respect, and certainly this helped his tribe. He was able to lease Comanche reserves favorably to cattlemen; he traveled to Washington, and met Presidents. Somewhere, he secured a picture of his dead mother and baby sister, which he kept with him at all times. He was no longer a warrior, but hardly less a man, until the end of his days.

Many years later, the government of the United States made Quanah Parker's reservation into a nuclear artillery range. But before that, he was buried beside the bodies of Cynthia Ann Parker and Prairie Flower, who were brought up from Texas. Over his grave was placed a monument, which read:

Resting here until day breaks and darkness disappears
is Quanah Parker, the last Chief of the Comanches.
Died Feb. 21, 1911, Age 64 Years.

31

THE LAST FRONTIER

As I walked out one morning for pleasure,
I spied a cow-puncher all riding alone;
His hat was throwed back and his spurs were a-jingling,
As he approached me a-singin' this song:
Whoopee ti yi yo, git along, little dogies,
    It's your misfortune and none of my own.
Whoopee ti yi yo, git along, little dogies,
    For you know Wyoming will be your new home.
Your mother she was raised way down in Texas,
    Where the Jimson weed and sand burrs grow;
Now we'll fill you up on prickly pear and cholla
    Till you are ready for the trail to Idaho . . .

Oh, a ten-dollar hoss and a forty-dollar saddle,
And I'm goin' to punchin' Texas cattle . . .
I'm on my best horse, and I'm goin' at a run,
I'm the quickest shootin' cowboy that ever pulled a gun . . .
I'll sell my outfit just as soon as I can,
I won't punch cattle for no damned man.

O bury me not on the lone prairie,
Where the wild coyotes will howl o'er me,
In a narrow grave just six by three,
O bury me not on the lone prairie . . .

They say that heaven is a free range land,
Goodbye, goodbye, O fare you well;
But it's barbed wire for the devil's hat band;
And barbed wire blankets down in hell.

The trail's a lane, the trail's a lane,
Dead is the branding fire.
The prairies wild are tame and mild,
All close corralled with wire.

FOLK SONGS OF THE CATTLE KINGDOM

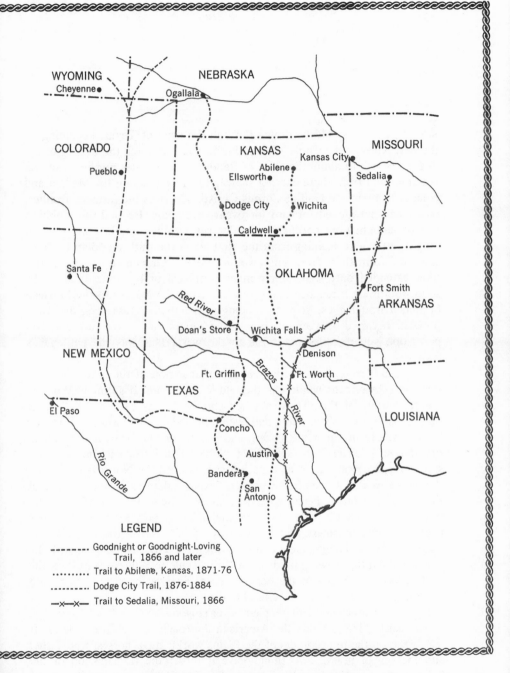

Cattle Trails in the Southwest, 1866-1884

Cattle trails changed somewhat with each season; those shown on the map are the more important ones. The trail through Austin to Abilene, Kansas, was known as the Chisholm Trail. Trails shifted westward with the population movement.

I N 1875 a line could be drawn through the state of Texas, beginning on the Red River at the Cooke County limits, south through the trading center of Fort Worth to about the town of Bandera, a few miles northwest of San Antonio, and from there curving sharply to the east along the Medina and Nueces rivers to the Gulf at Corpus Christi. This was the farmers' frontier, and it had not moved forward for twenty-five years. Beyond this stubborn line of scratched-out cornfields and dog-run huts lay another thin filter of Anglo settlement, running from the Red along the 98th meridian to Junction, and from there stretching away to the Rio Grande. In the north this filter extended only some thirty miles westward of the farm line; in the south-southwest it reached out 150 miles, from the Nueces to the Mexican border. Through these steppes, lapping at the Plains grass seas, the white population varied between one person per square mile in the east, and 100 per 1,000 square miles of prairie to the west. This was the cattlemen's frontier.

Here, in Texas, that abortive culture, that region of the map and mind that most Americans would call the Old West, began. It germinated as the planter culture of East Texas reached apogee. It was to have small effect on the institutions of the state, and even less effect on its lasting politics. Its impact was to be upon the Texan, and the American, heart and mind. In this thin strip of territory, something evolved that burned its image like a smoking cattle brand into the consciousness not only of North America but the whole world. A handful of border Texans, adapting to the realities of their time and place, began what was always essentially a small business, but they conducted it with a barbaric magnificence equaled nowhere. They exploded not a business, but a new way of life, across the entire North American West. They made a culture, with their business, that ran with the free wind and the bawling herds from Brownsville to Calgary, and from the Midwestern wheatfields to the Pacific slopes. They stamped a memory into America, and the world, that refused to die.

Say *Texas* anywhere, and people answer *cowboy*.

The cattle kingdom was the American approach to the Great Plains. It was based on the four corners of the Plains world: men, horses, wild cattle, and the sea of grass. Two things gave it birth: the transmission of the Spanish-Mexican cattle culture across the Rio Bravo; the attachment of Texas to the burgeoning industrial complex of the northern United States.

The seeds were plainly planted when Spain brought its tough, longhorned cattle across the Sonoran steppes. By 1774, at least 25,000 Spanish cattle dotted the Nueces Valley. The extension of Spanish latifundia, the Mexican *ranchos,* across the Rio Grande was no accident. This was a process, and a way of life, that Spain had worked out over generations in arid northern Mexico.

No country, and no animals, were ever better suited for each other than the Spanish strains and the grassy savannahs along the living Nueces. Here, in oak-studded natural parks, where it rarely snowed and some grass was always green, cattle could run wild and thrive. They multiplied without care. *Rancheros* who counted their lands not in hectares but in leagues had no concern for fences. They burned their property with their mark, counting each spring's increase, and in New Spain the brand was sacred. Their servants, *vaqueros* or cowmen, did their work on horseback. They sold a few hides, lived frugally but magnificently, lords of all the land they could ride. All observers agreed that the cattle kingdom—not the American industry of stock-raising—began in the Texas triangle below Béxar, between Laredo, Corpus Christi, and Brownsville on the Rio Grande.

In this pocket the Indian problem was remote; the Comanche trail to Mexico passed northwest of Laredo. The *pueblos* of northern Mexico were hard hit, while the lands between the Nueces and the Bravo went unscathed. The wild cattle—lean, tough, dangerous, some with horns that spread eight feet from tip to tip—bred phenomenally. They numbered in the hundreds of thousands, perhaps millions, when the Mexicans abandoned this land in 1842. To the Anglo farmers who breached this country, these animals were at first a pest. One farmer observed in 1849 that cattle were beginning to overrun the fields, and that out on the prairie lay rusting branding-irons "unrecognized by the people living there."

The bulk of the Anglo-Americans halted at the line where the water and wood ran out, which was where the Mexican cattle empires began. The prairies that would not grow corn year by year were covered with layers of rich, thick grass. Mexicans lived in this land by raising goats, sheep, and cows, on open range; this was a way of life Anglo-Americans knew nothing about. But in the 1840's and 1850's, some men moved across the line. Kinney, Kenedy, and King, all starting as traders on the coast, acquired land, and with the land *vacas* and *vaqueros.* Kinney, operating out of a trading post at Corpus Christi, began hiring men, both Mexican and Anglo, to work cattle and fight. He became, in Richardson's words, "a veritable lord of the marches." Richard King, the Pennsylvanian who cannily, carefully began putting together the million-acre Santa Gertrudis, was to become a king indeed. These men built empires, both of the earth and spirit, which gripped men's minds. They did not really create something new; they took over and built, with a few modifications, on a structure that had been erected in the century before.

The great change was the adaptation to the Mexican cattle culture by the Americans who filtered into the borderlands. Anglos had brought cattle to Texas; above the Colorado the predominant breed was the "Texas," or

American round-barreled stock. But these came as farm animals, handled as men had handled livestock for generations in the British Isles. They were herded on foot in the timbers and brakes, and grazed on small meadows; this was lowly work, left to children or even Negro slaves. Americans did not brand their cattle but kept them within fences; above all, they did not ride.

The Mexican horse complex was transmitted first. Hays' Rangers, without quite understanding it, began to think like Mexicans and Indians about man and horse. The horse was not mere transportation, but the most valuable possession the border Texan had. As the old joke went, the Texan's second most treasured object was his wife. Jack Hays and his boys could live without women; their hours were numbered without a fleet horse. But with a fast horse and a six-shooter, the emerging Texas borderer was monarch of all he surveyed. To learn to work cattle from horseback, in the Mexican fashion, was but a simple step.

The complex was transmitted entire: open range and cowboys, brands and language. The workaday words, lariat, hackamore, ranch, cavayard, and corral never derived from the British Isles. Even the spirit came through—the essential feudality of unreasoning fealty to owner and brand, the feeling of superiority of the menial on horseback to the free farmer with the hoe, the exhilaration of open vistas and the bedrock democracy of an armed society, that the gun made a fraternity of peers—here, in the years before the Civil War, something new was emerging, almost unseen.

The fringes of the Plains were fit only for cattle, but for some years, as the Americans adopted cattle ranching, the cattle themselves were of small use. Texas was remote and far from markets. In the 1830's, a few cattle were rounded up for beef. In the 1840's, some were driven to New Orleans; in 1846, about 1,000 head were delivered in Ohio. Texas cattle are recorded to have reached Chicago before the war. But the markets were uncertain, either in Cuba, the coastal cities, or Chicago; distances were too great and transportation means too poor. The few enterprises that tried to ship beef from the Texas coast by steamer failed.

Still, the cattle culture slowly spread. By 1860, estimates of the number of cattle in Texas range from 3,000,000 to 4,000,000. The savannahs below San Antonio were swarming. The laws of the Republic of Texas made unbranded stock public property; it was relatively simple for far-sighted or otherwise unemployed Texans to build a herd. From the still-Mexican ranches along the Bravo to the emerging Anglo-Mexican spreads around the Nueces, the kingdom slowly filtered up the borderlands. The men who moved out to the San Saba country, in Menard County, were ranchers; so were those who grimly defended Young County on the upper Brazos beyond Fort Worth. A few miles beyond the farmer, from north to south, the cattleman held a precarious sway. The business was restricted because the markets were few—the Army, the Indian reserves, a few settlement towns. Above all, however, the Plains Indians stopped the spread of this frontier. The cattleman went armed and defended himself and his herds as best he could. But, as Webb and several Texas writers have tried to make clear, the cowboy never thought of himself as hero. He did not destroy the Indians; he avoided them whenever and wherever he could. The Rangers were *samurai,* so much so that in later years the concept of the Western hero immediately and emotionally gripped the consciousness of Japan; the plots of American "Western stories" and samurai tales could be transposed. But the cowboy was a worker, a man trying to make a living in a harsh and still uncharted land. The Comanches were a summer pestilence, comparable to winter blizzards along Elm Creek. The cowman endured them, and begged the authorities back in comfortable civilization to do something about them. He carried a gun, for protection against Indians and his own wild beasts; a charging Texas bull could be the most formidable of foes. The cowboy was brave, like the *vaquero,* because he had to be. But he was a warrior by necessity, rather than choice. There will always be an argument in Texas whether the Army, the Rangers, or the hide hunters did most to exterminate the Indians. The cowboy fought battles, but he did not push the Indians back. In Texas, the cattle frontier did not materially expand until the Indians were removed.

Held between the cornfields to the east and the brooding expanses of Comanchería on the west, the cattle kingdom sideslipped the High Plains and spread along the slopes of the Rockies before the Civil War. Texas herds reached California in these years. Some famous Texas cowmen, such as John Chisum and Charles Goodnight, went from the northwest frontier of Texas to New Mexico, leaving the rich bison plains between. They were businessmen, not warriors waging holy war.

The explosion came after the War Between the States. Walter Prescott Webb, the historian of the Plains, wrote: "Then the cattle swarmed, passed out of the valley along the timber line, on the natural highway of the prairie, by San Antonio, Austin, Fort Worth, on and on, taking meat to the giants of the North—the first tie to rebind the North and South after the Civil War."

Suddenly, giant cities had arisen in the North, hungry for meat. The wild Texas cattle were not modern pasture steers; they could walk to market, over thousands of miles, across rivers and sands, through blazing droughts and Indian raids. They made their own roads, along the fringelands on the open plains. The rails, in an outpouring of American enterprise, came to meet them in Kansas; and their flesh, tough and stringy as it was, was too good to be fed to reservation Indians but good enough for the Northern laboring hordes, as the Texans said.

The story of how a few daring men blazed the northern trails, through Indian territory and even more dangerous and avaricious whites, has been told a thousand times. It was a business: in 1865 cattle in war-ravished Texas sold for $4 a head, but brought $30 to $40 in the booming North. In fifteen years, Texas drove 5,000,000 head north, while the herds at home increased. This was a business, which brought thousands of pouches of gold to ragged Texas. It fed hungry families, and made a few cow-millionaires overnight. But it was a businesss that was colorful and dangerous beyond all others; it was something new, and it left its imprint forever on the American heart.

From the first disastrous trials to move cattle through Misssouri, only to be met with warrants, floggings, robbery, and armed mobs, to the alliance with the Northern buyers and railroaders that led to the building of Abilene, far to the west, as the shipping point, this story has been too well told to be repeated here. The cattlemen learned they had to pass beyond the farmers' frontier. They put together vast herds, sometimes numbering 5,000, with slender crews. Ten men could drive 2,000 head. It was cheaper to drive than ship by rail, even after the railheads reached Texas. The best route was the famous Chisholm Trail, blazed by Jesse Chisholm, a Cherokee, which ran along the 98th meridian from deep in Texas to Caldwell, Kansas, then branched out to Wichita, Abilene, Newton, and other towns. Abilene was displaced by Ellsworth and Wichita by 1871, and these by Dodge City in 1876, as the rails extended west. In these towns, weary and battered men who had begun the trail at Brownsville, or San Antonio, or a hundred other Texas points, rammed their milling herds into loading chutes, received their pay, and created a thousand legends on the Plains. The months of grinding, eighteen-hour days in the saddle, the misery of rainstorms and endless dust clouds, the fright of Indian or cattle rustler attack, the sheer terror of a night stampede when lightning sparkled across the Plains, were dissipated in a few wild days, as gunslung Texans descended on the trail towns. "Abilene!" Webb wrote:

> Abilene was more than a point. It was a symbol. It stands for all that happened when two civilizations met for conflict, for disorder, for the clashing of great currents which carry on their crest the turbulent and disorderly elements of both civilizations—in this case the rough characters of the plain and the forest. On the surface, Abilene was corruption personified. Life was hectic, raw, lurid, awful. But the dance hall, the saloon, and the red light, the dissonance of immoral revelry punctuated by pistol shots, were but superficialities which hid from view the deeper forces that were working themselves out round the new town. If Abilene excelled all later cow towns in wickedness, it also excelled them in service —the service of bartering the beef of the South for the money of the North.

Here Texas cowboys tried to refight the Civil War with careful, deadly Northern killer-marshals, whom the town business interests sensibly hired. They rode horses into saloons; they galloped with six-shooters blazing along the dirt streets. Most of them spent their pay; a few died. After the horror of the trail some drovers foreswore the drive forever, but owners in Texas had no trouble putting together new crews. Some of these cattlemen, such as King Fisher and Shanghai Pierce, were as wild and tumultuous and dangerous as the surly longhorns they drove to market. But the majority were businessmen who came to get the Yankee dollar. They sold beef, drank whiskey, and made deals with Northern shippers and capitalists. They forged new ties. Webb exaggerated only a little when he asked: "Who can say that Abilene was less significant than Appomattox?"

For, on that ephemeral but immortal frontier, Texas replaced the cotton kingdom of the slave South with a cattle empire. In the West, for the first time in the 19th century, elements of North and South met and merged. The cowboy or the cowman, recognizable wherever he stood, was neither Yankee nor Southerner; he could be either, or both. The great majority of all Texans were then, and for decades remained, Southern farmers. But out beyond the 98th meridian the Plains sun burned through the fogs and lifted the burdens of Southern history. The Texas drovers set out to sell beef, but they recast the image of a state.

The Texans did not just ship cattle East through Chicago. Texas herds passed out of the historic triangle, north, northwest, and west. Round-barreled Texas cattle and Texas know-how passed across twelve Western states, from New Mexico to Montana. With the end of the Indians, the cattle business exploded. In 1876, the cattle frontier had barely arrived at the 100th meridian; five years later it had closed the High Plains and was established far beyond Texas, from New Mexico to the Cascades, and from the Panhandle to Alberta. Texas stocked the Western range, with stock and men. Some small modifications were made: a northern saddle could be distinguished from a Texas rig. But in the shadow of the Rockies, or on the semideserts of Oregon, cowmen were essentially the same.

This was because Texas shot not only a businesss but a form of culture across the American West. It was protean and adaptive, yet strangely uniform. The cow culture—and it was a genuine, if abortive culture—was the only Anglo-American process that adapted to, rather than developed and destroyed, the primeval land. The ranchers were nomadic, casting themselves out on the great sea of grass. They and their cattle moved from place to place. The cowmen built incredibly ugly ranch houses and raw corrals, and sometimes squalid shacks or sod huts that were as much forts as homes. But they built these miles apart, always out of sight of other human abodes, and otherwise they did not scar or modify the land. They used it, and perhaps loved it, much as the Indians had.

The range cattle were their buffalo; their spectacles and socializing acts were not the hunt, but the roundup, which was a form of hunt, and the cattle drive. Both required cooperation, and widely separated men came together briefly. In the early years, there seems to have been little concern for seizing strategic lands, such as riverbanks or water holes. In the developing culture a code worked out, which opened the range to all. In these years the land was not crowded, even by cattle, and the plainsmen looked upon the land something as sailors looked upon the sea, and gave as little thought to claiming its ownership.

Ironically, most of what was later looked upon by outsiders as Western lawlessness, came only when Eastern concepts and Eastern laws were forcibly imposed on the West. The Anglo-Saxon organic law was absurd as applied to water in the West, because it contained no useful precedents; it could not envision a land where rain fell only spottily, but surface water, wherever it happened to be, was needed by all. Anglo-American law thus gave full possession of all the water in a valley to whoever owned the surrounding land or riparian rights; it was centuries behind the pragmatism of the Hispanic-Mexican codes. This nonsense later led to bloodshed, but as most Western observers had little success in pointing out, the adherence to unworkable laws caused the violence in the first place.

The few years of the cowboys' West proved how quickly a new culture could germinate and explode. Of course, it was a transmittal direct from Mexico, but the adaptation and expansion were phenomenal. Cowmen came from everywhere, Scotland to New York. Many never got beyond the trail towns or the Eastern or British-owned cattle company's town offices, but others were as adaptive to the West as though they had been born in frontier Texas. The first wave learned the country's ways, rather than destroying the country to fit their own prejudicial judgments.

Cowmen came from everywhere, not only because the beef business was booming, but because something in its way of life called strongly to certain breeds of men; however obscured in romanticism and mythology this became, a core of truth remained. The new frontier culture that Texas blazed into America held a barbaric exhilaration; it affected some Americans as much as the transmittal of the horse exalted the grubbing mountain Comanches, more than one hundred years before.

Owners and capitalists might make quick fortunes on open range and free grass, while cowhands worked for $10 per month. But still they came, Scot financier and runaway farmboy, and both settled comfortably and grandly into the West.

The cowmen lived off different beasts and held by different totems—not the antelope, or the wasp, or the bear, but circle dots and flying L's, the sacred brands; but their society, in its great years, was as atomistic as the Indian. Their endless horizons were as culturally limited as the Kiowa's, yet their adaptations said something about the innate nature of the animal, man. They created the second American enterprise that became more than a business, and a way of life.

The terms used to describe the cattle explosion were always kingdom or empire, never the cattle business or the cattle industry. The home of the American cattle industry, in these years, never moved West.

In 1880, Texas and the Plains states and territories that Texas seeded produced only 28 percent of Americans' beef. Thousands of small farms and acreages in the East collectively marketed more meat. The East had its industry; the West its kingdoms. But the West, in a few short years, left its imprint forever on the American mind, because the West did its small business with sheer grandeur.

The cattleman was not an economic unit, but a man. His work—and it was work, not play—was arduous, danger-filled, and dirty. But he rode and roamed, and thus in his own cultural trap enjoyed great freedom; he fought for his own, and thus emblazoned living legends. Only a tiny handful ever sought this last frontier, but that handful captured the imagination of most men.

The cattle culture was logical; in 1870 there was hardly any other possible adaptation to the arid lands. The appurtenances of that culture—the horse, the pistol, wild cattle, the boots, chaps, big hats, and dust-catching kerchiefs or bandannas—were logical, too. They were necessary tools of a trade. But because, in their time and place, they seemed romantic to outsiders, they were to become as stylized, and eventually meaningless, as *toreros'* garb. Just as Spanish bullfighters adopted and clung to a degenerate form of 18th century gentlemen's dress, thousands of Americans would someday dress as cowboys, unconsciously hoping to assume the role of Western hero. They would wear cowboy boots while driving their automobiles to drugstores, and never quite know the reason why.

What happened in the Texas, and American, West was a small but powerful process of natural selection. This was a harsh land, and its pressing realities were hot and cruel. There was little real fat, either material or psychological. Inner convictions, developed in more rarified civilizations, could not stand unless they were practical. Logic was only logic in the West if it visibly worked. The man who held to a preconceived attitude toward Indians, and could not learn the Comanche reality, often saw his family killed; or he himself died in his own homestead's ashes. A little-noted but obvious fact of the long Texas frontier was that some men lived and some families prospered on the edge of Comanchería, while many others failed. and chance was not the major determining factor. Eternal vigilance, eternal hardness, was the price of success.

Observers wrote how old Rip Ford, weathered but not withered in his last years, squinted carefully down both sides of a San Antonio street—the famous, careful Southwestern stare, evaluating the men, the weather, the lay of the land—before he emerged into the sun. A Charles Goodnight could move early onto the far edge of nowhere, and hold his new range against all comers. Some men could not.

The successful cowman did not pray for rain so much as study the ways of the land, and learn when and in what cycles the rain would fall. Such men survived. Others, in whom wishful thinking was forever dominant, could not.

The Western selection was natural, but arbitrary, according to the needs of the land. No man who could not ride well fitted this country; he was a horseman, or he left. The society, atomistic as it was, could not tolerate physical cowardice; bravery was required. The coward not only died his personal thousand deaths, but he got better men killed as well. Again, the nature of the land worked strongly; timid men did not move into Indian country, nor did they ride mustangs and chouse longhorned cows. The syndrome of physical courage was a natural result. The Westerner could "ride the river" with some men; with others he could not. He saw no reason to tolerate the failures. Nature, and this land, did not tolerate its own. It was intellectually impossible for the Westerner to adopt a sense of the sacredness of life, because the evidence of his senses and his reason proved there was no such thing. On the Pleistocene Plains, nothing, neither man nor beast, had any inherent right to life. Some died, some survived.

The Indians were pests, and were removed, like cougars and range wolves. The buffalo was useless and stupid, in cowmen's eyes, and they welcomed their demise. Thus a definite Western psychology evolved, sometimes miscalled rugged individualism. The Westerner was brave and generous among peers, immensely adaptive to new ways and artifacts, anything that would help him live on the harsh frontier, but contemptuous to the edge of cruelty of ineptitude, and suspicious to hostility and beyond of unproved or undemonstrable ideas. The Westerner was as atomistic and self-reliant as the Indian, but in many ways almost as tribal, which was not understood. The same land called both breeds forth, and the land itself was dominant over man. No man could make it rain, though many tried, and no man, emulating Canute, could halt a blizzard howling across the wild frontier.

Nor could any man withdraw into his own empire of the mind. Such structures require an intricate civilization, far removed from the immediate realities of the soil. Thus the best-adapted Westerner was keenly intelligent and observant but at the same time highly unintellectual. Table talk, as writer after American writer has recorded, was of crops and cattle, markets and weather, never some remote realm of ideas.

This culture emphasized manhood, and it showed true feudal strains. The owner-cowman, the range boss, did not direct from his office, in the formative years, but from horseback. No wall of class or caste separated the wealthy cowman from his riders; he was more often than not a man who rose from their own mass. He was tougher, smarter, more capable of thinking or handling cows and men. Because of this origin, and this prejudice, a spartan atmosphere surrounded even the great and wealthy indigenous empires of the West. In Wyoming and other places, European and Eastern owners drank superb whiskey in local clubs, and enjoyed the amenities of wealthy, transplanted investors. In west Texas, and this was lasting, immensely respected and powerful cattle barons did not live any differently from the bunkhouse hands.

Their big houses were spare and without beauty; their sons learned to ride and shoot and curse like men, or were held in a certain, unspoken contempt. Just as a certain breed continually flowed to the frontier, the frontier continually threw its own detritus back. Some were men and women who could not live this life.

The life was peculiarly destructive of women, eternally the conservators of civilization. Few countries where men are men can be happy abodes for women. Good women, however, were partners and enjoyed immense respect, and not only because they were so few. But because they were rare, all women had a status beyond that in the East. No man respected a prostitute or dance hall girl, despite much romantic and anachronistic fictional maundering in later years, but a capable whore was a much more valuable commodity here than in the crowded, industrial, slum-town world, and thus enjoyed greater consideration.

Two things were remarkable historically in this ephemeral West. One was the evident early feudality. The cattle "baron" was a baron in the original sense of the European word: a man, not an aristocrat, who got things done, not from on high, but among men and at their head. With a water hole in danger, or free grass encroached upon by some farmer or "range hog," or if someone disparaged the totem of the brand, cowhands were known to ride at the cowman's back. American history will never be entirely expunged of the cow outfit: owner, men, and boys, clattering into town, or assembling on some disputed range. The tribe of sheepmen inspired horror beyond the destruction of cattle graze. Men who could not work from horseback, farmer or merchant, were regarded by the cowman with expansive contempt. The cow tribe came from many disparate parts and points, but it quickly fused into a tribe. Cowboys, from the Canadian to Canada, were one clan.

The other factor was how quickly this culture developed its own psychology and codes, not yet codified into laws, and how these lasted beyond the reality of their time. The imprint was immense in Texas, although the scattered cowmen never materially affected the lives of the vast majority of people in the state. It was a society of the young, because old men did not go West; and the young were more changeable and adaptive, while at the same time more tribal, and more inclined to be philosophical conservatives about fundamental things. Children's society, with its directness and its cruelties, was untrammeled, and so was the society of the West. The cowboy, as one observer wrote, was ready to sing, to ride, or shoot, at the slightest provocation.

Love was subordinated, though sexual gratification was not, a characteristic of young society. The horse and pistol were admired; "they filled the eye and purpose." They were a symbology of direct, uncomplicated action to satisfy the soul. The horse elevated men and increased their sphere of action; the pistol, a weapon, toy, and tool, increased men's democracy and individual sense of power and worth. "God made some men big and some men small, but Sam Colt made them all equal," the significant Texas proverb ran. The armed society was not necessarily democratic or free, except among the peer group, but it was imbued with the sense of being both.

It was a special social complex, in which men gave or took no orders except from the recognized leader. It was largely lawless, because in the explosive turbulence of the rapid advance across the Plains, law and the instruments of law could not keep pace. When 100 men lived in an area of 1,000 square miles, formal structures disappeared. But the West, in the great years, was not criminal, and this was to be a fact much misunderstood. Much of the so-called lawlessness of west Texas was a result of Eastern laws that made no sense in the milieu beyond the 98th and 100th meridians. Men had to make their own codes, because there was no authority otherwise to make them; and many of the codes of the crowded, organized counties to the East were in the West absurd. Police did not exist; and what courts there were frequently dispensed what few Westerners regarded as justice.

Theodore Roosevelt, who spent much time in the West, called the code of the West "a square deal," in other words, fair play. This was innate in the Anglo-Celtic nature; fair play was an Anglo-Saxon concept. Under fair play no man could bushwhack another, shoot an unarmed man, or shoot an enemy in the back. He could call a play, thus giving all a fair chance in ensuing duels or war. Some men were better shots, or faster, than others, but the code of the West did not call for equality, only for equal opportunity. All men had the right to defend themselves. His survival, as Webb said, imposed upon the Westerner certain obligations: courage, skill, and the ability to kill in self-defense. If he was too inept or bloodless to develop these, that was, in Texan eyes, his own tough luck.

Breaking of the code brought punishment, but not at law. The man who shot Robert Neighbors was not brought to formal justice, because formal justice could not, in Texas hearts, have given him what he deserved. The man who might shoot an Indian or a Mexican, even on dubious grounds, was not a criminal, because these were not social crimes. Nor could any man who did not live the reality of the bloody trail properly call them so; crime involves psychology as well as moral codes. The West evolved a different, but a very real, code of murder. Killing in an unpremeditated quarrel, or in a called fair fight, was not murder but an incident. It did not strike at the roots of society, and was tolerable. A hundred years later, the criminal codes of the state of Texas regarded casual killing as a relatively minor crime, drawing two to twenty years. The usual punishment set the killer in a fair fight free in two years or less. The penalties for burglary or robbery were more severe.

Crimes against property involved two kinds: horse theft and cattle rustling. There was almost no other kind of property in the West to steal, and petty thievery violated all social codes. In a horse-symbol society, and one in which the horse frequently meant the difference for survival, horse theft logically had to be punished by death. Cattle-stealing was less important, especially during the years when the price of beef on the hoof in Texas was low. In fact, some of the viciousness that centered on cattle-rustling in later years came because of the mildness of the law and public attitudes. Cattlemen who were being robbed blind and who saw juries deal leniently with cow-thieves, much as later juries dealt with drunk-driving and for the same reasons, were powerfully stimulated to take the law into their own hands, through cattlemen's associations, range detectives, or otherwise.

One distinction often misunderstood was between a branded cow and its unbranded maverick, or calf. An unbranded calf for many years was regarded as public property in Texas; most cattlemen gathered in any they came across and rarely considered themselves thieves for doing so.

The real wars between Americans in the West were over land and water, primarily water. Here the English laws were useless to promote justice, quick to foster range wars. Noticeably, when the sea of grass was still a sea, and cowmen moved on it, unwritten customs with the force of law emerged. Cowmen recognized each other's range and water rights, which were staked as miners in the West staked out gold and silver claims. The law did not understand certain realities in the West, almost certainly because the lawmakers and enforcers, all men of the regions farther east, did not understand them. These men thought in terms of purely private property, in which each owner fenced his own parochial plot, and water was available in some fashion to all. When the law allowed certain ranchers or farmers to fence off rivers, thus destroying everyone in vast valleys who owned no riparian lands, the law produced bloodshed. To the law, no one held range or water rights unless he owned the property itself. The Homestead Act of 1862, which was an immense but rarely admitted failure west of the 100th meridian, did not affect Texas, because in Texas there were no federal public lands. Other legislation, particularly on water, did. The only law that the various legislative bodies failed to pass to regulate land and water in the West, as one historian said, was a law requiring more rain. In the end, Texas, painfully, had to modify the English common law on waters, while most other Western states abrogated it entirely. But this was not easily or bloodlessly done. Texas was fortunate in having had experience with Mexican law, and the original Mexican-Spanish code of reasonable and prior use, and the code that available water belonged to a region, not just a single owner, eventually were used in much of Texas.

There was no solution to the basic problem, then or later, because west of the meridian there never was, and probably never would be, sufficient water for development on the usual American scale. All solutions were compromises and modifications.

This brief West was spectacular in its scenery and ways of life, lawless and hardy in its reputation; unfortunately, it was also romantic to many outside eyes. It was not the most important American frontier. It was a footnote compared to the advance across the Appalachians, and the strategic turn of the wheel at San Jacinto. Yet no part of American history, probably, received so much attention.

The reasons were probably several. The Civil War had ended, but left gaping wounds. The West was fresh and free, not only for settlement, but to catch men's minds. It was neither North nor South, but American, though a prejudice lingered against the Texas West in fact and fiction. The United States, as a nation, was strong now, but not yet caught up in its 20th-century role of imperial expansion. The nation looked inward, to its own receding frontier, and the immense success of that conquest "loomed high on the egocentric national horizon." There was a sense of closing the national destiny, and an awareness that, just as once the northern and southern streams of Anglo-Celtic migration met in the Allegheny-Appalachian foothills, the two mainstreams of American 19th-century movement met and fused on the Plains. The Texans who crossed the Sabine were still Southerners. The men who moved across the 100th meridian, and from there to Wyoming, were Western Americans.

The West had a common national tale to tell, just at the time when transportation and means of communication were being developed to carry its story across the entire nation. Both Chicago and Austin newspapers, almost the same day, carried stories like *All Hell Breaks Loose in Texas— Miles of Fences Cut,* when this frontier made its last stand once again, against the subtle but inevitable encroachments of the East. The last frontier was nationally advertised in the very days it ceased being a frontier; the impression was made.

Only a few Americans of many succumbed to Western psychology and Western mores, but they created a legend, with the aid of Eastern writers, which will never die.

As quick as its phenomenal expansion was the cattle culture's decline. The development flowered for a decade, then was extinguished on the Plains. The cow kingdom, the series of small empires, was always tributary and never sovereign, and it lasted for less than thirty years. It was moribund by 1885, dead by 1890. The Industrial Revolution, and the great mass of people to the East, subjected it as surely as they had destroyed the Indians, though they used different means.

Two inventions, the windmill and the barb-wire fence, destroyed the seas of grass. By themselves, each invention was imperfect; together, they made the cutting up of the Plains possible, and stock-ranching, rather than the cattle kingdom, profitable. The industrial society was endlessly inventive, endlessly destructive. With the air-driven, cheap, transportable windmill, wells could be planted on the semiarid prairies and stock tanks filled. Limited irrigation of pastures could be carried out. Each rancher could now stay in place, and cultivate his own parochial acres of land, to which he now must secure title. The wise cowmen had secured titles in Texas long before.

With the explosion of fence wire in the early 1880's, open range was done. Without cheap, transportable fencing materials, the Plains could not be sequestered; nor could the hardy but low-grade Texas stock be improved. The toughest and rangiest bulls, by natural selection, bred out the improved, weaker, fat stock. Behind barb-wire fences, the stockman could breed his expensive bulls and keep the range stock out. This was immense economic progress, but marked by certain failures. It was predictable that the ranchmen would overstock, and that the cattle, which cropped closer than bison, would eventually destroy the rich grass.

Meanwhile, there were no more trail drives or great roundups; wire enclosed the prairies and the rails pushed everywhere in the West.

Later Americans would never understand or sense the incredible vistas that inspired the first viewers to call the Great Plains an ocean. They were scarred first by stark lines of brutal metal wire, and iron windmill sentinels standing guard. Then the Plains disappeared in swirling duststorms, for which both the overoptimistic farmers who moved far west in wet years and the more economic-minded stockmen were jointly responsible. More people could live on the land, developing and destroying it, and that was the North American dream. The sun still shone, the winds still blew free, and only a handful of Americans heard a lament.

Now fully tributary to the economic cycles of the Industrial Revolution, the cattle culture withered; its bases were gone, engulfed in the continuing wave that devoured the First People. The boom and bust of the price cycles, the careful breeding of improved strains, the eventual development of vast farming operations, wheat and cotton, on some parts of the Plains, formed no part of history, except in books on economic development. The older, wiser, more good-humored stockmen sold off parts of their lands, helped develop towns, and usually served as directors of the first new banks. In one lifetime they had seen an abortive culture rise and fall. The lawyers were not far behind the Indians' demise; the men of the East insisted on making law and carrying it out for the men of the West.

The old-timers told old men's tales, of Indians, of fence wars, of good men and true, and bad men "mean as hell," as Dee Harkey wrote. Their descendants heard these tales, and were fascinated by them, but would never entirely understand.

They had not conquered the land nor bent it entirely to their will; they had cut it down to size.

The last stand of some, not all, of the cowmen was against the fences. The men who loved free range—free, if only a handful could enjoy or profit from it—saw the cruel wire come with horror. In Texas it was the large ranchers, above all the great cattle corporations, who fenced first. These people understood progress and stayed ahead of it. They fenced their huge acreages, which they bought cheaply from the state, and imported iron windmills along with the British cattle breeds. They crowded the small, reactionary, recalcitrant cowmen out. Some fought, some cut wires and tore down fences until it was made a felony at law. Behind these vast new preserves, and the small ones, ranchers raised cattle, rode horses, and wore boots, though they soon put their pistols aside. But the fenced pastures no longer resembled empires, nor were these men kings.

The land survived, immense, brooding, endless, its horizons lost in distant mountains, immensely old, yet somehow still young. There were places where men, and even the towns they built, were still specks of occasional ugliness upon it. New people came in and diluted old blood with new. Yet, something of the outlook, the psychology, and pragmatic directness of the Westerner remained along with the fading folk songs.

This land changed men, even Anglo-Americans, more than they ever changed it, and more, perhaps, than they would ever admit.

32

THE DARK
OF THE MOON

*I find that the killing of those parties has developed a most
alarming state of things on this frontier. The Mexicans on the
other side of the river are very much infuriated and threaten to
kill ten Americans for each of their Bravos. And then on this
side the Mexican residents of Brownsville (that is, the majority,
the canaille or lower class) are public in their denunciation . . .*
CAPTAIN L. H. MCNELLY TO THE ADJUTANT GENERAL
FROM BROWNSVILLE, JUNE 1875

What we want is about three good Rangers.
JOHN NANCE GARNER, JUDGE OF UVALDE COUNTY,
TO ADJUTANT GENERAL MABRY

VAST changes—more vast and more turbulent than the various explosions of the next century—took place in 19th-century Texas. Only in retrospect did the older times seem stable; and this was a false view. From the first arrival of Anglo settlers in the 1820's through the closing of the final far-west frontier in 1881, life was volatile and dangerous; there was very little security of life or property; the state was always living under some fear or threat.

These threats—Mexicans, Yankees, Indians—were primarily external. But the turbulence of the frontier wars created an almost equal turbulence immediately behind the lines. No observer, seeing the violence that flared continually on Texas' long frontier, can fail to understand the ensuing problems of law and order that beset the state. By 1835, Anglo-Texas was drawing men who sought violence like strong drink; if they could not find a

569

war, they were disposed to make one. It is an ironic fact that Stephen Austin's colony was one of the most orderly, with less crime, than almost any community in the history of the American frontier; but ten years after Austin's death, Texas had achieved an enduring reputation for lawlessness and bloodshed.

Austin's problem-solving was simple and direct, as it pertained to crime. By agreement with the Mexican authorities, he tolerated no unemployed, unpropertied, or people with dubious reputations on his lands. Gamblers and horse thieves arrived, along with duellists and gunmen. Austin saw to it that all such were rounded up, flogged if a lesson seemed judicious, and ejected from his colony. Expulsion was no difficulty; the criminals could always return to the States, or go beyond the confines of Anglo-Texas into Mexico. In terms of results, this system was almost perfect; it worked. Austin's Texas had no organized crime.

But with the immigration explosion of 1836 and ensuing years, the opening of headrights and free lands to any sort, and the eternal border violence that ensued, these conditions could not be continued. GTT—Gone To Texas—became a favorite entry, closing a case, in hundreds of American sheriffs' books. Along with the proud, stubborn pioneers Texas received many people of less wholesome cast. In 1842, homicides were common even in East Texas. The *Houston Telegraph* reported shootings and hangings, and observed that the frequency of both would "foster opprobrium upon the national [Texan] character."

The duel was not invented in Texas, but here it probably reached its widest use. At first these affairs were merely continuations of Southern custom; gentlemen shot each other for almost every conceivable affront. The Texas army was wracked by affairs of honor; officers put each other to the ultimate test almost with abandon. The end of the Republic, and the writing of an antidueling provision into the state constitution of 1845, halted most official frays. The old *code duello* brought across the Sabine fell into disuse, but the newer code of the West took its place. The informal, but no less bloody, duel in which the participants gave notice, drew, and shot it out—sometimes in a mass melee—was not recognized by the law as duelling, but as self-defense. It had the stamp of public approval; if a man went armed, he was expected to be able to defend himself.

But true crime also increased. The laws of the Republic were harsh: branding or flogging for theft, death for forgery, horse stealing, or equally opprobrious crimes. The state had no penitentiary until 1849, and these other methods were economical and direct. But already the laxity of law enforcement had become common, and this was to continue as a Texas trait. Local sheriffs tried to keep reasonable order, but not to stamp out crime. Texas juries were rough and ready, venomous when the public ire was aroused, but otherwise more disposed to set free than convict. Texans did not much like formal law or regulation, or the enforcement of codes that enjoyed no immediate popular support, and every state official knew this.

This condition, ironically, regularly created a real need for citizen action in defense of life or property. This again was an old American custom, the committees of vigilance, or vigilantes. The vigilantes normally only arose when the regularly constituted authorities refused, or failed, to achieve relief. When conditions became intolerable in certain areas, the citizenry did not want reasons, but results. However much vigilante action offended the concept of rule of law, it was more often than not effective. In 1852, after road deliveries and stock theft reached alarming proportions around San Antonio, the citizens hanged all suspected persons, some twelve or fifteen in all. Unquestionably some merely suspicious, not guilty parties, died, but crime in the vicinity temporarily ceased.

The majority of frontier communities organized vigilance committees at some point. A common practice was to give fair warning, usually through posted notices. If crime continued, the vigilantes rode. A high proportion of criminals, real or suspected, disappeared. Vigilantes were particularly active in Hill County, and further west. On one occasion, vigilantes shot one man in his jail cell. The fact that the court dockets were clogged, the jury system was venal—men biased in favor of the defense, or even relatives, were allowed by defense attorneys to serve—and sheriffs were somewhat inclined to live and let live where an arrest might start gunplay or a feud, all gave lynch law powerful impetus. The Texas frontier ethos, guileless and direct, demanded justice, not something the lawyers referred to as "justice under the law."

As often as not, justice was private and vengeance was personal.

The aftermath of the War Between the States created immense problems. Many of the thousands of deserters from the army in the last months of the war entered a twilight life of lawlessness and crime. Others were pushed over the line by the excesses of the occupation and carpetbagger administration. The line between a genuine criminal type, such as John Wesley Hardin or Sam Bass, an iron-fisted rancher building up his range by might and main or a rebellious frontiersman who hated Yankees, Negro police, banks, railroads, and all their works, was very thin. Some men went over the line of the law and made it back successfully. Some did not. The immense distances and open spaces along the frontier, and the lack of statewide, cohesive law enforcement, made criminality possible and profitable. In 1876, Adjutant General Steele compiled a roster of 3,000 known fugitives on the fringes of Texas. In a message of 1879, Governor Oran Roberts, the "Old Alcalde," told the legislature bluntly that the "amount and character" of crime in Texas was "entirely unprecedented" in the United States.

One newspaper estimated that 100,000 horses were stolen by white thieves between 1875 and 1878. Almost 1,000 men were engaged in running horses, but hardly more than one in ten was brought to justice. Private organizations such as the Northwest Texas Stock Association (later, the Texas and Southwestern Cattle Raisers' Association) discussed the problem continually, hired detectives, and tried joint action. They met two immense problems: men of some wealth or influence were often engaged in or behind the organized rustling, and they had insuperable difficulties getting convictions when they caught some rustler in the act. Juries had the habit of ignoring evidence, of being venal or being stacked by the defense, or, in case the accused had a family, was a Confederate veteran, or promised to go straight, of letting him go.

In northwest, west, and central Texas, the problem was internal, generated by the disorder in Anglo society itself after 1864. In the far south, along the Rio Grande, it took an ethnic cast. The protracted warfare with Mexico was still being carried on. Raiders regularly crossed the Rio Bravo; by the 1870's the lower valley's old nemesis, Cheno Cortinas, directed a huge rustling and cattle smuggling ring out of Mexico. Cortinas was a Mexican patriot and politico, but he shipped tons of Texas beef to Cuba and other points.

Meanwhile, something was being done to end the chaos. When the state government again came under Texan control after a lapse of nine years in 1874, the legislature moved quickly. It reconstituted the Texas Rangers, an act which Reconstruction and Carpetbagger policy had always opposed. Two separate and distinct paramilitary forces were created. The first, the Ranger Special Force, was designed to operate along the Rio Grande and bring Mexican depredations to a halt on that frontier. The second, called the Frontier Battalion, was to become the most famous constabulary in American history. The Frontier Battalion had two missions: a primary one to protect the Indian frontier in the west, and a secondary mission to clean up the state behind the frontier line.

Two disparate but entirely effective officers were put in charge of each command. Each, in his own way, was to blaze a legendary trail in Texas history, and leave a marked impression on the thinking of the state.

The old triangle in which the cattle kingdom was born fell into sheer chaos in the aftermath of the Civil War. Its upper fringes were scarred by intramural wars and feuds among Texas ranchers arising out of the disorder of the Carpetbagger years. More serious, large-scale cattle rustling and raiding was initiated from across the Rio Grande. Kickapoos, Mescaleros, Lipans, and other small bands of Indians took to riding across the river between Piedras Negras, opposite Eagle Pass, and Laredo. Further south, between Laredo and Brownsville, the lower valley's implacable enemy, Cheno Cortinas, organized and sponsored *vaquero* raids. There was a definite alliance, at least for the disposal of booty, between Indians and Mexican officials or powerful *rancheros*. The basic cause of these attacks was not so much the underlying hostility between American and Mexican as the eternal disorder in Mexico.

After heavy fighting in the north, between Republicans, French, Belgians, Austrians, and Imperialists, United States pressure—there were 52,000 Federal troops on the Mexican border in 1865—caused the French to withdraw from Mexico. Maximilian's empire soon collapsed in defeat and ruin. Despite international protests, Maximilian and his faithful general, Tomás Mejía, were condemned and shot to death at Querétaro in 1867. But this did not bring peace to Mexico. Two generations of internal disorder had fostered anarchy.

The government of Mexico, whether federalist-liberal or centralist-conservative, was not deliberately hostile to the United States. In fact, there was a considerable amount of goodwill engendered by American diplomacy against the French. The problem was that the regimes in the City of Mexico had no real control over the distant marches. There was no infrastructure of citizenry in Mexico. There was a governmental clique, always holding power by some resort to arms, and under this a group of varyingly powerful great landholders, *hacendados* and *rancheros,* who stood between the official government and the mass of common people. These *hacendados* in reality were the local governments, whether they held the titles of state governors, or merely generals; they commanded their own local armies, usually raised upon their own lands. These local warlords engaged in local power struggles; they were uncontrollable from the capital in the 1860's and 1870's; and in the north, few of them naturally had any love for Texas.

They permitted raiding, if they did not actually instigate it. Cortinas, who had become a powerful figure below the river, actually was the chief contractor supplying large amounts of beef to the Cuban market. This beef was all stolen from the American side. Significantly, on one occasion Cortinas entered a border town and hanged the *alcalde* and another man for interfering with the crossing of stolen cattle. This rustling was not a small business. The King Ranch alone lost thousands of head during this period.

General J. J. Reynolds, who commanded the U.S. Army in Texas in 1871, made the following report, in part:

> The gradual but heavy loss of property is very discouraging to the people; they are becoming restless, not to say desperate, and seeing the apparent determination of Mexican officials to retain the Kickapoo Indians in Mexico, as a cloak for the evil deeds of the Mexican people, they talk now quite freely of organizing themselves into armed bands and crossing into Mexico to recover their stolen property.
>
> . . . The ranchmen live from ten to thirty miles apart, and incursions from the south side of the Rio Grande . . . cannot be prevented by a reasonable force in Texas, unaided by any force, civil or military, from the Mexican side.
>
> It is believed that these depredations can be effectually and permanently stopped by pursuing marauding bands into Mexico with troops accompanied by owners of the stock and records of the brands.

In July, 1871, the *Daily State Journal* at Austin reported:

. . . The stock west of the Nueces is being driven over the Rio Grande by every available pass. At one crossing in Hidalgo County five thousand head of beeves have been driven since last June . . . for the merchants and traders in Mexico, who receive the stolen property and are the allies and sleeping partners of the thieves.

It is also charged that General Cortina[s], commanding the Mexican forces on the Rio Grande, protects and shelters this organized robbery, so that no redress can be obtained from Mexican law. Unless something . . . is done . . . the stock interest between the Nueces and the Rio Grande will be ruined. The thieves ride in companies, well mounted and strongly armed. They defy the resistance of the scattered ranchmen, and in broad daylight harry the country . . .

A federal commission made essentially the same report in 1873. It called strongly for "protection due citizens and residents whose members have been depleted by the arrow of the Indian and the knife and pistol of the Mexican assassin."

The raids were bloody and brutal. In Encinal County two ranches were besieged by bands of forty raiders, and Live Oak County was harassed; these areas were more than a hundred miles from the river. There were literally dozens of small depredations and individual killings. At Howard's Well, a particularly hideous event occurred in April 1872: twenty Mexican bandits, accompanied by some Indians, captured a group of American teamsters and tortured them to death by fire. In this border warfare, there was very little to distinguish between Indian and Mexican cruelty. The principal difference was that the Mexicans came during the dark of the moon.

The Texans responded to robbery and cruelty with characteristic brutality. Unfortunately, this fell primarily upon the ethnic Mexicans of south Texas; the white population was as little able to distinguish between a peaceable Mexican resident and a raider as it was between Cherokeees and Comanches. The "minute" companies around Corpus Christi staged counterraids, not across the border, but against suspected ethnic Mexican allies of the bandits. On one of these excursions, eleven men were executed. The Mexican population seethed with unrest, but this was even less heard in the United States than the protests of the ranchers.

The government did bring pressure on Mexico to remove the Kickapoo Indians, which both governments, by a sort of diplomatic fiction, decided were the main cause of the depredations. This did not relieve the lower valley. As one Texas editor, reflecting the viewpoint of all Anglo-Texans, wrote: "The State Department made a pretense of *protesting* and *protesting* and PROTESTING." The disgust for such protests, which received polite replies but accomplished little, was choleric and profound. But Washington believed the only solution had to be political, not military; Reynolds' and other officers' recommendations were not followed.

The military itself was powerless to defend the border. Two hundred and sixty miles of almost unsettled ranch country extended along the river from Eagle Pass to Brownsville. On dark nights raiders could ford the river in hundreds of places. The U.S. garrisons were composed of Negro infantry, whose radius of operations against mounted bandits was pitifully small. Robert E. Lee had written that 20,000 soldiers were required to police this frontier; the Congress had no intention of stationing such a number or even the requisite but much more expensive cavalry.

For logical reasons, but reasons no Texan accepted, the raiding and bloodshed went on, keeping blood feuds and mutual hatred alive on both banks.

In the spring of 1874, Captain Leander H. McNelly of the newly reconstituted Rangers had been diverted to DeWitt County, south of Gonzales, by an outbreak of the smoldering Sutton-Taylor feud. This, like all the county-wide feuds that erupted during these years, was beyond the ability of local peace officers to control. Sheriffs were intimidated, juries suborned, and witnesses, more often than not, murdered outright. If parties were arrested, jail breaks were common. Terror ruled, and a continual, guerrilla warfare ensued, drawing in more and more men on either side. Bands of armed men congregated, who in some cases degenerated into rebellious mobs. Court writs were powerless, because they could rarely be served; local officials had to move warily in counties almost evenly divided between two armed camps. McNelly did not accomplish much toward ending the Sutton-Taylor affair; only time could end blood-feud hatreds, but he damped it. Armed Rangers could serve writs and guard prisoners and make arrests; they created a climate in which the law could gradually reassume its place.

But the raiding situation further south was coming to a boil. In April, 1875, Adjutant General Steele received the following wire from John Mc-Clure, the Nueces County sheriff: "Is Capt. McNelly coming. We are in trouble. Five ranches burned by disguised men near La Parra last week. Answer."

Steele's answer was to send McNelly, with authority to form a Special Company of forty men, to the border region. Ranger captains, armed with the state's commission, recruited their own men, and like Ford, McNelly enlisted men on whom he could rely. They were young, horse-hardened youth; the youngest, Berry Smith, had had no experience; he was barely sixteen. Smith enlisted because his father was in the troop.

McNelly was a great captain. He was the epitome of the Texan in action, and he set a record of courage, cunning, and audacity that was never to be surpassed. McNelly himself was young, just thirty-one. He had been a partisan soldier for the Confederacy as a teenager in the Civil War, later served in Davis' State Police. Nothing was more revealing of his ability, honesty, and his reputation than the fact that he went from the State Police to the Rangers with equivalent rank. In Davis' service he had been blunt, outspoken, incorruptible, and had been seriously wounded in battle with outlaws.

He was a "tallish man of quiet manner, and with the soft voice of a timid Methodist minister," Webb wrote. There was very little braggadocio when men still went armed on the Texas frontier. McNelly ruled by example and force of personality; he was never a formal disciplinarian, but as Callicott, one of his privates said, there was no man in the Special Force that would not have stepped between the captain and death. McNelly was superbly equipped for his time and place. He left a legend that other leaders could never quite live up to.

McNelly rode into the triangle in May, 1875. He found a veritable state of war. Iron-handed, he ordered both groups of armed Mexicans and Texans who were coalescing to disband, and very probably averted a civil war. McNelly was not fooled as to the true situation; he wrote the Adjutant General: "The acts committed by Americans are horrible to relate; many ranches have been plundered and burned, and the people murdered or driven away." These orders were instantly obeyed. But McNelly also knew the source from whence trouble flowed. He rode on to the Rio Grande at Hidalgo, then to Brownsville.

Here he found much alarm in the countryside, and Potter, the commandant at Fort Brown, with only 250 Negro soldiers, admitted he could not control. McNelly reported this situation, and added: "I think you will hear from us soon."

McNelly believed in intelligence, and like most capable Rangers, he formed his own network. He learned that a ship stood three miles off Bagdad, awaiting beef for Cuba, and that a number of Cortinas' cronies were operating on the Texas side. He planned to ambush a raiding party, and he went about it coolly and efficiently. Everything that now happened did not enter his report, clear and concise as it was.

McNelly's methods can only be judged in the anarchy and terror of his times. He was not a law-man, but a guerrilla soldier, in a land where there the established formal law was a fiction. He had been sent to stop the raids, and his verbal orders were quite clear: to deal with cattle thieves as the Frontier Battalion dealt with Indians. He was empowered to kill any rustler caught north of the river, and to take no prisoners. He understood partisan warfare, and the Rangers were considered a military force, not policemen.

One of McNelly's Rangers was a Texas-Mexican cowman named Jesús Sandoval. The Anglo Rangers called this man "Casuse." Sandoval, along with an American, had some ten years before caught four Mexican bandits and hung them all to one tree, and thus began a blood feud with the Mexicans south of the Bravo. He could not live in his own house for fears of *la venganza*. He knew the country, and almost every inhabitant in it, and McNelly gladly enlisted him when he applied. Sandoval went on the rolls at $40 a month, the same as the Anglos, and he was issued a Colt .45 and a needle gun, or one of the new centerfire Springfield rifles with which the Rangers were armed. Sandoval was to prove invaluable.

On June 5, 1875, McNelly heard news that a party of cow thieves had crossed the river below Brownsville to round up cattle out on the Palo Alto. He took 22 volunteers from his camp and rode out on patrol. One of the volunteers was young Berry Smith. Smith's father went to McNelly and asked that some other man go in young Berry's place, since he was an only child, and if anything happened to him his mother "would die of grief." The Captain offered to leave the sixteen-year-old behind, but Berry protested. He had been "out for some time and hadn't had a fight yet." McNelly merely said that was the way he liked to hear a fellow talk, and let him ride.

McNelly's plan of operations was simple. He put out pickets or outriders, called "spies," with orders to bring in any suspicious-looking Mexican they came across. Whenever such a person was brought in, he was interviewed by old "Casuse."

Sandoval, who communicated through Tom Sullivan, a Brownsville boy, quickly identified the prisoners as citizens or "bandit spies." It was the practice of the bandit gangs to trail all American patrols, Ranger or military, with such scouts or spies, and up until this time bandit intelligence had been far superior.

One of McNelly's men later described the action when a Mexican citizen or otherwise unidentifiable Mexican was caught:

> . . . If the Mexican proved to be a citizen [of the U.S.] we let him go at once; and if he proved to be a bandit spy one of us would take charge of him and march along until we saw a suitable tree. The Captain would take Tom, the bandit, and four or five of the boys to the tree. Old Casuse would put the rope over the bandit's neck, throw it over a limb, pull him up and let him down on the ground until he would consent to tell all he knew. As far as we knew this treatment always brought out the truth.
>
> After the Captain had all the information he wanted he would let Casuse have charge of the spy. Casuse would make a regular hangman's knot and place the hangman's loop over the bandit's head, throw the end of the rope over the limb, make the bandit get on Casuse's old paint horse, and stand up in the saddle. Casuse would then make the loose end of the rope fast, get behind his horse, hit him a hard lick and the horse would jump from under the spy . . . Captain McNelly didn't like this kind of killing, but Casuse did. He said if we turned a spy loose he would spread the news among the bandits and we would never catch them. We caught several spies on that scout before we overhauled the bandits with the cattle, and Casuse dealt with them alike, showing no partiality—he always made them a present of six feet of rope.

McNelly hated hangings; "he could stand death better in any other form." But McNelly, even better than Jesús Sandoval, knew what he was doing. He found out where the bandits were, and what they were planning to do. A party of some dozen bandits were moving several hundred stolen cattle across the Palo Alto prairie near Loma Alta, a rise not far from Brownsville on the Point Isabel trail.

McNelly formed his men in line, then rode out in front and addressed them:

> "Boys, . . . we are likely to overhaul them tonight, and when we do I will order you all in line of battle, and when I order you to charge them I want you to charge them in line. Do not get ahead of each other and get mixed up with the bandits for if you do you are apt to kill one another. . . . Don't pay any attention to the cattle. The spy tells me there are seventeen Mexicans and one white man and that they are Cortinas' picked men, and Cortinas says they can cope with any Rangers or regulars. If we can overhaul them in open country we will teach them a lesson they will never forget. If they should stampede, pick you out the one that is nearest to you and keep him in front of you and keep after him. Get as close to him as you can before you shoot. It makes no difference in what direction he goes, stay with him to a finish. That is all I have to say. Ready! Form in twos! Forward, march!

McNelly did overhaul the bandits, driving a large herd, in open country after sunup. The cattle rustlers made an enormous mistake; they mistook the Rangers for U.S. soldiers and believed they could stand them off. Each one soon had a terrible nemesis riding on his tail. The fight broke into individual actions and swirled over six miles, through a mucky arm of the Laguna Madre, Spanish dagger clumps, and brush. The fleeing Mexicans were no match for the Texans' six-shooters; they left a scattered trail of bodies behind.

The last of the fight ended in the brush, where some Mexicans took cover. McNelly followed one man, who had emptied his gun, into a thicket. The Captain had a single ball left in his pistol. He stood outside the thicket and called out for help, saying his six-shooter was empty. The Mexican immediately charged with his knife, grinning; McNelly coolly placed his last round into the bandit's teeth.

This was young Berry Smith's first fight, and he was never to learn how. He dashed into the brush after a bandit, and was shot down and killed. He was the only Texan lost, against twelve Mexicans. The Rangers recovered twelve horses, guns, and gear, plus 216 head of cattle, many of which came from Santa Gertrudis, the King ranch. Thirty-three other brands were later identified, and the stock returned.

McNelly rode back to Brownsville and told Sheriff Brown that he was placed in charge of the bandits' bodies. The resident U.S. Marshal, O'Schaughnessy, went out with a detachment of soldiers and gathered up the corpses. Meanwhile, McNelly saw to it that his dead Ranger was given a military funeral. He allowed none of them to "touch a drop of anything" until afterward, and had one wear a captured sombrero to the funeral. McNelly said it would be good advertising, and a "fair warning to all bandits not to cross to the Texas side."

The Army trundled in the bandit bodies and dumped them in a single pile in the public square. McNelly passed the word for all to come and see how the Rangers handled cow thieves. This produced enormous indignation among the people of Matamoros, and much muttering among the canaille, as McNelly called it, in Brownsville. There were threats that Cortinas would gather his bravos and cross the border, killing ten Americans for every Mexican. The Rangers calmly agreed to "naturalize" all of them, if they showed up. None came.

Cattle theft in the Brownsville area stopped. A few more raids were attempted, but McNelly now had his own informants and spies. The mere word that the *Rinches* were riding out caused at least two parties to abandon their loot far north of the river and flee for Mexico for their lives.

The testimony of General E. O. C. Ord of the U.S. Army, in a report of this affair is perhaps significant: "The officer of the State troops in command had learned the whereabouts of this raiding party by means which I could not legally resort to, but which were the only means of getting at the actual facts. . . . No other official records refer to the torture or execution of prisoners. But whatever was thought of McNelly's methods on the Rio Grande, they were effective.

The period to October, 1875, passed quietly. But Mexican rustling operations had moved westward, upriver, and McNelly moved to follow them. He recovered some cattle eighty miles up from Brownsville. Then, the country being quiet, he left the border on a furlough to his home in Washington County. McNelly was actually dying of consumption, or tuberculosis, at this time, though no one knew it.

The theft of some 200 cattle from Cameron county soon brought him back. McNelly's actual thinking and planning in his next service will never be fully known, but the pattern of his actions was clear. McNelly did not believe all raiding could be stopped by passive measures, or counteraction, above the Rio Grande. Apparently, he actually planned to foment a war with Mexico, or at least that part of Mexico lying along the river. The United States had sent a gunboat to the border river, the *Rio Bravo* under Commander Kells, an old comrade of the filibuster, Walker. Kells apparently had latitude, and he and McNelly talked the same language. But Kells was in no position to do much, and the Army, under Ord and Colonel Potter, was wary of McNelly and all "State troops." However, reports of imminent action badly frightened officials on the Mexican side. They sent promises that the raiding would be stopped.

McNelly discounted this, because cattle now brought $18 per head on the Cuban market, a great sum of money for impoverished Mexico. He talked with Major A. J. Alexander, the senior cavalry officer along the border, and apparently got some kind of assurance that Alexander "would follow raiders anywhere" McNelly himself went. McNelly knew that an order had been placed for 18,000 head in Monterrey, and that the temptation to fill part of this order in Texas would be almost irresistible for

Cortinas. He openly told his men that with a little luck he would get some of the next band of thieves on the *other side* of the river.

When Mexican bandits did cross in November and pushed about 250 head south at Las Cuevas—known as a notorious headquarters point for stolen cattle—McNelly wired the Adjutant General of Texas he planned to go after them. He also said the Army refused to cross the border without further orders, but he would cross "tonight" if he could get any support.

He was attempting to get state officials to pressure Washington to release the Army.

Then, on November 18, he telegraphed Austin that he "commenced crossing at one o'clock tonight—have thirty men. Will try to recover our cattle. The U.S. troops promise to cover my return. . . ."

Las Cuevas lay about ten miles below Rio Grande City on the Mexican side, and about three miles back from the river. Between it and the Rio Grande was another ranch, called Las Cucharas, or "Cuchattus" in American accounts. Rancho Las Cuevas was presided over by General Juan Flores, who sold an immense number of cattle south and on the coast; there is no question whatever that thousands upon thousands of Texas beeves passed up the sandy banks onto Flore's pastures. Observers, both neutral and biased, left accounts of the brands seen on Las Cuevas cattle, most of which were registered Texas marks. McNelly intended to strike to the heart of the problem; his orders were to clean up the Rio Grande Valley; and if he had to start a war in the process, so be it. McNelly—and virtually everyone in Texas—felt he was in the right, and the Ranger code was that a good man who knew he was in the right could not be stopped if he "kept coming."

Interesting events led up to this crossing of Texas troops into Mexico. Shortly before, it became known to the Army command that Mexican rustlers were operating on the Texas side across from Las Cuevas. There were U.S. forces at Rio Grande City, at Edinburg to the north, and at Brownsville, many miles to the southeast. The detachment of 8th Cavalry at Edinburg was ordered into the field.

Colonel Potter at Brownsville ordered Captain Randlett, D Company, 8th Cavalry, to support the Rangers, to hit the cow thieves hard, and "if you come up with them while they cross the river, follow them into Mexico."

Randlett did catch up with some Mexicans crossing Texas cattle, fired on them and killed two, but then seems to have had a failure of nerve. He failed to cross in darkness, waiting until morning. With dawn, a superior officer, Major Clendenin from Edinburg, came up to him, approved his report, but countermanded the instructions to enter Mexico. Clendenin said this would be a warlike invasion of a peaceful country. Clendenin's real reason, apparently, was that he had opened negotiations with the *alcalde* at Las Cuevas and thought a crossing would show bad faith. Clendenin now received orders from Colonel Potter to do nothing until Major Alexander, from Ringgold Barracks, brought up more troops. The Army considered any move into Mexico as a major operation, requiring maximum force, though apparently all the officers involved did want to recover the stolen cattle.

In this situation McNelly, with thirty Rangers behind him, rode into the Army camp. He found the Army in paralysis, with two Gatling guns positioned to cover a crossing, but doing nothing. McNelly's troop covered sixty miles in something under five hours, and when they arrived next to the 100-odd regulars, McNelly sent one man to fetch a few muttons, while he tried to talk "the U.S. Captain" into doing something. The "U.S. Captain" refused to act, and McNelly said to his men, "We are going over if we never come back."

McNelly was about as foolhardy as a fox. His plan was simple: he would launch a foray into Mexico, seize a position in Las Cuevas, and force the Army to come to his assistance. McNelly did not believe the Army could stand by and let his men be slaughtered by the approximately 3,000 *vaqueros* and Mexican troops in the area. There is no question that Major Clendenin, although he was under orders not to cross until Alexander came down from Ringgold Barracks, promised McNelly this support. As his report to the Adjutant General read, he said, ". . . If you are determined to cross, we will cover your return. . . ."

McNelly's own report makes it clear he believed he had a firm promise of assistance in case he got cut off in Mexico, which, though he did not say this to the officers, he intended to let happen.

McNelly mustered his thirty at midnight. "Boys, you have followed me as far as I can ask you to go unless you are willing to go farther. Some of us may get back . . . but if any of you do not want to go over with me, step aside. . . . You understand there is to be no surrender—we ask no quarter nor give any. If you don't want to go, step aside."

All thirty shouted to go.

"All right, that's the way to talk," McNelly said mildly. "We will learn them a Texas lesson that they have forgotten since the Mexican War. Get ready." Then he gave his battle instruction, clear, complete, and simple, as McNelly's battle orders always were. On the Mexican side, when they arrived at Las Cuevas, designated men had designated jobs. He ended, "Kill all you see except old men, women, and children. These are my orders and I want them obeyed to the letter."

Everything went perfectly—except the Rangers descended on Las Cucharas by mistake. They struck a surprised group of Mexicans chopping wood for breakfast fires at dawn, and shot down everyone in sight. "We killed all we saw in the ranch," one of McNelly's people said later. But then, McNelly learned his mistake; he had hit an unimportant *rancho,* the real target was half a mile away.

"Well, you have given my surprise away," he said. "Take me to Las Cuevas as fast as you can," he told a Mexican guide. But at Las Cuevas,

250 Mexican soldiers had already assembled—the private, though official, army of Juan Flores. To attack this force, ensconced behind buildings, was suicide. Balked, McNelly took his Rangers back to the river.

But he did not cross back to the American side. L. H. McNelly was a determined man. He threw out pickets and began to fortify a position from which the Rangers could fight with rifles.

This caused the Mexicans, pursuing from Las Cuevas, to make a grievous error. Flores led some twenty-five horsemen at the gallop to the river, thinking that McNelly's men were swimming across, and hoping to catch them in midstream. The Rangers opened fire from the thickets, then advanced in line, shooting steadily. The Mexican force retreated in confusion, but not before General Flores took two Springfield balls. Marching in perfect battle order, four feet apart, McNelly led his men past Flores' body, picking up a gold-and-silver-plated Smith and Wesson revolver as he passed. Sandoval, with some awe, identified the body.

While this happened, Captain Randlett, figuring the McNellys were being massacred, plunged forty troopers over the river. McNelly tried to get him to resume the attack toward Las Cuevas, but Randlett refused. Soldiers and Rangers together took up a desultory battle with sniping Mexicans, and so the day passed.

Large bodies of Mexican soldiery were now arriving, with a flag and communication from the Chief Justice of Tamaulipas. A parley was arranged, but the request to vacate Mexican soil was so "mildly put" that neither McNelly nor Randlett saw fit to accept. Then, Major Alexander at last arrived from Ringgold. He shouted across to Randlett to "get out of Mexico at once."

Now, in negotiations with the Mexican authorities, the "officer commanding the forces invading Mexico," as communications to McNelly were addressed, displayed an audacity and coolness almost beyond belief. When asked to depart, McNelly stated he would go back only with the stolen cattle and the thieves. This prompted a request for a truce through the night, which McNelly refused unless his demands were granted. He then stated he would give an hour's notice before attacking, which was gratefully accepted.

It must be understood that the Mexican leaders were badly rattled. They had seen U.S. soldiers in regular blue fighting alongside the Rangers; the guidons and colors of the cavalry were clearly visible on the American side. McNelly had only a handful of men, but no Mexican could be sure that the U.S. Army was not poised for a major invasion, with the Rangers assuming their old chores as advance guards and scouts. There were veterans of the Mexican War along the river; and if in national mythology the word Ranger automatically conveyed the meaning hero to Americans, it symbolized monster to the south.

At 6 P.M. on November 19, 1875, the thirty Rangers were alone on the bank, calmly eating a cold supper, while the Mexicans took advantage of their promise not to attack. McNelly was by now disgusted. "Boys, it's all off. The U.S. Captain [a term McNelly used for all Army officers, regardless of grade] won't let me have any of his men and I know of no other Rangers in Texas except Major Jones' Rangers on the northern Indian frontier and they are too far away to get here. But we'll stay for awhile."

He had his men dig in thoroughly during the night and praised their work as equal to the Confederate army. He put pickets out in the bloodweeds, and counseled each man completely. It must be recorded that most of the Rangers were far from sanguine, as most later admitted, but the Captain was so cool and confident that the whole company would have followed him to hell if he had asked for it.

He professed to be more afraid of the Gatling guns that the cavalry might turn loose than of the Mexicans.

The next morning he sent the Adjutant General of Texas a telegram by runner. He stated the general situation, repeating the fact that the U.S. troops would not help, then asked: "What shall I do?" The wire was sent collect, datelined *Mexico,* and this document still rings with audacity and the roar of admiring amusement it brought from Texas can not now be fully understood.

But other wires were clicking the keys, from the border to Washington. Fort Brown queried San Antonio, and General Ord there requested enlightenment from the Potomac. He got it quickly: to carry on as if only cattle stealing were going on, and to inform the Mexicans that U.S. troops had orders not to cross the border.

With this instruction, Colonel Potter at Fort Brown sent a message to Alexander, "Commdg in the front," to advise McNelly to return, and to inform him that he was strictly ordered if McNelly were attacked by Mexican forces on Mexican soil not to render him assistance. The message ended, "Let me know whether McNelly acts upon your advice and returns." Potter was beginning to wonder.

Meanwhile, the U.S. Consul at Matamoros had been alerted. This man sent a representative to McNelly, advising him to surrender to "Mexican Federal Authorities," and that an American agent would stay with him for his protection. McNelly merely said, "The American consul at Matamoros arranged for our surrender . . . but I couldn't see it." The evidence indicates that the Consul was more terrified during these hours than the Captain.

Now, advised by the Army to retreat, and ordered by the State Department to surrender, McNelly took the action that would make him live forever in Texan, if not in all American, history.

He advised the Mexicans in front of him, who numbered at the least 400, as follows:

> So about 4 oclk (20) I notified them, that unless they accepted my proposition to deliver such of the cattle and thieves as they had on hand,

and could catch, to me at Ranch Davis, without waiting for the tedious legal forms that always ended in our receiving magnificent promises, in lieu of our property, that I would at once make an advance.

The Mexicans capitulated. They agreed to all McNelly's terms. With that promise, McNelly peacefully withdrew to Texas. Then, although the cattle had been promised, the Mexican officialdom resorted to further promises and delays.

Some cattle, not all the last-stolen herd but about half of it, were rounded up and driven to the river opposite Rio Grande City. Here, Mexican officials refused to see McNelly, and sent messages that they were too busy to move the cattle immediately to the American side. There was not only a real reluctance to return the property, but a determination to maintain Mexican dignity in the process, but this took forms that Texans found infuriating. McNelly took ten volunteers and went armed over to the Mexican shore.

A Mexican official, backed by twenty-five heavily armed men, informed McNelly that the cattle could not be shipped across without inspection. McNelly, through Tom Sullivan, told the officer that the cattle had been stolen from Texas without inspection by him, and they could damn well be returned without it. The official was insulted, but McNelly was finished with Byzantine politics, parleys, and devious duplicity. He ordered his ten men to form a line and ready their rifles. What happened next was told by one of the ten: "The Captain then told Tom to tell the son of a bitch that if he didn't deliver the cattle across the river in less than five minutes we would kill all of them, and he would have done it, too, for he had his red feather raised. If ever you saw cattle put across the river in a hurry those Mexicans did it."

So ended another confrontation of Teutonic directness and Latin subtlety, leaving a sour taste on each side. But McNelly left a stark and lasting memory on the border, for he got back the only stolen cattle ever returned to the Texas side.

The McNelly Rangers put a halt to wholesale stealing in the valley. But Washington's view that the solution was political rather than military proved true. However, Texans had more to do with solving it than the government of the United States.

The real problem was the governmental chaos in Mexico, that allowed men like Cortinas to hide behind border antipathies, and justify robbery with Mexican indignation toward Texans. Benito Juárez held a great reputation in the United States, but he was a disastrous President of Mexico. He was never able to rule the nation, and he died of apoplexy in 1872. His secretary, Lerdo de Tejada, took his place, during months of increasing disaffection. One of the greatest Mexican heroes of the French and Imperialist wars a Oaxacan named Porfirio Díaz took refuge in Brownsville. Díaz, who had defeated the French in 1862 and who had commanded all

Mexican armies in title later, enjoyed enormous support among the professional military.

Díaz pragmatically understood that Mexico needed good relations with its colossal neighbor; Mexico was too far from God and too close to the United States, as he said. His views were known to the prominent men in southern Texas. In his brief exile, the leading landowners, merchants, and political chiefs of the Rio Grande region of Texas sanctioned, abetted, and even financed his planned seizure of power in Mexico. This group included both Anglo and Mexican-Americans. Their names are not important; Díaz rewarded some of them well in later years.

In April, 1876, Porfirio Díaz crossed over to Matamoros; the garrison had already been subverted by prominent Mexicans operating out of Brownsville. Some 1,300 Guardia Nacional and regular soldiers declared for Don Porfirio, as he was called, and Lerdo de Tejada fled. Díaz entered Mexico in triumph.

Whatever the regime of Porfirio Díaz meant for Mexico, its effect on Texas was entirely good. Díaz, like Santa Anna, understood the church and landed interests were too powerful still to be abolished by Liberal ideology; like Santa Anna, he turned from liberalism to practical alliances. Unlike Santa Anna, this *caudillo* knew the balance of power in North America was irrevocably turned in the United States' favor. He began a centralization and consolidation of Mexico, a destruction of the still wild Indians, and the imposition of his power in all parts of the country. These measures, for the first time, brought an end to raiding by Indians and Mexican bandits north of the Rio Grande, and brought about a situation in which Mexican soldiers and American forces actually took the field together on several occasions, as allies. Díaz' handling of Juan Cortinas was significant. Although Cortinas declared for the new President, Díaz arrested him and ordered him shot. Strangely enough, his life was spared through the intervention of Rip Ford; but Díaz placed Cortinas, who was now a wealthy man, in virtual house arrest in the City of Mexico. Here, he could do no harm, either to Díaz or Texas, and he died in comfort in 1892.

Díaz was to rule Mexico until 1911. The dominant view in Texas, then and for many years later, was that this rule was a golden age. Frank C. Pierce, a historian of the lower Rio Grande Valley, summed up the Texan attitude accurately and honestly with these words:

> . . . He ruled Mexico with great wisdom, foresight, and patriotism. At the beginning of his administration he caused to be executed all those who in any manner attempted to foment an uprising, and even went to the extent of imprisoning those who criticized his administration. But, experience had taught that there was but one way to rule a people of whom 80% were ignorant, uneducated barbarians, and that was WITH THE IRON HAND. Under him the country soon took a place among the nations of the world. Every branch of industry was stimulated. The army was brought up to a high standard of patriotism so that when, during his

old age when his enemies sought to depose him the entire army stood loyal to him preferring death to dishonor. He granted concessions to foreign capital to build up railroads and kindred institutions of progress, just as the State of Texas had done and was doing at the very time. The indebtedness of the Nation was reduced to a minimum. . . . In fact, during the 31 years in which Don Porfirio administered the affairs of the Republic, every change which took place was destined to the uplifting of his people.

This statement should be read as revealing of dominant Texan attitudes, not as a description of Mexico in the 19th century. It was widely shared across the world, and by the upper classes, in Mexico itself. The choice in Mexico was not between freedom and tyranny at the time, but between order and chaos.

There was one final footnote to the McNelly Las Cuevas war. General Juan Flores, the *mayordomo* of Las Cuevas, had been considered a great man in northern Mexico. He had much of the same standing as a Goodnight, a Kenedy, or a King had in Texas. Up from the banks of the river where he fell, the citizens of Las Cuevas, later known as San Miguel, erected an elaborate, fifteen-foot monument, surmounted with a cross.

Its inscription read:

To Citizen

JUAN FLORES SALINAS

Who Died

Fighting for his Country

The 19th of November

1875

McNelly's Rangers returned some of King's cattle to the ranch at Santa Gertrudis. They said they had shot a cow thief, one of the worst of the lot. The real tragedy of the border country in those years was that both the Rangers and the words of the monument were right.

The choice in west Texas in these years was not between law and order and what would later be called police brutality, but between armed anarchy and a climate in which due process could take place. The story of the Texan Frontier Battalion, as well as the Special Force, must be viewed in this light.

Major John B. Jones, whom Richard Coke appointed to command in northwest Texas, was the least known of the great captains. This was not because his results were not even more spectacular than McNelly's, but because Jones was a type that west Texas took less easily to its heart. He was essentially an east Texan, whose father established a horse ranch in Navarro County, southeast of Dallas. He was a superb horseman, and a member of the very-Southern gentry, rather small but handsome, and altogether elegant. He was described by one of the neighboring Groce family: "I can see him now, the perfection of neatness; dark, well-kept suit, white shirt, black bow tie, heavy black moustache and hair, smooth olive skin, piercing, twinkling, sparkling, penetrating black or dark brown eyes that seemed to see through your very soul, and seeing sympathized as he understood."

The Major was the subject of many a fictional characterization, and altogether one of the most dangerous men to criminals who ever lived. Coke appointed him to command six companies of Rangers in 1874 because the Governor knew him from the war. Jones had enlisted in Terry's Rangers as a private and emerged recommended for major. He was older than the run of Ranger; McNelly was dead at thirty-three. Webb paid him the superb compliment, by saying Hays, Ford, McCulloch, and McNelly were captains only, while Jones was a great general.

He was a men of perception and education, who could see the whole frontier for what it was, and understand his over-all mission as clearly as the evils of the day. He took the field with his companies, riding through the dust of west Texas, drinking scummy green water from stagnant holes, which he boiled for black coffee. He did not drink or smoke; he never raised his voice, and his favorite beverage was reputed to be buttermilk. It is recorded that a few men mocked him, but all of them eventually ended up in jail or dead. He was not popular even with his own people, because, unlike the rough-and-ready McNelly and Hays, he was a disciplinarian rather than a camp democrat.

Jones' first problem was to protect the frontier from the Kiowas and Comanches; Quanah Parker and other chiefs were still at large when he took the field. Jones did this job with expertise. He stationed his companies, each with seventy-five men, in strategic sites affording maximum range and protection. He made them stay constantly on patrol; unlike the army, none of his force was tied up in fiddling detail or on barracks chores. He intercepted the small war parties the army could not prevent from slipping through. In six months, Jones' command fought fifteen actions, killed fifteen Indians and wounded ten, and recovered considerable livestock. On June 12, 1874, Jones himself, with twenty-six men, met one hundred Comanches at Lost Valley, near the Young County line. Jones did not try to be a hero; he sent a runner to Fort Richardson for help. He also contented himself with protecting white lives, while Mackenzie played the hero in the Far West. This was the measure of the man, and it only comes through in the magnitude of his decisive results.

The northwest frontier was safe by 1875. West of San Antonio, however, the Apaches still marauded, and the Rangers, in conjunction with General B. H. Grierson, moved southwest into the land of greasewood, buttes, and sage. During 1876 and 1877, Apache raids did much damage through the Big Bend country; but Rangers, the Army, and the Mexican army from below the border joined forces to pursue the marauding bands. In October, 1880, the last Mescalero war chief, Victorio, was killed below the line by Mexican troops. The sun of the eastern Apaches, like that of their ancient Comanche enemies, had almost set.

The society of Texas had been frayed by a generation of border war, the vast bloodletting of the Civil War, the moral and social erosion of Reconstruction, and now, by the explosion of the cattle kingdom into the vacuums left by the Indians to the west. Jones' Battalion's position needs clarification. The frontier, for thirty years, stood along a clearly defined line from north to south; suddenly, in 1875, this frontier acquired immense breadth and depth. The compressed cattlemen burst toward the west. The nature of the cow frontier did not bring immediate settlement, or cohesion, or anything approaching the orderly advance of civilization behind the farm line.

Overnight, the Rangers' mission changed from Indian fighting to a task of policing this turbulent frontier-in-depth. It was an infinitely more difficult job, and also more delicate, because now the enemy was not so clearly defined. Coke instructed both Jones and McNelly to be careful handling citizens; Jones, over-all, had the greater success. In March, 1877, Jones forbade the search for and pursuit of Indians, and ordered his captains to drive toward the "suppression of lawlessness and crime." Thus the Ranger force turned inward; it positioned itself generally between the farm and cow frontiers. At the time Jones planned his moves, these regions were actually more lawless and chaotic because of the sum of the years than they had ever been before.

In six years, the Texas Rangers closed the wild frontier. They did not entirely end all aspects of the Old West; no heritage of violence so deeply implanted could be so quickly erased. The Rangers changed the social climate from anarchy, where every man looked to himself for protection and his six-gun for judge and jury, to one that was simply violent, but over which the laws of organized society could preside. In this new war, Jones himself was more the general than the hero many of his individual troops became. He damped the terrible Mason County war, and the bloody Horrell-Higgins feud at Lampasas by a combination of diplomacy and force. Jones' policy was to arrest the leaders—men no sheriff dared touch —then hammer out a truce. He, like McNelly at Cuero, could not make complete peace between Germans and Anglos at Mason, or between the divisive political factions in Lampasas County. He could put a lot of angry people in jail, and produce an atmosphere in which the courts could arrest murderers and get them to the gallows in due time. He could send Lieutenant Dolan to Kimble County, which was run by thieves, arrest forty-one men, and scare the rest away. He could, and did, use brilliant generalship in plotting the demise of bandit Sam Bass, Texas' first popular Yankee following the Civil War. Jones kept his own counsel, made deals, worked through informers and spies. He even had his own man in Sam Bass' gang when he ambushed the outlaw at Round Rock. He did what he had to do, kept accurate records, and kept the Governor informed.

Three salient characteristics marked the Ranger force. First, in the border wars it had developed an enormous *esprit,* a genuine mystique. Every young Ranger, usually poorly educated and functionally illiterate, knew the legends of McNelly and Jack Hays. Their numbers were so few that in most cases, they were always beset by odds almost equal to those faced by McNelly at Las Cuevas. One Ranger sometimes had to cow a cattle camp, or three Rangers an entire town. They lived among a rough society, in which moved thousands of actual killers and thieves. Some Rangers were certainly killers and thieves themselves—but before they took the oath. No force, probably, was ever so little scarred by scandal in its great years. But the Rangers, widely spread, ununiformed, poorly paid, and with small gratitude from the state—McNelly was simply let go when his health failed, with a complaint from the Adjutant General filed for eternity with his mounting medical bills—lived by audacity as much as gun skill and wits. Their mystique, and growing legend, won them through, in situations where men lacking either would have given up or died.

Second, the Rangers were ruthless. Killing was almost casual on this particular frontier; almost every grown man had seen blood shed. The Rangers gave due notice, fair warning to the criminal kind, then they struck. They could not, in retrospect, have acted effectively in any other way. They did not worry too much about prisoners in some cases—the nearest jail and court was often a hundred miles away. They did not ride the range seeking war, but if someone offered it, they gave it back until strong men quailed. They were not bullies, unless demanding order was bullying. A favorite cowboy sport was riding off the range and shooting up a west Texas town. Horses were pushed into saloons, lights shot out, mirrors smashed by bullets. If a Ranger was present, he sometimes shot these joyous spirits out of the saddle; there were some who felt that this punishment was a bit severe for the crime.

On one occasion recorded in west Texas history, a group of cowboys showed ingenuity in treeing a town. They hopped aboard an incoming passenger train and arrived shooting from its windows. They were liquored, happy, and shouting they were the toughest hombres in the West. Three Rangers in this town, Toyah, told them once to quit, then opened fire. Four "town treers" bit the dust, and one was dead. The Ranger had three maxims: never wear a gun unless you know how to use it; never draw it unless you intend to use it; never shoot except to kill.

They rarely called the play, but their orders were to finish it. As officers of the law, they never issued an order twice.

Third, the entire frontier ethos gave the Rangers a great contempt for deviousness, including the deviousness of the Anglo-American law. A bullet cut a straight line. Local politics, and the law itself, hampered Ranger work in cleaning up the country. When McNelly, on one of his last missions, courageously brought in King Fisher and a half-dozen of his men, who had terrorized the entire country from Castroville to Eagle Pass, the courts set them free. Fisher and his men were certifiably guilty of murder, but not convictable under the technicalities of the law. The Rangers had no patience with this; and a great impetus was given an old Mexican practice, the *ley de fuga*. Rangers records indicate a large number of men killed trying to escape, or resisting arrest.

Direct action had always gotten the Texan, except during the sobering lesson of the Civil War, what he wanted and felt was right. McNelly's action at Goliad, where certain prominent cowmen in their range wars had taken to hiring killing done by strangers, was illustrative of the Ranger and the whole frontier-Texan mind. Even if the hired, nonlocal killers were apprehended, the real instigator of the crime went free. McNelly wrote one leading citizen, who was known to hire gunmen, that the next time such an incident occurred he would come to town and shoot the leading citizen dead within two hours. McNelly's contemporary good citizens slapped their thighs with glee. This attitude, and not anachronistic views arising out of later times and different conditions, must be applied. The Rangers brought order in the years between 1874 and 1880, and law could not be far behind. In bringing it, the records show they killed some scores of men, arrested some hundreds of others, and, as important, drove thousands out of the state.

When the big range country turned into the land of big pastures, the Ranger work was largely done. Public sentiment, rather than Rangers, finally halted fence-cutting, though Rangers did serve in certain counties where there was an outbreak of war. Local law could also handle the sporadic cattleman-farmer wars. By 1880, the task of ending the frontier—if not all frontier conditions and a lingering of the frontier mind—was almost over. Charles Goodnight had been ranching in the Palo Duro for four years. One of Captain Arrington's men, writing from Blanco Canyon, said that the Panhandle range was already crowded, with more herds and people coming in. New men brought jostling and some battle, but the numbers of people themselves inevitably brought in discipline and law.

The bandit gangs and stage robbers that had thrived in west-central Texas west of the farm line were fast disappearing. Crime itself would never be ended, because crime was a part of civilization itself—but significantly, throughout much of Texas, men were beginning to put their old pistols away. Ironically, one of the last Apache depredations in far West Texas ended in the easy murder of a number of stage travelers because none of the men were armed.

This incident came in 1880, when General Grierson, General Buell, Baylor's company of Rangers, and General Joaquín Terrazas of the Mexican forces were following the last Apache war trail. It was a coordinated campaign, ranging from the Diablo Mountains to New Mexico, and deep into Sonora. The Apaches moved with the dark of the moon, but there were hundreds and thousands of Americans and Mexicans to watch their water holes. The American forces drove Victorio south of the Rio Grande, where Terrazas caught him and killed him with sixty of his warriors. The survivors of this band fled back to Texas. They numbered twelve warriors, four women, and four children. They were defiant to the last.

Early in January, 1881, these Indians killed two Americans in Quitman Canyon. Jones wired Baylor to take the bloody trail. The Rangers began a systematic, deadly manhunt; one party lost the Apache trail, another found it. Past Chili Peak to Rattlesnake Springs, and into the Sierra Diablos, well-mounted Rangers gave the band no rest. Their Pueblo scouts clung to the trail, and the fleeing Indians dared not sleep. Finally, high in the Rockies, they stopped.

At last, in the Diablos, or Devil Mountains, Rangers came down on the Apache camp. The Indians were afoot; they had eaten some of their horses, and the rest had been worn out. Baylor and Nevill surrounded the camp in the dark on the morning of January 29, crawling to one hundred yards through the Spanish dagger thickets, waiting for the sun to rise.

With the cold light, nineteen Rangers opened fire. Apaches, unlike Comanches, did not turn at bay and fight; these tried to run, but nothing could save them. When the shooting died away, four warriors, two squaws, and two children were dead; most of those who crawled away had bullets in them. One woman and two children were captured; the squaw had three wounds and one child, a baby, was shot through the foot. Lieutenant Nevill took this prisoner to Fort Davis, commenting that every time "it hears a gunshot . . . it begins to scream." Baylor made no apologies for this action, none was asked. As he stated, "The law under which the Frontier Battalion was organized don't require it."

There were two pools of water in the camp. One was so filled with blood the Rangers could not use it; they made their morning coffee from the other pool.

Captain Baylor's report to Major Jones concludes:

> We all took breakfast on the ground occupied by the Indians which all enjoyed as we had eaten nothing since dinner the day before. Some of the men found horsemeat pretty good whilst others found venison and roasted mescal good enough. We had an almost boundless view from our breakfast table; towards the north the grand old Cathedral Peak of the Guadalupe Mountains; further west the San Antonio Mountains, the Cornudas, Las Almas, Sierra Alta; at the Hueco Tanks, only twenty-four miles from our headquarters, the Eagle Mountains. The beauty of the scenery [was] only marred . . . by . . . the ghostly forms of the Indians lying around.

The last settler had been killed by Indians in Texas. In the chill rare air and stark shadows of the Rockies at this daybreak, Texas Rangers had shot down their last Indian. The vast Pecos drainage was secure; this same year the last free range disappeared, and rails had almost reached El Paso.

In 1881 Jones died, and the principal captains of the Frontier Battalion resigned. The Battalion lived on for many years, but it was a living anachronism.

The frontier was closed. Texans at last stood the masters on their chosen soil.

Part VI

THE AMERICANS: NEW DREAMS FOR OLD

33

THE STUBBORN SOIL

The fertile lands, delightful climate, and wonderful resources of Texas, all combine to attract within her borders the intelligent and enterprising of every State, and indeed of almost every land.   THE Vicksburg Times, 1870

Shall we gather at the river,
The beautiful, beautiful river;
Shall we gather at the river,
That flows by the throne of God.
                    TEXAS SETTLER HYMN

THE parameters of Texan life were set by the outcome of the Civil War; no restoration of 1874 could alter certain basic facts. Texas was subject to the revolutionized theory of government that destroyed all state sovereignty over politics, money, and social organization. The Industrial Revolution triumphed, turned the United States into a common market, and established economic development as the primary goal in American life. The cotton kingdom was aborted with much pain and blood; the cattle kingdom vanished because it never embraced enough people even to make a fight. Americans, like most peoples, accepted the inevitable as good. It would have been healthier for the nation, however, to have looked upon the contest for what it was, and to have recognized that while the greater and better organized population of the industrializing North could subordinate the South and Southwest, it did not effect for many years any solutions for the social and economic problems that made those regions different. Cotton and cattle were made tributary to the industrialized society, on its terms. The emergence of a new mercantile elite in the South, the building

595

of rails, and the domination of Eastern finance did not industrialize Texas. These gave the state some new problems in exchange for old.

The wholly agrarian society in Texas was to suffer from severe problems and tensions in the last quarter of the 19th century. The greater nation dragged it along certain courses it did not want to go, and forced it to abide by laws and rules few Texans saw as working for their own best interests. There were continual prejudices and bitternesses on each side. Social and geographical factors slowed industrialization in Texas compared with the U.S. as a whole; meanwhile, the economy, oriented as much or more to Europe as to the North, suffered from enforced national tariffs and hard-money policies. Texans saw these impositions as a part of the pattern of conquest; Yankees looked on Texan protests as rebellion.

The agrarian problem—and most, if not the most powerful Americans, were agrarians in the 1870's—was consistently misunderstood or ignored by dominant government after the Civil War. Industrialism was an ideology, even if not well articulated. Once the United States adopted the Texan solution to the Indian problem consciously, and agreed to the reordering of the Negro tacitly, economics were to dominate Texas politics and federal-state relations. In these fields Texans were not to have their way.

For about two decades after the restoration of nominal state sovereignty, however, the agrarian society of Texas was successful. In these years the state developed enormously. The development, however, was like the previous Southern advance, along static lines. The two reasons for the great increase in over-all wealth and state revenues during the 1870's and early 1880's were, first, a heavy immigration, mostly from the South, and second, a cycle of wet or rainy years throughout even the central and western areas of the state.

Life in the 1870's was very little different for the average Texas farm family than it had been in 1860. The planters were gone, and the new landowners who took their place tended to live in towns, but the thousands of small farms throughout eastern and central Texas still raised cotton and corn, and were surrounded by a few cows, sheep, hogs, and noisy flocks of domestic fowl. The more industrious families had gardens now and a few fruit trees for home use. Corn was eaten or fed to the stock; cotton was sold for cash, needed for taxes and always desperately scarce. Much trading, even at the local settlement stores, was still by barter: bacon for denim, smoked hams for flour. Each fall hogs and beeves were killed, hides sold, and the meat cured. Game was still abundant in most regions of Texas, and venison, duck, squirrel, turkey, and quail supplemented every farmer family's diet.

Land was still plowed with oxen, seeds planted by hand. Husbands still made implements and furniture, wives clothing, soap, candles, and bedding. Spring or well water supplied each farm; logrollings, house-raisings, and quilting parties continued as they had for a hundred years. The school

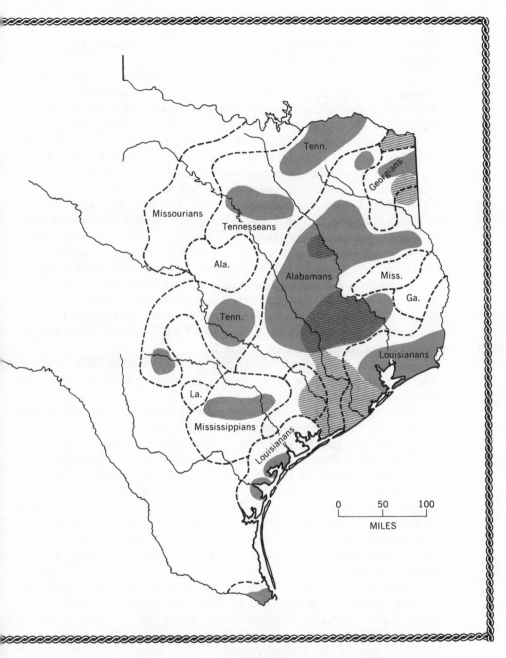

Origins of the Southern Population of Texas, 1880

According to the U.S. Census of 1880, natives from the state named in the areas marked were more numerous than those of other states (excluding Texas). The slanted lines indicate the region in which slaves numbered more than one-half the population in 1860; shading of certain regions indicates that out-of-state natives named were at least 150 percent more numerous that the next largest group.

system, after the destruction of the Radical innovations, was the old, largely private, little red house system of old.

The countryside was overwhelmingly rural. Washington County, with the largest population of any county in Texas, had no important towns at all. But county seats and settlements were important centers; the farms radiated around them. The Texas farmer was still in no sense a peasant, affixed to his soil. He moved frequently, always seeking better land, and while the towns, in an era of limited transportation, were inhabited solely by business or professional classes, the farmers went in and out of them. They provided centers for communication, and such business as the farmer did.

A typical Texas town contained a courthouse, several general stores, at least one drugstore, and inevitably, a number of saloons. The general stores sold a limited number of goods: a few groceries, such as cured meats, sugar, syrup, cheese, coffee, crackers, dried fish and fruits. Canned goods could normally be found only in larger towns. Dry goods could always be bought, such as denim cloth, calico, gingham, and hats. Furniture or hardware was rarely sold; men made their own. Guns and ammunition always filled one counter; though the farm families almost always owned an old percussion rifle or shotgun—old "Tin and Tack"—handed down, and for which they manufactured their own shot.

Luxuries in this ragged South were few: peppermint stick candy at Christmas time, to make children's eyes grow wide; lemon crackers, and not much else.

The drugstore was as important, perhaps more so, than the general goods store. Patent medicines were plentiful, and guaranteed for almost any ill. Despite glowing statements, and vehement denials, health conditions in much of eastern Texas, particularly near the Gulf, were not good. The actual incidence of the dread diseases, cholera, typhus, and yellow fever, is hard to determine, because Texas newspapers vigorously suppressed such news. However, in the early years of the Republic, cholera epidemics were frequent, at Goliad, Nacogdoches, Indianola, Brazoria, and San Antonio. Typhus, certainly brought in from Central Europe, ravaged the German settlements at New Braunfels and Fredericksburg in their formative years.

Cholera was combatted among the Spanish-Mexican population by the wearing of copper amulets, and by lime, laudanum, and boiled peyote water taken internally. Anglo-American cures such as large doses of brandy, cayenne pepper, and mustard were probably equally effective and euphoric. Almost all educated people, however, connected Asiatic cholera and filth, and by the 1870's actual epidemics were rare; a few outbreaks were still caused by polluted wells.

Yellow fever, with endemic malaria, caused havoc along the coasts. U.S. Army records are more informative than Texas newspapers, which printed little that might inhibit immigration. Some two thousand soldiers died of yellow jack at Fort Brown, with the worst outbreak coming in 1882. This hazard was not removed from the Gulf coast until these fevers were finally associated with mosquitos.

For most assorted chills and fevers Texans took large amounts of quinine. Doctors prescribed quinine and calomel for most ills and advised against milk.

The numerous doctors in the state were generally poorly trained and educated, and their practice was hardly brilliant. No Texas doctor ascribed to the theory of germs in the 1870's, nor could any perform abdominal surgery or remove an inflamed appendix. Many frontier doctors served also as dentists; a medico who could set broken limbs while someone held the patient down could also pull teeth by the same method. One brilliant exception to the rule was Dr. Ferdinand Ludwig von Herff, who practiced distinguished medicine at San Antonio. Herff brought German medicine to Texas, used chloroform as early as 1854, and founded a medical dynasty that kept in touch with Vienna.

The hotels in Texas, except in the larger towns like Galveston and San Antonio, hardly changed; they served up rough fare, well water, and common, vermin-infested beds. The saloon, however, had grown into a genuine Texas institution. It was a social and political center for a considerable part of the population. Heavy drinking seems to have been common, and in an armed society, particularly in the frontier regions, politics, strong drink, and strong opinions produced frequent gunfights. The saloons were already producing a certain reaction, however. The American temperance movement entered Texas in the 1840's, and it made considerable headway among the puritanical farmers. By the 1850's the question of alcohol had entered politics; under a local option law later found unconstitutional, thirty-five counties restricted the sale of liquor. Agitation to close the saloons was growing, but this was not yet a dominant force.

One great change in postwar Texas was the emergence of the churches. All historians seem to agree that they were the single most important cultural and social force behind the Texas frontier. The more institutionalized churches, Presbyterian, Episcopalian, Lutheran, and Roman Catholic, were among the first to build edifices, but these were mostly confined to the towns. They were influential, particularly the Presbyterian, but they did not have the effect on politics or life that the Methodists and rapidly growing Baptists did. Methodists and Baptists carried over the old Anglo-Celtic puritan ethic almost intact. Baptists recognized only the authority of the local congregation in matters of religion; they supported no other; and they could organize a church without authority or ordination. They were slow to erect church buildings, but by 1860 they already had 500 congregations in Texas. The Methodists were still a majority in 1870, but losing ground fast. These, and other evangelical bodies, enjoyed a rapid growth in Texas. By 1870, there were 843 churches, with some 200,000 members.

These fundamentalist congregations were evolved by the frontier; they met its conditions most perfectly; and they were saturated with the American frontier ethos. All were puritanical, sectarian, and enormously democratic; they were brotherhoods rather than institutionalized organizations. They bore very little resemblance to the urban Presbyterian, Anglican, or other churches. They filled a much larger void in rural life. The evangelical assemblies provided the frontier with its social cohesion; they were the only cultural and socializing agencies Anglo-Texas had.

Their puritanism, also, was not quite the same as that of the urban middle class. Frontierspeople never quite adopted the Victorian urban furor over sex. Texans were much too close to the soil. Conversely, they chose alcohol as a more violent battleground. But the puritan ethic had the same root, and therefore the same basic effect. It made both Texan farmer and Northern businessman utterly functional, and severely limited the cultural vision of each. Both saw work as the greatest virtue; both expected material success.

Church meetings were as much social as ideological. They were held in open groves or brush arbors. Here families came from miles around, dressed in Sunday best. They included suppers, bazaars, and basket parties; they lasted all day, with religious services in the morning and at night. There were two-hour sermons, delivered by circuit riders or local laymen; men and women listened from separate benches. Here women and girls, starved for companionship of their own kind, could grasp at news and gossip, and men discussed crops, common problems, and politics. This meeting was the only place large numbers of people ever assembled regularly on the harsh frontier. The enormous, socializing, tribal effect on thought and custom is easily understood. What was discussed, and thundered from the crude pulpits, set the moral standards and much of the thinking of farming Texans across the whole frontier.

Some of the preachers were cultivated men. The great majority were men of God called from the people, well-meaning but unlettered, who understood their people and the essential evils to which all flesh was heir. This was a cruel, hard, atomistic place, where great wrongs were done and received. The preachers tried to battle the world and the devil; they thundered against sins of every kind. They did not regularly prevail; nor was it possible for any clergy, in this or any other time or place, to alter the facts of human nature or be substantially different from their own people in thought and deed. The preachers were sometimes harsh, stubborn, intemperate, intolerant, like their flocks; but they made the pulpit the center of their world, and they probably left the world a bit better than they found it.

The frontiersmen were Old Testament-oriented. The land they lived in had many parallels with the land of Canaan, and they themselves with the children of Israel. They were beset with dangerous heathen enemies. The land was scourged by ravaging insects and burning drouth; the imagery of the Israelite deserts struck home in the Texan heart. The farmer endured plagues of grasshoppers; he lost sheep and cows to cats and wolves; he saw green crops die and wells run dry. The Old Testament had a relevance it would have for no later American generations.

The lives of the farmers hung on acts of God, who made rain fall from the heavens and the rivers swell. Their best-loved hymns, with which they made the arbors shake, sang of cool and beautiful rivers they would some-day cross, and of glorious showers of blessing upon the land. These people, especially near the 98th meridian, were locked in gigantic battle against Nature's God and their own weaknesses; like Israelites, they chose this soil; like Israelites they had to fight for it, with faith. They developed an Is-raelite chauvinism and intolerance, which sometimes gave them callous cruelty, but with it, a Hebrew strength.

Fresh immigration swelled the tribes; families filling up the land tended to be absorbed quickly. The scattered, lonely life, with its barren society centered on the meetings, permitted few enclaves, integrating all.

The true cities were still small. Galveston, enjoying a flush of seacoast prosperity, had temporarily become the largest settlement in the state. It had about 14,000 inhabitants in 1870, and 22,000 ten years later. It was briefly beautiful, with six public squares, two parks, two miles of espla-nade, street railways drawn by horses, thirteen hotels, three concert halls, and an opera house. Half of the cotton grown in Texas was exported; it went through Galveston, and the profits erected splendid mansions and financed insurance companies and banks. Galveston, unique in Texas, had 23 stock companies, with capital exceeding $12,000,000. It was a sea-coast, Southern city, with gas lights and theaters; on its island it was remote from the earthy heartland.

San Antonio, like Galveston outside the body of rural Anglo-Texas, was only slightly smaller, with 12,000 persons in 1870. The Spanish-Mexicans were outnumbered by the Germans, though the Spanish had given a certain character to the town. San Antonio had become an important military center, headquarters for all Army troops in Texas, and this function it was never to lose. The military, the Europeans, and the Spanish all brought a peculiar cosmopolitanism, which in the 1870's began to be submerged. The rails first reached the city then, and they brought in an influx of Anglo-Americans for the first time. In these years, also, San Antonio became a headquarters for prominent ranchers from the south and southwest, who fled the arid *brasada* as the Spaniards had. It became a mecca and retiring place for prominent Texans from all parts of the state. Here Rip Ford, other Ranger captains, Confederate generals, past governors, and big cat-tlemen from the Rio Grande met at the Menger or on the plaza and made talk.

Houston, with nine thousand people, was third in size. It was not yet a port; it lay fifty miles inland up Buffalo Bayou. But it was an important rail and steamboat terminus, and already had begun to make such things as steam engines, rail cars, wagons, cigars, and soap. It had twelve sawmills, for the vast timberlands of east Texas, with seemingly endless stands of pine and cypress, were coming into their own. Out of this ravaging, Houston steamed and prospered.

Austin, the capital finally confirmed to it in 1872, now had its rail line, and reached five thousand. It was an attractive town, overlooking the wide channel of the Colorado, set in rolling hills. It lived primarily off the government; it was orderly and clean.

The next largest center in Texas was an ephemeral boomtown, Jefferson. In the far north, on Cypress Bayou, Jefferson counted four thousand souls. It had sixty brick stores, built in a single year, an ice plant, a brewery, gas lights, and all-night trade. But the rails pushed on through east Texas, and in the 1870's Jefferson began to fade.

In these years Dallas, Fort Worth, and El Paso were all small frontier towns. Waco, on the Brazos, was larger. But the people of the state were now rapidly pushing west. The last great tide of immigration into Texas had arrived.

In bringing this immigration a number of factors converged. The first was the dilemma of the planters, and their successors in the ownership of the land, in finding labor. The landed groups in the older parts of Texas all tried to find new people to replace the newly freed, and temporarily euphoric, slaves.

One landowner, in an unsigned piece in the Texas Almanac of 1870 wrote prophetically: "Competition will dissipate many of the freedmen's conceited notions and lower their growing pretensiousness." Having learned nothing from the Negro problem in the South, this same writer urged the importation of Chinese. Although a few Chinese were brought in, they proved too clever to work on the farms. Some worked for railroads, others as cow-camp cooks. As soon as they could, most became small merchants in the cities. Much more successful were the efforts to get ruined whites from the older South to move to Texas.

Committees met in various places, agreed to transmit favorable information about the state, above all, concerning the healthful climate, the richness of the soils, and the availability of unused lands. Southern newspapers agreeably printed such intelligence as landowners in Texas supplied.

The state government also widely encouraged immigration, which was felt essential to strengthen the Indian-riddled western frontier. The state had two ends: to settle white labor, as tenants, on the idle cotton plantations in the east; and to encourage homesteading on the far frontier. A homestead act, similar to the federal law of 1862, was passed, and also a law exempting 200 acres of homestead land from foreclosure for debt. These state laws were unusual, and since approximately half the state was still unsettled by whites, seemed to offer enormous opportunities. Besides open lands in the west, there was an abundance of slave-deserted plantation acres, and very cheap acreage all through the farm-line counties on the edge of the Great Plains. Articles were printed all over the South that a family head needed "no money to secure him a good farm in almost any part of Texas"; all a man needed was "good character, industrious habits, and one or two boys . . ."

All through the blasted South people were ready to hear this call. Old memories stirred. Every family knew someone who had gone to Texas and made it rich—either in truth or legend. Everyone knew the rails were pushing west, and that the Indians had been exterminated or driven off. Thousands upon thousands of Southern poor whites, seeing the hopeless landscape around them, determined to move to Texas.

This was to be the last major immigration into the Texas heartland. Significantly, almost all of it came from old American stock, primarily from Georgia and Tennessee. However, every Southern state sent people, and sizable numbers arrived from Kentucky, Iowa, and even Illinois. European immigration renewed, but this was small, and also, unlike in the North, it was rural. The groups who arrived from Germany, Scandinavia, and the Austrian Empire took up farms instead of flocking to the towns.

More than 10,000 persons, bound for Texas, passed through Memphis in 1870–1871. Some 100,000 newcomers arrived in 1872, and because of the depression the next year, more came in 1873. The cost of living in Texas was less; land terms were better; and many families abandoned old debts.

The immediate effect of this influx was a flush of prosperity in Texas, reflected in public revenues. Large areas of the state that had been very thinly settled were filled up. From 818,175 inhabitants in 1870, of which some 51 percent were native-born and of which some 250,000 were black, the population almost doubled in ten years, and climbed to 2,235,527 by 1890. The Negro proportion rapidly fell, since the new arrivals brought no slaves. Cotton production jumped from about a half million bales in 1874 to 1,514,000 in 1886. Railroad mileage in the same period more than tripled. Property on the tax rolls increased enormously. All this, although the vast majority of Texans were very poor, gave the state a new impetus and activity different from the ruined economic and social scene of the rest of the old Confederacy.

The immigration generally separated into two broad streams. One filled up the vacant or unused lands in east Texas, replacing the old plantations with hordes of tenant farmers. Now, the freedmen had competition indeed, as they were forced back on the land. Many of the newcomers were forced to take up sharecropping, since they lacked all capital; virtually free lands were available in many areas of the state, but families needed seed money and something to get them through the winter. The other stream spread into the western counties, filling up the sections along and around the old frontier of 1850, and pushing even further west, eventually to the 100th meridian. These families were freeholders, but they also needed money, and almost all of them were forced in some manner to go in debt. Some borrowed money; more took advantage of credit at the general store.

Here, in this hopeful immigration, the seeds of much human tragedy were laid.

Both the cattle and the farming frontiers had been static for a generation until 1876. In five years the cattle kingdom exploded to the very limits of the Texas line; it filled the Panhandle in the high northwest, pushed past the Pecos and preempted the vast Big Bend country. Now, hundreds of miles separated the cattle and farming frontiers, but the hoemen were not far behind. The farm line punched out westward. Generally, it followed the rails into the west.

In this settlement, the rails played a new and controversial role. As in the eastern United States, the first rail lines merely connected already settled points. They served an obvious purpose and enormously increased commerce and industry. But west of about the 98th meridian, the tracks were moving into virtual desert, and deserted lands. The cattle kingdom would not support them; for many years the cattlemen consciously avoided the nearest railheads, because a trail drive was far cheaper than shipping cattle as freight. Texas cattle still went to Abilene and Dodge; also, it had been discovered that cattle pastured on the northern range put on weight.

The tracklaying in the west was more an exercise of ideology than a commercial enterprise. In retrospect, the arid regions of Texas, and other parts of the American West, did not possess sufficient economic potential at the time to justify the expense of railroad building. It was clearly seen at the time the rail companies required subsidies. They got these, from both the federal and Texas governments. In the great, gaudy era of corruption and rail expansion in Texas, the state alone gave assorted railroad companies 32,150,000 acres of public lands. This was a total acreage equivalent to the state of Alabama. Historians have shown that the total cost of rail-laying in the West amounted to a tax of $28 on every American citizen between 1865 and 1873. Even then, most railroad companies were under-capitalized, their lands were sold for a few cents per acre, and most ended up in receivership. It is fully understandable that C. P. Huntington, Jay Gould, and General Grenville Dodge, who built rails across Texas, pushed the tracks with a conviction amounting to élan. What is not so understandable is that they pulled legislatures and the general population along behind, not by corruption alone, but by that magic Anglo-American word, progress.

Rails connecting cities made sense. The rails reached San Antonio in the 1870's, and pushed on to Laredo by 1881. El Paso was reached by 1883. At Laredo, the rails connected with the commerce of Mexico, and both El Paso and Laredo, then tiny hamlets, began a rapid growth. Significantly, Brownsville, which had been the queen city of the Rio Grande, was now bypassed. Harassed also by a yellow fever epidemic and the silting of the pass at Brazos de Santiago in 1882, Brownsville stagnated. Its Northern capitalists went elsewhere; the lower river valley retreated into a stunted cattle culture that did not end until the rails came at last in the next century.

But while rails joined El Paso and San Antonio, Fort Worth and Denver, and El Paso and Fort Worth, this laying of track across the dry Plains was disastrous. There was nothing for the rail lines to feed on in between. They ran into money troubles. The failure of Cooke's Northern Pacific in 1873 is credited with causing the national financial panic of that year. Built at enormous cost, these rails did not really serve their purpose; as studies at the University of Chicago later revealed, they increased the gross national product by only 4 percent.

The rails held great power in the West, because they could focalize settlement or commerce, what little there was, along their routes. But they lacked one necessary power to develop the country: beyond the 98th meridian they could not make it rain.

So strong was the philosophy that increased population meant progress —and rapidly increasing population was necessary to a credit economy, which Texas always was—that Rupert Richardson, noting the anguish and controversy caused in Texas by the railroad subsidies, wrote that the question was moot. He insisted "the railroads promoted rapid settlement and development of the country, the goal of every Anglo-American commonwealth." The railroads were indeed forced to promote settlement once they had laid track into the desert; they did their best to induce farmers to go where no 19th-century farmer should have gone. Not the rails but development of widespread irrigation techniques in the 20th century allowed cultivation west of the 100th meridian. By this time, new methods of transport had developed; and the automotive engine eventually caused a great retraction in Texas railroad mileage.

The rails cannot be blamed for bringing the people to the arid West; they would have come in any case. If they promoted thousands of individual and collective tragedies, the people were eager to be promoted. The problem was twofold: the optimism of the Anglo-American that he could conquer any country, and the fact that there was almost a conspiracy to conceal the fact that in the West there was little water and rain. Texas papers rarely commented on the dryness anywhere. Official pressure even caused regions where rainfall was fifteen inches annually to be described as "less humid" in reports and geography books. The term "arid" was angrily avoided. This is understandable psychologically, when it is realized that climatically speaking, the arid, semiarid, and subhumid regions of Texas comprise exactly one-half the entire state. These were conditions with which the Anglo-American had no experience. The cattle culture, borrowing heavily from Indians and Mexico, had adapted to the dry Plains. The swarm of later immigrants did not intend to adapt to the country but to adapt the country to their use.

They considered themselves the harbingers of civilization; they thought that all former occupants had put the land to small, and thus, immoral, use. They came filled with moral and personal courage, but with no money, to do battle with the "cattle barons" and the not-really-believed eternal drouth.

Water was and still remains in the West the last unconquered frontier. It was so little understood because in those years it was not yet an American problem; the entire East had so much water it was contemptuous of it, and was busily polluting and ruining a plenteous supply. But west of the 98th meridian there was never enough rainfall for farming. Irrigation, so-called scientific dry farming, and the use of well water were no real solutions. Subsurface water did not exist everywhere; and before the development of powerful pumps it could not be extracted anywhere in adequate supply.

Then, it tended to be exhausted rapidly. There was not sufficient stream water anywhere for widespread use. Storage was impractical because of a horrific evaporation rate; in any event, the distances were too great for impounded waters to be used except in limited areas.

Between the 98th and 100th meridian some places, some years, had rain. Here there existed another phenomenon not experienced by Anglo water and woodlanders: the Pleistocene-like, cyclical climate. This actually extended far to the east beyond the 98th meridian; rainfall was not even, but came in irregular cycles. There might be seven good years, but inevitably, despite protests and prayers, good years were followed by the dry and lean. People pushed into these expanses of rolling plateaus and high plains; they found them covered with buffalo grass, or saw them beautiful with red and yellow wildflowers in the ephemeral spring. They did not realize that the grass was a cover of eons, or understand the full horror of the brassy sun of summer, sucking moisture from plowed earth, or the wild winds that warred from north to south and soon began to carry aloft tons of dirt.

These were boom psychology years. All Texas history is connected in some fashion to a land rush, and the psychology of development and profits ran deep. What was later called "boosterism" was already fully born, and in Texas, despite a massive battering, this feeling never really died. This was a basic American affliction, not invented in Texas, but nowhere was it to emerge stronger. Just as local papers ignored the evidence of the fever coast, they avoided mention of storms, drouths, hard water, or the lack of any water at all. The grim "water jokes" of this frontier gave more real information than all the propaganda and comfortable reports of bounteous crops.

"I seen snow once," a sixteen-year-old told an immigrant in one joke. "Yeah," his ten-year-old brother chimed in: "And it rained once, too." Only later, much later, did Texans universally see humor, and take a grim sardonic pride, in such jokes.

The early 1880's began a series of wet years, with greater than average rainfall. "The country is becoming more seasonable," sensible men reported, believing what they wanted to believe. They had not been on the 98th meridian long enough to know that the weather cycles were often long. The records of old ranches, such as the McAllen ranch in deep south Texas, and the information available from government geographers was deliberately ignored. The government in fact gave warnings, to no avail. Government never stopped Anglo-Americans from doing what they wanted to do. A stream of immigrant settlers went west, spreading across the "less humid" lands until they reached the edge of the High Plains.

Here began a war, between Nature and man. As Webb, other historians, and countless novelists have tried to explain, it was fought with grim determination against cattlemen and Nature. The cattlemen were largely brought to heel, but in the end Nature won.

Even before the immigrants arrived in large numbers, the cowmen had already begun to fence. Glidden's barbed wire was perfected in Illinois in 1873, and a few years later it was already enclosing the frontier. This wire was perhaps the single most important factor in the final development of west Texas. With the concurrent arrival of the iron windmill and the rails, which transported both easily and cheaply into the West, it spelled the death of open range. Formerly, neither cowman nor farmer could fence lands in the West, because there was no suitable material, and hedges failed to grow. To import rock or wooden rails cost more than the cost of the land. In fact, until the continuing Industrial Revolution gave an answer, fencing had become a major American agrarian problem. Farm fences cost more than all the stock in the United States, and more than the rails themselves. The annual amount spent on fence repair came to more than all the taxes collected in Texas. The long, flat, Glidden's patent wire, and its dozens of imitators, performed a technological revolution. The wire was foolproof; stock could not cross it or tear it down. In fact, wire killed much stock, by screw-worm-infected scratches, until cattle and horses acquired an ancestral, instinctive awareness to avoid it. A rampaging bull could butt down a rail, but no bull could cross barbed wire. The farmers' fields were made safe as they could not have been in cattle country; and the cowmen themselves, aided by windmills tooling up water, could create pastures and begin painfully to improve their runty range stock. An expensive English or French bull was not a folly, but an investment, when cows were protected by the cruel wire from the combative and usually victorious native stock.

The cowmen themselves turned the open range of the High Plains into the big pasture country. Wire cost from $150 to $200 per mile of fence, and the largest outfits generally commenced enclosing first. By 1883 most of the huge latifundia in south Texas were fenced and patrolled. In the northwest, the movement began along the farm line—farmers protecting their fields—but rapidly spread among the larger cow outfits on the High

Panhandle Plains; above all, among those ranches owned or financed by Eastern or British interests. These Easterners saw the future more clearly; they had never been exposed to the abortive culture of the Plains. They were managing businesses, not acting out manhood roles between sun and sky, awed by the immensity of the earth. The water and best lands were fenced off first. The big interests also generally had title to their lands, which the average cowman did not.

In 1876, Texas still held 61,258,461 acres of unappropriated public domain, mostly in the west. It had another 20,000,000 acres in the state school lands. The state was eager to dispose of both. Although the state continually favored farmers over cattlemen in its sales policies, for years writing homestead codes that made no sense in the grass country, it also sold off much land in huge chunks.

The largest, and most famous, deal was the sale of 3,050,000 acres on the High Plains, which became the XIT Ranch, to finance the erection of a new state capitol at Austin in 1879. The new granite building was imposing; so was the enormous ranch. Other cattle syndicates, drawn west by the cattle boom of the 1870's and early 1880's, had multimillion-dollar investments: the Matador Land and Cattle Company, the Hansford Company, the Espuela, or Spur, and others. These companies had the capital to fence, and they did so. Quickly, they transformed cattle raising from a wild and woolly career into a stable business. The terrible blizzard of 1886, and the drouths of 1886–1887, which killed thousands of cattle and forced other thousands on the market, also destroyed many hip-pocket cowmen.

Early fencing was done with arrogance; rivers were fenced off that other men's cows had used for years; the Eastern lawyers never heard of range rights. No such thing existed under the law. Public trails and roads were also fenced. The small cowman, who had never bothered to ride to Austin and secure his lands, was fenced out. He fought, as did cowboys forced out of work and rustlers whose work was now made more difficult. By 1883, fence cutting was an epidemic in west Texas; it was worst along the farm line, but essentially it was a war between large cattlemen and small. This destruction of private property had much sentimental support throughout the state, not to preserve the romance of open range, but because sale of public lands and fencing was "creating principalities, pashalics, and baronates among a few capitalists and arousing a spirit of agrarianism among the poorer classes," as one newspaper printed. In a few counties things became so bad that something like civil war ensued, and the Rangers were called in. In 1884, fence cutting was made a felony at law, even the concealment of cutters in saddlebags was a crime. But at the same time the law required gates to be opened at every three miles along a fence, and made fencing land not owned or leased illegal also. The fence wars gradually sputtered out, and in the end, virtually all west Texas was fenced.

Everyone, large or small, had to fence in self-protection. The range baron turned into a peaceful stockman, whether he owned hundreds of acres, or millions. A long era of ranch consolidation began with fencing. Cattlemen bought up land from the state, the railroads, school lands, generally at from twenty-five cents to one dollar per acre. Ranchers were limited in their purchase of school lands, since the state officials favored farmers. This policy brought "nesters" into cow country in the 1880's, and also forced cattlemen to buy through agents and in other illegal or extralegal ways. It took many years for the big ranches to consolidate and prove title. Despite Land Commissioner Terrell's famous statement, that ". . . a few good homes are worth more than many ranches, one good home for one child is worth more to a country than many ranches with a thousand cows upon every hill and in every valley; the cry of one child is more "civilizing" than the bleat of ten thousand calves. . . ." in Texas, west of the 100th line, the ranchers won. They could not beat the law, but the lawmakers could not legislate the climate. The wholesale misrepresentation, fraud, and perjury resorted to by cattlemen, as well as occasional force, are almost universally excused by Texan historians on the grounds that the government was dominated by men who tried to impose upon the West a social pattern unsuited to its needs. The farmer prejudice lingered, however, in song and story, long after the passing of the wars.

Cultural life and death was still being enacted on the prairies, with profound effects on the Texas mind and soul. The triumph of wire, which destroyed the longhorn and made it as extinct as the bison, also enormously enhanced the concept of private property in Texas. When every man wired and patrolled his land, fighting off encroachments, the big pasture country became a country of endless enclaves. The ranches were still empires of a sort, but remote and secluded imperial domains. In Texas, men crossed somebody's fence at peril.

The feeling for property right, and against trespass, grew more deeply and emerged more ferociously than in almost any other state.

The fences gave the last blow, in a largely unseen way, to the status of the cowboy, the underpinning of the cattle culture. Thousands were turned loose from jobs; without roundups on open range, and without long trail drives, fewer hands were required. A series of cowboy strikes against the large Eastern cattle combines in the 1880's failed, because of a surplus of such labor. Loading pens and loading chutes, with fences, forced the buckaroo to become a cowhand. Now, he had to do laborious work on foot— "wade in cowshit" as one rider contemptuously snarled—to hold his job. He drove fence posts, strung wire, wrestled cattle up chutes; he no longer did almost all his labor from the saddle. His proletarianization was far advanced. On the trail, he had been a *charro* hero; he was now only a poorly-paid ranch hand.

Even while cowman was opposed to cowman over fences, the intrusion of the hoemen went on. Thousands of immigrants followed the wet years of the early 1880's, buying farms from public domain, the railroads, or homesteading on unappropriated land under the laws of the state. Experimental colonies again came in vogue. Carhart founded his Christian colony near Clarendon in 1879; 400 Germans settled in Baylor County (Texas in 1876 "organized" fifty-four counties in the west even before the necessary 150 people lived in them), and there were groups of Quakers from Ohio in Lubbock county before 1880. What happened to these colonies makes tragic reading. Totally ignorant of the country and its demands, these people failed miserably. They collapsed under drouth and swarms of grasshoppers and disappeared. But by about 1890, almost all the territory between the 98th and 100th meridian, especially along the trail tracks, had been plowed.

Here millions of dollars were lost and thousands of lives blasted. Men sweated themselves to death, anguished as their plants withered; their sunblackened women grew gaunt and died. The old joke told a grim tale: the tracks west, littered by tin cans; the tracks east, marked only by lark feathers and jackrabbit bones. Thousands of families retreated finally back to other regions, broken and bitter in spirit, radicals in embryo. A human detritus was scattered across the whole Texas frontier. This had happened before; but on this arid frontier, even the strong failed in the face of hostile nature.

Yet they came on in wave after wave, hopeful, determined to win their own destiny in the west. The Anglo-American psychology was tough; he held on and fought, tearing what the cowmen had left of the seas of grass to bitter dust. American literature, for years afterward, would show the profound scars on the social thinking of those Americans brought up in this environment.

Ridiculous theories were tried: tree-planting, to make rain where Nature forbade trees to grow; turning the earth, to gather clouds. Evidence was plain, but not believed. The farmer stood on the edge of nothing, figuratively shaking his fist, demanding the earth succumb to his desires. Every so-called solution he tried treated symptoms. None of them struck at the real problem, which was the lack of water in this stubborn soil, and which made it unadaptable to certain kinds of use.

Part of this determination was based on the Anglo-American ideology of inevitable progress; solutions would be found, because they had always been found. The Industrial Revolution produced the six-shooter, barbed wire, and windmills just in time, or so it seemed. The Anglo-American was bred to the expectation of triumph in the end.

Unhappily, the frontier farmer in Texas was continually encouraged by politicians, who catered to his prejudices and hopes as unrealistically as had Calhoun. No governmental agency in Texas attempted to discourage men from farming on the harsh, arid frontier. Instead, blinded by its own ideology and credit economy, the state enticed more to come.

Families staked out their lands with hope, breathed the dry, clean air of early spring. They put in crops, threw up sod dugout huts—there was no timber here for dog-runs—or erected flimsy shacks out of lumber laboriously hauled in. Some failed the first year despite generally favorable conditions. Then, the long drouths of 1886 and 1887 came. These years wrought sheer havoc all across the wide new farm belt. Some families actually starved. Private agencies and counties gave what aid they could; the state voted $100,000 in relief to feed the hungry. This was only token help; most families lived on their own slim resources, their dwindling credit, or whatever aid more fortunate neighbors could afford.

Thousands left the country for good, creeping eastward in defeat to humble jobs or tenantry. The bad years of the 1870's were followed by a brief revival, then the bad times of the 1880's. Only a people essentially devoid of history would have kept at the struggle so long. Cultural life and death, though no American would call it that, went on.

The passage was observed grimly by the older, hardier, or luckier survivors in the west. Throughout this half of Texas the cattle people, some of whom soon turned to certain kinds of farming themselves, with new grains and new machines, developed a certain prejudice against the boosterism that kept newcomers pouring in. The farmers and the new townsmen, and the older landholders, saw things with different eyes. Much time would pass before the cowman, ensconced behind his wire walls, saw any value to successful settlement. Populating up the country in the years before 1900 only brought the old hands new problems.

The survivors saw the weak and poor, the stupid and inept, arrive with bright theories and slink back in bitter defeat. What happened was that a large, representative human mass was simply not able to populate this Texas west. There was a brutal form of natural selection once again. All did not depend on courage or energy; adaptiveness and capital were equally important. The laws and social theory of the eastern half of the state, that towns and farms meant progress, could not repeal the rules of climate; the state could give a man 160 acres, or later, four sections for grazing, but it could not guarantee that his crops would grow. Only a limited few succeeded. Year after year, stockmen, or farmers turned farmer-stockman, bought the failures out, in a process that went on for many years, and was accelerated with every recurrent, hideous drouth, from 1887 to 1917, and from 1918 to 1933.

Nothing in the frontier ethos conditioned the Texan to cope with the unsuccessful. The Westerner was not immune to pity, or totally without compassion, as some charged. Rather, he considered pity in some cases misplaced. He saw no reason to try to cope with the inept, the foolish, the incapable, and unlucky. They should "go back where they came from," as the old ranch saying went. If they stayed, like the Indian they faced extermination, or lower status, like the Mexican. Texans on the frontier were strongly democratic, but it was the old Anglo-Celt democracy among peers.

Indians, Mexicans, and nester trash were pitiable, but only tolerable under certain terms.

The long barbarism of the frontier created something akin to a barbarian ethos in parts of Texas. The strong were respected, even if they might be hated; the weak, or late-comers clamoring for "their share" tended to be despised. In the enormously difficult, enormously demanding West, the idea that everyone had an inherent seat at the dinner table did not, and could not, evolve.

The Anglo-Celt arrived on this last frontier without a sense of social organism, and nothing in his long experience there developed it. This would become apparent when he began to move to cities in later years.

34

THE PEOPLE'S PARTY

It is undoubtedly true that liberal intellectuals have in the past construed a flattering image of Populism. They have permitted their sympathy with oppressed groups to blind them to the delusions, myths, fables, and foibles of the people with whom they sympathized. Sharing certain political and economic doctrines and certain indignations with the Populists, they have attributed to them other values, tastes, principles, and morals which the Populists did not actually share.

C. VANN WOODWARD, SOUTHERN HISTORIAN

When men suffer, they become politically radical; when they cease to suffer, they favor the existing order.

WALTER PRESCOTT WEBB, PLAINS HISTORIAN

TEXAS, along with much of the American South, already alienated by the War Between the States, was further alienated by economic developments in the last quarter of the 19th century. Four out of five Americans still lived on rural farms at the beginning of this period; the Texas proportion was much higher. But under the impact of the Industrial Revolution the growth of towns and cities was to be the dominant trend of the next forty years. This was a world trend, creating problems everywhere, but nowhere more ferociously than in North America. The United States was not destined to pass easily or painlessly from a rural to an urban culture, or from the freehold farm into industrial capitalism. The earliest and most acute pain was felt in the agrarian South, and in some parts of the far Midwest.

In these regions urbanization and industrialization had been delayed.

Texas, because of the Civil War, the interminable frontier, and the problems of the arid western half, was about two generations behind the dominant Northern tier of states in social trends and developments. Conquest had been done, but conversion lagged. Texas still had an 18th-century economy, property-oriented, but in no sense capitalist. The only capitalist class in Texas, the planters, had been destroyed. The new mercantile and banking groups that rose in the shambles of Reconstruction were not industrial or productive; they tended to acquire control of the resources of the land, or the land itself, but without increasing the creation or flow of material wealth. New industries were not created, or were created very slowly; towns did not grow quickly, and this was an essential difference from the North and East.

A combination of economic and financial factors, from 1873 onward, tended to destroy the viability of the American small farm. Increasing mechanization of life and rising expectations eroded subsistence agriculture; the farmer needed cash. The opening of vast new lands in Texas and the Midwest, coupled with the static money supply enforced by the gold standard, generally caused farm prices to fall. Governmental policy favored hard money; recurrent financial panics tightened credit painfully. Commodity prices on world markets were generally higher, in terms of the same money, at the close of the 18th century than 100 years later. There was more than enough capital to finance industrialization. But—and this was to become a worldwide trend, also—there was not enough to capitalize both industry and agriculture, and under the dominant philosophy agriculture suffered.

This was long regarded in Texas and the South as a plot against the Southern people to keep them in economic bondage to the North, producing cheap fibers and food for the industrial mass. While the situation was certainly agreeable to the burgeoning capitalists and industrialists, now consciously making their headquarters in New York City, there seems to be irrefutable evidence against a regional conspiracy.

Freight rates were discriminatory, and deliberately kept so for competitive advantage, but falling prices, expensive money, and rising expectations also wreaked genuine havoc among the small farmers of the North and Northeast, and the Republican-voting allies of the industrialists in the West. In the years following the Civil War the rockribbed farms of New England were depopulated. The Eastern farmer could not compete with the production of endless miles of prairie soils. But the Northern farmer, and to some extent the Midwesterner, possessed an escape valve. He could move to town and join the growing industrial proletariat; he had certain advantages in competing with the Irish and other immigrant city masses and could rise into the industrial middle class. Industry, in the North, kept general pace with the flight of people from the farms, and urbanization created its own new markets for labor and goods.

This long movement had a profound effect on the mind of America, making a rural nostalgia almost too great to bear, keeping alive a rural mythology for many years. Whether the movement was good or bad was immaterial; it was irresistible and inevitable. Concentrations of wealth and people were accruing to the cities, and they were to become dominant over the countryside. Historically, the better organized and more powerful always became dominant, whatever their philosophy.

Farther west, in states such as Nebraska, overproduction began to grind the small homesteader down. It took exactly three times as many bushels of wheat in 1885 to pay the fixed cost of a mortgage acquired in 1865. Enormous amounts of land passed into the hands of railroads, insurance companies, and other corporate mortgagees, who resold them at increasing unfavorable terms for the farmer.

In Texas, where farming in the east was in the deep-South pattern and in the west similar to the freehold homesteads of Nebraska, the trends were equally disastrous. Texas was one-crop country, and the crop was cotton. The Texas market was entirely in the industrial world; half the crop went to Europe, and half to the Northern states. In both markets the price of raw cotton continually fell: thirty-one cents per pound in 1865, eleven cents between 1875 and 1884, followed by an irregular decline to five cents by 1898. In 1887 a harvest of 1,600,000 bales brought Texas farmers $88,-000,000. Three years later, in 1890, they produced 2,000,000 bales but received exactly $20,000,000 less.

Behind these figures lay an era of social demoralization and heartbreak.

The Texas farmer was not able, in these years, to change to different crops. He was bound to cotton; it was the only marketable commodity he knew. He could not, with the technology of the time, greatly increase production on his individual acres; tragically for him, the over-all increase in production due to the opening of new farms drove all prices down. His taxes, which had to be paid in hard cash, stayed level. The costs of the industrial products he increasingly needed or wanted rose. His income fell. He could not quit his farm, even had he been willing to. There were no cities, and no industrialization, to absorb him, and he had no money to go elsewhere. Thus, the hundreds of thousands of impoverished poor whites who fled the older South for frontier Texas, with high hopes and considerable courage, merely fled one frying pan for the fire.

The cheap prices of land, the easy terms and outright gifts of farms offered by land companies, railroads, and the state government through homestead laws, were not so generous in reality as they seemed. The great mass of new farmers in west and central Texas arrived poor. They had to borrow money to live, and to put in a crop. They had to mortgage their soil—the Texas homestead law made it impossible for the small farmer to get credit in this way—or their crop. Credit became increasingly harder to get. This was the result of no general conspiracy; the poor farmer was a poor risk. But the over-all result of conditions was to drive the Texas farmer into a form of peonage. Virtually all white farmers were freeholders in 1860. A majority were tenants a generation later. Those who were not farming for shares on someone else's soil worked all year for almost no return. Merchants extended credit at interest rates that rose to 60 percent, and this was still hazardous for the seller.

In the 1870's, and again in the early 1880's, the destruction of land values caused by the war and generally decent climatic conditions made farming profitable. But the continual decline of cotton, corn, and wheat prices (about thirty counties in the north-northwest grew wheat, and corn was used extensively as a feeder crop) was a hazard, like the weather, utterly beyond the farmer's control. Men could resignedly accept the burning drouths of 1886–1887 as acts of God. But the enormous erosion of income that followed was something else. Texas farmers, generally poor, were being ground into something resembling debt peonage, and a race that traditionally thought of itself as free, equal, and middle class, was fast becoming a new American peasantry.

The Texas government was in no sense hostile to commerce or business, although it took an agrarian approach to the theory of government. The idea that business and industry and farming were mutually hostile, or even that railroads were not inevitably paths of progress was something that grew rather slowly. Texans, like many other 19th century Americans, had a historic antipathy to corporations, not so much because of what corporations did but because the idea was strongly held that no "soulless enterprise" should be equated with human beings and given the full protection of the laws. Texans found the extension of the Fifth and Fourteenth Amendments to corporations by the courts abominable, and in a very real sense, the 19th-century judiciary tended to put the human beings behind corporate fronts above the law. When the farmer became increasingly anguished, his attention was increasingly drawn to the fact that the agents, if not the authors, of his misery were corporate land companies, railroads, and banks. His suspicion was certain, and his hostility inevitable.

The basic miasma of monetary discontent was even more historic. Texas had always been part of the traditionally credit-economy, inflation-favoring American frontier West. From the early-18th-century English colonies to the age of Jackson, the Western regions, always in debt and always dependent upon necessities from the East, demanded more paper money and looser credit. There was tension between Massachusetts farmers and Boston merchants; Pennsylvania frontiersmen and Quaker financial interests; Texas farmers and the men enforcing hard money, based on gold, in New York.

In coming to demand greater regulation of corporations and increased credit, Texas agrarians were attacking symptoms, rather than the basic cause, of their discontent. But it was already an American practice to misunderstand basic causes and become emotionally involved with sym-

bols. If the Texas farmer was generally ignorant, and incapable of understanding the whole picture of what was happening in the world, the Eastern
capitalist and worker who joined together to defend the system fully as
hysterically as it was attacked showed no greater intelligence. The Texas
agrarians were not trying to foment a social revolution; they were attempting a last stand against one which was already in full swing, and which was
not to be stopped, then or later.

What occurred in Texas in the last quarter of the century was a great
upsurge of interest, rather than class or status, politics. The farmers began
to seek political means of defending themselves. W. W. Lang, master of the
Texas Grange, which was a strong force in the 1870's, was nearly nominated for governor in 1878. The Democrat convention finally nominated
Oran M. Roberts, who won election that year and again in 1880.

Meanwhile, the first new protest party had appeared on the Texas scene.
This was the Greenback Party, which grew out of the Grange as a political
arm, and which fused with the Republicans in 1882. The Greenbackers
were powerful only in the western counties, which had been recently settled
by freeholders who arrived poor and stayed poor, as Richardson said. The
principal platform of the Greenbackers, as their name indicated, was a
demand for more money, issued by the federal government in the form of
paper notes, and for all treasury notes and bonds to be redeemed by the
same. The poor farmers suffered from a lack of purchasing power and
credit; their demand was that the government change this through printing
more money by fiat.

But certain other planks of the Greenbackers were to have more general
significance. These were: the income tax, to supplement the raising of all
revenues through property levies, falling most heavily on the farmer; an
improved school system for rural areas; the abolition of some state offices
and a general reduction in salary for all; the repeal of taxes on farm
commodities—the "smoke-house tax"; and the strict regulation of railroads.

The platform of "more money, and cheaper money," had immediate
appeal. The stated program of protecting the little man against the banks
and corporations and bondholders made the Greenbackers the second
largest political party in Texas in 1878, displacing the Republicans. The
Democrat Party, though dominated by farmers, was still inherently conservative on all things at this time.

The Greenbackers scored some local successes, electing ten state legislators and one Congressman, who left the Democrats. In 1882, the Greenback Party and Republican Party fused, running candidates for governor
and lieutenant governors as "independents." This was a rather remarkable,
and probably an utterly cynical alliance, as the two parties had nothing
whatever in common except dislike of Democrats. Their candidate, Jones,
polled 102,501 votes to the Democrat Ireland's 150,891.

Democratic loyalties in east Texas were entirely too strong to be upset. But the enormous opposition vote pushed the Democrats into adopting some Greenback planks. This, and the temporary prosperity of the early 1880's, caused the protest party to wither away and disappear. Agrarian complaints continued, however. When national depression, drouth, and disastrous prices combined to make things intolerable again, it was inevitable that some such political movement would again arise.

The Farmer's Alliance began in Texas about 1875. It reorganized in 1879 and exploded into a national body in 1887. It claimed between 1,000,000 and 3,000,000 members; figures were not, and could not, be exact. The Alliance, like the Greenbackers, was a product of the farm-line west, where a good worker could at best make 30 bushels of corn on the uplands, 60 on the river bottoms, and half a bale of cotton per acre was considered a splendid crop. Here, dryness, thin soils, and rampant capitalism combined to bring the sweating, sunburned people together in shouting protest. Most Americans tend to think of Populism, or the People's Party, the great third party movement of the century, as a Middlewestern affair. But it was born in Texas, at Lampasas, almost exactly on the old farm-line frontier. It picked up supporters to the north where conditions were similar, but the heart and soul of Populism were always in the South.

At first the Alliance did not organize as a political party, although one purpose of the group was to "labor for the education of the agricultural classes in the science of economical government." But in 1886, the Alliance made certain demands upon the state and nation. Among these were the following: the sale of school lands only to bona-fide settlers in small lots; the assessment of all railroad property at full value; the regulation of interstate commerce. In 1888, a demand for an antitrust law was added to these. The sentiment of the Farmer's Alliance was made clear by the wording of its protests against "the shameful abuses that the industrial [working] classes are now suffering at the hands of arrogant capitalists and powerful corporations."

The Alliance was kept out of active political organization in these months and years because the ruling Democratic Party continued to seize upon these planks. The Democrat platform of 1886 echoed most of the Alliance's demands, and even more extreme, called for a law requiring stockholders of a corporation to be made financially responsible for all debts incurred by the corporation. This would have obviated the usefulness of corporations, of course, but in these years corporate enterprise was being much abused. Railroads and others could incur obligations with élan and go bankrupt with impunity, some men making fortunes in the process, while the general debacle and panic that ensued damaged everyone. In 1888, the Democrats of Texas added anti-trust legislation and railroad regulation to their list.

More and more Texas farmers had come to believe that the best land was being "hogged" by monopolies and railroads, forcing them to scratch a

living on the rest; that the interest demanded by whatever corporate entity
that held his mortgage was exorbitant and immoral; that the railroads
charged too much for everything; and that every middleman, whether merchant or cotton ginner, was out to gouge him and suck his blood. In certain
respects, all of these charges were true. But the real problem was that the
small farmer simply could no longer earn a living in Texas at this time. He
could not even raise enough cotton by his own efforts to pay his debts.

The "system" was surely at fault, but it was a system beyond anyone's
real control. This did not prevent the farmer from suspecting vast conspiracies, hating all capitalists, or believing fervently that a little manufactured credit would save his world. Mixed up in this welter of beliefs and
views was a rising prohibitionalism, an agitation for the abstinence from
alcohol by law.

Statewide prohibition, backed by the Grange and Alliance, was only
beaten back in 1887 after a prolonged and amazingly bitter political campaign. Prohibition was supported strongly by the fundamentalist, puritan
churches, which had their membership among the farmers. Although the
movement to ban liquor was defeated at the polls, it was carried on by the
preachers and would not die.

The rising tide of protest in Texas had some national effect. Congressman Roger Q. Mills, who fought prohibition, was chairman of the House
Ways and Means Committee; his anti-tariff bill died in the Senate in 1888,
but became a plank in the national Democratic platform. Conservative
Texans realized that a one-crop commodity economy, which increasingly
sold more and more of its product abroad, was disastrously tied to the
industrializing, protectionist North, and that a destruction of tariffs would
do more to restore the South than a flood of regulation and credit. However, Senator John H. Reagan, the past postmaster general of the Confederacy, had better success with his own bill, which created the Interstate
Commerce Act. Business regulation—but nothing that actually tended to
dismantle industry—was beginning to have some currency in the North.

Meanwhile, the fact that the great mass of people were impoverished
and resentful, while the new class of business leaders, the "Burbons," were
neither a gentry nor a political elite, had its inevitable effect. A new type of
politician appeared in Texas; the same sort were cropping up in many other
areas of the cotton South. The first prototype in Texas was Attorney General James Stephen Hogg, elected to statewide office at the age of thirty-
five. There will always be some controversy whether Hogg was a statesman, democrat, or demagogue.

Hogg was born in east Texas, the son of a Confederate brigadier; he was
well-born but orphaned in the terrible Reconstruction years at twelve. He
obtained almost no formal schooling. He worked ambitiously as a typeset-
ter and printer until he could enter the practice of law. Flamingly ambitious, he chose politics as his field. Brilliantly intuitive, he chose the "soulless corporation" as the burning issue of his day. As Attorney General of

Texas, he declared war on big business, wherever it might be found. He became the center of attention and won a million farmers' hearts.

In office, Hogg struck first against insurance companies and drove some forty from the state. His main target was the railroads. The constitution, which made rails common carriers, was adequate to allow their regulation, but until Hogg's time, no state official had really tried. The railroad corporations, usually undercapitalized and in serious financial trouble, had gotten away with much. They were not particularly unlawful or unethical in Texas for the day, but they were certainly, in this age of unrestrained corporate and money power, behaving no better. Hogg attacked this with reforming zeal, so much so that he was accused of driving capital from the state.

Hogg forced one line that had quit running trains to recommence. He forced a giant pool of nine carriers (directed from outside the state) which was in control of all but a single Texas line to cease and desist from setting common service standards and rates. He brought suit after suit to disentangle Texas roads from out-of-state control, no matter where their ownership lay. Hogg was instrumental in getting every company that operated rails in Texas to establish a general office within the state. The out-of-state money might look upon Texas as merely one cog in a gigantic common market, but Hogg and the citizens of Texas did not. He asserted state control of every track that lay within Texas' borders.

None of this was really effective, because Texas lacked any kind of commission or bureau to regulate the roads. Theoretical power under the constitution was not translated into day-to-day control. Showing that the rail companies set rates to favor foreign interests, not residents of Texas— one line shipped lumber from east Texas more cheaply to Nebraska than to Dallas—Hogg plumped for a railroad regulatory commission as his major issue when he ran for governor in 1890.

His platform also called for abolition of the national banking system and free coinage of silver; two things on which most Southerners and Westerners agreed. He captured the Democratic nomination, and the farm associations were jubilant; they had their champion close to the seats of power at last. Charles A. Culberson joined Hogg's ticket for the attorney-generalcy. These two men were to set the tone of dominant Texas government for many years to come.

Hogg campaigned with awareness that there were more common people in Texas than any other kind, and he suited his merchandize to the market. He was a great commoner. He knew the dirt farmer's soul, and which allusions grabbed his mind. Hogg was earthy in his speech, inventive in his epithets—though "by gatlings" was the worst he essayed when ladies were around. Hogg was a flaming reformer on the hustings, standing against everything the embattled farmer hated, inventing some things the farmer had not yet imagined. But Hogg was no fool, nor was he really radical. He was a flamboyant, but deeply folk-conservative man; he knew how to survive in party politics, whom to fight, and with whom to make a deal. He was a hoeman champion, but no farmer himself; he ended up quite rich. Hogg had a keen mind, and he proved it more than once in court against some able outside legal talent. Above all else, however, in the public eye he was a stump man.

On the stump, he could hold a crowd of Texas farmers for hours, blasting railroads, bloated capitalists, insurance companies, gold; he extolled the simple life and the virtues of the men who tilled the soil. He threw off his coat and worked up sweats; he dropped his suspenders and splashed water over his brow, got his second wind, and went on to new heights amid cheers.

Hogg and his railroad commission plan won by a huge vote.

The new body created so much interest and attention in Texas that John Reagan resigned from the U.S. Senate to chair it. It had power to fix freight rates and passenger fares, and even more important, by a later act, gained the power to control the issuance of railway stocks and bonds. The immediate action of the commission was to order a general reduction of rates. The carriers fought back in court, and lost. Their next fight was in the elections of 1892.

The carriers, joined by a variety of corporate interests fearing regulation, charged the commission was wrong in principle, undemocratic, and unrepublican. Hogg again carried the day against powerful opposition from conservative elements within the Democrats, against George Clark of Waco, who was a railway lawyer.

The Railroad Commission was there to stay, and generally, over the years, it was to do good work. It did correct many abuses; here Texas succeeded earlier than many other states.

Hogg continued in action in the governor's chair; he was a powerful executive, not because of the state constitution but in spite of it, because he had overwhelming popular support. His next step was the strengthening of a state antitrust law. The railroads were cowed, but the "cotton-bagging trust," the "beef combine," and the great land companies remained. As attorney general, Hogg had secured the United States' second antitrust law, following the state of Kansas by about one month.

The Texas law emerged with teeth. It carried heavy penalties against any combination restricting trade, fixing prices, or limiting production. It carefully exempted farmers or laborers, but was extended to insurance companies and virtually every other enterprise. It was, and remained, far more severe than all the antitrust legislation enacted in this century or the next by the federal government.

Another law prohibited the ownership of Texas soil by foreigners. This was thrown out by the supreme court, then revised within the limits of constitutionality. In 1893, an act of the legislature was intended to prevent the formation of corporations to deal in lands; it provided that such entities already in existence divest themselves of all holdings within fifteen years.

The land company had a historic bad name in Texas, but there was no prohibiting its operations. This law, and another requiring all corporations to own only such land as was needed in their business operations, were faulty and easily contravened.

The trends of the century, and the coming one, ended the dream of a state of small freeholders. In fact, large landholdings were to become one of Texas' most characteristic patterns, while in many other western states, under the impact of the Federal Homestead Act and the fact that the general government did not sell off its lands, the vast ranches disappeared. In Texas, there was a tendency for the large cattle ranches of the 1870's and 1880's to consolidate and grow much larger in the next decades, as the less lucky and less hardy operators were squeezed out. Large landholdings in the East were also the rule; however, this was obscured by the fact that, tenant-operated, these holdings were cut up into thousands of small farms. The large farms and ranches in the West, because they were more business-like and capitalistic in concept, were more efficient. This did not make them more popular among their smaller neighbors.

Hogg remained a popular hero in these bad times. His public acts were always calculated and performed to make him appear colorful, and a friend of the common man. One such act was his ultimatum to the Southern Pacific to provide transportation for 700 members of Coxey's Army across Texas in 1894.

Hogg, however, was Governor of Texas. He had to serve the legitimate demands and interests of all citizens, some of whom were inevitably more equal than others. He could relieve the farmers' tensions a bit by scratching assorted fat cats, either actually or rhetorically. But his powers had definite limits. And the practicalities of politics limited any intelligent man as well.

The Texas Democratic Party was folk-conservative in thought and tone, but it representated the local "interests" as well as debt-ridden farmers. It was, like all successful American political organisms, composed of various sorts of men. Its conservatism was preindustrial and antimonopoly or trust, but among its powerful figures it included beef buyers and cotton ginners, landlords, lawyers, and bankers. It represented land and money as well as angry 'croppers. Almost all Texas voters agreed in regulating the powerful, "foreign" railroads, and in singeing outside capitalists, or any-thing else touched with a Yankee taint. The farmers groups, however, began to grow too radical for the essentially sensible Hogg. Increasingly, they attacked the "middlemen," as the local business groups were called. It was understandable that farmers who had not seen real money for years began to hate merchants and buyers, who seemed to work less yet took everything they earned year after year. But such attitudes went beyond Hogg's poli-tics.

The Alliance demanded the confiscation of railroads, moving radically beyond mere regulation. This offended a great many people on principle, whether they owned railroad stock or not. It was socialism, or worse. This was undoubtedly more an emotional reaction and not so fundamental as the basic Alliance demand for federal credits, to be made at nominal interest and secured by crops. But like free silver and the abolition of national banks, it got more attention.

Almost all the Alliance's demands were eventually to be worked into United States law. The federal credit scheme became the basis of American farm policy in later years. But it was neither a panacea nor a solution, then or later. The demands and dreams of the American small farmer, which wormed themselves ineradicably into American myth and United States government, were all based on one fundamental false assumption: that families should, or could, support themselves in an industrializing society on freehold farms. Probably extensive credit to the farmer of the 1890's would have done him no more good than the credit he finally got in later years. In any case, he would have had to leave the land. Few farmers could see the root of their troubles; they demanded symptom-treatment to ease their pain.

Hogg and the Alliance leadership fell out. Then, the national Democratic Party chose Grover Cleveland, a sound-money conservative, for its Presidential candidate in 1892. The Farmers' Alliance felt betrayed. In the emotional backwash, Hogg snubbed the Alliance men, and the chairman of the state Democratic committee read them out of the party. They followed the course of the truly alienated in American life: they joined a hitherto unheard-of group, the People's Party of Texas, newly formed among the hardscrabble, limestone hills of Lampasas. Here, on the exact edge of the old farmline frontier, third-party Populism was born. Quickly, the People's Party exploded, via the already formed Alliance, from Texas to Nebraska, from Arkansas to Virginia.

The crushing depression of these years fed its growth. But Populism was to be relatively unimportant in the West and upper South, despite the adoption of some of its planks by the national Democrats and William Jennings Bryan. Third-party Populism, the only real Populism, sprouted fully only in the far South. It was to be a bitter and debased continuance of the Civil War, dividing not only North and South, but this time Southerner and Southerner. In Texas, in 1894 and 1896, the People's Party did not fuse with the Democrats. Instead, it developed its own leaders and own platforms, and fought a bitter, hardly understood internal political war.

The basically amiable faction politics, without ideological divisions, disappeared in a welter of bitterness and turmoil not seen since Reconstruction days. Interest politics arose, dividing farmer and businessman, owner and tenant, debtor and creditor, with intolerance on both sides. The Populists mounted their attack on the "system" with evangelistic fury, flaying now the national scene of uncontrolled capitalistic orgy, now the "middlemen" who were the system's local lackies. They had, certainly, sufficient to be bitter about. Their reaction, and actions, were logical in their time. They also were rather frightening, as all such American movements are from time to time.

The Populists proclaimed the old doctrine of Jeffersonian equality, shouted that the common people were the salt of the earth, that labor was holy, and the tree of American liberty withered in too-dry soil. The attack caught fire. Seventy-five Texas papers supported the third party; one, the *Southern Mercury* at Dallas, was influential. The Populists evolved their own pantheon of stump men: Tom Nugent, Jerome Kearby, Cyclone Davis, and T. P. Gore, who later had some success in Oklahoma.

A high number of Populist leaders were fundamentalist preachers from the frontier. Populist meetings took on a camp meeting, revivalist style. Hymns were sung; sermons preached; this was not a campaign but to some men, a holy crusade. The new evangelists found much inspiration in the Bible, against money-changers and self-proclaimed scribes and Pharisees. Caught up and bewildered by eroding economic change, over which they had no control, the farming people listened and agreed to high-sounding, if ridiculous, financial panaceas, and roaringly agreed that their manhood must not be sacrificed up on a cross of gold.

Rhetorical hatred was directed toward the East, the source of all evil, the place from which Yankee money flowed. Wall Street, whose workings not one farmer in a million understood, became an enduring, odious symbol. The shadowy figure of the "Jewish banker" became involved, although not one Texan in a thousand had ever even seen a Jew. Shylock had been a respectable, despicable English-speaking symbol for three hundred years— something later, and Jewish, observers forgot. Shylock the banker was an allusion every farmer immediately understood, and every farmer had figuratively, with great anguish, been relieved of his pound of flesh.

Someone, inevitably, had to serve as scapegoats for this long pain. The rancor against the Shylocks was to remain rhetorical, because the Jews remained out of reach. But also inevitably, scapegoats nearer to home were found, despite the earnest, and apparently honest, efforts of the Populist leaders.

Easterners made a number of errors about this lot. They did identify Populism with the fundamentalist Bible Belt, and considered it anti-Eastern, anti-intellectual, anticapitalist, anti-Semitic, and anti-aristocratic. They reacted rather violently. Major magazines, such as the *Nation* and the *Atlantic Monthly* and *Harper's Weekly,* were as hysterical in denunciation as the preachers on the stump. Theodore Roosevelt accused Populists of plotting social revolution and subversion of the Republic, and actually proposed shooting twelve of their leaders dead by firing squad. Joseph H. Choate argued before the Supreme Court that the demands for an income tax were "beginnings of socialism and communism." The members of the Union League Club apparently were so frightened that the estimable Mark Hanna, the coolest if not the most lovable head around, rebuked them for acting like scared chickens.

Somehow, Wall Street had its own myth: that the People's Party were anarchists, frothing to burn the nation out.

All this requires some inspection. Actually, Populism was neither the beast the corporate capitalists thought it, nor anything like the true reform movement later Eastern anticapitalist intellectuals lovingly longed for.

Populist thinking was provincial and Southern, because its supporters were provincial and generally uneducated. It was also imperfect, over-emphasizing the importance of ready money, and believing a few dollars could offset a long-term trend. It was also simplistic, trying to separate mankind into producers and drones, farmers and workers, and "greedy interests living off them." This was then and later emotionally satisfying, if socially insane. An industrial society had to be complex, and in no tightly organized society would human psychology afford much honor or reward to manual labor. Populism also succumbed to the American agrarian myth, but far better educated Americans succumbed to it, also. The People's Party invented its conspiracies and its inevitable Golden Age. It was composed mostly of ignorant people, and heir to all the superstition, folklore, and prejudice of inner America, which was considerable. However, few of these foibles were in any way worse than the biases and hypocrisies of other American regions. The industrial upper classes in the East were more than rhetorically anti-Semitic, although they were too genteel to shout about it from the pulpit. The insistence upon rampant capitalism and gold, as sort of religions, bears no more inspection than the farmer's naïve trust in government credit and free silver.

For better or for worse, most of the Populist programs came to pass in later, neo-Populist times. The Populist charge that private banking was stacked against the farmer was true, as was his belief that only the general government could provide adequate credit on the farms. Given his mistaken assumption that there was a place for the family farm, much Populist thinking was eminently logical.

American intellectuals could view the historic passage of the dinosaur, or the collapse of the European feudality under economic factors, with greater assurance than they could view the demoralization of the farmer. The American ethic did not have an agrarian origin, but Americans had spent too many generations on the farm. Populism, and its myths, were to infect the coming years with deep nostalgia.

The Populists in Texas were theoretically and rhetorically opposed to the monied East. But distant capitalism was out of reach; they waged their bitterest battle against what they considered the agents of capitalism and industrialism at home. The farmers rebelled against the pretensions to breeding and social superiority of the new-rich, post-1860 mercantile and business classes, but not against private property or the concept of wealth itself.

Many outsiders confused this attack as an attack on aristocracy, but then they confused the new industrial upper class in the United States with aristocracy, too. In parts of Texas—and much more strikingly in Virginia, where there was more available gentry—some of the most honored names supported the Populist cause. The landowning, or former landowning, groups shared many of the beliefs and hurts of the small farmer.

The Populist assault on the state government was not intelligent but emotional. They turned a political struggle into a crusade and made it "them" or "us." They were too simplistic, forgetting the essential of American political success, the pragmatic alliance between disparate groups. They tried to form a great alliance composed only of the poor. There were more poor than rich or well-off in America, but in America, with its cause-and-effect ethic, any such alliance was doomed. Locally, they drove the Democratic Party with all its historic strengths and associations in the Southern mind entirely into the business-conservative camp. Instead of creating a new North-South battleground, Populism scarred new battlefields in the South itself, on which some poisonous mushrooms were allowed to grow.

The farmers hoped to enlist the Northern proletariat, to create another New York-Western axis as in the Jacksonian age. They had no real routes of communication, nor any ideology or leadership palatable to the North. Mark Hanna, master craftsman that he was, was certain that silver could not be sold to Indiana farmers, and he was right. The whole tier of states that went for Lincoln in 1860 went for McKinley in 1896. The Northern farmer remained unconvinced, and the McKinley people, with enormous success, convinced the Eastern workers that Southern agrarianism threatened their whole house of cards. It was still a near-thing; the Republicans won because they yet retained the initiative in American life. The Populist-Democrats, on the national level, were a reactionary wail of protest for a passing way of life.

The second great alliance sought by the Populists was with the impoverished and quiescent Negro mass. The Populist leaders knew they could not offset the Democrats in Texas without black allies. Negroes still voted in Texas in the 1890's; there were no legal restrictions in their way, though they faced intimidation in many counties. After Reconstruction, the Negroes, always outside the money economy, drifted outside the political scene. Populist evangels determined to bring them back in.

There was no real difference between the lot of the black tenant and the white. Both faced and suffered from the same conditions. But here the Populist leadership stepped on dangerous ground. Blinded by their own logic, they failed to remember the illogic ways men think and act. They made their second great mistake. First, they had turned "interest" politics into class politics in Texas; now, they infused status politics with disastrous results.

Black and white workers were sent among the Negroes. These were paid workers, generally called " 'fluence men." They distributed bribes and favors, and their mission was to influence votes. They enjoyed considerable success, because the Negro vote was ripe. The Democrats, for twenty years, had left it strictly alone.

With its melange of factions, traditions, and expertise, the Democrat Party fought back. Hogg and Culberson built tight south-Texas machines, dragooning the Mexican vote; at this time the Mexican vote in Texas was brought almost entirely into the conservative camp, not by ideology but through the use of local Anglo leaders and superb machine politics. The Democrats had the scared support of most businessmen and virtually every corporation or interest within the state. They also had control of the apparatus of government, and they used it well.

The Populists had aroused class and caste hatreds. Now, they met with practices not seen since Reconstruction: the stuffed ballot box, packed courts, hostile election boards. They also found economic boycotts, social ostracism, and severe retaliation. Preachers who favored Populists were turned out; both white and black Populist workers were evicted from their tenant farms.

The black alliance made the People's Party terribly vulnerable to the South's most sensitive charge: race treason. The Populists were branded with the accusation that they were disloyal to both Texas and the white race, and this was one they simply could not throw off. The Civil War was still a burning event. All voters either remembered the conflict, or had been born during Reconstruction.

The Republican patronage party in Texas made things worse, by publicly supporting Populism. Hoping only for a McKinley victory in the North, local Republicans plotted further wreckage among the Democrats. They did more damage to the Populists.

The Democrats survived. Culberson, Hogg's successor, beat Tom Nugent in 1894 for governor. In 1896, the year the national Democrats undercut Populism by adopting its planks, Culberson beat Jerome Kearby by only 58,000 votes out of more than half a million. The election was resplendent with counting-out and other forms of fraud.

The People's Party did elect a bloc of state representatives and many local officials, but not enough to win influence; 1896 was their high-water mark. By now, the national Democrat Party had destroyed third party Populism by incorporating it, and in Texas the stubborn third party, by battling the Democrats, had strangled themselves.

Populism aroused an enormously hostile reaction both in the North and South. Much of its approach was irrational, but its method scared more men than its madness. Pragmatism, not evangelism, was the root of American politics. There was still a shuddery sensitive spot left on the American soul by the irrationalism of the Civil War.

More remarkable than the People's Party's rise was its quick demise. By 1898 it was fading fast, and by 1900 it had disappeared. There were a number of reasons. The most important was that Populism had never had a genuine ideological base. It was interest politics, waged by men who wanted dollars more than social reform. As historians noted, silver dollars were the real goal, not the theory of free coinage of silver. Populists rose because they were hard-working men and women who were pushed to the wall by changing systems; when they could make it again under the American system, all their protest would dissipate. Populists in Texas had very little, if anything, in common with the Progressivism of the high Midwest, with which they were often confused. They were not liberals, but reactionaries—looking not forward but backward, to the mythical agrarian democracy over which Tom Jefferson was supposed to have presided. Their cause was lost forty years before.

Few Texas farmers in their smelly overalls had deserted the American ethic, or the folk-conservatism deeply implanted in the American Protestant mind. The great wail of political protest heralded no change of outlook or ethic, or any European infusion of notions of political theorism or class. The Texas farmer revolted, within the strict limits of political action, because his middle-class attitudes and status were eroded by economic forces beyond his control, but the erosion did not continue long enough to have a permanent effect. He did remain essentially anticapitalist, but this was nothing new. The Southern farmer had always been basically anticapitalist.

By 1900, the economic outlook for farmers brightened immeasurably. Cycle followed cycle; due to increased urbanization in the North and improved European markets, all farm prices rose. The desperation of the 1890's was followed by ten fat years. The farmer had dollars to jingle, and his protests subsided, if they did not entirely go away. The Democrats learned something from Populism. They incorporated much of it, in Texas and nationally. If the adoption of the silver plank was political idiocy, there were other aspects of Populism that had more lasting appeal.

Although much genuine myth, and much later political practice, lived on after the great crusade, one part of it turned sour. The People's Party germinated the racism that was simply waiting for irrigation in the South.

An understandable reaction of the dominant Democratic local parties was to demand that the large, unlettered, and alien Negro vote be placed without the pale. The attempt to fuse blacks with poor whites scared every business and property interest in Texas. It also, in a humanly understandable if not entirely palatable reaction, turned many Populists' stomachs. A phenomenon of the collapse of third-party Populism was its retreat into virulent racism, perhaps brought on by Democratic charges, perhaps a result of failure and frustration. The attempted political alliance between white and black sharecroppers did psychological damage to the status-minded white. The black man performed one definite service in Texas besides labor; he provided an unmistakable social floor. Few white men could equate their lot with the Negro and maintain an American self-esteem. No men willingly accept a loss of caste.

The Democrats, first by *de facto* practices, then by written law, denied the Negro the privilege of voting in the Democrat primary. In one-party states, this disenfranchised the race. The former Populists approved this fully, as if frightened by the brink they had almost passed. The former Populists, even more strongly, demanded that the blacks be defined and be legally separated socially at law. The polls were closed; the signs went up. Here the restoration was finally consolidated in caste, and both interests and "the people" rid themselves of a bad scare.

These years again showed that relations between white and black depended upon the Negro not impinging upon the white. The white's tolerance was geometrically proportional to his distance, real or imagined, from the black. This of course was a common human reaction, by no means confined to Texas or the American South.

Cotton-kingdom Texas' mood was to ensure continued subordination of the race. The new western counties tended to be more liberal; the cattle kingdom's dominant feeling was to keep the Negro out. One incident in Lubbock County in 1900 was significant, and told much of American race relations beyond the limits of the South. Farming was at this time coming experimentally to the High Plains and along the lower Rio Grande, based on new ways of irrigation and new crops. One immigrant seeded cotton in the far northwest. A horde of cowhands, when they learned the nature of the crop, roped the farmer, and at gunpoint made him plow it up. "Cotton brings niggers, and this is white man's country," they said.

The black belt was never to spread successfully much beyond the old cotton line. White—and unseen but equally important, Mexican—hostility kept it out.

Texas seemed half-radical in 1896, but in 1906 it was comfortably conservative again. Populism and neo-Populism, as in the New Deal, had great vogue in depressed times. Reform got short shrift if proposed during prosperity, which was a fact that some Populist allies in other places never understood. Texas was split, not between liberals and conservatives but between functional liberals and functional conservatives. Both camps were philosophical conservatives at heart. They saw nothing wrong with Anglo-Saxon civilization as it had grown up in Texas, as a whole.

Although there was a brief, consciously genteel reaction about 1900, the traits of Populism triumphed in the debacle of its politics. The dominant Democrats found expediency lay in stealing some People's Party thunder. Hogg and Culberson were prototypes of a most recurring breed: "common" men, insistent that no one mistake their commonness, spouting and perhaps believing much neo-Populist doctrine, while pragmatically making deals with "the interests" on the side. The Populist debacle damped the desire for class politics in Texas. Afterward, few evangelistic demagogues, spouting reform and radical doctrine, actually cultivated any trend toward genuine social change. What was confused with and taken for democracy and reform was a massive injection of vulgarity. Voters who liked deep-burned, catsup-splattered steaks and distrusted any elegance in manners or dress, gave birth to an enormous total of candidates with the same displayed tastes. The trick was to be common, and solid in support of all social bias, but not to offend any locally dangerous interests in the process. This confusion of vulgarity-cum-folk-conservatism was often guileless. Nor was it by any means restricted to Texas, although in Texas it was usually highly successful at the polls.

In these years there was a general retreat from the high-mindedness and gentility of the older South in many places. Anglican Senators were replaced with earnest, gallus-snapping Baptists; former brigadiers in gray were supplanted by new men who escaped the crumbling family farms. This was an inevitable evolution, a logical response to basic trends in American society as a whole. There was an enormous aversion to, and a conscious gravitation away from, elites of any kind. The importance of family crumbled rapidly; ephemeral, constantly changing status took its place. The status society was even more functional than the old one had been. Now no Texan could be properly identified until it was learned "what he did"; who he was, or where he came from, made less and less difference. The dominant American social system, if not all the dominant American ideas, was to triumph completely.

Certain trends clung in politics. It was always safe, and in fact, sensible, to be against the "interests," especially the foreign ones. For many years interests active in, but headquartered outside Texas took heavy blows. Culberson's attorney general, Crane, levied an enormous fine against the Waters, Pierce Oil Company and drove it out of the state. He had good reason; the company had broken the laws. But similar companies, in this era, were behaving the same way with impunity in most parts of the nation. A few years later, twenty-one major life insurance companies left Texas, appalled by the so-called Robertson law, which required them to invest 75 percent of the reserves on lives of Texas citizens inside the state. For many years any Yankee interest was fair prey. The severe antitrust codes, which were far more severe and enforced with greater effort than the federal laws, possibly hampered industry and business development. However, their major effect was to hold certain national corporate empires at bay, in a series of Shilohs in this new war, while Texas could grow native corporate octopuses of its own. The large, powerful, indigenous insurance and corporate utility companies were Texan beneficiaries of the fights against Eastern capital.

While Texas was succumbing to American society, it had some success in maintaining federalist notions of its own. Local money was less evil than foreign.

The antitrust laws probably affected banks and financial trusts most of all. Texas was to develop immense wealth out of natural resources, but the growth of major financial institutions was very slow within the state. Nothing like the major, spreading New York or California banking systems could evolve.

The business climate, although there were few pressures for industrialization, was quite good. Reality forced government to live and let live with "the interests." The dual quality of some Texas politicians, ultrademocratic but also ultraconservative in some ways, was puzzling to outsiders, but founded on the single-party politics of the state. Business, of all kinds, took an active part in politics in Texas; corporate lawyers attended every party convention. They had to, in self-defense; some chicken farmer always came up with some new anticapitalist idea. The so-called interests had money, and spent it, which gave them two advantages over the reformers. Money was important to politics, especially in a one-party region. No matter how democratic his image, or how commonfolk his manner, the first requirement for any successful politician was to line up adequate financial support. The primary was decisive, and candidates ran in the primaries on their own or their supporters' resources. There were no "party funds," or a system by which promising young politicos were brought along.

However, to pretend that the amiable corruption that often occurred in Texas was worse than the American norm, would be nonsense. Texas was a simpler society than the mainstream North. Its corruptions, like its racism, were simply more easily seen. More sophisticated states had greater success in obscuring both. The Texan mind was always too direct, out of the frontier, to learn the true possibilities of hypocrisy.

"Interests," as such, protected themselves rather than attempting to run the state of Texas. They made no attempt either to enlarge or depress the parameters of society or thought. Yet some hostility to them remained, in a survival of neo-Populist suspicions in the average man, whether worker or university professor.

Texas politicians, after the time of Populism, were Democratic, popular, and pragmatic. They had to find issues, which were sometimes grotesque, sometimes profound. Factional fights were sometimes bitter. But an old Texan political proverb told more of internal affairs and ruling officials than pages of discourse. It ran, "Don't spit in the soup; we all got to eat."

Burned by the War Between the States and Populism, the Texan political mind rejected the notion of destroying a structure just because it could not be controlled to one's fancy. The Texan, pushed toward violence by one aspect of his history, pulled toward mercilessness by another, was pragmatic within the limits of his peoples' folk biases. Too many people have despised the Texan politician too much. Most of them, at home and abroad, were effective; they did what they set out to do.

No Texan in the 20th century would try to spit in the nation's soup. All would try to get a large share, but that was the real essence of the American Dream, which the Populists, Jim Hogg, and the men in Wall Street equally shared.

35

THE TWENTIETH CENTURY

... In the New World things make haste;
Not only men, the state lives fast ...
One demagogue can trouble much:
How of a hundred thousand such?
And universal suffrage lent
To back them with brute element
Overwhelming? What shall bind these seas
Of rival sharp communities
Unchristianized? ...

                                    Know
Whatever happens in the end,
Be sure 'twill yield to one and all
New confirmation of the fall
Of Adam. . . .
Myriads playing pygmy parts—
Debased into equality:
In glut of all material arts
A civic barbarism may be: . . .
An Anglo-Saxon China, see,
May on your vast plains shame the race
In the Dark Ages of Democracy.

                        WALT WHITMAN

Texas entered the 20th century with its basic society a full two generations, or about sixty years, behind the development of the American mainstream. Industry was in its infancy; among the people themselves the norms and patterns of the industrial society had no root. Texan speech was already becoming picturesque, because it retained earthy allusions forgotten by Northern city dwellers. The early 19th-century American values were in no way eroded in Texas. There was no reason why they should have been. During a century of explosive conquest and settlement, the land changed very little, and the people not at all.

The United States was far from a unitary nation, although it was moving steadily toward a unitary general government. For some years, however, Texas and its Southern allies maintained an acceptable stabilization and compromise. The Supreme Court of the United States disappointed Texans severely by its gentle attitude toward corporate combines and rampant capitalism. It satisfied them, however, by its full acceptance of the caste imposed upon Negroes by the "separate but equal" codes and black disenfranchisement.

The Supreme Court was hardly an Olympian institution, despite American reverence for organic law. In these decisions, as in so many others before and afterward, the justices tended to rule presently on the ideals or myths of yesterday. They were more apt to see problems in terms of the ideas or thinking of their formative years than in terms of current realities. Thus the Court had made its Dred Scott decision, ignoring the fulminating crisis of slavery; at the turn of the century, and again in the early New Deal years it refused to accept a reasonable regulation of the American industrial machine. In its 1896 decision on caste it failed to see the implications of continuing subordination, just as in the 1950's, when it rescinded the earlier decision, it failed to take into account the reality of American race relations, and when the problem of civil disorder had become the most serious one facing American society as a whole, the Court continued in terms of the preceding generation, enlarging civil liberties.

The Texan view that the Court was fallible was a deep-seated 19th century conviction, stemming from the actions of the Court in the Reconstruction decade. The Court had followed changing popular prejudice faithfully in those years. Also, the enormous alienation caused by the Civil War and the Populist-Democratic revolts against capitalist industrialization never completely faded away. A sense of Texan separatism, which the Iowan did not share and could hardly compehend, continued.

Also not clearly seen was the fact that Texan parochialism tended to increase for some years after the turn of the century. There were two primary reasons. Texas was a vast province, with most of its community remote from the rest of the United States. It was not yet mercantile or industrial, and thus not in continuous contact with other states. Second, after the final quarter of the 19th century, there was no significant outside immigration into the Texas heartland. Knots of Northerners and Midwesterners did develop the High Plains agriculture and the lower Rio Grande Valley, while Pennsylvanians drilled wells and organized the early Texas oil companies. But no people, either American or foreign, immigrated into the politically dominant, most heavily populated, agrarian regions of the state. This was to have its immense effect, not only on the farm but in the Texan cities when they arose. There were to be no non-Anglo-American influences, and since urbanization came late, Texans in the 20th century would be far closer to the land.

At the close of the century, Texas entered a brief, tranquil twilight of the Old South, probably a reaction to the turmoil of the Hogg-Populist years. The leadership, as Richardson saw, was "unusually adroit" in avoiding or damping issues that tore the people apart. Behind this leadership was one of the most skillful and adroit political movers the American nation produced. This man was a well-to-do planter who made his own compromise with changing times by becoming a railroad magnate. He never ran for office or appeared upon the public scene. He took up state politics as an avocation, adapting new ways and means to the basic thinking of the Old South. He passed into American history not so much as the most important man in Texas for many years, but as President Woodrow Wilson's mysterious Colonel House.

Edward M. House moved behind Governor Hogg, and managed his campaign for reelection in 1892. House put together the great machine that staved off the Populist revolt; while at the same time drawing Hogg and Culberson into the Establishment. In fact, House created the conservative Texas Democratic establishment; from his time its outlines, through good years and bad, tend to be clear. He was the Texan answer to the Republicans' Mark Hanna of Ohio.

House was a supreme backroom politician, who knew how to pick and work with the most influential men: W. T. Gregory of Austin, Andrews of Houston, and the powerful Jim Wells of Cameron County in the south. Wells faithfully delivered the ethnic Mexican vote through an alliance of ranchers and local politicos in a great patronage machine. These men, with House, successfully engineered the essential compromise between the native "interests" and the mass voters of the Democratic Party. They were anti-Republican, antitrust, anticapitalist as Northern capitalism was then construed—but definitely not hostile to the developing corporations and business interests in Texas. It was a pragmatic and generally successful compromise, in the best tradition of Anglo-American politics. If it was unidealistic in most respects, it worked.

Colonel House masterminded both of Culberson's campaigns, and after Culberson was sent to the Senate in 1899, where he was to remain twenty-four years, House engineered the Sayers-Lanham era of good feeling. Joseph Sayers and W. T. Lanham were the last Confederate soldiers to hold the governor's chair. They were older men, mature, stable, and appeared to live by the ideals and ethics of the former, long-gone age. Both had served in Congress; neither was involved in the controversies of the Hogg-Culberson years. They did not become deeply involved in the day-to-day politics of Austin; in turn, they presided with high-minded gentility between 1899 and 1907. These were the last completely genteel governors of the state.

By 1906 Colonel House dropped out of state politics, but he was soon to be heard from on the national scene.

The improved farm prices did not reverse the long trend of farmer discontent, although they damped it. The underlying hostilities remained. All important or successful state officials shared the same basic views: hatred of national combines or trusts, dislike of corporate lobbyists, a desire to reform taxation by taxing more intangibles, but with an underlying support of the state's basic institutions. Although the Sayers-Lanham administrations had put through numerous reforms, including heavier taxation of railroads, pipelines, and utilities—which raised property on the state tax rolls from $1,221,159,869 to $2,174,122, between 1906 and 1908—they were vulnerable to the charge they had been too favorable toward big business. Two-thirds of the entire tax burden still rested on property, and two-thirds of this on real estate. The farmer was eager to shift his burden elsewhere, since the costs of government continually rose. But the great problem for many years was that there was really nowhere else to shift it within the state.

Campbell, who became governor in 1907, revived some of the Populist wars; all Texas officials tended to be neo-Populists in some degree. Campbell engineered a light inheritance tax, but failed to win his major goal; a state income tax. Against this too many landowners, as well as big businessmen, combined. One of the first states to propose such a tax in the 1960's still had not imposed it.

The prohibition issue was now coming to the fore. This was to be a potent, and at times dominant issue in Texas politics. The farming counties of the heartland and the upper west had prohibitionist majorities; the towns, and south Texas, with its Germanic-Mexican influx, had much less enthusiasm. A great deal of the old Populist fervor was siphoned off into Prohibition, which then and later often kept state politics in turmoil. The governor who followed Campbell, Colquitt, was a Hogg man, hard on rails and trusts, but obstinately partial to hard liquor. Ironically, Colquitt's opposition to prohibition threw him over to the functional conservative camp, because the prohibitionists captured the reformers. Afraid of legal abolition of alcohol, Colquitt insisted upon legislative rest.

The Democrats for a period of years divided into prohibitionist-anti-prohibitionist wings. Confusing things completely to outside observers who forgot the agrarian nature of Texas was the fact that the prohibitionists were reformers and "liberals," as they were beginning to be known nationally, while the antiprohibitionists were in general Establishment and business conservatives.

Texas had adopted local option on liquor and a number of other things, a logical compromise in a region so sharply divided between rainy east and arid west. The heartland farmer wanted prohibition; much of the west and southwest did not. Likewise, pistol carrying was unnecessary and abhored in the east in the last quarter of the 19th century, while it was still a necessity of life beyond the farm frontier. In farmlands, a requirement that all stock be fenced made sense. On the vast sweeps of west and south Texas, where in dozens of counties there was not a single farm, it did not. On a number of essential issues Texas had begun to show a viable pragmatism, a federalism within a federal system, by which the needs and interests of vastly disparate regions could be served. But whenever emotion was injected into an issue, the notion of leaving it up to local option disappeared. As with slavery, the idea that something was immoral or wrong made a pragmatic approach impossible. The reformers confused morality with liberal politics, probably to the disadvantage of both.

The election of 1911 was fought almost entirely on the alcohol issue. Democrats of each faction condemned each other with more virulence, in many cases, than they had ever attacked E. J. Davis. The brewery industry, which had become an important interest in the state, raised more than $2,000,000 in campaign funds, supporting drinking candidates no matter what their other politics. Conversely, when a poll tax amendment went through after the beginning of the century, requiring a head tax in order to register to vote, this was heralded by the prohibitionist reformers as a great triumph for morality. It would hold down the Mexican, beer-bibbing vote; prohibition was another Anglo-American frenzy utterly incomprehensible to the Latin Catholic mind.

On statewide referendum, prohibition was defeated only by about 6,000 votes. It was to triumph a few years later, when prohibitionism found a happy combination with patriotism. First, saloons selling liquor to soldiers were closed; then, in a burst of wartime feeling, in 1918, the whole state voted out liquor. This, of course, was a national phenomenon, and Texas quickly ratified the Eighteenth Amendment in 1919. Thus the controversy was ended for some years.

The year 1914 marked the appearance of the most colorful governor since Jim Hogg. This was James E. Ferguson, who was to be at or near the center of Texas politics for thirty years. Ferguson threw up a completely confusing image to some people, but the pattern of his own career was quite simple. He was typical of a whole breed of Texas politicos in the 20th century. Ferguson liked office, but was a man without a mission; having no particular program, he tailored his campaigns to the electorate's foibles and desires.

Ferguson was a banker, a deep conservative on most matters, and by no means unfriendly to corporate stocks and bonds. At the beginning of his campaign for governor, he pacified "the interests" by declaring as a business-man's candidate. He told city newspapers that there was room in Texas for both the rich and the poor, and that the rich had a right to the protection of their money. He also shied away from the prohibition issue. In both these ways, Ferguson gained important support, and, as later investigation was to turn up, important funds.

Then, Ferguson took his campaign to the country. He made 145 speeches in the cotton belt, only 10 in cities or towns. He knew exactly what he was doing.

The continuing commodity price cycles were hastening the erosion of family freehold farms. Each bad period destroyed a few more farmers; each drouth put more farmers in debt from which they could not escape. The figures on the percentage of farmer-owners in Texas tell the sordid tale of social destruction. In 1860, almost all Texas farmers owned their own land. In 1880, the percentage had fallen to 63 percent. By 1900, 49 percent of all farm families were sharecroppers; ten years later the percentage rose to approximately 53 percent. A vast mass of people through the Southern states were approaching the status of peasantry. There were other cruelties not shown by the price cycles and percentages of tenants.

Custom fixed the landlord's shares at one-fourth on cotton, one-third on other crops. But as the country grew more crowded and good land was taken up, in parts of Texas landlords demanded cash bonuses beyond the customary shares before leasing their lands. Even in good years the tenant could not get ahead.

After ten good years—the time that was fixed in American minds as the era of "parity," when the farmer earned his fair share of the national income—the agricultural cycle again went down: 1911 was a bad year for prices; it was followed by the national depression of 1913–1914. Drouth returned, and worst of all, the European war. Cattle and cotton prices tumbled when the foreign markets were cut off. At this time hundreds of cattlemen and thousands of farmers went bankrupt.

Two-thirds of the Texas cotton crop was exported to Europe in 1913; it comprised the major value of all U.S. exports. The American fascination with industrialization produced a blindness to the value of agricultural exports; Americans thought of themselves as industrial people, although mass production of agricultural products was one of the things at which they excelled. The cotton economy had been entirely viable in 1860, de-spite the military weakness of its society. The Civil War and the lack of capital in the South forced the unhappy arrangement known as sharecrop-ping; the pro-industrial policies of the next two generations continued depression in the South through hard money and tariffs. When amelioration finally came in the policies of the New Deal, it was too late. The family farm was already doomed, although the myth of its social viability survived. The future lay in large-scale, capitalistic farming, with markets both at home and abroad, but in the years it took to reachieve this, terrible damage was done to people in the South. Few Americans saw that for the first two generations following the war, Texas would probably have prospered more had it not been attached to and dominated by the United States.

The final erosion of small-scale agriculture in the 1930's has been clearly seen, if not entirely understood. The enormous damage done fifteen years earlier was not seen. Cotton prices dropped to eight cents. The rash of local solutions, such as better storage, more cooperative credit, and the desperate, patriotic "buy a bale" program launched among businessmen and townspeople were all failures, as they had to be. The sad fact was that no amount of "credit" and delay could salvage an economic enterprise that was not able to stand on its own feet. The cooperatives that lent farmers credits in lieu of the general stores themselves went bankrupt; the agrarian myth that held family farming to be socially beneficial ignored the basic problem of long-term trends. The federal government, later trying the same artificial symptom-treating, spent vast billions, with no better results.

However, the terrible process of poverty and social erosion had definite political results, then and later. Candidate Ferguson could do nothing about drouth and bad markets, but he could promise sympathy and legislative succor for the "little man." Ferguson galvanized the rural areas of Texas by promising to fix rents at the customary shares by state law. He had found an "issue," the one thing most avidly sought by officeseekers. With this program, he swamped a prohibitionist candidate through Texas' fundamentalist cotton-growing Bible belt. He took office in January, 1915.

The legislature was impressed sufficiently by his total vote so that it enacted his promised law. But the law was not effective. It could not be enforced—there was no way to police private contracts in which nothing was written down. In the end the supreme court threw it out. But Governor Ferguson, without spending a cent of state funds, established himself as a hero to the little man.

Ferguson was as canny as Hogg. In office, he tried to be spectacular, and he seized attention by beginning a massive pardons program, freeing convicted felons by the hundreds. This served two purposes; it was not unpopular with the rank and file, and it served to cut state expenditures. The problem of what to do with the crowded prisons had been a serious one since the Rangers had begun to fill them after 1875. Convicts had been treated barbarously for a great many years. Ferguson's pardons policy was far more popular than many people realized.

Like Hogg, Ferguson appalled lawyers, city dwellers, and the like, but

Ferguson was never under any illusion that his electorate was genteel. Actually, he presided over a considerable amount of genuine reform. Ferguson, and governors like him, did not hold Texas back from the 20th century; they were probably a necessary transition. They did not damage the institutions of the state, while they did keep the minds of many suffering people off their troubles. The sharecroppers had to have an outlet, and one enormous satisfaction was to have a man they thought their own in the governor's chair.

Flamboyant and colorful, Ferguson got into trouble because he did attack one institution of the state, the developing University of Texas at Austin. In 1915, he became embroiled with the University administration over appropriations. The argument developed personal animosity on both sides. Inevitably, there was hostility between any conservative official and the officers of any state-supported institution; this university-governor quarrel was common to many other places. Ferguson made an error; he tried to have the University president dismissed.

When the regents refused to do this, Ferguson vetoed the next university appropriation bill. This joined him in heated battle with virtually every lawyer, professional man, and Texas University alumnus in the state.

While this battle was emerging, meanwhile, the legislature had been investigating Ferguson's affairs. Certain things the governor had done did not appear in an entirely wholesome light. There apparently was some misuse of funds; state monies had been deposited to a bank in which Ferguson held stock; and most spectacular of all, it appeared that the governor had an unrepaid loan of $156,000 from the Texas Brewers' Association, contracted in 1914. There was, of course, no intention on either side that this "loan" be paid. Such things were a regular manifestation of American politics, which most candidates hoped would never see the light of day.

Significantly, the investigating committee recommended that no charges be brought, and the case against the governor pragmatically be dropped. No one wanted to "spit in the soup." Then, Ferguson began his vendetta against the university, and he angered many powerful men within the legislature. The charges were made public. The revelation that Ferguson had accepted a fortune from the "beer trust" paralyzed his horde of Baptist tenant-farmer allies. The University-educated lawyers in the legislature tore the governor apart.

In July, 1917, Ferguson was impeached by the Texas House on twenty-one counts; the state Senate upheld ten charges. The governor was dismissed from office, with the proviso that he never hold office in the state of Texas again.

In the cotton-farming democracy of the South, however, this would not deter James E. Ferguson for very long.

About the turn of the century, Texas moved strongly into national Democratic politics. Texas was becoming the largest habitually Democratic state, and the fusion with Populism by the national party had important effects. National officeholders, like Senators and Congressmen, could give the national alliance wholehearted support, even while the local party took a somewhat different course at home.

Thus, while the Democrats battled the People's Party in Texas tooth and nail, and trampled it under, fair means or foul, a long succession of representatives in Washington were free to take a definite neo-Populist tinge. The old-line conservatives like Roger Mills, who supported Cleveland— "both a Democrat *and* a gentleman"—were replaced with men like Culberson and Bailey. Bailey, who like Ferguson had personal affairs that could not bear inspection, soon foundered in controversy and was forced to retire. But Culberson, sent to the Senate in 1899, remained there twenty-four years. This was not to be an unusually long stay. A number of other Texans, such as Garner and Rayburn, were to reside there many more years. One-party politics, in which officials built personal, not party, machines kept the same men in national office interminably.

Texans gained great seniority in the Congress, an institution in which power largely depended upon seniority. Joseph Bailey was minority leader of the House before his elevation to the Senate, and a long succession of Texans followed as party leaders in each house. Others inevitably reached the vital committee chairs, where they could exercise real power, when the Democrats won control. One-party politics allowed Texas far more leverage than, for example, Illinois or New York, where the voters tended to be divided between two parties, and regularly threw one set of rascals out.

Bailey, in the House, advocated cheap money, regulation of Eastern capitalism, bedrock support of Old American institutions, and overseas belligerency. All these, in more or less degree, became the hallmarks of the Texan neo-Populist in national politics. Bailey was aggressive and influential in goading the McKinley Administration into a war in Cuba in 1898 that McKinley obviously did not want.

When this war came, Texans reacted very much with the old Southwestern belligerency, a feature of every U.S. war since 1812. The Texan response was enthusiastic. Ten thousand men enlisted immediately, and this fact brought a regiment recruited largely at San Antonio into national prominence. The Rough Riders, under the command of the regular army's greatest hero, Leonard Wood, gained a national reputation by charging up San Juan Hill on foot behind their lieutenant colonel, Theodore Roosevelt. Whatever the merits of their victory, this cowboy regiment made Theodore Roosevelt President in time. They engaged in a great triumphal parade in Washington, during which some of the more ebullient amused the audience by roping Negroes among the crowd. National sentiments and Texas feeling were in general confluence at this time.

The northern United States was strongly influenced by the ideas of social Darwinism, and this had much in common with the Texan unarticulated sense of natural selection on the frontier. Senator Beveridge of Indiana eulogized U. S. Grant in 1898: "He never forgot that we are a conquering race and that we must obey our blood and occupy new markets and, if necessary, new lands. He had the prophet's seer-like sight which beheld, as part of the Almighty's plan, the disappearance of debased civilizations and decaying races before the higher civilization of the nobler and more virile types of men."

With this the great majority of Texas could agree. Generals Grant and Sheridan had wiped out the bitter stains of the Civil War with their final Indian campaigns; in their last years they toured Texas as heroes, and by the turn of the century Texans again could wear bluecoats with pride. They also agreed solemnly with Admiral Alfred Thayer Mahan, who wrote: "Self-interest is not only a legitimate but a fundamental cause for national policy, one which needs no cloak of hypocrisy . . . Governments are corporations, and as corporations they have no souls."

The whole history of Anglo-Texas was a history of conquest of men and soil, and with the closing of the last frontier no such powerful thrust and impetus could merely die.

Those few Texans who played parts on the national scene entered fully into the spirit of the first premature American expansion overseas. They, and the Texas population behind them, exhibited those characteristics that some observers believed were true of Anglo-Americans: buoyancy, enthusiasm, exuberant idealism combined with a certain naïveté. But these supposedly characteristic American traits were surface manifestations masking deeper currents. The true, fundamental Anglo-American temper, whether Texan or Yankee, was something else. Bedrock seriousness of purpose, canny calculation, shrewd understanding of times and men, and implacable determination to surmount or destroy obstacles were much more deeply imbedded in the nature of the Anglo-American who conquered the continent.

Some Latin observers called American buoyancy and idealism "deliberate escapes on the plane of imagination." Americans, and Texans, preferred to take their apparent traits at face value; no people is easily able to recognize or face its real hypocrises. But running through the Texan people and their representatives on the national and international scene was the barebones realism of men who had learned profound distrust of all abstractions and ideologies, but who retained a deep respect for power and the uses of power. Thus Texans in Congress could indulge in hypocritical oratory on the floor without taking their expressed hypocrises seriously. This empiricism, and sense for the roots of power, made many Texans, naïve, ignorant, and parochial as they seemed, more than a match for many other men.

The Texan's thirst for empires was guileless and natural, his distrust for theories profound. In foreign affairs, this seemed to translate into belligerency, before and during the 20th century's wars. But Texans, instinctively, saw struggle at the root of life. Doctrines of quietism that influenced other American regions never penetrated the stark puritanism of Texas.

Grover Cleveland, the conservative Democrat, was eventually regarded in Texas as another hard-money Republican in Democrat disguise. Texans found Theodore Roosevelt, the first President to come from the gentry since early in the 19th century, much more palatable. Roosevelt thought and talked the Texans' language; he was West-seeing and imperial; only his Republicanism and his Eastern origin kept him from becoming a major hero in the state. It was significant that Roosevelt raised his volunteer regiment during the Spanish-American War mainly in the West, and made recruiting headquarters at San Antonio.

Theodore Roosevelt was a man of action, untrammeled by ideology in the best American tradition, but with an awakening social conscience. He understood that the rampant industrial machine that was making the United States a world power was also creating internal chaos. His greatness lay in his realization that the machine could not be turned off, nor the clock stopped, but that somehow events must be brought under control. In this appraisal Roosevelt appeared far superior in pragmatic realism to Woodrow Wilson, who always gave the impression he would have preferred to turn the clock back to preindustrial times.

Yet, since Wilson's heart and mind were closer to the hearts of Texans, Texas took Woodrow Wilson, with his genuine mistrust of capitalism much closer to its collective heart. The Southern-born President's speeches aroused deep, nostalgic pulls in the American middle-class breast. His protests echoed the protests of farmers forced into a new form of peasantry, and of small merchants losing out to powerful concentrations of energy and wealth. Beneath the Texan empiricism lay a reactionary mood. If Wilson did not quite see that the destruction of the America of small towns, corner drugstores, and family farms was inevitably in progress, neither did Texans. It was impossible to transmit a soul to corporate America; in 1912 Wilson could attempt to regulate it, or try to destroy it. Texans, in the majority, would have preferred the latter.

In 1912 the Texan delegation to the Democratic convention at Baltimore held out for Wilson, first and last. This support assured his nomination as the Presidential candidate, and Wilson never forgot it. Surprisingly, the strong Texan flavor of Wilson's Administration has sometimes been overlooked.

Albert Sidney Burleson became Postmaster General. W. T. Gregory, the central Texas political boss, was appointed Attorney General. David Houston, Texas-born, was Secretary of Agriculture, and Tom Love was Assistant Secretary of the Treasury. More important than any of these men, and the horde of lesser officials of Texan extraction Wilson brought to Washington, was Wilson's most trusted friend and confidant, the backroom politico Colonel E. M. House.

How much House influenced Wilson's thinking is not easily determined.

Yet, strong signs of Texan attitudes appear in Wilson's relations to Latin America. The Wilson Administration was eager to move into Haiti, Santo Domingo, and Mexico, either to uphold the flag, or "clean the places up." The Texan attitude toward Hispanic America, born out of long and unhappy experience with Mexico, was not essentially hostile; it was rather one of considered domination. Texas agreed vociferously with Theodore Roosevelt that "the contemptible little creatures in Bogotá" should not expect to deal on equal terms with the masters of the Hemisphere. Once domination and security were assured, the Texas—and generally, the American—attitude was one of amiable contempt.

Wilson's Administration exercised the North American prerogative vigorously, carrying on the Large Policy to the south. It also stirred up a generation of fear and hatred below the Rio Grande. It is certain that Colonel House saw nothing wrong in trying to end the European war by buying off Germany through offering it annexation of parts of Brazil.

Partly because of German machinations in Mexico in 1916, partly on general principles, Texas was ahead of the nation as a whole in belligerency in 1917. The support for Wilson's declaration of war was overwhelming. Volunteers came forward in huge numbers, and there was very little draft evasion—this, primarily, among ethnic Mexicans living near the Rio Grande. Almost 200,000 Texans served in the armed forces between 1917 and 1919. Because large areas of the state were well suited to military camps, with a mild climate and open territory, the war saw the emergence of important military camps in Texas. At Kelly Field, Texas became the home of United States military aviation. More than 5,000 Texans died in World War I, a full 10 percent of all combat casualties, and vastly more than the Texan share by population percentage.

The entire country mounted World War I as a great crusade rather than an empirical choice of violence in self-defense. The Texas reaction was not greatly different. Since 1900 Texas had increasingly fused back with the nation in foreign policy, especially when foreign policy was basically imperial—whatever name was put on it. Texans instinctively sustained anything that seemed to support American power and prestige. Both the domination of the banana republics and the destruction of Imperial Germany were parts of the same policy, blended of self-interest, self-defense, and an arrogant form of goodwill, that all through the 19th and early 20th century convinced most Texans that an American conquest of Mexico would be in that nation's own best interests. This drive, throughout the American, as well as the Texan, heartland, was more profound than many Americans in the essentially unimperial East ever understood. Men who would have left the Indians in possession of their lands, and Mexicans in possession of the Southwest, were not historically inclined to seek new adventures. Those who had in some part carried the American flag West did not metamorphose overnight when they had no new worlds to conquer on their shores.

In 1917, Texas fused with the American nation in a tremendous burst of

American-flag chauvinism, behind a government and President who spoke the Texan language even better than Theodore Roosevelt, that Westerner at heart. While the destruction of the Kaiser was enthusiastically pressed, the legislature made criticism of the flag, the government, its officers, its policies, and even the Yankee uniform a criminal offense. Here it followed the general government, which passed similar laws, in one great act of fusion. The legislature recommended that all books favorable to Germany or Germans be destroyed; study of the language was dropped in schools. There was a brief, but rather nasty, persecution of families with Germanic names, some of which were fifth-generation Americans out of 18th-century Appalachia. This extended to all foreigners in general.

The election codes were amended to stop voting by the foreign-born for the first time in Texas. Shortly following the war, the Constitution of the United States, and of Texas, was required to be taught in all schools, by teachers who were citizens, and English was made mandatory. Up to this time, Spanish had been permitted in most border schools. The same legislature wrote the "white primary" codes, which excluded Negroes from the Democratic Party by formal law. This was all part of a whole; Texans honestly believed that Negroes could never be effective citizens of the United States, though hope was still retained for ethnic Mexicans.

All crusades, from the Civil War to 1917, produced an aftermath of prejudice and frustration. While Attorney General Palmer hunted out Communists and anarchists from Washington, other forms of hysteria invaded Texas. In Texas, the national mood logically took a local coloration. About 1921, the Ku Klux Klan reappeared throughout most of the eastern portions of the state.

The 20th-century Klan had no real connection or historical root in the old one, though both movements were white-supremicist. The early Klan was a political group, formed only to try to control the black vote dragooned by the Radical Republicans. The revived Klan arrived out of Georgia, where it came to life in 1915. This new movement was much closer in form and spirit to the old Know-Nothing party, nativist, Protestant, and secretive. It merely borrowed the hoods and mysterious trappings of the 19th-century Klan, which had been adopted to terrify superstitious Negroes. The early Klansmen did not believe in this foofaraw, but hoped the blacks would.

The rise of such a movement was logical, particularly among the lower elements of American society. The massive immigration of the early century had been more than the country as a whole could gracefully absorb. The turn of the century notion of the melting pot was still in vogue, but it obviously was not working; all of the vast masses were no longer being Anglo-Americanized. The Republican-backed policy of encouraging labor immigration aroused deep suspicions and hostilities among native Americans. It was a logical outgrowth of these years that the labor movement took advantage of the prevailing mood to cut immigration down. If this was a tribal movement, some of its results were logical and perhaps, even necessary.

The 1917–1918 war suddenly made the nation aware of vast numbers of so-called hyphenated Americans. The disillusioning aftermath of the crusade, which did not and could not make the world safe for Anglo-American democracy, somehow sharpened resentment against all "foreigners." There were not many foreigners in Texas, but this did not prevent a great upsurge of the Klan in the rural areas, with much of the old Populist rhetoric against the Jews. Anti-Catholicism was strongly revived; and a natural, and not rhetorical, target was the Negro. The fundamentalist, Protestant-oriented Ku Klux Klan, however, had one other drive, which perhaps has not been given sufficient attention. It enlisted thousands of men who knew no Catholics and had rarely seen a Jew, because it stood for "law and order," and against corrupt officialdom. Of crime and corrupt officials Texas had its share.

By 1922 the Klan was deeply involved in local politics, and Klansmen had captured many local offices. In 1924, the organization opened a drive to win control of the state, with Felix Robertson of Dallas as its candidate for governor.

In these years the organization, mysterious, with secret membership, seemed to permeate the farms and towns from San Antonio to the Sabine. Reports of hooded men, riding by night, came from everywhere. The Ku Klux Klan—or men acting in its name, since the organization itself denied violence—took up another old American custom, vigilantism. Masked groups acted as prosecutor, judge, and jury toward people they did not like. In many communities, men and women were terrorized: criminals, real or supposed; people of supposedly loose morals; uppity niggers who strained the barriers of the caste system. Men and also women were dragged into the woods at night, tried by flaming torch light, flogged or otherwise punished. The victims of these courts were warned not to talk about them, and few did. Unlike the true vigilantism of earlier days, however, there were few leaders of society within the Klan. This made its aim of stopping crime untenable. There is no evidence that the mass persecutions of certain elements improved the air, as the mass hangings at San Antonio in the 1850's had; few, if any criminals were apprehended, and certainly no corrupt officials smelled out. Noticeably, a large number of various officers, including sheriffs, judiciously joined the Klan, though it is doubtful if many were active.

The effect on society was not very great. Those punished invariably came from the lowest dregs—waitresses, prostitutes, drifters, Negroes, Mexicans, halfwits. The Klan, through its organization, mystique, and anonymity, could move against these with relative impunity. It dared not move against anyone in the real power structure, corrupt or not. It could paralyze sheriffs through implied political threat, but it could in no way touch the so-called little rich, who were widely thought to be running local governments in Texas. In these groups, the Klan also aroused an immense hostility, both by its assault on law and order and by the obviously proletarian origin of its members. In its greatest era, the Klan was far less powerful than it was feared. Governor Pat Neff was hostile, and while some politicos tacitly let it be known they were members, a violent political reaction was at hand.

In this volatile, confused democracy, the next move was unexpected, but not illogical. James E. Ferguson smelled the wind, and scented an "issue." Ferguson was barred by the terms of his impeachment from ever again holding office in Texas, but barred from politics, he was a man in pain. He had formed the American Party, and had been its candidate for President in 1920; its fiasco at the polls convinced Ferguson to return to the Democrats. Showing an ingenuity that would later be remembered by men with similar problems of being barred from office by law, Ferguson entered his wife's name in the Democrat primary as an anti-Ku Klux Klan candidate. Mrs. Ferguson, in a bitter contest, wrested the primary away from Klan candidate Robertson by some 100,000 votes.

Things were completely confused in the general election of 1924, in which Ma Ferguson, as she was universally known, opposed George Butte, dean of the University of Texas law school, who ran as an independent candidate with liberal, Republican, and despite his dismay and disavowal, Klan support. The incongruous and unpopular mélange behind Butte ruined him, and Miriam Ferguson became the first woman governor of Texas.

Ma Ferguson provided the color the Ferguson type sought and had to have. She was news, merely by being in office. But Ferguson himself was the governor of Texas, in everything but name. He was appointed to the powerful highway commission, which let juicy contracts; he dominated the executive office from the bedroom. All this provoked criticism in responsible quarters, but in others it provided Texas with endless fun. It took the mind of the common man off his troubles. No small portion of Ma Ferguson's support came from people who consciously or unconsciously believed in cutting "the powers" down to size. Ma Ferguson, and her husband, focused much resentment among those people who equated commonalty with real democracy and professed to see social value in being "common as an old shoe."

The second Ferguson administration was not only conservative, it was legislatively inert. The Fergusons did not even fight the Klan. They did not need to, because, like the Know-Nothings, the Klan, simply faded away. All such movements seemed to follow a similar pattern; they made sound and fury and caused much fright; they had no real effect on society's mainstream. The woman governor was to be remembered primarily for one thing: the most extensive use of executive clemency in Texas history. Ma

Ferguson pardoned, furloughed, or otherwise freed 2,000 convicts in twenty months, in some cases before the individual even reached the penitentiary. Her husband, as she admitted, made these decisions. He was accused of corruption in this, as well as his letting of contracts through the highway commission. The state attorney general, Dan Moody, declared war on the Fergusons, and in 1926 entered the Democratic primary against the governor.

Moody defeated Mrs. Ferguson. At thirty-three, he was young, able, earnest, and reform-minded. Moody was a progressive who had made his reputation fighting the Klan in Williamson county. Like almost every serious-minded governor of Texas, he understood that the state constitution, with its separation and limitation of powers, was an enormous obstacle to public action. In office, Moody argued that the fact that all major state officers were independent of the governor was unworkable; he made what was to be a frequent demand: that the governor be permitted to appoint his own administration. He also asked for other reforms, including a civil service system for the state and changes to the constitution that would make tax bills easier to enact.

Moody was popular and had no trouble in winning two terms. But the legislature and the people ignored his recommendations; Texans like limited government. In referendum after referendum, the public showed that it refused to use the means of strengthening the state government even for generally approved ends. Texans kept their local governments much closer to the original American framework of 1789 than the nation, or most other states.

Moody, like the Fergusons, was a recurring type of governor. There was a certain pattern. The candidate whose campaign centered around a gimmick was followed by a more dignified man who promised better government. Hobby, who replaced Ferguson in 1917, called for a "new era." Pat Neff, following Hobby, declared the "New Democracy." Regardless of who was elected on what program, very little changed. The people liked fun and fury in political campaigns, but the forces gravitating against real change were massive. The "interests" could be blamed, and were, but the basic inertia lay in the genuine conservatism of the Texan race.

In prosperous times, there was almost no chance for any kind of political change. The 1920's were generally prosperous, although agriculture was still on very shaky ground. Low prices were offset by good harvests, however, and meanwhile, the automobile had begun to eliminate the distinction between town and farm. Texas was urbanizing, and the towns began to drain off some of the misery from the cotton fields. Instead of holding mass meetings, ruined farmers headed for town, where a developing economy could absorb them.

Richardson saw a pattern in the 1920's, which could actually be applied to the entire 20th century:

> Thus for business and industry the decade . . . did constitute a new era;
> but in politics and political institutions the historian finds little to dis-
> tinguish it from the years that preceded it. A few new government agencies
> were added, and some of the old ones were enlarged, but there was little
> suggestive of the "new era." . . . The political history of Texas is largely
> the story of governors who sought reforms which were in the main
> moderate and reasonable and generally needed, but which indifferent
> legislators and a still more indifferent electorate would not accept.

This *was* to be the political history of Texas through the first seven
decades of the century, though in many cases the word "hostile" should be
substituted for Richardson's use of "indifferent."

What happened was a continuing, almost explosive economic change, as
agriculture was continuously improved, more lands developed, and the
mineral resources of Texas discovered and extracted. This development,
which followed the pattern of all American history in the century, did not
cause great changes in the ethic or outlook of society. The farmer, with his
inherently urban 17th-century ethic, easily made the move to town, but he
did not become an urbanite in the European or even Eastern sense. Because of the peculiar form of industrialization in Texas, the fabric of
society barely changed. The old practice of gerrymandering kept the legislature under rural control. Economic reform did not mean social or psychological change; the Texan had little difficulty in remaining a 19th century man.

This did not and could not prevent constantly rising costs of local government, increasing bureaucratization, and demands for new services. Here
Texas was no different from the other American states. With the constant
economic changes began the long, tawdry cycle of constant financial crisis
in local government. This was nothing new. Needs rose faster than the
process of raising revenue could follow; also, government, as government
everywhere, showed the common tendency to expand under its own dy-
namism unless it were severely shocked, as in the restoration of 1874. The
trend was universal, in other states and in the general government. The
industrial states, with far greater sources of revenue to tap, simply spent
more money than Texas, and, with more social pressures to spend than
Texas, generally spent far more than they could afford. State governments
lacked the credit resources available to the federal apparatus, and were
also everywhere under much greater actual control by taxpayers and the
people than the distant federal giant.

As one governor of Texas stated, the practice at Austin was for the
legislature to vote expenditures in May, but refuse to raise the monies in
December. Summer appropriations were rarely accompanied by winter
taxes. Then, when financial crises were acute and could no longer be
avoided, new sources of revenue were painfully searched out. For several
decades, state expenditures were severely limited in Texas because the

brunt of all taxation still fell upon the land. No agrarian society with a dominant ballot power ever allowed itself to be taxed heavily.

Texas did change, in accordance with the general changes across the United States. All public services and administration were regularly improved. Prisons were reformed, old-age pensions instituted, welfare payments began. The "little red schoolhouse" began to disappear in the 1920's, and after 1930 school district consolidation was widespread. Public services of all kinds in Texas found a general level, considerably above that of the other states of the old Confederacy, but far below those of the industrialized regions. Public services were calculated to a grudging minimum in almost every case.

One great exception was roads. Transportation and access was a necessity in a state where the population was scattered across immense distances; at the start of the century some farmers had to haul cotton more than 100 miles to gins or markets. Towns and cities lay hundreds of miles apart. The automobile, in a very real sense, replaced the horse in both social function and symbology; Texas went from a horse culture to something resembling an automobile culture in one swoop. One public service Texas spent enormous sums of money for was roads; on this, rural and urban interests all agreed. Although the progress was hardly uniform— some Texas counties got their first paved roads in the 1940's—by the 1950's even the rural, farm-to-market roads in underpopulated areas were superior to most U.S. highways in the East.

Roads hastened economic improvements, urbanization, and school consolidation in almost every region of the state. Just as every poor farmer had owned a horse, every poor tenant living in a tarpaper shack in Texas owned some kind of car. The auto arrived before efficient public transportation—rails had always been limited and unprofitable in such a thinly populated expanse—and thus had far greater economic and social importance than in the more compact East. The auto expanded Texas horizons, and consolidated communities at the same time.

In 1928, two things of political interest occurred. This year, for the first time since 1860, national politics overshadowed local state campaigns. Local affairs had always absorbed Texan politics and passions more than the national scene, from Reconstruction through the Bryan-McKinley confrontation and beyond. The Populist-Democrat fight in 1896 and the prohibitionist-antiprohibitionist wars of the 20th century were more important to Texans than national policy. But the nomination of Alfred E. Smith of New York, a Roman Catholic, an Eastern conservative, and an avowed antiprohibitionist for the Presidency by the Democrat Party started reverberations through the heartland.

The rural belts were Southern and fervently Democratic in loyalty; Republican to most Texans was still a dirty, capitalist word. But Smith's Catholicism and views on liquor hit the loyal Democrat farmer where it hurt most. Governor Moody was able to hold the state party and most party officialdom to Smith, but he could not hold the voters from the "Constitutional Democrats," who were now defending the Constitutional provisions of prohibition. The three P's of Protestantism, prohibition, and prosperity combined to give Herbert Hoover, despite his Republican and business labels, a plurality of 26,000 votes. This same election sent another long-term Senator, Tom Connally, to the capital.

The immense crisis of capitalism that began in New York October 23, 1929, did not at first affect Texas. The real pinch only began in 1931, when the financial collapse engulfed central Europe, rebounding westward. European markets dried up; cotton fell from 18 cents a pound in 1928 to 5 cents in 1931. Texans descended with the whole nation into depression and economic chaos. But there were two very marked differences to the Great Depression experience in Texas compared with the industrial North and East.

The Depression was taken more calmly; there were few of the funks that affected businessmen elsewhere. Relatively few Texans owned corporate stocks or bonds; all of them had lived through excruciating commodity-price crises before. Texan morale and fundamental concepts of society were undamaged by 1929, because the majority of all Texans had never believed in Wall Street, or the capacity of the industrial machine to lead Americans to a better way of life. They faced no crisis or crossroads of capitalistic belief. The mass of Texans were still poor in 1928; they were more adapted to relative poverty than the American groups now hit the hardest. Since there was almost no industry, there could be none of the industrial unemployment and crushing fear that pervaded other regions. In fact, a striking phenomenon of this era was that more Texans remembered the disastrous drouth and dust storms of the 1930s than the Depression itself; the savage dry spell that once again gripped Texas and adjacent Plains states did more fundamental damage, and evicted more families from the soil, than the fiscal and financial crisis.

In 1930, Ross Sterling of Houston defeated Ma Ferguson for the Democratic nomination, although she led in the first primary by some 100,000 votes. Sterling campaigned for governor as a businessman candidate; he was a successful businessman who promised a businesslike administration. This did not prejudice him in Texas; success in business was admired, especially if the succeeder began poor. Always, the man who won success by personal enterprise, whether in ranching, farming, selling, or whatever, remained probably the most respected type in the state. Professionals were rarely, if ever, accorded the same respect.

But whatever Sterling's expertise, his administration was battered and swamped by the continuing collapse that no man, even the President of the United States, could halt. Farm prices, mineral production, and the infant industrialization of Texas, all stagnated. Demands for expenditures continued, and actually rose, while revenues fell; taxes in effect became almost uncollectable. Sterling had to veto measure after measure passed by the legislature, simply because the state treasury had no money and no prospects of raising any.

By 1932, economic discontent spilled strongly over into politics. Sterling tried for reelection, but this time the Fergusons sniffed the wind correctly. Ferguson again offered his wife for the governorship, with two often-quoted statements: "Two years ago you got the best governor money could buy; this year you have an opportunity to get the best governor patriotism can give you;" and "When Ma is governor, I'll be on hand picking up the chips and bringing in water for mama."

Despite violent efforts by Sterling, former governor Moody, and the Democratic establishment, Mrs. Ferguson won in the second primary by a few hundred votes out of a million cast.

Again, the Ferguson regime has been difficult for observers to evaluate. People reacted to "Fergusonism" emotionally; and in truth, the Fergusons kept real issues thoroughly confused. Miriam Ferguson went back to pardoning and paroling prisoners; the legislature, by and large, was hostile, and although regular appropriations were reduced about 20 percent, the financial crisis deepened. County governments were collapsing under relief costs and bonded indebtedness everywhere, and the state had to assume this burden. It was aggravated by the fact that the people demanded tax relief at the same time needs for public support became acute. By constitutional amendment, all homesteads were freed from taxation to the value of $3,000, which removed millions of dollars from state revenues. Provisions for a sales tax were emphatically turned down.

The problems were so crucial, in fact, that the Fergusons, for the first time in twenty years, withdrew from politics in 1934. James V. Allred, the more conservative candidate, defeated oilman Tom Hunter in the Democrat primary and became governor in 1935. Allred's program did not envision vicious taxation of the wealthy and the utility, oil, and chain store corporations that was in these times proposed. His problems would not have been solvable, except for the fact that, with the coming of Franklin Roosevelt's New Deal, Texas was able to transfer approximately 70 percent of its social costs to the Federal government.

There are strong indications that many outsider observers did not understand Texan attitudes and politics during the era of the New Deal. The New Deal proposed to regulate corporate capitalism, which was blamed for the general economic debacle that reached hideous proportions by early 1933. There were many Texas business interests opposed to Roosevelt's neo-Populism, but the great mass of people were miserable and certainly enthused. One thing must be remembered: Texans had no real love for corporate capitalism as it had grown up in the United States between 1862 and 1929. They believed strongly in private property and *personal* free enterprise, which were two somewhat different things. Roosevelt, like Wilson, appealed enormously to the farmers, and to the desperate middle class. His reform measures in no way destroyed the Texan's concept of American society. In fact, the strong bias of many theoretical New Dealers in Washington for the depressed agricultural areas of the nation permitted a joyous alliance. Texans, in office and out, had a long habit of accepting any Yankee dollar they could get.

These reforms, in general, greatly ameliorated the conditions of life for the depressed, though they did not end the great malaise nor alter the increasing social domination of the industrial way of life. In fact, although this was not immediately seen, the 1930's gave the growth of national corporations, both of labor and industry and government itself, a powerful push. It was inevitable, perhaps, that the national Democratic Party would move gradually from hostility to a live-and-let-live attitude toward corporate enterprise, and finally seek a tacit partnership, much as the state Democratic Party in Texas had already done. While the New Deal poured in outside money, and mounted no attack on private property or social organization in Texas, the homesteaders of Texas, large and small, were enthusiastic Democrats.

In this era, the influence of Texans in the capital increased, as it normally did with Democrat regimes. John Nance Garner, who had served in the House since 1903, became Speaker in 1931; he was Vice President through Roosevelt's first two terms. In the Senate, as presiding officer, Garner aided greatly in pushing many of the New Deal reforms, as did many other basic folk-conservatives from the South and West.

Jesse Jones, the Houston magnate, exercised much influence as chairman of the Reconstruction Finance Corporation, Administrator of the Federal Loan Agency, and Secretary of Commerce, in turn. By 1933 Texans held the chairs of a half dozen committees in the House: Agriculture, Interstate Commerce, Judiciary, Public Buildings and Grounds, Rivers and Harbors, and last but not least, Appropriations. In the Senate, Texan influence on military affairs and foreign relations was strong, through Sheppard and Connally. In general, these men continued the old tradition of the Texan in Washington: support for cheap money, regulation of Eastern capitalism, bedrock belief in all the 18th-century American social institutions, and when the occasion offered opportunity, overseas belligerency. Texans liked many New Deal measures, but, like Harry Truman of Missouri, they generally had a strong distaste for most New Dealers. The Texan distrusted the predominantly intellectual or theoretical man, out of ancestral memory, as they distrusted anyone who offered criticism of the conquering Anglo-American race. As a group, the Washington representatives were remarkably successful in one goal. They secured to their state, in various ways, money and appropriations far exceeding its population's proportionate share. One study showed that this, over a period of thirty years beginning in the 1930's, topped the national average by 27 percent.

The keen empiricism of most of these men, behind their sometimes folksy image, made them effective operators behind Congressional doors.

Every redneck from the cotton belt, and every Senator with a big hat and flowing locks, or dry, lean cowman in boots, was not stupid. Some men learned this to their sorrow. In the Texas caucuses, there was a general, if unspoken agreement: their state and region had gotten a dirty deal from most Americans since the Civil War. Garner, Rayburn, and Lyndon Johnson all felt this keenly, as insiders knew. But since the War, Texas leadership had learned not to show it.

The coming of crisis in Europe in 1939 showed that President Roosevelt's cautious policy of American commitment enjoyed huge support in Texas. Texas sentiment, generally, called for more than the President's careful interventionism. Some of this could be, and was, explained by the fact that Texas was more aware of its European markets than other areas. But even this fell short, because as both *Fortune* and Gallup polls showed, Texans were the most belligerent people in the United States toward Germany and Japan. Texan interventionism far outran even that of the South.

Nor was Anglophilia a reason. This was more a phenomenon of the Atlantic states. Texans had little sense of British origin; their ancestors had hated Britain worse than most Americans, for its aristocracy, its corruption, its culture, and its Indian-arming policies in the War of 1812. New York contained more true Anglophiles than all of Texas, but New York was the least belligerent region in America, despite its keen awareness of Atlantic civilization.

The crisis of world democratic states in the 1930's and early 1940's—their inability to react to totalitarian aggression effectively—was simply not reflected in Texas. Instinctively, apparently, Texans sensed Nazi Germany as an enemy, and once the enemy was defined, they believed it should be destroyed. The ideology of Nazism had little effect on this belief; any ideology carried by a power obviously hostile to the interests of the United States would have been, and was, hated without much evaluation. Texans hated the Soviet Union as much as Nazi Germany, which, to their own surprise, caused some observers to deem them fascists. But their reaction was no more fascistic than the belligerence of the Southwest in 1812, or the reaction of Texans at the onset of the Mexican and Civil wars. Unpalatable as it might be to some Americans, had Texas directed policy between the wars, Adolf Hitler would have arrived at Valhalla earlier.

A barbarian awareness of true danger can be an asset to any society, as well as a barbarian willingness to believe that straight action, not interminable moral confusion, is sometimes required. A majority of all classes in Texas believed that eventually Hitler must be destroyed. They held the same hot anger, yet cold clear awareness toward the defiance of Japan. In a very real sense, contemptible little men in Berlin and Tokyo replaced those earlier "contemptible" figures in Mexico and Bogotá. Texas attitudes refuted those who insisted that ideology rather than instinct lay behind human wars.

Many Texans, in 1941, writhed at what they considered the cowardice of their nation as a whole. There is no evidence that Texans liked war; there is evidence that they had apparently much less fear of it than was held in other places. They never shared the agony of many liberal Americans, who realized Hitler was a menace, but who hoped there was some way to get rid of him short of killing him. Long before the war came out of the sun at Pearl Harbor, Texans were enlisting in the armed services, and a significant number had gone to Canada.

The air service was popular, because Texas, with a clear-skied climate, was its training center. However, an entirely disproportionate number of Texans enlisted in the U.S. Marines; men from the brushlands exceeded the proportion population-wise from the eastern maritime states. Texans tended to be combative. In the war years, Texan casualties were the clearest indication.

Texas held 5 percent of the U.S. population; it provided 7 percent of the total armed forces; and its war dead exceeded 7 percent of the total killed in action.

Texas was the army's largest training ground, training 20 combat divisions between 1940 and 1944. Other facts probably had no real significance, but hardly went against the trend:

A cotton farmer from Farmersville named Audie Murphy gained more combat awards in World War II than any other man in the U.S. Army; Sam Dealey, another Texan, was the Navy's most decorated man. There were still Anglo-Celts seeking a far war frontier. A Texan from German Fredericksburg, Chester Nimitz, commanded the U.S. Pacific Fleet. A Texan-born general, raised in Kansas but still a product of the inner American frontier, held the Supreme Allied Command in Europe.

Following this massive outpouring of belligerence, the evidence shows clearly, in private reactions and opinion polls, that Texans as a people heartily disapproved the long picketing of Nazi Germany's ruins, as well as the determination to democratize Japan. The notions behind the Nuremberg trials had small currency in Texas. Texans neither understood nor approved Hitler's bloody rancor against the Jews, which was subtly different from their own determination to subordinate internal groups considered inferior. The Texan attitude toward colored races, probably, was closer to the Nazi view of eastern Europeans, who seemed to provide a ready-made laboring mass. Anti-Semitism was far less a Texan than a Northern American trait, which, much evidence shows, was given impetus by European immigration. No mobs in Texas ever attacked a Jew; few, if any, clubs, ever blackballed an otherwise qualified Jewish applicant. New York and Chicago could not say the same. The Texas violence toward blacks, which at times could be very violent, was provoked and condoned not by any desire to wipe Negroes off the earth but to keep them conquered and in their appointed place. Anti-Semitism, historically, often was provoked by a very real superiority, in certain things, shown by Jews, as well as the obvious religious intolerance of many ages.

The Texan attitude was that armed Germans had been dangerous; they needed to be, and had been, removed. So long as they stayed conquered, or amiable, there was no need to punish them. Privately, a number of Texans stated that the Germans had only carried certain basic, recurrent drives to disgusting extremes; moralizing over it—although few Texans could articulate or rationalize their feelings—produced a somewhat incoherent disgust. The Germans had tried to conquer the world, and got their heads kicked in by better men. Maybe they would learn.

The specter of Jewish genocide, which haunted many other people, never impinged strongly on the Texan mind. It had not much more relevance to Texas society than the once-famed Armenian massacres by the Turks. Thus the Texan was more ready to go to war, but quicker to drop its aftermath than some Americans. As for reshaping Germany and picketing its ruins, this disturbed uncomfortable ancestral memories. A great many American Southerners, including Lucius Clay, expressed similar doubts, born of handed-down family tales, during Germany's reconstruction.

The South had committed its own horrendous crime of losing a war.

In the late 1930's, the love affair between the intellectuals of the New Deal and Texas leadership began to wane. So long as the New Deal poured money into Texas and punished capitalists according to neo-Populist biases, all folk-conservatives, from Texans to Harry Truman, could approve. This was functional liberalism most Texans had wanted for a long time. But reforms beyond the ones grasped in the pain of the worst Depression years were not desired. Anything that suggested a broad movement of the parameters of American social institutions drew immediate hostility and fear. John Nance Garner, the Westerner from Uvalde County, became disillusioned with FDR, long before Roosevelt aborted Garner's own drive for the Presidency in 1940. Just as Cleveland's policies appalled Texan officeholders in 1892, Roosevelt's later proposals were anathema, and the national and state Democratic Parties began to separate. Texans joined in the Republican-Southern Democrat Congressional coalition that formed in 1938. This Texas trend was not confirmed until 1944. That year, with Northern Democratic approval, the Supreme Court struck down Texas' white primary law. Increasing prosperity, which flooded all America during the war years and increasing interest in the North to dabble in social, rather than economic reform, split the state Democratic Party when Roosevelt was renominated in 1944. Smarting over the *Smith v. Allwright* decision, and Garner's aborted candidacy for President in 1940, the Conservatives (as they now came to be called) organized the "Texas Regulars." The state party convention split between "conservatives" and "liberals" in 1944. From this time forward, there were to be two Democratic parties within Texas. One was a nationally oriented party, which loyally supported the national Democrat aims. The other loyally supported the desires of the majority within the state and normally won major offices and power.

Each fought the other bitterly in the summer primaries, but usually fused in November of general election years to assure continued Democratic patronage control.

The delegations in Washington had to step warily between these factions, now voting money bills that pleased everyone, now filibustering racial legislation or other bills that clearly appalled the majority vote.

In Texas, the most conservative candidate, Allred, again won the governorship in 1936, advocating greater pensions but equally avoiding calling for new taxes. The legislature's penchant for approving new expenditures while hanging back on revenue bills did not change. Allred's last term expired in a legislative logjam and fiscal crisis.

Inevitably, color returned in the race of 1938. The Fergusons were passé, but a new hero was on the horizon. In a thirteen-man first primary —multiple candidacies were normal in one-party states—W. Lee O'Daniel of Fort Worth came in first, polling more than half the votes. O'Daniel, a flour merchant who sold by radio, had discovered a substitute for promises to tenant farmers: playing country music over the air waves. Despite anguished howls that he sold politics like flour, O'Daniel reached more people than all the other candidates combined. O'Daniel's major program was borrowed from similar candidates in other states, a variable of the popular ham-and-eggs plan, by which every aged person would receive a state pension.

In office, O'Daniel dropped the bait and switched. The proposal was watered down, to offer pensions only to needy old folks over sixty-five, and then only enough to raise their income from all sources to $30 per month. But even to put this through O'Daniel had to propose a sales tax, which, though it had a different name, was recognized all the same. In the end, pensions were voted, but the legislature destroyed all revenue bills. O'Daniel, like every Texas governor, wallowed in vetoes and increasing red ink, adding more than $5,000,000 to the deficit in the general fund.

However, in 1940 he won again, largely because he had never stopped his regular homey broadcasts to the people of the state. O'Daniel was better known than any other politician. Also, the pension issue had become so popular that no candidate, even those who opposed it privately, dared attack it from the stump. Pappy O'Daniel promised more, and he was over-whelmingly reelected.

The new legislature faced a financial brink; unless some money were raised Texas would lose its federal welfare funds through not providing its matching share. After much controversy, the burden was at last—as had been earlier proposed—shifted heavily onto gas and oil. Taxes were also placed on tobacco and alcohol. This trend produced the wry joke in later years that a citizen who neither smoked nor drank nor drove a car was unpatriotic; he did not support his state.

Morris Sheppard died, creating a Senate vacancy in 1941. When the interim appointee, Andrew Jackson Houston, the eighty-seven-year-old son of the hero of San Jacinto also died, Pappy O'Daniel chose to run for this vacancy himself. He entered confidently, but Texans' fancy for the flamboyant had about expired. O'Daniel defeated a serious-minded young candidate, Congressman Lyndon Johnson, by only a few hundred votes. His prestige suffered, and although the next year he beat Allred and Dan Moody for the full term, his influence was on the wane. It was said widely that the Establishment supported Pappy O'Daniel for the Senate simply to get him out of the state.

Coke Stevenson, the lieutenant governor who moved up to O'Daniel's office in 1941, was a deeply conservative man. When war came, Stevenson was able to lever important reductions in spending as a patriotic measure. Rigid economies were enforced in all departments. Appropriations for most state agencies, including the University system, were substantially cut. A no-strike covenant was secured from labor, which prevented stoppages during the war. These measures, coupled with the boundless demand for Texas raw materials caused by the war, swelled the treasury. Texas produced half the nation's gas and oil, much of its cotton and food, while family incomes rose by an average of one third.

Coke Stevenson retained popularity at home by feuding with the Federal rationing program. Distribution, more than actual shortage, caused unbalanced supplies of gasoline and beef in the East; Stevenson, and most Texans, saw no valid reason why they, in a region awash with refined petroleum and overrun with cattle, should share the distant Yankee woes. After a near-confrontation, when federal agents took note of thousands of automobiles parked outside football games and Stevenson hinted he might turn the Rangers loose on every federal snoop in the state, the matter was nicely compromised. The gasoline problem—the auto was no longer a luxury but a necessity to the Texas way of life—was solved by tacitly permitting local ration boards to issue every rural family car a higher priority card. This was not as selfish as it sounded to the East; the federal guidelines of three gallons per week for nonfarm or nonbusiness autos hardly got the average housewife to and from the grocery store, and throughout most of Texas, there was no effective public transport, even in the towns.

The rationing of meat, sugar, and other items was solved in a purely local way in many areas. Most Mexicans and Negroes were unaccustomed to consuming the allotted share, or could not afford it, and thousands of rural white families were able to take advantage of these cards.

By 1945, Texas had not only paid off $42,000,000 in arrears, but was enjoying a surplus for the first time in memory. This surplus, as anywhere in America, immediately produced a desire to spend. The minimal payments offered by various state agencies were increased substantially. Unfortunately, inflation soon wiped out these gains, and the old round of deep-in-debt began again.

Stevenson turned his office over to an approved successor, Buford Jester, in 1946. The election of 1946 brought the governorship into contention between the Texas liberals and conservatives for the first time. Homer Rainey, who had been dismissed as president of the state university after a violent quarrel with the conservative regents, took his case to the people. Jester won, with the support of the "regular" or now anti-Truman party.

Jester, more a moderate than a real conservative, had a considerable taste for new spending bills. Unlike his predecessors, he vetoed little, and in his first term many appropriations doubled. Happily, inflation and increased prosperity continued to swell state revenues even faster, and much progress with hospitals and schools was made. Some money was found by tapping the now defunct Confederate veterans' pension funds, taking advantage of an already existing tax. Jester's regime, however, was most noted for the eleven labor laws the legislature enacted in 1947. This followed a national pattern and mood, which, more than the industrial states, Texas was able to exploit.

O'Daniel had reacted sharply to the labor unrest that spread across the nation during the great industrial expansion and retooling of 1940–1941. In Texas, there was not much of this militancy, which was more for union recognition than for wages at the time. The Texas mood, highly belligerent and patriotic, did not support this wave of strikes. O'Daniel called for, and got, a law making it a penitentiary offense to commit any act of violence while on strike.

In the 1947 spate, which followed the 1946 spate of Northern walkouts, Texas forbade the check-off of union dues, made it unlawful to require union membership of employees, or conduct secondary strikes, picketing, or boycotts. Picketing of utilities was outlawed, and unions were brought under the antitrust laws. The law also abolished strikes by public servants and restricted picketing severely: no mass picketing, no picketing on private property, and pickets must maintain a set distance between themselves. These codes prevented the legalized violence their absence allowed in many other states. In 1951, they were strengthened further, to close loopholes that Northern corporations with plants in Texas had relied on to allow the closed shop.

The 1947 laws were bitterly attacked by organized labor leaders as destructive of all progress. The evidence is clear that they did two things: they had little effect on prices, incomes, or wages, except these rose as industrialization was given new impetus; they made organized labor much more active in state politics.

Jester, through careful footwork, kept the state party from splitting during Truman's race with Dewey in 1948. The majority was anti-Truman, but the Republican Dewey offered nothing, in either image or program, that any substantial number of Texans admired. The Dixiecrat candidate carried one county, Houston's Harris, the biggest metropolitan area in the state. No one ever discovered exactly what this signified.

The same year saw a primary election that was later fraught with national importance. Former governor Stevenson opposed Congressman

Lyndon Johnson for Pappy O'Daniel's Senate seat. O'Daniel, who found his broadcasts from Washington ineffective, chose not to stand. Both candidates were conservatives; both had important support from various interests throughout the state. In an acrimonious campaign, each man tried to prove he was more conservative than the other. In the end, personal spite settled the contest. A south Texas political boss switched his controlled Mexican vote from Stevenson to Johnson, who won by a delayed report from the famous "Box 13." This vote was probably manufactured. The U.S. Senate, with a certain wisdom, refused to interfere, and a federal court gave the race to Johnson by eighty-odd votes. There was probably no injustice involved. As in most close races in Texas, Johnson men had not *defrauded* Stevenson, but successfully *outfrauded* him. In office, Johnson healed the breach somewhat by gathering the Stevenson interests into his own camp.

Jester died in office, and Allan Shivers succeeded. Shivers' administration was marked by the continual tug of war between expenditures and income. Shivers, a pragmatic, somewhat enigmatic conservative, had a taste for politics his wealthy wife did not share. Possibly because of this, Shivers did not seek the national offices he might have had.

The national Democratic choice for the Presidency in 1952 finally brought the smoldering liberal-conservative feud into the open. Truman was already in trouble in Texas. His policy of limited war in Korea smacked to many Texans of Grant's early handling of the Indians. More important politically, Truman dismayed every officeholder in Texas by his veto of the Congressional tidelands bill. This bill would have given Texas title to the mineral deposits along the Gulf marginal shores, which Texas claimed out to ten and a half miles, using Spanish law. The Supreme Court in 1950 had declared the federal government had paramount right and power over this region, which Texas had already leased for $10,000,000 in bonus revenues. The Congressional action to overturn the Court was not sustained over veto.

Despite pleas, Adlai Stevenson showed no sympathy with the Texas claims. Shivers, as party chief, denied the Illinois governor his support. This caused the loyalist Democrats to bolt—but they had nowhere to go, since Shivers kept complete control.

If Dewey's image was unappealing, Stevenson's was appalling. He seemed to carry liberalism far beyond the functional limits of a Roosevelt or Truman. Whatever he stood for, it was something that to most Texans was suspect. When Eisenhower declared for state ownership of the tidelands, Shivers threw the party organization over to him, by letting every local Democrat do as he pleased. Shivers was easily reelected; Price Daniel, by declaring against everything Truman had ever done and Stevenson proposed to do, drove Tom Connally out of the Senate race and defeated the moderate Lindley Beckworth for Connally's seat. The "Democrats for

Eisenhower" raised more money for the Republican candidate in Texas than the Republican organization itself. Stevenson posters and propaganda, sent into the state, gathered dust in warehouses. Eisenhower, the first Texas-born President, carried the state by 100,000 votes. During the 1950's the division between the Democrats deepened. The so-called liberal, or loyalist wing, was composed of organized labor, ethnic Mexican, Negro, and other elements that regularly favored the policies and imperatives of the Northern Democrats. The conservative wing, much larger, represented most financial and business interests, and the great bulk of the middle class. It was socially conservative, states-rightist, and in the broadest terms, antigovernment. It continued to be better financed and organized. It retained control, though only with bitter party in-fighting.

Frustrated over thirty years, the liberal faction of the Democrats tended to become more and more illiberal in pronouncements and attitudes, and to look more and more to the federal government for support than to the people.

During the Eisenhower years, a small, rather patrician native Republican leadership emerged in the cities. Republicanism gained a respectability it had not enjoyed since the demise of the conservative Republicans, although the party itself remained small. A majority of conservative Democrats might vote for the national Republican ticket, as they did in 1952 and 1956, but, in local control, this same majority felt the one-party system adequately served their needs. Republicans contested few local races, and won even fewer, but there was a steady, noticeable growth, fed by the continually unpopular policies of the nationally dominant Northern Democrats.

A feature of Texan politics became the fusion of Republicans and conservative Democrats in the Democratic primaries, which frequently defeated the liberal faction even in its own strongholds. Then, in November, the nominees of the victorious conservative wing usually played effectively upon partisan loyalty and drew the liberal vote against Republican candidates. By pulling Republicans into the Democratic primaries—where the action was—and by holding the liberal vote in the fall, Texas conservatives kept both factions whipsawed. Both minorities knew what was happening to them, but found it impossible to ally; a great weakness of the liberal Democrats and conservative Republicans in Texas was that both tended to be more ideological than practical; they preferred programs to power, and thus surrendered both to the ruling faction.

If there was any single trend in the entire period following World War II, it was that Texas, despite drouth and oil gluts, grew increasingly more prosperous. The middle-income groups grew richer, though there was relatively no gain or much social mobility among the underclasses after 1944, following a national pattern. This was directly reflected in politics in two ways: the dominant electorate grew increasingly more conservative as a whole (though less virulent on racial matters, thus separating from the Old

Confederacy) while the protests of the minority grew more bitter and strident.

In 1952 and 1954, Allan Shivers, the conservative Democrat, easily defeated the liberal Ralph Yarborough in the governor's race. In 1956, the labor-liberal faction mounted a great show of power and actually won control of the state Democratic convention through a heavy attendance of its members at precinct and county party conventions. This was a hollow victory; the liberals could not consummate it at the polls; Shivers and the Democrats for Eisenhower swept Texas with twice the margin of 1952. Again and again the conservatives displayed better organization. Shivers, and afterward, John Connally, were able to build firm power bases among the heavily Mexican and largely impoverished counties in south Texas.

Patterns of fiscal irresponsibility continued. The conservative Texas Democrat was no Whig or Republican in his attitudes toward money; the legislature kept on voting money bills but refusing to tax. This of course was now a strong national pattern; every state was fiscally bankrupt, or nearly so. In Texas public needs continued to be met, but barely; government proceeded to grow larger, but slowly. In per-capita public expenditures Texas ranked in the bottom tier of states. Taxes did remain comparatively low.

Political corruption apparently increased in the 1950's. During the investigation of a spate of insurance company failures, the legislature uncovered the fact that nine state senators were in some way on the payroll of insurance corporations. Regulation and audits of such corporations had been lax. This pattern was not new; it had prevailed since the last century, because Texas politics had remained essentially 19th-century politics. Texas had no conflict-of-interest code; lobbying and the bribery of state legislators were carried on almost openly both at Austin and in their home districts.

In the public furor spawned by the collapse of insurance companies, one legislator was convicted of accepting bribes. The state land commissioner, a nine-term veteran, was sent to the penitentiary. In all, 300 indictments were returned. However, when the furor ended, there had been no real reform.

The legislature adamantly refused to pass lobby-control bills, or to effect any kind of scrutiny of state officials' personal financial affairs. The legislature did vote itself a substantial pay-raise, using the argument that this made members less susceptible to corruption. This pattern was hardly Texan; the United States Congress set an impressive example along these lines.

Price Daniel, a conservative who showed some demagogic traits, defeated Yarborough for the governorship in 1956. The next year, however, Yarborough, in a sweepstakes race, gathered some 37 percent of the total vote and captured Daniel's vacated Senate seat. A conservative Democrat and a Republican divided two-thirds of the vote. Belatedly, the legislature outlawed sweepstakes races, just as, because of the abuses of the Fergusons, Texas eventually took the pardoning power out of the govenor's hands and gave it to a commission. Daniel was forced to preside over the imposition of a limited sales tax; this, and the fact that he made a fatal error in denouncing the insurance industry over settlement of claims following the hurricane of 1961, led to his downfall. He was replaced by John Connally, a conservative of the Johnson camp in 1963. Connally, like Shivers, was fairly young, handsome, intelligent, and pressed for reasonable reforms. He was to enjoy the same limited success. Requests for such measures as modernizing Texas' higher education to meet the needs of an industrial society, and liberalizing of liquor laws to permit the sale of liquor by the drink, languished. The legislature voted new expenditures, but put off adding revenues until actual crisis ensued.

The selection of Lyndon B. Johnson as John F. Kennedy's runningmate in 1960 blurred the partisan and the liberal-conservative picture. The state party remained under conservative control; Connally, though in moderate terms, denounced most of Kennedy's liberal programs. Meanwhile, because of Johnson's presence, the state party supported the national ticket in 1960. Although a majority of white voters favored Nixon, the Republican, Kennedy and Johnson carried the state by a marginal 46,000 votes, out of 2,000,000 cast. The law had been changed to permit Johnson to run for both the Vice Presidency and his Senate seat; Johnson ran far ahead of the national ticket. Perhaps significantly, a very conservative Republican took Johnson's vacated seat in a special election of 1961.

The confusion between national and local partisan politics had created a situation in which both Texas' Senators were political sports, representing minority factions in the state. Both, however, in true Texas fashion, were able to build and hold personal coalitions of power, and win reelection.

One pattern was not clearly seen outside the state. Kennedy's Catholicism and liberalism did not damage him in traditional, Southern Democrat sections of the state. McLennan County on the Brazos, which was dry and had a Baptist majority, went heavily, like most such regions, for the Easterner. Kennedy most disturbed the increasing urban middle class. After his election, considerable numbers of former Democrats went over to the Republicans. This trend was stemmed, but not entirely stopped, by Johnson's candidacy and Connally's skill and hero status (he was almost killed with Kennedy at Dallas). With changing economies, shifting populations, and new problems, politics became more volatile, with rapidly shifting alliances, and much erosion of former partisan loyalties. This was akin to similar reactions everywhere in the nation. In Texas, however, the swing was more to conservative than to Republican party politics.

Some broad patterns did not change. The relative vote in most Texas communities was always small; less than half the qualified voters normally cast a ballot even in national elections. In local races, small blocs prevailed. Even after the abolition of the poll tax by federal action, voting registration increased very little. The dominant wing of the Democrats, with Republican and general approval, took pragmatic steps to keep the electorate small. Registration for voting in November was cut off in January. Political apathy was apparent in the large ethnic blocs, and few politicos of the major party wanted to arouse it.

A major factor in this trend was the fact that the Texas government was limited in its powers, and politics simply did not impinge heavily on private life. The successful officeholder, from James Hogg on, followed a remarkably similar pattern. He had to attract voter attention among various factions with campaign promises and oratory, but at the same time arouse no deep uneasiness among any powerful economic interests or pressure groups within the state. This caused considerable color, action, and even at times violence during campaigns, but the fight was decided more often on personalities than policies. Politics was more a game of seeking office than pushing programs. No matter who was elected, few real changes came about. All candidates, for example, might promise to raise teacher salaries (Texas in 1968 ranked about 34th in the nation in public school pay scales) but such promises did not usually count once the polls closed. Gubernatorial candidates were free with pledges, secure in the knowledge that the legislature would never let most of them be kept.

Texas politicians, great and small, fitted a broad pattern. There was an utter lack of anything approaching a genteel tradition in Texas politics after the turn of the century. The vast majority of officeholders and office-seekers needed the pay or emoluments of the office; those who did not were invariably self-made men who never ceased bragging about it. Politicians were expected to work their way up the ladder of public service through succeeding elections. The image of the poor boy who made good comforted the ethic and outlook of the dominant middle class. The vulgarization of politics that persisted was illustrated by an incident during one election in the 1960's in San Antonio's Bexar County. When one faction was able to show that all of the members of an opposing slate lived in one elite section of the city, both sides, probably correctly, believed that the revelation had a decisive, deleterious effect.

The Texas officeholder tried to avoid elegance of any kind, along with intellectuality, out of necessity. He generally closely followed the imperatives of powerful interests and catered to the biases of his electorate. He was realistic; he could adjust. Lyndon Johnson was a prime example, but far from the only one.

Johnson was first elected to Congress from an impoverished, hard-scrabble hill country district in the 1930's. Socially conservative, his people still wanted every dam, credit, subsidy, and stray Yankee dollar they could get. Johnson therefore was neo-Populist and New Deal; he cultivated President Roosevelt with general approval. FDR's endorsement, however, could not gain him office in his first try for the Senate. He succeeded in this only after he had convinced many Texans he was actually a deeply pragmatic conservative.

In the Senate, Johnson rode with increasing prosperity and increasing Texan conservatism. He ably represented the anti-Negro attitudes of east Texas, and skillfully defended the oil and mineral interests. His remarkable cloakroom ability, the force, energy, and empiricism that made him perhaps the most effective Senate majority leader in history, were only fringe benefits to his electorate; they enjoyed his prominence and power, and the more he gained, the more he could do and did for the state. But leaping to the national stage as Kennedy's Vice President, Johnson instinctively sensed and followed the imperatives of the national Democratic Party, catering to his broadened electorate, while holding his old contacts and alliances so far as possible. An enormously effective President at first, his failures would probably be attributed by history less to his mistakes than to his style. Johnson did things for people, but the Presidential image, in the national mind, required more. Most of the very traits that made him a superb Texas Senator hampered him in the White House. "Something for everyone," an utter lack of ideology, and the judicious use of power behind the scenes was excellent Texas politics. But Johnson's whole stance smacked of chicanery to many Americans; his instinctive Texan approach to world power politics involved him in world problems beyond his depth.

It was felt and resented deeply by many Texans of both parties that the Texan President who had secured more far-reaching legislation than any Chief Executive since Roosevelt, was forced to step down because of his Texan style. He was part of a pattern many elements across the nation distrusted or despised.

This pattern in no way changed or damaged the essential interests of Texas society or the nation. Historically, it had one flaw. The Texas system threw up men who instinctively could make the correct political decision, but only rarely a great moral decision. In Texas politics, gaudy as they seemed, there were ethics, but morality really had no place.

Twentieth century Texas, like 20th century America, was primarily concerned with economic development. There were enormous economic changes, but little true history was made. The changes in Texas, as in the nation, were so rapid and so pervasive that they escaped perfect definition. The only major differences between Texas and the majority of other states were that, in Texas, the development seemed more explosive because it started late, and such industrialization as occurred took peculiarly regional forms.

The automobile accelerated urbanization by obviating the distance between farm and town. Most farmers always preferred to live in town if they could. The urbanization, however, did not create manufacturing on the Northern scale. Heavy industry was not feasible in Texas because of a basic lack of water, coal, and iron. Remoteness and transportation problems hampered the growth of light industry. The truly spectacular development (which many Texans mistakenly called "industrialization") was the exploitation of Texas' enormously rich natural resources of lumber, mineral earths, aluminum, petroleum, and, as always, land.

Large lumbering concerns rose in the eastern pine woods. These followed the national pattern by first ravaging the timber, then, gradually, beginning to use conservation practices in their own interests. This industry was purely exploitive, as were the new businesses that blossomed wherever oil, natural gas, sulfur, and an assortment of rare earths were uncovered.

Extensive agriculture in west Texas, on the Plains and in the south near the Rio Grande, came only in the 20th century. These regions could only be farmed profitably after new techniques had been developed. The basic, small-farm agriculture of the cotton-growing heartland could not survive in the south and west; it took the invention of new crops, such as hardy grains, and new heavy machinery to exploit these regions. Ranchers began the basic experiments before the turn of the century; after 1900 many ranchers began to sell off large tracts for developments other than cattle-raising. The trend was led by, but not confined to, Eastern or British owners who were determined to refute the notion that this land was suitable only for grazing.

Tractors, disc plows, steam-powered brush-clearing equipment, and giant combines and harvesters, all products of the 20th century, permitted the last land rush on the old frontier. Grain sorghums were discovered that would grow where the over-grazed buffalo grass once grew. The red North Central Plains were proved suitable for wheat, and the South Plains, once extensive irrigation and fertilization techniques were employed, were the best cotton lands in the state. Parts of Northwest Texas began to resemble Kansas in their economy; the strongholds of the North American cattle kingdom, where fences had once been planted only with bloodshed, were to become the major cotton-growing counties in the United States, surpassing the Mississippi delta.

Rails reached far south Texas, arriving at Brownsville in 1904. The remote birthplace of the cattle empire was opened to settlers and development for the first time; the old merchants who had made fortunes supplying the army and trading with Mexico were gone; new kinds of men arrived. The old families sold much of their vast land grants to land companies whose executives talked of irrigation and drainage schemes. With new machinery, immense networks of canals were dug, bringing water to areas miles away from the Rio Grande. Soon orchards of citrus fruits, vegetable farms, and cotton plantations drove the dark, lean Mexican cattle out of what was now called the Magic Valley.

By the third decade of the century, thousands of Texans, Midwesterners, and many Northerners were engaged in developing huge acreages in south and west Texas. The cattle kingdom was pushed back to the truly marginal regions—which still were immense in the state. New uses, such as the raising of sheep and goats, were found for lands too poor to run cows.

In these newly developed areas the pattern of Texan society changed radically. They required a different form of pioneer. Few, if any, share-croppers or tenant farmers could emigrate to the Rio Grande Valley or to the wheatlands of the Panhandle. Land costs, because of the required development investment, were high; large acreages were necessary and the rule, and large acreages required some mechanization. The new settler-farmer had to have capital, in the form of money. In the south, a further trend discouraged the tenant farmer; the new capitalistic agriculturists needed cheap stoop labor, and deliberately began to import workers from Mexico. The new farming regions of the north-northwest and the Rio Grande delta, together with the Southern Plains, saw the first revival of capitalistic agriculture in Texas since the Civil War. Inevitably, these regions were to produce the major part of Texas' cash crops during the century.

Despite the cattlemen's fears, the spread of cotton south and west on newly irrigated farmlands did not bring Negroes. It brought farm machinery and Mexicans. In the northwest, where machinery predominated, the country began to resemble other regions of the American Midwest in appearance and economy; while along the Rio Grande, a great many of the earlier Spanish patterns remained, side by side with an economy resembling the corporate farms of California. Baronial beef empires gave way to remarkably similar baronial cotton and vegetable empires. Outside observers studying the economy and society of the Rio Grande delta, with its large, capitalistic landholdings, its purely mercantile towns and cities, and its large and largely depressed ethnic Mexican underclass, frequently described the region as "feudal." This was semantically inaccurate but conceptually understandable term to American minds.

A small, relatively rich landowning group accounted for most production, and, together with shipping, processing, and mercantile interests in the towns, held most influence in the region. Without industry or large-scale commerce, a true middle class grew slowly. Both class and caste distinctions separated Mexican ethnics from the Anglo owners; and since the economy was 90 percent agricultural, there were few means of escape from the dominant social pattern. This remained stable until the 1950's; then, machinery rapidly replaced most farm labor, changing the countryside again, and also creating enormous problems in south Texas cities. In 1948, Hidalgo County in the Rio Grande Valley was recorded in the top three counties in agricultural income in the United States. In 1968, however, this general region contained the lowest per-capita-income urban areas in the entire nation, Brownsville and McAllen.

The economy of these regions produced very conservative politics—over a deep well of protest—for the same reasons that much of Latin America was dominated by conservative politics. In fact, South American observers in south Texas often were struck by its many similarities to lands below the Rio Grande.

Despite all this economic growth in the south and west, two-thirds of all Texans continued to live east of the old 1850 farm line. These people, still holding to most of their old mores, continued to dominate the state. They set its dominant patterns, and ruled its politics. But here there was a gradual erosion of agriculture in the old, post-Civil War pattern, to an economy overwhelmed by mushroom cities, set among pasturelands and oil fields.

The great factor in Texas's spectacular growth after 1920 was the discovery of some of the largest petroleum reserves on earth. Oil made Texas different from the other states of the old Confederacy; it provided wealth and employment other agrarian states lacked. It caused the peculiar form of industrialization that took place; it was the major factor in the growth of most metropolitan areas; and it too shaped and colored Texas social patterns and politics.

The first great field was brought in at Spindletop at Beaumont on the Gulf coast in 1901. Other discoveries followed: Petrolia in 1904, Electra in 1911, the Ranger field in 1917, until finally, petroleum was found under a majority of Texas counties. By 1928, Texas led all other states in oil production, with more than a quarter billion barrels. The historic East Texas strike in 1930 literally swamped the state, and the nation, with oil, leading to stringent state production control. Great fields were brought in in far west Texas after World War II. Exploration and development became continuous. In the war years Texas accounted for one half the nation's gas and oil; afterward, due to increasing use of cheaper foreign imports, the percentage dropped to about one third. This was still an enormous business, in an exploding national economy in some ways based on petroleum products.

Oil made the base for the industrialization that followed. Progress was not immediate after the discovery of oil, because oil, like beef and cotton, was tributary to the national industrial machine. As the industrial, oil-using society expanded, so did Texas production and wealth. After some decades, the state was able to shift the major burden of new taxation to gas and oil; royalties, meanwhile, swelled the state's educational endowments to immense sums.

The petrochemical industry, which produced 80 percent of the total U.S. output, became the largest true industry in the state. In some ways oil, and the industries based on oil, changed Texas, but in other ways oil only reinforced old trends.

One immediate effect was to enrich thousands of landowners across the state. By 1955, almost $500,000,000 was paid annually to farmers, ranchers, and other landholders in rentals, royalties, and bonuses. As the Texas saying went, a few oil wells made ranching a fine business. This great inpouring of outside money in exchange for petroleum added enormously to the over-all economy.

Most great fortunes of the 20th century have in some way been based on oil. Petroleum created in Texas something similar to the Eastern industrial upper class of the 19th century; a group of immense wealth, whose rise was aided by the provisions of a depletion allowance in the federal income tax.

It created the Texan new-rich oilman, who became something of a personi-
fication of ostentatious vulgarity, replacing the industrial barons of the
American East. This image made an impression around the world more apparent than real, however; the oilman did not assume that much importance
in Texan life, though some oil corporations did. The oilman, like the second-
generation industrial rich, was freed from economic worry and responsibility to pursue whatever form of social disintegration he preferred. His
ethic, in most cases, did not adjust to anything else. There were, as always,
important exceptions, especially where beef or cotton money had preceded
new oil wealth. The tendencies of the most spectacular type of oil-rich man
was to pursue more wealth, often around the world, enjoy it in the same
places as well as his limited cultural vision permitted, and frequently, to
indulge in Presidential politics by writing checks.

The individual oil-rich family, again with important exceptions, tended
more to remove itself from daily life and politics in Texas, following the
characteristic pattern of the Northern class. It had less influence on the
customs, mores, and even social life of Texas than supposed, because it
was not fully engaged. Great wealth tended to close as many doors as it
opened, where no ethic such as dominated the early American gentry appeared.

In the cities, from Dallas to San Antonio, the older, mercantile families
exercised more influence on life and business.

The industrialization caused by oil was not quite all it seemed. Oil was
extracted wealth, based on land, and thus it fitted easily into the old patterns of land speculation and development. For many owners of producing
wells, it was merely another salable crop, and the great majority of oil-
producing landowners were small. Oil was extracted by machinery without
much labor; it was hauled to market, and sold. The lease of oil lands was
similar to the lease of graze, or the contract harvesting by machinery of a
wheat or cotton crop.

Further, the great refining and petrochemical industries were not labor-
intensive. Refining, for example, by the 1950's employed less than 50,000
workers; it did not create an extensive new proletariat. Because of the
wealth involved, people employed in petroleum projects were highly paid.
Oil and attendant industries made an industrial base, with characteristic
concentration and organization of labor, in only a few areas, mostly cen-
tering around Beaumont-Port Arthur-Houston on the Gulf coast. Oil did
not, unlike the making of autos and shoes, erect a considerable industrial-
mercantile-labor complex similar to that of the North.

Other extractive industries, such as mineral earths for pharmaceuticals
in east Texas, employed similarly highly skilled people, without heavy
industrial production lines. These, like the aluminum, aircraft, and insurance industries that centered in a complex surrounding Dallas, actually
gave a huge impetus to the growth of an urban middle class, and not nearly
so much thrust to organized labor as was supposed. Thus oil, both through

concentrations of money and little change in social structure, strengthened rather than damaged the existing power structures across Texas.

The domestic effect of attacks on the oil industry by outsiders was not well understood. These intensified and strengthened political conservatism at the polls. Adlai Stevenson's courageous, and politically stupid, stand on the Texas tidelands did him damage that could not be retrieved, because it cut him off from both the most powerful interests and the Democratic power structure of the state. Eisenhower lost no Northern votes by promising to override the Supreme Court with legislation; he gained the support of most officeholders, schoolteachers, and taxpayers in Texas. Anything that took oil money away from Texas hurt the small man as well as the so-called big rich. Oil provided a great ocean of public money; it made interest politics, performing the same function in Texas cotton once did.

Cuts in the 27 percent depletion allowance in federal taxation had little Texas "liberal" support. Anything that tended to cut production or exploration hit everyone's pocketbook in some degree.

Petroleum was the largest factor in shaping the urbanization of east and west Texas, affecting the middle band of distribution centers the least. The explosive surge of oil from the earth made it possible for the tenant farmer to begin deserting his eroded acres in 1920. The old Texas saying that a city dweller was a farmer crossed with an automobile using oil was humorous, and true. By 1933, when a second plague of depressions and drouths scourged the land, only 33 percent of all Texans lived on farms. Within another generation this percentile had dropped to eight. Meanwhile, as everywhere, research and mechanization and the growth of capitalistic agriculture allowed this smaller group to produce vastly more food and fibers than the hordes of yesteryear. The land did not go out of production; in fact, more lands were opened, especially in the west. People recongregated in the towns, and found new work.

All the efforts of government, and the billions spent by government agencies, had little effect on either trend; histories would record that when the agrarian mythology and the farm vote were completely dead. In fact, government policy, unwittingly, assisted the growth of capitalistic enterprise; large, efficient operations could actually exist, where small ones could not, on minimum subsidies. Acreages continued to increase, and valuations of land to rise, from 1910 through the 1960's, with only a short break during the utter paralysis of the Great Depression years. In the long process, farmers became fewer, and of these, only a handful produced 80 percent of the total marketable output. Similar processes in industry, perhaps, were easier to assimilate and accept, because industry held no ancestral "feudal" memories, such as were stirred up in some Americans by farms comprising thousands of acres of cultivated land.

The trend was firm, no matter who was Secretary of Agriculture in

Washington or what theory of commodity credit, parity, or crop restriction was the current fad. The opportunities offered by new industries, the weariness of farm labor, the loneliness of farm life started the trend before 1900, even in good years. Government certainly affected the trend by delaying it at times. Two factors that were more important than national policy and all the neo-Populism combined were the brilliant successes scored in universities with research on new chemical processes and crops, and the influence of private enterprise, looking for its own markets on the land. The axiom that more stubborn farmers listened to seed, fertilizer, and tractor salesmen than to all the earnest, helpful members of various governmental agricultural agencies appears true. One reason for the success of one group over the other was that the salesmen confined their efforts to the farmers most likely to succeed, while government was determined to help the others, with the usual historical result.

Figures show what became of the impoverished, socially destructive tenant farm. The small farmer, who far into the century outnumbered every other social group in Texas, began to disappear; the surviving farmers, large and small, entered a gradually strengthening partnership with government. Both trends were deplored publicly and widely, by farmers and non-farmers alike. Some Americans looked on the farmer as the salt of the earth and society's ballast; others held to the notion that the farmer had once been successful and independent on his own terms. However, truly profitable agriculture in Texas had been colonial since colonial days; the movement of farmer to town was a worldwide trend, and the new subsidies and ties between agriculture and government only followed similar patterns in other enterprises.

Between 1930 and 1957 the number of tenant farms decreased by half, while the average size of Texan farms doubled. In 1930, there were more than 300,000 tenants, including sharecroppers. By 1950, tenants numbered only 75,000, of whom only 10,000 worked on shares. During the next years, the remaining tenant farmers themselves changed; the tenant farm grew much larger. Some tenants were now successful operators, with huge investments in machinery, sometimes renting thousands of acres. The old-style sharecropper all but disappeared. With him went a way of life.

The changes, like all change, made new problems. The white tenant was able to make the transition to city worker, and more often than not, enter the urban middle classes. The black sharecropper went to town at his side, but the black's passage was far less successful. The white Texan found a place in the nearest city or town which caste and lack of education denied the Negro. Large numbers of Texas blacks gathered in poverty, taking menial jobs, on the outskirts of the towns. In the 1940's, they began their great migration north and west to their dark cities of destruction. The end of tenant farming in Texas, and other regions of the South, was thus both a social improvement and the start of an immense national social problem.

Due to technological changes, one farmer on the land could now keep several city-dwellers fed, and employed as well. The processing of foods and minerals took the place of agricultural work.

On the coast, Beaumont, Port Arthur, and Houston (Texas' first great metropolis) were almost wholly creations of oil and other rich mineral earths. Houston, for the first time, and finally, passed San Antonio as Texas' largest city in the 1930's. That this took so long—San Antonio had no oil or mining and developed very little industry of any kind—showed the lag of industrialization in the state. Far into the century, Texas cities and towns were distribution centers, unchanged from the century before.

On the Plains, where no cities had been able to rise at all, Abilene, Lubbock, Midland, and San Angelo grew. These doubled in population every decade, depending for their gains on greater discoveries and extraction of oil.

Extraction and processing allowed the total population to grow; Texas never lost population, like many agricultural states. Oil not only shaped population, it expanded it, by holding fecund farm families and bringing new immigrants in. In 1920, Texas had about 4,000,000 people, more than its farms could support. Forty years later it passed 10,000,000, achieving Sam Houston's dream at last. Something Sam Houston never dreamed of made it true.

Other natural resources contributed to the growth. This was a rich empire. Sulfur, salt, limestone, oyster shell, gypsum, talc, helium grew up with the hunger of the industrial North. Texas contributed 80 percent of the world's sulfur, and a full quarter of the total United States' mineral supply. It produced 20 percent of the nation's aluminum, and all of its domestic magnesium ingot and tin. Texas made 70 percent of all American carbon black.

It led all other states, and most nations, in cotton, wool, and mohair exports. Eight million head of cattle dotted the world's greatest pasture lands. Texas was also the shrimp processing capital of the world, with more than 400 boats based at the mouth of the Rio Grande.

This was industrialization, but only of a certain kind. Most of Texas' industry, with the exception of the aero-space complex around Dallas and a few other scattered enterprises, was based on the processing of agricultural products and the extraction and processing of raw materials. The economy could be described more accurately as a vast agricultural-mining complex than that of a true industrial state. Every Texas industry was based upon, and tied directly to, the land on which it sat. Almost all such industries depended not on local, but on distant markets, whose fluctuations in virtually every case were beyond the producers' control. The nature of these industries, fixed to the soil, and depending in most cases upon the ownership of the soil, automatically continued a basically nonindustrial type of society. They produced great variations in income and real wealth, which were often obscured by the determined egalitarianism of Texan social practices. The fortunes they produced more nearly resembled landed or mining fortunes; the new technicians required to run the new enterprises had a status more like that of the mining engineer of the 19th century, or the overseer of a plantation. Such men had to have skills, and were well paid, but a sharp division between owner and manager, such as was disappearing in most of corporate America, remained. Men and large companies, owning a fortune in the ground, hired managers and technicians to extract it and to process it once it was out. Many of these technicians came from somewhere else. In Texas, however, they did not, and were not yet beginning to, form a sort of diploma-mandarinate such as officered top national corporations, and was beginning to be thought of as the new American elite.

The society of Texas was still based on private property, not skills; the recognized elite were owners, not executives or managers. Here was a great difference not usually noted, though the marked maldistribution of natural wealth in Texas was usually seen by all.

Texans crossed the Sabine convinced that the land was the source of all riches, determined to build new empires, and for some of them this came true. For all, the land and what lay under it shaped their lives from beginning to end.

Even the educational system of Texas in the modern age remained fixed to the land. It did not, as Governor John Connally fruitlessly warned, prepare Texans to compete in an increasingly conceptual and technical industrial society in the greater nation. In agricultural techniques and mass-scale farming, Texas excelled, both in university and farm. It had the finest school in North America devoted to petrochemicals and oil. It turned out sufficient technicians of the kind its society needed: accountants, drillers, geologists, repairmen, distribution executives, and engineers. Beyond this, Texas higher education, unconsciously, fitted men for the old careers, the pulpit, school, the battlefield, and bar. Though the whole gamut of education was available, the Texan mind failed to grasp, or to value, most of the developing psychology of the more advanced industrial societies. The Texan status system had hardly changed in a century; its values were based on private property, ownership, not employment. The idea of a society based on social role was yet foreign. While the lower social classes, from laborers to the rapidly proletarianizing schoolteachers, clerks, and other so-called white-collar workers, thought in terms of education as a means of improving social station, the genuine Texan social elite continued an imperial, rather than social, outlook. In the highest levels of society, and to reach the highest levels, men worked for, and had to attain, property.

Instinctively, the majority of Texans tended to admire or envy a family that owned 100,000 acres more than one that produced two great surgeons, a fine musician, or a new theory of relativity. This definite, if sometimes denied, value system inexorably colored all Texan education. The practical outweighed the conceptual; things were more important than ideas; education was to fit children to society, not change them or produce inherent confusion by educating too many students beyond their station.

The Texan educational system, and the Texan mind, produced superb trial lawyers, good soldiers, keen politicians, excellent ranchers and businessmen. It did not turn out boys apt to invent the mathematics for a new space drive—though any intelligent Texan would probably be able to grasp and use the finished product with eagerness and skill.

Education and enterprise were still suffused with the old Protestant frontier ethic; society was as realistic, narrow-minded, and as disciplined as a century before. The ethic was strongest in the politically dominant middle strata, which approached both education and business with discipline and determination. Actually, the great problem of adaptation to Texan society, for those who had the problem, was that of acquiring the dominant outlook.

Texan politicians had become widely recognized, for their abilities if not their style. But oddly, the Texan was not thought of as a superb businessman in many areas of the nation. This, probably, was due to the confusion in the national mind of the businessman with the corporate executive. Texas, with the American Southwest, remained the nation's last great pool of entrepreneurial spirit. Here was found an urge and drive now noticeable only among more recent immigrants to America; in the grandsons and great-grandsons of the original Northern industrialists entrepreneurism seemed dead. But there were Texans who still held the old American imperial dream.

Men such as Young, Ling, Hughes, Thornton, Murchison, and scores of others, all Southwesterners, all asocial, atomistic products of the frontier ethic, could still grasp the essentials of action, dream huge dreams, and erect conglomerate business empires, stand or fall. They were the kind of American, whether from Louisiana or Connecticut, who instinctively hit the road for Texas years before. Texas was noted for financial giants—and not just "oilmen"—who escaped the definition of corporate executive. These giants worked alone or with small teams, but they were no more "team" or "company" men than had been Richard King or Mifflin Kenedy. They were never cells in some great organism, where one set of hired hands wrote reports for another hired-hand echelon.

These men stood out against a society falling more and more into the functions of social role, determined by education and credentials. The Texan entrepreneur rarely owned credentials; some could hardly read or write. But they were dynamic; they were self-reliant, free men with no real use for either gentlemen or beggars, free as few men in a compressing society could still be. They did not work inside companies or with companies; they bought companies and piled them one atop the other, like the old cattle baron had once built up his range piece by piece.

Any examination showed that an utterly disproportionate percentage of this kind of man derived from, or congregated along, the vanishing outlines of the last frontier.

In these traits, however, there were certain dangers. While some of these men reshaped cities, and even affected the entire American economy in certain ways, they tended to remain out of tune with the dominant notions of the nation as a whole.

The urbanization of Texas, starting late but proceeding faster than the American norm after the 1940's, proceeded on several planes. The automobile sent the first growth to the small cities and towns. Then, suddenly, the new metropoli started to suck the countryside dry. This trend was at first obscured, because as the farmers and ranchers moved from country to town, all towns in Texas gained population. But then, as the counties became more and more depopulated, many of the small, rurally situated towns began to wither. Their market area was drying up. When the total population of an agrarian county shrank—and the 1960 census revealed that two-thirds of all Texas counties were losing people—the trade base of the smaller cities was eaten away. In most Texas small towns established businesses declined; young men looked for opportunity elsewhere; numbers stagnated, then slowly declined. Across Texas, some smaller cities were dying. This caused something akin to panic in many places, because, from the very first, the idea that growth was good was almost an Anglo-Texan religion. Sinking property values frightened Texans as nothing else could.

The larger cities, and above all the five great metropoli, Houston, Dallas, San Antonio, Fort Worth, El Paso, together with a dozen other burgeoning centers showed explosive growth. They gained what the counties lost.

One of the most depopulated regions was the long stretch of the old farm-line frontier, where men tested nature to the limits, and where the People's Party rose. Here, the pasture country was moving eastward; stock ranching had moved out of the arid regions onto good east Texas graze, a genuine but not unhappy regression. Meanwhile, stock farming within the old cattle kingdom declined under a wave of new consolidations. Big ranches were coming back. A growing, major worry among cattlemen by the 1960's was the problem of passing on their holdings, unemasculated by the state and federal estate taxes.

The Texas metropoli, fast-formed, were not cities in the European sense. They were more accumulations of individuals than communities. They contained huge, efficient economies, filled with the material abundance that was the hallmark of all 20th-century America; they were visibly similar to the American cities of the North and especially the West and Midwest. They were beginning to consume culture, though not yet to create it; in this Dallas resembled Kansas City or St. Louis. But inwardly these great cities were different from the cities of the North, and even those of the heartland Midwest.

They were populated from different human sources. Very few Texas urbanites ever arrived out of Europe, or even from the other American regions. They poured in from Texas' own heartland. Paris, Texas, was populated in the beginning exactly as was Paris, France. The great majority of Texas cities had no foreign enclaves, or any non-Anglo-American communities, except for Mexicans and Negroes, and these two groups formed distinct societies.

The politics of Dallas, Houston, and Lubbock therefore could not be similar to those of Minneapolis or Chicago. The outlook of the larger Texas cities was predominantly conservative, in economics, ethic, and social attitudes. These cities had to be put in true perspective of time and place. The shining towers thrusting up from the plains, rising over miles of green fields and oceans of subterranean oil, were filled with old-stock, Anglo-American Protestant pioneers. This ethnic strain was not an elite, or an enclave; it was the majority, homogeneous throughout all classes except for the Mexican and black subordinate castes. This strain survived here. These people brought their attitudes and value systems across the wide Atlantic, through the Appalachian chain, onto the savage, sunlit plains. They held it intact, finally transmitting it to the cities, where, finally, they migrated as individuals. In the cities there was small erosion; they stayed hard-working, disciplined, wholly economically-oriented as before. Because of the sprawling nature of the Texas metropoli, the pioneer stock was almost as atomistic and uncompressed as when it filtered through the Texas prairies. All this showed through, beneath some superficial veneers.

People who criticized Dallas in the 1960's were really criticizing Anglo-America in 1900. The changes in America, for better or worse, were still taking place elsewhere, not in Texas. Education did not, and would not, change the basic ethic. Under stress, everywhere, human beings react according to their basic value systems, never according to acquired education. Anthropologists knew this, but it was a fact most educators and sociologists preferred to dismiss.

Texas, with its gleaming, spreading cities and its leagues of primordial, slow-changing landscape, presented a pattern common to many parts of the 20th century world. Texas began as a colony, with a colonial society and economy. It was still bound by unbreakable cords to the vaster world community the Anglo-Celt never quite escaped. Here the most modern enterprise and technology lived side by side with elements of crushing poverty, with age-old drives, and with unchanged ideas. Texas was rich, and poor, tributary to a distant civilization, paying its tribute for money and artifacts in cotton, beef, and oil. The Texan took everything from that distant world he thought he could shape or use: the German rifle, the Yankee six-shooter, the Pennsylvanian know-how in drilling for oil. The colonial, and the frontiersman, always needs the artifacts of civilization.

But he always resists domination. Texans, again and again, now successfully, now hopelessly, rejected ideas and changes that seemed to have no relevance to their land or to their history, or which brought about social situations few Texans desired.

Societies changed internally; they rarely could be changed by pressure from without. The white man exterminated some Indians, conquered the rest, but in three centuries he could never destroy the Amerind's own concept of man, society, and the world. On sullen, squalid reservations, thousands of Amerind remnants held to the old ways still; probably, they always would. The Indian knew the white man had won; this did not mean he himself had to become an imitation Caucasian or commit race treason by adopting European ways.

The Texan society, brawling, vulgar, expansive and expansionist, with a simmer of violence beneath its surface, and a cool, empirical view of its own and other men's worlds, thus like certain other basically colonial communities remained static on one plane in the 20th century while it exploded dramatically on another.

36

THE LIGHTS
OF SAN ANTONIO

*Once you were master of all you surveyed, and your head of
cattle were countless, in south Texas. As adventurous, carefree,
and pleasure-loving Dons, you dealt with the friendly Tejas and
the savage Apaches. A Nordic cloud appeared in the north, and
slowly but unremorselessly, grew into monstrous proportions.
. . . Your pleasure-loving ways, your good nature, have been unable
to cope with the energetic, wealth-seeking characteristics of the
Nordics.*   FROM AN ARTICLE FOR TEXAS MEXICANS
                                 BY RODOLFO DE LA GARZA

At the core of the violence and warfare marking Texas history was a
series of ethnic problems, the situation developing when two or more
sharply differentiated peoples are brought under a single government. As
the ethnic consciousness of all peoples increased enormously in the 20th
century, ethnic troubles have come increasingly to the fore in America.
Both in Texas and in the United States, these problems have been met with
a combination of indifference, lack of perspective, and naïveté.

In world terms, ethnic troubles were neither new nor unusual. Historically, they came about in only three general ways: conquest of one race or
culture by another, the imposition of arbitrary boundaries combining
different groups within one political entity, or the importation of foreign
stock by a more highly organized society for labor. Canada's ethnic problem came through the British conquest of French Quebec; black Africa's,
and Belgium's, through the arbitrary combination of different peoples

677

within common boundaries by outside powers; while the Texas situation strongly resembled the chain of events in Algeria and South Africa.

Like Algeria and the south African region, Texas was a large, almost unpopulated land when the first highly organized and determined European settlers arrived. The Texan experience with the Indians was similar to the French, and Boer, experience with certain savage, primitive tribes. These were fought, beaten, and pushed back into marginal lands the conquerors did not want. In the 1850's, American observers compared the state of the Great Plains, with its chain of protective forts ringing the Amerinds beyond the 98th meridian with the French policy in North Africa. There a similar chain of military posts guarded the agricultural regions, where Europeans settled, against the wild tribesmen of the desert, while no real effort was made to subdue or settle the less fertile regions.

The nature of the Plains Indians, who could be conquered but not civilized in white terms, determined the nature of the North American contest. The Indians could not bend, so they were broken. They were useless to the Texans, and dangerous. They were killed or driven out. In 1900 there were only 1,000 Amerinds living in the entire state. The Indian wars in Texas obviated a later Indian ethnic problem.

However, just as European settlers in North Africa and on the southern tip of the continent could not refrain from importing huge masses of cheap, unskilled, and exploitable labor—Muslims in the north, Bantus in the south—the dominant Anglo-Texans proceeded with a similar lack of vision. The Muslim population of North Africa, and the Negroid population of a South Africa that had been almost deserted when the first Dutch arrived, exploded under the opportunities and improvements the conquerors made. It was inevitable that, sooner or later, a contest for control of the land would begin.

The Spanish-Mexicans had imported Anglo-Americans into Texas for their own reasons, and they suffered a logical result. When Anglos outnumbered Mexicans in Texas, they controlled the province; they frightened the government of Mexico long before the Texas Revolution began. These Texas settlers were the catalyst that provoked a Mexican-American war, though some such war was probably inevitable, since the Anglo civilization was dynamic and expansive, the Mexican nation static and even regressive, unable to exert power in the borderlands.

The conquest of Texas, and even the extension of the American border to the Rio Grande, did not create a large ethnic conflict within Texas, because the Mexican population was too small. There were only about 12,000 ethnic Mexicans in Texas the year before the Civil War, and during the rest of the century the figure did not proportionally increase. There was no reason for Mexicans to enter Texas; in fact, there was ample reason for them to leave it; and even discounting heavy Anglo immigration, the Anglo-Texan rate of population increase, at least until 1880, exceeded the ethnic Mexican. German immigrants, who Americanized rapidly, outnumbered

Mexicans in San Antonio by 1850, and Anglos outnumbered both soon after the railroad arrived in 1877. The ratio in the border counties was about fifty-fifty at the end of the 19th century, and the total population figures were small. The ethnic Mexicans were being engulfed, and it was widely believed they were being absorbed. Although there were bitter troubles on the border, a happy solution, in the American tradition, seemed in sight.

The first, and most serious, ethnic problem in Texas centered around the Negro. The Negro was never a prime mover, but always a dangerous catalyst in American life. The institution of black slavery—originally imported to solve the most vexing problem facing a developing North America, labor—determined the course, and the fate, of the South. The industrializing North solved its own labor problems through massive European immigration: Irish, then Germans, later Italians and Eastern Europeans. The majority of these immigrants were not noticeably differentiated from the original Anglo mass; many of them were already urbanized and arrived with important skills; and those who were accustomed to urbanization and possessed skills, such as the Germans who flooded the Midwest, integrated into American society within several generations with immense success. The Irish tended to freeze on lower social levels, but still, because of political skills and the fact they already spoke English, made the transition with minimal cultural pain. The latter-day, 20th century immigration from Eastern and Southern Europe was too culturally different, and too massive, to be easily absorbed, but massive problems were eased with the choking off of unrestricted immigration after the First World War. After that, troubles in Europe enormously increased the quality of immigrants—refugees tended to be skilled, urbanized, and valuable additions—and the flow was still ample to provide New York, Chicago, and other cities with an indispensable supply of labor in certain fields.

The nature of the European immigration into the United States, and the fact that most immigrants deliberately dropped most of their history and culture during their passage, arriving as individuals determined to Americanize, blinded American society as a whole to the normal nature of ethnic difficulties. The American process in the North was not average; it was almost unique. A growing, amorphous, rapidly expanding and industrializing society provided tremendous opportunities for any immigrant who could meet certain basic social parameters, whether he was Jew or Greek.

The society of the American South was neither growing nor amorphous, though it was expanding in static form toward the West. Except for the one large wave of European agrarian migration to Texas in the 1840's, Europeans sensibly sought the urban centers of the North. White immigration could not compete with the horde of Negro slaves; even the old Anglo stock was not competing economically with the slaveholders of the planter class. Thus there were two enormous differences between the Northern laboring groups and the Southern depressed class. The slaves were black, and noticeably different; static social forces, among whites of both the upper and the middle and lower classes, gravitated strongly against social change. Planters faced economic loss; marginal whites feared competition.

The blacks were brought into Texas for only one purpose: to provide essential labor. The myth that the slave system was economically unviable was about as valid as the myth that white men were unfit to labor in the coastal climate. Both grew from rationalized desires. The myth of white supremacy was also a normal, in fact, a required rationalization to prevent social change no Southerner wanted. In 1860 the slave economy was producing enormous profits, though at dangerous social cost, and it was guilty of the greatest social sin of all, military weakness. But when it was destroyed by war, the purpose of the Negroes' existence in Texas was destroyed with it.

Tragically, in American history it was impossible to provide the millions of black human beings who labored, and whose backs built so much of the economy, with individual faces. Their situation was analogous to the faceless hordes who sweated out their lives in Sicilian wheatfields or Thracian mines under Roman overlords, or the millions of serfs upon whose labors the cathedrals of medieval culture were raised. History records that the brilliant culture of Renaissance Europe had to eat, and that someone provided menial work and food. It records the name of no serf, unless he entered history through rebellion.

In Texas, the black man faced a combination of class disadvantage, differentiation, and imposed caste. After a logical Emancipation, American society as a whole faced all these problems with naïveté.

The black could not be made an effective citizen overnight, because in voting democracies the one essential was that a majority of the citizens be at least theoretically equal. The Negro was unequal, in education, social conditioning, and in the white mind.

Nor was he integratable, in the manner of the immigrant Rumanian or Jew. Miscegenation was rejected in theory and practice by the Nordic white, and rejected even more ferociously once the Negro was free. The Negro could not meet one essential parameter: a white skin. President Lincoln and a host of Americans of his generation, before they fell into dangerous experimentation for political purposes, recognized that some form of social polarization must result. A tiny, almost insignificant Negro minority was brought into white society in the North with reasonable success. In Texas, where one-quarter of the total population was black, this was impossible. Political democracy had to grow up from the basic social institutions of the people, to rest on a firm base of consensus. It could not be imposed. The Southerner could not willingly allow the former slave to vote, because he considered the freedmen's ballot dangerous to his own status and institutions.

There was no historical precedent for a society's basic institutions being overturned by ballot; democracy possessed very real limits. Neither George III nor Jefferson Davis were deposed in America by elections or legal writ, but by war.

The Negro in Texas had always lived in a separate country, with separate laws, from the dominant white. The change from slavery to elaborate caste was probably as inevitable as a similar situation inevitably created caste in India, Ethiopia, and Hispanic America generations earlier. The tragedy, and error, was that the new caste system provided no means for eventual social elevation and change; it did nothing to provide the Negro the means for eventual entrance into American life on an equal, if separate, basis with white society. But then few caste systems ever do. The faceless slave became the faceless sharecropper and handyman, whose name history continued to ignore.

The existence and the function of the freedmen under tenantry was always anomalous. Most landowners always distrusted ex-slaves, preferring whites. For some years, the system was workable, if not very viable, because there was no other solution at hand. The Negroes were thinly scattered, and even more controllable than they had been as slaves but never so profitable. Then, with the agricultural revolution that began in the last quarter of the 19th century, even the meager security of the sharecropper began to disappear. Slowly but inevitably, the Negro farmer failed to serve any useful purpose, like the tenant white. But the white farmer had avenues of escape, which to the Negro were closed.

Texas agriculture was more pragmatic and adaptable than that of the older South. The squalor of the sharecropper's shack provided his landlord with no measurable profit, and while there were reactionaries in the deep Brazos bottoms who took a sort of paternal pride in the Negroes on their lands, the majority of landowners, sooner than the rest of the South, began to let their Negroes go. Mechanization was not possible for the Negro, who lacked capital and credit; those tenants who survived financed themselves and emerged as respectable farm operators in their own right. The owner who farmed himself, or let his acres to efficient white tenants, made money. From his Negro sharecroppers, in many years, he collected only a few pounds of cotton or a bag of beans. Thus arose a Texas saying in the 1930's, to the effect that "the last one saw of niggers, the first one saw of money again." By 1930, the majority of Texas Negroes were already living in the small cities and towns.

The great boom caused by the exploitation of mineral resources passed the Negro by. Texas had instituted a public school system for blacks in 1870, but in a region where the white rural schools averaged in the bottom third in national ratings, the Negro schools were poor indeed. The black school was marked by untrained teachers, substandard buildings, short terms, and few funds for such things as books. There was no social pressure among the bottom caste for education; education did not fit into their world. They lacked motivation, and the white structure logically saw no reason to educate them beyond their expected station. The majority of Negroes were functionally illiterate at best. They could not compete with the more aggressive, American-ethic-stimulated white farmer in town in any case. In specific cases, both Negroes and whites took the caste system to town; the vast majority of Negroes found employment only in menial jobs.

The black settlements formed almost separate towns beside the white communities. They were rigidly segregated and endured rigid poverty, not so much on the world scale but on the American. Again, in these "nigger towns" scattered throughout the old heartland, the Negro lived in a separate nation, under separate laws. The civil and criminal codes were not enforced rigidly within the black communities by the dominant white power structures, unless the Negro and white man impinged. Here, not earlier, a considerable trend toward Negro crime and violence emerged. The sharecropper was among the most peaceable of men; the compressed town dweller exploded more easily. Texas took an entirely empirical view toward this trend. Negro violence was not severely punished, nor did it much concern white society or politics, so long as it was directed at the Negro community. If a Negro crossed the invisible line—much like the old deadline drawn by the western frontier towns—by harming one of the upper castes, his punishment was usually swift, heavy, and sometimes horrible.

In the first three decades of the 20th century, in which 60 percent of the Negro population congregated in municipalities, Texas—with Oklahoma and certain border states—was peculiarly noted for racial violence. There were several historic uprisings, both white and black. Negro soldiers in the federal service rioted at Brownsville and shot up the town with some fatalities. The national government refused to turn the suspects over to the state authorities, as one Ranger captain demanded, but whole units were dismissed under unfair conditions from the service. A similar rebellion erupted among Negro soldiers in Houston in 1917, and several of the participants were executed by the military authorities at Fort Sam Houston at San Antonio. In the era of nativism of the 1920's, there were several white lynch actions and innumerable smaller persecutions. In one incident, which served as a model for studies in mob psychology, the residents of a Texas town burned down their new courthouse and jail in order to incinerate one Negro prisoner. Actual mob violence was far more prevalent in Texas than in the Deep South, where lynchings were conducted with greater decorum. While all observers stepped warily in explaining this phenomenon, the greater democratization of Texas urban life in these years, with the influx of dirt farmers, probably was a factor. There existed no power structure with either the ethic or the power to deny mob action. Something like the great fear wave of 1860, when western counties lynched slaves whom the planters protected in the east, occurred.

However, the Texas picture changed sharply in the 1940's, from one of the worst situations in the South to perhaps the best. One reason, certainly, was that the burgeoning economy and rapid metropolitanization of Texas —more than half of the population was metropolitan by 1950, almost three-quarters by the late 1960's—broke the patterns of Southern society. All of Texans' biases remained, but the social necessity of maintaining them disappeared. Powerful economic interests became increasingly important in the state; these interests, unlike local municipal officials and country sheriffs, were determined to force law and order even against the prejudices of the white lower and middle classes. Probably more important in the long run, the black population itself began rapidly to decrease.

With World War II, and in the decades that followed, Negro emigration out of Texas became a flood. Some went West, most went northward up the Mississippi Valley. The higher wages in the North and West in those years, plus the hope of escaping the pervading caste system, drew Negroes in torrents. The Northern and Midwestern cities had thousands of openings for unskilled workers, at a time when the Texas Negro's usefulness at home had almost vanished. In time, after millions had gone, the social utility of the Southern Negro in the North also vanished; he had traded the Southern fields of degradation for the Northern cities of destruction. But that, as several Texans commented, was the North's problem; now the North could apply its own morality to it. A growing, horrifying national racial crisis each year, paradoxically, affected less and less the region where it had all begun.

At the end of the Civil War, about one in three residents of Texas were black. By 1950, Negroes comprised 12.7 percent, by 1955, 11.6 percent. The figure stabilized in the 1960s at about 12%, with areas of high concentration rarely reaching more than 20%. With each announced decrease, the amiability of the white society toward the Negro problem tended to increase. Unlike many parts of the South, and now, almost all great cities in the North, the Negro offered the Texan politician nothing to fear. Thus, in Texas there was little resistance to the long, uneven trend of interference in state affairs by the Supreme Court and federal administrations that now aroused resentment and won few adherents in the South generally.

Texans disapproved of the so-called civil rights movement; few were badly disturbed or frightened by it.

The destruction of the Democratic Party's white primary law in 1944 at first aroused consternation; one reason the Negro had been quiescent in Texas, if far from content, was that since the turn of the century no officeholder had ever made him promises. But the fears of a new wave of demagoguery faded in the census figures. Unlike many states of the old Confederacy, few regions in Texas put up any obstacles to Negro voting. If a Negro paid a poll tax, he could vote without hindrance or let. His vote, except in a few areas, could not be decisive, particularly in a one-party state. Black votes could swing close state elections, as in 1960, but little else.

In 1949, Texas moved strongly, for the first time, to improve Negro education. This effort was designed to justify the 1896 "separate but equal" doctrine of racial segregation. It came too late, and would not have affected the Supreme Court's decision in any case, since the Court was now operating under the theory of the desirability of social integration of the Negro with the white. However, most Negroes continued to attend segregated schools after 1954, and these were much improved. Equally important, by 1957 there were eight independent colleges, and two state institutions of higher education for Negroes. The level of average education rose dramatically, although the quality still left much to be desired.

The 1954 Supreme Court integration decision again caused consternation, but significantly, little defiance. Polls and referenda and statewide elections, year after year, showed an overwhelming Texan disapproval of federal civil rights enforcement. In 1956, the Democratic primary revealed huge majorities in favor of strengthening laws against racial intermarriage, exempting white students from attending schools with blacks, and interposition of the state laws to offset federal court decisions. Later elections favored retention of the poll tax. But, as each social, educational, and political barrier was dismantled by the national government, the state accepted the changes with a remarkable amount of grace.

Threats of violence attending school integration were quickly stifled by the state government. Governor Shivers sent Rangers to Mansfield in 1956, with orders to remove any troublemakers, black or white. A mob action to bar Negroes from Lamar State College at Beaumont, in deep east Texas, failed miserably. The power structure that had grown up in modern Texas had no belief in integration, but even less belief in civil disorder. In this, Texas resembled Virginia and South Carolina, where the vulgarization of society in the 20th century had become somewhat reversed. Law, not popular sentiments, prevailed.

In 1957, Texas went through the painful, somewhat farcical process of legal interposition, trying to interpose its own laws between its people and the federal apparatus. A law was passed requiring a local election before Texas schools might be integrated, and another, closing any school at which troops, state or federal, had to be stationed. Important progress, however, was made with the 1957 local option law. School segregation under state laws had long worked a hardship on many western and southern Texas counties. Some had been required to build and maintain separate schools for only a handful of students. The vast majority of Negroes had always been found in the older counties of the east, and west Texas generally welcomed the end of segregation with relief.

The single biggest factor causing the general amiability with which the state desegrated was the metropolitanization that had taken place. There were still deep-Southern, diehard counties, predominantly rural, east of the Brazos, but these no longer had much political power. Desegregation here worked a social revolution of a sort. But in the cities, desegregation did not mean integration, and it had almost no effect on society at large.

Texas cities, unlike many of the older South, were rigidly segregated by wards and precincts; the Negro population invariably lived only in certain parts of town. The new, largely 20th-century metropoli were structured on the American plan of city building; neighborhoods and surburbs were defined by income. Education was still divided among local boards, local school districts. When San Antonio desegregated in 1954, without waiting for state sanction, the change moved only a handful of students from former schools. More important, perhaps, the end of legal segregation seemed to give actual impetus to *de facto* segregation. Where there was any large proportion of black students in a school, the white population tended to move out, following a nationwide pattern from Washington, D.C., to Chicago.

The same pattern took place when public segregation or discrimination was barred by law in 1964. Some cities, notably San Antonio, had already largely taken down the bars quietly long before. Fears continued to decrease when the white population realized it would in no case be overrun. In a region noted for its violence in the past, now there was almost none.

Again, several factors were at work, besides the small proportion of black people, almost everywhere below critical mass. One was that the vast majority of unemployed Negroes, or families with no stake whatever in Texas society, had emigrated. Behind remained a far more able and responsible Negro community than most white Texans realized. It was still socially remote, living in its own part of town if not entirely in its own country; nowhere in Texas did or could whites and Negroes intermingle, except in political affairs, or in enclaves around universities. A rising proportion of this residue were middle class, in income and also, immensely more important, in ethic. Houston contained more Afro-American millionaires than any city in the United States. One of these families was descended from the slave who had made shoes for ten cents per pair before the Civil War.

There were also several important Negro business organizations in Texas, including an insurance company. These provided balance. The great expansion and upgrading of Negro higher education was another large factor in providing an indigenous black middle class. Many of this group found more opportunity working within the black community at home than those who emigrated only to crash against the unadmitted caste barriers in the North.

This middle class did not turn into what the black community called "niggers"—successful Negroes who tried to become imitation whites, by living and working within the white community. Here, the Southern social ethos, and the clear understanding that race barriers existed, prevented the flight of middle class blacks from their own people, and prevented much of the destructive ghetto atmosphere of the North. There was little fragmentation of the black elites into white suburbs. This might do damage to the integration theory, but it seemed to provide greater stability.

Certain characteristics of Texas cities made them less prone to racial tensions than elsewhere. They were all products of the automobile age, and mostly built on open prairies; they lacked compression. Dwellings were overwhelmingly composed of single-family units; the crowded apartment houses and tenements originally erected to house immigrants in the Northern cities did not exist. While blacks were segregated, there were no tight neighborhoods, of either whites or blacks. The black areas generally had almost unlimited room to expand; the Texas annexation laws prevented most cities from being choked off by suburbia.

There were some recorded—and many more unseen—instances in which Negroes from outside Texas tried to rouse interest in demonstrations or public protests in the 1960's. In virtually every case, the local black power structure was hostile to these, and prevented any such action. Significantly, following the assassination of Martin Luther King, Jr., in the spring of 1968, only one racial incident occurred in the entire state, and this was a single instance of breaking and entering.

One final factor was a generally clear understanding between both black and white communities that the Texas economic and political power structure would not tolerate civic disorder. Few Texas leaders on any level were likely to be gripped by the paralysis that agonized and immobilized Northern political structures in the face of riots. The white community did not believe in social integration, and therefore felt little guilt or hypocrisy about the situation of the races. The white elected officials were rarely dependent on black votes. Texans by and large obeyed the desegregation and antidiscrimination laws because these were the law; they were prepared to enforce local codes as well.

Caste barriers could not be disposed of by fiat in Texas, any more than the Republic of India could abolish untouchability by legislating against it. There were still hatreds, frustrations, and a thousand reminders of the past, for both races. But many enormous changes were occurring with remarkable ease. The Negroes were emerging rapidly, not into the white community, but into the total community as a strengthening entity. Blacks served on police forces, argued on city councils, sat in the legislature, all without dangerous friction. This was not true integration, but a strengthening of one polarized community vis-à-vis the other. It was the most that was possible at the time.

The whites had never believed in true integration; significantly, perhaps, the Texas black community was moving rapidly away from it as a goal. Leadership in both communities, with a general realization that the total society was racist and polarized on both sides and would remain so, struggled for empirical working relationships with each other. They might or might not be hammered out. No society in human history had solved the problems thrown up when two highly differentiated populations were forced to live side by side.

Meanwhile, federal studies described Dallas, Fort Worth, Houston, San Antonio, and other Texas cities as those least likely of any large metropolitan areas in the United States to experience major disorders.

Seventy percent of the black population of America had emigrated into some dozen industrial centers, where tragically, the Negro, with his limited skills and remaining caste handicaps, was almost as obsolete as he had become on the sharecrop farm. Texas had not solved its Negro problem, but the state had exported most of it.

In the same years that the historic Negro migration out of Texas was taking place, another great folk movement was happening. This was also largely unseen. While Texas exported one potential crisis, it was deliberately importing another one, which was inherently more serious. The 20th century saw the beginning of a huge Mexican immigration into Texas.

The new migration was misunderstood by most Texans and almost all other Americans, because there had always been ethnic Mexicans in south Texas. But statistics reveal a startling pattern. In 1860, there were about 12,000 ethnic Mexicans in all Texas, all in the south-southwest. Between 1861 and 1900, approximately 334 Mexican nationals entered the United States annually; as many departed as entered. By 1900, immigration averaged 100 Mexicans per year. In 1900, 70,000 ethnic Mexicans lived in Texas, or less than 5 percent of the total population; only 5,000 lived in San Antonio, where they were still less numerous than ethnic Germans. By contrast, Arizona contained 14,172 Mexicans, California 8,096, and New Mexico 6,649. No other state had as many as 500.

The first decade of the 20th century brought an enormous reversal of the trend. The reason was the new development of massive agriculture and the processing of agricultural products in the American Southwest. In Texas, the combination of spreading rails, organized land companies, and extensive irrigation projects invaded the old cattle enclaves along the Rio Grande. Surveyors, in the last great American land rush, laid out vast tracts through the brushland where Rip Ford and Cheno Cortinas once rode. New cities were laid out, too, some on old settlement sites, some on new, such as the Western Land Company's bright new town of Weslaco, in rich alluvial soils a few miles from the Rio Grande. With diverted water, the *brasada* and the *ebonal* began to bloom with fields of fruits and vegetables. The Texas citrus industry began; millions of acres were cleared and plowed.

Until this time, economic gravity along the border lay with Mexico. Matamoros was a rich city; Brownsville, after 1882, had reverted to a sleepy small town. The border, separated by the arid country between it and San Antonio, lay outside the economic boundaries of the United States, except for cattle, and more cattle were shipped abroad than sent North. Mexican money was even dominant; border merchants continually complained as falling silver prices depreciated their stocks of "adobe dollars," or Mexican silver pesos, vis-à-vis United States gold. The new development changed all this; it brought the Southwest back firmly into the United States. Tons of vegetables, fresh and canned, were shipped North by rail; towns and cities swelled. New blood came in, because here was a lusty new frontier, where a man with capital could make his fortune out of crops and land.

This entire development was based on Mexican labor. In fact, none of it would or could have taken place without a great mass of low-paid workers from south of the border. Much of the new lands was marginal, and since irrigation and drainage was required, it took enormous investments in capital to develop them. Further, these croplands were separated by immense distances from their markets, almost entirely in the far North and East. The cost of land, irrigation, and crushing freight charges could only be met by using labor cheaper than any other in the United States. Without Mexican labor, the Southwest could no more have been developed agriculturally than the huge cotton plantations could have produced their surpluses for the antebellum South without the Negroes.

Day wages, even for low pay, offered the Mexican lowest class opportunities it did not enjoy at home. Thousands of Mexicans were recruited below the border; others, sensing a new frontier of their own, poured north. The Anglo-Americans had solved the problems of Indians, transportation, and large-scale agriculture in old Spanish Texas, and until all this had been done, mass Mexican immigration into Texas simply could not take place. In each year after 1900, more Mexicans emigrated into Texas than had gone there during all the generations of Spanish rule.

These new workers, hardy, gregarious, polite, accustomed to savage suffering, long bound to the soil, arrived not only as adventurous individuals but in whole family and extended family groups. Very few of them were *vaqueros* from northern Mexico. They poured up from the immense central plateau, where the Spanish had first established the *encomienda* and *hacienda,* from the states of Michoacán, Guanajuato, Jalisco, and Nuevo León. They were predominantly Indian by blood, but long Hispanicized, and they fled from the Mexican regions where landholdings were the largest and conditions for the *pelados,* "the skinned ones," were the worst. Thousands fled to escape debt peonage, as once European peasants fled from manor to town, or took ship for America. These Mexicans entered a new country where most of the land and almost all the means of production were owned by Anglos. They were subjected to fierce exploitation, by American, but not Mexican, standards. Mexican laborers took jobs at 50 cents per day, but still, in a month, some earned more cash than they had seen in their entire lives. No Anglo-Texan could exploit this *pelado* class to the extent it had been exploited in Mexico for four hundred years.

They poured in, increasing the ethnic Mexican population of Texas between 1900 and 1910 by 76 percent. In ten years, between 1910 and

1920, 264,503 arrived, and 165,044 in the next decade. Most of this immigration was utterly informal. There was no quota placed on immigration from the Western Hemisphere; in many cases Mexicans simply crossed the river. Years later, there were hundreds of thousands of Mexican nationals living in south Texas who had been residents for three or more decades, but who had never taken citizenship. After a certain period of residence, or the birth of children, they were not deportable.

Because they came *en masse,* to an area where there was already a Mexican presence, they failed to assimilate culturally as did other groups; further, there was a deep racial barrier between the dark-skinned Indian-blooded peasant and the color-conscious white Southerner. Mexicans, like Negroes, entered with certain problems not faced by other national groups. The acute problem was only recognized nationally in the 1960's, when the migration, running now at some 50,000 per year, aroused fears in Washington.

The fact that Middle America was expanding its population faster than any region on earth, with people far outrunning economic development, caught attention. Mexico would have a population of 70,000,000 in the last quarter of the 20th century. This realization resulted in the first quotas ever placed on Western Hemisphere immigration, 100,000 per year. But by 1950 there were already 1,500,000 ethnic Mexicans in Texas, comprising 17 percent of the total population. Increase and steady immigration pushed the percentage to approximately 20 by the 1960's, and all projections, even figuring in the immigration quotas, predicted an increase. One in five of all Texans was Spanish-speaking. This was hardly mere immigration; it was colonization.

Studies published by the University of Texas as early as 1920 warned of immense ethnic and social problems to come, unless this *Völkerwanderung* were stemmed. It was already recognized that the Mexican immigrants were not assimilating, in fact, had no desire to assimilate or adopt Anglo culture. The second generation was not learning English. But the developer and farmer in the Rio Grande Valley, the pecan sheller and cigar maker in San Antonio, thousands of housewives wanting maids, were as adamant as the South African Boer would have been, if told he should send his Bantu boys back to the veld from which they came.

The immigrants were rural Mexicans, and their exodus was very similar to the exodus of rural Negroes out of the Mississippi drainage to the North. The reasons behind both movements were identical. The great social and political revolution that shook Mexico beginning in 1910 affected the rural masses least. The old feudal *hacienda* system was at last destroyed, allowing the beginnings of social reform and modernization of the state, but as in the United States, the beginnings of industrialism did not mean an immediate improvement for the people on the land. The revolution did little to stem emigration; the slacking of south Texas development during the Great Depression halted it for a time, but only briefly.

Meanwhile, the Mexican Revolution caused increased problems between Mexico and Texas.

Relations between Texas and Mexico had always depended in large degree upon whether order or chaos reigned below the Rio Grande. In 1910, a long period of chaos began, and this revived old troubles on the border. The Mexican Revolution, like most revolutions, was markedly antiforeign in tone; it upset the old empirical relationships Porfirio Díaz had hammered out, and inevitably embroiled Mexico in serious conflicts with the United States. The U.S. troop-landing at Vera Cruz and the dispatch of Pershing's army on a fruitless chase of Pancho Villa were not part of Texas history. But a tragedy of these years was the revival of the old racial war along the Rio Grande.

This region, even after the coming of the land companies, was always violent. Rangers and peace officers, for example, killed sixteen Mexicans between 1907 and 1912 in Hidalgo and Cameron counties alone. But the Mexican Revolution, which turned bloody when Felix Díaz, Reyes, and Huerta revolted against Madero in 1913, and Venustiano Carranza led his own revolt in the north, brought more Texan and American troops and fighting to the border than had been seen since the Civil War.

As government in Mexico again collapsed, and the ephemeral reigns of a series of warlords began, conditions in south Texas returned to something very much like the old days of the 1860's and 1870's. Large numbers of refugees crossed the border. Some very bloody battles were fought along the Mexican side, from Piedras Negras to Matamoros. The river was open and the country was still brush-choked and wide, and soon large parties of Mexican raiders, owing allegiance to no authority, rode looting and killing across the Bravo. This war was almost unnoticed in the thunder of greater conflict in Europe at the time.

This provoked a violent reaction against all ethnic Mexicans in the Rio Grande Valley. President Wilson sent large numbers of regulars and National Guardsmen to the Valley, and the Governor of Texas dispatched approximately a thousand Rangers, most of whom were recruited especially for the mission.

At this time, the loyalty of ethnic Mexicans was genuinely suspect; generally, it did not yet exist. Many Texas-Mexicans went south to avoid military service in 1917; at this time, even old families had not yet decided where their true nationality lay. German propaganda circulated among the Spanish-speaking, and the famous Plan of San Diego, signed both by natives of northern Mexico and some residents of the Texas side, aroused violent fears and reprisals.

Under the Plan of San Diego (named for San Diego, a town in south Texas, where one of the signers taught school; this same man, under another name, later served in Carranza's secret service in Mexico), ethnic Mexicans were to rise in Texas and proclaim their freedom from the Anglo-Saxon race. The independence of Texas, California, New Mexico,

Arizona, and Colorado was to be proclaimed, ending the settlement of the Treaty of Guadalupe Hidalgo. Two army corps of Mexicans were to be raised, under the Supreme Revolutionary Congress headquartered at San Diego. No one was to be enrolled in this army unless he was Mexican, Negro, Indian, or Japanese by blood. The revolutionary regime was to reestablish a new government for all captured Texas and Southwestern American towns, while every *gringo* male over sixteen was to be taken prisoner until all his money could be extorted, then shot. The Apaches of Arizona were to be promised the return of their old lands in return for joining the race war.

When the revolution had carried the five target states, they were to request "annexation" by Mexico, if this seemed "expedient." The six states adjoining the Southwest were to be forcibly severed from the United States and given to the Negroes, who would then form a buffer between the expanded Mexico and the United States east of the Mississippi.

When a copy of this glorious fantasy, which in truth aroused certain fevers in the Mexican breast, was found on a Mexican national captured in McAllen, Texas, by a deputy sheriff, the fat was in the fire. It is almost certain that no Spanish-speaking person authored it; although written in Spanish, certain usages were unidiomatic and wrong. Most authorities, later, suspected the Plan of San Diego was devised either by a German agent to stir up trouble at the United States' back door or by one of the many wealthy American landowners who were being dispossessed in Mexico at this time. But the description of the Plan as a "sublime" undertaking, and the reference to Anglos as "white-faced hogs from Pennsylvania" in other papers taken with the Plan, prepared the Anglo-Texans for race war.

Not long after the Plan was uncovered, the Zimmerman note was made public, in March, 1917. This "note," from the German Secretary of State for Foreign Affairs to the German ambassador in Mexico, through the German ambassador in Washington, proposed that an alliance be formed between Germany and Mexico to wage war on the United States. As part of the deal, Mexico was to reconquer Texas, New Mexico, and Arizona. The sum result of both the Plan and the note was to unleash Texan vengeance on numerous hapless and indiscreet citizens of Mexican or German descent. Many sought asylum in Mexico.

The events along the border between 1915 and 1919, like those of 1859–1876, had been almost consciously put aside by all concerned. It is a part of American history Texans take no pride in, and no one likes. Rangers and local posses, in retaliation for real crimes against American lives and property, committed other crimes. The Rangers, out of tradition, history, and the emotions of the times, "shot first and investigated afterward." This action, serious as the times were, was no longer called for, as dozens of local law enforcement officers later testified. The United States, and Texas, with 35,000 troops on the border in 1917, was in no danger from Mexico.

The Rangers, as still constituted, were something of an anachronism. Captains were appointed by the governor through the adjutant general, and these officers enlisted their own companies. Such state troops were essential during the frontier wars, but the Rangers had enjoyed less and less success as an internal police force. They performed numerous functions beyond the scope or powers of local authority, but the old partisan traditions, and politics, increasingly got in the way. The 19th century had called for Hays, Ford, and McNelly in Texas. The 20th century presented different problems, in an altered milieu. When one Ranger captain, in the 1920's, shot the tires off the car of a state official who had refused his command to halt, Texans smiled at his toughness. But this man, and those Rangers who still solved law enforcement problems by squaring away and requesting the other party to draw if he dared, were relicts of a frontier that, although it loomed large in Texans' minds, had disappeared.

Between 1915 and 1917, many Rangers emulated Captain McNelly, in altered circumstances. Instead of genuine partisan warfare, they waged persecutions. They by no means bore the whole guilt; local citizens and sheriffs, and even the army, shared in it. There were numerous cases of flogging, torture, threatened castration, and legalized murder. Even some of this was justified by events, since the Rangers faced some of the cruelest outlaws who ever lived. But enough of this reprisal fell on people innocent of any crime but the one of being Mexican to discredit the whole.

One incident testified to by Sheriff W. T. Vann of Cameron County was illustrative of some hundred others. On October 18, 1915, Mexican bandits wrecked and looted a passenger train six miles north of Brownsville. Sheriff Vann and a party of Rangers captured four men suspected of having taken part in the attack. The Rangers decided to take the captives into the brush and shoot them, since they had had poor experience in getting convictions at trials. Vann refused to take part in this and was told by one Ranger: "If you do not have the guts to do it, I will." The four Mexicans were shot. Vann, however, commended many Rangers; they were more effective than the army in this brush fighting. But with the good men, there were some vicious misfits in the force.

R. B. Creager of Brownsville, Republican National Committeeman from Texas, testified later that about 200 Mexicans had been executed without trial by Rangers, local officers, and citizens. He estimated that 90 percent of these had committed no crime. At this time, every male in these counties of Texas went armed with six-shooter or rifle. If an ethnic Mexican were found armed, however, he was sometimes accused of banditry and shot. No record exists of these executions, which were estimated to number between 200 and 5,000, because obviously no records were made or kept. Accounts do exist of the finding of many bodies here and there, and the burial of these. A good estimate, by old hands, suggested that about 300 ethnic Mexicans were summarily executed in reprisals. Most of these were Texas

Mexicans; hundreds of others fled to Mexico, where Carranzanista officials extorted large sums from them before permitting them to stay.

In 1919, J. T. Canales, state representative from Brownsville, introduced a bill in the legislature to reorganize and upgrade the Ranger force. Canales was a member of an old landowning family; he professed no desire to destroy the Rangers, but to rid them of unqualified and vicious men and to remove the force from politics. An exhaustive investigation ensued, and at the end of it, the Rangers were badly discredited. A bill passed the legislature that in effect abolished the Texas Rangers as the principal state police force and sharply reduced their numbers to 76 men. A few years afterward the Ranger functions were given to the new state highway patrol. The Rangers lived on, but as a small, elite force of 60 men, whose work was primarily investigative, but who were available for duty during disorders and situations in which local officers could not keep control. Mexican complaints alone did not destroy the Rangers, though this was commonly believed. The force was intensely disliked by many local law officers and citizens, especially during the Prohibition years. Rangers, operating free of local pressures, smashed illegal gambling casinos, destroyed liquor, and generally harassed some illegal operations that many sheriffs and local powers preferred to have them leave alone. The Hays-McNelly tradition, dear to every Ranger heart, made them respected and loved at large, but in many quarters hated and feared. No Ranger was in the habit of issuing the same order twice.

Between 1911 and 1920, race hatred was reinflamed along the border, where it had never completely died. Unknown to most Anglo-Texans who took pride in their famous Rangers, *Rinche* again assumed the proportion of a bugaboo in Spanish-speaking minds. Children were frightened with the term. Almost every lower-class ethnic Mexican alive in those years carried a violent, superstitious fear of Rangers, and the folk-hatred had permeated so deeply into all Mexicans that even third- and fourth-generation citizens, who had never actually seen a Ranger, reacted with an instinctive phobia toward the name.

Senate investigators, including Edward Kennedy of Massachusetts, who held hearings on labor disputes in the Rio Grande Valley in 1967, were puzzled and perhaps given erroneous impressions by the violent reactions of ethnic Mexicans to the sending of a Texas Ranger to the area. This was an ancestral race hatred that Kennedy and even most Texans, with little knowledge of the past, could not quite understand.

The triumph of the Mexican Revolution ended the bloody skirmishing along the border, but it did not halt continual Mexican immigration. The Party of Revolutionary Institutions, which took power and held it afterward, modernized Mexico in great degree, but the PRI had no real place in its plans for peasants. Industrialization of Monterrey and other centers was pushed and capitalized, while agriculture, at least until the 1960's, languished. Some Mexican peasants in 1960 were poorer than they had been fifty years before, and there was actually less food in Mexico to eat. This continued to force a stream of migration north, both as temporary laborers, or *braceros,* and as permanent residents.

However, the restabilization of Mexico gradually eroded the old fears and hatreds along the frontier. While Mexico remained in disorder, it was impossible for Americans to regard the nation with respect. As Mexico began to modernize and, more important, send thousands of new-rich urban shoppers into Texas cities, respect increased. By the 1960's, in some Texas cities the Mexican trade during the Holy Week vacation was as important as the local trade at Christmas. The average Mexican tourist, coming from a society where all manufactured goods were high or scarce, spent more than $1,000 per visit, against the average American expenditure south of the border of $400. Of course, the tourists were of a different type. The Americans were largely young people and schoolteachers; the Mexican shoppers almost entirely from the new-rich, industrial upper and middle class that arose with revolutionary Mexico. In the 1940's, all of the old border forts were closed. Relations among the United States, Texas, and the Mexican nation entered their friendliest era in history. Once again the dominant groups in Mexico were empirically nonhostile to the northern neighbor, as in Díaz' day, and the United States, so long as neither its borders nor its interests were threatened from below, was entirely amiable. Unless some new, unforeseen cataclysm tore either nation, relations had entered a long, stable, and happy phase. Only a newer Mexican revolution, or a violent leftist swing in that progressively more conservative country, could undo this trend.

But as historic hatreds damped, the emerging ethnic problem in south Texas far from disappeared. The Mexican problem in Texas had shifted its center of gravity from Mexicans in Mexico to ethnic Mexicans in the United States. Here ground was both gained and lost.

Until 1920, the Mexican population was rural, stable, and inert. Then, it began to move, first into local towns, crowding into noisy neighborhoods, moving out in the fields each day to work. It kept being sucked north, drawn by the lights of San Antonio, until it made San Antonio the capital of that part of Mexico that lay within the United States. Mexicans were inherently urban. This was part of a great worldwide trend; similar groups of rural laborers were streaming to the large cities of South and Middle America, piling into smelly slums and rickety shacks. Sometimes they found work, often they did not. But life was still better in the city. Gradually, those who had citizenship discovered social services and welfare, and ultimately, the great discovery of all urban masses since the time of Rome, political power.

The Mexican Revolution, and the events of World War I years, produced a decided swing among the older immigrants, and the old Spanish-Mexican stock, toward becoming genuine citizens of the United States.

After World War I, and the turmoil and shock of 1915–1917 on the border, Texas Mexicans opted strongly toward fusion with the Anglo society. Radicalism and counterreligious activity to the south offended many, while the shock of renewed persecution made most realize they had to take a stand. From 1920 onwards, the basic loyalty and patriotism of the overwhelming majority of ethnic Mexicans could not possibly be suspect. Just as Anglo-Texans responded in disproportionate numbers during World War II, Hispanic Texans responded with even greater élan. They made valiant soldiers. They won a high proportion of the Medals of Honor granted to citizens of the state. They threatened no more revolutions nor spoke of the injustices of the Peace of Guadalupe Hidalgo. They were basically hard-working, and remarkably law-abiding, considering their background and economic class.

However, they were different. Because most of them came to Texas for economic opportunity, not to become *agringado* ("Americanized"), they colonized; they did not assimilate. They wanted to live and work and improve their lot in Texas but not to become Anglos in any way. In this they resembled faithfully the Anglo-Saxons who had entered Texas in the preceding century. The Anglos also came for opportunity, with no intentions to Mexicanize. Few Anglos in the old days ever bothered to learn Spanish; few Mexican immigrants ever adopted English as their primary language. The Mexicans, however, did not enter an empty province, which they could develop and dominate. They rapidly became the most numerous group throughout all south Texas—in some communities 90 percent of the total inhabitants, about 70 percent over-all—but they entered a society totally owned by previous conquerors, and run under very non-Mexican concepts and rules.

The Anglo attitude progressed through a number of gradual changes. During the long years of border stagnation, the few Anglos, who had complete economic control, continued to look on Mexicans as a useful underclass. Mexicans were small, superstitious, ignorant, and dark by Nordic standards. They performed a function similar to that of the slave caste. Inevitably, the first Texas reaction was to equate ethnic Mexicans, almost unconsciously, with Negroes.

This Texan attitude was not so arrogant as it seemed; it followed very closely the attitude of the native Spanish elite. Between 1836 and 1880 there was much intermarriage between incoming Anglos, particularly Roman Catholics, and the older families. Some of these families became *inglesado* or *agringado;* they Anglicized. Most did not, retaining their profound belief in the aristocracy of lineal descent and superior culture. All through south Texas existed a small but tightly knit aristocracy of which the majority of Anglos were not even aware, even though many of these families retained lands or wealth. After the turn of the century, there was less and less association, for two reasons.

The horde of lower-caste farm laborers injected a sour note, at a time when original war antagonisms had had time to die. Anglos tended to equate all people with Spanish names, unable to distinguish between a Harvard or Sorbonne graduate named Terrazas and an Indian with a similar last name. The idea of an elite based on culture and family descent was enormously repugnant to the dominant Anglo middle class in any case. They were intensely suspicious of both things. Many older Texas residents of Spanish ancestry looked on the invasion of farm labor with much the same horror that the tiny group of well-integrated Northern Negroes must have seen the coming of the sharecropper millions to Chicago and New York. They dragged down the whole definable group. Most Americans refused to believe that there were class distinctions between Mexicans based on family and descent, or any Mexican culture besides Indian artifacts and folk music accompanied by guitars.

The apocryphal story of the Texas artistocrat who asked an Anglo doctor if he had read Cervantes' classic, *Don Quijote,* and was answered, "No, but I believe I saw the picture," was illustrative of an enormous gulf, even greater than smiling Anglos who heard the story realized. The value systems of *Don Quijote* were not translatable into the English tongue. Between Anglo-Saxons and *la raza* lay a greater cultural ocean than almost any ethnocentric American understood. Americans shared more values with Germans and Japanese than they did with Hispanic neighbors to the south; yet this, apparently because of geography, was most vehemently denied.

The Spanish elite had its choice; it could assimilate or not. It did not provide ethnic leadership for the great Mexican mass. The Cheno Cortinases were rare. This class, the *hacendados,* never provided any sort of political leadership in Mexico, before or after independence. This was simply not a characteristic of the *criollo* upper class. The political dominance of Mexico came into the hands of the *mestizo* middle classes, first as military leaders and finally, when enough of them existed to inject a revolutionary fervor and provide leadership for the part or wholly Indian mass, as leaders of the whole society. The old elite in Texas tended to withdraw to itself rather than inject itself into public affairs. This was why the Anglo leaders of the Reds and Blues had no trouble taking control of the politically inert Mexican lower class.

The Texans in the 20th century applied the same parameters to the Mexican as they did to the Negro, and found him wanting in most respects. Mexicans were segregated officially in almost all south Texas public schools, in separate classes from Anglo students. This segregation was not applied to the Spanish, or almost-Spanish, elite, who were recognizably white. The term "white" was rarely if ever used for ethnic Mexicans by native Texans, although officially the Mexican race was designated as Caucasian—this, in itself, a reverse form of racial arrogance. The terms "white man" and "Mexican" aroused bitterness among those Mexicans proud of Indian ancestry,—because it forced the Mexican to equate himself in Anglo esteem with the Negro, whom the Mexican, if truth be told, also despised.

Ethnic Mexicans were almost universally residentially segregated. The new towns in the Rio Grande Valley were laid out with designated Mexican quarters across the railroad tracks. Following the pattern of the Negro, except for voting rights, almost every form of discrimination applied, making the ethnic Mexican another, separate depressed caste. The Negro-authored Texas jinglet presented a truer picture of the real social situation than pages of official study:

> If you're white, well, all right!
> If you're brown, you can stick around.
> But if you're black—stand back.

Mexicans provided useful services to the burgeoning economy; they were encouraged to stick around. They were not encouraged to meddle in the white folks' business. Intermarriage was not illegal—but unthinkable. It should be understood, however, that this incipient caste system was most pronounced among the old-line native Anglo-Texans. It was never fully adopted by Americans who came from other states. They were more likely to regard Mexicans as somewhat like Italo-Americans or other non-Nordic immigrants.

This understandable, and finally abortive, effort to equate Mexicans of the lower class with blacks confused much of the real problem in Texas. A great many Texans of goodwill, understanding the Mexican contribution to Texas following World War II, believed that the removal of such arbitrary caste barriers would cause Mexican-Anglo assimilation. They did not understand that the Mexican notion of *la raza* was a concept held at least as deeply by Mexicans as the Anglo-American preoccupation with the color line.

The concept of *la raza* did not translate into English adequately, like Cervantes' elegant language. It did not mean "race" as Anglos thought of race. It was as much spiritual as physical; it stood for a great gamut of almost mystical Hispanic values, most of which were antithetical to the Anglo-Saxon's much starker world. The Mexican, of all classes, was as differentiated in mind and soul and history from Anglo-Americans as the European Jews entering 20th-century Israel were from Arabs. Here, the great American assumption that all peoples were, or should be, more or less like Americans in their desires and values, broke.

Texas destroyed Mexican segregation—except for some local diehard insistence here and there, and the segregation imposed by income and residence among all races—in both schools and homes. This was done following World War II. At the same time, a great many social barriers eased, if they did not disappear. This did not make an immediate difference, because the great mass of ethnic Mexicans were still lower-class laborers, but it did seem to offer opportunity for the coming generation.

The Texas Mexican who had matured prior to 1949 on the average had just three years' schooling. He was functionally illiterate, in any language. His opportunities to rise above farm worker or city garbageman were rare. There were so many of him, and he was so disorganized in a strange society, that the lot of the whole could hardly be improved. Unionism was not practicable on farms and it had no support in American law, unlike unionism in industry. The glut of immigration, further, flooded the market; the organization of labor was not possible in a state like Texas, without vast industry, where there was a large surplus of black and brown laborers for most jobs. This glut of indigent people not only drove the whole group down economically but also logically intensified racial prejudices.

There did grow, slowly, a considerable ethnic Mexican middle class. But this only further polarized an already separate society. By 1965, studies showed that the Mexican resident of Texas had fallen far behind the Negro in acquired education. Schools were open to him; the laws, so far as they could be enforced, encouraged him to attend them. While the average Texan Negro had received almost twelve years of schooling, the Mexican still had acquired seven years or less. The problem was language. The Mexican, overwhelmingly, whether he was first, second, or sometimes even fifth generation, entered the first grade unable to speak English. If he progressed, he was always behind. Too many grew discouraged and dropped out. These joined the hordes in menial jobs, speaking English badly, with strong accents, or took up migrant farm work, homing in Texas, but ranging as far as Michigan.

It was found almost impossible to induce the Mexican to surrender Spanish, as Italian-Americans consciously gave up Italian or German-Americans soon forgot the ancestral tongue. Spanish was the language of friendship, race, family, home. It gave him comfort; but it also codified his mind, and value system, into ways alien to an English-speaking society long before he emerged into the world. The educators and planners and social workers in Texas crashed, with great frustration, into a cultural problem few Americans even believed to exist.

The Mexican-American remained too much Mexican to move, or compete, in a social system that stayed foreign to him. He became unique in the United States: a native-born citizen, often of many generations, who was still a foreigner in his native land. Only Europe, with its myriad of ethnic groups, offered a similar aspect, and the example of Europe, where cultural groups clung stubbornly to ancestral customs and languages despite minority status and discrimination within the boundaries of foreign states, could only be depressing.

In this milieu, the growing Mexican middle class reacted much as did a similar emerging middle class in the province of Quebec, engulfed in an English-speaking sea. This group primarily provided services for its own people, as storekeepers, lawyers, doctors, and, more and more, politicians. With its emergence, political interest also emerged among the Mexicans. In the 1930's, very few ethnic Mexicans held political office, even in areas where they predominated. By the 1950's, this radically changed, as new lawyers, medics, and businessmen began successfully to stand for office, offering leadership to their own race.

The new middle class was not more Anglicized—although it did, from necessity, speak English—but tended to be more ethnically aware than either the elite or the depressed working class. It felt discrimination more keenly. Educated, it clung to Hispanic values more fervently than the illiterate mass, who sensed them rather than intelligently understood them. It did not learn English with a native accent, and spoke Spanish at home by choice. Above all else, the majority of this new group, like its counterpart in old Mexico, wanted to raise the whole standard of the race. It wanted equality, not Americanization; a sort of fusion, not assimilation, in which both Hispanic and Anglo values would be equally respected and recognized.

What it wanted was not impossible, but almost impossible to obtain, because the two value systems did not easily fuse. Elena Landazuri, in trying to explain to Anglo-Americans why Hispanic Americans were different, wrote:

> We have a different mental or perhaps spiritual reaction to the world . . . Other peoples, perhaps, desire the means to live, money to build, to do good, to spend. They want to impress themselves upon the world; our treasure is time. We must think, we must chat, we must see, we must enjoy ourselves, we must be.

Nowhere in the Mexican ethos were the bedrock assumptions, the value system that lay so close to the Anglo heart that no Anglo bothered to rationalize or think about it: work as a virtue, transcending all necessity; wealth as a desirable, if not the only desirable, basis of status; the drive for status itself. The incessant drives of Anglo society struck most thinking Mexicans as barren and inhuman. The incessant argument that to be was as important as to do of the Mexicans struck most hard-working Anglos as pure shiftlessness, if not something far more subversive.

A Mexican-American, thrown into a dominant society suffused with the American frontier values, trying to compete in an atomistic, consciously struggling, fragmented social fabric whose apex was not honor but success, carrying along not only a mental attic full of organic values but often an extended family group as well, started with impossible handicaps. English-speaking persons owned 80 percent of the property and production means of Quebec, although the French-Canadians had long ruled the province politically. The reason was not discrimination or conspiracy, although these did exist, but something the utterly Latin soul kept trying to reject. The Protestant ethic, whether held by Protestants, Catholics, or Jews, drove its possessor to lengths with which no humanistic thought could

compete. The Mexican found it hard to depersonalize. He could not gracefully swim in America's vast, impersonal industrial-financial seas.

The differences, and the aspects of these differences, were endless; they
could not be obviated unless the Mexican either consciously or unconsciously rejected his heritage. Americans offered him the chance to do so, as
they offered all other immigrants, and Texans' contempt was extreme when
the Mexican, still complaining bitterly because his own values were not
accepted, let the offer pass.

The manifestations of discontent that in the 1960's began to appear—
strikers bearing emblems of the Virgin of Guadalupe, union leaders demanding improvement of the workers' lot—were not nearly so important,
or so dangerous to the whole society, as the new, sudden demands of the
rising classes: bilingual education, instruction in Hispanic civilization, the
fused society. These aroused little alarm, because their implications, in the
practical and pragmatic, noncultural Anglo society, were not understood.
Many people were inclined to grant them, thinking this might make Americans of Mexicans at last. Politicians who needed Mexican votes, and could
no longer take for granted a group shaking off its inertia, were inclined
even more so to go along.

The Texas Mexican could make it more easily politically than he could
economically, in his new chosen land.

In the 1960's, when more than half of the nearly 750,000 people in San
Antonio were Spanish-speaking, the outlines of the emergence, through
political power, of a new Quebec were clear. Few Americans saw this,
because few Americans enjoyed perspective. There was a grudging feeling
that the Mexican had to be given a better break. Experimental classes in
bilingual education were already under way; there were strong pressures to
give Mexicans at least ceremonial membership on all public boards and
offices, whether they were qualified or not. The day of the Anglo political
boss was almost over; the Democratic Party writhed in concern, while the
Republicans sniffed the signs of major overturn. It was beginning to be
widely said, and believed, that the ballot was the American way to equality
and respect. Few dared say that it was also the way to confirm a Mexican
nation living entirely within the United States. Less concerned than any
were a new horde of American-Anglo businessmen, many from the Northern states, who had realized that the "unique Spanish culture of old San
Antonio" held glorious opportunities for profit. "Old Spanish culture," like
spicy Mexican food, could be endlessly purveyed, above all to an increasing Northern American mass losing its own sense of identity and roots.
Whatever came of this new confluence of cultures in Texas, it could no
more be stopped than the original invasion had been, because out of it some
men made money.

The Mexican could make a new Quebec in south Texas, but it was not
likely he could remake the greater society to which he, like the Anglo-Texan
himself, was irremediably attached. He was probably always doomed to feel

somewhat a stranger in his own land, for which he had a profound love. Already, a new Mexican mythos was coming forth: the Mexican had always been there; the land had always resounded to the Spanish tongue; this land was theirs. All of this was true, but only in limited degree.

A defeated Anglo politician, driving past the Alamo, was perhaps more bitter than profound, when he said: "Next time, that place will not fall by bullets; they'll use the American way." In this, perhaps, was still a profound hope. At worst, the polarization into powerful Anglo and Hispanic societies could produce new trouble; it was not likely to create worse trouble, or more injustice, than there had already been before. At worst, it could create a Mexican Quebec. At best, it could make, instead, an American Alsace. This much was certain. The world was not made, nor was the great game of cultural life and death upon the planet done.

37

THE AMERICANS

After all these things do the Gentiles seek;
After all these things do the Gentiles seek.
FROM THE CHORUS OF
THE CANTERBURY WOMEN IN
"MURDER IN THE CATHEDRAL,"
T. S. ELIOT

WHILE the wagons were moving westward, and the sun rose on endless vistas of unconquered, almost empty land across their continent, Americans were fortunate. The American nation did not have to seek its mission or rationalize its conduct. It possessed two instinctive goals: to expand across its chosen continent and to become predominant upon it. Any dynamic human society would have attempted to do the same. Americans succeeded, almost too easily, because the cultures they met were static and unable to adapt. Unlike the reconquest of medieval Spain, the conquest of North America did not involve the minds, bodies, and souls of all those who came to inhabit America; therefore, the hearts of those Americans who took part in the great movement would be different, in the world that followed, from those who did not.

The history of Texas was unique in North America, but never unique or even unusual in the world of man. It was an old, old story: new peoples, new civilizations impinging upon the old. The reactions of these peoples— Caucasian, Amerind, and Hispanic-Mexican—were in no sense aberrations. The treatment of one culture or one race by another was always determined by relative strengths and weaknesses, and by the nature of the cultures themselves, dynamic or regressive. It was never, and probably never will be, so long as men stay men, determined by internal ethical or moral ideas and institutions. More Texans understood this, out of their history, than their compatriots who never physically or spiritually left the safety of the sheltering Appalachians.

The open frontier was a great, unifying, imperial experience, and one that was continued for generations with only minor pain. But when the words of the song "Across the Wide Missouri" were no longer a call to action or a spur to dreams but touched a profound nostalgia in the American mind, and the image of the Rio Grande recalled faded moonlight rather than hot blood, a certain sense of purpose departed from the American soul. At the very hour Americans stood at last predominant upon their continent and emerged as a power into the world, they showed the first signs of incoherency, ultrarationalism, and frustration. Their world policies grew confused. Europeans who called America an immature power had it wrong: American society was showing the signs of immense success and age. Only new societies had a deep and simple sense of mission or could move after predominance and power without having to rethink their uses.

The search for new missions and new myths was certain to be prolonged and painful. The first fatuous hope that the world was made collapsed in the recurrent assaults by other powers upon the political structures erected during the previous century. The United States oscillated between self-satisfaction and disillusionment, with others and itself, between powerful thrusts out into the world and abrupt retreats. Like Rome, during and following the Carthaginian wars, America had to hammer out a new form of advance, and a new world view. It had made itself an island, or more accurately, a continental power, but no nation could remain an island in a reclosing ecumene.

The great power possessed by Americans would be used, wisely or disastrously. No people possessing power ever completely eschewed its employment. The American idealists who felt a sense of mission to protect or improve the earth, and the American cynics who weighed every use of power in self-defense, essentially followed the same course. Both found frustration, and nowhere was this frustration more apparent than in the frontier-conditioned regions, because never again was the United States apt to achieve such decisive results as it won on its own shores, against the kind of obstacles it met.

As always, the end of the expanding frontier and the refinement of civilization behind it forced the nation to feed upon itself. Increased internal organization, compulsion, and control were inevitable; the relatively tribal frontier society would coalesce into classes and then bureaucracies, with increasing social distinctions, whatever they were called. The outcome of the War Between the States prepared inevitabilities, but it did not end all resistance. Texas conducted a long, and losing, series of delaying actions and last-ditch campaigns. But as the planter economy was destroyed, so was the cattle kingdom, and finally the bedrock social institution, the family farm. As the better-organized Texas society exterminated Indians and cowed Mexicans, Texas itself was made subject by greater organization and power. Nothing could prevent this, not even Wilson's and the second Roosevelt's nostalgic reforms. The pressures on frontier society were as pervasive as the pressures on the Norman-conquered Saxons. For all the Populists' complaints about the immorality of their millions of individual crucifixions, better organization always won, not only by brute power but by conversion.

Texas was always torn by the historic East-West tension in Anglo-America, the tension that existed from the time Anglo-Celtic frontiersmen found their policies dictated in Pennsylvania by men with incomprehensible Quaker ideas. The tension was based more on regional outlooks and interests than status or class. The Westerners always seemed more "democratic" because they were relatively classless in the social sense; the Anglo-Celt was more tribal than hierarchical. This enabled the Westerner to build a society with immense inequities, but which appeared egalitarian. Andrew Jackson lived in a great mansion, surrounded by thousands of acres and hundreds of slaves, yet appeared a "common" man, because the Westerner clung to his tribal vulgarity through many stations in life. He even rejected the notion that there were stations in life. The planter society did infuse incipient aristocracy, but it was abortive.

Because neither Kentucky nor Texas could have survived without assistance and artifacts from the Atlantic slopes; no matter how vigorous or violent the West became, it had to be subordinate. The West invariably held less people, and numbers determined dominant law. Because poor people settled the West, the frontier was always in debt. Even the capitalistic farmer, the cotton planter, and the wheat or citrus man in later years depended on money that had its wellsprings in the East. A certain form of colonialism always colored American history during the winning of the West. The West fought back, at times successfully, through politics. Alliances, however, like the New York-Virginia axis or the Boston-Austin deal, were generally fragile.

The East was structured, the West consciously if falsely classless; the West was imperialistic; the East was Atlantic-looking; the East was money-holding; the West held the cheap-money beliefs of the land-poor. All these conditions were enough to preserve lasting differences between the regions. But all these were the basis of interest politics, for which the federal apparatus had been invented. There were certain other differences between the Texan and most other Americans that were harder to define and even more difficult to obviate.

The people who moved remorselessly into the frontier, who destroyed the great Amerind hunting preserve with a glacial advance developed certain weaknesses and strengths. Their first great strength was the sense of moral superiority, which gave them a crushing advantage over the Amerind, the Mexican, and the Negro race they dragged along. Austin, Houston, Hays, and McNelly struck the Hispanic-Mexican culture with a force like that of the *conquistadores* who struck the Aztecs. They, and the hordes behind them, rarely doubted the essential rightness of their kind and ways.

The feeling at times led to a high nobility, and frequently to a valor, like that of the *conquistadores,* almost beyond belief. When the Texians decided "to hold these ditches or die in them," this was not fatalism or courage born of desperation. It was the sort of combative will that more often than not carries all before it. Cortés wanted at the Amerinds. Travis wanted at the Mexicans, and so did Ford, McNelly, and Hays. The men who beat the Comanches were the ones who sought them out.

This same sense of superiority also produced self-satisfaction, chauvinism, and brutal prejudice, traits for which Texans and Spaniards became equally famed. The feelings were guileless and therefore guiltless. The Texan never doubted he was superior to the Indian, the Mexican, and Negro slave; all the other races excelled in something, but the Texan could count his superiority in obvious ways. He was able to exterminate the Indian, conquer the Mexican, and the black man was already his slave. To have expected people with an empirical cast of mind to adopt an ideology of equality was in itself beyond belief.

Another great strength of the Texan was his very empiricism. He carried few ideologies to the West. The Spanish conquest broke on the bitterly husbanded belief that the Texas Indians could be civilized, the trampling of reality under old ideas. The mission and presidio served on the Mexican plateaus; both were useless on the Comanche frontier. The Texan brought some equally useless experience with him when he entered onto the seas of grass. But he possessed a remarkable ability to see the real world, shed old baggage quickly, and change. Any useful tool, any new technique, exploded across the whole frontier. He seized the horse like any Spanish *caballero,* saw the superiority of repeating firearms before any tradition-bound army in the world, and, in the west of Texas, even restructured his dirt-farming society and law. The horse, the pistol, and the unwritten code of the West were not laughable in their day. They left an impress that lingers still.

The codes and actions of the Texans showed that all men seek moral and temporal order, but not necessarily the same kind. If Charles Goodnight, Jack Hays, and L. H. McNelly had waited for someone to make law for them or hand down precedent-justice, the intolerable conditions of the frontier would have lasted longer. Hays and McNelly, judged against their own times, were not murderers but warriors; the charge fails to stick in their white hats. The taking of life could not and did not develop the stigma in Texas it already had in the more sedate regions of America, because the Texans were at war. Hays, who shot down many a squaw outside her tepee, was no more a killer than the bombardier who dropped his armament on crowded tenements in World War II. Both consciously worked to defend his own people by breaking the enemy's will.

In the same milieu, the shoot-out was an incident rather than murder, if it was carried out according to the rules. On the frontier, the burden of self-defense lay on the individual; it was a burden that could not be denied. If it was one he could not bear, this was his tough luck. No one forced anyone else to come to the Texas frontier.

Many of the emulators of L. H. McNelly and Jack Hays were killers. Codes tend to live on in debased form, often long after the necessity that called them forth is dead. McNelly shot a dozen Mexican bandits and left them where they lay. But the Cameron County of 1875 was not the county of 1915, when other Rangers left other hapless Mexicans littered through the brush. Like the gentleman's sword in Europe and Ireland, the pistol lingered very long after it had ceased to be a necessary tool. Men wore pistols on the border until the middle of the 20th century, and no few of them got in trouble for it. In the 1960's, all Texas had a high shoot-out, now called murder, rate. The laws dealt with unpremeditated killing more leniently than those of any other American state.

The lawlessness of Texas was generally misunderstood. At least half of it came because of continual attempts to impose law that did not fit the place or times. No intelligent people obey laws that contradict their society or otherwise make no sense. The Texan was not so much lawless as law-making, bending his own concept of law to fit conditions few Easterners, even east Texans, could comprehend. The notion that the border must live by the same legal codes as bound the streets of New York seemed logical to some. But to the Texan, an Indian policy written by Easterners that permitted Kiowas to flaunt blond hair or an army policy that made commanders adhere to instructions on how to catch Mexican cattle thieves coming by Washington telegraph, was incredible. The policies and instructions were often ignorant, because they came from men ignorant of local conditions or affairs.

The cattlemen, fence-busting, and nester wars do not fit simply into patterns of aggression or greed. The West was able to handle the range hog, until the Eastern law interfered. Land laws were broken because the Homestead Acts made no sense, except to farmer legislatures who could not even envision what the country beyond the 98th meridian was like. Congress never agreed to make the homestead base 2,650 acres in the West, although this was intelligently proposed. This amount of land was the basic minimum a stockman needed to survive, but in the face of all such evidence the small-farm-heritage Easterners refused to pass such laws. Like Indian policy, Eastern law often broke down in the West, because it absurdly failed to take local conditions into account.

Lawyers failed to recognize such on-the-spot solutions as range and water rights. They gave those with legal title to the ground the right to fence it off, even if this fencing barred other men's cattle from grass or water. Millions of dollars in damage was done, and many lives lost, before certain compromises were made. The cattleman gained his ground by hook or crook, often falsifying before the law, but he gained it. The law recognized that public roads could not be fenced and that openings had to be left each three miles. The English common law was amended to recognize that all the people living in a watershed, in arid country, had rights to flowing water, not just those who owned the river banks. None of these things were easily done, because men think in preset ways. In the course of such troubles, Texans understandably came to hold many reservations about the infallibility of laws.

One important Texan discovery and usage was local option. Texas had wide divergences in climate, topography, and the way men earned their livings; it soon occurred to legislators that some statewide laws could not apply. Texans allowed counties to opt on pistol-wearing, open range, and later, on school segregation and the sale of alcohol. It was firmly established in the Texan mind that men make laws to their need and satisfaction, as Webb said, and for no other reason. To impress a Texan with the notion of a "higher moral law" outside of use and wont was like impressing a Comanche with the wisdom of the Great White Father in Washington. Both Indian and Texan bent, because they had to, before superior force. But men convinced against their will remained of the same opinion still.

Texans had few self-doubts. No conquering race could, and proceed to conquer. Here was an enormous strength in action, a strength most Americans exhibited through the 19th century on their way west. The Texans were purposeful, almost to a man. They came to Texas because they wanted land. Men like Rip Ford, who, unlike some of the men he showed up in the field, never was able to acquire land, keenly felt the bite of failure in their old age. This terrible, psychological sense of failure could not easily be understood in more stable societies, where men were not expected to acquire property come hell or high water. Honors meant very little in Texas. The successful Ranger captains, who left few if any legends, were Armstrongs and Tobins who did have the pragmatic sense to acquire ranches while they could. This tradition did not end. Land acquired a prestige value in Texas not unlike the landed estate in 18th-century England. Almost universally, successful politicians bought ranches, which had a symbolic value far beyond any possible income that might be derived from them. Senator Lyndon Johnson and Governor John Connally, both of whom began poor, instinctively sought large tracts of land. Their offices did not mean as much to their Texan souls as the ownership of thousands of acres. When they possessed miles of ranch lands, they had arrived.

It was very noticeable that the most prestigious people, in the Texan mind, were the owners of visible property. The corporation executive, who might make far more actual money, lagged far behind. Old-line Texans put their capital in real estate as well; even wealthy men from old families kept a certain distrust of Yankee stocks and bonds. Noticeably, customers' men or stock salesmen in Texas, though they developed a large market in the metropoli, usually originated somewhere else. Texans thought in property, not financial terms; they preferred land to paper values.

Much of the old cheap-money philosophy survived, in a way incomprehensible to the substantial people of the East, who could not understand the separation of private property and paper money in the Texas mind.

Money, to the substantial Texan, was a commodity used to buy property; of itself it had no mystic value.

The Texan ethic and Texan society, both inherited, rewarded enterprise. The Southern American outlook was generally as puritan and enterprising as that of New England, although its outlets took different forms. The frontier made Texan society far more atomistic than that of the East or North, however, and this, while it allowed individual men to break patterns and do great things, was an inherent social weakness. The strongest Texans, remarkably, could think and act for themselves. But there was an enormous tendency to what Texans called "jackleggism," too.

Texans were independent. No man put his nose in his neighbor's business, unless asked. They could act in concert, but not for long. Few Texans could subordinate their dreams and desires for any length of time to the group. The frontier did not draw that kind of men, and the kind it drew had less sense of community than the people in the North and East. Significantly, the Ranger companies coalesced, then disappeared. It was difficult for Texans to sustain a campaign; each man had better things to do. Collective action, or group discipline, grated on the Texan frontier soul. In retrospect, the Texan defense of its frontier was poorly done. It was mounted as thousands of individual efforts, while a few years of sustained, collective struggle would have solved the problem quickly.

The refusal to act in concert slowed the frontier. Jackleggism also affected Texas and Texans in later times. It was a strong bar to unionization of labor; the native Anglo-American, even where he could see unions might help him, maintained his distrust of collectivization. Farmer unions, though they were tried again and again, usually foundered. Noticeably, cooperatives in Texas were never so strong or so successful as in other states. Thousands of Texas farmers, large and small, suffered from price discrimination and other practices that their counterparts in California or Wisconsin alleviated by concerted action. The Texas frontiersman, stubbornly, even bitterly independent, refused to cooperate. This was a weakness as society grew more crowded and organized. But it was a source of strength in the early days, because no organic-thinking people could possibly have scattered across the wide and wild frontier, fighting a thousand separate, successful battles, winning a million separate plots of soil.

The Mexicans were lacking in both independence and entrepreneurism, and until the stubborn Anglos had tamed the country, their colonization failed.

As conditions changed, and Texas was drawn more tightly to the larger nation, the very Texan empiricism of mind also became a weakness. The average Texan could not quite grasp the meaning and the reality of the industrial society, where men worked and lived in relation to other men, not to Nature and the land. Thinking in straight material, not social, terms, Texas continued to produce men who were prepared to exploit and process the resources of the earth, while it produced few people prepared to offer the services society more and more required. By the middle of the 20th century, Texas was importing the vast majority of its technicians, in management, medicine, and such new industries as television, from outside. Texas metropolitan society was rapidly taking on a Yankee patina in public communications, sales management, business and finance. Northern minds and Northern techniques even conceived and exploited the urban development, and found the gold in Texas history. Immigrants smelled profit in the Spanish heritage while the practical Texan mind yet failed to see any glories in it. There were more foreigners, inevitably, directing and shaping San Antonio's world's fair in 1968 than natives.

Texans were not in the vanguard on the newer industrial frontier. They were still entirely purposeful, but their internal society and its education were not fitting them to exploit fully many newer avenues of American life. In fact, the messy meritocracy that seemed to be evolving on both American coasts had little appeal for Texans. It was not attached either to private property or the soil, and its very intellectualism to minds as hard and dry and practical as Texans' was inherently suspect. Texans could conceive of a society based on cotton, cattle, citrus, and oil, but not of a structure resting on techniques and ideas, in which intellectual capacity merited as much attention and respect as a ten-thousand-acre pasture or title to a city block.

Northern businessmen and students flocking into Dallas sometimes referred contemptuously to turn-of-the-century attitudes among the natives, and in the calmer, sun-splashed San Antonio, despairingly sensed a lingering of the 18th century. In all this there was a certain truth. The old American ethic was not eroded in Texas. Nothing had occurred to cause such erosion.

Ethics were more tenacious than ideologies or ideas, which changed to meet changing conditions. An ethic comprised an unconscious outlook or motivation; it was so fundamental it was rarely consciously thought of or discussed. The Texan still believed subconsciously that work was the real virtue, and acquisition of property its reward; that ceaseless, aggressive action was the proper sphere for man, and God had given him the world for his arena; that social classification was wrong but status all-important; and that the only logical, or moral, basis for status was acquired wealth. It was a cultural tradition that was literally civilized; it tore down forests and plowed millions of acres of virgin soil; it extracted billions of tons of petroleum and spread great cities over the land; it erected massive dams and paved countless highways to connect the whole. It was a cultural ethos that had no room for culture. Texans were not responsible for it; their ancestors brought it from the British Isles.

The American frontier was superbly fitted to the puritan ethic, which was only minimally devoted to certain attitudes towards alcohol and sex. The puritan ethic drew a straight line between cause and effect. On a frontier embattled with aboriginal natives and hostile Nature, cause and effect reigned, and had to reign, supreme. Ideas did not overpower the earth; unless man was in ceaseless action the earth overpowered him. The vast sweep of land and sky, the great plateaus, the savage drouth and frequent, howling storms, stripped man of intellectually conceived notions. Men succeeded, or lived and died, not because of what they believed but how they applied themselves. The Texan was predominantly a fundamentalist Protestant Christian, but his religion was fundamentally different from that of the earliest Christian centuries.

Texans had a hard time visualizing the Christian martyrs. They had to dismiss the hagiocracy of saints, because the first Christian saints did not live in the real world, but created their own. Texans could understand the rejection of the values of the Roman Empire, but not men who dismissed the Empire and proceeded to dwell in their own minds. A few such men arrived on the Texas frontier, but blizzards or Indians usually got them.

The parts of the Bible in which the children of Israel saw the sweetness in a harsh land, and piled up the foreskins of their enemies, to the Texan made more sense.

The movement to the cities failed to erode the old ethic quickly. For one reason, it came late; the Texas metropoli did not really grow until the fourth decade of the 20th century. The cities grew linearly, not upward; they grew statically, much as the Old South spread west. They were entirely creations of the auto age. In 1920, San Antonio, with 161,000, was the only large city in Texas, but in 1920 both Boston and St. Louis were larger than they would be in 1960. The Texas cities were planned for the automobile, thus avoiding certain enormous problems. In Dallas or Houston in the 1960's, three-quarters of all employed people rode in automobiles to work. This figure far exceeded the ratio in Detroit, the automobile center of the world.

The cities also grew in the age of the single-family dwelling, the outlying shopping center, the small plant with its parking lot, the drive-in theater, and drive-in bank. In the same era the downtown church waned, because the new city dwellers built their own on the periphery. Thus Texas did not build genuine cities, in the European sense, but atomistic accumulations of people. The metropolitan Texan lived in far greater comfort but socially not much changed from the way he had lived on his scattered ranches and farms. Nothing like the European or Northern city neighborhoods evolved. Strikingly, the Texan retained more loyalty to his region than to his city. He called himself Texan, not Dallasite or Houstonian. Dallas, San Antonio, Houston, Fort Worth, sucked millions of scattered Texans from surrounding areas, in a general pattern. North of the Brazos, in east Texas, most families moved toward Houston. South of the Colorado, they tended to move southwest, to San Antonio, or in unending fragmented streams, up from the Rio Grande. Dallas pulled its hundreds of thousands from the old corn and cotton fields of the post-oak belt and from along the ancient farming line. These people drove to the metropoli, often moving less than two hundred miles through country without much change. They kept their roots. They were at most second generation urbanites, not yet urbane, and they all had relatives or property back in the small towns or farms.

Since they were all of the same stock, and Texas had flexible annexation laws, they did not suburbanize as did people in other places. The cities kept spreading out, making continual new islands of commerce in the sprawling mass. Urban sprawl Texas had, but as yet not much real urban decay. By the 1960's, a pattern was emerging in several Texan metropoli: large numbers, even majorities, no longer went to the city center for any purpose, either to shop or work.

Thus the economic effect of cities was enormous, but they provided very little cultural force. The resident of Dallas could live, work, and think, suspended between streets and the surrounding land, almost exactly as he had lived, worked, and thought on his cotton fields or shady small-town lanes. The great Texas middle class merely moved from farm to town, and found conditions basically unchanged. They still lived off the land. In San Antonio, in fact, in 1960 more people lived in the city than worked there. Nowhere was there a flight of the business or professional class.

Texans, as on the frontier, had different social characteristics, and different problems, from other metropolitan Americans. One effect was that the Texas urbanite remained inherently conservative in politics, while the masses in Northern cities, composed of different kinds and classes of people, did not.

The great difference between Texas and every other American state in the 20th century was that Texas had a history. Other American regions merely had records of development. This made, and had to make, certain subtle differences between the Texan and the average Anglo-American soul.

Seventy percent of the people of Texas moved only a few miles, and did not change their culture, to become metropolitanites. By contrast, the urban majorities in the North came thousands of miles, most of them dropping, or trying to shed, their history on the cattleboat. Millions of Germans, Englishmen, Irish, Italians, or Poles started their American experience in Chicago, Omaha, Milwaukee, Baltimore, or New York, bringing with them certain traits and cultural patterns but no discernible past. When they became middle-class Americans, they twice severed their ancestral roots. The inhabitants of "Winesburg, Ohio" had no sense of the great American conquest, the battle between North and South, East and West, the mystic feeling that comes with having buried one's own dead in one's own soil. As a sensitive Jewish writer once remarked, he could never sing "Land where our fathers died" without feeling a stabbing qualm. Millions of modern Americans, who became definable Americans, bypassed the frontier experience altogether.

There was nothing bad in this, except some tried to deny the frontier experience.

The distance from Chicago to Dallas, or from Omaha to San Antonio, where the gloomy Alamo stood, was not measured merely in miles but in years and blood.

The Texan did not shed his history in the 20th century; he clung to it. Texas history was taught in Texas schools before the study of the United States began. The Anglo held to his history; the Mexican to his; only the Negro faced an immense psychosis in Texas, because the black man's history was not defined, and unbearable when it was. This Anglo history was shot through with the national myths all such histories have; it had its share of hypocrisy and arrogance. Parts of its mythology made both ethnic Mexicans and Negroes writhe. But in essence, it rang true. *We chose this land; we took it; we made it bear fruit,* the Texan child is taught. History, and the fact that he has never really left the land, made the 20th-century Texan the most "European" of all American stock.

They had had the longest frontier in America; they had battled in close combat with foreign races; they had subjugated other peoples, and had been conquered themselves. They had learned that all peoples were not the same; parochial inside America, they were yet less parochial than those Americans who thought all the world was essentially the same. The great majority knew where their grandparents lay buried. They were as provincial as Frenchmen, as patriotic as Russian peasants. They put not their trust in governments, but in holding to their soil. These were things all Texans felt or sensed, though few could articulate well.

Noticeably, while thousands of Texans sojourned around the world, and Texas millionaires found pleasanter havens in which to live, few completely broke their ties with home. A frequent phenomenon was the return of the Texan prodigal from Los Angeles or New York. Much more common, but less noted, was the refusal of the Texan to leave. Literally thousands of Texans surrendered better-paying jobs in order to remain where they were, something few other Americans could really understand. The average American's pride in his state of birth was more normally shown by his alacrity to leave it forever, given the chance.

In a number of ways, then, rising out of his past and present, the Texan was different from the mainstream American, even beyond the obvious Southern variation from the norm. He carried the ancient American ethic untrammeled and unchanged; he was apt to be as mercilessly middle-class as his ancestors on the long-erased Scots-English war frontier. Warrior values, rapidly diluting in America, also survived.

The cult of courage was obvious; cowards never sought out any dangerous frontier. But like all warrior-colored societies, the Texan despised cowardice in a way more secure societies could not understand. The physical coward, the man who rode away when the Comanches poured along the Brazos, leaving his womenfolk behind, was not tolerable for obvious reasons. But the cult of courage was mercilessly applied much further: the man who did not accept combat when it was offered, for any reason, was suspect.

Warrior values made Texans respectful of the rights of peers, much as all Indian braves were essentially equals when not on warpath. L. H. McNelly, in a recorded incident, shocked the officers of the U.S. Cavalry when he invited one to dine with him, because he ate, smoked, and squatted among his Ranger privates on terms of perfect equality when not on patrol. But McNelly would have shot dead on the spot any Ranger enlisted man who disobeyed a combat order. McNelly was a leader, like Hays and Ford, not because of any military hierarchy, or some governor's written commission, but because he was recognized as the best thinker under stress, the deadliest man around. The Ranger bands were almost perfect microcosms of the Texas frontier concept of democracy. Leaders were leaders, because they first proved they could act.

The reverse of the coin was that no warrior society was respectful of the rights of those outside the peer group. McNelly never told a Mexican twice to do something. Hays, either personally or in the name of his regiment, took no insult from any man, either disrespectful citizen of Mexico City or General Winfield Scott. *Samurai* could be touchy men.

Texans appeared to be courageous and self-reliant; the majority were. They could also be contemptuous and brutal, if not cruel. Webb, perhaps better than anyone else, summed up the Western hero as he really was, and remained: "Gracious to ladies, reserved toward strangers, generous to friends, brutal to enemies." The Texas partisans could just as easily have wielded claymores or led men in armor on more ancient forays. They would apply the same values in other times, with weapons far more lethal than Jack Hays' Colt; values are slow to change.

The Texan was different also in his psychological conservatism. Every major social change that came in the 20th century was forced upon the State of Texas by outside pressures. Texas, from the Eastern, Southern influence, did not follow the Western pattern of granting female suffrage. This came by federal amendment. A host of restrictive laws applying to women remained. They were barred from jury duty, restricted in doing business in their own name, and could not transact property without their husband's consent. Some of this derived from Spanish law, but survived many referenda at large. Texans were indeed gracious to ladies, but perferred not to have the ladies dabbling in warriors' business. The Texan image, everywhere, was dryly and assertively masculine; this, too, shaped the native culture.

Votes for Negroes, desegregation, welfare, and various forms of the so-called civil rights for the non-peer group were forced down the Texan throat from outside. These trends, in a region where New England libertarianism did not dilute the essential puritanism, kept Texas in continual collision with the dominant forces in Washington. The Texan bitterly attributed all such agitation to politics, and was outraged when politics were used to alter the basic parameters of social life.

The mass migration to cities, because of its nature, did not alter the Texan concept of the inept, the foolish, the unlucky, or the weak. Nor was he enamored with these when they congregated and clamored for attention. The frontier ethic and experience laid no groundwork for such accommodation. The intelligent Texan realized that something had to be done; these people could not be "sent back where they came from," but most subconsciously wished they could run the new welfare reservations in their cities into Oklahoma.

Texas was relatively a rich state, although enormous differences in wealth and income continued between its citizens, white and white, black and brown. Such differences were bound to persist in a cause-and-effect society, based on action. But inevitably, the survival of its value system, and the strengthening of that system particularly in the west, led Texas to deal with its poor, its handicapped, its colored, and its blind, insane, and aged less compassionately than any comparatively wealthy state. Texans were decent, Protestant people, but the concept of public welfare beyond the starvation level violated every ancient Protestant ethic they possessed. God helped them who helped themselves. Those who could not cope deserved second class, or worse, status.

The entrance of the United States Supreme Court into such matters, and the slow, but massive assault on private property and tribal concepts of law that the modern Court took up, offended Texans not only in the pocketbook but in the soul. The Texan trend had always been to modify the law to fit conditions on the ground, and from this struggle Texas had evolved the stiffest concept of, and defense of, private property anywhere in the United States. Trespassing in Texas was no small offense. Fence-damaging was a felony; so being caught in someone's orchard with the *prima facie* evidence of holding a fruit bag was a crime. Stray stock could be impounded; pickets had permission to walk a public street, but not set foot on private ground; any hunter or fisherman who invaded another's property without express permission was subject to arrest. All this was a logical outgrowth of land-hunger and land-struggle, and as one splendid side effect it preserved Texas' last great herds of game; Texans invented the game ranch because they found it profitable, not because they loved the deer they hunted. But because under many circumstances a landowner could shoot a trespasser and be absolved, it showed that Texans instinctively put the defense of property above notions of humanistic law.

The pressures out of Washington to regulate and control the individual's use of private property, whether his acres or his factories, offended Texans. This conflict created interest politics, as with the tideland oil. Above all, the movement of the Supreme Court into the destruction of state boundaries by an overriding, expanding federal law, aroused anger and fear. This went far beyond the mere opposition to imposed civil rights.

The Court's decisions on criminal procedure and law enforcement convinced Texans that the Court was trying to change conditions to fit ideas, rather than making law to fit the dominant majority's needs and mood. The pressures for civil rights Texans could understand; there was a Negro vote. But other moves smacked of the triumph of ideology over the way things were. Successful Texan politicians, more often than not, ran on platforms pledging greater opposition to the ideologue reformers in the North, who were called much worse terms.

All of this opposition was not pure reaction or stupid stubbornness. Texans were far closer to the heart and mind of 19th-century Anglo-America than others. Frequently, the greater nation telegraphed orders to Texas to change, when local conditions had not been taken into account. This was on occasion like trying to fight Indians, or defend the border, from preconceived notions in Washington. Laws that made sense for the industrial society did not always make sense in a preindustrial ethos. There was a parochialism in Washington thinking, which held that all parts of the United States were, or ought to be, the same. A certain colonialism continued. Texans could not resist a longing for the Yankees to let the natives in the hinterlands run things for themselves, whether the Great White Father liked the way they were run or not.

In some ways the Texan, out of his history, was far more tolerant than other Americans. Having no real ideology, he could not ride ideological horses or get worked up over things that did not personally affect him. No Texan really cared what kind of government Spain had; that was for Spaniards to decide. Nor did he care what kind of laws were passed in New York—so long as New Yorkers did not try to apply them to him. If the Texan had none of the New England libertarianism, he had little of the moralistic American penchant for meddling. He was far more tolerant of Germans or Russians, in the 20th century, than his apparent belligerency revealed. When Germans or Russians appeared to menace his interests, then he reacted with the frontier attitudes; otherwise, he could not care what they did. His ancestors had burned their bridges to any notion of a world society when they crossed the Atlantic; they deserted the British Isles because they found Europe, and all its works, intolerable.

It was impossible to imagine a protest emanating from Texas over some other nation's internal affairs—or even a protest march in atomistic Anglo-Texas. Mexicans did it, and Hungarians, but those were foreigners with a more organic view.

Such attitudes were natural; there would always be interest politics, because the United States was not, and probably never would be, an entirely unitary nation.

Yet the Texan was nothing if not an American.

All his traits of heart and mind and action were American traits in some degree. Nothing the Texan did, or believed, or thought, was foreign to

America, though some of it was foreign to some Americans. No American, from anywhere, felt he was crossing a border when he stepped across the Texas line. He was moving into different country, yes—foreign, no.

The American ethic was hardly dead in Chicago or New York, where men struggled to gain status, though not land, with the same intensity, though in different ways. The two most prominent Texans of the 1960's— Governor John Connally and Lyndon Baines Johnson, new-rich, capable, successful, boastful as only men with a sharecropper mentality who have made it big can be, buying ranches, and dressing like Chamber of Commerce presidents—had their counterparts from San Francisco to New York, where men made money from the garment industry or television, investing it in stocks or bonds. The oldest cities in America had plenty of men who wore diamond jewelry and boasted about their money, though admittedly few had Anglo-Saxon names. Between the farmer gone to town and the European newly across the Atlantic, there was an enormous bond, despite the occasional suspicion and hostility. America and its unspoken ethic made strong cement, for both Anglo-Celtics and Rumanians.

The bleak and unlettered view of God and God's earth, the stark and impoverished cultural tradition, the burning interest in what men do, or own, but not what they are, or might be—the motion, the pursuit, the ceaseless imperialism of the pragmatic mind—what American could deny these? All had a deep root in the English-speaking world, above all in America. Texas, from Stephen Austin to Sam Houston to L. H. McNelly to Lyndon Johnson, was only a boldly drawn example of Anglo-Saxon society, showing what any English-speaking community would do, under similar conditions. Between frontier Australia and frontier Texas there was an affinity that almost amounted to brotherhood: Down Under was one place Texans went to stay. A Texan became the most popular American ambassador to Australia that country has had. There was an essential vulgarity and violence in both souls.

If the Texan was little worried about what he was, and must obscure all thought in action, resting his case for greatness on great works, good or bad, most Americans were the same. If Lyndon Johnson chose to stand or fall on what he did in the vitally evil arena of public action, he would stand higher among Americans in many things than other men who chose to conceptualize and talk.

If Texans were man-centered, and to them the earth was nothing if not to be exploited; if God was not a God who died upon a cross but a smiling uncle who accepted a junior partnership while suffering little children to eat candy on his knee, what American would not destroy a river, or demolish a hundred forests, or create a dust bowl, if doing it provided a thousand jobs? What American was not a wholly economic man?

All Americans, in one way or another, had grasped their chosen land, out-Goded God, made a blaspheming, materialistic, burgeoning—and yet *decent*—society. They worked much kindness with their evils, much good with their gains. Texas was not a better place when the Comanches had it, killing Apaches with the torture and themselves barely living thirty violent, squalid, brutish years. Nor would the Spanish have erected a Garden of Eden, had their arms prevailed. The Spanish left enough evidence of that behind, in other places, other times.

The Texan despised the Mexican. But the Mexican problem, the race's real problem, was one Texas did not invent. Never exposed to the frontier ethic, he moved doggedly into a society saturated with the beliefs that life's a fight, that man must get ahead, bend nature to his will, even if he must destroy nature in the process. The *pelado* came from a culture where no man for four hundred years gained anything by slaving harder for his master; where his gentle hope that God might yet provide was still alive. He was unequipped to step into the whirlwind, against which other-driven men cannot stand. He thought "just like a Meskin—work eight hours, then payday, and hit the beer halls"; he *was,* but he could not march across that bleak puritan landscape and become an entrepreneur. Men who exist get overrun by men who act.

It was no different in San Antonio or New York.

What was the great drive toward new playgrounds, clean streets, better housing, better schools, and more bloodless bureaucracy that gripped 20th-century Texas metropoli but part of a last outburst of the American frontier heresy, the Pelagianism that had such deep roots in the Anglo-Saxon soul? The efforts to forge a single society out of many pillars, to improve the race of man by educating his mind: these heresies gripped the Texan as surely as the American mind.

He was an American, first and last.

Those who tried to reject the Jacksonian advance to the West, the policies of James Polk, and the Sheridan-Grant solution to the Indian problem as American aberrations themselves committed aberrations by not seeing things, and themselves, as they really were.

The history of Texas, and the people of Texas, were American history and American people, and in part, a part of the story of the world.

As the raw scar of the frontier fades and the frontier values evaporate, as they must; as Texan society grudgingly grows genuinely metropolitan, as it mixes and amalgamates with fresh waves of human stock, patterns change. The people change, as they must change. The first settlers called themselves Texians, and their descendants, and all those who took part in the great conquest, are properly called Texans. There are already several million non-Texan residents of Texas, and their numbers must increase. In another hundred years, perhaps, the reality of the frontier will be as remote to Texas residents as the American frontier is to residents of Massachusetts, where not one in seven people is descended from stock that killed an Indian. The Anglo conquest of the American West will become a distant thing, perhaps to be despised, certainly to be misunderstood, even if admired. Already certain Texas chauvinisms are dying; Texans are revising their own mythology.

When they have lost it altogether, and when the office-working, car-

driving Texan is completely indistinguishable from his Northern counterpart, the history of Texas, as Texas, will be done.

In the end, perhaps after all people, will be the land. It was stubborn
soil, and it was difficult to destroy. Men tore it, gouged it, cut down its
forest cover and plowed up its shielding grasses, yet most of it remained.
The rivers were dammed, but they were still there. The seas of grass were
cut by endless pasture fences, but the land itself, and the sweeping, rising,
majestic plateaus were bedded in limestone too solid to remove. Nor would
cities ever cover all of them, because when God made Texas, He made
water scarce. Already, under the plateaus, the deep-driven wells were running dry. More plowed fields would shrink, more thick green-and-brown
grass grow over the humus made by eons of bison bones. In many places,
man had already begun a long retreat.

Most places had little changed. On Palmito O. G. Jones could still plant
his guns where no one lived, and sweep the Yankees back to Boca Chica.
The thicket where Rip Ford sat his horse and sounded the charge was still
there. A few miles away, a rusting cannon marked the lonely prairie where
Taylor crashed into the Mexicans. Taylor, and Arista, would have recognized the ground. Through much of Texas, only the ubiquitous paved
roads, and fences, and telephone and powerline poles had changed the
surface of the land.

The Coahuiltecs would have found their old hunting grounds as inhospitable as before. More cactus and mesquite grew on them, spread by the
overgraze of cattle. But the *brasada* shimmered in the sun, much as it had
for a thousand years.

The old Comanche trace to Mexico, near Fort Clark, lay still ephemerally green under the Comanche moon. Blue gentians grew in the headwaters of the Brazos, as they grew to the sound of Kiowa flutes. The bones
of men and buffalo were gone; the land took them, and remained.

The vast stretches of the fraying limestone plateaus above the Balcones
Scarp remained also; clear shallow streams playing over deep brown beds,
the oaks standing ocher and solemn against the fading meadows after the
first fall frost. Anywhere, across hundreds of leagues, the horizon rose clear
against low hills for miles.

This land shaped those who lived upon it more than they changed it.
Hostile, yet with a beauty the second generation came to love, with crashing meteorological changes that punished man and beast, with winds that
made them uneasy, yet volatile and free, it somehow aroused a sense of
music in the Spanish-Mexican soul. In Americans, it made feelings they
could not articulate.

The land, the climate, the sense of endlessness yet constant change made
all who came there hospitable, patriotic, violent, and brave. In the Indian it
produced mysticism, as he wailed his death songs to the earth, the cold
moon, and sun. In the Hispanic breast it made a communion with Nature,

a poetry, a willingness to ride the broad vistas, pause under moss-hung oaks, and be.

The Anglo had no eye for beauty, less feel for rock-ribbed soil. Yet the land was too big even for big men to develop and destroy. He fenced it, dammed it, threw his cattle over it in prodigal hordes; he farmed it, and in drouth and shattering hail and cold, cursed Nature and Nature's God. Yet all these acts were in their own way acts of love. The Anglo-Saxon laced this soil with his own and other men's blood; it would take his bones, and monstrous artifacts, and still remain.

The sun would remain, while men must die. The moon would rise again, while civilizations fell. In the end would be the earth. Texas, under any name, would go on forever.

BIBLIOGRAPHICAL NOTES AND SUGGESTIONS FOR FURTHER READING

The most important sources of Texas history are found within the following broad categories, all of which I have drawn on heavily:

GENERAL HISTORIES

The best of the older books is Henderson K. Yoakum's *History of Texas 1685–1846* (New York, 1856). Another standard in every Texas library is Hubert Howe Bancroft, *History of the North Mexican States and Texas* (2 vols., San Francisco, 1884–1889). These contain excellent coverage of the French-Spanish periods and reflect American moral certainties of the 19th century. Dudley G. Wooten, *A Comprehensive History of Texas* (2 vols., Dallas, 1897) reproduces Yoakum's text with additions. John Henry Brown, *A History of Texas, 1685–1892* (2 vols., St. Louis, 1892–1893) and Frank White Johnson, *History of Texas and Texans* (Chicago, 1914) are compilations of men and events with contemporary views. Johnson's work, largely written by editors E. C. Barker and E. W. Winkler, is a superior history, published a generation after his death. Interesting, but of lesser value, are William Kennedy, *Texas* (London, 1841; Fort Worth, 1925), and David B. Edward, *History of Texas* (Cincinnati, 1836).

Louis J. Wortham, *A History of Texas* (5 vols., Fort Worth, 1924) is very readable but lacks index and some accuracy in details. Clarence R. Wharton's *Texas Under Many Flags* (Chicago and New York, 1930) consists of two volumes of history and three of Texan biography. H. S. Thrall, *Pictorial History of Texas* (St. Louis, 1879) is also valuable for biographical sketches.

General histories on the later periods of Texas history are few. Ralph Steen, edited by F. C. Adams, *Texas Democracy* (4 vols., Austin 1937) is primarily a political study; Steen's *Twentieth Century Texas, An Economic and Social History* (Austin, 1942) covers only the early decades. The most modern, and widely used, general history is Rupert Norval Richardson, *Texas, The Lone Star State* (Englewood Cliffs, N.J., 1943; rev. 1958).

PERIODICAL LITERATURE

There is widespread agreement that the best, and most useful, writings on Texas history have been published in the *Quarterly of the Texas State Historical Association* (Vols. I–XVI, Austin, Texas, 1897–1912) and its successor, *The Southwestern Historical Quarterly,* continuing from July, 1912. These articles and monographs cover every field and period, and in innumerable cases each is the definitive work on the subject. Unfortunately, these gems of research and writing are scattered over the years and have reached too small an audience. Similar valuable Texas material is included in *The Journal of Southern History* (Lexington, Ky., quarterly since 1934), and the quarterly *Mississippi Valley Historical Review,* (Lincoln, Neb.) issued from 1914.

Newspaper archives provide perhaps the best reflection of contemporary attitudes. Editorial writing in the 19th century was both a florid and a violent art and probably revealed genuine sentiments and ideology much more clearly than the bland dissertations of today. Newspapers, scattered about the state, also contain an enormous amount of historical trivia for the student inclined to search it out.

The Texas Almanac, which first appeared in January, 1857, and had a combined antebellum distribution of perhaps 100,000 copies, has been and is the single most valuable reference work on Texas. Suspended between 1873 and 1904 and published irregularly from 1904 through 1925, *The Texas Almanac* is now issued biennially by the *Dallas Morning News.* Of special interest to student, historian, and general reader is a compendium of the years 1857–1873 published by the Texian Press (Waco, 1967), placing heretofore rare material in easy access.

MANUSCRIPT AND OTHER PRIMARY SOURCES

There is a trend among professional historians to seek out more and more original sources, producing a tremendous flow of antiquarian mosaic-fitting. Manuscript material, in several languages, is plentiful. The archives of Spain and Mexico are rich, but unfortunately not easily accessible even to on-site research by bilingual students. Like early Texas newspapers, manuscripts of the Spanish-Mexican period are highly colored, reflecting strong clerical or anticlerical bias. It is possible to explore material on the Texas missions, for example, which utterly ignores their secular situation and purpose. These must be balanced with the equally fervent—but often brilliant and incisive—reports of civil and military officers.

The best (and certainly most accessible) Hispanic library on Texas is at the University of Texas at Austin. This, with the University of Oklahoma at Norman, is the richest repository of unpublished source material on the Southwest.

Important source material on Texas in the German language has generally been translated into English and published in this country.

One of the most heartening trends of recent years has been the continuing publication either of manuscript material or the reprinting or reissue in facsimile of old, and often quite rare, writings. These projects have been carried out by Texas publishers such as the University of Texas Press, Texian at Waco, Steck at Austin, and by the Rio Grande Press of Chicago and others; in this way an enormous amount of firsthand information has been made available not only to the student but also to the general reader and Texas history buff.

Usually avoided, but clearly important for the serious student, are the several government archives. Those of Texas and the United States hold civil and military reports, data, and pertinent information available nowhere else. Not only for accuracy but also for enlightenment, official data may be compared against newspaper and other published accounts. U. S. Army records, for example, often contain facts and figures contemporary Texans ignored, such as the death rate from yellow fever on the coast.

For the 20th century, the historian must use much fragmentary material. Subjects such as industrialization, agricultural revolutions, immigration, race relations, politics, and the like are rarely covered adequately in general accounts. Here specialized writings, in newspapers and periodicals (and ethnic periodicals, such as the League of United Latin American Citizens bulletins, as well) must be searched out; a clipping file is basic. Until the focus of Texan historical interest moves beyond the 19th century, students and historical researchers will have to draw heavily on scattered and specialized material and synthesize it through their own outlooks and experience.

SUGGESTIONS FOR FURTHER READING

This list, from most of which I have drawn in some degree, by no means forms a complete bibliography. I have deliberately restricted it to recent works, books in print, or volumes easily found in good Texas libraries; and I have excluded the often definitive publications of the historical quarterlies, which are highly specialized and scattered. This selection does offer an enormous insight into the Texas past, and should provide any serious reader with more material than he can easily exhaust.

PART I. COMANCHES AND THE KING'S MERCIES

The land of Texas is well laid out in Frederic W. Simonds' *The Geography of Texas* (Boston, 1914), a standard. *The Natural Regions of Texas* (University of Texas Bulletin 3113, Austin, 1931) clarifies the sharp differences between east and west. Roy Bedicheck, *Adventures with a Texas Naturalist* (Garden City, N. Y., 1947; Austin, 1966) remains a popular and interesting book.

The best archeological reference on Texas is contained in Dee Ann Suhm and A. D. Krieger, *An Introductory Handbook of Texas Archeology,* published by the Texas Archeological Society, Austin, 1954. E. H. Sellards, *Early Man in America: A Study in Prehistory* (Austin, 1952); H. M. Wormington, *Ancient Man in North America* (rev., Denver, 1957); and Fred Wendorf, A. D. Krieger, Claude C. Albritton, and T. D. Stewart, *The Midland Discovery* (Austin, 1955) reveal some of the excitement and controversies concerning the mysterious first settlers.

There are countless books on Amerinds: Clark Wissler's *Indians of the United States* (Garden City, N. Y. 1940, 1966); Mary Jourdan Atkinson's *Indians of the Southwest* (rev., San Antonio, 1963), also general; the best one-stop source is W. W. Newcomb, Jr., *The Indians of Texas* (Austin, 1961). The Comanches are thoroughly explored in E. A. Hoebel, *Comanches, Lords of the South Plains* (Norman, Okla., 1952). The industrious will find useful the *Handbook of American Indians North of Mexico*, Bureau of American Ethnology Bulletin No. 30 (2 vols., Washington, D. C., 1907, 1910).

The early European explorations of Texas are well covered in Paul I. Wellman's narrative history of the Southwest, *Glory, God, and Gold* (Garden City, N. Y., 1954), Bancroft's history (cited under "General Histories," above), and Herbert E. Bolton, *Spanish Exploration in the Southwest, 1542–1706* (New York, 1925). Because of the glamour that attended these searches for glory and gold, an enormous literature exists.

Spanish Texas is comprehensively covered by Carlos Eduardo Castañeda, *Our Catholic Heritage in Texas* (6 vols., Austin, 1936–1950). Castañeda also translated Fray Juan Agustín Morfi's *History of Texas, 1673–1779* (2 vols., Quivira Society, Albuquerque, 1935); this, with Charles W. Hackett's edition of *Pichardo's Treatise on the Limits of Louisiana and Texas* (3 vols., Austin, 1931, 1934, 1941), opens a mine of Spanish information. For a thorough treatment of all aspects of the time, see Herbert E. Bolton's scholarly but superb works, *Texas in the Middle Eighteenth Century* (Berkeley, 1915) and *Athanase de Mezières and the Louisiana-Texas Frontier 1768–1780* (Cleveland, 1914). Walter P. Webb, *The Great Plains* (Boston, 1931) and Max L. Moorhead, *The Apache Frontier* (Norman, 1968) throw light on the Spanish Indian Problem.

PART II. BLOOD AND SOIL: THE TEXANS

Theodore Roosevelt's *The Winning of the West* (4 vols., New York, 1889–1896) reflects the views of a westward-looking President at the flood tide of American imperial thought. A paperbound volume of excerpts, edited by Harvey Wish, (New York, 1962) presents the student with a brilliant picture of the Western frontier through the Louisiana Purchase.

The filibuster and early Anglo-Saxon colonial periods are adequately covered in most general histories. Eugene C. Barker, *The Life of Stephen F. Austin* (Nashville and Dallas, 1925) and *Mexico and Texas, 1821–1835* (Dallas, 1928) give in-depth treatments of the empresario age. The best descriptive book of the period is Mary Austin Holley *Texas* (Baltimore, 1833); the author was a cousin of the great empresario. Noah Smithwick, *The Evolution of a State* (Austin, 1900) is rich in firsthand experience and observed detail.

The general histories devote enormous space to the Texas Revolution; all 19th century historians considered this event the heart of Texas history. Further detail is endlessly presented in the historical quarterlies. The student will find interesting the *Diary of William Barret Travis* (Waco, 1966); Marquis James,

The Raven (New York, 1929), and John Myers Myers, *The Alamo* (New York, 1948). Antidotes not without merit to the Texan mythology are Carlos Castañeda, *The Mexican Side of the Texas Revolution* (Dallas, 1928) and Richard G. Santos, *Santa Anna's Campaign Against Texas, 1835–1836* (Waco, 1968). *The Eagle: The Autobiography of Santa Anna* (Austin, 1967), edited by Ann F. Crawford, presents another differing view.

PART III. STAR LIGHT, STAR BRIGHT

The compendium of the *Texas Almanac 1857–1873* (Waco, 1967) contains the bulk of eye-witness reports and documents of the 1836 campaign; the student will find these nowhere more accessible. Llerena B. Friend, *Sam Houston: The Great Designer* (Austin, 1954, 1965) and *The Writings of Sam Houston,* A. W. Williams and Eugene C. Barker, editors, (8 vols., Austin, 1938–1943) reveal the often enigmatic mind of Texas' first President.

For a complete view of the Republic, see Stanley Siegel, *Political History of the Texas Republic 1836–1845* (Austin, 1956); William R. Hogan, *The Texas Republic: A Social and Economic History* (Norman, 1946); and Joseph W. Schmitz, *Texan Statecraft, 1836–1845* (San Antonio, 1941). Mary Austin Holley, *The Texas Diary 1835–1838* (Austin, 1965) is descriptive. The adventurous may want to explore *The Papers of Mirabeau Bonaparte Lamar* (6 vols., Austin, 1921–1927) and *Memoranda and Official Correspondence Relating to the Republic of Texas, Its History and Annexation 1836 to 1846,* by Anson Jones (New York, 1859; reprinted, Chicago, 1966). Almost all of the biographies of the men of this period are useful.

Again, the 19th century general histories deal adequately with the early statehood period. Valuable information is contained in the Houston papers. The boundary controversy is explored in W. C. Binkley, *The Expansionist Movement in Texas, 1836–1850* (Berkeley, 1925).

For information on immigration, see the *Texas Almanac* for 1857, 1858, and 1859; *German Seed in Texas Soil,* Terry G. Jordan, (Austin, 1966); and the U.S. Census, 1850 and 1860. The historical quarterlies richly supply information on settlers and colonies.

There is a huge total of writing on the life and institutions of Texas between 1836 and 1861, both published and unpublished. The following contemporary accounts are recommended: Mary A. Maverick, *Memoirs* (San Antonio, 1921); Frederick L. Olmstead, *A Journey Through Texas* (1857); Ferdinand Roemer, *Texas 1845–1847* (Bonn, 1849; San Antonio, 1936); August Santleben, *A Texas Pioneer* (New York, 1910); Francis R. Lubbock, *Six Decades in Texas* (Austin, 1900); J. C. Duval, *Early Times in Texas* (Austin, 1892; facsimile, Austin, 1935); Melinda Rankin, *Texas in 1850* (Boston, 1850; reprinted, Waco, 1966); *Gustav Dresel's Houston Journal,* translated and edited by Max Freund (Austin, 1954); *William Bollaert's Texas,* edited by W. E. Hollan and Ruth L. Butler (Norman, 1956). Also useful are Joseph W. Schmitz, *Texas Culture 1836–1846* (San Antonio, 1960); Marilyn M. Sibley, *Travelers in Texas 1761–1860* (Austin, 1966); Samuel Wood Gerser, *Naturalists of the Frontier* (Dallas, 1937); D. W. Winfrey, *Julien Sidney Devereux and His Monteverde Plantation* (Waco, 1966); and Dorothy R. Bracken and Maurine W. Redway, *Early Texas Homes* (Dallas, 1956).

PART IV. THE CONFEDERACY AND THE CONQUERED

There is so much literature on the War Between the States, both national and in scores of local Texas histories, that only a few representative accounts are recommended to the student: Oran A. Roberts' account in Wooten, *A Comprehensive History of Texas;* Frank W. Johnson, *The History of Texas and Texans* (both cited in "General Histories," above.); Governor Lubbock's *Six Decades in Texas* (cited above). These are Confederate accounts, but nine out of ten Texans were Confederates. Claude Elliott, *Leathercoat* (San Antonio, 1938) presents the life of James W. Throckmorton; August Santleben, *A Texas Pioneer* (cited above) gives the story of a Texas-German Union volunteer.

The student will easily find published accounts of most of Texas' fighting legions, from Terry's Rangers to Ross' Brigade. A useful compilation of Texas Confederate troops is Col. Harold B. Simpson, *Texas in the War 1861–1865* (Hillsboro, 1965). Col. John S. Ford's journals detail the Rio Grande Valley campaign; the most useful compilation is *Rip Ford's Texas,* edited by Stephen B. Oates (Austin, 1963). Another contemporary account is *Rags and Hope,* the memoirs of a survivor of the 4th Texas Infantry (Hood's Brigade), edited by Mary Lasswell (New York, 1961). For authoritative data, there is no substitute for *The War of the Rebellion, An Official Compilation of the Records of the Union and Confederate Armies.*

The definitive work on secession and reconstruction is Charles William Ramsdell, *Reconstruction in Texas* (New York, 1910; reprinted, 1964). W. C. Nunn, *Texas Under the Carpetbaggers* (Austin, 1962) is less scholarly but full of detail. The *Texas Almanac* between 1867 and 1872 is useful, as is D. Richardson, *Texas as Seen in 1870* (Shreveport, La., 1870).

The failure of reconstruction and the restoration has been explored most thoroughly by Seth Shepard McKay, *Making of the Constitution of 1876* (Philadelphia, 1924) and a number of other papers. The constitution itself can be found, with amendments, in the *Texas Almanac.* Other works of value are Governor Lubbock's memoirs (cited above); L. E. Daniell, *Types of Successful Men in Texas* (Austin, 1890); S. H. Acheson, *35,000 Days in Texas* (Dallas, 1938); and James T. DeShields, *They Sat in High Places: The Presidents and Governors of Texas* (San Antonio, 1940).

PART V. UNTIL DAY BREAKS AND DARKNESS DISAPPEARS: THE LAST FRONTIER

Just as the Texas frontier itself was fragmented and scattered, so are the writings on its aspects. Joseph Milton Nance, in *After San Jacinto* (Austin, 1962) and *Attack and Counterattack* (Austin, 1964) presents exhaustive studies of the Republic's Mexican wars. T. H. Wells, *Commodore Moore and the Texas Navy* (Austin, 1960) covers one little-known aspect of Texas frontier defense. George W. Kendall's *Santa Fe Expedition,* (London & New York, 1846) is hard to find; John Russell Bartlett's *Personal Narrative of Explorations and Incidents* (New York, 1854) has been reissued (Chicago, 1965). These contemporary books show attitudes and flavors of the Anglo-American in the Mexican Southwest.

The truly monumental work on the warfare on both the Mexican and Indian frontiers is Walter Prescott Webb's *The Texas Rangers: A Century of Frontier*

Defense (Austin, 1935, 1965). Webb is flavorful, folkloric, and detailed, and incorporates most of the useful sources. For those who wish to go beyond Webb, accessible accounts are *Rip Ford's Texas* (cited above); *Recollections of Early Texas: Memoirs of John Holland Jenkins* (Austin, 1958); *Now You Hear My Horn: The Journal of James Wilson Nichols 1820–1887* (ed. Catharine W. McDowell, Austin, 1967); *Robert E. Lee in Texas*, by Carl Coke Rister (Norman, Okla., 1946). Biographies are available of all of the important Rangers, from Big Foot Wallace to the McCullochs.

Mildred P. Mayhall, *Indian Wars of Texas* (Waco, 1965) incorporates many valuable original sources.

The northwestern Texan frontier is exhaustively covered in the following: Carl C. Rister, *The Southwestern Frontier* (Cleveland, 1928); *Fort Griffin on the Texas Frontier* (Norman, Okla., 1956); with Rupert N. Richardson, *The Greater Southwest* (Glendale, Calif., 1934); Rupert N. Richardson, *The Comanche Barrier to South Plains Settlement* (Glendale, 1933), and *The Frontier of Northwest Texas 1846 to 1876* (Glendale, 1963); J. Evetts Haley, *Fort Concho and the Texas Frontier* (San Angelo, Tex., 1952).

Col. Richard I. Dodge, *33 Years Among Our Wild Indians* (reissued, New York, 1959) and W. S. Nye, *Carbine and Lance* (Norman, 1937) are both interesting and valuable.

Mari Sandoz, *The Buffalo Hunters* (New York, 1954) describes this animal butchery. T. C. Battey, *The Life and Adventures of a Quaker Among the Indians* (Boston, 1945) presents a non-Texan view, from the Indian side.

Historical literature about the cattle frontier is endless and increasing. Suggested reading includes Ernest S. Osgood, *The Day of the Cattleman* (Minneapolis, 1954); Lewis Nordyke, *Cattle Empire* (New York, 1949) and *Great Roundup* (New York, 1955); C. L. Douglass, *The Cattle Kings of Texas* (Dallas, 1937); and Wayne Gard, *The Chisholm Trail* (Norman, 1954). The cowboy is covered in A. R. Rojas, *The Vaquero* (Charlotte, N. C., 1966); Charles A. Siringo, *A Texas Cowboy* (New York, 1950); and Joe Frantz and J. E. Choate, *The American Cowboy: The Myth and the Reality* (Norman, 1955).

Works about the great Texas ranches and ranchers form an important class of this literature: J. Evetts Haley, *The XIT Ranch of Texas and the Early Days of the Llano Estacado* (Norman, 1953) and *Charles Goodnight, Cowman and Plainsman* (Boston and New York, 1936); W. C. Holden, *The Spur Ranch* (Boston, 1934); Tom Lea, *The King Ranch* (2 vols., Boston, 1957).

PART VI. THE AMERICANS: NEW DREAMS FOR OLD

The student will find the general histories weakest beginning with modern Texas. Compared to earlier periods, there is an actual scarcity of good published material, especially at the turn of the century; fully caught up in the battle against the frontier, Texans tended to ignore its aftermath in literature. In addition to the more or less general works listed below, for much factual data the student must consult public documents, newspapers, and specialized studies. Much political writing is either superficial or emphasizes the grotesque. The few good writings on Texas' race and ethnic problems are generally found in magazines usually published nationally or outside the state. The *Texas*

Almanac is invaluable.

General political studies: Steen and Adams, *Texas Democracy,* and Steen, *Twentieth Century Texas* (both cited in "General Histories," above); Wilbourn E. Benton, *Texas, Its Government and People* (Englewood Cliffs, N.J., 1966); Caleb Patterson, Sam B. McAlister, and George C. Hester, *State and Local Government in Texas* (New York, 1961); James C. Soukup, Clifton McCleskey, and Harry Holloway, *Party and Factional Divisions in Texas* (Austin, 1964); Fred Gantt, Jr., *The Chief Executive in Texas* (Austin, 1964); Paul Casdorph, *The Republican Party in Texas 1865–1956* (Austin, 1965).

Also valuable are S. H. Acheson, *35,000 Days in Texas* (cited above) and the scattered writings of Seth S. McKay, the latter especially covering the Depression period; his *Texas Politics, 1906–1944* (Lubbock, Tex., 1952) is recommended.

C. E. Evans, *The Story of Texas Schools* (Austin, 1955) is a comprehensive work on education.

Settlement of the last frontier and the problems of the Southwestern farmer are shown in Carl C. Rister, *Southern Plainsmen* (Norman, 1938). W. C. Holden, *Alkali Trails* (Dallas, 1930) covers west Texas. The politics of Populism can be found in R. C. Martin, *The People's Party in Texas* (University of Texas Bulletin 3308, Austin, 1933); broader insights are in S. J. Black, *The Agrarian Crusade* (New Haven, 1920) and John Hicks, *Populist Revolt: A History of the Farmer's Alliance and the People's Party* (Minneapolis, 1931), two national studies. For individual lives and trials on the late nineteenth and early twentieth century Texas farm frontier, read Edward Everett Dale, *The Cross Timbers* (Austin, 1966) and William A. Owens, *This Stubborn Soil* (New York, 1966). J. Lee Stambaugh, *Lower Rio Grande Valley of Texas* (San Antonio, 1954) provides much data about the scene of Texas' last land rush.

Minor K. Kellogg's Texas Journal, 1872, edited by Llerena Friend (Austin, 1967) gives some tenor of Texan life.

For studies of Mexicans in Texas, see John H. Burma, *Spanish-Speaking Groups in the United States* (Durham, N.C., 1954); Pauline R. Kibbe, *Latin Americans in Texas* (Albuquerque, 1946); Arthur J. Rubel, *Across the Tracks, Mexican Americans in a Texas City* (Austin, 1966); William Madsen, *The Mexican-Americans of South Texas* (New York, 1964); F. J. Woods, *Mexican Ethnic Leadership in San Antonio* (Washington, D.C., 1949). Cultural insight into Mexican society is provided by Julia Waugh, *The Silver Cradle* (Austin, 1955).

Various publications on the Negro in Texas tend to be out of date. The ferment of the 1960's in both Negro and ethnic Mexican affairs is best reported in current newspapers, periodicals, and other media. Both situations are not only controversial but very much in flux.

The major oil corporations, like the major ranches, have their individual published histories. For an authoritative study of the whole subject of petroleum, see Carl C. Rister, *Oil! Titan of the Southwest* (Norman, 1949). *The Texas Business Review,* published monthly through the University of Texas, is a rich source of business and industrial information for recent years. For a bitter view of the Texan's (and American's) economic obsession and destruction of his country through exploitation, see William O. Douglas, *Farewell to Texas*

(New York, 1967).

There are many books which attempt to explain or illustrate Texas life; most of these are superficial, more travelogs than studies. Among recent publications recommended is Stanley Walker's *Home to Texas* (New York, 1956), which captures the feelings of a successful expatriate on his return to native soil.

The following are not purely Texas works but regional treatments of the American Southwest of special interest:

The writings of J. Frank Dobie, including *Coronado's Children: The Longhorns* (Boston, 1941); *The Mustangs* (Boston, 1952); *A Vaquero of the Brush Country* (Boston, 1943 rev.); *Texas and Southwestern Lore* (Dallas, 1927) are folkloric and filled with the mystique and flavor of a vanished way of life.

Paul Horgan's *Great River* (New York, 1954) is a superb study of the culture of the entire Rio Grande from the Rocky Mountains to the Gulf of Mexico.

Bernard De Voto, *The Year of Decision* (Boston, 1950) presents a discerning history of Manifest Destiny, the Mexican War, and the explosion of the American nation to the Pacific.

Finally, in *The Great Plains* (Boston, 1931) Walter Prescott Webb wrote the definitive history of man's approach to the plains of North America. This book is timeless, readable, and probably presents more insights to the American West than anything in print.

INDEX

INDEX